# families
## developing relationships

SECOND EDITION

# fAmilies

## developing RelAtionships

232966

**lAURA S. SMART**
*Northern Illinois University*

**Mollie S. SMART**
*University of Rhode Island*

MACMILLAN PUBLISHING CO., INC.

New York

COLLIER MACMILLAN PUBLISHERS

London

Copyright © 1980, Macmillan Publishing Co., Inc.

Printed in the United States of America

Earlier edition copyright © 1976 by Macmillan Publishing Co., Inc.

Macmillan Publishing Co., Inc.
866 Third Avenue, New York, New York 10022

Collier Macmillan Canada, Ltd.

Library of Congress Cataloging in Publication Data

Smart, Laura S
    Families: developing relationships.

    M. S. Smart was the first-named author of the 1976 ed.
    Includes bibliographies and indexes.
    1. Family.   2. Marriage.   3. Sex.   I. Smart,
Mollie Stevens.   Families.   II. Title.
HQ728.S57 1980     301.42     79-11176
ISBN 0-02-411930-X


Printing: 1  2  3  4  5  6  7  8      Year: 0  1  2  3  4  5  6

To ELLEN

# pReface

In the four years since we wrote the first edition of this textbook, the world has seen many changes that have had impact upon families. Our economic position has worsened in relation to other countries. In the first edition we discussed the problems stemming from overpopulation and depletion of natural resources. Now those problems are made obvious through the fuel shortages, unemployment, and high prices that affect American families, and in the agonies inflicted upon refugees all over the world. Many of the current changes in American family living are responses to changes in other sectors of life, economic, political, and environmental. In studying family life, it often seems that improvements or solutions require changes in one of the other sectors, rather than in the family itself. At other times family members are able to learn better ways of controlling their operations and of providing greater fulfillment for themselves. This book is concerned with the interactions between families and their physical, economic, and social environment, and with interactions within families.

The book is planned to meet the objectives of students in a family and marriage course, but we want to say in the beginning that it does not provide a direct path to a happy marriage. Nobody can do that, nor can a book. Books and teachers can give information, raise questions, and direct a student's efforts. Students also learn through discussions with one another, both informal ones and guided discussions.

Students' objectives include the following. They want to gain an understanding of their interactions and relationships with the people who are important to them in the contexts of love and home. They would like to integrate different points of view and value systems for themselves. They seek skills in communicating, relating, planning, and carrying on home living. Many students will use such a course in their professional work in fields involving service to people, teaching, and research in human development and relationships. While considering all these purposes, we have also thought about the conditions under which present and future students will be learning. The world is shrinking and changing very fast. How can we learn today in such a way that our efforts will be productive for tomorrow as well? If students are taking a "marriage course" in order to learn how to have happy marriages, they can learn about the conditions under which many happy marriages are created and maintained. They can identify and acquire appropriate skills. A book can open up choices to students. We hope that our readers will gain freedom to decide what kinds of persons they want to become and what kinds of relationships they want to develop with the people they love.

Through time and space, families have been and are organized in an amazing variety of patterns. Whatever the structure and function of a particular family type, it arose in order to fill certain human needs. It exists as long as it fills those needs, and often longer. Human beings are very talented at inventing new forms of everything —languages, clothes, houses, vehicles, foods, gadgets, roles, and relationships. And yet, as someone invents a new pattern and some joyfully adopt it, others are satisfied with the old ways and feel anguish at the possibility of having to relinquish them. Conflict is inevitable. Each person affects other people through what he or she does. Even when a couple flees to the wilderness or a South Sea island, they are not merely living their own lives, but are influencing the networks of people from which they are trying to extricate themselves. We are all involved in continuity and change.

This book reports many research studies on the various ways in which human beings interact and some of the results of their behavior. Starting with North Americans, whom we know best, we bring in material from many other cultures. We use many examples from India, a place where we lived for three years. Some historical material is also used. The purpose of this cross-culture discussion is to consider the many social inventions that human creativity has produced and to show that human problems of love and living can be solved in a multiplicity of ways. North American problems seem very threatening when a person considers destruction of the earth's resources, family violence, poverty, inflation, crime, divorce, racial conflict, and drug problems. Looking beyond national borders, one sees widespread starvation, war, terrorism, and population explosion. All of these represent human failure and cry out for solutions that transcend nationalism and parochialism. In introducing students to modes of living and values that differ from their own, we are trying to prepare them for the near future. They need to be able to think flexibly, to consider many different points of view, to discard what is rendered obsolete by new conditions, and to create better ways of being human.

Through understanding the ways in which individuals interact in family and societal settings, a person can judge what is most worthwhile, change his behavior in a direction he really wants, and communicate more clearly with others. He thus develops a justified feeling of being more in charge of his own life and of being able to cooperate and build with other people. In being more able and more free to decide, he experiences liberation. Thus a student of family life will become freer from the fetters of his own past, even while he builds upon all of his experiences to incorporate new knowledge.

FAMILIES

The two of us, daughter and mother, aided by our father/husband, have looked at the state of human relationships as we now see them in North America, as we have observed them in other parts of the world, as we have learned them through our parents, siblings, grandparents, nephews, nieces, and other relations, and as we interpret them from reading research. Because the two of use are of different generations, we have brought to bear two very different life experiences, and yet we have a vast amount in common. In putting this book together, we feel that we have grown. We hope that our readers, while using it, will grow, too.

During the time since we wrote the first edition of this textbook, the diversity of American families has been acknowledged not only by professionals, but also in government circles. The title of our book, *Families*, rather than *The Family*, reflects the current point of view that there is no typical or correct American family form, but rather a multiplicity of forms. Some of the subjects discussed in the first edition, such as work, health, and sibling relationships, were not commonly found in family texts. They have recently received more attention from teachers and writers of textbooks. We have developed such topics further in this edition. There is a whole new chapter on divorce. We include the most recent information on values and technology in family planning, health, and disease. Living together, aging, and crises are treated more fully. All chapters have been thoroughly revised. The majority of the photographs are new, and taken expressly for this book.

We continue to be indebted to the colleagues who helped us to understand and express the subject matter of the first edition. We are grateful to Patricia Daly, Pamela Dole, and Janice Prochaska for their assistance with the present edition. We thank the college and university professors who so generously answered a questionnaire about the first edition and our plans for the second: Harold R. Bergen, Dorothy Brengarth-Jones, Carole M. Carroll, Vera Channels, J. Kenneth Davidson, Jr., Dorothy Fruit, G. Fremont, Kathleen Gorman, Harold D. Grotevant, Bobbie A. Henderson, Charlene LeFebre, Bruce Pringle, R. M. Rodgers, Donald Schneller, M. E. Shelley, Delores R. Sykes, James Walters, Ralph Wedaking, and the Family Living Teachers of Central Missouri State University. We thank Emily Brown for the use of her title "Splitting and Splicing" for Chapter 9. We also thank our photographers: Barbara N. Armstrong and Cynthia Oziomek and their students, Robert Burgess, Ray Clayton, Mush Emmons, Zette Emmons, Donna Harris, Joseph Hornick, Robert J. Izzo, Fred Kellman, The Narragansett Times, Tina Sanghvi, Ellen S. Smart, Denis Stock, Stanley Summer, Craig M. Szwed, Townsend Studio, Rhode Island Housing and Mortgage Corporation, and Robert L. Wilkie.

Russell C. Smart, although not listed as an author, is a partner in the production of this book. He discussed ideas, edited, corrected mistakes, typed, read proof, made bibliographies and indexes, wrote letters to our editors, and enjoyed shocking male colleagues by telling them that he was our secretary. He lived androgynously before the term was adopted by contemporary professionals.

L. S. S.  
De Kalb  
Illinois

M. S. S.  
Saunderstown  
Rhode Island

# CONTENTS

**1** This Is Where You Start     **1**

**2** Love, Love, Love     **24**

**3** Communication: Where the Interaction Is     **49**

**4** This Grows on You: Sex     **77**

**5** It Keeps on Growing: More about Sex     **118**

**6** Two Find Each Other     **151**

**7** Partnerhood     **185**

**8** Partners at Work     **227**

**9** Splitting and Splicing     **257**

**10** Parenthood: A Matter of Choice     **295**

**11** Living and Learning with Children     **332**

**12** Sisters, Brothers, and All the Rest     **365**

**13** Health Is More Than Brushing Your Teeth     **392**

**14** Coping with Crises and Problems     **419**

**15** Down the Road and Around the World     **455**

Appendix A    Premarital Questionnaire     485

Appendix B    Basic Sex     494

Appendix C    Budget     499

Appendix D    Venereal Disease     502

Appendix E    Glossary     509

Author Index     515

Index of Subjects     525

# CHAPTER 1

# THIS IS WHERE YOU START

We, the authors of this textbook, are daughter and mother, members of a family. We use life experiences with families, both our own and others that we have observed, as examples in this book. Most of our readers have also grown up in families (their **families of origin**), and some may have started families of their own (their **families of procreation**) through marriage, bearing children, or both. Your and our experiences with families are valid starting points upon which to build a more complete knowledge of families.

The family in some form is basic to most, or perhaps all, societies. There are many possible definitions for the family, and we wish to take a broad rather than a restrictive view. Therefore, throughout the book we include many types of families, both in our own society and outside of it, within our conception of the family.

## USE OF TERMS AND FRAME OF REFERENCE

Because of our own experiences in countries other than the United States, we include examples from other cultures. We do not dwell at great length upon the many ethnic and class differences within our own society. By "our society" we mean the United States of America and the Dominion of Canada, or for short, North America. We exclude Mexico from our use of the term *North America,* considering it part of Central America instead. Our choice is arbitrary, and we realize that Spanish culture, including Mexican, is very much a part of certain areas in the United States. As with most of life, cultural groups and the geographic areas that they inhabit form a continuum.

Not wanting to overemphasize either the male or female members of families, we have broken with the tradition of referring to an individual who might be male or female as "he." At times we call such an individual "he" or "him," at other times, "she" or "her." If this choice seems strange it is only because we were all brought up taking for granted that the use of the male pronoun is correct.

We also break with the tradition of referring to ourselves as "the authors." We are two people, individuals who have had some common experiences and some unique experiences. When we wish to express a common experience or belief, we use the pronoun "we." However, when we wish to speak as individuals, we do so. After the use of the word "I," we often place our initials in parentheses to show which author is speaking. Conveniently, from my (LSS) point of view, my Mother's initial is an M. In this way, you, the reader, may be able to remember more easily which one of us is the elder author (MSS) and which is the younger (LSS).

## Values

We believe that it is impossible to write a value-free book, and we do not claim to have done so. However, we have tried to make our beliefs clear. We do not expect you to agree with us on all counts; how dull that would be! We hope to challenge you, not to tear down your beliefs, but to give you a new perspective from which to view them. We see such a challenging of values as a part of our own growth as individuals: this statement in itself is a value-laden statement with which you may disagree!

## Tools of the Trade

A person encountering a new experience or environment needs to learn new ways of coping. This may mean adapting old ways, or learning to use new tools or concepts. In this book we use concepts and terms from a number of related fields, including human development, home economics, psychology, sociology, and anthropology. Some students will be familiar with some or all of these terms; to others, the terms will be new. In this chapter we introduce a number of these basic tools of the trade; we bring in more later. For quick reference, the terms may be found in the Glossary (Appendix E) at the back of the book. The learning of new terms may be dull to most students, but once they are understood, they greatly simplify the communication process.

## WHY STUDY FAMILIES?

Although the elders in many societies have always had some concern about what young people were doing, people of all ages are now wondering what is happening to the family in North America. Some people fear that the family will disintegrate and disappear, but it is most unlikely that the fundamental foundation of society will disappear. The family is changing and will go on changing. Many people worry about the high divorce rate, the unwillingness of some couples to get married, adolescent parenthood, the birth of unwanted children, rejection of parenthood, family violence, and isolation of the aged. A study of the family can offer not only insight into such problems, but also some understanding of how positive, healthy relationships can be built and maintained.

Young children take their own family behavior for granted. As a child grows older, she notices differences between her own family and those of her friends. She sees that Sally's grandmother lives with Sally and her parents, that Jeremy lives with his father and not with his mother, that Joanne's parents buy very expensive clothes and toys, that Amy can get her way by having a temper tantrum after her parents have said "No." These small variations between families can give a child the notion that there are many acceptable modes of family living, even though she may still think her own the best.

Through studying the family in a course, a person gains not only a deeper understanding of his or her own family, but also of the "family of man" or people throughout the world, and the processes underlying the ways in which people relate to one another. Both types of knowledge make a person better able to control his or her own life, to resist pressures, to make intelligent choices, to deal with problems, and to live creatively as a family member.

## Personal Choices

When I (LSS) was an undergraduate in the early seventies, many girls suffered from Senior Panic. They felt a terrific pressure to become engaged or even to marry. No doubt some of the pressure came from parents who felt that college was the best place for finding a husband. Peers who were already engaged added to the anxiety of those who had not yet found their partners. Some of the steam has been taken out of Senior Panic, since young women have more choice than they have ever had as to what they will do with their lives and when they will do it. Even so, many real and difficult choices must be made. Having to live up to definite expectations produces one kind of pressure (or even panic), but being free to make very important choices can also result in anxiety. The difficult choices include whether to commit oneself to another person; whether to marry; and, if so, when; whether to have children; and, if so, when and how many.

Most people probably still think that "falling in love" is the basic reason for getting married, but the choice whether to marry should be an active one, and not the passive one implied by the concept of falling in love. Where a person will go as an individual, or as one of a couple or family depends upon many factors, including choosing a compatible partner at the right time under the right circumstances. No one can foresee the future, but by investigating what has happened to others in similar circumstances, one has a better idea of one's own chances. This book raises questions about human interaction that may give the reader more insight into her own behavior.

Never before has the question of the active development of oneself as an individual been more pertinent to family relationships. The human liberation movement, born of women's liberation, has caused many individuals to question their goals. Men are giving up responsible, high-paying jobs in order to learn a trade or profession that they believe will be more personally satisfying. Women are venturing forth from their homes, and some men are returning joyfully to theirs. For others, traditional roles continue to provide sources of satisfaction. Human liberation means that the individual can search for what he believes to be right for him. But it may also encourage selfishness. Emphasis on self-fulfillment can diminish a person's willingness to contribute to other individuals and to social groups, including family and society. A woman can thus justify leaving spouse and children because she felt that while being a wife and mother she was not "growing" or developing *herself*. An aged person is put into a nursing home because his presence in his son's home would curtail the children's freedom and would place a burden of responsibility upon the wife and husband. A volunteer in a social agency decides that she is being exploited, resigns, and gets a job that will reward her with money.

Everyone needs social groups to belong to, including an intimate, familylike group and a community or societal group. Exclusive pursuit of happiness and self-development would be bound to fail, because it would leave a person without family and friends, with nobody who cared and supported. Families and societies would disintegrate as everyone tried to fulfill himself. There has to be a middle way, one in which individuals can enjoy considerable freedom while still meeting some societal demands and feeling bound by certain responsibilities.


## APPROACHES TO THE STUDY OF FAMILIES

Although one's own life experiences are a valid starting point, they are very limited. Research done by social scientists provides a way of distilling the experiences of many persons. The scientific method of study is a value orientation not shared by all persons. It forms the core of this book, because what we have written here is in large part based upon scientific social research. There is considerable room for error on a number of counts, the most important of which is the errors that can be made by the researcher. We have tried to interpret research as accurately as possible.

The following sections of this chapter describe different types of families, starting with the kind most familiar to North Americans. Although this plan may seem like a roundabout way to get to the personal and family questions that most concern students, we think it the soundest route. While the traditional extended family or the polygamous family may look unconnected with present-day life, these structures serve some of the same purposes for which the most modern forms of living are designed.

## The Structures of Families

Every society has its own particular regulations and expectations that show people how to behave in different situations. Each person acquires a set of behavior patterns or **roles** that go with the **positions** he occupies. In each position, his behavior dovetails with that of the other person in that position. In the mother-daughter position, a girl is in the role of daughter to the woman in the role of mother. In one **sibling** position, the girl plays the role of sister to the boy who is playing the role of brother to her. The type of family in a society is the result of the way the positions and role are defined. When we speak of the **structure** of a family, we mean the pattern of positions and roles in it.

Whatever the structure of the family in a particular society, it seems natural and right to most of the people living within it. At first glance, the family structures of other societies may look peculiar, wrong, or inferior. Every form of the human family, however, demonstrates solutions to human problems and represents human creativity. Occasionally students of family and marriage can deepen their awareness by examining nonhuman family forms. Humans are primates, and the other primates, their closest animal relatives, also live in a variety of family forms. These range from promiscuous troops to more limited pairings of males and females to raise their young [10, p. 250].

**Nuclear.** Father, mother, and children make up a unit found in almost all societies, known as the **nuclear family.** When this unit is called the **conjugal family,** it means that the husband-wife relationship is of primary importance. The nuclear family is established and regulated by marriage. There are many different ways in which the nuclear family is attached to other family units and members, sometimes as part of an intricate large family structure and in other times and places as an isolated unit. Throughout Western Europe, the United States, Canada, Australia, New Zealand, and in many other parts of the world, the nuclear unit of a married couple and their children is the most important and usual family form.

Nuclear families are decreasing as a proportion of United States families. Table 1-1 shows types of households in 1978 and 1970 and the extent of changes during the 8-year period. The Census Bureau defines a family as two or more persons, related by blood, marriage, or adoption, and living together [7]. As Table 1-1 shows, households maintained by a married couple have increased by 5.9 per cent, while nonfamily households have increased by 59.7 per cent [21]. There are about 60 million children under 18 living in families with both parents or one parent. Ten million, or 17 per cent, live with their mothers and 1.5 per cent with their fathers.

Living in a nonfamily household does not mean that a person is without family.

ELLEN S. SMART

Many individuals who live alone or with unrelated persons have attachments and warm relationships with their parents, siblings, children, aunts, uncles, and so on. Nuclear families and other family households often have close connections with individuals and other units called the **kin.** Included under kin are grandparents, grandchildren, uncles, aunts, nephews, nieces, cousins, grown brothers and sisters, and their spouses, North American society exerts little, if any, pressure on nuclear units in regard to how much attention they pay to uncles, aunts, nieces, nephews, and cousins, although it is expected that parents and children and brothers and sisters act and feel in certain ways toward each other.

A nuclear family lives only as long as its two focal members, the husband and wife, since the conjugal relationship is what holds the group together. Sometimes a

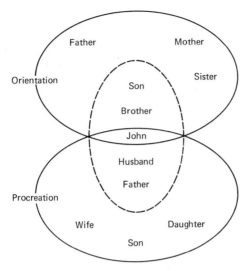

**FIGURE 1-1**    John's two nuclear families. John holds positions of son and brother in his family of origin; husband and father in his family of procreation.

nuclear family is called a *broken family* when one of the conjugal pair dies or leaves the family through divorce or desertion. There is some disagreement as to whether **nuclear** should be applied to a family consisting of one parent and a child or children. The term *one-parent* family makes it quite clear. When children move out of their family of orientation and marry, they start new nuclear units.

**TABLE 1-1**    **Types of Households in 1978 and 1970 (Numbers in thousands)**

| Type of Household | 1978 | | 1970 | | Change, 1970 to 1978 | |
|---|---|---|---|---|---|---|
| | Number | Per Cent | Number | Per Cent | Number | Per Cent |
| Total household | 76,030 | 100.0 | 63,401 | 100.0 | 12,629 | 19.9 |
| Family household | 56,958 | 74.9 | 51,456 | 81.1 | 5,502 | 10.7 |
| Maintained by a | | | | | | |
| Married couple | 47,357 | 62.3 | 44,728 | 70.5 | 2,629 | 5.9 |
| Man, no wife present | 1,564 | 2.1 | 1,228 | 1.9 | 336 | 27.4 |
| Woman, no husband present | 8,037 | 10.6 | 5,500 | 8.7 | 2,537 | 46.1 |
| Nonfamily households | 19,071 | 25.1 | 11,945 | 18.8 | 7,126 | 59.7 |
| Maintained by a | | | | | | |
| Man | 7,811 | 10.3 | 4,063 | 6.4 | 3,748 | 92.2 |
| Woman | 11,261 | 14.8 | 7,882 | 12.4 | 3,379 | 42.9 |

*Source:* U.S. Bureau of the Census, *Current Population Reports,* Series P-20, No. 327, "Households and Families by Type: March 1978" (Advance Report). U.S. Government Printing Office, Washington, D.C., 1978.

Many people think of the typical American family as a nuclear family in which the father goes out to work and the mother stays home to take care of children. Actually, at any given time, only 16 per cent of American families are like this [11]. During their life careers, many more than 16 per cent of people have the experience of living in such a family. A person may have lived thus as a young child. Then the mother goes out to work, or the parents get divorced. The person may set up such a family as a young parent, and maintain it only a few years. Thus during the lifetime family career, an individual lives in several different types of families.

**Extended.**   When nuclear units are integrated into more complicated family structures, however, the resulting families may last for generations. The traditional family of Asia, the **extended** family exemplifies this type of family. An extended family includes two or more nuclear units living in one home, most often an older parent couple with their married sons and the sons' wives and children. Or it may consist of several brothers, their mother, and their wives and children. Many extended families live in India today, especially in rural areas and in the more traditional, smaller cities; the extended family is the ideal, but not the most common, type of family. A study of family types in Ahmedabad, one of the most modern industrial cities, showed about 20 per cent to be extended families [12]. Because 80 per cent of Indians live in rural areas, the total percentage of extended families in India must be considerably larger. About a third of families in Thailand are extended families [18]. An investigation of childrearing in extended Indian families dealt with families that ranged in size from 10 to 28 members, with an average number of 16.5 [1]. We have visited an extended family consisting of more than 40 members. In an extended family, the emphasis is on parent-child bonds, and relationships between siblings, especially brothers. Since "blood ties" hold the family together, it is called the **consanguine** family.

In modern Iceland, after public announcement of betrothal (engagement), a couple may or may not live together, but sexual intimacy is expected [17]. During engagement the pair often live with the parents of one of them, while they save money and prepare for marriage. Therefore, during this period of time, they live in an extended family.

Extended families are similar to communal families in that they are more complex in structure and can perform more functions than the nuclear family. An extended family is usually organized, as some communes are, around a business or occupation that provides work and income for everyone. For example, the Patel family of India owns a textile manufacturing business, in which three adult sons divide the responsibilities of personnel, technology, and sales. Their father, although titular head of the business and the family, has retired from active work. The mother devotes herself to volunteer work while one daughter-in-law runs the household, another is responsible for all the children, and another is a graduate student. In the large, rambling Patel house, each nuclear unit has some private space, but all cooking is done in one kitchen and all eating in one dining room. Thus husbands and wives have some time alone together at night, but during most of the daytime hours,

they are with several members of the consanguine family, sharing work, leisure, and food. The conjugal relationship is diluted in concentration and intensity, in contrast to the husband-wife relationship in the nuclear family, where much of daily life is shared by only the pair. Childrearing is different, too, in both aims and methods.

Most extended families are **patrilineal,** with a father at the head and descent going through the male, as in the Patel family. (Many long-lasting communes are also headed by a strong man.) **Matrilineal** families, those headed by mothers and descended through the female line, also exist in India, Africa, and other places. Since relationships along blood lines (either patrilineal or matrilineal) are very important, terms for relatives are much more exact and numerous than those available in the English language and other Western European languages. In Hindi, one does not say merely, *aunt,* but *bua, thaii, chachi, masi, ma,* or *mami,* depending upon whether the woman is on the paternal or maternal side, whether she is a blood relative or not, and whether she is younger or older. Here there is not merely one role of *niece;* there are six.

Extended families also exist among lower-class ethnic groups in North America where several generations may live in one house. Upper-class extended families, although they may not live in one house, often have joint property. They may build their houses in a cluster, particularly their summer houses. On the seacoast of Rhode Island, there are still clusters of nineteenth-century cottages in which large extended families used to spend their summers and a few still do. Upper-class North American families share some characteristics with Asian extended families. Blood relations are important and the conjugal pair less central than in the middle-class nuclear family. The upper-class family traces its ancestry far into the past and includes present, secondary, and even tertiary members as important. The child in this family would have little choice as to whether he associated with his cousins and behaved warmly to his aunts and uncles. Older members have power and status. Since women normally outlive men, the leader or highest status member of an upper-class family is likely to be a woman with considerable financial power. To the children, it may be a grandmother, great-grandmother, or even a great aunt. The upper-class family controls the choice of marriage partners much more than does a middle-class family, although not as completely as does an Asian extended family. With any extended family, a marriage is a family affair, since it is a link between two ongoing families.

**Polygamous.** When one person has plural spouses at the same time, the marriage is polygamous. The most common form of **polygamy** is **polygyny,** in which a man has more than one wife. **Polyandry,** wherein a woman has more than one husband, is practiced by only a few societies. Polygamy, of course, makes for a family larger than the monogamous, conjugal nuclear family.

Common in Africa and the Middle East, polygyny most often occurs in places where the Islamic religion and culture dominate. The Bible records some polygynous families, such as Jacob's. Polygyny was practiced in pre-Communist China and by Hindus in India before 1957. In the United States, the Mormons used to be polygynous.

Polygamy occurs in the form of group marriages in the United States, but it does not have the support of the law and other institutions. Larry and Joan Constantine [3], who have studied group marriages, say that there may be fewer than one hundred, and certainly less than a thousand such marriages in the United States. Many or most North Americans have little understanding of polygyny; perhaps its being illegal makes it seem immoral. Probably the most common concept of a polygynous family is based on a visual image of an oasis, a harem, a handsome sheik, and a large number of beautiful young women in filmy, full trousers and floating veils. We ourselves admit to surprise and disappointment on first entering the harem (women's quarters) of a Muslim family in India. Secluded from the entrance and the rest of the house, it was an ordinary courtyard with ordinary rooms opening off it. The women's clothes were no different from those of women on the street, just everyday cotton saris. Rather than dancing and playing instruments, the women in the harem were preparing the next meal and taking care of the young children.

In polygynous families, wives are friends, sometimes sisters, often with close, affectionate feelings toward each other. The first wife is likely to have status and authority. Although there are sure to be some disagreements, clashes, or even jealousies when people live together, in the polygynous family there is nothing like the intense jealousy or sense of failure that many a North American wife feels when her husband takes a mistress. In the Yoruba tribe of Nigeria, when over 6,000 wives were asked how they would feel if their husbands took another wife, 60 per cent said that they would be pleased [23]. They would enjoy sharing the care of house, husband and children, and gossiping and playing with the new wife. Only 23 per cent would be angry. The rest were ambivalent.

Among the polyandrous tribal people in the Himalayas, the ideal type of family consists of one woman with several husbands. Often the husbands are brothers. This custom occurs also in South India and among some Eskimo tribes. Where life is very hard and earning a living takes a great deal of effort, it may work out best to have several men supporting one woman and her children. Thus, the population is controlled, since one woman can bear only a certain number of children, no matter how many husbands she has. Female infanticide is often built into the polyandrous family system since the sex ratio will be upset if some women have plural husbands.

**Communal.**   About the only generalization to be made about communal families is that they consist of cooperating groups of people who are committed to their group [15]. Members are not necessarily, but may be, related by blood or marriage. Communal families have lived in various parts of the world in times past, often as Utopian societies. The Oneida Community of New York State, established in 1846, is an American example that has been studied extensively. Much has been written about communal childrearing in the U.S.S.R. and in kibbutzim, communes that have flourished in Israel for half a century. Information on Chinese communes is now available.

**One-Parent.**   Since nearly 17 per cent of children live in one-parent families, a large number of parents and children are represented in this type of structure. Most one-parent families are the result of death, marital breakup, and unplanned unwed motherhood. There are also single women and even a few single men who choose to become parents and to live in one-parent families.

Although many people view one-parent families as merely incomplete or deviant *conjugal* families, a look at the structure reveals something quite different. One adult performs the functions usually shared by two, including earning money, keeping house, and caring for children. The great majority of single parents are women, and many of them are poor. Of the 8.2 million families headed by women, 2.6 million, or 31.7 per cent, are living below the official government poverty line [22]. Of black families headed by a woman, 1.2 million, or 51 per cent, are poor. Because one person must do the work of two, the economic liability of this type of

structure is serious, to say nothing of the limitations on affection, communication, emotional support, helping, and teaching. On the other hand, there are a few one-parent families with adequate income and in which friends and other adult family members give love, support, and help.

**Homosexual.**   When two people of the same sex live together, they may consider themselves a family. Although it seems fairly certain that the majority of North Americans do not think of homosexual pairs as families, this kind of living arrangement makes possible many of the functions and relationships carried out in the conjugal family. Of course the pair cannot reproduce as a heterosexual pair can, but several means of parenthood are open to them: bringing children from former heterosexual partnerships, adoption, artificial insemination, and brief heterosexual relationships for reproductive purposes. Homosexual couples can perform the nurturant socialization of the newborn, the one function that Reiss (see page 14) considers the universal function of the family. Homosexual behavior occurs in all parts of the world among human beings and also among other primates. Of the 76 societies studied by Ford and Beach, 49 societies, or 64 per cent, considered homosexuality acceptable. Some of these societies have an institutionalized form that is a homosexual marriage. Resulting families are structured according to the norms of society. For example, the Kodiak, of Alaska, rear some of their baby boys to play the female role [6, p. 131]. These boys learn women's crafts and wifely homemaking skills, eventually becoming wives of important members of the community. Such a wife is given great respect.

## The Functions of Families

Just what does a family do that makes it a family? Because sociologists have written a great deal about this topic, a group of our students set out to find out what ordinary people thought to be the functions of a family. They tried to secure equal numbers of men and women, distributed between three age groups, under 30, 30 to 60, and over 60. They got answers from 117 people to the questions, "Why do you think people live in families? What are the important things that families do for their members?" Most people (101 out of 117) mentioned *love, affection,* and *emotional security.* All but two of the under 30's mentioned love, as did all of the women between 30 and 60. The next most frequently mentioned function had to do with children, their protection, care, and socialization or upbringing.

**Many Possible Functions.** The number of functions a family might perform are almost unlimited. In fact, one of the marvelous and unique characteristics of the family is that its fields of action are not strictly defined and it can specify new roles, duties, rights, and actions as needed [24]. A list of functions performed by families in various places and times includes the following: love and affection, sex, reproduction, childrearing, health care, education, religion, recreation, production, consumption, and status-giving.

Sometimes all of these functions are performed by a nuclear family. Pioneer families and other isolated families, such as sheep ranchers in New Zealand, must do almost everything for themselves. Sue and Ross, who are in their twenties, live on 120 acres of mostly wooded land in northern Maine. They live in a one-room house without plumbing or electricity. They built this themselves from timber taken from fallen-down barns. Their only source of cash income is ten colonies of honey bees. They have a small garden, an apple orchard, and several hens. In the winter, they are entirely snowed in, and must snowshoe three miles to pick up their mail.

Many functions are more easily carried out by an extended family or a communal family than by a nuclear unit. Where the *conjugal* family is the usual type, other institutions take over a large part of education, religion, production, recreation, and security. In North America, where kin relationships are often optional and nuclear families are largely on their own, families use schools, churches, stores, factories, and recreation facilities. Not long ago families did more and other institutions did less. When faced with modern social problems, a number of people suggest solving them by returning to an older era of multiple family functions. With this mind set, people often complain that the schools are usurping parents' rights, the parents should teach their children to work and be productive in the home, that family religion should be given more attention and that parents should be able to control their children's bad behavior. Letters to the editor still place the blame for delinquency on parents. Public school sex education programs are still hotly debated.

**Universal Functions.** A generation ago, Murdock [13] claimed that the nuclear family is universal and that it always has four functions. Ever since that time, sociologists have been looking for exceptions. Although they have discovered a few, it is still true that the nuclear family can be found in almost all human societies and that it almost always fulfills four functions. These are sexual relations, economic cooperation, reproduction, and **socialization.** One could argue, then, that a celibate commune is not a family, or even that a childless married pair is not a family. The truth is that definitions of family and marriage vary with place, time, and the orientation of the person stating them. Sociologists try to define the family as an institution, in terms that can be tested scientifically. For example, Reiss [16, pp. 18–26] having disproved Murdock, stated the only universal function of the family (nuclear, extended, or otherwise) to be the **nurturant socialization** of the newborn. The group that **nurtures** the newborn, the family, does not have to be biologically related in any particular way, but the society defines its relation to the newborn and views it as right, proper, and obligatory that this group nurture and socialize its infants. The Bureau of the Census, in contrast to the sociologist, defines family in concrete terms that American census-takers can use to decide whether a group of people should be counted as a family.

Although numbers of singles and one-parent families are increasing in North America, the majority of children are born into conjugal families and brought up in those families. A large proportion of conjugal families do provide for sexual relations, economic cooperation, bearing children, and bringing them up. Our students were pleased to see that their findings on the most frequently mentioned family function were in agreement with what their textbooks said about the major function of the family in the United States, the provision of love, affection, and emotional security. Discussing the nuclear family, Udry [20] states, " . . . it provides the major source of emotional security for adults and children during most of life. Marriage is the longest and most significant relationship in life." Udry also points out that the nuclear family is the main consumption unit of our society and that it gives the child a place in the community, determining his opportunities for development and achievement. There are, however, other structures through which people relate to each other in ways that are very important to the participants. Very often love and emotional security are involved, but one or more of the four "universal" functions may be lacking. Some of these structures are legal and socially accepted; some are not. Some are changing status, such as the custom of living together before marriage, which is becoming more and more accepted by society. The Family Impact Seminar, a group of authorities working in Washington, recently defined a family as "any group of two or more persons related by blood, marriage, or adoption." [9]

## Developmental Approach

**Family development** usually refers to the changes that take place in individual nuclear families over time. A nuclear family begins with marriage and ends with the death of one member of the couple. Studies of two or more generations are also done. There are at least two other ways in which the term **family development** might be used. It could be applied to an ongoing family to study generation after generation. Or, the term could refer to changes in the family as an institution in a given culture or society, as is done in the historical study of the family.

**Nuclear Family Development.** A family goes through different stages, each of which has its particular tasks, problems, hazards, and rewards. Thus, families in the same stage of development share many similar conditions and concerns. Researchers usually divide the life of a nuclear family into stages according to the coming, growing up, and departing of children. Evelyn Duvall [4, pp. 113–114], who has written a great deal about family development, points out that there are two main divisions, the *expanding family stage* and the *contracting family stage*. The expanding stage lasts from marriage until all the children are grown; the contracting stage begins when the first child leaves home and ends when one of the pair dies. These two main stages can be split into smaller and smaller stages. The couple without children must be considered in different terms. The family development framework is not so suitable for them.

**Lifetime and Lineage Families.** Because the word *family* has several meanings, Margaret and Harold Feldman [5] have suggested the terms **lifetime family** and **lineage family.** The lifetime family of any individual begins at her birth and ends at her death. During that time she moves into and out of various postions and roles. She is a daughter until her parents die. She may become a sister, niece, cousin, wife, mother, aunt, and grandmother. Movement is always forward in time, never backward and hence the individual does not experience cycles. **Career** is the term used to describe the forward movement. Just as in an occupational career, where events are not repeated, in the parent-child career (one of the family careers), the mother experiences child A's infancy only once. He then becomes a preschool child and a school child, and is never a baby again. The marital career progresses onward, even though the couple may joke about having a second or third honeymoon. The lifetime family career includes, in addition to the marital career and the parent-child career, two more careers, the sexual experience career and the adult-parent career.

The **lineage family** is the family that lasts through time, going on and on through generation after generation. When the family is viewed in this way, the positions remain, but different people move into and out of them as they live their individual careers. "The Heyward family has lived in this house for seven generations!" The Heyward family is a lineage family whose members were born in a particular house. The first male born in each generation lived his lifetime family careers and his occupational career in the house and the surrounding fields. When his lifetime career ended, he went to a nearby cemetery, while the lineage family continued in cycles of births, careers, and deaths. The term *cycle* is appropriate to use with the lineage family, because the events of family living occur over and over again, as new casts of characters play the old roles of baby, sister, brother, father, and so on up to great-grandmother. Although the best-known lineage families are royal or very wealthy families, everyone belongs to lineage families whose cycles stretch back endlessly.

In Europe and North America the patrilineal line forms the base for a family life cycle investigation. In Africa, the matrilineal line is often the base of the family life cycle, as it is among the Akan people of Ghana [14].

**Usefulness of the Developmental Approach.** The developmental approach is useful for doing research on family and individual behavior, changes, crises, strengths, and weaknesses. The practical uses of this approach are great. A young couple can look ahead in order to plan wisely, knowing something of the demands they will encounter in future stages or categories. In teaching college students, we have found that the concept of family life stages helps young women to look beyond finding a husband and living happily ever after. Both sexes learn that the role of parent-of-young-children requires a special set of skills, knowledge, attitudes, and strengths. They come to realize that the parents of school-aged children take on new social roles in regard to the community, that vocations and careers outside the home have their ups and downs in relation to the various family careers. Appreciating how much of life goes beyond the wedding, they tend to see some of their studies as potentially important to later vocations and others as useful in specific aspects of family living. Individuals can gain self-understanding and be better understood if the ebb and flow of their various careers is considered [19]. Persons grow and change with the development, interaction, and decline of careers in family, community, vocations, recreations, religion, and so on. In fact, another example of a helpful developmental point of view is that of a family facing problems peculiar to a certain stage. Even though the solution may be hard to find, it helps to know that other families in their stage face similar dilemmas or that families grow beyond such difficulties.

## The Family as a System

A family can be thought of as a complex system, an organization of people who interact with one another and influence one another in many ways. Their communications with one another are very important in their interactions. A large part of the concern of this book is with interactions within the nuclear family, especially between the husband and wife. Interactions between nuclear family and kinship system are also of interest. The family is only one social system, however, and it operates in connection with many other systems, social and nonsocial.

**The Family's Connection with Nonsocial Systems.** Although we are mainly interested here in the family's interaction with human social systems, we should mention some of the other systems that are significant to family functioning. The survival of the family, in fact human life, is threatened because the ecological system of the world has been changed by man. The family function of reproduction has had a lot to do with upsetting the ecology. And now, food shortages, energy problems, crowding, and pollution are affecting families. One can even go outside the earth to note a system that affects the family system. The solar system affects the family interactions of all who believe in astrology or of all of us, if the believers are correct. The configuration of the stars at the moment of birth is thought to affect the child's personality and his potentialities. Astrologists assert that the stars influence the person continually. Marriages must therefore be made between couples whose horoscopes fit auspiciously and weddings must be performed at the proper moment for heavenly powers to work benignly upon the pair. (Although we ourselves do not use the principles of astrology, we believe that there is something valid in it that remains to be identified scientifically.)

**The Family's Relation to Other Social Systems.** Families are deeply affected by the following: the economic system that determines their level of living and its stability or instability; the occupational system that may dictate where they live, when they move, and how much self-esteem the husband and wife derive from their jobs; the education system that directs learning and self-concepts; the religious system that influences their philosophy of life, morals, social involvement, and perhaps their number of children; the legal system that defines the responsibilities of parents, children, community, and state; the health care system that makes for more or less freedom of choice on family limitation, methods of childbirth, and use of hospitals. Families also affect these other social systems through their interactions with them. Sometimes families organize into a new social system for the purpose of influencing

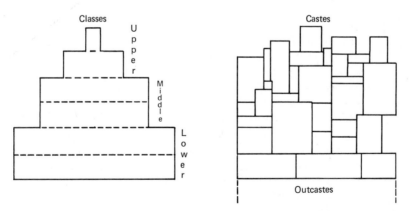

FIGURE 1-2   Schematic representation of class system and caste system. Dotted lines between class divisions indicate that individuals can move from one class to another. The upper class is smallest and hardest to enter. Closed lines around castes indicate that movement is impossible or extremely difficult. There may be a great many castes of varying size. Outcastes are people not included in any caste.

THIS IS WHERE YOU START

**17**

another system. For example, a group of parents formed an organization that changed a hospital's pediatric department by adding a play program and liberalizing visiting regulations.

**Influence of Social Stratification Systems; Caste, Class, and Ethnicity.** Almost all societies organize their members so that some rank higher than others socially and thus have more power and influence. The type of work that people do and the amount of income they receive are often the basis for their social positions. Caste and class are two modes of social organization through which statuses are assigned and maintained. Some differences between class and caste are shown in Figure 1-2.

A **caste** system locks certain people into a particular kind of work or function through inheritance or birth. The Indian caste system still operates to a large extent even though Gandhi and his followers have tried to get rid of it. A child born in a caste of leatherworkers is most likely to become a leatherworker and a child of cloth merchants will most likely go into the family business, each child retaining the same social standing as their *community,* as caste is now called. Most likely they will marry within the community. Some people are outcastes, placed below all the castes. In a caste system, there is often some distinguishing feature of the various castes that enables people in the society to tell one caste from another. Skin color may be such a feature. It has been argued that black people have been in the position of a caste in the United States, since they have been held to a certain status and they can be distinguished physically from the rest of the people.

A **class** system places people into higher and lower groups within the society, giving the higher people more rewards. Older societies, such as the British, are quite strict about keeping individuals in the classes into which they were born, although some movement takes place. In the United States, it is easier to move from one class to another, but not as easy as many people think. New Zealand and Australia are less class-bound than the United States, having fewer divisions and fewer restrictions on social mobility. Class structure also differs from one region of the United States to another, being more rigid and complicated in New England and more open in the West. The class sytem goes against the ideals of democracy and restricts the opportunities of many people. The class system, however, is a reality, although unjust by democratic standards.

The **ethnic group** is an important part of the social structure in North America, Europe, and many other parts of the world. The people in an ethnic group share a culture. Usually they have a common language, religion, and history. They often have distinctive food patterns, music, crafts, and social customs. Different levels of social class can be seen within ethnic groups. For example, there are upper-class, middle-class, and lower-class Blacks, Anglo-Americans, and Jews. Family life, especially child rearing, is influenced by both social class and ethnic group membership. Relative importance varies with both class and group [8].

A family's class and ethnic group are very important in determining the structure and function of that family and its relation to the other social systems. A great deal of American research has been concerned with contrasts between lower- and middle-

NARAGANSETT TIMES

class families, their marriage patterns, sex behavior, childrearing patterns, nutritional intake, learning behavior, and intelligence. Relatively few studies have dealt with the upper class, although it is a favorite topic of novelists. "Privileged Ones: The Well-Off and Rich in America" is a report on the ways in which upper-class parents teach their children how to think and behave as they do [2].

Class and ethnic group can be broken down into a number of more precise components. Instead of trying to compare, for example, middle- and lower-class behavior in general terms, the trend now is to ask the relation of a certain income

level to a certain childrearing practice or to study how families in a certain occupational or residential situation solve a particular problem.

**The Systems Approach to Family Study.**   We have mentioned some of the systems outside the family that influence it and the individuals who comprise it. The systems approach to the family is a theoretical approach that some authors use exclusively. In this book, we do not follow one theoretical orientation to the exclusion of others. We use an approach when it seems to explain best what we are trying to say.

## UNIQUENESS

Every family is special, even though there is much that can be said about families in general. Since every human being is different in some way from all others, the married pair and their family must be a unique combination. Each family is unique in the expectations of the people in various roles, in its patterns of interaction, its history of development, and its relationships with other systems.

Because each family is special, there are no formulas for coping with its crises and problems. A marriage counselor cannot simply turn to page X of his manual and tell his clients to follow prescriptions 5, 8, and 14. A family is continually creating new ways of coping with the situation of the present. When problems are too difficult and a friend or professional is called in to help, that person draws upon what he knows about families and people in general and also creates something new when he applies it to this particular family.

A sense of uniqueness makes a pleasurable bond between family members. Newlyweds, or newlybondeds, often make a big thing out of their uniqueness, having secrets, sending coded messages, communicating with private looks and gestures. As the family life careers progress for a pair, they and their children may develop solidarity through a private communication system with invented words, family rituals, or jokes that are not funny to outsiders. Our family has many cherished special words that we use in private conversations and letters to each other. Thus we laugh, we remember shared incidents, we acknowledge past immaturities, and we affirm our membership in our own very special family.

**SUMMARY**  Personal experiences, observations, and research are all valid sources of information about families. This book is primarily concerned with persons and families living in the United States and Canada, but draws upon supplementary information from many parts of the world. We have chosen and defined certain terms, approaches, and values. Family studies lead to understanding of self and others, promoting personal liberation by extending the individual's choices. Family-related social problems require scientific study as part of the efforts to solve them.

Families consist of persons acting toward each other in certain expected ways, with some leeway in creating new interactions. Although every family is unique, certain types predominate in various parts of the world and in various positions in each society. The most common or basic unit is the nuclear family, consisting of a married couple and their children. Nuclear units are, in some places, incorporated into extended families. Monogamy and polygamy are variations in marital customs. Communal families include many different types, organized in a variety of ways, but committed to their groups and working together in some way. One-parent families, also varied in structure and behavior, constitute a sizable proportion of North American families. Homosexual pairs may be considered families.

Families perform few or many and varied functions, according to the demands on them and the opportunities for action. Changes in family functions reflect changes in the whole society.

The developmental approach to the study of the family focuses on changes that take place in a family and its members, over a span of years. Stages are defined according to the birth, maturing, and departure of children. The careers concept is helpful in studying individual development. *Cycles* refers most accurately to the generational or lineage family. The family can be thought of as a social system, related to the other systems in society and also to biological and physical systems. Ecology and economics are of concern to many people today as they face problems facing individuals and families.

The status and power held by each family bear some relation to the whole society of which that family is a part. A class system organizes social placement, but allows some movement from one class to another. A caste system is more closed. Ethnic groups, important determinants of behavior, cut across social class divisions.

**REFERENCES**

1. Ames, E. W. Family structure and childrearing in India. Paper presented at meeting of the Society for Research in Child Development, Minneapolis, 1971.
2. Coles, Robert. *Privileged ones: The well-off and the rich in America. Children of crisis:* Vol. 5 Boston: Little, Brown, 1977.
3. Constantine, Larry L. and Joan M. Constantine. The group marriage. In Michael Gordon (Ed.), *The nuclear family in crisis: The search for an alternative.* New York: Harper, 1972.
4. Duvall, Evelyn M. *Marriage and family development.* (5th ed.) Philadelphia: Lippincott, 1977.
5. Feldman, Margaret and Harold Feldman. The family life cycle: Some suggestions for recycling. *Journal of Marriage and the Family,* 1975, **37,** 277–284.
6. Ford, Clellan S. and Frank A. Beach. *Patterns of sexual behavior.* New York: Harper, 1951.
7. Glick, Paul C. and A. J. Norton. Marrying, divorcing and living together in the United States today. *Population Bulletin,* **32,** No. 5. Washington, D.C.: Population Reference Bureau, Inc., 1977.
8. Havighurst, Robert J. The relative importance of social class and ethnicity in human development. *Human Development,* 1976, **19,** 56–64.
9. Institute for Educational Leadership. *Family impact seminar: An introduction.* Washington D.C., 1977.
10. Jolly, Alison. *The evolution of primate behavior.* New York: Macmillan, 1972.
11. Kahn, Alfred J. Policies for families: What can we do? Paper presented at meeting of the Groves Conference, Washington, D.C., 1978.
12. Khatri, A. A. The Indian family: An empirically derived analysis of shifts in size and types. *Journal of Marriage and the Family,* 1972, **34,** 725–734.
13. Murdock, George P. *Social structure.* New York: Macmillan, 1949.
14. Oppong, Christine. *Marriage among a matrilineal elite.* Cambridge: U.P., 1974.
15. Ramey, James W. Communes, group marriage, and the upper-middle class. *Journal of Marriage and the Family,* 1972, **34,** 647–655.
16. Reiss, Ira L. *The family system in America.* New York: Holt, 1971.
17. Rich, George W. The domestic cycle in modern Iceland. *Journal of Marriage and the Family,* 1978, **40,** 173–183.
18. Smith, Harold E. The Thai family: Nuclear or extended. *Journal of Marriage and the Family,* 1973, **35,** 126–141.

19. Spence, Donald L. and Thomas D. Lonner. Career set: a resource through transitions and crises. *Aging and Human Development,* 1978, **9,** 51–64.
20. Udry, J. Richard. *The social context of marriage.* 2nd ed. Philadelphia: Lippincott, 1974.
21. U.S. Bureau of the Census. *Households and families by type: March 1978* (Advance Report). Current Population Reports, Series P-20, No. 327. Washington, D.C.: U.S. Government Printing Office, 1978.
22. U.S. Bureau of the Census. *Money income and poverty status of families and persons in the United States: 1977* (Advance Report). Current Population Reports, Series P-60, No. 116. Washington, D.C.: U.S. Government Printing Office, 1978.
23. Ware, Helen. Polygyny: Women's views in a transitional society, Nigeria, 1975. *Journal of Marriage and the Family,* 1979, *41,* 185–195.
24. Zimmerman, Carle C. The future of the family in America. *Journal of Marriage and the Family,* 1972, **34,** 323–333.

# CHAPTER 2

# LOVE, LOVE, LOVE

The most ancient of written records show mankind as involved in love, but nobody, ancient or modern has been able to define *love* exactly or to tell just how it operates. Many great religious documents deal with the love of God, and also with brotherly and neighborly love. Because this book is focused on family interaction, we deal with the individual's development as a loving being and with the love between partners and family members.

Being **in love** is one kind of love, important in itself and in forming partnerships on which families are established. Love is important at every age and stage, since everyone needs to love and be loved. Love is different at each age and stage, since it expresses what a person has learned and experienced. Love is viewed differently in various places and at various times. By describing its development in several settings, we hope to give a perspective from which the reader can better understand himself and his love relationships. A broad understanding of love is basic to gaining insight into the significance of love in finding and choosing a partner and building a marriage or a lasting, meaningful relationship.

## EVOLUTION OF LOVE

Love includes actions and feelings or inner experiences. Some of the behavior characteristics of human love can be observed in many living things. Attachment and care behavior are ways in which human love is expressed and developed. When one creature makes repeated efforts to gain and keep the proximity of a certain other creature, he is **attached** to that creature. When the attempts are mutual, there is an

**attachment** between the two. Attachment is a part of love, a basic, essential part, but not all of it.

Attachments occur in nonhuman creatures as well as in people of all ages. Lorenz [16, pp. 32–36], an ethologist, tells about a chichlid fish that seemed to be attached to a special female. Geese and gannets mate monogamously for life. Beach has shown that dogs show preferences for specific individuals as mates, retaining these attitudes for as long as 66 months [3]. Attachment in dogs and people does not have to be sexually based. Nick, a dog we had while I (MSS) was a child, had a dog friend called Mac, who lived across the street. As soon as Mac was let out in the morning, he came to our front steps and sat on his hind legs, watching the door until Nick was let out. The two dogs played and stayed close together all day.

Primates show a large variety of attachments between individuals [14, p. 254]. A chimpanzee, Flo, who has been studied in her natural habitat for many years, maintained close relationships with her four children. A family photograph shows

Flo grooming eleven-year-old Faben while four-year-old Fifi plays with the new baby, and Figan, age seven, sprawls nearby. Studies of Japanese macaques have revealed extended families. In one, a mother and her brother lived in close proximity and the brother helped to take care of his nieces and nephews.

Mammals and birds take care of their young, feeding, grooming, warming, and protecting them from injury. Mates perform some of these functions for each other, too. Monkeys, especially young females, enjoy baby-sitting, taking care of infants belonging to other females. If a mother dies, her infant may be adopted.

Attachment and care behavior are elements of human love that combine with other behaviors and feelings. Through growth and learning, the individual develops complex modes of loving that are distinctively human.

## A LOVE CAREER

This section, deals with the development of loving through personal interaction. The human baby is born with great potentialities for loving, some of which he shares with animals, birds, and fish, others of which are especially human.

The life of an individual starts in a very small social world and expands to include more and more people, more types of social interaction, more ways of loving, learning, and growing. Figure 2-1 is a diagram that shows seven stages in the expansion of life and love. The self, a dot at first, becomes a cone that expands as the individual interacts with other people. The mother is the first of the other people,

**FIGURE 2-1**    Stages in the expansion of life and love.

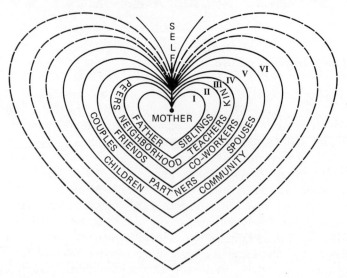

represented in a heart-shaped space with the baby's self filling the top of the heart. Concentric hearts represent the significant people as they are added to the child's social world. As the baby's world expands, he interacts with more people and more categories of people. In this process, he and the others learn to love. The following sections deal with the first six stages of this process.

## Infant-Mother

Under ordinary circumstances, the baby's first relationship is with his mother. She cares for him and they become attached to each other.

**Attachment.** A newborn is equipped for building attachments to other persons. Since there is another person especially equipped to build an attachment to this baby, the result is certain, unless something goes wrong with the natural process. The infant and mother become attached to each other through their own actions, pieces of behavior that fit together like keys and locks. (This process is described in detail by the ethologists, particularly Ainsworth.)

Ainsworth defines attachment as "an affectional tie that one person forms between himself and another specific person, binding them together in space and enduring over time" [1]. Bowlby, the originator of the use of *attachment* in this sense, says, "No form of behavior is accompanied by stronger feelings than is attachment behavior. The figures toward whom it is directed are loved and their advent is greeted with joy" [4, p. 209].

A mother and baby begin to form bonds of attachment when they interact immediately after birth. After a normal birth with little or no medication, a baby is alert, looking at what falls within his gaze, with eyes especially attracted to faces and eyes. The mother looks into the baby's eyes. She touches her baby's fingers and toes, arms and legs, and finally moves her whole hands from limbs to trunk [15]. These experiences are known to have lasting effects on the mother's attachment to her baby. When fathers take part in birth, or even when they are included in the early hours and days of postnatal life, they quickly develop attachment to and tenderness toward their babies.

The newborn infant can root (move his head to find the nipple) and suck, thus taking part in finding his mother's breast and obtaining milk from it. When held against another person's chest, with his head at the shoulder, the baby cuddles. He looks at faces more than at other objects and at eyes more than at any other part of the face. He listens to sounds, especially to voices. He cries. Within the early weeks, he smiles and vocalizes, soon doing so to particular people and in response to particular actions. Human infants also grasp and cling, although not as strongly as do other primates. All these behaviors serve to bring the parents close to the baby, to make them respond to him, care for him, feel pleasure in him, and become attached to him. As the parent and child respond to each other, their attachment grows stronger.

A baby shows that he is attached to his parents by crying when they leave, trying to follow them and looking for them. When a baby is with his parent, he derives security that enables him to explore strange places and toys and to allow strange people to come close to him. Perhaps this security is a reflection of his experience of *care*, his knowledge that his parent cares for him.

**Respect.** There is another aspect of infant love that Ainsworth and her associates have demonstrated. By one year of age, babies tend to obey and to cooperate with the people to whom they are attached. The more harmonious the infant-mother relationship during the first year, the more the baby tries to do what he perceives his mother as wanting him to do [27].

In infant obedience and cooperation, we can see the origins of *respect,* one of the elements of love. Respect involves realizing that the other person is an individual with needs and wants, letting the other person be himself, helping him to grow in his own ways [11, pp. 26–29]. In suppressing his impulses and trying to cooperate with what his mother asks him to do, the baby is respecting her as a person with wishes separate from his own. Thus, the care and respect that a baby receives in the first budding of love is in the attachment process, which is biologically based and set to go at birth. In the context of attachment, the mother's care and respect for the infant give rise to the infant's respect for her.

## Infant-Father

Section II in the diagram (Figure 2-1) includes father, siblings, and any other members of the household.

A father may be very close to his baby, or very distant from her. Among all the interactions that mothers can have with infants, breastfeeding is the only one that a father cannot also have. And because many mothers do not breastfeed, the possibilities open to both parents are about the same. Several studies have shown fathers to be just as interested and nurturant as mothers, but more playful [21]. Fathers tended to be more physical and exciting than mothers in playing with babies. Mothers were more likely to talk to babies and to play conventional games, such as peek-a-boo. Babies often showed that they had more fun playing with fathers. Several studies seem to show that in most homes the father's main role is that of playmate to the baby, while the mother is the main caretaker. However, there are a few fathers who share caretaking equally and some who are the main caretakers of infants. A study of these fathers, called primary caretakers, showed them to behave more like mothers than do secondary caretakers (that is, most) fathers [10]. Primary caretaker fathers included play that was like mothers' play more than did secondary caretaker fathers. The former and the mothers did more smiling and mimicking in high-pitched voices, probably because they knew their babies so well and realized that babies enjoy and respond to this kind of behavior. When fathers participate in infant care, then, they play in a greater variety of ways, using the typical repertories of fathers and also doing what mothers typically do.

## The Home Circle

If there are older children in the family, the baby ordinarily becomes attached to them as well as to the father and to other household members or people who often come in and out. The baby is most likely to build attachments with people who play with her and pay attention to her, offering interesting stimulation.

## Self

Figure 2-1 shows a wedge that represents the self as part of the individual's development in love. This portion begins as a small part of the infant-mother circle and increases as the child grows and encounters more and more of the social world. Love of self includes *knowledge, respect,* and *care* [11, p. 26]. The infant comes to know herself through her own senses and actions and through the ways in which her parents and siblings see her. If they show her that she is lovable through their enjoyment, care, and respect, she knows she is lovable. Through testing her own powers of mind and muscle, making some decisions that turn out well, she comes to *know* herself as a person in her own right, an autonomous, lovable person.

## The Neighborhood Circle

Peers, kin, and teachers make up Section III of Figure 2-1. Much of the action is outside the home but is still closely related to it. Grandparents, aunts, and uncles may give **unconditional love,** acceptance of the child for who she is (grandchild, niece). Peers and teachers are more demanding and selective, rewarding her when she fits their expectations, punishing her when she does not.

At home and in the neighborhood, young children explore love relationships through play, pretending to be mommies, daddies, and children sorting out ideas and feelings. In doll play and dramatic play with peers, the child rehearses attachment behavior, care, and even respect and knowledge of the beloved. Sex play between peers is common at this age, because of a desire for knowledge of self and others and of the processes of life itself. *Care* is shown in efforts to help at home and to give to friends and family. *Respect* for the wishes of others (parents, teachers, siblings) shows in cooperation. Love-oriented behavior can be dampened by shame, guilt, and feelings of powerlessness.

## Friends and Co-Workers

Section IV corresponds to the school age and early adolescence. The personnel of previous stages continue to interact with the child but now the important new influences are friends and work. Both help the child to develop that part of loving that is knowledge.

**Friends.**   At this age, friends are likely to be the same age and the same sex. The strength of attachment between the pair determines the closeness of the friendship. Attachment behavior is not so biologically based as it is in infancy, but rather depends upon proximity, shared activity, and communication.

Through long talks with close friends, a child reaches into the deeper parts of the human personality and gets new insight into love. The love is for the child's own self as well as for others, because the most pressing task at this point is to achieve better self-understanding. The problem is to develop a strong sense of identity, as Erikson has explained and most young people well know [9]. The adolescent has to recognize himself as the child he was, anticipate himself as the adult he will be, and accept himself as he now is, to feel that his family, friends, and community are worthwhile and that he fits into the whole scene. Thus, he needs to know and respect himself in connection with all the people in his life and to know, respect, and care for them too. Through his attachments to a few friends, he works on these problems.

**Work.** Through work, both at school and in jobs, the young person learns *responsibility* for himself and others. He *responds* to social needs by becoming competent and producing. He also contributes to his self-knowledge and self-respect and to the feelings of being an important part of his society. Teachers are key figures in helping young people to be worthy workers, both in the way they see their students and in the skills they teach. Parents and other adults do likewise. And although the students do not feel love from teachers in the same sense that they feel it from family and friends, they know respect, care, and knowledge to the extent that teachers offer them.

## Lovers and Spouses

By the time a person can become a committed member of a pair, that person has loved his or her way through four sections of our diagram and has piled up a good deal of experience. He or she has formed attachments to parents, siblings, kin, and friends. Within the context of various attachments, the boy or girl has cared for other people, respected them, responded to them, taken responsibility for them, and sought to know and understand them. Childhood family attachments do not end as a person grows up. Bonds to parents, and often additional family bonds, remain strong throughout life, although attachment behavior may change. During the teen years, a new kind of love relationship appears. Books addressed to lovers usually begin here, often with the question, "How do you know you are in love?"

**In Love.** Being in love is usually easy to recognize. It includes the very strong feelings that Bowlby (see page 27) recognized as accompanying attachment behavior, efforts to attain and keep proximity to the loved one (attachment behavior), and sexual response. The combination of all these strong feelings often blocks out other perceptions, feelings, and actions, even affecting breathing and heart rate.

> How does Love speak?
> In the faint flush upon the telltale cheek,

And in the pallor that succeeds it; by
The quivering lid of an averted eye—
The smile that proves the parent to a sigh
      Thus does Love speak.
      How does Love speak?
By the uneven heart-throbs, and the freak
Of bounding pulses that stand still and ache,
While new emotions, like strange barges, make
Along vein-channels their disturbing course;
Still as the dawn, and with the dawn's swift force—
      Thus doth Love speak.[30, p. 9]

The state of being in love is often temporary. The word *infatuation* is frequently used to refer to what we have called being in love, but we object to this word because it implies deception, or that the relationship is shallow and will remain shallow, and is therefore doomed. Rather, some couples who are in love progress to a more stable, less exhilarating kind of love; others "fall out of love" or cease to be in love with each other. When looking back upon their now defunct love, many couples declare that they never really loved each other; it was only infatuation. The next time they feel the same way about a new person, they again say that they are "in love."

What we have called being "in love" is not enough to build a lifelong relationship upon, but it is a beginning. Furthermore, as the years progress, the excitement, desire for closeness, and sexual response that one feels in the early stages of being "in love" add sparkle to a relationship that has become more concerned with day-to-day life than with the exhilaration of courtship.

For some couples, the "in love" feelings appear to give way completely to another kind of love.

After the fierce midsummer all ablaze
Has burned itself to ashes and expires
In the intensity of its own fires,
There come the mellow, mild, St. Martin days
Crowned with the calm of peace, but sad with haze.
So after Love has led us, till he tires
Of his own throes and torments and desires. [30, p. 21]

Being in love usually involves two people of opposite sexes, since the sexual behavior system is activated, along with attachment behavior. After the arousal of attachment behavior and sexual response, what happens depends upon both the loved one and the social setting. Sometimes only one person is in love and the other person does not respond in like fashion. Mutuality is essential for the development of a relationship and unrequited love usually fades away, though not without pain. Many popular songs deal with the sadness of one who was loved but is no longer, such as the classic "Smoke Gets in Your Eyes." Trying to hide his tears, the singer pretends that the dying flame of his love has enveloped him in smoke.

The role of family, kin, friends, and society is so important that we devote the next section to it, under the heading *Lovers in Time and Space*. First we must discuss the next step in the love career—partnership love.

When couples ask, "How do we know we are really in love?" what they often mean is, "Do we love each other enough to get married or to set up housekeeping together or to make some sort of commitment to each other?" They are not asking whether their hearts are beating fast enough or whether they are sufficiently breathless. They wonder about whether their desire to be with each other will last and if it will be satisfying for them to live as partners.

Partnership love includes being *in love* (attachment plus sexual response) and the elements that Fromm [11, pp. 7–38] has called *care, responsibility, respect,* and *knowledge*. In previous stages of growth, the individual has learned something of these aspects of love, through receiving them from other people, through practicing them in simple ways and rehearsing them in dramatic play. If the childhood and adolescent learning of love have gone well, the person in love has some substance with which to anchor ephemeral feelings.

Partnership love is obviously mutual. Each feels that together they are a couple. The are **pair-bonded,** Fromm says. Two people care for each other and take care of each other. Respect is reciprocal. Both are responsible and responsive to one another. Each continually seeks to know the other. Fromm suggests that man's need to love and be loved in this full sense arises from his feeling separate and alone. The only way to escape continually from aloneness is to love. In knowing another person deeply, one feels united. "Love is the only way of knowledge, which in the act of union answers my quest. In the act of loving, of giving myself, I discover us both, I discover man" [11, p. 31].

Erikson's concept of the **sense of intimacy** is a similar insight into knowing as loving. The main problem of growth for the older adolescent or young adult is to learn how to know another person deeply and to be known by him or her. The process is a two-way interaction, in which each person tries to experience the other person deeply, to know and understand the other's thoughts and feelings, and in turn to allow the partner to experience, to know and understand him. Lack of intimacy means *isolation* [8]. Murstein's research confirms Erikson's ideas on intimacy [19]. Progress in courtship was correlated most highly with being understood by the partner and understanding the partner. Courtship progress was also related to sexual compatibility and to couple agreement on self-perceptions and ideal perceptions.

A mature person establishes intimate interactions with the people he or she loves, close (intimate) friends, as well as family. When a sex relationship is part of love, the intimacy is more complete. Fromm [11, p. 33] goes on to say that man and woman are aware of sexual polarity, division along sex lines, and also know that each carries both male and female characteristics. Union between a man and woman therefore carries a sense of unity that yields the deepest knowledge of others and self. Erikson [8, p. 265] also regards heterosexual mutuality as the deepest sort of intimacy.". . . . the total fact of finding, via the climactic turmoil of the orgasm, a supreme experience of the mutual regulation of two beings in some way takes the edge off the hostilities and potential rages caused by the oppositeness of male and female, of fact and fancy, of love and hate."

Much of this book is concerned with the development of the sense of intimacy, with knowing and responding. The chapter on communication is about the process of knowing and being known. The theme of knowing and intimacy as emphasized in this book also runs through discussions of family interaction, sex relationships, family problems, and therapy.

To return to the question of what kind of love is adequate for marriage or commitment in Western culture, we suggest that partnership love is the right kind. Since nobody is perfect in ability to feel and give care, respect, responsibility, and knowledge, partners keep working at all this. But love is not enough. Love partners interact with other people, and families with other social systems.

We discuss the process of selecting a partner further in Chapter 6, and the process of maintaining the partner relationship is discussed further in Chapters 7 and 8. Love plays an important role in both processes, but can neither explain the processes or keep them functioning by itself, as we show.

## LOVERS IN TIME AND SPACE

People fall in love everywhere. They have done so since, and probably before, the beginning of recorded history. The development of the love affair depends very much on where and when it takes place. The behavior, feelings, and beliefs of the pair are heavily influenced by the beliefs and values of the people around them, by the customs and laws of their community and society. All cultures recognize the situation of attachment-and-sexual-response that we call being in love. It may be regarded as universal or exceptional, delightful or deplorable, sweet or sick. In the examples that follow, we start with our own culture and go on to some others that illustrate various attitudes toward lovers and the functions of being in love.

### Here and Now

In North America it is commonly believed that everyone, child or adult, is entitled to love. As mentioned in Chapter 1, love is thought to be the most important function of the family. The state of being in love is also highly esteemed. Being in love is the basis on which to choose a marriage partner. Although it is acceptable to give thought to other considerations, such as moral character and religion, to marry for money is considered despicable. Of course, there are exceptions to this general picture. Property and lineage are important in the upper class, where parents and the

A Rajput prince and princess are depicted smoking (hashish?) together in this eighteenth century Indian miniature.

extended family have considerable control over partner selection. Some ethnic groups also permit parental control and stress mate selection factors other than being in love.

Being in love is also the basis for continuing a marriage, as the **high** divorce rate suggests. There is some difference of opinion on whether a marriage should be broken if the couple fall out of love, but it is acknowledged as highly desirable that the in-love state should be maintained throughout a marriage. Attachment and sexual response are not the only salient aspects of love and marriage, as shown by columnists such as Ann Landers, and by articles in popular magazines that deal with partnership love and the technologies of family living. The in-love state is nevertheless of tremendous importance, since it is stimulated and sustained at a high pitch by the romantic love complex.

**Romantic Love.** Many North Americans and Europeans believe strongly in romantic love, although there is evidence that romantic love is declining [31]. A complex of feelings and ideas make up romantic love: attraction and attachment to one particular person, excitement, depression, mystery, possessiveness, jealousy, idealizing, perfection in the other and unworthiness, yet hope, in the self. There is one true mate for each person, and if people are lucky, they find their ideal loves. Romantic love is blind. It thrives on not perceiving reality and is therefore enhanced by beautiful clothes, makeup, moonlight, candlelight, firelight, perfume, music, and strange places. Participants remain mysterious and therefore attractive by holding

back information about themselves or even deliberately creating false impressions. Each can then believe what she (he) wants to believe about the other, creating the person in the image of the ideal.

As some later examples will show, romantic love occurs more often in some times and places than in others. One condition that seems to promote romantic love is the blockage of sexual expression [31]. There is evidence that romantic love thrives more in cultures that restrict nudity and premarital sex than in those where sexual freedom is the norm. Since permissiveness for nonmarital sex has been increasing in the United States, one would expect romantic love to decline, and indeed, it seems to be doing so. One piece of evidence is the decrease in popular songs dealing with romantic themes. For example, song hits in the 70's contained words such as *heavenly* and *angel* only half as often as songs in the period from 1954 to 1958 [2].

**Exploitation of the Romantic Love Complex.** Other systems in our society impinge upon the courtship and marriage system at the point of falling in love and on the basis of staying in love. The economic system zeroes in on lovers through the advertising industry and the entertainment industry. Both industries play shamelessly and successfully upon themes from the romantic complex.

Advertisements proclaim that attachment and sexual response will reward those who groom and adorn themselves with certain products, including tooth paste, tooth polish, mouthwash, soap, deodorants, razors, shampoo, hair rinse, hair dye, face creams, moisturizers, cuticle cream, and nail polish; medicate themselves with aspirin, stomach-settlers, laxatives, appetite depressants, vitamins, and sleep-inducers; consume or make use of soft drinks, cigarettes, cars, and mattresses. There is some validity to claims that beauty and health will make a person more fall-in-lovable, but it is farfetched to say that a particular shampoo will make a person irresistible to the opposite sex. Therefore, advertisers cleverly refrain from saying just that, but build up a picture that strongly suggests it. Linking a mattress with sexual response is more easily credible. There is necessarily more innuendo in regard to soft drinks and cars, since direct statements about inducing attachment and response would be even more absurd than in the case of tooth paste. I (MSS) can remember back to adolescence when an ad for a beauty mask parted me from a week's allowance, giving me hope of enchanting the boy who sat across the aisle from me.

The entertainment industry shapes everyone's ideas about love, through songs, films, and television. The desirability of being in love is stressed, with directions on how to achieve it and how to feel when things go right or wrong, when it does not happen, and when a love affair breaks up.

**Counter Themes.** Although romantic love is a strong influence, there are contemporary themes that do not fit the romantic picture: equality between the sexes; honest communication; emphasis on the immediate present; the importance of individual development and self-expression. There seems to be a growing acceptance of such ideas as that being in love can be very temporary, monogamy is too restricting, and everyone is entitled to entertainment through sex, either as observer or participant.

Another theme in North American concepts of love is a realistic view of marriage as a partnership. The ideal is a strong love of the type we have described as partnership love. Cooperation, communication, and application of homemaking knowledge are seen as keys to satisfying family interaction and personal development. Romantic love contributes important threads to the fabric of a marriage. This is the point of view shown in some magazines and newspaper features.

**Studies on Attraction.** Psychologists and sociologists are doing research to find out what makes a person like, love, dislike, or hate certain other individuals [5]. This topic is discussed further in Chapter 6. Here we are especially interested in what makes people fall in love. If falling in love is romantic, then, according to definition, it has little to do with knowing and understanding the other person, but is much concerned with an attractive exterior. Although research has shown that similarity in certain personality characteristics, attitudes, and opinions stimulates liking, studies also show that physical attractiveness is indeed important in choices made by both men and women.

Some insight into loving as different from liking can be gained by looking at the items in a scale that measures loving and liking [25]. The scale was derived from answers given by college students who checked the questions once in reference to a girlfriend or boyfriend and once in reference to a platonic friend of the opposite sex. In the following questions from the love scale, the respondent marks in one of 9 points, from *not at all true; disagree completely* through *definitely true; agree completely*. The girlfriend's or boyfriend's name is to be put into the blank. Some of the items from the love scale are these:

I feel that I can confide in __ about virtually anything.
I find it easy to ignore __'s faults.
I feel very possessive toward __.
If I were lonely, my first thought would be to seek out __.
I would forgive __ for practically anything.
I feel responsible for __'s well-being.
When I am with __, I spend a great deal of time just looking at her (him).

Scores on the love scale were highly related to the respondents' reports on whether they were in love and whether they expected to marry the person. Liking scores were only moderately related to being in love and intending marriage.

Another attempt to distinguish between loving and liking met with some success [20]. College students checked statements referring to another person whom they identified as being the object of dating, friendship, or love. The love group indicated that they felt more attachment, altruism, and physical attraction for their partners than did the friendship group. The love and friendship groups were about the same in their expressions of respect for the other person.

Studies such as these indicate that careful questioning can distinguish between loving and liking. Such questionnaires can help individuals to judge the depth of their feeling for potential partners. The questionnaire in Appendix A in this book is intended to stimulate discussion between couples, not to help the individual to decide whether his feeling is loving or liking.

## Evolution of Love in the West

The study of the history of the family is in its infancy. Available research has little to say about love, but plenty to say about sex and marriage [7, 13, 24]. Other cultures have provided varying amounts of information regarding love. In this section, we briefly trace the development of love in Western culture. Then we look at three contrasting cultures, Samoan and ancient and modern Indian.

**The Ancient World.** The Old Testament tells some stories about couples falling in love, but on the whole, it treats being in love as of little importance. The Song of Solomon is a romantic expression, but the biblical focus is usually on God and upon playing one's proper role in human affairs. The New Testament teaches much about spiritual and brotherly love, but little about falling in love or erotic love. The Greeks and Romans were interested in love, including romantic love and homosexual love. They contributed some ideas that survive today.

**The Middle Ages.** Romantic love developed to a high degree in Europe, beginning in the twelfth century, as courtly love. Love was a favorite topic of conversation at court. The *Treatise on Love,* by Andreas Capellanus is a report on what Queen Eleanor of France (later of England) and her courtiers thought to be the nature and proper conduct of love. Love affairs were not preludes to marriage, nor were they between spouses. They were extramarital affairs. The woman was married to someone else and sometimes the man was also married [6].

Capellanus starts with a definition of love that includes several romantic notions. "Love is a certain inborn suffering derived from the sight of and excessive meditation upon the beauty of the opposite sex, which causes each one to wish above all things the embraces of the other and by common desire to carry out all of love's precepts in the other's embrace" [6, p. 28].

Attachment was explained by Capellanus. The very word *love,* in Latin *amor,* comes from the word *amus,* meaning "hook" or "capture." Thus, the attachment aspect of love is contained in its name. " . . . the man who is a captive of love tries to attract another person by his allurements and exerts all his efforts to unite two different hearts with an intangible bond. . . ." [p. 31].

The treatise includes a list of 31 rules on how love is to be conducted. In the rules can be seen many of the romantic ideas that persist today: it is possible to fall in love with someone other than one's spouse; lovers are always jealous, and jealousy stimulates love; everyone is entitled to love; no one can love two partners at once and a true lover does not seek other partners; greed and love are incompatible; love fades when made public and changes easily anyway; frustration enhances love; seeing one's lover causes paleness, heart palpitations, lack of appetite and sleeplessness; being in love means thinking constantly about the beloved and trying to please him. Courtly love was definitely for the royalty and nobility. Capellanus tells just how a would-be lover should approach someone from a class lower or higher than his own and what she should answer. As for peasants (farmers), they should not be instructed in the theory and practice of love, lest they neglect their work. However, if a nobleman should be so foolish as to fall in love with a farmer's daughter, Capellanus' advice was, " . . . be careful to puff them up with lots of praise and then, when you find a convenient place, do not hesitate to take what you seek and embrace them by force."

**The Puritans.**    In contrast to the nobility of the Middle Ages, the Puritans who settled this continent did not have the time or resources to make an art out of love. They certainly did not leave great treatises on love for us to read. Their religion emphasized work in the service of God, and there was much work to be done. Love was probably taken for granted as one small part of life. Sex was to be enjoyed within the confines of marriage, but neither sex nor love in marriage was supposed to infringe upon man's or woman's love for God. " . . . Husband and wife must not become 'so transported with affection, that they look at no higher end than marriage it self (sic) [18].

Some sermons published in Boston in 1712 mention the duties of husbands and wives to each other.

> They should love while detailing endeavor to have their affections really, cordially and closely knit, to each other. . . . (God) requires Husbands and Wives to have and manifest very great affection, love and kindness to one another. They should (out of Conscience to God) study and strive to render each other's life easy, quiet and comfortable; to please, gratify and oblige one another, as far as lawfully they can . . . yet let this caution be minded that they dont (sic) love inordinately, because death will soon part them. [28]

**The Victorians.**    Historical material from the nineteenth century, the Victorian period, shows a very different attitude toward the relationships between men and women. Prudery and double talk were the order of the day. Women were supposed to be pure (sexually), strongly virtuous, weak, inferior to men, superior to men, competent, incompetent, and pious. Writings of women and about women of this period show that the love of her husband and the privilege of loving were supposed to be full and sufficient rewards for all sorts of self-denigration and self-suppression on the part of the woman. Women's duty was to resist men's sexual advances before marriage and to submit to them quietly after marriage [29].

The romantic theme dominant in the Victorian era is that of idealizing the woman, of putting her on a pedestal, and never viewing her as a person. Probably women did not really see men as persons either. Each sex maintained a large fiction about the nature of the other. Although women were supposed to provide the utmost in care and respect for men, there was little chance for mutual response and knowledge, for true intimacy, to develop. The honest communication of today's partners must have been very rare in the Victorian couple.

On the other side of the ledger, the Victorians believed that romantic love was very beautiful and that true lovers had a special, unique experience. Poems, music, and art were created in the expression of love. One of the legacies from this period is the high regard for love that exists. The present belief in the uniqueness and value of a love relationship owes some of its foundations to the Victorian attitude toward love.


## The South Seas: Source of Romantic Fantasies

To a North American couple, Samoa looks like a perfect setting for romantic love. Cocoanut palms shade silken sands. Warm, clear water covers coral reefs where millions of bright fish swim. Giant ferns fringe the mountains. It is easy to assume that the beautiful Samoan youths and maidens, in their colorful lava-lavas, hibiscus flowers behind their ears, are involved with love that is overpowering, idealistic, monogamous, faithful, and jealous. Samoa is a perfect setting for Samoan love affairs, too. Margaret Mead made observations here in the 1920's [17]. We use it as a contrast, making no guesses as to whether Samoans are the same today. Like Western-world romantic lovers, the Samoans sing love songs, write love letters, and call upon the moon, stars, and sea in their talk of love. However, they see nothing amiss in carrying on more than one love affair at a time. Teen-agers usually have a number of casual love affairs that include sexual intercourse. The only girls who are to be virgins at marriage are the daughters of chiefs. "Samoans rate romantic fidelity in terms of days or weeks at most, and tend to scoff at tales of life-long devotion. (They greeted the story of Romeo and Juliet with incredulous contempt)" [17, pp. 155–156].

The South Sea islands have long been regarded as a sexual paradise by the Western world, and with good reason. There is little restraint on young people's choice in love affairs, although marriage is controlled. Boys are expected to learn techniques that will make them proficient lovers. Sex is considered an art. " . . . there are no neurotic pictures, no frigidity, no impotence, except as the result of severe illness, and the capacity for intercourse only once in a night is counted as senility" [17, p. 151].

The Samoan child grows up in a large, strong, extended family from which he derives his identity and security. A deeply intimate relationship with one person is not needed in the way that it is needed by a relatively isolated North American couple.

Ancient India is intriguing to everyone interested in love because of the records that are available, both written and graphic. Present-day India is interesting as a contrast to Western romanticism.

**Ancient India.**   The Kama Sutra, written around A.D., 400 is known to American students who are fascinated by its explicit instructions on how to perform sexual acts in ways that produce the most pleasure. Similarly, American tourists in India are eager to see the erotic temple sculpture. These artistic works, verbal and visual, are expressions of the unity of religion, love, and sex in Hinduism. The Kama Sutra is not only a book of instructions on how to enjoy sex but on how to show love in sexual expression. *Kama* means both love and pleasure. Love and the enjoyment of all the arts are believed to contribute to the well-rounded personality. Love is a basic sentiment and its expression is an art. The longing of lovers for each other was used by Sanskrit poets and artists to depict the love of God. In fact, a whole system of human relationships and behavior was designed in terms of religion. Very little was left to spontaneity or to chance. Every family position, including husband and wife, had obligations, and the performance of those duties had religious overtones.

Lovers were supposed to be married to each other. The joy and goodness of love expressed through sex were not permitted to be sampled before marriage. Grooms, as well as brides, were expected to be virginal at marriage. There was allowance for the possibility of a young couple falling in love and wanting to get married for love. Eight forms of marriage were known, a love marriage being sixth in desirability. The most approved forms, the first four, brought purification to ancestors, but the sixth form did not [22, p.152].

**Modern India.**   Dating and casual contacts between young Indian men and women are infrequent, and generally disapproved. Adolescents are usually segregated by sex in schools and in social life. Since families exert control over the choice of marriage partners, it is necessary to keep boys and girls from becoming strongly attached to partners of their own choice. Occasional love marriages occur, but unless parents approve the match, general social disapproval ensues. Because women are expected to be virgins at marriage, and sex urges are recognized as powerful, young people find few opportunities to be alone together. Gossip and social disapproval are strong forces that keep them in line.

Among traditional Indian families, the love between mother and son may be stronger than the husband-wife bond. The young wife has very low status until she has borne a son. She pours out affection on the baby who becomes very attached to her. Religion and social approval strengthen the tie between mother and son and maintain it throughout life. An example is Ramdas, a young man who came from the head family in a village. His first absence from home was a business trip of two months, which meant leaving his parents, wife, and five children. He described his return, "As I came in, the whole family was there. I went to my mother and put my arms around her. All I could say was 'Mother.' We both stood there, crying."

Love between a man and woman is supposed to develop after marriage, when courting begins. Traditionally, the groom does not see the bride until the wedding. However, a procedure sometimes followed today is for the parents to set up matches for the boy and girl to accept or reject. They might then start to fall in love when the match had been arranged and approved. The assumption is that love will naturally follow if the important conditions are right, horoscopes matching, families in proper relationship as to caste and affluence, the couple adequate in health, character, competence, and good looks. It often works out as intended.

# CONCLUSIONS

## Universal Aspects

Falling in love can happen anywhere, and it often does. The in-love condition is biologically based behavior that is shaped by the culture in which it occurs. The most mysterious aspect of falling in love is the question of why a specific person is chosen rather than any other person. The romantic complex promotes the notion that for each individual, there is only one other with whom the best in-love relationship could be established. Where the *one ideal lover* concept is lacking, as in Samoa, people also fall in love but there they are very free to change the love object. The *one ideal lover* seems to be losing ground with youth today, as evidenced in more frequent and agreeable divorces, more premarital love affairs, more extramarital sex. Not all lovers believe in monogamy, faithfulness, permanence, or jealousy.

Attachment behavior has a biological base in youth and adulthood, as it has in infancy. Looking and clinging are common to both stages. Infants gaze at their mothers' faces especially their eyes; lovers gaze at each others' faces, especially their eyes [25]. In fact, a study on looking showed that both men and women preferred individuals who maintained eye contact with them. What is more, they liked opposite-sex individuals with wide dilated pupils better than those with small pupils [26]. Girl babies look at faces and eyes more than do boy babies; women look at men more than men look at women [25]. Puberty brings development of secondary sex characteristics, which become additional focuses of lovers' gazing. We need no research to prove that men tend to look at breasts and hips, and women at broad shoulders, slim waists, and long legs. Lovers put their arms around each other and cling to each other, just as infants cuddle and cling. The term *lovemaking* is very apt, because sexual intercourse often (but not always) creates powerful bonds of attachment between lovers.

## Societal Regulations

Cultures set forth a variety of ways of expressing love. Every society regulates love-making, not only because sexual intercourse produces children but because of the bonds it creates between couples. Thus, the Puritans were supposed to keep the joy of loving within bounds lest it interfere with the society's greater duty to God. Ancient India, also concerned with duty to God, emphasized joy in lovemaking because it was thought to be a manifestation of universal love and energy. Three main areas of social shaping of love behavior can be seen.

**Choice of a Lover.**  Freedom to choose a lover varies enormously from one society to another. In the examples given here, Samoa is very free and modern India is restricted. Capellanus' writings showed the role of a strong class system in regulating love, denying instruction in love behavior to the workers.

**Attachment Behavior.**  A society may teach its young attitudes toward love-making and techniques for it. The Victorians taught the beliefs of the romantic complex and taught attitudes but not techniques relating to sexual intercourse. They, like the courtly lovers of Europe, concentrated on how to behave during the first stages of falling in love. In contrast, the Kama Sutra taught every detail of lovemaking. The present situation in North America is similar in the availability of vast information on how to conduct sexual behavior. Sex therapists concentrate on enhancing sexual pleasure, the ultimate goal usually being orgasm through sexual intercourse.

**Importance of Heterosexual Love.**  In contemporary American society, tremendous emphasis is placed upon fulfillment through heterosexual love. It is doubtful if any society has ever taken love more seriously. Although in the days of courtly love, royalty and nobility were much involved with love, romantic love was not considered appropriate for the lower classes. The Indian attitude, both ancient and modern, is that love has its place and that sex is important, but man and woman have many duties to perform and life involves a great deal more than lovemaking.

## Fulfillment of the Individual versus Welfare of the Group

Our society is greatly concerned with the rights and fulfillment of the individual. This emphasis can be seen in the freedoms guaranteed by the Constitution of the United States. Interest in individual fulfillment is just as great today, or even greater. This attitude stands in contrast to that of most Asians and Africans, who consider family and group welfare as more important than the individual.

American youth have embraced Kahlil Gibran because he expresses the notion that one can have a marriage that is based on being in love and loving, and at the same time, individual development is possible. "Let there be spaces in your togetherness . . . eat not from the same loaf . . . the oak tree and the cypress grow not in each other's shadow" [12, pp. 15–16].

Carl Rogers also maintains that a couple can be in love, married, and growing.

> When a person is making progress, in all the ways I have described, toward becoming his own separate self, then he/she is a worthy partner—not a slave or slave owner, not a shadow or an echo, not always a leader nor always a follower, not a person-to-be-taken-for-granted . . . it is so rewarding to be in process of becoming one's real self, that it is almost inevitable that you will permit and encourage your partner in the same direction, and rejoice in every step that he or she takes. It is *fun* to grow together, two unique and intertwined lives. [23, p. 208]

We, too, believe that it is possible for two people to be in love, to show mutual care, respect, responsibility, and knowledge and to grow as individuals. Probably a limited number of couples actually achieve all this. It is much more difficult to build and maintain this dynamic relationship than to play traditional wife-husband roles as prescribed by society. The dilemmas involved include the following.

**Permanence and Stability.**  Is the marriage to last "as long as we both shall live" or "as long as we both shall love?" What degree of in-loveness must be maintained in order to keep the partnership?

**Dependency versus Self-Sufficiency.**  How can two people be a team and yet be individuals?

**Exclusiveness.**  How much can this relationship dominate the emotional lives of the pair? Can there still be love and loyalty for children and kin? For friends? For other loves?

**Synchronized Growth.**  How can two committed people continue to grow at the same rate and change in the same direction? Two people brought together by similar circumstances may find that as their experiences become more different, they no longer grow as a pair. This problem has been common when one partner works to support the other through school, or when one partner works exclusively outside of the home and the other stays at home and cares for children.

**SUMMARY**  Concepts of love vary between cultures and between individuals. Attachment, an element of love, is an affectional bond that ties one person to another, making him try repeatedly to gain the presence of the loved one and to stay near her. Attachments are seen in animals and birds, as well as among human beings. Care, another element of love, also occurs in subhuman forms of life. Through care, a person tries to promote the well-being of another.

At birth, an infant has behavior patterns through which he builds an attachment to his mother, at the same time stimulating attachment behavior in her. The result is a bond between the pair. The infant also builds attachments with other people. Fathers vary greatly in the amount and quality of their interactions with infants.

As his social world expands in people and space, the young child experiences love expressed in different modes, conditional and unconditional love. The child explores and rehearses love through play. Friends play important roles in the adolescent's identity and intimacy, both of which require knowledge of himself and others. Friends also give opportunities for care, respect, and response.

The state of being in love includes very strong feelings, efforts to gain and keep the presence of the beloved person, and sexual response. Heart rate, breathing, and perception are affected. An intense level of being in love is usually temporary. Couples in love often wonder if their love is sufficient for commitment of a somewhat permanent sort.

Partnership love (love appropriate for commitment to a partnership) includes being in love plus care, responsibility, respect, and knowledge. Love that comprises these elements offers the experience of intimacy and some escape from loneliness. When sex is included with the other elements of love, the possibility for deep intimacy is especially great.

Falling in love occurs everywhere, but the conduct and meaning of a love affair are shaped by the culture in which the couple live. At present in the United States and Canada, being in love is highly valued and considered to be the main factor in mate selection. Romantic love is cherished but it seems to be declining. Based on centuries-old ideas, romantic love is a complex of beliefs, attitudes, and values. Romantic love is exploited by industry, especially the advertising and entertainment industries.

As an example of historic American views on love, the Puritans held marital love and sex in great esteem. They insisted, however, on keeping mortal love under control so that it would not interfere with the love of God. Another era, the nineteenth century, embraced romance, prudery, and the double standard. Expectations of women were contradictory. Courtly love, a flowering of romantic love, began in the twelfth century.

The non-Western world has not incorporated and does not incorporate the romantic complex. In Samoa, sex is an art, jealousy is muted, and commitment is weak and temporary. In ancient India, love and sex were blended in designed expression of religious love. In modern India, most marriages are arranged by parents, and falling in love is not considered an adequate method of choosing marital partners. Love is supposed to come after marriage.

Sexual intercourse is an adult equivalent of attachment behavior, being biologically based upon complementary behavior patterns in two people. Thus, *lovemaking* is an appropriate term.

Every society regulates lovemaking because of its bonding properties as well as its reproductive role. The regulations often differ from one social class to another and in subcultures. Regulations are placed upon the choice of a lover, upon the when and how of attachment behavior, and upon the degree of importance accorded to heterosexual love and to self-expression and development. The fulfillment of the individual has always been important to Americans and is becoming even more so. The modern approach to love and marriage includes the notion that the bonds of love not only permit freedom to the individual but that a full partnership love actually promotes growth in both partners. Dilemmas of modern love partnerships include permanence and stability, dependency versus self-sufficiency, and exclusiveness.

**REFERENCES**

1. Ainsworth, Mary D. Salter. The development of infant-mother attachment. In Bettye M. Caldwell and Henry N. Ricciuti (Eds.). *Review of Child Development Research,* Vol. 3. Chicago: U. of Chicago, 1973.
2. Anderson, W. Song hits of the super 70's. Conn.: Charlton, 1976. (Quoted in Wilkinson [31].)
3. Beach, Frank. Beagles and locks. *American Psychologist,* 1969, **24,** 971–989.
4. Bowlby, John. *Attachment and loss.* Vol. I. *Attachment.* London: Hogarth, 1969.
5. Byrne, Donn and William Griffitt. Interpersonal attraction. *Annual Review of Psychology,* 1973, **24,** 317–336.
6. Capellanus, Andreas. *The art of courtly love.* Trans by John J. Parry. New York: Norton, 1941.
7. Carlier, Auguste. *Marriage in the United States.* New York: Arno, 1972. (Reprinted from the 1867 edition.)
8. Erikson, Erik H. *Childhood and society.* New York: Norton, 1963.
9. Erikson, Erik H. *Identity and the life cycle.* New York: International Universities, 1959.
10. Field, Tiffany. Interactions of primary versus secondary caretaker fathers. *Developmental Psychology,* 1978, **14,** 183–84.
11. Fromm, Erich. *The art of loving.* New York: Harper, 1956.
12. Gibran, Kahlil. *The prophet.* New York: Knopf, 1965.
13. Gordon, Michael (Ed.). *The American family in social-historical perspective.* (2nd ed.) New York: St. Martin's 1978.
14. Jolly, Alison. *The evolution of primate behavior.* New York: Macmillan, 1972.
15. Klaus, Marshall H. and John H. Kennell. Parent-to-infant attachment. In Joseph H. Stevens, Jr., and Marilyn Mathews (Eds.). *Mother/child father/child relationships.* Washington: National Association for the Education of Young Children, 1978.
16. Lorenz, Konrad Z. *King Solomon's ring.* New York: Crowell, 1952.
17. Mead, Margaret. *Coming of age in Samoa.* New York: Morrow, 1928.
18. Morgan, Edmund S. The Puritans and sex. In Michael Gordon (Ed.). *The American family in social-historical perspective.* New York: St. Martin's, 1973.
19. Murstein, Bernard I. A taxonomy of love. Paper presented at meeting of the National Council on Family Relations, San Diego, 1977.
20. Pam, Alvin, Robert Plutchik, and Hope Conte. Love: A psychometric approach. *Proceedings, 81st Annual Convention, American Psychological Association,* 1973, 159–160.
21. Parke, Ross D., and Douglas B. Sawin. Fathering: It's a major role. *Psychology Today,* 1977, **11:**6, 109–112.
22. Prabhu, Pandharinath H. *Hindu social organization.* (3rd ed.) Bombay: Popular Book Depot, 1958.

23. Rogers, Carl R. *Becoming partners: Marriage and its alternatives.* New York: Delacorte, 1972.
24. Rothman, David J. and Sheila M. Rothman (Eds.). *The colonial family in America.* New York: Arno, 1972.
25. Rubin, Zick. Measurement of romantic love. *Journal of Personality and Social Psychology,* 1970, **16,** 265–273.
26. Stass, A. W. and F. N. Willis, Jr. Eye contact, pupil dilation and personal preference. *Psychonomic Science,* 1967, **7,** 375–376.
27. Stayton, Donelda J., Robert Hogan, and Mary D. Salter Ainsworth. Infant obedience and maternal behavior: The origins of socialization reconsidered. *Child Development,* 1971, **42,** 1071–1082.
28. Wadsworth, Benjamin. The well-ordered family: or relative duties. Boston: B. Green, 1712. In David J. Rothman and Sheila M. Rothman (Eds.). *The colonial family in America.* New York, Arno, 1972.
29. Welter, Barbara. The cult of true womanhood: 1820–1860. In Michael Gordon (ed.). The American family in social-historical perspective. (2nd ed.) New York: St. Martin's, 1978.
30. Wheeler, Ella W. *Poems of passion.* Chicago: W. B. Conkey, 1883.
31. Wilkinson, Melvin L. Romantic love and sexual expression. *Family Coordinator,* 1978, **27,** 141–148.

# 3

# COMMUNICATION: WHERE THE INTERACTION IS

In the previous chapter, we discussed knowledge as one of the basic elements of love. Knowing one's beloved and letting oneself be known are essentials of loving, of developing an intimate, caring relationship. And how does a person know another person and be known? By communication, sending messages and receiving them. Vital though communication is to lovers, it is not their monopoly. Every living creature communicates. In fact, every system does. In this book, we are especially concerned with communication between lovers and between family members and, to some extent, between all human beings.

## SOME BASIC USES FOR COMMUNICATION

Without a good communication system, human society would fail utterly in many processes.

### Socialization

Through communication, the infant and child become a part of the culture into which the baby is born. No newborn knows how to speak the language of his parents and community, but no one is surprised when within a year or two the child begins to use it. The infant arrives into a setting in which the older members speak with each other. They talk to the baby in this language and use it when addressing each

other in the baby's presence. On reaching a certain level of mental and physical maturity, the child begins to speak the language that she has heard since birth.

Exactly how a child acquires language is not known. What is important for our purposes is that in normal children, this learning takes place without causing much trouble to those who do the "teaching." When a child cannot hear, see, or both, he has more problems than a normal child in learning the language, and in becoming a part of the family and community. Such a child's tremendous need to communicate is illustrated by the story of Helen Keller, who became deaf and blind at the age of 19 months because of illness. Helen remembered feelings of terrible frustration because she was unable to communicate with those around her. At the age of six, she made the discovery with the help of her teacher, that every thing has a name. Having learned this, the rest of the world opened up to her, although it was difficult for her to grasp the meaning of abstract concepts such as "love" and "think" [19].

A newborn baby could fit equally well into an American, Indonesian, or Nigerian family, or any other human family. He becomes a member of a particular society through the content and style of communication he experiences. He becomes socialized into that society. What the child sees and understands will be largely conditioned by the language. In Chapter I, it was stated that the Hindi-speaking child has six different kinds of aunts, depending upon the age of the aunt, relation to his parent, and whether or not the aunt is a blood relative. This child would find it hard to understand how North Americans can lump together six totally different types of relative into one category.

## Societal Adaptation and Stability

Communication is necessary if a given society is to survive, because it allows both change and stability. Any society (or person) must be able to change if it or he is to live. If life were completely unpredictable, however, nobody could function. Most social interaction is probably concerned not with change but with the ordinary demands of daily life in a group. Communication between people thus maintains equilibrium, or a relatively steady state [4, p. 14].

Change, rapid or slow, is always with us. Changes in technology, the economy, and the political structure all exert an influence upon each of us. Social change has become more rapid since the beginning of the industrial revolution. In former times a boy would grow up to resemble his father in occupation and philosophy of life; a girl knew that her life would most likely center around her husband and her children. The girl might marry someone whose occupation differed somewhat from her father's. She might be a butcher's wife rather than a tailor's wife, as her mother had been. But the girl would have learned how to cook, sew, keep house, and care for children.

In earlier eras, when a couple married, each had ideas about what a husband and wife should be like, both in terms of what each should do to keep the family functioning, and in terms of how each should feel about their interaction, their tasks, and their children. Most of the other people of the same social class in the community felt the same way. Discussion of women's and men's roles in the family was not important, because it was understood by all.

In a society that is undergoing technological and social change, more communication becomes necessary. First, it is not as likely that all persons, particularly those of different generations, will have the same expectations concerning what life should be like, what a man should do and feel, what a woman should do and feel, and so on. A girl may get some ideas of what it is like to be a woman from her own mother, but she can no longer model herself on her mother as closely as did a girl of a century or two ago. Furthermore, a girl has more diverse models today, for example, her teachers and television personalities. Her mother may have spent more years bearing and raising children and fewer years working outside the home than the modern girl wishes to do. Jobs that did not exist twenty or thirty years ago may appeal very much to the young woman and man of today.

Compared with their counterparts in former generations, a young couple at the present time needs more discussion of their desires and expectations. We do not wish to imply that communication was unimportant in the past, but only that it is more necessary now, because roles are less clearly defined.

Communication is increasingly significant for another reason as well: Our society is tremendously complex, made up of many different groups with varying interests. In order to maintain a degree of cohesiveness, groups separated by geography or philosophy must be able to air their views before each other. Through communication, a society (or small group, such as a family) is able to adapt to new situations, while maintaining some sense of cohesion and continuity.

In a very real sense, we are evolving toward becoming a global society. Worldwide communication systems already exist, but need to be improved. The actual existence of human life may depend upon adequate worldwide communication.

## Building Relationships

Discovery of others and defining of relationships are necessary before building intimate relationships.

**Discovery of Others.**   It is through communication that one learns about other people, and in so doing, learns more about oneself. Communication is an antidote to isolation and loneliness.

> Communication . . . has a creative power. It gives self-awareness to each speaker in the reciprocal relation with the other. . . . Each . . . recognizes the other and receives from him that same recognition without which human experience is impossible. For, reduced to himself, man is much less than himself; whereas, in the light of openness to the other, the possibility of unlimited growth is offered to him.[11, pp. 67–68]

People get to know each other in the first place by exchanging information. If the relationship is to continue to grow, communication must continue. Letters to "Dear Abby" from socially unsure individuals ask the question, "How do I get to know———?" The reply is, "Take an interest in him (her)." Get the person talking about himself.

There must be a certain amount of reciprocity in such communication, however. I (LSS) spent the evening with a young woman who would tell me nothing of personal interest about herself, although she was skilled in keeping me talking. When a pause would come, I would try to find out some information about her, but she would cleverly turn things around and get me talking once more. The one-sided flow of information was apparently comfortable for her, but it was not for me.

**Defining a Relationship.**   Related to the discovery of others is the use of communication to define a relationship. When two people begin interacting, they have a wide range of behaviors from which to choose. The kinds of behaviors they select will define the kind of relationship that develops. The "agreement" concerning the kind of relationship is in a constant process of development [12]. One does, however, get clues concerning how she should interact with another person from the way he dresses (in a mail carrier's or nurse's uniform, faded blue jeans and t-shirt, a conservative business suit), or wears his hair, or speaks (accent and grammatical structure), his skin color, and so on. Some of these clues put the individual in a particular category that is more reliable than others: the uniform of a mail carrier or nurse clearly identifies a role for us about which we have certain expectations that are more than likely to be proven correct. When in uniform, certain behaviors can be expected from these individuals in relation to others. For a religious ceremony, one goes to a priest or minister; if injured, one calls a nurse or doctor.

> The roles and status of receivers and senders in a network of communication indicate to the participants how a message ought to be interpreted. . . . In communication theory, therefore, roles have a double function: they identify the participants, and they represent silent messages about communication which constitute instructions of the receiver to the sender about the way he should be addressed and from the sender to the receiver about the way his message ought to be interpreted.[29, p. 223]

The role and status of a person with whom we are communicating help us to interpret what the person is saying, and help us know how to respond. We get an idea of whether the conversation is one between equals, or between unequals; of how similar we are to the other person; and of how intimate the communication should be. Nonverbal as well as verbal communication plays a part here. Martin is sitting in his office with his feet on his desk, smoking a cigarette as he looks over an intraoffice memorandum. A man walks in. Martin keeps his feet on the desk, and says, "Hi, Charlie, have a chair." Is Charlie of the same or lower status as Martin, or of higher status?

**Intimacy.**  In the previous chapter, we discussed knowledge of one another as part of love. Intimacy results when each member of a pair tries to learn how the other thinks and feels, and permits that other person to know how he or she thinks and feels. And how do the two people go about exchanging knowledge of one another? By communicating, of course. Many of the problems of lovers arise from faulty communication. Countless stories and plays feature dilemmas resulting from communication failures. The rest of this chapter is an effort to make communication more understandable and to show its importance in developing relationships between partners and family members.

## Self-Expression

Clarification of thoughts and expression of feelings can result from self expression.

**Processing.**  Not only do people need to communicate with others; they need to communicate with themselves. Sometimes, the two uses of communication may be fused, and at other times, separated. Frequently, when I (LSS) am confused about my feelings about a particular person at a particular time, I write what I call an "imaginary letter" to the person. I try to express all of my feelings on paper, pretending that I am going to send the letter to the person, but knowing that I will not. Putting the words down on paper helps me to clarify what I feel, and frequently when I read the letter over a few times the feelings of stress and confusion go away. While pretending to communicate with another person, I hold a deep conversation with myself. A diary may serve the same purpose as an "imaginary letter."

At other times, a person may need to talk about a problem with other people, not so much for the purpose of conveying the information to someone else, but in order to sort things out much as I do when I write "imaginary letters." Talking about a problem helps the speaker to clarify what happened that is now troubling him. It may be hard for the person with the problem to put a sequence of events in order in his mind and attach labels to the feelings that the events evoked. Talking to another person who listens acceptingly can begin this sorting-out process.

Even thinking, or talking to oneself, can be helpful in processing events and feelings. A person who cannot communicate adequately within himself—that is, label his own feelings and be honest with himself about what he is thinking and feeling—will have a hard time communicating with those outside himself. The young child talks to himself out loud, and gradually becomes able to talk silently—to think [33, pp. 16–24].

**Tension Release.** When a person feels angry, an outpouring of angry words can sometimes release some of the tension. If angry feelings are not released through words or action, but kept inside, they may intensify in a spiral of emotion.

> Emotionally poisoned speech often floods through our being in waves. We seldom say, "Oh, how I hate him" just once to ourselves; we say it again and again. We almost hypnotize ourselves with the refrain. Like Tam O'Shanter's wife, we "nurse our wrath to keep it warm." The circling statements intensify as they spiral. Irritation turns to anger and anger into fury as the hypnotic self-suggestion dulls our critical powers. . . . [6, p. 24]

In a study done on a college campus, a thousand samples of emotionally toned utterances were collected by students in dormitories. Over 70 per cent of them expressed anger. Slightly more than 10 per cent reflected anxiety. One per cent expressed guilt, and 19 per cent had to do with happy or joyful experiences. Rather than indicating that college students feel angry 70 per cent of the time, the findings in this survey indicate that it is more acceptable in our culture to express negative, angry feelings than it is to express other feelings. These angry feelings were most frequently expressed in terms of ejaculations rather than verbalizations. Subjects showed anger more through cries or groans than in words. "Even the curses were colorless, trite, and without real meaning or pertinence . . ."[6, pp. 24–25]. If the angry *words* meant little, how, then, did the researchers get such a clear picture of anger? From the cries, groans, and accompanying gestures. These human behavior patterns are understood universally. They are more primitive than words, less intellectual, more emotional, emitted spontaneously, and understood immediately. Verbal conflict between partners and family members is discussed on pages 69–70.

## Controlling Others

Communication is also used to manipulate and control others. The infant learns this quite early in life: when a baby cries, someone will usually attend to him. Later, when the child learns how to use words, he has even a greater tool with which to control the actions of others. Instead of crying in order to get a drink of milk, the child says the word *milk*—and is given milk. A bit later in life, the mother asks if the child would like to go outside, and he says "No"—not because he doesn't want to go out, but merely to have control of the situation. Words have a magical quality, because they give the toddler a power far beyond his small size.

Most people are not aware of how often they use speech to control or persuade others. Some control speech is a part of most human interactions. Any request that is made has the potential of controlling. The tone of voice, or nonverbal behaviors accompanying speech, can influence the behavior of the listener. At the more extreme end, speech, such as political speeches or sermons, can be used to whip up strong feelings. Control speech can be used for good or ill [6].

# THE NATURE OF COMMUNICATION

**Communication** refers to the sending and receiving of messages through both words and nonverbal behavior that occur in a social context.

## Nonverbal Communication

Although talking may come to mind first as a means of communicating, messages can be sent through any of the senses. Looking and other forms of bodily behavior are powerful, although often unintentional, especially when carried on during speaking and listening. Communication can also be carried on through writing and other symbols.

**Looking.**   As mentioned in the previous chapter, looking is a form of attachment behavior, and gazing between lovers has a special quality. In some cultures, the eyes are thought to have evil power. Even in our own, we say, "If looks could kill!" Societies have unwritten laws about the ways in which people look at each other, and people understand them [2]. Looking conveys messages and provides feedback in most situations where people are together.

**The Language of Behavior.**   It is often easy to tell how a friend is feeling just by looking at him. If he approaches with a grin on his face, his posture erect, and his steps bouncing, the person who is "tuned into" these nonverbal cues readily assumes, *without even thinking about it,* that this friend is in a good mood. If he walks slowly, eyes downcast, posture slumped, the perceptive friend assumes that he is unhappy or perhaps tired. The person who picks up a friend's nonverbal cues will react differently in each case. People do not always have to speak to communicate how they are feeling; they can do so nonverbally. When two or more people are interacting, it is impossible for them not to communicate. Even silence can send a message from one person to another.

Not all persons are equally sensitive to nonverbal cues. I (LSS) was once sitting in a tight circle with two friends, talking about a problem and trying to keep from crying. A third friend, Fred, came up to us, sat down, and started talking about a small aggravation of his. The three of us looked at him in disbelief, but Fred kept right on talking. I found out later that this behavior is characteristic of Fred: he is usually unable to pick up nonverbal cues that other people notice. Although Fred is less perceptive than most men, he did illustrate the gender difference that has been found by researchers using the PONS test, or Profile of Nonverbal Sensitivity [13]. Women usually score moderately higher than men.

Bodily behavior told observers a great deal about two groups of couples who agreed to discuss a marital problem for research purposes [10]. One group was made up of couples who felt their marriages to be unsatisfactory; the other group considered their marriages mutually satisfying. The nonverbal behavior of the two groups differed more than did their verbal behavior. Nonverbal behavior was judged by the observers on items such as these: smile, head nod, eye contact, frown, sneer, fear, cry, angry face; voices that sound warm, tender, affectionate, cheerful, happy, cold, tense, fearful, impatient, whining, sarcastic, blaming, angry, hurting, mocking, depressed; bodily behavior that includes touching, relaxation, forward lean, arms akimbo, neck or hand tension, inattention; and hand movements of pointing, jabbing, and slicing.

Usually, human beings use a wide assortment of cues given off by a person with whom we are conversing. We hear the words, listen to the tone of voice and the emphasis placed on words, and observe the speaker's facial expression, focus of eyes, body postures, and gestures. When an author wants to report the context in which words are spoken, he must do so with more words. Note the difference in the meaning in the following sentences:

"You're a good friend!" she snapped, her eyes blazing with anger.
"You're a good friend!" she said, smiling and reaching over to touch his arm.

We can distinguish between the two sentences on the basis of the *nonverbal cues* accompanying the words (ex. 1: blazing eyes; ex. 2: touching the listener's arm); and also on the basis of the *tone of voice,* that one only can infer from the way words are written. The nonverbal cues that accompany the first example imply a lack of sincerity: the speaker does *not* think the listener is a good friend. But the sentence implies even more than that: it suggests that the speaker had expected the listener to be a good friend, but had been disappointed. In the second example, the touching of the listener's arm implies that the speaker really *does* think the listener is a good friend and that she wants to emphasize this point.

The sense of touch plays a particularly important role in nonverbal communication. Kisses and hugs spell love or at least liking, and they feel so good! Clinging gives comfort. A pat on the hand means encouragement, a pat on the back, congratulations. Shaking hands means acknowledgment of the other person, acceptance, agreement, or a contract. Stroking, petting, and sexual intercourse are lovemaking. There seems to be a human need for communication through touch. In fact, it goes deeper than that. The need for mutual touching is part of our biological inheritance. Animals and birds relate to their mates and offspring through touch. The following description of nonhuman primates leaves no doubt as to the vital role of the sense of touch in social life.

> Tactile communication plays a major part in primate life. . . . Mothers carry the young for long periods on their bodies. Adults frequently sit or even sleep together in furry clumps. Above all, primates groom each other. . . . There is a huge repertoire of patting and nuzzling lumped as greeting behavior—as well as the agonistic contact of cuffs and bites and even kicks. Chimpanzees, particularly, pat each other's hands, faces, and groins, lay a hand on each other's backs in reassurance, and kiss in affection. [16, pp. 153–155].

**Symbolic Messages.**   What does a picture of Cupid, with bow and arrow, mean? Or a halo? Or a skull and crossbones? Or a bunny with colored eggs? North Americans understand the messages carried by these symbols. Every culture has its own set of symbols. In using symbols, a person shares in the feelings, as well as the ideas, of his family, community, and society. Children and lovers seem to make special use of symbols.

Falling in love is a stimulus to all sorts of creative expression, as lovers try to communicate with each other in attractive, original, and artistic ways. "I love you" and "You are beautiful" may seem inadequate, and a love poem or song may seem more appropriate. Flowers, gifts, special settings, and music are all used to communicate "I love you." Some symbols carry generally recognized meaning, for instance, a diamond ring. Other symbols may be invented by the pair to carry messages that are not put into words. For example, Dick expresses special tenderness by ordering the kind of wine he and Helen drank on their first date.

## Congruent and Incongruent Messages

When nonverbal cues that a person is giving are relaying the same message as the verbal cues, we say that his message is **congruent.** If a mother picks up her child and hugs him, and says, "I love you," the two messages sent by the mother are the same, or congruent. But if a mother hits the child and says, "I love you," the message is

**incongruent.** It may be that the mother is hitting the child in order to make him stop doing something that is dangerous, such as running out into the street. By keeping him from running into the street, she is showing her love for him. Saying "I love you" at that time might be accurate. However, the actual feelings that the mother has *at that time* are probably feelings of *fear* that the child will be hurt by running into the street, or perhaps *anger* that she has been disobeyed again. A more congruent message to say to the child at that time would be, "I am afraid that you will get run over! And I am angry that you keep running into the street when I have told you many times that you must not!"

The following examples further clarify the distinction between congruent and incongruent messages:

1. Congruent message: Joan says to Sam, "I love you, darling," and draws him close, kissing him.
2. Incongruent message: When her husband tells her that he won't be home for dinner that night, Gloria says curtly, with tight lips, "Oh, that's all right."
3. Incongruent message: George, who is trying to diet but loves to eat good food, says while gulping his second helping of pie, "Mom, why are you such a terrible cook?"

Gloria may or may not want her husband to know that she is angry at him for planning to be out for dinner. If he wishes, he can ignore her nonverbal message and insist to himself and to her that she had told him it was all right to stay away. George, on the other hand, wants his mother to know that she is a good cook, but his feelings of discomfort about eating pie when he knows he should not are also evident in what he says.

An incongruent message may also be used when a person wants to convey a negative message through the use of sarcasm. Gloria might also say to her husband, "I can tell you really care about me," with tones of sarcasm that make the words mean, "I can tell you *don't* care about me." Should her husband get defensive, and reply, "What do you mean, 'I can tell you really care about me!'" (repeating her intonation), "I *do* care about you!" Gloria then can repeat her message, using intonation which removes the sarcasm: "All I said was, I can tell you really care about me. You're giving me warning that you won't be home for dinner" [24, p. 41].

A person may be unaware that he is sending nonverbal messages that are not congruent with his verbal messages. The young woman who wears a short skirt and tight top, with no bra, may be unaware that she is sending a message of sexual availability to a particular man. If he makes sexual advances, she may be incensed at his forwardness, and say something to that effect. The man, meanwhile, may be confused and angered himself by her messages that *he perceives* as conflicting.

On the simplest level, when communication occurs between two individuals, A sends a message (verbally, nonverbally, or both) and B receives it. However, as indicated by the above example, the message that A intends to send may not come through to B as A had intended. The young woman did not intend to be sexually provocative to the man; from her point of view, her clothes were comfortable and perhaps stylish. He understood her physical appearance to be an invitation for his advances. When he slid his hand around her waist, he gave her the chance to clarify her message to him. Had she accepted his advances, he would have been assured that his assumption was correct. However, her rebuff showed that he had interpreted her appearance incorrectly.

Within the context of the family or some other close relationship, we usually have more information about the person with whom we are communicating than we do when we are relating to a stranger or acquaintance. A husband might know from previous experience that when his wife puts on a certain negligee, it means that she would like to make love. However, on a particular night she might put on the negligee only because all her other nightclothes are dirty.

## Representations of Reality

Verbal and nonverbal communication is a representation of reality. If I describe to you a person throwing a ball, you will form a mental picture of someone engaging in that activity, based on your previous experiences. You do not actually see a person throwing a ball, however: you only conjure one up in your mind. The description is only a representation of the event: Each event is unique, even when we are watching a pitcher practice his curve ball over and over again.

Virginia Satir, a family therapist, has seen the problems that can be caused when a person fails to realize that words are representations of reality. A person may assume that something which occurs once is an example of all instances: a young woman is mistreated by a man whom she loves and so assumes that all men mistreat women. Or, a person may assume that all people think the way she does: I like carrots, so everyone must like carrots. Or, she may think that what she perceives is final, and will not change: I don't like Sandy because she seems selfish. Instead of observing her in other situations, or finding out why she is behaving the way she is, I will write her off as a lost cause.

Another problem encountered by the person who does not realize that words are abstractions, or representations of reality, is that she tends to think in terms of "black and white." Such a person believes that each individual is either good or bad, and not a combination of the two. For example, she may believe that it is not possible to love and hate the same person. The person who does not realize that words are abstractions assumes that the characteristics that she names in things or people represent the complete reality of the thing or person. By calling someone a name, such as coward, bully, devil, sexpot, or pollyanna, one may give the impression that the particular name describes the whole person, all of him. For instance, Joe calls Sally a *cripple*. He might have said that Sally is crippled or disabled. The term a *cripple* suggests that Sally is just that and no more. In reality, Sally is a person with many attributes, abilities, and assets. She cannot walk smoothly and cannot run at all, because one leg is shorter than the other. Joe saw Sally's limited locomotion, gave the condition a name, applied the name to Sally as an individual, and left the impression in himself and perhaps in others that Sally's disability was a total picture of Sally. When Sally hears herself called a *cripple,* it makes her think that others perceive her as nothing but a person who can't walk well and it diminishes her concept of herself.

Another source of misunderstanding is the assumption that another person can understand what is going on inside the speaker's head and that the speaker also knows what the listener is thinking. A wife asks her husband, "Did you bring the whachamacallit?" If he asks her what she means, and she gets annoyed, she was assuming that he could read her mind [31, pp. 66–67].

The person who realizes that words represent reality will be more able to express herself meaningfully to a listener. She will understand that there is room for a tremendous amount of error in the sending of messages and in comprehending them. She will also more readily understand the complexity of communication and of the world.

## Different Kinds of Meanings

Clarity of communication suffers because words often have two kinds of meanings: a literal, or **denotative** meaning, and a **connotative** meaning. If you look up a word in a dictionary, you will find its different denotative meanings listed. For example, the word *bail* has a number of different denotative meanings, including the following:

1. Security given for the due appearance of a prisoner in order to obtain his release from imprisonment.
2. To deliver (property) in trust to another for a special purpose and for a limited period.
3. A device for confining or separating animals.
4. To clear water from a boat by dipping and throwing over the side [34].

We can usually tell which denotative meaning is intended by the context in which the word is found. Misunderstandings can and do occur when the context does not make the meaning clear.

Another kind of meaning that words have is the *connotative* meaning, which is a more personal meaning. What kind of reaction do you get to the word *liberation?* Liberty is a basic value in our society; if this were the only association of the word liberation, one would expect that only positive (good) feelings would be aroused by the word. For some, the word liberation is associated with women's liberation or black liberation. Such connotations might stimulate feelings of anger, pride, anxiety, or hopefulness.

## Not a Simple Two-way Process

It is tempting to think of communication between two persons as a simple, two-way process, in which one person sends a message, the second one receives and processes it, and sends one back. We tend to think that people in real life talk and communicate in turns the way people do on television or in a novel [4, p. 12].

> Speech communication is a two-way process, not to be conceived as one where a verbal ball is being tossed back and forth, but as one where at least two, and often many, balls are being tossed in both directions at the same time [6, p. 51].

Even though we are not usually aware of it, when we are conversing with another person, we are constantly giving off cues to which the other responds. We smile, look surprised, our eyes widen, we grimace, we move closer or farther away, we cross our arms or legs, or relax our bodies completely. The person with whom we are talking may interpret our nonverbal cues correctly or incorrectly, but whichever is the case, an effect has been made upon the interaction.

Imagine, for example, that you are talking with a friend about an issue that is emotionally laden and difficult for you to discuss. You are concerned about your friend's reaction: will he *accept* you and what you are saying, or will he think you wrong, odd, immoral, and so on? As you are speaking, you see your friend stiffen a bit. He is trying to look unruffled, but you detect tension. How do you feel? Would you have a different reaction to a response that is decidedly warm and accepting?

Jane is talking about her boyfriend. Can you tell how she feels by looking at each photo?

CRAIG M. SZWED

To *accept* what another person does or says is not the same as *agreeing* with it, *condoning* it, or *wanting it for oneself*. Debbie, a woman with a career, accepts her sister's wanting to be a housewife as right for her sister, but not for herself. Ted feels that he is incompetent. Kevin accepts his feelings, but does not agree with Ted's evaluation of himself when he says, "I know that *you* think you're not doing a good job, but *I* think you're doing fine."

**Interference from Within.**  The message that is sent to us by another can become garbled by interference from our own needs and desires, and by our anxiety. The man who wants to get to know a woman better may think that her casual, "Hello, how are you?" means that she is interested in him the way he is in her. Perhaps the most harmful interference to communication is feelings of anxiety and fear [6, pp. 70–71]. Negative feelings about the person with whom we are attempting to communicate can distort our perceptions and understanding. Mutual distrust between whites and blacks or chicanos is a barrier to communication and cooperation. People with widely varying life styles and values may fear each other. Individuals on each side of the chasm may label their feelings as dislike or hatred, but behind these feelings are likely to lurk anxiety, fear, and misunderstanding.

# EFFECTIVE VERSUS INEFFECTIVE COMMUNICATION

Just because a message is sent does not mean that the same message is received by the listener. Both the speaker and the listener need particular skills if effective communication is to take place.

## Empathy versus Sympathy

In order for effective communication to take place, the listener must be able to "put himself in the psychological shoes" of the speaker [7, p. 318]. In other words, the listener must have **empathy** for the speaker. The listener must not, however, lose himself in the words of the speaker, and forget that it is the speaker who has a particular feeling and not himself. The person who experiences real empathy has been described as a pendulum that swings between his own identity and feelings and identity with the speaker [18]. Although the empathic listener can feel and understand the emotions expressed by (or behind the words of) the speaker, he understands that he is a separate person from the speaker.

When we were in India, we were told by a person whose first language was Hindi that "Hindi is the sweetest language and easiest to learn." At that point, we were struggling with Hindi lessons five days a week, and found many of the sounds impossible to articulate, and the grammar troublesome because it was so different from English grammar. One of us replied that perhaps Hindi was the sweetest language to him, but to us, it was difficult. A look of disbelief crossed the face of our acquaintance, and he repeated: "Hindi is the sweetest language." At that moment our acquaintance was entirely lacking in empathy. He could not put himself in our shoes; he could not believe that even a foreigner would not immediately recognize Hindi, which he had learned at his mother's knee, as the sweetest language in the world.

If he had responded instead, when we insisted that Hindi was difficult, "Oh, goodness, I meant that Hindi is the sweetest language to *me* because it's my mother tongue!" he would have given an indication that he realized that we might feel differently. If he had also said, "I can understand how Hindi might be difficult for you, because the sounds and grammar are different from English," his response would have been empathic.

In contrast to empathy, a person who feels **sympathy** cannot distinguish his own feelings from those of the speaker. This frequently happens when the listener's experience is similar to the speaker's. Dennis is telling Jerry about his feelings concerning his (Dennis') divorce. Jerry was recently divorced, and still has a lot of tumultuous feelings concerning his own divorce. As Dennis becomes more emotional, so does Jerry. Jerry finally says, "I can really understand what you're saying, man, but I don't think I can help you sort out your feelings. This is hitting too close to home for me— it makes me think about Barbara and me." Jerry recognizes that he is feeling sympathy, not empathy.

Suppose that Jerry does not have disturbing feelings about his own divorce and says instead, "Wow, man, you're really making me feel sad. Seeing you upset like this really affects me, too. You really feel torn by this whole thing. You're glad to be rid of the pressure of living with Tish, but you still feel that you have failed." In this case, the feelings behind Jerry's words are empathic ones, because Jerry recognizes that the problem of the divorce is Dennis' problem and not his. Jerry's understanding of Dennis' feelings may have come in part because of Jerry's own divorce, but Jerry can keep the two events and the accompanying feelings separate in his own mind.

## The Problem of Not Hearing

Very frequently a breakdown of communication occurs when two people do not "hear" each other. "Nonlistening" is unfortunately a very common practice in our society; parents don't listen to their children, so the children do not learn how to listen to their parents. Nonlistening can also come from a kind of verbal sparring in which each person is more concerned about what *he* is going to say next rather than what the other person is trying to communicate [21]. Preschool children will often hold a mock conversation, each one speaking in turn, but the second child's sentences have nothing to do with the first child's. Adult conversations can be remarkably similar.

| *Tom:* | "Guess what! I got the promotion! Just one other guy and I got it!" |
| *Joe:* | "Yeah, well my boss says some of us will be coming up for a promotion soon. I think I've been doing a pretty good job." |
| *Tom:* | "With the raise in pay, we'll be able to get out of the financial hole we're in. But the best part of it is that he finally recognizes that I've got something to offer." |
| *Joe:* | "Yeah, well it's been a long time coming for me. I've been putting in extra hours for over a year now." |

How do you feel when another person cuts you off in the middle of a thought, or starts each of his sentences with a quick "yes" and then goes on to tell his own story? When their own needs are overpowering, even the most skilled listeners transgress in this way at times, but to do so frequently is bound to frustrate the speaker, to make him feel unimportant and unheard. This can happen when one or both people are playing a game of one-ups-manship (who can tell the funniest story? who had the worst experience? who caught the longest fish?), or it can happen when one or both conversants feel threatened by what the other is saying.

In contrast, a person who really listens to another is at the same time communicating that he cares about the speaker as a person. At times, we all need simply to talk about a problem with another person; sharing the burden somehow makes it lighter. The listener need not always have a verbal response: a concerned facial expression, or a calm, warm hand may say to the speaker, "I hear you, and I care."

Not hearing can also occur because the listener is too close to the problem, or too emotionally involved in it. Alice R. is pregnant by mistake and not married. When she tells her mother, who is a social worker, her mother's response is, "How can you do this to me?" Instead of supporting her daughter when her daughter has a difficult problem, Mrs. R. ignores Alice's feelings. Because she is a social worker, Mrs. R. frequently deals with women who have problem pregnancies. As a professional, she is effective, but when her daughter needs help, she is unable to give it because she is overwhelmed by her own feelings. The problem is too close to home.

**Clarification of Messages.** Even when two conversants are attending to what the other is saying, they may not "hear" each other. Because of the different denotative and connotative meanings of words, and because of interference from anxiety and one's own needs, the message sent may not be the same message that is received. If one person is not sure what the other means, he may ask for clarification by saying, "Do you mean———?", "What I hear you saying is———. Is that right?" or, "What does 'it' refer to?" Sometimes, putting what another person has said into one's own words, and saying these words back to the original speaker, can help clarify for both parties what the first speaker was trying to say. Doing this exercise for each thought expressed by each party in a conversation would take up an extraordinary amount of time, and would probably confuse rather than clarify. But if a particular statement is difficult for the listener to grasp, putting it into his own words *out loud* can save time and confusion in the long run.

# COMMUNICATION IN THE FAMILY

Because of the nature of the family, communication between family members has some special characteristics.

## Roles and Expectations

The kind of communication that exists in a family is intimately bound up with the kinds of roles and expectations in the family. In a family in which the members relate to each other mostly in accordance with the status of each member, the members will communicate in a much more restricted way than will families in which the members relate as persons [5, pp. 95–96]. If a person's role is clearly set out for him, then his relationship to other people does not have to be discussed. If the father makes all the decisions about how the family will function, and the other family members accept him as the decision-maker, he will do more talking than listening. Thus, if a family is more *status-oriented* than *person-oriented,* then members are treated according to the positions they occupy. A child is supposed to act in certain ways simply by reason of being a child, and very often those role prescriptions include being obedient, polite, and quiet. The eldest child may be required to mind the younger ones and wash the dishes simply because he or she is the eldest. Likewise, a wife has her slot to fill and a husband his.

In status-oriented families, children, in particular, are not permitted to express their feelings. When the child in this kind of a family asks why he must do something or may not do something, he is more likely to be told, "Because I said so," rather than the reason. Such a reply does nothing to clarify for the child the reason an act is demanded or forbidden, but it does clarify relationship to his parent. It shows who is more powerful. When mothers' discipline techniques were person-oriented rather than status-oriented, girls and boys were found to be more likely to take people's intentions into account when they were judging the morality of actions [26].

The person-oriented family makes opportunities for each member to act as a unique person. The feelings of each member are important to the others, as means of understanding and planning appropriate actions for each. Person-oriented families carry on much discussion. Everyone talks and everyone listens.

**Family Communication Patterns.**   Couples and families have **communication patterns**, which are typical ways of relating to each other in various situations [25]. For example, Tom is comfortable with expressing gratitude when Peggy saves him from an awkward situation, but Peggy is uncomfortable about thanking Tom when he rescues her. However, Peggy is more able to express love spontaneously to Tom than is he to her.

Family rules cover the kind of topics that can be discussed, and the ways in which conversations about various topics will go. In some families, it is expected

that issues will be dealt with directly; in others, communication codes provide an indirect but mutually understandable way of dealing with issues. It may be taboo to express anger or disappointment openly.

## Honesty

"Open and honest communication" seem to be bywords of the young generation. Turned off by what they see as hypocrisy in their parents, many young people want to do away with what their parents see as tact and good taste. Having taken an introductory course on counseling skills, James decided that he should tell his parents that he was having sexual relations with Maria, whom he wanted to marry. To James and Maria, their sexual experiences together were good, and terribly important. James' instructor had stressed the importance of honesty in communication. Therefore, when James went home from college, he told his parents about himself and Maria, and let them read some passionate letters that Maria had written to him.

Instead of loving Maria as much as James did, his parents were horrified. To his parents, Maria was a slut. Girls who have intercourse before marriage could be nothing else. The marriage of James and Maria has done nothing to change their opinion of Maria.

James later realized his mistake. Honesty does not always require that hurtful realities be laid bare. James and Maria's sexual relationship was not something that his parents needed to know. The knowledge wounded his parents, and their rejection of Maria hurt her very much.

**Honest and Direct Questions.**   The issue of honesty is concerned not only with the kind of answers one gives but with the kinds of questions that one asks. An honest question is one to which the person asked can respond without penalty. A dishonest question, in turn, must be answered the way the asker wishes, or the person asked will be penalized in some way. For example, if a person asks me, "Do you mind if I smoke?" and I respond, "Yes, I do," and the smoker gets annoyed or lights up anyway, he asked a dishonest question. Dishonest questions unfortunately are very much a part of our everyday life. The words "Do you mind if . . ." very frequently introduce a dishonest question. Other examples are, "Are you busy?" "Is it all right if we are half an hour late for dinner?" "May we bring the children?" The person asking a dishonest question often has an answer in mind [23].

Related to honest and dishonest questions are direct and indirect questions. A direct question "asks it like it is"—there is no hidden meaning. "Would you like to have dinner with me Saturday night?" is a direct question. An indirect counterpart, so frequently used, is "What are you doing Saturday night?" The problem with an indirect question is that the listener can never be sure what is really on the asker's mind. If a husband asks his wife, "Are you tired tonight?" when he really wants to know if she would like to make love, the wife can't be sure whether her husband is really concerned whether or not she is tired, or if he has something else on his mind (watching the late show? going out for a drink?).

## Communication Codes

It is possible for a group of people to develop an elaborate code that is mutually understandable. For instance, the Lacey family has a hospitality code that can result in sadly overstuffed guests among those who do not understand. Conversations like these are common:

| | |
|---|---|
| *Mrs. Lacey:* | Do have some more strawberry shortcake. |
| *Harriet:* | No, thank you. |
| *Mrs. Lacey:* | Oh come on. You had such a small piece to start with. |
| *Harriet:* | Really, I've had plenty. |
| *Mrs. Lacey:* | I'll think you don't like my shortcake! |
| *Harriet:* | You make the best strawberry shortcake of anyone I know, and I just love it. But I simply can't eat another bite. |
| *Mrs. Lacey:* | Oh, all right Harriet. Now Horace, let me give you some. |
| *Horace:* | No thanks, Mrs. Lacey. |
| *Mrs. Lacey:* | Why Horace, you had such a small first course. I thought surely you would like the dessert. |
| *Horace:* | I've had plenty of everything, thank you. |

> Mrs. Lacey: Surely a big man like you can eat more than such a small dinner. Let me give you just a sliver.
>
> Horace: Well, all right, just a wee bit.

Harriet obviously understood the code and Horace did not. Mrs. Lacey had to keep pushing food until she had exhausted all possibilities of having the guests accept more. She may even have hoped that there would be a piece left for tomorrow, but hospitality required her to make sure that her guests were not refusing from politeness rather than satiation. Harriet properly reassured Mrs. Lacey that she was a marvelous cook and hostess. Horace, not understanding the true meaning of Mrs. Lacey's comments, did not elaborate enough on his pleasures, satisfaction, and approval concerning the meal. For his ignorance of the code, Horace was punished by an overloaded stomach.


## Planned Communication

Fruitful communication requires *respect* for the other person's integrity and feelings.

Ben Ard, a marriage counselor, underscores the need for careful communication between parents and children, and others who are close to one another. He writes:

> In many serious marital discussions, considerate, thoughtful, and even planned communication can frequently be more helpful than merely saying whatever one "feels" like saying. When important matters are being discussed between married couples, I would go so far as to suggest . . . that some thought be given to the questions raised, to possible alternative positions and why one "feels" the way one does. I have even suggested something akin to "position papers" being written out before an important discussion (e.g., whether or not to get a divorce, or have another child, or indulging in a bit of wife-swapping, or moving one's mother-in-law into the family home, or moving to another state, etc.) [1]

Too frequently people treat those close to them in a way in which they would not treat an acquaintance or a stranger. Intimacy is seen as a license to be rude or cruel in the guise of honesty. The harried mother, who has asked her daughter many times to clean her room, finally explodes in anger: "Why do I have such a slob for a daughter? Your room is always a pig pen!" This kind of character defamation is not likely to motivate the child to change her habits. If a guest breaks a dish, a hostess will usually respond (perhaps untruthfully) that the guest shouldn't worry; it is nothing. But the same woman, when her child breaks a dish, accuses the child of carelessness.

Miller and associates [25] point out that honest and skillful communication is not sufficient for the building and maintaining of relationships. A person can use communication skillfully with the intent of damaging her partner's self-esteem. Esteem for self and partner is built when each partner takes responsibility for what is said, how it is said, and in which context. Each partner also needs to be in control of the way he or she responds to what the other partner says. According to Miller, "This is a critical choice point which, over time, distinguishes esteem-building partnerships from esteem-diminishing relationships."

Timing of communication is important. Children learn at a young age to make requests of their parents at times advantageous to the child. When the parent is busy and doesn't want to be bothered by the child, the parent is likely to say "yes" to a request that will keep the child occupied. When tired and hungry, it is usually best to avoid topics of discussion that are likely to cause disagreement, unless one wants a fight! A particular time of day may be an impossible time for a certain individual to communicate effectively; for example, before breakfast. Nonverbal cues are important aids to determining a time for fruitful communication. The slamming of a door that is usually closed gently can alert the listener to the possibility that the person entering or leaving is in a bad mood. A furrowed brow, slumped shoulders, or a frown can signal that now is not the best time to begin discussion of certain topics.

## Handling Disagreements

Unnecessary blowups can be avoided through the use of tact and good timing. Conflict and disagreements are not always harmful to relationships, and, in fact, may be necessary for continued growth in the relationship. Some couples who remain married to each other even seem to thrive on continued conflict [9]. One of our students, when asked why people live in families, replied with a sparkle in her eye, "So they'll have someone to fight with."

Bach and Wyden wrote a book devoted to the subject of marital fighting. They maintain that since fighting is inevitable in marriage, couples might as well learn to do it effectively [3]. What they are really talking about, however, is communication in marriage, rather than fighting. Disagreements are inevitable between people who are truly intimate and can be used to deepen the relationship and the intimacy. Problems and disagreements should be aired regularly, and not stored away in a "gunny sack" and later dumped upon the hapless partner when the burden becomes too great. Bach and Wyden recommend honesty during marital "fights." However, when extramarital sex, real or fantasized, is discussed, they recommend that extreme tact be used.

Many people think that verbal fighting, or verbal aggression, prevents physical fighting and aggression. The notion is that the expression of anger is cathartic, that letting it out makes it go away. From his studies of family violence, Straus thought that the idea of catharsis was misleading and so he set out to test it [32]. By asking college students questions about their parents, he got information about 385 families' use of verbal and physical aggression and how they settled conflicts and differences. Straus found that the greater the amount of verbal aggression carried on, the greater amount of physical aggression. Physical aggression was less when people tried to

discuss the issue calmly, did discuss calmly, got information about the issue, and brought in someone to help them settle things, or tried to.

Can the ideas of Straus and Bach and Wyden be reconciled? It looks as though constructive "fighting" is not aggression, verbal or physical, but a controlled statement of feelings. A person could say, "When you're out late at night, and I don't know where you are, I feel afraid and then I feel angry at you for making me feel afraid." This statement describes feelings, but it does not attack the other person as does the following one. "You sneaky rat, next time you'll find the bolt on the door and I don't give a damn where you sleep."

## Partners

As our readers must know by now, we have strong personal values concerning communication between married partners. We believe that deep communication is necessary for pair intimacy and for the growth of partners as a pair and as individuals.

Common sense, as well as a number of studies, holds that marriage partners get along better and enjoy marriage more when they communicate with each other [8, 15, 17, 22, 27]. Researchers are presently concerned with how partners actually carry on communication, what they think and feel about it, and what influences them toward more or less success. There seems to be a widespread desire for knowing and understanding, for the sort of intimacy that we have described on pages 33–34.

There is evidence that husbands and wives differ in their skill levels. In an Australian study, husbands' and wives' interactions were videotaped. Wives sent more accurate messages to their husbands than their husbands sent to them, and wives were also better at interpreting what their husbands said. Wives interpreted neutral messages more positively than husbands did. While wives were more skilled in communicating than were husbands, the husbands' skills were more related to happiness in marriage [27a].

Husbands and wives of varying educational levels have been found to place a high value on talking things over calmly [14]. But believing in something does not always mean that a person can do it! A study of preferences and actual behavior suggests that although all the partners would like to communicate honestly and deeply, the better-educated people have more facility in talking, listening, and controlling negative feelings. The groups studied were those with more than 12 years of schooling and those with less. All believed in the importance of expressing, accepting, and taking account of the feelings of both partners. By observing the couples discussing a marital problem, the investigators found two main differences between the educational levels. The group with more education carried on discussions with more tentative explanations and more openness to other points of view. This group made fewer controlling comments, in which the speaker strongly states what he thinks or feels, and gives the other person no chance to present a different idea. This study, done in a laboratory, gives numerical results that are shown to have statistical significance. A complementary study, done through intensive interviews, offers a deep understanding, communicating with the reader through vivid word pictures.

Lillian Rubin's book, *Worlds of Pain*, [30] is a report and interpretation of married life in the working class. Her treatment of husband-wife communication bears out the results of the laboratory study just mentioned. There is a new dream of companionship, intimacy, and sharing, in both the middle class and the working class, but it is newer for the working class, and it is sought more by the women than by the men.

"I'm not sure what I want. I keep talking to him about communication, and he says, 'Okay, so we're talking; now what do you want?' And I don't know what to say then, but I know it's not what I mean." [30, p. 120].

"I get scared sometimes. I always thought I had to think things to myself; you know, not tell her about it. Now she says that's not good . . ." [30, p. 121].

When Komarovsky studied working-class couples in the 1950s, she found that they neither expected nor desired close communication between marital partners [20]. These couples believed that men and women were *unable* to communicate effectively. Therefore, they were not distressed by the fact that they did not communicate with their partners. A generation later, Rubin's subjects had a different idea and they were indeed distressed by lack of communication, because they believed it was possible.

## Childrearing

Parents and newborn baby communicate through touching, looking, crying, talking, feeding, and gestures, especially smiling. Even the beginnings of verbal communication exist, because infants react selectively to human speech. The sounds of a baby's babbling are shaped within the first year by his parents' language. Through all these modes of communication an infant gets messages from which he builds expectations of himself, his family, and the world. A sense of trust, in Erikson's terms, grows as the child receives prompt attention to his own signals. The baby is fed when hungry and comforted when distressed. The baby's smiles bring smiles from others. His cooing results in others' talking to him. Using his own abilities, the child causes events, makes things happen, and experiences himself as capable. Thus it is important for the personality development of an infant to communicate with the family.

With the beginning of true language, at the end of infancy, parents and children can communicate more precisely. Nonverbal messages are still important, and will be throughout life, but the use of words adds enormously to the exchange of information and ideas. Parents, in fact, all adults, intuitively adjust their language to a young child, talking in shorter, simpler sentences and in words that children are most likely to understand. Parents, from their day-to-day experience, usually fit their words to the particular child's understanding. Sometimes it is hard to resist the impulse to talk baby talk and to imitate a toddler's mistakes, but to do so very often is to hold back the child from learning the language. Sometimes a family will get and keep special words from their infant's baby talk. In our family, we say *bianna* for *banana,* because the first grandchild said *bianna,* and we thought it was cute. We have other such words, too, and they make a way for us to communicate intimately and jokingly in our immediate family. However, we made sure that the originator of *bianna* learned to say *banana,* and now she, too, reserves the former term for fun within the family.

Language serves many purposes in childrearing. In addition to giving information and sending messages of love and attention, parents use words to help children anticipate and reflect, and to control behavior. At the same time that a child learns to talk in sentences, she can recall past events and think about future ones. A parent can prepare a child to cope with what is coming next by communicating. "Shana and her mother are coming to see us. Let's find a toy for Shana to play with." Later, positive social behavior can be consolidated by recalling with approval. "Shana liked playing with your little cars. You and Shana both had fun playing together with the cars, didn't you?"

Limits on behavior and reasons for them can be set verbally. Rewards and punishments can be verbal, not only physical. Even if physical punishment is given, reasoning increases its effectiveness [28]. Listening, the other side of the coin, is also an important part of discipline that helps the child to become socially responsible. The most constructive kind of listening is not merely keeping quiet while the child talks, but helping him to explore his feelings and reasons. Thus the parent communicates an attitude of really wanting to understand how the child was feeling and thinking when he did whatever he did, even though the parent disapproves of the action or its results. All these methods of discipline, reasoning, listening, approval, disapproval, anticipation, and reflection are most effective when used by a loving parent who has built trust with the child. The topic of discipline is discussed further in Chapter 10.

**SUMMARY**     Essential on many levels, communication is important in love relationships and thus in marriage and family relations. The child is socialized as parents and other people communicate to her in the context of their culture. The language used constitutes a particular interpretation of reality.

Communication is basic to social adaptation, permitting both change and stability. The more rapid the change taking place, the greater is the need for communication between people in the society. Partnership roles between men and women undergo social change and thus require increased communication in order to maintain the relationship. Communication is used to discover self and others, to develop intimacy and understanding, to release tension and to control others.

Communication involves sending and receiving verbal and nonverbal messages. Nonverbal (neither spoken nor written) messages include facial expression, looking behavior, touching, gestures, posture, and other aspects of physical appearance, as well as tone of voice. Symbols are shared carriers of meaning that may be understood by a group or privately by a pair or a few people.

Congruent messages are messages that agree. Sometimes verbal and nonverbal messages are incongruent, making it difficult for the receiver to know just what the sender meant. Sometimes the sender is not aware that he is sending incongruent messages. When he communicates, a person is sending a message about what he thinks is real. The recipient may be confused because he has a different interpretation of reality. Confusion may come from an individual's thinking that all other people share his values or that an interpretation he has made is true for all people. Sometimes people assume that they can read each other's minds.

Communication is complicated, since many messages are sent and received in one social encounter. Thus, there may be confusion in the sending, in sorting what is sent, and also in distractions arising within the recipient. Anxiety and fear and preoccupation interfere with the individual's ability to receive the messages that others are trying to send. Communication can be made more effective when the listener uses empathy, imagining himself into the place of the other person but still remembering that he is himself. In contrast, in feeling strong sympathy, a person may lose his sense of self. Nonlistening is another detriment to communication. A speaker can tell when other persons are really listening by the attentive expression on their face and by their not interrupting, as well as by comments that show they are trying to understand. Communication is improved when participants try to clarify their interpretations.

The role orientation of a family strongly influences the kinds of communication patterns that develop. Less effort is required when status and role determine interaction; more communication is needed when each family member is regarded as a unique person. Questions, as well as answers, can be either honest or dishonest, depending upon the intention. Sometimes a communication code appears dishonest to an outsider but is, in reality, understood by the participants. Positive communication involves respect as well as honesty. Family members may fail to respect each other's feelings, often because they do not plan the content and timing of what they are trying to communicate. Disagreements can be used constructively to deepen understanding. The depth of communication required for marital success depends upon the couple's expectations of marriage and of each other.

Infants are born with ability to communicate. Through these processes, they build attachments and trust and develop controls of mind and body.

**REFERENCES**

1. Ard, Ben N., Jr. Communication in marriage. *Rational Living,* 1971, **5,** 220–222.
2. Argyle, Michael. The laws of looking. *Human Nature,* 1978, **1**:1, 32–40.
3. Bach, George and Peter Wyden. *The intimate enemy.* New York: Morrow, 1968.
4. Birdwhistell, Ray L. *Kinesics and context: Essays on body motion communication.* Philadelphia, U. of Pa., 1970.
5. Britton, James. *Language and learning.* London: Penguin Books, 1970.
6. Brown, Charles T. and Charles Van Riper. *Speech and man.* Englewood Cliffs, N.J.: Prentice-Hall, 1966.
7. Brownfield, E. Dorothy. Communication: Key to family interaction. *Marriage and Family Living,* 1953, **15,** 316–319.
8. Corrales, Ramon. The influence of family's life cycle categories, marital power, spousal agreement, and communication styles upon marital satisfaction in the first six years of marriage. Unpublished doctoral dissertation, University of Minnesota, 1974. Cited in Sherod Miller, Ramon Corrales, and Daniel Wackman. Recent progress in understanding and facilitating marital communication. *Family Coordinator,* 1975, **24,** 143–152.
9. Cuber, John and Peggy Harroff. *The significant Americans.* New York: Appleton, 1965.
10. Gottman, John, Howard Markham, and Cliff Notarious. The topography of marital conflict: A sequential analysis of verbal and nonverbal behavior. *Journal of Marriage and the Family,* 1977, **39,** 461–477.
11. Gusdorf, Georges. *Speaking.* Evanston, Ill.: Northwestern U. P., 1965.
12. Haley, Jay. An interactional description of schizophrenia. In Don Jackson (Ed.). *Communication, family and marriage.* Palo Alto, Calif.: Science and Behavior Books, 1968.
13. Hall, Judith A., Robert Rosenthal, Dane Archer, M. Robin DiMatteao, and Peter L. Rogers. Decoding wordless messages. *Human Nature,* 1978, **1**:5, 68–75.
14. Hawkins, James L., Carol Weisberg, and Dixie L. Ray. Marital communication style and social class. *Journal of Marriage and the Family,* 1977, **39,** 479–490.
15. Hobart, Charles and William Klausner. Some social interactional correlates of marital role disagreements and marital adjustment. *Marriage and Family Living,* 1959, **21,** 256–263.
16. Jolly, Alison. *The evolution of primate behavior.* New York: Macmillan, 1972.
17. Karlsson, Georg. *Adaptability and communication in marriage.* Totowa, N.J.: Bedminster Press, 1963.
18. Katz, Robert, cited in Charles T. Brown and Charles Van Riper. *Speech and man.* Englewood Cliffs, N.J.: Prentice-Hall, 1966.
19. Keller, Helen. *The story of my life.* New York: Grosset, 1904.
20. Komarovsky, Mirra. *Blue-collar marriage.* New York: Random, 1962.
21. Lederer, William J. and Don D. Jackson. *The mirages of marriage.* New York: Norton, 1968.
22. Locke, Harvey, Georges Sabagh, and Mary Margaret Thomes. Correlates of primary communication in empathy. *Research Studies of the State College of Washington,* 1956, **24,** 116–124.
23. Madsen, C. cited in David Knox. *Marriage happiness: A behavioral approach to counseling.* Champaign, Ill.: Research Press, 1972.
24. Mehrabian, A. *Silent messages.* Belmont, Calif.: Wadsworth, 1971.
25. Miller, Sherod, Ramon Corrales, and Daniel Wackman. Recent progress in understanding and facilitating marital communication. *Family Coordinator,* 1975, **24,** 143–152.
26. Montemayor, Raymond. Parental disciplinary techniques and the development of chil-

dren's moral judgment. Paper presented at meeting of the Society for Research in Child Development, New Orleans, 1977.

27. Navran, Leslie. Communication and adjustment in marriage. *Family Process,* 1967, **6,** 173–184.

27a. Noller, P. Marital communication & sex differences in the sending & receiving of messages. Paper presented at meetings of the Australian-New Zealand Association for the Advancement of Science. Auckland, N.Z. 1979.

28. Parke, Ross D. Effectiveness of punishment as an interaction of intensity, timing, age, nurturance, and cognitive structuring. *Child Development,* 1969, **40,** 213–235.

29. Reusch, Jurgen. Synopsis of the theory of human communication. *Psychiatry,* 1953, **16,** 215–243.

30. Rubin, Lillian B. *Worlds of pain: Life in the working class family.* New York: Basic, 1976.

31. Satir, Virginia. *Conjoint family therapy.* Palo Alto, Calif.: Science and Behavior Books, 1967.

32. Straus, Murray. Leveling, civility and violence in the family. *Journal of Marriage and the Family,* 1974, **36,** 13–29.

33. Vygotsky, Lev S. *Thought and language.* Cambridge: The M.I.T. Press, 1962.

34. *Webster's seventh collegiate dictionary.* Springfield, Mass.: Merriam, 1965.

# CHAPTER 4

# THIS GROWS ON YOU: SEX

This chapter starts with a brief look at the biologically based characteristics of male and female. A larger part of the chapter is devoted to the acquisition of masculine and feminine role behavior and attitudes toward gender roles. Sex education, human sexual response, birth control technology, and birth control use are also discussed. The topic of sexuality continues in the next chapter.

## MALE OR FEMALE, MASCULINE OR FEMININE

What determines whether a human organism becomes a woman or a man? What determines whether a person is masculine or feminine? What are masculinity and feminity? The answer to the first question is biological; the answer to the second is that being masculine or feminine is the result of the experiences of the person in interaction with the environment. The third question is the subject of much debate today, because concepts of masculinity and femininity are changing and confused. The roles of woman and man in our society are not clear-cut. Relationships between males and females are consequently in a state of flux.

Sexual differentiation is a fact of life. This chapter deals with how males and females actually differ in behavior and with how those differences arise. Some differences are due to teaching and learning as structured by family and society. Both benefits and deprivations result to individuals, families, and societies as boys and girls are taught to behave in accordance with gender roles.

DENIS STOCK, MAGNUM PHOTOS, INC.

## GENDER DIFFERENTIATION

Gender is determined at the moment of conception, when either an XX or an XY sperm wins the race to fertilize the ovum. From this moment onward, the genes organize interactions with the environment to produce a developing body that we call male or female, and changing behavior patterns that we call masculine or feminine. At six weeks, a male embryo looks just like a female embryo, because their **gonads** (sex glands) have not yet differentiated into **testes** or **ovaries**. At birth, boys can be told from girls by their genitals, but otherwise, they look very much alike. Young children become easier to sort into boys and girls as they grow older. At puberty, the development of secondary sex characteristics—breasts, hair, voice changes—makes most young people unmistakably seen as male or female. In the meantime, behavior patterns have been following the same path of differentiation. Baby boys and girls act more alike than do adolescent boys and girls.

The physical differences are easy enough to agree upon and to assign to the influence of the genes. (Really, though, genes are always expressed in an environment.) Behavior patterns are much harder to study and to explain. For one reason, they vary more. For every characteristic generally considered masculine or feminine, an exception can be found, either in another culture, or in individuals in our own society. (Some men are homemakers; some women are engineers.) For another reason, the topic of gender differences arouses emotions and prejudices. The inferior position of women has been and often is excused on the grounds of real or fabricated sex differences. Some persons of both genders assume fixed behavioral gender differences in order to defend their own life styles.

Differentiation continues into maturity, but during old age, it reverses in some ways. Old men and old women look more alike than do young men and young women. As their activities become restricted, they may also resemble each other more in behavior.

## Gender Differences

Differences between the sexes exist in physical and behavioral characteristics, but most of the differences are between the average of characteristic large numbers of boys and girls or men and women. (See Figure 4-1 for an example.) The reproductive system is the only area in which any man differs from any woman, and even in that, a very few people are hard to place in one sex or the other. Behavioral differences based on the reproductive system are very definite gender differences. For example, hormones influence feelings and actions, as shown in a study of college women, who were least likely to feel self-confident and self-assured during their menstrual period [40].

More males are conceived than females (120 males per 100 females), but males have a higher mortality rate from conception on than do females. For every 110 males born, 100 females are born. But for every 106 live male births, there are 100 live female births. Throughout life the male's higher vulnerability to disease slowly chips away at this ratio. By age 60 or 70, women exceed men in prosperous countries. In environments of extreme poverty, childbirth takes a great toll of women.

At birth, males as a group are heavier and longer than females as a group, but they are less developed. A newborn female functions as maturely as a four-to-six-week-old boy. At puberty, the average girl's growth is about two years ahead of the growth of the average boy: her bones ossify earlier. Girls learn to walk and talk before boys do. The male newborn exhibits more spontaneous movement, consisting of larger bodily movements than the female, whose movements are finer, concentrating around the facial area [26].

Sex differences in brain organization have been demonstrated in children and adults by tests of differential use of the right and left hemispheres. Boys and men, as compared with girls and women, make more use of the right hemisphere in processing spatial information. Women are more likely to use some of the verbal processing

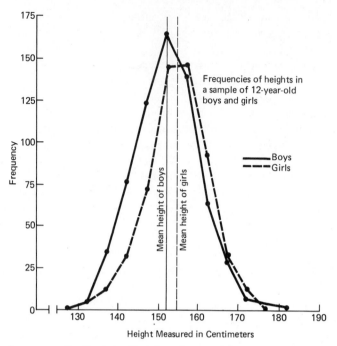

**FIGURE 4-1a**    Frequency distribution of heights of a sample of 12-year-old American youths.

*Source:* Health Services and Mental Health Administration. Height and weight of youths 12–17 years. United States DHEW Publication No. (HSM) 73-1606. Rockville, Maryland: U.S. Department of Health, Education, and Welfare, 1973. Table 1.

system, located in the left hemisphere, when they try to solve spatial problems. On the average, females are more fluent than males, suggesting more use of the left hemisphere [35]. However, these sex differences in brain organization are only differences between group averages, and very slight differences at that. There are many women who exceed the average male score on spatial tests and many men who are more fluent than the average woman. In the case of most characteristics, individual differences are larger than group differences. Even with the timing of puberty, where the difference between the averages of boys and girls is larger (about two years), the range in timing in each sex is greater than the sex differences. Thus, 11-year-old John, who has reached puberty, and 14-year-old Tamara, who has not, are both normal. Figure 4-1 shows distributions of heights of boys and girls at ages 12 and 17. At 12, the girls' mean height is slightly greater than the boys', but there are still some girls who are shorter than the average boy. At 17, the boys' mean height exceeds the girls', but there are still some boys who are shorter than the average girl.

After reviewing and criticizing hundreds of studies on sex differences, Block [5] lists some for which there is strong evidence: boys and men do better than girls and women on spatial problems, quantitative problems, and problems requiring restruc-

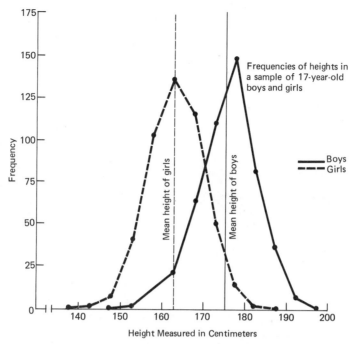

Frequency

175 —

150 —

125 —

100 —

75 —

50 —

25 —

0 —

140    150    160    170    180    190    200

Height Measured in Centimeters

Mean height of girls

Mean height of boys

Frequencies of heights in
a sample of 17-year-old
boys and girls

——— Boys
----- Girls

**FIGURE 4-1b**    Frequency distribution of height of a sample of 17-year-old American youths.

*Source:* Health Services and Mental Health Administration. Height and weight of youths 12–17 years. United States DHEW Publication No. (HSM) 73-1606. Rockville, Maryland: U.S. Department of Health, Education, and Welfare, 1973. Table 1.

turing; girls and women score higher on tests of verbal ability; men and boys are more aggressive, dominant, curious, active, exploring, and impulsive; men and boys have stronger self-concepts; girls and women express more fear and anxiety; girls and women have less task confidence; girls and women seek more help and reassurance; girls and women stay closer to friends; girls and women score higher on social desirability; young girls score higher on compliance with adults. Most of these studies say little about whether the sex differences were learned as a part of a culturally given gender role, or whether they arose from male and female genes expressing themselves in environments conducive to the development of gender differences. In other words, there may be a natural tendency for boys to learn aggressive behavior more readily than girls when an opportunity for such learning is provided.

In thinking about gender differences, it is important to remember that behavior patterns are learned (some easily, some with difficulty), and that most sex differences overlap in distribution. Especially in the realm of psychological differences, the average differences between the sexes are so small that they are completely useless in predicting what any individual can do. There is thus no basis in reality for restricting women or men from any occupation on the grounds of sex differences.

THIS GROWS ON YOU: SEX                                                            **81**

# GENDER-ROLE LEARNING IN CHILDHOOD

Only gradually does the young child become established as a boy or a girl, as he or she learns to feel, think, and act in these terms. Different theories have been developed to explain the process of gender-role learning. We briefly describe psychoanalytic theory, social learning theory, cognitive theory, and dialectical theory. Each contributes something to the understanding of gender-role learning and behavior. Our presentation of the theories does not mean that we believe that either is totally correct. Psychoanalytic theory especially has been under attack by many social scientists. The fact remains, however, that it has been a tremendous influence upon the thought of social scientists and the public as well.

## Psychoanalytic Theory

According to psychoanalytic theory, the infant begins life seeking pleasure through his mouth (through sucking). The first year of life is called the *oral* stage, and both male and female infants have as their love object their mother. However, the infant cannot at this stage distinguish himself from his mother, whom he views rather as an extension of himself. Around the beginning of the second year, the child becomes focused upon the anus and eliminatory functions as a source of pleasure (the *anal* stage). During this stage the child must learn to control his elimination of urine and feces. Beginning around age three, the third stage is the *phallic* (from *phallus,* meaning penis) stage, when the child focuses upon his or her genitals as a source of pleasure.

It is during the phallic stage that the child has important experiences in regard to sex-role learning. The girl becomes aware that she has no penis, and the boy, noticing that females lack a penis, becomes fearful that he will lose his (the "castration complex": It is called this in spite of the fact that true castration does not involve the removal of the penis, but the removal of either male or female gonads). During the phallic stage the boy develops the Oedipus complex, and the girl develops the Electra complex: He or she sexually desires the opposite-sexed parent. For the boy, the Oedipus complex also involves a fear of his father, who he thinks might harm him physically. The boy manages to overcome his fear of his father by identifying with him. The girl learns to substitute for her desire for a penis the wish for pregnancy and the child that results.

According to the theory, around age six the child's interest in sexuality drops off, and he or she enters the *latent* period that lasts until puberty. During this stage, the boy or girl is not interested in sex, nor in friends of the opposite sex. The boy is consolidating his knowledge of himself and feelings about himself as a member of one sex, affirming his gender identity. The girl is going through a comparable process, affirming her gender identity as a girl. As the child begins to mature sexually, he or she enters the *genital* stage, when once again the pleasure zone becomes the genital area. During the genital stage, the child becomes interested in members of the opposite sex.

## Social Learning Theory

A second theory of gender-role learning is social learning theory. The child learns appropriate feelings, thoughts, and behavior through interaction with other people, who instruct, reason, reinforce, and act as models. For the young child, parents are the most powerful of the social influences on gender-role learning. However, siblings are also important, as are peers. Teachers and other adults also may have influence.

**Parents as Socializers.** Most studies have shown parents as active teachers of gender identity and gender-role adoption, fathers being more concerned than mothers about sex-appropriate behavior. Even though mothers reported that they did not treat infants differently according to sex, they behaved differently with one infant dressed as a male and as a female [54]. Parents treated toddlers differently according to whether the child was a boy or a girl [11]. They gave more positive responses to boys playing with blocks than to girls, and more to girls than boys when playing with dolls. Fathers gave more negative responses than mothers when boys played with dolls or other soft toys. Parents criticized girls more than boys when they were running and jumping. Parents encouraged girls more than boys to ask for help, to help with tasks, and to stay close. A group of New Zealand parents in another study thought that preschool children showed more sex-typed behavior than their own preschool children were observed to exhibit [33].

The topic of differential treatment of boys and girls was raised in interviews with a national probability sample of 1230 families [55]. Seventeen per cent of parents (21 per cent of fathers, 14 of mothers) agreed definitely that boys and girls should be raised differently, and 35 per cent of fathers and of mothers agreed partially. Six per cent of parents were uncertain, and 42 per cent disagreed. In the following account of how parents teach gender identity, it must be remembered that some parents teach it purposely and consciously, some teach it while not intending to, and perhaps some differentiate little or not at all between boys and girls.

Gender identity is established as the baby learns "I am a boy" or "I am a girl." This piece of learning is normally a firm conviction. *Myself, a girl* or *myself, a boy* becomes incorporated into the self-concept. The lesson is so thoroughly learned by 18 months of age that when a mistaken sexual assignment needs to be corrected, authorities urge that it be done no later, and preferably several months earlier [38, p. 13]. Children as young as two have knowledge of gender-role stereotypes [29]. This knowledge is correlated with realization that gender identity is permanent and irreversible. Parents themselves learned when they were very young that boys and girls are different in important ways and that they should be treated differently. Part of every cultural heritage is an interpretation of what it means to be male and female.

When parents stray far from their culture's usual ways of teaching babies to regard themselves as male or female, those infants may grow up with some disturbance in gender identity. The classic example is the longed-for boy who turns out to be a girl but is treated as a boy, especially by the father. Her conviction of being a girl is likely to be weak.

Initial socializing for gender identity includes speaking to and of the baby as *she* or *he,* attaching words and tones of approval to sex-defining terms (my good boy, our clever daughter). Dressing the child as a boy or girl probably contributes to the establishment of gender identity, but in the cultural context. In 1895, my (MSS) father and his peers went to kindergarten in Canada dressed in blouses and pleated skirts, their hair in curls. They apparently had no problems of gender identity, because everybody knew who was a boy and who was a girl, even though the current fashions did not differentiate between male and female clothes for young children.

As the child grows from infancy, parents continue to affirm gender identity, or, as it is also called, gender-role orientation. Theories of identification hold that young children strive to incorporate some of the essence of their parents into themselves, a process that is both conscious and unconscious. In acting and feeling as she (he) perceives her (his) mother (father) to feel, the child becomes more firmly a girl (boy). Different theories impute various motives to the child's efforts to imitate parents.

Parents call attention to the ways in which Sam looks and acts like Daddy and Katie looks and acts like Mommy. Older brothers and sisters or kin may also be held up as models for Sam and Katie. Many studies on father absence, summarized by Biller indicate that fathers' influence on boys' gender-role orientation is profound. When fathers were absent or unavailable during the boys' first five years, and especially during the first two years, boys later showed less masculine self-concepts. Fathers may also exert influence on girls' gender-role orientation, as studies of father absence and unavailability have shown [4, pp. 110–114].

After the young child has established a firm gender identity, there is still much to do in sex-role development. *Gender-role adoption* is the acquiring of behavior patterns that are culturally accepted as sex-appropriate. Both parents, of course, define to children what is masculine and feminine behavior. They make it clear by what they *do,* as well as by words, rewards, and punishment, serving as models of male and female in clothing, grooming, coordination, tone of voice, work, play, interests, sensitivities, attitudes, and values. The parents' interactions with each other show children a powerful model of male-female interaction. The young child ordinarily goes along with much of what his parents ask of him. He incorporates some of the demonstrated behavior and rejects some, in favor of other models and other behavior that gratifies him more. Siblings, peers, and other adults are also models. In fact, preschool children's knowledge of culturally accepted adult male and female roles seems to be little affected by father absence, social class, race, and sex. Using appropriate pictures, young children were asked questions about who performed certain roles in a pretend family and in their own families. Father-absent children knew very well that fathers ordinarily earned wages, exerted power, and made decisions, even though they were not observing their own fathers doing so [1].

It is in *motivation* to use the knowledge that fathers exert special influence on children. Boys are generally pushed toward masculine gender-role adoption and preference for the male gender role by fathers who are warm, nurturant, and involved with the boy, and who are strong decision-makers [4].

A mother reinforces masculine behavior by direct approval and also by defining the father to the son as worthwhile, whether he be present or absent. Girls seem to be motivated to adopt gender-typed behavior by fathers who offer nurturance, acceptance, interaction, and approval for that behavior [15]. One study of father-absent, brotherless girls indicated that such young women behaved inappropriately with men, being anxious and shy or too assertive [23]. However, a recent attempt to replicate the study, using a slightly older sample, did not show such differences between father-absent and father-present girls [19]. The authors suggest that if father-absent adolescent girls do show inadequate heterosexual interaction, they may be able to compensate for father-absence through further social experiences. Another recent study showed no differences in sex-role identification between father-present and father-absent black girls and white girls [25].

A woman's ability to attain orgasm may be related to her trust in the important men in her life. Since consistently orgasmic females were found likely to have had strong, stable fathers, it is likely that trust in their sexual partners was built upon early trust in their fathers [7].

**Siblings and Other Kin.**   Gender-role learning is, of course, influenced by other family members, in addition to parents. A younger child is affected by the sex of the older siblings. When fathers are absent, older brothers' influence is likely to be heightened. (The teaching and learning functions of siblings is discussed further in the chapter on siblings.) In cases of father absence, a grandfather or an uncle sometimes takes on more responsibility with children, especially with boys. The purpose, of course, is to supply the male influence that seems to be essential for smooth gender-role development.

**Teachers.**   Both purposefully and unintentionally, teachers also play a part in gender-role learning. Like everyone else, teachers have concepts of appropriate masculine and feminine behavior. They also are either men or women, chiefly women in North America. In all the other countries where we have worked and observed in schools, the proportion of men teachers was higher in the grades and high school. In nursery schools and kindergartens the world over, women are in charge. When fathers are absent, as they are from six or seven million American families, children have a highly feminine environment. Even when fathers come home at night, many or most are away all day, and few take their children for an occasional day at work with daddy. Therefore, both younger and older American children are likely to be under the influence of women much more than of men.

ROBERT J. IZZO

A nursery school observational study revealed that young children are more likely to imitate teachers of their own sex. In the predominantly feminine school world, young girls can see more congruence between their sex roles and school goals than can young boys [32]. Women nursery school teachers have been found to reinforce feminine behavior in both girls and boys. (Feminine behavior was defined as the play activities preferred more by girls than by boys [11].)

A few years later, however, a replication of this study yielded different results [49]. Although gender preferences in the children's choice of activities were evident, and children reinforced like-sexed peers, the teachers did not differentially reinforce boys and girls. Neither did they make reinforcement contingent upon sex-appropriate play. Perhaps these teachers had consciously eliminated sex biases from their behavior with children.

A third observational study revealed nursery school teachers responding more to boys than to girls, giving boys more reprimands for aggression, and twice as much praise, hugging, and instruction as they gave to girls [47].

When nursery school teachers attempted to promote selection of sex-inappropriate toys, as they did in an experiment, young boys resisted more vigorously and *anxiously* than did girls. This finding was consistent with earlier research that has shown boys to be under greater pressure than girls to assume sex-appropriate behavior patterns [44].

There is abundant evidence that the school experience is structured very differently for boys and girls. In the later elementary grades, boys receive more than their share of low marks, grade retention, special class placement, referral to specialists, and teacher disapproval [32]. It is not surprising that boys respond with more aggression and negativism.

In a comparison of male and female teacher behavior, observations and pupil interviews were analyzed. Boys did indeed receive more disapproval than girls, but although both men and women disapproved more of boys, the men were less disapproving than the women. When choosing leaders, teachers more often chose children of their own sex. Boys saw themselves as closer to male teachers, but girls had similar feelings of affiliation toward both male and female teachers. The experimenters concluded that male teachers established a classroom atmosphere that was more congenial to boys than was that established by a woman teacher. Having a male teacher was little or no detriment to girls, and an advantage to boys [32].

**The Media.**  Gender-role learning is also influenced by toys, books, television, films, and similar experiences. Since adults design and control the media, their ideas of gender role are translated to the children by these means. Toys intended for boys are mechanical and spatial, stimulating the boy to take them apart, put them together, and fix them. Girls' toys are oriented toward "domestic development" and learning to be nurturant and social [37]. Girls often want to play with boys' toys and are usually permitted to do so. Because pressures on boys are greater, they are not often so eager to play with girls' toys. Although many books portray rigid sex roles to children, there is a trend toward humanly oriented books. *William's Doll* is a refreshingly different story of a little boy who wants a doll to love and care for, so that he can practice being a father. He gets one in the end, thanks to an understanding grandmother. But it wasn't easy [58].

A count of characters on Saturday morning television programs showed males outnumbering females three to one [39]. Males gave and received more approval and disapproval than females, suggesting, according to social learning theory, that boys are more significant persons than girls. Another analysis of children's programs showed that female characters were deferrent to the wishes of males, and more likely to be punished for action than are males. Males are portrayed as both good and evil, but females are almost always shown as good. Females are more likely to use magic; it seems that only through magic can they achieve anything. Males are shown as not deferring to the wishes of others, and not expressing admiration for others [48].

## Cognitive Theory.

Through his own thinking and reasoning, the child structures his gender role, just as he is active in building other parts of himself. Cognitive theory complements social learning theory, which focuses on the ways in which other persons influence the child's learning. Since growth and development are results of interactions of the child with his world, his own actions, as well as the actions of others, are salient in sex-role development.

The crucial establishment of gender identity, discussed under the previous topic of social learning, depends not only upon what parents and other people tell the child, but upon the child's cognition. Before three years of age, probably between one and two years, the toddler thinks something like, "I am a girl" or "I am a boy." Then she and he try to fit their behavior to what they perceive as girl behavior and boy behavior, respectively. They get the necessary information from direct statements by family and others, by observation and reinforcements for appropriate behavior. It can be as subtle as physical teasing and rough play, followed by smiles and laughs when the baby boy participates, or as an approving nod when the baby girl hugs her doll. Although the smiles and nods may act as rewards, they also act as feedback that informs the baby that the behavior actually was girl behavior or boy behavior.

Nursery school children, ages three to five, showed play preferences that had been rated sex-appropriate by adults. Boys' and girls' verbal intelligence, and boys' visual-spatial ability were correlated with choice of sex-appropriate activities, suggesting that intelligence plays a role in children's learning to conform to gender stereotypes [8].

As the child grows up, even after gender identity is firmly established and irreversible, she continues to observe, discuss, and reason about the gender roles in her family, community, and society. Eventually, if she goes to college, she learns about gender roles in other cultures. She thinks about those too and about her own self, her behavior and relationships. She develops moral values of which sex and gender role behavior are a part. She makes goals and plans for reaching them. Thus the individual exerts control and direction over her own self-development, through interaction with other people and through her own thinking.

## Dialectical Theory

Individuals and societies develop continually through experiencing conflicts and resolving them. Gender-role learning is seen as having three phases [22]. During the first phase, the child has an undifferentiated concept of sex roles and behavior. As we have already mentioned, the youngster enters the next phase very early, learning that there are girls, boys, women, and men, and that certain activities are appropriate for each. Social learning theory and cognitive theory spell out the kinds of learning and concepts that are achieved in phase 2. Most persons stop here, as do most, probably all, societies.

The next step is into phase 3, or sex-role transcendence. The conflict between masculine and feminine roles, between sex-appropriate behaviors, between men and women, is solved by discarding behavioral requirements on basis of sex. Men and women are both free to use all their abilities and to express themselves in ways that used to be restricted to one sex or the other. This condition of not being confined by gender-based restrictions is called androgyny. Androgynous men may sew and be tender; androgynous women may repair the car and ask men out on dates. Some couples try to live together in an androgynous life style.

## Changing Attitudes Toward Rigid Gender Roles

Is it necessary, as dialectical theory suggests, to go through a phase of rigid gender-role definition before achieving the freedom of sex role transcendence or androgyny? Probably a child needs to integrate into his self-concept some notion of being a boy or a girl, but surely it could be done with less vigor. Indeed, there have always been some adults, often nursery school teachers, who believed that all children should be allowed and encouraged to explore activities and materials freely, to develop all their talents, and to grow fully as human beings. Women's liberation and other social forces have sought to rescue women from the bondage of strict gender roles and in so doing have raised questions for men and women, boys, and girls. Farrell has suggested that men may be more restricted than women in terms of the range of emotional behavior allowed them and the choice between paid employment and homemaking [14].

BARBARA N. ARMSTRONG AND CYNTHIA A. OZIOMEK, THE UNIVERSITY OF AKRON

Sex-appropriate behavior is no longer clearly stated in the Western world, or even in the world as a whole. Who can now say with certainty that it is masculine to be aggressive and feminine to be sensitive? Along with the loosening of stereotypes of gender-role behavior, we see more emphasis on individuals as human persons, rather than as women or men. There is increasing latitude for all persons to acquire executive competence and assertiveness that used to be considered masculine, and attitudes of caring, knowing, and responding that used to be considered feminine. Concrete indications of these changes include unisex clothing and hair styles, men sewing and knitting, and women fighting for financial and occupational equality. In the face of these changing attitudes and practices, we wonder how many parents continue vigorous efforts to promote clear sex-role adoption by saying, "Boys don't cry," or "Little ladies don't swear," or, later on, by encouraging girls to be nurses, not doctors, and boys to be doctors, not nurses.

Because the terms *feminine* and *masculine* are emotionally tinged and associated with notions of propriety and restrictions, it is difficult to think about all persons having both masculine and feminine characteristics (as indeed they do). Therefore, the more objective terminology of Bakan [3] is helpful in learning to think about and accept the wide ranges of behaviors that are truly human and possible for both sexes. Bakan suggests that all living forms have a balance of two fundamental modalities, *agency* and *communion*. Agency has to do with the organism as an individual and is manifested in the protection, assertion, and expansion of the self. Communion has to do with the organism as a part of a larger whole, and is manifested in the sense of being one with the larger whole. Agency is what has been traditionally conceived as "masculine traits"; communion is "feminine." By getting away from the terms *masculine* and *feminine,* however, it is easier to conceive of these traits as being fundamentally human.

Bakan emphasizes that in the normal person, agency and communion are tempered or mitigated by each other, and that unmitigated agency or communion is pathological. The wholly agentic individual would think only of himself, and obviously could not function as a social being. The wholly communal person would be equally at a loss socially, because he would always defer his needs to the needs of others.

## SEX EDUCATION IN THE FAMILY: THE EARLY YEARS

When an infant is born, he begins to learn about his environment. He cannot at first distinguish himself from the things that surround him, including the person who cares for him. However, he begins to learn lessons about himself at an early age. He is quick to sense whether the person holding him is tense or relaxed.

The sex education of the child cannot be held off, as many North American parents believe, until the child is ten or eleven. It begins when the child is still an infant, and is nonverbal in the beginning. A baby enjoys being touched and tickled, he enjoys being bathed gently. When the infant's genitals are washed, he responds with pleasure. If the person bathing the infant responds with displeasure to his squirms of delight, the baby begins to learn that he is doing something wrong.

As the child grows, the parents continue to provide an education in sex, whether or not they intend to do so. Parental acceptance of family nudity, whether or not parents kiss and cuddle in front of the children, adult and child toileting practices, parental acceptance of child masturbation, and other sex exploration practices, all begin to form the child's ideas about sexuality. The little girl pictured on this page is learning how her parents express their love for each other. When the child starts to ask questions about herself and her world, she will include some that the parent may interpret as being sexually oriented. The parent's reactions to these questions will also shape the child's sexual attitudes. If the child senses that the parent gets upset

By watching, Kisandra learns that her parents believe that loving and touching go together.

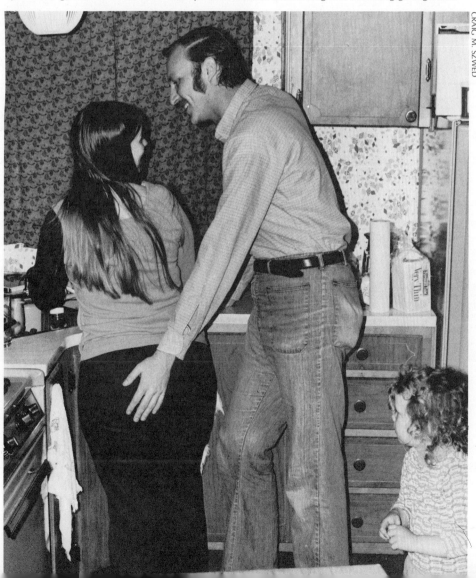

or nervous when certain topics are brought up, the child will invariably feel that there is something wrong with these topics.

The parent, of course, is not the only socializing agent. I (LSS) suffered from an early age because of my knowledge of sexual matters. At the age of three or four, I informed my four-year-old boyfriend that his "piddler" was really called a penis. His mother was horrified at my "dirty talk" and said that I could no longer play with him if I did not stop. I was perplexed. Why did my mother and father tell me to say something that upset my friend's mother so much? Parents need to be sensitive to the reactions of their children to such situations.

If the parents and child have a trusting relationship with each other, the child will probably continue to bring questions to the parent who has answered them (or honestly tried to) in the past. The child may eventually pick up the cultural taboos concerning sexual activity and development and stop asking questions of the parent, especially around adolescence. We return to the subject of sex education in the home later in this chapter (see page 96).

## SEXUAL BEHAVIOR IN CHILDHOOD

In some societies, parents will kiss or stroke their infant's genitals in order to comfort him or her. Whether or not the young child is stimulated by those older than himself, he will discover his own genitals just as he discovers his fingers and toes. However, the American baby is likely to learn from his parents that it is considered wrong to play with his genitals. Some parents may slap the child or say, "Don't do that!" in a desperate tone of voice; others may give the child a toy to play with instead. For some children, the mere fact that the parent does not respond with a comment such as, "That feels good, doesn't it?" is enough to give the child the idea that all is not right.

The child's feelings of shame may or may not stop him from sexually stimulating (masturbating) himself. Girls as well as boys **masturbate,** although they may not be aware that they are doing so. The male usually masturbates by moving his hand up and down the shaft of his penis, but he may also stimulate himself by pressing his penis against a bed or other object, or by rubbing it on his thigh. A female's self-stimulation techniques may vary widely. Some females masturbate by pressing their legs together, or by rubbing against a pillow, bed, and so forth. Others stroke, tickle, or press their vulvas with their hands. Some tickle or press directly on or next to the clitoris in a rhythmic motion, either gently or with more vigor. Another method is to insert an object in the vagina and simulate sexual intercourse.

It used to be thought that masturbation caused a number of maladies, including insanity and acne. It is now known that masturbation does not become harmful to the individual unless he (or she) experiences a large amount of guilt, or masturbates to the exclusion of all interpersonal activities. Masturbation can be an extremely useful way to release sexual frustrations at times when other releases are not available or are not appropriate.

Children also play sex games with each other, in like-sex and opposite-sex groups. They examine each other's genitals and may attempt and succeed at sexual intercourse—without ejaculation on the part of the prepuberal male. Depending upon the attitudes of his society or parents, the child will be encouraged, ignored, or punished for his sexual behavior.

## PUBERTY AND ADOLESCENCE

The stage of development at which sexual maturity is reached is **puberty.** A series of bodily changes called **pubescence** lead to the point of puberty. Pubescence lasts about two years, on the average, but some children reach puberty in less than two years, while others take longer. There is evidence that pubescence begins when the body reaches a critical weight. **Menarche,** the first menstruation, is commonly taken as the indication of puberty in a girl. Boys have no event that corresponds to menarche, but male puberty is indicated when a boy first produces sperms. The timing of puberty is genetically controlled, but is influenced by nutrition and possibly by other factors.

The term **adolescence** refers to a cultural invention, a time of life that is socially defined. It begins with pubescence and ends, vaguely, at adulthood. Since adulthood has many definitions, even within North American culture, it is hard for an individual to know whether he or she graduates from adolescence to adulthood when first getting a driver's license, when graduating from high school, when getting a job, or when getting married.                                                                •

### Female Physiology

The average age of menarche for American girls is around 12.5 years, which means that pubescence begins around 10.5. A group of malnourished American girls began to menstruate at 14.4 years [17], although their weight, 43.5 kg., was almost the same as the menarchal weight of the well-nourished girls (44.6 kg.) who were 12.5 years old. Critical weights for menarche are different in different races, the Japanese weight, for instance, being about 6 kg. less than the American. The age of menarche has declined throughout the Western world for over a century, most likely because better nutrition has made girls bigger at an earlier age.

Pubescence usually begins with the appearance of the breast bud, although sometimes the pubic hair is the first sign [51]. The uterus and the vagina develop further at the same time. The height spurt begins and picks up speed, reaching its greatest velocity at about six months before menarche and then slowing down.

About two years after the first pubic hair appears, circumanal hair and then axillary hair begin to grow. The internal organs also spurt in growth, each having its characteristic timing of the peak in growth velocity.

During the first years or months after menarche, a girl is less capable of conceiving than she will be later, but conception may be a possibility for her. Her menstrual periods may be erratic for a year or two, and she may skip periods altogether.

In a mature female, the tissue within the uterus is built up each month prior to **ovulation,** the release of an egg from one ovary. Rich in blood vessels, this lining is sloughed off each month if the egg is not fertilized. This sloughing-off of the blood-rich uterine lining is called **menstruation.** Menstruation occurs generally every twenty-eight days and lasts from two to seven days. However, it is considered normal for women to menstruate every twenty days, or every forty days. Each woman has her own individual cycle, which may vary as much as ten days (five days early or late) and still be considered a normal cycle. It is quite common for women to have emotional ups and downs connected with the menstrual cycle. The few days before menstruation are likely to be difficult ones for those women who experience cyclic effects. Around age fifty, the woman experiences a change in physiologic functioning that is known as **menopause,** the **climacteric,** or the "change of life." Her ovaries gradually stop producing eggs and hormones over a period of about two years. When menopause is complete and no ova are being released, the woman can no longer become pregnant. We discuss menopause further in the next chapter, pages 131–132.

## Male Physiology

Pubescence begins, on the average, at about age 12, with the testes and scrotum increasing in size [51]. Pubic hair may also begin, but its growth is slight until the time when the penis begins to grow fast. Height also spurts at this time. About two years after the first pubic hair, circumanal, then axillary and facial hair appear. The voice begins to change, because of the enlarging larynx, at the time when penis growth is nearly finished. Strength spurts when height is nearly complete. About midway through the series of changes, about a third of boys have some breast development, which lasts about a year. The pubescent growth spurt lasts longer in boys than in girls, resulting in greater average height in men than in women. Although the sequence of pubescent growth is quite consistent, the timing varies considerably from one boy to another. There is great variation in a group of 13- and 14-year-olds, ranging from prepubescence to maturity.

A few months after the beginning of pubescence a boy will experience his first ejaculation, either through self-stimulation or when he is asleep (a "wet dream"). From infancy, he has been capable of having an erection and probably also an orgasm [16], but no ejaculation has occurred. Ejaculation is made possible at puberty when the male begins to produce sperm.

# PUBERTY: A CROSS-CULTURAL PERSPECTIVE

By the time a person reaches puberty, he or she already has acquired many feelings and ideas about the culturally accepted manifestation of sexuality. The body is seen as something to be covered up or displayed in various types of social situations. Members of the opposite sex and the same sex may or may not touch in public, and if they do touch, the contact may be approved or disapproved. An American man living in India scandalized the citizens of a medium-sized city by wearing short-shorts and kissing his wife good-bye at the train station. An Indian holy man, naked or wearing a loincloth, was "decent" but an American in short-shorts was not. In our society, a bathing suit is "decent" when worn at the beach but not in the office.

Some societies permit children to engage in sexual play before puberty, because of the belief that if a child does not experiment, he will never function adequately in the sexual realm as an adult. Others forbid sex play until puberty, but permit limited or relatively unlimited sex play after puberty has been reached. Other societies restrict full sexual activity until marriage [16]. Whatever the correct childhood behavior in a particular society, the members of that society believe that the behavior contributes to proper adult attitudes and behavior [16].

In many preindustrial societies, adulthood follows quickly on the heels of child-hood. Before menarche, a female is a girl, and afterwards, she is a woman. She may, however, have to go through ceremonies known as **puberty rites** in order to be fully admitted to womanhood. This usually means that she is secluded from most of the people in her group, especially the men. She may receive special instruction from older women regarding sex and marriage. In some societies, she is tattooed, or her ears are pierced, or her hair is cut off. Generally, at the end of her time of seclusion, she is bathed or goes through a ritual purification, after which she dons the clothes of a mature woman.

For the male in such societies, puberty rites may be even more important than for the girl, because he does not have the dramatic beginning of menstruation to mark his passage from childhood to manhood. His puberty rite may be very simple: on the island of Truk, when a male's facial and pubic hair become noticeable, he puts on a red loincloth and goes to live in the men's dormitory.

Some societies pay attention to the appearance of facial or body hair or to the boy's first ejaculation as an indication of his manhood. In other societies, boys are initiated in groups when enough boys in an age group have become sufficiently mature. In many societies, male puberty rites include seclusion of the boy and a test of his endurance through ordeals or some kind. He may undergo circumcision or other bodily mutilation [16]. If he successfully completes the initiation rites, it is proclaimed to the world that he is a man.

In modern industrial societies, it is extremely difficult to pinpoint exactly when an adolescent becomes an adult. There are a number of occasions that may serve as **rites-de-passage,** such as graduating from high school, becoming 18 or 21 years old, joining the military, graduating from college, or getting married. However, some grown-up children are still dependent upon their parents in some way for support, perhaps even after military service is over, or when college has begun and ended, or even after the children have married and borne children of their own. Likewise, some "children" who are still in school or who have dropped out of school before age 18 are full-fledged members of the working force, supporting themselves and perhaps their parents or brothers and sisters as well.

Adulthood, then, cannot be easily defined in our society as it can in a society where there is a recognized break between childhood and maturity. The end of adolescence, the time between the end of childhood and the beginning of adulthood, comes at different times for different people.

## SEX EDUCATION IN THE FAMILY: PUBESCENCE

When the child's body begins to mature, she (or he) has to adapt her self-concept to her changing form. How a child reacts will depend in part upon the family's attitude toward the changes. The girl who is told nothing in advance about menstruation, or the boy who has been told nothing about ejaculation, may be frightened when the evidence first appears. Not all parents understand their own sexual "plumbing" and its workings, but there are ways for parents to find out: through books, from the family doctor, Planned Parenthood, or a local family service agency. Sexual anatomy and reproduction are taught to children in many schools, but the basic attitudes and feelings about sex are acquired long before pubescence. The biological changes that herald sexual maturation make sex information even more important at this time.

## SEXUAL RESPONSE

In order for a woman to become pregnant, she does not have to be sexually aroused. All that is necessary is that a man become sexually aroused enough to have an erection and an ejaculation in or very close to her vagina. The female's contribution to the new life depends upon her own biological clockwork. For the male to contribute to a new life, a complicated series of responses must take place.

### Male Response

When a male becomes sexually aroused, the spaces in the spongy tissue of his penis become engorged with blood, making the penis firm and erect. Arousal may be caused by fantasy, by viewing a person or object, by touching another person, or by being touched by someone. The erection may be lost if the individual is startled in some way, by a sudden noise, change in lighting or temperature, or other environmental changes [34].

Once the penis is erect (the *excitement* phase), it may be inserted into the female's vagina or other means of manipulation may be employed in order to induce orgasm. During sexual intercourse, the penis is plunged into the vagina, drawn partially out again, and then plunged in again. This in-and-out activity may last only a second or two, or many minutes. Many men learn to delay the completion of their response cycle, increasing the likelihood of their partner's reaching orgasm. After the penis has become erect, the male experiences a *plateau* stage that is a time of high sexual excitement. Usually, the plateau stage is followed by the *orgasmic* phase, when ejaculation occurs. At times, however, a man may not be able to reach the orgasmic phase; instead, his penis will gradually lose its hardness.

When an individual is about to have an orgasm, he or she knows that it is imminent, much as a person knows when a sneeze is coming. The exact mechanisms that trigger an orgasm are not known. A simple explanation, however, is that neuromuscular tension is released [36]. A normal orgasm may be mild or extremely intense.

Immediately following orgasm, the male ejaculates, releasing about a teaspoonful of semen, which is thick and milky and contains millions of sperm. The ejaculate may spurt from the end of the penis or it may dribble out. After ejaculation, the penis returns to its flaccid state. Before a male can be sexually stimulated again, he must pass through a refractory period that may last for a few seconds to any number of hours. Unlike the male, the female does not have to experience an orgasm in order to contribute her part to the creation of new life. She is, however, capable of *multiple* orgasms, whereas the man must undergo the refractory period before he may experience a second orgasm (See Figure 4-2).

## Female Response

Freud made a distinction between a woman's having a clitoral orgasm, through stimulation of the clitoris, and a vaginal orgasm, through sexual intercourse. The former was his definition of an infantile woman, and the latter he defined as a mature woman. Masters and Johnson's laboratory research has demonstrated that there is no physiological difference between these so-called types of orgasms. There is only one kind of orgasm, triggered by direct or indirect stimulation of the clitoris. The orgasm is located and *experienced* by the woman in or around the vagina [27]. Some women require direct stimulation of the clitoris in order to reach orgasm; for other women, such stimulation is painful. Similarly, women vary in the amount of vaginal sensitivity that they report.

Many women fear that they are abnormal if they do not easily achieve orgasm through coitus. Recent clinical evidence indicates that many, perhaps most, women who are able to reach orgasm are *not* orgasmic through coitus alone. A surprising

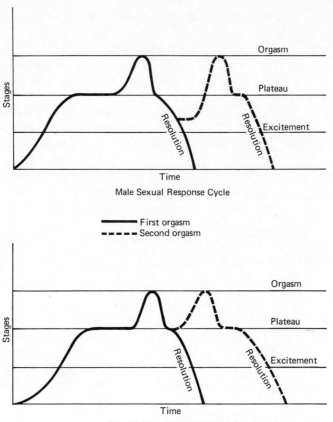

Orgasm

Plateau

Resolution

Resolution

Excitement

Stages

Time

Male Sexual Response Cycle

First orgasm
Second orgasm

Orgasm

Plateau

Resolution

Resolution

Excitement

Stages

Time

Female Sexual Response Cycle

**FIGURE 4-2**    Male and female sexual response cycles, showing that the female is capable of multiple orgasms, whereas the male must undergo a refractory period before experiencing a second orgasm.

*Source:* Adapted from William H. Masters and Virginia E. Johnson, *Human sexual response.* Boston: Little, Brown, 1966, p. 5.

number of women who complain of never having reached orgasm are able to climax when they are given sufficient stimulation, either through masturbation or from their partners [27].

The first sign that a female is becoming sexually excited is the "sweating" of the vagina: ten to thirty seconds after the beginning of effective sexual stimulation, vaginal lubrication appears within the vagina, preparing the vagina for penetration by the penis. Although the early embryonic development of the clitoris is parallel to that of the penis, and although in some ways the clitoris resembles a miniature penis, it does not respond to sexual stimulation in the same way as does the penis. The glans (head) of the clitoris will engorge with blood, but this engorgement may not be noticeable. The clitoris does *not* "erect" the same way as does the penis [34].

As the female becomes sexually aroused, during the excitement stage, her vagina, which is normally shaped like a tube, balloons out at the top so that it looks more like an inverted pear. As she proceeds to the plateau stage, the width and depth of her vagina increase a bit more. When a female experiences an orgasm, rhythmic contractions occur in her uterus and vagina. Unlike the male, who can experience only one orgasm before he must go through a refractory period, the female can experience a series of orgasms before dropping into the resolution stage [34]. (See Figure 4-2.)

Kinsey found that women increased in sexual responsiveness (ratio of orgasms per coital contact) up until around age thirty, and then dropped off somewhat [28]. Part of the reason for this increase may be that in our society a woman has to overcome her girlhood socialization that sex is wrong. She has to learn full sexual responsiveness. Another reason is that her body becomes more responsive with more sexual experience.

When a man becomes sexually aroused, his penis becomes engorged with blood. Similarly, when a woman becomes aroused, the tissue surrounding her sex organs become full of blood. The clitoris has aptly been described as "the tip of the iceberg" [46]. During sexual excitement, it takes longer for the woman's network of blood veins to engorge with blood, partly because there are more veins. Sexual activity and pregnancies increase the complexity of this network, and increase a woman's sexual capacity [46].

## Individual Differences

Sexual responsiveness is highly complex. It depends upon a person's anatomy, innate capacity, and experiences. In the nineteenth century, it was thought that men had a greater sexual capacity than women; today opinion is swinging in the other direction. Because women can have more orgasms in a shorter period of time, it is said that they have greater capacity than men.

Not all persons have an equal interest in, or desire for, sexual activity. A male or female may feel inadequate or disabled sexually because he or she does not feel able to measure up to a standard of sexuality, or feels that he or she has exceeded it. The girl who was interested in sex used to feel abnormal, as did the boy who was not interested in sex. Today, the girl who can't have multiple orgasms may feel that she is different. It should be remembered that there is a wide range of normal behavior, and that individual differences are much greater than the differences between averages of two large groups.

Some couples may find that they are instantly compatible sexually, but for most couples, sexual adjustment takes time. North Americans are not trained in sexual techniques, as are the Mangaians of Polynesia. The young Mangaian male learns about female sexual anatomy and learns the difference between a fully covered clitoris and an exposed clitoris, a high clitoris and a low clitoris, differently shaped labia, and so on. Different types of anatomy require different types of stimulation, and the Mangaian youth learns these techniques expertly [46]. By contrast, the Western male and female have to discover their own idiosyncracies by themselves, and may worry when they appear to differ from a standard set forth in their marriage manual.

According to Kaplan [50], a sex therapist, a highly prevalent sexual problem that affects couples today is lack of sexual desire or an imbalance of desire between members of a couple. When sex therapy fails, the lack of sexual desire on the part of one or both partners is frequently the cause. Lack of desire may come from boredom with one's partner, which may be the result of making love in the same way for months or years. Sometimes lack of desire indicates that there are other conflicts in the relationship. In other cases, sexual problems can be helped by getting accurate information. For example, it may help a particular middle-aged couple to know that a man at 40 or 50 requires more direct stimulation in order to achieve and maintain an erection than he did 20 years before, but that women's sexual responsiveness generally peaks around age 40. Kaplan reports that men are more likely to want to make love in the morning, and women are more likely to want to make love at night. When partners want sex at different times of the day, a compromise needs to be worked out. In order to solve a couple-centered sexual problem (which most sexual problems are), verbal communication about sex is essential.

## COMMUNICATION AND SEX

Sexual behavior that occurs between two people is itself a form of communication. The same message, however, is not always inherent in all acts of sexual intercourse (or breast-fondling or oral-genital intercourse) even between the same people. A specific sex act may mean, "I love you" or "I enjoy you" or "You turn me on," or "I abuse you." It can, of course, mean one thing to one partner and something else to the other. Sexually intimate behavior can be an expression of feeling that already exists, or it can cause a feeling to grow larger or smaller. Verbal communication is needed to clarify the development of feelings.

Communication about sex is important for the enhancement of the sensual and sexual aspects of the relationship, as well. Masters and Johnson [34] emphasize the importance of each partner letting the other know what feels good. What is most enjoyable to one person may be dull, painful, or repulsive to another. The quality of communication is important: saying "You're clumsy—stop it" would not be as help-ful as asking for a gentle touch.

Communication about sex can also avert unwanted pregnancy. Before the invention of highly effective and nonvisible female contraceptives (that is, the Pill and the I.U.D.), the careful male used a condom. Now, many males assume that their female partners have protected themselves. After all, the men reason, it *is* the female who gets pregnant. Both may be reluctant to discuss contraception before

coitus. The female may fear that if she mentions that she is unprotected, intercourse will not take place. If pregnancy results, it is the fault of both. It is to the topic of birth control that we now turn.

## BIRTH CONTROL

Through birth control, couples, but especially women, gain more control over their lives. In this section, we discuss birth control methods.

### Some Historical Methods

Many people today seem to think that the subject of birth control is relatively new. However, birth control was mentioned in Egyptian records dating back to 4,000 years ago, and it was discussed by the Greek philosophers 2,400 years ago. The earliest surviving records on birth control from India are about 1,600 years old. The first Chinese record of birth control is in a medical text written 1,300 years ago, although the idea is probably much older [21].

Some of the ancient contraceptives were more useful than others. Magic charms might be worn, or brews drunk from roots or leaves. The World Health Organization is currently conducting research to determine the effectiveness of herbal contraceptives that have been used for centuries in various parts of the world [42]. The vagina might be washed out by means of a douche, or other substances such as pepper might be inserted in the vagina after coitus. More sophisticated methods included the forerunners of modern mechanical barrier methods: Egyptian women used plugs made of crocodile droppings; other people have used plugs made of seaweed, beeswax, cloth, and other substances. Aristotle recommended the use of oil of cedar or frankincense mixed with olive oil inserted in the vagina before intercourse.

Romans used the forerunner of the modern condom, which is a sheath placed over the penis to catch the ejaculate fluid. However, the first condom-like devices were used by women who placed a loose pouch made of animal membrane in their vagina. Condoms worn by men were probably a later invention, and it is not until 1844 when rubber was first vulcanized that the use of condoms became widespread [21].

## "Natural" Methods

The most effective method of birth control is **abstinence.** This method is more widely practiced among the unmarried than the married, although certain religious groups have practiced abstinence. Gandhi, the political leader who fought for India's independence from the British, advocated abstinence as the solution to India's growing population problem, with disastrous results.

**Continence,**  like abstinence, is a method of birth control that requires no special devices. In this method, the male penetrates the vagina with his penis, but does not achieve orgasm or ejaculation. This method was practiced by the Oneida community in New York State in the midnineteenth century. It is not recommended medically, because male sexual release is not attained. When the individual is sexually aroused, his or her genitals become engorged with blood. When the individual has an orgasm, tension and blood buildup are released. If there is no release, painful congestion may result, sometimes known as "blue balls" or "lover's nuts," in the male. The female may also suffer from congestion, although she may obtain release through orgasm without fear of pregnancy. Another hazard of this practice is that it is possible for a woman to become pregnant even if her partner is capable of practicing continence. A few sperm may be contained in the preejaculatory fluid that may ooze from the end of the penis during sexual excitement. If these sperm are deposited in the vagina, it is possible that pregnancy will result.

**Withdrawal** (also called **coitus interruptus**) is similar to continence, except that the male withdraws his penis from the vagina just before he ejaculates. As with continence, sperm in the preejaculatory fluid may cause pregnancy. Another danger is that during orgasm the male's natural reaction is to thrust deeper into the vagina, not to withdraw. This method may cause considerable anxiety on the part of both partners, but especially the female, wondering whether the male will be able to withdraw in time. Out of 100 women whose partners use this method for one year, 20–25 will become pregnant. (For every 100 sexually active women using *no contraceptive method* for one year, 80 will become pregnant [20].)

**Rhythm** is the only method of birth control presently sanctioned by the Roman Catholic Church. The rationale behind the rhythm method is that a woman may become pregnant only a few days of each month, just before and just after she ovulates. Therefore, if she restricts intercourse to only her infertile days, she will not become pregnant. In theory, the rhythm method should work well, but unfortunately it is difficult to determine for sure when the fertile days are. If a woman's menstrual cycle is perfectly regular each month, she is more likely to succeed with the rhythm method. Only 8 per cent of women have cycles that are regular [20].

If a woman's periods are not regular, it is impossible to determine in advance when ovulation will occur. Even a woman whose periods are regular may ovulate early or late because of sickness or a change in routine.

A second method of determining the time of ovulation is by taking the woman's temperature every morning before she gets out of bed. A day or two before ovulation, her temperature will rise about 0.6° F. When this occurs, she should refrain from sexual intercourse for three days. The temperature method is not foolproof, either, because illness or distress may also cause temperature fluctuations that have nothing to do with the presence or absence of ovulation.

Another rhythm birth control method uses as an ovulation indicator changes in the mucus in the cervical opening. The cervical opening is protected by a "plug" of mucus that changes in viscosity throughout the menstrual cycle. Women can learn to detect changes in the consistency of their cervical mucus, and avoid intercourse when the viscosity of their cervical mucus indicates that ovulation is about to occur or has recently occurred. Care must be taken not to confuse changes in vaginal secretions with changes in cervical mucus [20].

Effectiveness of the rhythm method is generally not high, around 25 to 40 pregnancies per 100 women per year. Women who are properly trained to use changes in cervical mucus have better results. One study reported that only two to three per cent of women using this method became pregnant in a year [20].

**Breastfeeding** reduces the risk of pregnancy among a large population of women, but should not be relied upon by the individual nursing mother. Women who breast feed are less likely to ovulate and to have menstrual periods than are women who have recently given birth that do not breastfeed [20]. However, since ovulation precedes menstruation, it is possible for a nursing mother to ovulate and to become pregnant before her menstrual periods resume after she gives birth. By twelve months after the birth of a baby, the contraceptive effectiveness of lactation is considerably reduced [13]. Among 100 mothers who rely solely upon breastfeeding as a contraceptive, about 40 will become pregnant in a year [20].

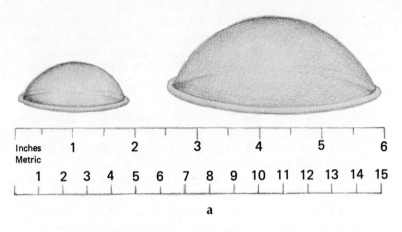

| Inches | 1 | 2 | 3 | 4 | 5 | 6 |
| Metric | | | | | | |

1  2  3  4  5  6  7  8  9  10  11  12  13  14  15

a

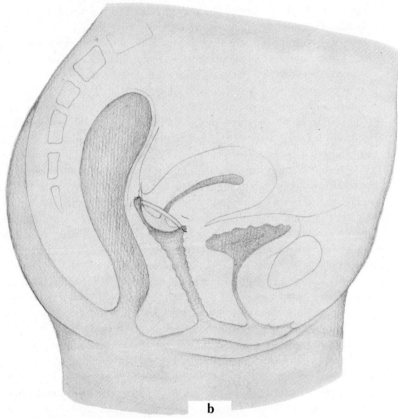

b

**FIGURE 4-3**      Diaphragms. a: Scale shown by ruler. b: Diaphragm in place.

## Preventive Methods

**Mechanical Methods.**   The **diaphragm** is a shallow rubber or synthetic rubber cup that is inserted into the vagina and fitted over the cervix, preventing sperm from entering (see Figure 4-3). It ranges in size from about two to four inches in diameter, depending upon the size of the woman's internal organs. A flexible rubber-covered metal ring helps hold it in place. The diaphragm must be properly fitted to the individual woman by a physician or other trained medical person. The diaphragm must be used with a spermicidal (sperm-killing) jelly or cream, which is smeared around the edge of the diaphragm and placed in the center of the cup. To be most effective, the diaphragm should be inserted before the woman becomes sexually aroused. Proper placement of the diaphragm is more difficult in a sexually aroused woman, since at this time the top part of her vagina is expanded and the cervix does not protrude as far into the vagina. When the diaphragm is in place, additional cream or jelly may be inserted into the vagina with an applicator. Additional cream or jelly *must* be used prior to each subsequent ejaculation. The diaphragm must be inserted not more than two hours before coitus, and must be left in place for at least six hours afterwards. Properly inserted, the diaphragm may be left in place for 8 to 24 hours without causing discomfort.

Over the period of one year, among women who use the diaphragm every time there is a penile-vaginal contact, two or three out of 100 will become pregnant. Since diaphragm users occasionally fail to use the devices, the actual rate of pregnancies among diaphragm users is nine to 13 per hundred women per year [14]. The diaphragm is an excellent method for most women who feel comfortable touching their genitals and who are strongly motivated to avoid pregnancy. A study of 2,175 diaphragm users found a 2 per cent failure rate in a year's time [30].

The **condom** is a sheath worn on the penis that prevents the sperm from coming into contact with the female (see Figure 4-4.) It may be made of animal membrane, or more usually, very thin rubber. The condom is almost as reliable as the diaphragm; its effectiveness may be increased by placing a small amount of spermicidal cream or jelly in it before it is put on, or by the woman's using contraceptive foam. Condoms are available in drugstores, and sometimes in vending machines in men's rooms. It is advisable to buy them only from drugstores, since the quality is probably higher. Condoms may deteriorate if exposed to heat; therefore, one should not keep them in a pocket or wallet next to the body.

Condoms may be reused. If they are the rubber kind, they should be washed after use, dried with a towel, powdered with talc, and rerolled. If they are made from animal membrane, they should be washed out and stored in rubbing alcohol. One should be sure to rinse condoms very carefully before reusing those stored in alcohol. Before reuse, condoms should be tested for holes by filling them with water.

It is important to leave a space at the end of the condom for the semen. If worn too snugly, the condom may burst. The male should withdraw after ejaculation so that the shrinking of the penis does not cause semen to leak out of the edge of the condom. For every 100 women whose partner uses condoms each and every time

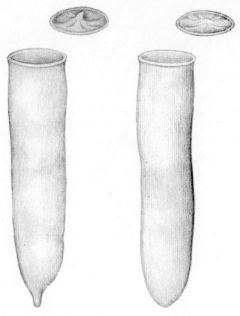

**FIGURE 4-4**    Condoms.

there is penile-vaginal contact for one year, 3 will become pregnant. This number may be reduced if contraceptive cream or jelly is used in conjunction with the condom. The actual rate for condom users is 10 pregnancies per 100 women per year [20].

   **Chemical Barriers.**   Chemical methods include the use of jellies and creams that are inserted into the vagina prior to intercourse, forming a barrier that both prevents sperm from entering the uterus and kills many of the sperm. A chemical barrier is aerosol foam, which is sold without a prescription in drugstores. Chemical barriers must be reapplied before each act of coitus. The length of time that may elapse between application of the foam and coitus varies with type and brand. Other types of chemical barriers are tablets that dissolve on contact with the vagina and suppositories that melt in the vagina. For every 100 women who use contraceptive foam each time there is penile-vaginal contact for one year, slightly over 3 will become pregnant. The pregnancy rate among actual users of contraceptive foam is 22 per 100 women per year [20]. Relatively new in this country is a suppository that produces a contraceptive foam when placed in the vagina (for example, Encare Oval). Although its manufacturers advertise extremely high rates of effectiveness, many family planning specialists believe that the effectiveness is about the same as that of other chemical barriers [20]. With any chemical barrier, family planning specialists recommend that condoms be used in addition during midcycle when risk of pregnancy is greatest.

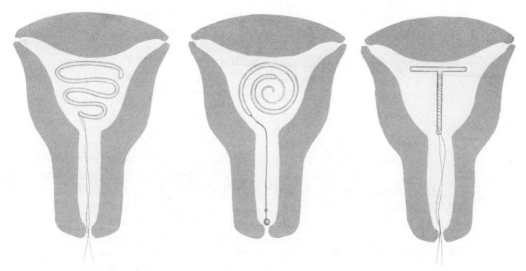

**FIGURE 4-5**    IUDs in place. Left to right: Lippes loop, coil, copper T.

**The Intrauterine Device (IUD).** The first known "IUDs" were pebbles placed in camels' uteruses to prevent the camels from being burdened by pregnancy or young while crossing the deserts. Modern IUDs are made of steel, plastic, or plastic and copper, and come in a variety of shapes (see Figure 4-5). The device is inserted by a doctor or trained technician into the woman's uterus, usually during her menstrual period when the mucus plug is thin. The cervix is slowly dilated; this process causes some cramping. The IUD is then inserted. There may be some cramping and bleeding after the insertion, and the IUD may be expelled from the uterus by means of muscle contractions. Many women experience no discomfort; others experience mild discomfort during their menstrual periods. For still others, pain may be severe at times. If the bleeding and pain become intolerable, a woman may have to have the device removed. However, if she is able to retain the device, it may remain in place for about two years.

IUDs have a small string that hangs down the through the cervix, and may be felt by the women's fingers when she inserts them in her vagina. She should check each week to make sure that she can still feel the string.

It is not known exactly how IUD's work. Different shaped IUDs work better in different women. Popular kinds are the Lippes loop, Saf-T-Coil, and the copper 7. The copper 7 is shaped like a 7 and has a very thin copper wire wrapped around the shaft. Shaped like a T, the Progestasert-T has the unique feature of containing a small amount of progesterone, a hormone that is released slowly into the uterus.

The IUD has the advantage of being coitus-independent; that is, since the IUD remains in the woman's uterus all of the time, she does not have to be concerned with applying a contraceptive device when she is about to have intercourse. Disadvantages of the IUD include greater risk of infection and ectopic pregnancy (a pregnancy that occurs in the Fallopian tube or within the body cavity instead of in the uterus). Some IUD users report heavier menstrual periods and more menstrual cramps than they had before the IUD was inserted. Out of every 100 women using IUDs who do not expel the devices, between one and three will become pregnant in one year. The longer a woman uses an IUD, the less likely she is to become pregnant [20].

**Oral Contraceptives.**  Birth control pills have freed between 80 and 100 million women in the world from the fear of unwanted pregnancy. In the United States, there are about 10 to 15 million "Pill" users. There are three kinds of female oral contraceptives, all of which work by preventing ovulation, by making the uterine lining hostile to any fertilized ovum that "tries to implant," or both. Exactly how pills work is not completely understood; other factors as well may prevent pregnancy.

The most commonly prescribed pill is made of a combination of estrogen and progesterone. The first pill is taken on the fifth day of the menstrual period, and pills are taken for a total of 20 or 21 days. A few days after the last pill is taken, menstruation begins again.

The sequential pill is also taken for 20 to 21 days, beginning on the fifth day of the menstrual period. The first fourteen pills contain only estrogen, and the last six or seven contain estrogen and progesterone.

The "minipill," which is less effective than the combination pill, contains a small dose of progestin and is taken every day. The minipill is more effective in previous users of other oral contraceptives. Among women who have never used other oral contraceptives, the pregnancy rate is about 3.5 per 100 women per year, but among previous users of other oral contraceptives, the pregnancy rate is just under two.

Birth control pills should not be used without consultation with a doctor. The woman should ask the doctor for a complete physical examination, including a test for cervical cancer. If there is a history of breast cancer or blood clotting in the woman's family, she should tell her doctor so that he can take the information into consideration. She *must* not use birth control pills if she has any history of blood clotting disease, breast cancer, undiagnosed genital bleeding, undiagnosed breast lumps, severe impairment of the liver or kidney, or any undiagnosed uterine mass [20].

The metabolic processes and nutritional requirements of normal women have been found to be affected by oral contraceptives [6]. In women taking oral contraceptives, requirements for vitamin B 6 were raised considerably and the level of vitamin A in the bloodstream was increased. The glucose tolerance level has been changed [56]. (Glucose tolerance refers to an individual's ability to metabolize carbohydrates, or starches and sugars. A woman who uses oral contraceptives has a higher blood glucose level than a woman who does not use oral contraceptives. Therefore, diabetics and other individuals with glucose tolerance problems should avoid using oral contraceptives.) Effects of oral contraceptives on metabolic processes are heightened in women who smoke [56].

A number of side effects are associated with the use of birth control pills. For most women, however, the side effects are minor. Some women become nauseous when they first begin to take pills. Others gain or lose weight. Some may have an increase in size and/or tenderness of their breasts. If a woman is troubled by side effects from the pill, she should consult her physician. When properly used, the combined type of birth control pill is the most effective method of birth control that is reversible. For every *thousand* women who use birth control pills for one year, between one and ten will become pregnant. Between 50 and 60 per cent of women who try birth control pills discontinue use during the first year [20].

**Sterilization.**   The most common kind of male and female sterilization uses the same technique: in both cases, the tubes through which the sex cells travel are severed and tied off, or burned. The male operation is called a **vasectomy,** and may be done in a doctor's office. Usually, the parts of the vasa deferentia that are in the scrotum are cut and each end is tied back upon the tube. A few stitches are all that is necessary to sew the slit in the scrotum. After the operation, the sperm can no longer escape from the testes, but are resorbed into the body. However, sterilization is not effective until the sperm stored outside of the testes are ejaculated, in a few weeks to a few months. Since sperm make up only a tiny fraction of the ejaculate fluid, it is impossible to detect the difference between the semen of a sterilized man from a fertile, nonsterilized man unless a microscope is used. The man does not have any impairment of his sexual functions, unless he is affected psychologically.

Because the woman's Fallopian tubes are located deep within her body, a **tubal ligation,** the female counterpart of a vasectomy, is harder to perform. There are several ways in which a tubal ligation may be done. If a woman has delivered a baby by means of Caesarian section, the tubes are readily available and may be cut and tied. Although this kind of sterilization is easiest for the doctor to perform, it has the highest failure rate. An incision may be made in the vagina, or in the abdomen, and the tubes cut and tied. Another method of severing the tubes is cauterization (burning). When this procedure is used, the tubes may be approached either through an incision in the abdomen, an incision in the vagina, or through the cervix. The third approach is not used in the United States, but the first two are commonly used in this country.

Although the chances of pregnancy are extremely small once one partner or the other has been sterilized (between 4 and 15 women in 10,000 would become pregnant in a year if the woman or her partner had been sterilized [20]), sterilization is not the ideal method for everyone because it is usually not reversible. Some skilled doctors claim that they may reverse a high proportion of vasectomies that they perform; others claim that vasectomies are not reversible. However, a baby has been born to a woman who ten years previously had a successful tubal ligation, and men who had vasectomies reversed have fathered children. Among men in one study who had been sterilized fewer than ten years before the reversal, 91 per cent regained a normal sperm count. Forty-seven per cent of men whose vasectomies had been performed more than ten years before the reversal operation also regained normal sperm counts [43].

Sterilization is one of the most popular methods of birth control among Americans over 30. It is not recommended for those who might want to have children in the future, since reversibility is not guaranteed. It is also important that the individual feel comfortable with the idea of sterilization. While a vasectomy does not directly affect male potency, if a man becomes worried that after vasectomy he may not be able to maintain an erection, his fears may cause him to fail.

**Experimental Methods.**   At the present writing, there is talk of two methods that are not yet available to the public. One is a device that would enable a woman accurately to determine the viscosity of her cervical mucus. Another is a once-a-week pill for men [41]. Progress in developing the male pill has been very slow, but some reserachers are optimistic that solutions can be found to the problems that are involved.

**Douching: Not a Contraceptive.**   The myth still exists that douching (cleansing the vagina with water or water with other substance dissolved in it) is a form of birth control. Douching is not only too late to prevent pregnancy, it may actually harm the female's delicate tissues. A douche with carbonated soda might even kill a woman, if the carbon dioxide dissolved in the liquid should enter the woman's bloodstream.

## After-the-Fact Methods

A couple has intercourse with a condom, which bursts during coitus. What can they do then? The best thing to do is to call the woman's physician. Some doctors will prescribe what is called *"The morning after pill"*—a massive dose of estrogen taken over five days. The "morning after pill" must be taken within 72 hours after intercourse at the very latest, but preferably treatment should begin within 24 hours. It is a drastic measure that would not be safe for all women, and may cause severe nausea in others. It should not be repeated often.

Another after-the-fact method is morning-after IUD insertion. The device should be inserted as soon as possible after coitus. This method is not recommended for women who are at high risk to infection: those with any kind of vaginal infection, those who have had many recent sexual partners, or those who have been raped [20].

**Menstrual Extraction.**   Menstrual extraction is a method very similar to abortion, except that it is performed before a pregnancy is confirmed. The cervix is dilated, and the contents of the uterus are sucked out.

**Abortion.**   A spontaneous abortion (also known as a miscarria[ge]) [is the termi]-nation of a pregnancy by natural causes. Usually, there is something wr[ong with the] fetus when it is spontaneously aborted. Contrary to popular belief, a woma[n cannot] bring on a miscarriage by falling down a flight of stairs or by taking hot and [cold] showers: if she has a spontaneous abortion after a fall, the abortion was not caus[ed] by the fall and would have happened anyway.

Abortions may, of course, be performed medically in order to interrupt a preg-nancy that will be harmful to the woman, or that the woman does not wish to carry to term. As a birth control device, abortion is a last resort. As we have seen, no method of preventive birth control is completely foolproof: even sterilizations may prove to be ineffective in some cases.

Until the 1973 U.S. Supreme Court decision that struck down state laws prohib-iting abortions before the twenty-fourth week, women in most of the United States could not get legal abortions. Current laws restrict poor women's access to abortions. Desperate women have always sought abortions, whether or not they were legal or safe. A dramatic drop in maternal death rates in areas with liberal abortion laws indicates the value of medically supervised abortions.

Opponents to abortion believe that it is wrong to purposely terminate a preg-nancy because it is taking a life. Those who believe that women have the right to choose whether or not to have an abortion believe that women have the right to control their own bodies, and that every child has a right to be wanted by its parents.

Abortions performed up to the twelfth week of pregnancy are safer and less expensive than those performed later. The preferred method for an early abortion is the suction method. The cervix is dilated, sometimes under general anesthesia and sometimes under local, by inserting a tapered metal rod into the cervix until the opening is large enough for a thin metal tube to be inserted. A vacuum pump is attached to the outer end of the tube, and the embryo and the lining of the uterus are gently sucked out. The entire operation including preparation takes about 15 to 20 minutes, and is usually accompanied by cramps. For up to two weeks after the abor-tion, a woman will have intermittent spotting or light bleeding.

After the twelfth week of pregnancy, the cost of the operation and the risk involved increase. Between the thirteenth and sixteenth weeks, there is a great risk of hemorrhage with suction and most doctors believe that the uterus is still too small for the late abortion method, saline abortion or "salting out." To perform an abortion by this method, the physician removes some of the amniotic fluid from the woman's uterus by inserting a needle through the abdominal wall, under local anesthesia. He replaces the fluid by a concentrated solution of salt water. The salt water kills the fetus, and labor usually begins within 12 to 48 hours.

The decision to have an abortion is often a difficult one, involving complicated feelings and relationships. Counseling is highly desirable for the pregnant woman, her partner, and any of their family members who are involved with the problem pregnancy. Adequate abortion clinics provide emotional care and support before, during, and after the procedure. Women who choose not to have an abortion can

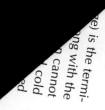

from organizations such as Birthright, which offers alternative methods of
ith problem pregnancies.

thirds of Americans in a nationwide random sample taken in 1976 said
believed that the decision to have an abortion should be left up to a woman
doctor [2].

Plato and Aristotle approved of infanticide for limiting the population and eliminating deformed and diseased babies [31]. Infanticide was common in Europe during a period of rapid population growth, from 1750 to 1850. A higher death rate in girls results from the Indian practice of giving scarce food and other resources to boys before girls. Severe child abuse and neglect cause infant deaths in the United States, at present, but the killing of children is regarded with horror and infanticide is not acceptable as a method of population control. Many of the deaths from abuse and neglect could be prevented by a birth control policy that protected people from unwanted births.

## Decision Making

The question of whether or not to practice birth control is one that is left up to the individual in our society. Nonetheless, a method of birth control is used by virtually all married U.S. couples, except for those who are pregnant or trying to become pregnant. Only about 4 per cent of non-Catholic and 7 per cent of Catholic couples (who are not pregnant or trying to become so) do not use birth control [53].

Birth control is less widely used among unmarried teen-agers. Among a national sample of 15- to 19-year-old females in 1976, 26 per cent reported that they never used contraceptives, 44 per cent said that they sometimes used contraceptives, and 30 per cent said that they always used contraceptives. Whereas older respondents were *less* likely than younger ones to report that they *never* used contraceptives, there was no difference by age in the percentage of respondents who said that they *always* used contraceptives [57]. High school and college females who are in a committed relationship are more likely to use contraceptives [18; 24]. One study of high school and college women found that contraceptives were used by 94 to 100 per cent of middle- and upper-middle-class respondents who had been in love more than once and who were presently in a committed relationship. (The respondents in this study were at least 16 years old) [24]. Thus, it seems clear that contraceptives are widely, almost universally, used by North American couples who are not young teenagers, who are in committed relationships, and who wish to avoid pregnancy. When contraceptives are made available to teenagers, their birth rate is lower [12].

However, as we have seen, no birth control method except abstinence is without failures. Human error accounts for many birth control failures, and some methods are subject to failures even when used correctly. In a study of wives [9], 12 per cent of whites and 18 per cent of blacks had an unplanned pregnancy in a 12-month time period. Not surprisingly, women who used the more effective contraceptives were least likely to have an unplanned pregnancy. Use of the pill, IUD, and sterilization help couples to have no more than the number of children that they want [45]. Among pill and IUD users, unplanned pregnancies are usually the result of the woman's discontinuing use of the contraceptive without replacing it with another [52].

There is no such thing as a birth control method that is perfect for everyone. The most statistically effective method may be dangerous medically to a particular person. A method may be objectionable because an individual finds it difficult or unpleasant to use, or it may be objected to on moral grounds. In order for a birth control method to be effective, it must be used properly. Birth control pills must be taken as directed. Condoms, diaphragms, and chemical barriers must be used every time that the erect penis is near the vagina. It *is* possible for a woman to become pregnant if a man ejaculates near her vaginal opening, even if there is no penetration by the penis.

Since it takes two to make a baby, each partner to sexual intercourse has a responsibility to plan for birth control or the care of an infant should one result. Taking such responsibility requires communication and planning. A man should not assume that a woman is using contraceptives if she does not mention it. A woman should not assume that she cannot get pregnant, unless she knows for sure that she is sterile. Pregnancies can occur even with the safest methods of birth control. Neither marriage nor abortion is an easy solution if an unplanned pregnancy results.

**SUMMARY**    Differences between the sexes are rooted in physical structure and elaborated by interaction between the individual and sociocultural forces. Chromosomal content, fixed at conception, determines sex. During embryonic life, the reproductive system, as well as other systems, differentiates. This differentiation continues through infancy, childhood, and adolescence, making males and females increasingly different in appearance.

Males, conceived in greater numbers than females, are more vulnerable to destructive influences in the environment, both before and after birth. Females mature more rapidly, both physically and psychologically. Although sex differences in brain functioning have been demonstrated, the differences between averages are so small as to be meaningless for individuals. The most salient of sex differences is that between the reproductive systems, since the two are complementary. During the embryonic period, the undifferentiated gonad develops into either a testis, whose endocrine secretions direct the development of male external genitalia, or an ovary.

Through learning, the young child develops a self-concept that includes being a girl or a boy. Several theories contribute to understanding how individuals develop the psychological aspects of femininity and masculinity. Psychoanalytic theory bases learning more strongly on bodily experiences and emotional interaction with parents. Social learning theory stresses more cognitive and social interaction, with reinforcement as an influence and modeling an important process. Gender identity or sex-role orientation (thinking of oneself as a male or a female) seems to have a critical period for establishment, during the first two or three years. Gender-role adoption, or acting like a male or female, is a longer, more gradual process. Both processes are strongly influenced by fathers, who are likely to take more interest than mothers in motivating children toward sex-typed behavior. Siblings, teachers, and the media also influence sex typing.

According to cognitive theory, the child structures his own gender role through thinking and reasoning. Before the age of three years, the child has a concept of his or her self as "boy" or "girl." The child then fits his or her behavior to what the child perceives as boy behavior or girl behavior. Dialectical theory holds that in the first stage of gender-role development, the individual is undifferentiated. In the second stage, gender roles are distinguished by certain behaviors appropriate for males and other for females. In the third stage, androgyny, each sex is free to use all of its abilities.

Cross-cultural comparisons reveal great variety in the patterning of sexual expression. Childrearing methods are articulated with societal norms of sexual behavior. Masturbation and sex play in childhood are interpreted in various ways, and thus restricted or encouraged. In later childhood, when growth is slow and the reproductive system is immature, some societies keep boys and girls quite separated. Pubescence is the period during which the body grows fast, changing in all its systems while the genital system matures. Adolescence is a socially defined, culturally variable period between childhood and adulthood. Although sex education in early childhood is largely handled by parents, adolescents often need sex education beyond what is offered in the home.

Sexual interaction involves responses that are both physiological and psychological. Erection, the male physiological response, is essential for intercourse, but female arousal is not. Ejaculation marks the completion of the male physiological response, and orgasm is its psychological counterpart. Female response also includes genital enlargement and orgasm. Interaction involves mutual stimulation. There are wide cultural and individual differences in sexual techniques, since learning, teaching, and natural endowment are all factors in performance.

The use of birth control requires decision making and management and results in giving people, especially women, more control over their lives. Methods that are reliable when properly used include the mechanical, chemical, intrauterine, hormonal, and surgical. Rhythm has a high failure rate. Douching is not a contraceptive. Conceptions can be interrupted by immediate medication, morning-after IUD insertion, menstrual extraction, and abortion. Early abortion performed by qualified personnel is safe and simple, although emotions are also involved. An adequate abortion includes counseling and emotional support. A later abortion is more difficult physically, emotionally, financially, and philosophically.

Infanticide, although strongly disapproved at present, has been used widely throughout space and time, and persists today, even in North America. Adequate birth control would prevent most infanticide.

**REFERENCES**
1. Aldous, Joan. Children's perceptions of adult role assignment: Father-absence, class, race and sex influence. *Journal of Marriage and the Family*, 1972, **34,** 55–65.
2. Arney, William Ray and William H. Trescher. Trends in attitudes toward abortion, 1972–1975. *Family Planning Perspectives*, 1976, **8,** 117–127.
3. Bakan, David. *The duality of human existence*. Chicago: Rand McNally, 1966.
4. Biller, Henry B. *Father, child and sex role*. Lexington, Ma, Heath, 1971.
5. Block, Jeanne Humphrey. Conceptions of sex roles: Some cross-cultural and longitudinal perspectives. *American Psychologist*, 1973, **28,** 512–526.
6. Butterworth, Charles E. Interactions of nutrients with oral contraceptives and other drugs. *Journal of the American Dietetic Association*, 1973, **62,** 510–514.
7. Chilman, Catherine S. Some psychological aspects of female sexuality. *Family Coordinator*, 1974, **23,** 123–131.
8. Connor, Jane M. and Lisa A. Serbin. Behaviorally based masculine- and feminine-activity-preference scales for preschoolers: Correlates with other classroom behaviors and cognitive tests. *Child Development*, 1977, **48,** 1411–1416.
9. Cutright, Phillips and Lyle Peter Groeneveld. Birth planning success: Motivation and contraceptive method. *Family Planning Perspectives*, 1978, **10,** 43–48.
10. Fagot, Beverly I. The influence of sex of child on parental reactions to toddler children. *Child Development*, 1978, **49,** 459–465.
11. Fagot, Beverly I. and G. R. Patterson. An in vivo analysis of reinforcing contingencies for sex role behaviors in the preschool child. *Developmental Psychology*, 1969, **1,** 563–568.
12. *Family Planning Perspectives*. Available contraception lowers teen birthrates. 1978, **10,** 160–161.
13. *Family Planning Perspectives*. Most nursing mothers run risk of becoming pregnant by 12th postpartum month if contraception is not used. 1977, **9,** 231–232.
14. Farrell, Warren T. *The liberated man*. New York: Bantam, 1975.
15. Fish, K. D. and Henry Biller. Perceived paternal relationships and college females' personal adjustment. *Adolescence*, 1973, **8,** 415–420.
16. Ford, Clellan and Frank Beach. *Patterns of sexual behavior*. New York: Harper, 1951.
17. Frisch, Rose E. Weight at menarche: Similarity for well-nourished and undernourished girls at differing ages, and evidence for historical constancy. *Pediatrics*, 1972, **50,** 445–450.
18. Furstenberg, Frank Jr. Birth control experience among pregnant adolescents: The process of unplanned parenthood. *Social Problems*, 1971, **19,** 192–193.
19. Hainline, Louise and Ellen Fein. The correlates of childhood father absence in college age women. *Child Development*, 1978, **49,** 37–42.
20. Hatcher, Robert A., G. K. Stewart, F. Stewart, F. Guest, P. Stratton, and A. H. Wright. *Contraceptive technology 1978–1979*. New York: Irvington, 1978.
21. Havemann, Ernest. *Birth control*. New York: Time-Life Books, 1967.
22. Hefner, Robert, Meda Rebecca, and Barbara Oleshansky. Development of sex role transcendence. *Human Development*, 1975, **18,** 143–158.
23. Hetherington, E. Mavis. Effects of father absence on personality development in adolescent daughters. *Developmental Psychology*, 1972, **7,** 313–326.

24. Hornick, Joseph, Louise Doran, and Susan Heffernan Crawford. Premarital contraceptive usage among male and female adolescents. *Family Coordinator,* 1979, **28,** 181–190.
25. Hunt, Janet G. and Larry K. Hunt. Race, daughters, and father loss. Does absence made the girl grow stronger? *Social Problems,* 1977, **25,** 90–102.
26. Hutt, Corinne. Sex differences in human development. *Human Development,* 1972, **15,** 153–170.
27. Kaplan, Helen Singer. *The new sex therapy.* New York: Brunner/Mazel, 1974.
28. Kinsey, Alfred, Wardell Pomeroy, Clyde Martin, and Paul Gebhard. *Sexual behavior in the human female.* Philadelphia: Saunders, 1953.
29. Kuhn, Deanna, Sharon C. Nash, and Laura Brucken. Sex role concepts of two- and three-year-olds. *Child Development,* 1978, **49,** 445–451.
30. Lane, Mary E., Rosalinda Arceo, and Aquiles J. Sobrero. Successful use of the diaphragm and jelly by a young population: Report of a clinical study. *Family Planning Perspectives,* 1976, **8,** 81–86.
31. Langer, J. W. Checks on population growth, 1750–1850. *Scientific American,* 1972, **226,** 93–100.
32. Lee, Patrick C. and Annie L. Wolinsky. Male teachers of young children: A preliminary empirical study. *Young Children,* 1973, **28,** 342–352.
33. Lott, Bernice. Behavioral concordance with sex role ideology related to play areas, creativity, and parental sex typing of children. *Journal of Personality and Social Psychology,* 1978, **36,** 1087–1100.
34. Masters, William and Virginia Johnson. *Human sexual response.* Boston: Little, Brown, 1966.
35. McGlone, Jeanette and Andrew Kertesz, Sex differences in cerebral processing of visuo-spatial tasks. *Cortex,* 1973, **9,** 313–320.
36. Melton, Alfred. Human sexual response. In Carlfred Broderick and Jessie Bernard (Eds.). *The individual, sex, and society.* Baltimore: Johns Hopkins, 1969.
37. Mitchell, Edna. The learning of sex roles through toys and books: A woman's view. *Young Children,* 1973, **28,** 226–231.
38. Money, John and Anke A. Ehrhardt. *Man & woman boy & girl.* Baltimore: Johns Hopkins, 1972.
39. Nolan, John D., Joann P. Galat, and Mary A. White. Sex bias on children's television programs. *Journal of Psychology,* 1977, **96,** 197–204.
40. Patty, Rosemarie A. and Marcia M. Ferrell. A preliminary note on the motive to avoid success and the menstrual cycle. *Journal of Psychology,* 1974, **86,** 173–177.
41. *People.* Once-a-week pill for men? 1977, **4:**2, 31–32.
42. *People.* Seeking new methods. 1977, **4:**4, 31–32.
43. *People.* Sterilization reversed. **4:**4, 32–33.
44. Ross, Dorothea M. and Sheila A. Ross. Resistance by preschool boys to sex-inappropriate behavior. *Journal of Educational Psychology,* 1972, **63,** 342–346.
45. Ryder, Norman B. The predictability of fertility planning status. *Studies in Family Planning,* 1976, **7,** 294.
46. Seamans, Barbara. *Free and female.* Greenwich, Ct: Fawcett, 1972.
47. Serbin, Lisa A., K. Daniel O'Leary, Ronald N. Kent, and Illene J. Tonick. A comparison of teacher response to the preacademic and problem behavior of boys and girls. *Child Development,* 1973, **44,** 796–804.
48. Sternglanz, Sarah H. and Lisa A. Serbin. Sex role stereotyping in children's television programs. *Developmental Psychology,* 1974, **10,** 710–715.

49. Stewart, Mollie K. Sex-typed behaviors of boys and girls in preschool activities and the reinforcements of these behaviors by peers and teachers. M.S. thesis, U. of Rhode Island, 1973.
50. Switzer, Ellen. The sex problem that nobody talks about: An interview with Dr. Helen Singer Kaplan. *Family Circle,* 1977 (October), 54–60.
51. Tanner, James M. The adolescent growth spurt and developmental age. In Russell C. Smart and Mollie S. Smart (Eds.). *Readings in child development and relationships.* New York: Macmillan, 1972.
52. Vaughan, Barbara, James Truseel, Jane Menken, and Elise F. Jones. Contraceptive failure among married women in the United States, 1970–1973. *Family Planning Perspectives,* 1977, **9,** 251–258.
53. Westoff, Charles F. and Elise F. Jones. The secularization of U.S. Catholic birth control practices. *Family Planning Perspectives, 1977, 9,* 203–207.
54. Will, Jerrie A., Patricia A. Self, and Nancy Datan. Maternal behavior and perceived sex of infant. *American Journal of Orthopsychiatry, 1976,* **46,** 135–139.
55. Yankelovich, Skelly and White, Inc. *Raising children in a changing society.* Minneapolis: General Mills, Inc. 1977.
56. Yeung, David. Personal communication. Guelph, Ontario, 1975.
57. Zelnick, Melvin and John F. Kantner. Sexual and contraceptive experience among young unmarried women in the United States, 1976 and 1971. *Family Planning Perspectives,* 1977, **9,** 55–61.
58. Zolotow, Charlotte. *William's doll.* New York: Harper, 1972.

# CHAPTER 5

# iT kEEps ON GROWiNG: MORE AbOUT sEX

In this chapter, we continue the discussion of sexuality and gender roles that was begun in the previous chapter. We follow male and female sexual development and behavior through adolescence, adulthood, and old age.

## CROSS-CULTURAL COMPARISONS

In all societies, expression of sexuality is restricted in some ways. What is and is not permitted, however, varies widely from one society to the next. A person is not born with sexual attitudes; these must be developed as he grows up. Ford and Beach's description of the sexual behavior of 190 societies throughout the world illustrates how many variations there can be in beliefs about what is proper and right regarding sex for human beings [19]. In the United States, for instance, a man is permitted by custom and by law to have only one wife at a time; a wife is permitted to have only one husband. Westerners tend to think that monogamy is normal and natural for all human beings. Ford and Beach, however, found that less than 16 per cent of 185 societies studied prohibited all members from having more than one spouse. Most of the societies that permit marriages of more than two individuals permit only the husband to have more than one spouse, and he is allowed this privilege only if he can afford to support them. Only two societies studied by Ford and Beach permitted a woman to have more than one husband.

Societies also take different stands concerning premarital and extramarital sexual relations. Only about 5 per cent of the 185 societies for which this information

was available wholly disapproved of premarital and extramarital sex relations. This does not mean that all individuals in the permissive societies could have intercourse with whomever they pleased; most societies place restrictions on which people are available sexual partners.

## PREMARITAL HETEROSEXUAL ATTITUDES AND BEHAVIOR

The question of the existence of a "sexual revolution" may be approached in two ways. One may look at changing attitudes toward sexual behavior, or one may look at changes in behavior. Both sexual attitudes and behavior have changed rapidly in recent years.

By premarital heterosexual behavior, we mean sexual behavior between members of the opposite sex that occurs between puberty and the first marriage. (We realize, of course, that not all persons marry.) Sexual behavior includes kissing, touching, petting, and coitus. Coitus has been the most frequently used index of premarital sexuality, but more recent studies have taken into account the fact that amount and kind of sexual experience varies widely even among virgins.

## Four Sexual Standards

In 1960, Reiss wrote a book that dealt with the major sexual standards in the United States as he saw them [45]. These standards are *abstinence, permissiveness-with-affection, permissiveness-without-affection,* and the *double standard.*

The sexual standard that is upheld by many religious organizations and by the law in some states is *abstinence before marriage;* that is, no sexual intercourse prior to marriage for either men or women. The traditional sexual standard of our society, abstinence, is losing ground to the permissive standards, described below. Some people who hold the abstinence standard think that sexual intercourse is too cherished and intimate an act to be performed outside of marriage. However, there are various subdivisions of this standard that allow differing degrees of intimacy. A person who believes that coitus before marriage is wrong may believe that only kissing is acceptable, or may believe that petting is acceptable.

Of course, not all virgins hold the abstinence standard. There are reasons for refraining from intercourse other than feeling that it is wrong before marriage. For many, the time has not yet come, for a number of reasons. Unfortunately, growing numbers of sexually inexperienced young women and men are feeling socially pressured into having premarital coitus, or are feeling abnormal if they are abstinent. Virginity is seen as a burden instead of something worth saving for the right time and person.

Research on college campuses indicates that among college students *permissiveness-with-affection* is becoming the dominant sexual standard [23, 42]. For persons who hold this standard, premarital intercourse is acceptable for both men and women as long as the couple feels mutual affection. This standard is the traditional standard in Sweden [45] and Denmark. The Danish standard, however, may be changing toward promiscuity, as the American and Canadian standards become permissiveness-with-affection [12].

*Permissiveness-without-affection* has traditionally been the least commonly held standard in the United States, but there is evidence that it is becoming more popular [43]. Adherents of this standard feel that both sexes are entitled to indulge in premarital coitus for the pleasure that it brings. Couples need not be in love.

Like the abstinence standard, the *double standard* is losing ground as the permissiveness standards gain acceptance among college students. The traditional double standard holds that premarital sexual relations are permissible for males but not for females. Because men were considered to be more in need of sex than were women, not all men were expected to remain abstinent before marriage. In order to save the chastity of their sweethearts, double standard men engage in premarital coitus with permissive women. Traditionally, double standard men would go to prostitutes, but in the late nineteenth century more women who were not prostitutes began to have premarital intercourse. At that time, most men probably considered these permissive women to be "bad." Not surprisingly, the traditional double standard has been more popular among males than among females. Recent evidence, however, suggests that among male and female college students, a single standard of sexual permissiveness has emerged [18, 29].

Later, Reiss [45, 46] elaborated his method of measuring premarital sexual permissiveness and the theoretical explanation of it. Within any one of the standards previously mentioned there is room for a great deal of variation. As defined, an abstinence standard individual may believe that only kissing is permissible before marriage, or may believe that everything except penile-vaginal intercourse is permissible before marriage.

Furthermore, Reiss reasoned that sexual permissiveness would vary for individuals not only in the amount of physical activity, but also in the conditions under which such activity would be acceptable. Kissing, petting, and coitus were physical acts that Reiss studied, and the conditions of affection were no affection, strong affection, love, and engagement. Reiss also asked his respondents whether they thought that a certain act under one of the conditions was acceptable for females, and also for males. For example, respondents were asked whether their agreement or disagreement was strong, medium, or slight to the following question: "I believe that kissing is acceptable for the male before marriage even if he does not feel particularly affectionate toward his partner." Both men and women answered this question and eleven more that dealt with the three physical acts under the four conditions of affection. Then, men and women answered the same questions again, only the word "female" was substituted for the word "male" in each case. By comparing an individual's answers on the male and female questions, it could be determined whether a person held a double or single standard, as well as how permissive he or she was under various conditions [45].

If one defines a permissive sexual standard as referring only to premarital coitus, then those who engage in petting but not intercourse would be considered nonpermissive. It seems more realistic to conceptualize as permissive individuals who engage in genital petting. Certainly the person who believes in petting is more permissive than the person who does not.

## Choosing a Sexual Standard

In some societies, traditional standards are still upheld by the majority of people. The person who deviates from the rest of the group is likely to be punished in one way or another. Because virtually everyone that he knows upholds the traditional standards (at least in public), the deviant will be cut off from all his friends and family if he does not live by their standards. In North America, however, there are many different groups of people holding different standards. If a person wishes to change his attitudes and beliefs, he often can find another group of people willing to accept him even if his family refuses to associate with him. Although changing basic attitudes is often a long and painful process, it can be done.

During the teen-age years, the individual's friends become increasingly important to her; their opinions often mean more to her than those of her family. Eventually, if the individual becomes fully an adult, she is able to make up her own mind about what is right and wrong for herself. She may choose traditional values handed down from her parents, or she may choose some new values and keep some old ones, As an adult, she is responsible not only for her own actions but also for the welfare of the people whom her actions affect. A responsible individual will carefully consider all of the possible consequences of her actions, both for herself and for other people.

Choosing a sexual standard for oneself is rarely easy in the United States. Because of the varying opinions and standards, it is difficult to put sex into perspective. Is sex something dirty or disgusting? Is it the most wonderful thing in the world, but only in marriage? Is it bargaining currency for getting what you want from another person? Is it a way to prove your adulthood? Is it fun? Is it sacred? Is it a lasting bond between two people? Is it a moment's pleasure?

A person looking for the answers to these questions would do well to consider the possible consequences, positive and negative, of either engaging in or refraining from sexual intercourse before marriage. He should weigh each consequence in terms of his own personal beliefs regarding right and wrong. Some consequences, however, are unforeseen. No person can predict his own reactions perfectly.

**Negative Consequences of Premarital Sex.**   The most commonly noted consequence of premarital sex is an unplanned pregnancy. With the availability of contraceptives, unwanted pregnancy is theoretically avoidable. However, as we saw in the previous chapter, use of contraceptives seems to be more difficult outside of a stable, committed relationship. Furthermore, all temporary means of avoiding pregnancy still entail some risk of failure. Sexually active persons who are not sterile or beyond the childbearing years should give some thought to a plan-of-action to be taken in the event of pregnancy.

Keeping a baby born out of wedlock has lost much of the disgrace that it traditionally held for white females. Giving up a baby for adoption was, of course, much more common in the past than it is today. Between 1957 and 1969, the percentage of children born out-of-wedlock who were adopted varied between 45 and 50 per cent. This ratio began to decline in 1970, and by 1974 had reached a low of 36 per cent [7]. Most of the mothers who choose to keep their babies are not yet out of their teens. A large number continue to live at home with their parents. As we will see in Chapter 11, parenting cannot be done effectively by a mother who is still a child herself.

Where legal abortion is readily available, more women with problem pregnancies choose to terminate them. In 1971, two in five pregnancies among whites aged 15 to 19 ended in abortion or "miscarriage," but in 1976, three in five pregnancies in this age group were so ended [63].

Deciding whether to keep an unplanned baby, to give the baby up for adoption, or to have an abortion involves choice that is usually extremely difficult to make. Both men and women very often have unhappy feelings later on regarding their choice, regardless of what it is. Parents who give up their child for adoption wonder about the child's welfare. Those who keep their child may wonder at times if the child might have been better off adopted by someone else. Some who have abortions (or whose partners have them) feel guilty later on. The man may worry that he did not support his woman enough, and the woman may later feel that she did not give enough consideration to her man's feelings.

Venereal disease is a very real possible consequence of premarital intercourse. It, too, may usually be prevented by the careful use of a prophylactic. Some double-standard men protect themselves from venereal disease by the use of a condom ("rubber") and consequently protect their partner from pregnancy as well [44]. Venereal disease is discussed further in Appendix E.

A third consequence of premarital intercourse is social condemnation. This consequence usually is felt more keenly by the female than by the male. For the double-standard male, premarital intercourse is a cause for boasting to his friends. A way to avoid social condemnation is to make sure that no one finds out. The female who has intercourse with a double-standard male will usually find that he does not respect her request for secrecy. For couples with an egalitarian permissive standard (permissiveness with or without affection), it may be easier to keep their activities a secret. To maintain secrecy, care must be taken to prevent pregnancy and venereal disease, for if either of these conditions is discovered, it will provide proof of sexual activity, and a basis for condemnation.

A fourth consequence may be guilt feelings. If the individual is acting against his own sexual standard, it is very likely that he will feel guilty. In our society, women are especially susceptible to guilt feelings, but men are certainly not immune either. A person who forces or encourages another to engage in activities that are contrary to the second person's values may do that person a great injustice. In a moment of passion, a person may agree to do something that he will later regret. This is why communication between possible sexual partners is important, and why issues of "how far to go" are best discussed before the passions begin to boil. Such cool-headed discussions are probably rare, because our popular culture puts such an emphasis upon being swept off one's feet.

Premarital sex can lead a couple into premature commitment to a partner or to concentration on heterosexual relationships at a time when friendships with the same sex would be more growth-promoting. In societies where boys and girls are kept apart during middle childhood and early adolescence, individuals build close friendships with members of their own sex, usually have a few "best friends," and belong to a group of like-sex friends. It is at this time of life that the sense of identity is developing fast. Friendship contributes to identity by providing a noncritical person who shares the same experiences, doubts, puzzlements, and projections to the future. A friend listens to confidences. In the very process of *expressing* to a sympathetic, trustworthy person, the adolescent gains insight, solves problems, and gets a feeling of connection to the social group and to the past and future. All this is more possible when sexual activity is not part of the picture [16]. Although it is conceivable that boys and girls help one another to establish the sense of identity, it is much more likely that the very exciting emotional experience of sex prevents or shatters the cognitive and mildly emotional progress of identity development through discussion. In terms of time, it is reasonable that the boy and girl who are together daily are not going to be spending hours with like-sex friends. When a pair-involvement results in a teen-age marriage, the boy and girl (or one of them) may still be involved in establishing a sense of identity and therefore be unable to develop the intimacy that a partnership requires. Thus they fail with each other, perhaps because they are not suited as partners or possibly because they simply are too immature in their personality development.

With the delay in the age of marriage, more people are entering young adulthood still unmarried than was true in the past. In 1978, 47.6 per cent of women aged 20 to 24 were unmarried, compared to 35.8 per cent in 1970. The corresponding percentages for men were 65.8 and 54.7 per cent [59]. It is important to make a distinction between unmarried sexual activity among young adolescents and young adults. Sexual intercourse among young teenagers is associated with more psychological problems, but by the college years nonvirginity is not so closely related to such problems [10, p. 194].

Sorensen [53, p. 341] has argued that the concept of premarital sex is becoming outmoded because "young people are not scheduling marriage on their life agenda simply to gratify their sexual needs or in order to legalize their sexual relationship." It seems to us that Sorensen is right in many cases, but for many other individuals, he is not correct. There is a wide divergence of sexual standards in North America today, with many young persons still adhering to the abstinence standard, but with greater numbers than in the past adhering to the permissiveness standards, especially permissiveness within a committed relationship.

**Positive Consequences of Premarital Intercourse.**   The most obvious advantage is physical satisfaction. An additional advantage is what Reiss calls "psychic satisfaction—non-sexual, lasting, emotional rewards yielded by a sexual relationship . . . such as security, warmth, and emotional satisfaction" [45, p. 18]. A satisfying sexual relationship can help to form a bond between unmarried as well as married lovers. The degree of satisfaction that lovers get from their sexual relationship is to some extent dependent upon other aspects of their relationship, and the absence of fear from unwanted pregnancy. Premarital coitus may help sexual adjustment in marriage. Women who experience orgasm in premarital sexual intercourse are more likely to experience orgasm through intercourse after marriage than women who have not had premarital intercourse. However, premaritally orgasmic women may be more capable of orgasm than those who did not experience premarital intercourse, and orgasmic women probably would have experienced orgasm sooner or later regardless of their premarital activity [45].

Another argument for premarital sex is that it helps a couple to determine whether they are sexually compatible. However, for some people sexual responsiveness is difficult to achieve if they are married (or if they are not married). A couple with a good sexual relationship before marriage may find that sex isn't so good once they are married—or vice versa. Lovers who have difficulty relaxing early in a relationship may relax later on and enjoy sex tremendously. Others who were very excited at first become bored later on. Nonetheless, having a sexual relationship before marriage does help some people to uncover sexual incompatibilities that would otherwise have come to light only after marriage. With adequate sex therapy, such couples often can become sexually compatible. Other couples may be unable to adjust, and may choose to part.

## Factors to Consider

When deciding whether to choose a permissive or restrictive standard for oneself, the individual should carefully consider his motivations for choosing a particular standard, and the consequences of each. Will he go against beliefs that are important to him? Is he motivated by a desire to be popular, or to prove his autonomy? Will sexual involvement increase the emotional intensity of his relationship to levels that he cannot or is unwilling to handle? Will sexual involvement be a meaningful addition to the relationship, from which both partners will benefit? Do both partners agree on the meaning of the relationship? What about contraception? If a pregnancy results, what action will be taken? Also, the possibility of contracting venereal disease should not be overlooked. Although the careful and well-informed person's chances of causing a pregnancy or contracting or giving venereal disease are very small, and although medical intervention is possible in both cases, the individual should not dismiss either consequence as being impossible for himself.

## Female Sexual Revolutions

Kinsey's data showed that an early revolution in female sexual behavior occurred among women born in the first decade after 1900. Of women born before 1900 who were unmarried at age 25, 14 per cent had experienced premarital coitus. The women born in the first decade after 1900 reached sexual maturity between 1915 and 1925, and during these years a rise in female premarital coitus took place. Of those women born between 1900 and 1910, 36 per cent who were unmarried at 25 had premarital coital experience. The increase continued at about the same rate until 1929, and then leveled off [30, pp. 298–299]. The first female sexual revolution, in terms of a rise in premarital coitus, took place between approximately 1915 and 1929. During this time, the male premarital intercourse rate showed virtually no increase.

A more recent female sexual revolution began in the late 1960s. The availability of the birth control pill, the feminist movement, and the publication of Masters and Johnson's book *Human Sexual Response* [39] all contributed to the popularization of a new code of sexual morality [10, pp. 106, 114–115], which spread to mainstream college and working-class youth in the early 1970s [10, p. 122]. Figure 5-1

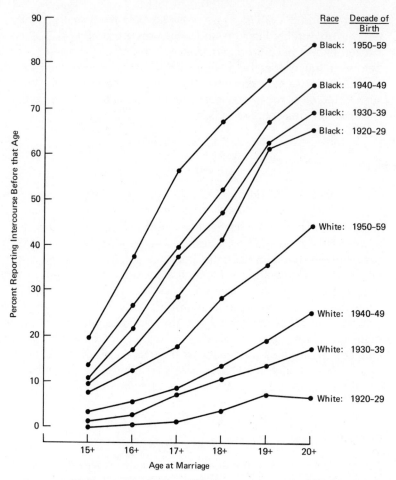

**FIGURE 5-1**   Per cent black and white women marrying at a given age or later who reported first intercourse at an earlier age, by decade of birth.

*Source:* J. Richard Udry, Karl E. Bauman and Naomi M. Morris. Changes in premarital coital experience of recent decade-of-birth cohorts of urban American women. *Journal of Marriage and the Family*, 1975, **37,** 783–787, Figure 1. Used with permission.

shows the increase in reported premarital intercourse rates among black and white women born during the 1920s, 1930s, 1940s, and 1950s by age at marriage. It can be seen that among married women of both races there is an increase by decade of birth in having experienced sexual intercourse before marriage. For example, among white women born between 1940 and 1949, around 23 per cent of those married at 20 or later were nonvirgins. Of women born in the 1950s and married at 20 or later, more than 40 per cent were nonvirgins at the time of marriage [58].

Premarital sexual intercourse has increased among college students [5, 18, 37, 60] and among high school students as well [64]. Zelnick and Kantner questioned young women aged 15 to 19 throughout the United States about their sexual experiences and use of contraceptives. In 1971, 14 per cent of 15-year-olds, and 47 per cent of 19-year-olds were nonvirgins. In 1976, 18 per cent of 15-year-olds and 55 per cent of 19-year-olds had experienced sexual intercourse [64].

## Increased Acceptance of Premarital Coitus

Increasing numbers of young women approve of premarital intercourse [42, 47, 61].

## Increased Number of Coital Partners

Although females are more likely than a generation ago to have had intercourse with more than one partner [58], most limit their sexual activity to one partner at a time [10, p. 171]. Because age at first intercourse is lower than it was in the past, and age at marriage is higher, over time there may be a series of partners.

**Sex and Love.** Although the behavior of women is becoming more liberal, a number of studies have found that women tend to equate sex with love, whereas for men, love and sex are more easily separated. For example, in a study of Canadian high school students it was found that 74 per cent of the females and 36 per cent of the males reported that they had been in love with their first coital partner [26].

## Male Evolution

Changes in men's sexual behavior have been less dramatic than in women's. Reflecting a greater concern about how many women are "doing it," more is known about rates of female coital activity than male. Nonetheless, it is safe to conclude that females' reported rates of premarital intercourse have risen more dramatically than have males', since the latter were much higher to begin with. In the 1920s, when the first female "sexual revolution" took place, male rates of premarital coitus did not rise [30]. During the late 1960s, the prevalence of sexual intercourse among college men began to rise. In one study, men who were freshmen in 1970 were more likely to have had coitus than were men who were *seniors* in 1971 [18]. This study demonstrates that a generational change had taken place even within a relatively short period of time. It is more difficult to determine how many more high school males are having premarital coitus now than was true a given number of years ago, because of a lack of data. Hornick [26] found that 27 per cent of eleventh- and twelfth-grade males from a rural Ontario town were nonvirgins. Sixty-seven per cent of undergraduate college men were nonvirgins. Ross [50] reports that in a sample of 13- to 19-year-old males in New York City, 84 per cent of Hispanic, 80 per cent of black and

68 per cent of white respondents were sexually active. Using a partial national United States sample, Sorensen [53] reports that 49 per cent of 16-year-old males, 55 per cent of 17-year-olds and 57 per cent of 18- and 19-year-olds had had premarital coitus. As can be seen, the figures vary widely.

The attitudes of young men have become more permissive over the past generation [46]. The double standard is declining among men in favor of a single permissive standard [18].

## Other Group Differences

Males and females, of course, are not the only groups that differ in sexual behavior and attitudes. Premarital coital behavior varies by region of the country, by race, and by social class. Southern black male college students were more likely to have had premarital coitus than were their white, midwestern counterparts, both in 1968 and 1973. Among both races, individuals in the 1973 samples were more likely to be nonvirgins than were individuals in the 1968 samples [13]. In another study, sexual permissiveness attitudes of black and white college students living in both Florida and California were compared. In both states, blacks had more permissive sexual attitudes than did whites [54].

**Influence of Peer Group.** The adolescent peer group is thought to have a tremendous influence upon the adolescent individual. In the sexual realm, there is evidence that the perceived behavior of the peer group is related to the individual's behavior. Studies have found that high school and college students who believe that their friends are sexually active are more likely to be nonvirgins themselves than are their classmates who believe that their friends are virgins [56, 61].

Using as subjects patients at a venereal disease clinic in New Zealand, investigators found that similarity between the individual's sexual activity and his friends' varied by the age of the respondent. Forty-four per cent of those persons who had their first coitus at age 14 or under reported that their friends were sexually active at the time, as compared with 80 per cent of those age 15 and 16, and 64 per cent of those age 17 and older. The author suggests that the media are a potent socializing force for some individuals, and that their influence has not been adequately researched [14]. Certainly, television, advertising, movies, and magazines do exert a tremendous influence upon our behavior in many ways, and sexual behavior is no exception.

## MARITAL SEX

A survey of readers of *Redbook* magazine [34] reported that 70 per cent of wives who responded said that their marital sex was *good* or *very good*. Among women who had orgasms all or most of the time from intercourse, 81 per cent said that their marital sex was good or very good, and 13 per cent said that it was fair. Among women who were occasionally orgasmic, slightly more than 50 per cent said that their marital sex was good or very good. Sixty per cent of the women said that they initiated sex at least half of the time, and 90 per cent said that they were active in lovemaking at least half of the time. Ninety per cent of the women under 40 and 80 per cent of those over 40 said that they practice oral-genital sex. Kinsey [30, p. 375] found that women's reported incidence of coital orgasm increased over the first 20 years of marriage. Similarly, the *Redbook* study reports that women between 35 and 39 were most likely to be highly orgasmic, and those under 20 were the least likely to be. Wives who discussed their sexual feelings with their husbands were more likely to rate their sex lives as *very good* or *good*. Among women who always discussed their sexual feelings with their husbands, 58 per cent said that their sex lives were very good, and 30 per cent said that their sex lives were good. Among women who *never* discussed their sexual feelings with their husbands, only 9 per cent said that their sex lives were *very good,* and 21 per cent said that they were *good*.

## SEXUAL STANDARDS AFTER MARRIAGE

Marital sexual fidelity is not required by all societies. In polygamous societies, individuals (more usually men than women) are permitted to have more than one spouse. In other societies, sexual liasons are permitted for married persons. In some cases, "wife-lending" or "wife exchange" is encouraged as a part of the hospitality code. Among the Chuckchee of Siberia, the host offers his wife to a man who is traveling away from home, and has the favor returned when the guest is in turn in the host's role. Other societies lift the restrictions on extramarital sex on specific festive occasions [19].

The Christian marital vow usually includes the words "forsaking all others." These words are a promise of emotional and sexual fidelity to one's partner. But as we all know, the formal standard of marital fidelity is not adhered to by all persons in our society. Persons who disapprove of premarital intercourse are more likely to disapprove of extramarital intercourse than are those with more liberal attitudes toward premarital sex [52].

### Illicit Extramarital Sex

Traditionally, extramarital sex in our society has equaled "the affair." An affair is an extramarital sexual involvement that is carried on without the knowledge or consent of the spouse of at least one of the parties to the affair. Both persons involved in the affair may be married, or one may be married and the other single. An affair may be a one-night stand, or it may continue for years.

It is difficult to determine how many people actually engage in extramarital affairs, since this topic is obviously a sensitive one. Kinsey found that 26 per cent of the women in his study had at least one extramarital coital experience by age 40 [30]. Male extramarital coital rates were reported to about twice as high [31]. A more recent study of women found that 26 per cent of married women had experienced extramarital intercourse at least once by the age of 35 [6]. A survey of *Redbook* readers found that 25 per cent of 20- to 24-year-old wives, and 38 per cent of 35- to 39-year-old wives, reported having had extramarital intercourse. The longer a woman was married, the more likely she was to report having had extramarital sex (EMS). College-educated women were less likely to have had EMS than those without a college education, until age 40, after which they were more likely to report EMS. Wage-earning wives were most likely to have had EMS (47 per cent), followed by women who worked as volunteers (32 per cent) and housewives (27 per cent). Those who reported strong religious convictions were less likely to report EMS experience. [33] No doubt more people have a desire for having an affair at times during their married lives than actually carry through with their fantasies. In his book *The Affair*, Morton Hunt [27] claims that nearly every married person has the desire for an affair at least once during his marriage.

## Consensual Extramarital Sex

Not all persons who engage in extramarital sex do so without their partner's knowledge or approval. *Swinging* and *sexually open marriages* are life styles that condone sexual infidelity.

> Swinging generally involves two or more pair-bonded couples who mutually decide to switch sexual partners or engage in group sex. Singles may be included either through temporary coupling with another individual specifically for the purpose of swinging or as a part of a triadic or larger group sexual experience [44, p. 436].

A sexually open marriage is a marriage or marriage-type relationship in which the partners agree that each has the right to form intimate relationships with others that may involve sex. The spouse's other partners may or may not be personally known. We deal more with consensual extramarital sex in Chapter 15.

## Postmarital Sex

What happens to the person who loses his or her partner through death or divorce? Sexual needs do not end when the relationship ends. Little is known about the postmarital sexual activity of the widowed, but divorced persons generally do not wait very long before becoming sexually involved with someone. Sexual activity among the divorced is covered in Chapter 9.

## AGING AND SEXUALITY

The work of Masters and Johnson [39] has refuted the myth that sex is only for the young. Kinsey [31] noted a decline in male coital rates, starting from the time of marriage and continuing throughout the man's lifetime. A similar decline was noted for females [30], but it was concluded that the decline in female behavior was a reflection of a decline in male capacity, rather than that of the female.

### Menopause

The cessation of menstruation is called **menopause.** Menstruation does not merely pause, however. It stops, usually after some irregular periods, but sometimes with no warning. Since most women have a span of a few months or a year or two during which menstruation signals its approaching end, menopause is commonly considered to be a period of life. *Change of life* is often a term for it. Some of these signals are menstrual periods are shorter and then longer; periods are less frequent; periods are skipped; bleeding is profuse; hot flushes or hot flashes, sudden waves of heat with perspiration and then chilling, lasting from a few seconds to half an hour and occurring once or several times a day; emotional disturbances of irritability, nervousness, depression, frigidity, lack of memory, and problems in concentrating.

Menopause occurs when the estrogen level sinks to a certain point. A woman's ovaries produce estrogen from before she is born until she dies. Estrogen is produced also by the adrenal glands in both men and women. A woman's ovaries are especially active during her prenatal life and during the period between menarche and menopause. Production of estrogen by the ovaries begins to decrease in the late twenties and continues to decrease. Menopause may occur any time between the ages of 35 and 60, the average age of menopause being around 47. Removal of both ovaries will bring on the physical symptoms of menopause. Being the result of a lack of estrogen, menopause is like a deficiency disease [21]. (Not all physicians would agree with us.) In some women, the adrenal glands begin to produce more estrogen at some time after menopause is reached. Although the production of adrenal estrogen does not bring back a woman's menstrual periods, it does mitigate some of the negative aspects of menopause, such as the masculinization of body contours and the coarsening of facial hair.

An occasional complication of menopause is pregnancy. It is rare for a woman to become pregnant one year after her last menstrual period, but it has happened. In the beginning stages of menopause, when periods are merely lengthened or skipped,

pregnancy can occur. Healthy children have been born to women of 60 or even 70, but the odds of a menopausal woman producing a mongoloid or deformed child are high [8].

## Postmenopause

Most women live for many years after the menopause. After menstruation has finally stopped, many discomforts disappear, including the hot flashes and many emotional complaints. If a woman has had a hard time with heavy bleeding or painful periods, she usually welcomes freedom from these burdens. Why, then is this time of life considered problematic by some people?

Some of the symptoms of insufficient estrogen continue to be annoying and even debilitating [8]. General skin tone slackens. Breasts shrink and droop. Bones become porous and brittle, because of a loss of calcium. There is an increased risk of coronary heart disease and cancer. Numerous physical problems include insomnia, headache, fast-beating heart, vertigo, loss of appetite, and weight gain. Estrogen therapy often improves or even removes these problems. In the case of loss of bone tissue, however, estrogen therapy may prevent deterioration but will not reverse the process. The vagina becomes less acid, increasing the likelihood of infections. The walls lose elasticity and may bleed because they are easily eroded. Thinness and dryness of the vagina may make intercourse painful. Local application of a cream containing estrogen counteracts the negative effects on the vagina of lack of ovarian estrogen. Estrogen creams are available by prescription.

## Emotional Aspects of Menopause and Postmenopause

Some of the problems attributed to menopause stem from the self-concept and its relation to the parent-child, marital, and occupational careers. Since menopause often coincides with the children's departure from home, the mother may be then faced with problems of how to occupy herself in ways that seem worthwhile to her. Feeling useless and low in self-esteem, she may attribute her problems to menopause. Another example comes from the sexual career. If a woman has not had a satisfactory sex life up to this time, she may use menopause as an excuse for avoiding sexual intercourse. If untreated menopausal symptoms are also making intercourse unpleasant, then she will be thoroughly convinced that she should not participate.

Emotional aspects may be very positive. Some women report no negative symptoms at all and many more have no symptoms when they have adequate medical supervision. Many such women comment that it is wonderful to be relieved of the nuisance of monthly periods. Some report improved sexual relations because they no longer have to worry about getting pregnant. Even women with mild negative symptoms may think that the benefits of menopause outweigh the problems. Since menstruation no longer serves any useful purpose to the woman who does not want to have any more children, menopause may be especially welcome to women who are eager to get on with their jobs and occupational careers. Menopause marks the beginning of a period of life that can be very fulfilling in terms of companionship in marriage and advancement in personal development.

**The "Male Menopause."** Although men do not experience a change as dramatic as menopause, the level of testosterone gradually drops until around age 60, when it then stabilizes for the rest of the man's life [28]. Lower levels of testosterone mean that a man needs more tactile stimulation to develop and maintain an erection, production of less semen, production of fewer sperm, a less intense orgasm, and a longer refractory period [28, 38]. It is interesting that in traditional China, where old age was revered, a man was considered to be at his sexual peak in old age, because by then he was able easily to control his ejaculation. During a particular incidence of coitus he might not ejaculate at all, but would nonetheless experience great pleasure, while at the same time satisfying his partner by bringing her to orgasm a number of times.

# GENDER ROLES IN ADOLESCENCE AND ADULTHOOD

In the previous chapter, we described how early gender-role learning takes place. By the age of two or earlier, the child has a conception of herself or himself as female or male. As the child progresses through childhood, she continues to learn her culture's conception of the proper gender role. This learning continues through life.

## The Question of Malleability

Some feminists argue that *all* sex differences beyond the anatomical are learned. It is our belief, however, that one's maleness or femaleness provides broad ranges for behavior, but that there are some differences beyond genital differences [27-a, Parts I and II]. Socialization has a large influence upon the innate differences, in most cases enlarging upon them.

The case of the transsexual indicates that this socialization process occasionally does not occur. A *transsexual* is an individual, usually male (we use the male example), who believes that he was born into the wrong body. From early childhood, he identifies strongly with women, and is very unhappy as a boy. He wants to have relationships with men, but not man-to-man. Rather, he sees himself in the female role. The homosexual, by contrast, sees himself as a man, a man attracted to other men. The only solution for the true transsexual is a sex change operation; the body is more easily changed than the mind.

Studies of male transsexuals suggest that an individual can be effectively socialized as a member of the opposite sex [23]. However, the role of altered brain states upon transsexualism has not been ruled out.

In the normal individual, as we have stated before, heredity sets the stage for environmental influences. Sutton-Smith puts it this way: "Masculinity and femininity are . . . forms of adaptation towards which the individual is assisted by inheritance and training" [55].

**Continued Reorganization of Gender Roles.** As dialectical theory teaches (see pages 88–89), the learning of gender roles continues throughout life, responding to changes in the culture and situational changes of the individual. In a traditional society, male and female roles are generally more distinct, so that behavior that is defined as "masculine" is also "not-feminine," and behavior defined as "feminine" is also "not-masculine." In modern societies, however, it is more difficult to make these distinctions. For example, as more and more men in a society become involved in the nurturing of their children, we would expect "nurturance" to become defined less exclusively as a feminine attribute, and come to be seen also as a masculine attribute in that society.

As people move through their life careers, their behaviors and attitudes change. One stage in a person's life career calls forth more or fewer "masculine" and/or "feminine" behaviors and attitudes. In a study of men and women at four life-career stages (living together, newlywed, expecting their first child, and parents), it was found that gender-role self-concepts varied by sex and by stage of life career [1]. At all stages, men saw themselves as more "masculine" than women saw themselves, and women saw themselves as more "feminine" than men saw themselves, but the differences were largest among the parents. Women saw themselves as increasingly feminine from the earliest stage, living together, through the stage of parenthood. At the same time, they saw themselves as most masculine when in the living-together stage, as least masculine when they were newlyweds, and as somewhere in between during the expectant and parent stages. Men's masculinity self-concept scores paralleled the women's, but were higher. In terms of their femininity, men saw themselves as increasingly feminine from the living-together stage through the newlywed and expectant stages, and then as less feminine in the parent stage.

## The Women's Movement: A Brief "Herstory"

More than a century and a quarter has passed since the first Women's Rights Convention, held in Seneca Falls, New York, in 1848. The women who met there wanted to be released from bondage to men, who controlled their lives as husbands and fathers. The movement to free the slaves was growing in the United States, and some women clearly saw the parallels between their condition and that of the slaves. A woman belonged to her husband, who could abuse her as he wished. She could not be a minister, a doctor, or a lawyer. She could not vote. A different moral code existed for women. Furthermore, within the Abolitionist movement, women were clearly second-class to men. During the Civil War the activities of the women's rights movement ceased, but they began again once the war was over [25].

The opening of the West also had an effect upon women's rights. Women were scarce in the West, and this gave them a bargaining power that they did not have in the "civilized" East. It was impossible for women to be sheltered and protected in the West the way they had been in the East. They often had to do the work of men. It is significant that Wyoming led the way in 1869 in giving the women the vote.

During the 1800s, women began to go to college in greater numbers, and more women also began to earn their own living, largely because of the industrial revolution. Women were paid less than men; working conditions and wages were deplorable; but women began to gain another bit of bargaining power that was previously denied them. Groups of feminists fought for equal rights for females, with varying degrees of success, but did not receive the right to vote in national elections until 1920. About the same time, the first revolution in female sexual behavior was taking place. During World War I, the services of women had been needed in the labor market, and their working experience changed their lives and status in a way that could not be completely undone.

Following World War I, more women went to college and entered the professions than ever before. The Equal Rights Amendment (ERA) was first introduced into Congress in 1923, and has been introduced in all sessions of Congress since that

GEORGE & FRANCES FELDER SONS & DAUGHTER

time. During World War II, women worked in huge numbers. But after the war was over, drastic changes occurred for women. Women's place suddenly became the home once again. Books and articles in women's magazines promoted the idea that the ideal woman stayed at home, making and caring for lots of babies and keeping her husband happy. It was all right for her to go to college, but she should not consider having a career unless she were unfortunate enough to remain single.

**The Rebirth of Feminism.** In 1963, Betty Friedan published *The Feminine Mystique* [20]. It tells the rise and fall of the first women's movement, and it helped to start a new movement. The National Organization for Women (NOW) was founded in 1966. Since that time many other women's rights organizations have been founded, some of them highly structured, such as NOW, and others at the grass-roots level. Women want equal pay for equal work; they want equal job and educational opportunity; many want day care facilities for their children. Before the 1973 Supreme Court decision that struck down the antiabortion laws, many women lobbied for the individual right to choose whether or not to end a pregnancy. As it had more than a century before, racial politics had implications for the feminist movement. Women who worked in the Civil Rights Movement in the 1960s found that they were not considered as equals by the men in the movement.

In 1967, an amendment to the Constitution made it unlawful for a person to be discriminated against on the basis of race or sex. At the time, some legislators took the ''sex'' part as somewhat of a joke, but women took it very seriously.

Since industrialization began in this country, women's nonfamilial work has responded to the needs of the economy. When women's labor was needed outside the home, women worked away from their families, but when the economy slowed down, it was back to the kitchen. However, the rebirth of the feminist movement coincided with a technological change that has far-reaching implications for the autonomy of women: the development of contraceptives that give women control over their reproductive function. Women have responded by having fewer children, thereby spending a shorter portion of their lives on childrearing. Women also are more likely to resume work when their children are small. As we shall see in Chapter 9, work commitment is higher among women than it was 20 years ago. Thus, it seems unlikely that women will return willingly to the kitchen even when the economy puts pressures on them to do so.

**The Equal Rights Amendment.**  The Equal Rights Amendment would give men and women equal protection under the law. Although the House and Senate have approved ERA, at this writing the amendment has not been ratified by a sufficient number of states (thirty-eight) to make it law.

At the present time, in most states laws exist that apply differentially to men and women. Sixteen states have their own ERAs that apply within their borders. One of the first states to adopt an ERA was Pennsylvania, in 1971. Since that time a number of court cases in that state have indicated what ERA would mean for the nation. For example, parents in Pennsylvania have equal responsibility to support their children, taking into account financial and nonfinancial contributions. A wife may now sue a third party for "loss of consortium" (loss of affection, companionship, and help with home and children) if her husband is incapacitated in an accident for which the third party was at fault. Husbands have had this right for centuries. Opponents of ERA argue that under ERA the divorce rate will go up, that public toilets will be integrated, and that women will lose protective labor legislation. Evidence from Pennsylvania contradicts these predictions. Pennsylvania's divorce rate has not gone up as fast as has the divorce rate in most states, the Attorney General has said that the right to separate toilets is protected by the constitutional right to privacy; and most protective labor laws have been extended to men [2].

**Black Feminism: Some Contrasts.**  The early feminists saw their position as being similar to that of the slaves. Although some black women today join the feminists, others believe that they can have no true liberty until all blacks have real equality. They feel that black women should not join with white women in the white woman's struggle against male dominance, because black women are not dominated by black men. The black man is even more controlled by white society than is the black woman, who has traditionally been more able to get work than has the black man [40].

**Requirements for Women's Self-Esteem.**  Before we assess some of the changes that the women's movement has made on the lives of both men and women, we would like to note some requirements for woman's best functioning and self-esteem, as proposed by Whiting [62]. She studied family life in simple subsistence societies in which women still participate in the production of goods, and/or control resources. Female economic roles complement male roles.

In such societies, the men are herders and women usually tend gardens that are close to the house, but when gardens are far away they become the male's responsibility. In this case, the woman stays at home and tends the fire. Women sell excess produce, cooked food, or cloth if there is a market nearby. When the woman goes to the market she may take her babies or leave them at home with a relative or an older child.

In societies that are changing from pastoralism to agriculture, woman's work is usually heavy. As land becomes scarce and herds dwindle, the man's work becomes less and the woman's responsibility becomes greater. Men fail to help in agriculture if it is considered "woman's work."

In these societies, whether or not the man still has a viable economic role, the woman is contributing to the welfare of her family. Her role is not limited to cooking, cleaning, and child care. She controls economic resources, and this gives her power and prestige. Furthermore, there are relatives nearby with whom to interact and to take care of her children; she never spends the entire day in housework and child care. When children reach the age of five to seven, they begin to care for younger

STANLEY SUMMER

siblings and help with other family tasks. This gives the children a sense of being worthwhile and gives them direct experience in adult roles.

Whiting proposes that in order for a woman to be happy she must have self-esteem, and in order to have self-esteem she must (1) "be involved in productive work—cooking, cleaning, and childrearing is not sufficient." (2) She needs to have control of some resources so that she is not totally dependent upon her husband for material goods. (3) "She needs to be away from her children four or five hours a day and at some period to be in the company of other adults." (4) She needs a flexible schedule and a work day no longer than five hours. (5) She needs other women nearby to help her in emergencies.

The American housewife spends more time than ever before in child care and housework. As labor-saving devices are invented, housework standards go up. Although children do need the attention of their parents, too much parental attention can be damaging. The feminine mystique that extolled the glories of full-time housewifery and motherhood is apparently on the wane. Not all women should work outside the home; many really are fulfilled as homemakers. Nor are paid jobs essential to all. But Whiting's research supports and explains Friedan's thesis that many women are discontent in the homemaker role.

### Men's and Women's Gender Role Attitudes

Gender-role attitudes are defined as "liberal" when men's and women's roles are thought to be the same or similar, and as "conservative" when they are thought to be different. There is considerable evidence that among college students, gender-role attitudes have become more liberal for both sexes, but that women's liberality has increased more than men's [42, 51, 61]. It seems that childrearing decisions are the most problematic area for both men and women. When couples don't want children, it is easier for men to support nontraditional roles [57]. But when there are children, wives are expected (and themselves expect) to do most of the child care [41]. Liberal women are therefore more likely to reject the idea of becoming mothers, and consider the parenting role to be relatively uncreative. By contrast, liberal men and conservative women see the parenting role as more creative, and want to take an active role in childrearing [35, 36]. Men who share childrearing equally with their wives free the wives to pursue employment of some kind. We return to the subject of work and family roles in Chapter 8.

### Implications of Gender Roles in Adulthood

Although only a small proportion of women at any one time are actively involved in the women's movement, the movement has touched the lives of most women in our society. Equal pay for equal work is endorsed by most Americans. The women's movement has touched the lives of men as well. When a wife works, her husband must make some changes in his life style, however few. Some men are responding to feminist ideology by taking an active part in the men's movement, or what some call the human liberation movement. A major goal of this movement is to lessen the impact of gender roles.

We ourselves believe that gender roles, like all roles, have a function for a society. Although individuals sacrifice freedom when they adhere to roles, a society may benefit. When roles are rigidly prescribed and adhered to, members of a society know what they are supposed to do and do it. We are not here advocating a return to rigid gender roles, but we want to point out that they do serve a function. Rather, we would prefer that more role choices be open to individuals, while still taking into account the needs of the larger group (the family, the community, and the society).

Family gender roles ideally change to meet the needs of the family at a particular time. For one family, having the wife stay at home and care for the young children may be the best solution. For another family, the husband may wish to fill this role, and in yet another, the role may be shared. When the children are older, parental roles would probably shift to take into account the changing needs of family members. If economic necessity dictates that both parents work, fairness requires that family roles reflect this reality. Androgyny does not work for many families in the stage of childbearing and rearing young children. The reason is not that men are naturally poor caregivers, but that many men think they cannot take care of little children or that they don't want to. Parents, friends, and society have socialized them to think this way. A second set of reasons is that societal supports are lacking. Men cannot get enough time off from their work. By staying home to be parents, they may lose the wages and promotions that they need in order to earn money for their families.

## HOMOSEXUALITY

Homosexuality may be defined as feeling sexual attraction to the same sex. It may or may not be accompanied by the overt expression of these feelings. Kinsey defined a homosexual as an individual who had at least one homosexual experience at some time in his life [31]. Even a person who had had one homosexual experience in childhood would be considered a homosexual by this very broad definition.

Some individuals are attracted to members of both sexes, and these may be termed **bisexuals** or **ambisexuals.** To further clarify the distinction between hetero-, homo-, and bisexuals, we make the distinction between them as follows: a **heterosexual** is a person who, throughout all or most of his adult life, is sexually attracted to and possibly has sexual relations only with members of the opposite sex. A **homosexual** is a person who throughout all or most of his adult life is sexually attracted to and possibly has sexual relations only with members of the same sex. In either case, an occasional "switch" to the other sex would not change the individual's basic sexual preference orientation. A *bisexual* is an individual whose erotic and love interests are divided between men and women. The bisexual may have concurrent relationships with men and women, or may change back and forth throughout his or her life.

Our definitions would not be accepted by all clinicians, social scientists, heterosexuals, homosexuals, or bisexuals. There is much controversy as well regarding the causes of homosexuality, and whether it is a disease or a normal condition. In 1973, the American Psychiatric Association's board of trustees voted to remove homosexuality from the mental illness category. Not all psychiatrists agree with this decision, however. This move by the American Psychiatric Association reflects a softening of public opinion in this country regarding homosexuality.

## Causes of Homosexuality

The ancient Greeks believed that each person was originally created from the splitting of another individual. Some persons came from an all-male whole, others from an all-female whole, and others from a half-male, half-female whole. The resulting mortal searched for his "other half," an idea kept alive in our society today in the romantic notion that people are made for each other. We have tended to forget about the homosexual pairs, thinking only about the heterosexual. The Greek explanation of homosexuality, of course, is not accepted today. But it has not been replaced by a completely adequate explanation.

**Freud's Explanations.**   Freud never developed a coherent theory of homosexuality, and his writings on this subject have been subject to many interpretations by other psychotherapists. Freud considered all persons as having both male and female qualities but did not regard homosexuality as normal. The child's failure to resolve the Oedipal conflict could be manifested in a number of ways, including homosexuality. Homosexuality wasn't thought by Freud to be treatable by therapy, because it was a "perversion" and not a "neurosis" [22].

**Disease Theories.**   A number of psychiatrists still view homosexuality as a disease. Some claim that there is no such thing as a happy homosexual, that all homosexuals are depressed, guilty, and fearful of the opposite sex. The family is sometimes seen as the cause; in the case of the boy, the father is detached, absent, or brutal, and the mother is overprotective or domineering. The female homosexual (Lesbian) may come from a similar family, or the girl's mother may regard all men as brutal or no good, and teach this attitude to her daughter. Other explanations for homosexuality include a deep fear of assuming adult responsibility, extreme competitiveness with one's own sex, the child's awareness that her or his parents wanted a child of the opposite sex, or, in the case of the male, a search for maleness that the individual feels that he lacks [22].

**Normality Theories.**   Other psychiatrists view homosexuality as a normal variant of the human behavior spectrum. They note that not all homosexuals come from disturbed families, and that not all persons from father-absent, mother-dominated families become homosexuals. Some argue that homosexual behavior is normal for mammals. Several studies have found groups of homosexuals to be as psychologically healthy as matched groups of heterosexuals. The homosexuals who go to psychiatrists for help are troubled people, but psychiatrists rarely see the "invisible" nontroubled group of homosexuals. Members of the Gay Liberation movement who lobbied to have homosexuality removed from the mental illness category have pointed out that nothing makes a person feel mentally sick more effectively than constantly being told that he is sick. They contend that now that the "sick" label is being lifted, more and more homosexuals will come "out of the closet" and declare themselves to be homosexuals. This appears to be happening.

**Influence of Hormones.**   There is some evidence that hormonal imbalances may be a part of the explanation for at least some homosexuality. The Masters and Johnson Sex Research Institute reported in 1971 that young men who were predominantly or exclusively homosexual had lower levels of testosterone than did normal men. A very small group of Lesbians was found in England to have lower estrogen levels than normal women. These findings have not been consistently supported by other researchers, and in some cases have been refuted. Administering testosterone to male homosexuals does not change the orientation of their sex interests, but does increase their sex drive [22].

It is possible that prenatal influences of hormones could influence an individual's later sexual orientation. Severe prenatal protein deficiency has been found to cause estrogen feminization of human males, resulting in enlarged breasts, atrophied testes, and a more feminine cognitive style, with higher verbal ability and lower spatial skills [15]. Whether or not the individual's sexual orientation was also affected was not determined by this study. However, prenatal effects have not been ruled out as yet.

**Learning Theory.**   From a learning theory approach, homosexuality is behavior that is learned as a result of a series of positive homosexual experiences and few negative experiences. An individual would become a homosexual when homosexual experiences were more numerous and more gratifying than heterosexual experiences. From this theoretical viewpoint, early-maturing boys would be more likely to become homosexuals than would late-maturing boys, because the former are ready for sexual experiences at an earlier age than is generally accepted by society. Frustrated in establishing sexual contacts with girls, such boys would turn to other boys for sexual gratification [10].

**Some Tentative Conclusions.**   Homosexual behavior cannot be explained by one factor or one series of events [32]. Gould [22], a psychiatrist, suggests that there are three types of homosexuals: "Those who are disturbed and whose homosexuality

reflects that disturbance symptomatically,'' for example, those persons with an intense fear or hatred of the opposite sex. Such fear, however, need not be manifested in homosexual behavior, but can also be manifested in sadomasochistic heterosexual behavior (that is, enjoying inflicting pain on one's partner or enjoying having pain inflicted on oneself).

A second type of homosexual is the disturbed individual "for whom homosexuality is not related to the psychiatric problem" [22]. The disturbance in this case is not sexual, but has to do with some other aspect of the personality.

The third type of homosexual is the well-adjusted kind, who is not a psychiatric patient. This kind of individual lives a comfortable, productive, and happy life, and is often committed to long-lasting, intimate, one-to-one relationships, as is the normal and healthy heterosexual.

**Homosexual Behavior.** Kinsey noted that persons with homosexual experience vary in the ratio of homosexual to heterosexual experiences [31]. A more recent study of homosexuals in the San Francisco Bay area, carried out by the Institute for Sex Research that was founded by Kinsey, came to similar conclusions [3]. Homosexuals were asked to rate themselves on their present sexual behavior and feelings, and also on their sexual behaviors and feelings during adolescence. Three quarters of the males, and two thirds of the females, rated themselves as currently exclusively homosexual in behaviors and attitudes. However, only around half of men and women said that they were currently exclusively homosexual in their feelings and covert sexual responses. During adolescence, even more of the respondents had experienced both heterosexual behavior and feelings. Males were equally divided among those who had been exclusively homosexual in behavior, predominantly heterosexual in behavior, and mixed. A quarter of the males had been predominantly heterosexual in feelings during adolescence, and a third were exclusively homosexual in feelings. More than half of the men reported a discrepancy between feelings and behaviors during adolescence.

Women, too, were likely to have had heterosexual experiences and feelings during adolescence. Forty-four per cent said that they had been predominantly homosexual in feelings, and 43 per cent had been predominantly heterosexual in their feelings. A third had been exclusively heterosexual in behavior during adolescence, and fewer than a quarter had been predominantly homosexual in behavior. Thus, among a group of men and women who identified themselves as homosexual, many had current or past heterosexual feelings and experiences.

**Homosexual Life Styles.** Homosexuals, like heterosexuals, have varying kinds of relationships with each other [4]. Some live with their partners in close, bonded relationships, and are well-adjusted in their relationships and in other aspects of their lives. Others who live with a partner continue to seek outside relationships. This life style is less frequent among women, but is the usual type among males. Still others maintain a life style that is similar to a "swinging singles" style. Rather than maintaining paired relationships, these men and women seek large numbers of sexual partners. Their lives are organized around their sexual experiences; there is much involvement in the "gay" world and few regrets about being homosexual. Another group, called "dysfunctionals" by Bell and Weinberg, fits the stereotype of the "tormented homosexual" [4, p. 225]. These are the individuals who wind up on the psychiatrist's couch. Dysfunctionals report more sexual problems and a great deal of worry about their sexual inadequacies and what they perceive to be their own lack of attractiveness. Other aspects of their lives were equally problematic. Another group of homosexuals, although identifying themselves as such, had few social contacts. Unlike the "dysfunctionals," who were quite active sexually, "asexuals" had few sexual contacts. Although they complained of loneliness, asexuals were not very interested in establishing relationships with others. Bell and Weinberg conclude that homosexuals, like heterosexuals, are a diverse group. Some are interested in having large numbers of sexual partners; others want to settle down with one person, and still others appear to wish to remain fairly isolated. The stereotype of the homosexual in much psychiatric literature is based upon clinical observations of homosexuals who were unhappy enough to seek help, and not upon observations of all kinds of homosexuals.

Many homosexuals have noted the stresses that accompany their sexual orientation [17]. They are different; they are not allowed in some restaurants and hotels; they are forbidden to work for the government; they are discriminated against in jobs and housing; they are not allowed to claim the benefits of marriage. Living a double life is another strain on them. Some male homosexuals date women or marry in order to hide their sexual orientation and thereby avoid discrimination. The Lesbian also is under pressure to marry, although generally she is less suspect than the male if she chooses to live with a friend of the same sex.

"Coming out," or recognizing and ceasing to hide one's homosexuality, can lift the burden of living a double life but it means opening oneself up to the other pressures described. Many homosexuals from small towns feel unable to "come out," or may not even recognize that they are homosexuals. Some are desperately lonely, unaware that there are others like them. The city offers a degree of anonymity and tolerance that is not available in one's small home town. Cities, therefore, attract many homosexuals. The college campus also may offer a more tolerant atmosphere for homosexuals, as evidence by "Gay" or "Homophile" groups, especially on larger campuses.

As the gay scene continues to come out farther into the open, it is likely that one will hear more about changes in the homosexual world, both in terms of increases in promiscuity and increases in long-term relationships among homosexuals. However, the homosexual who wishes to enter a stable relationship does not receive the same support that a heterosexual does, and is, therefore, less likely to be successful [9]. The heterosexual who marries receives legal and social support. It is harder for him to get out of marriage than it is for the cohabitor to break a relationship, whether or not the cohabiting partners are of the same sex. When considering the degree of promiscuity among gays, one should keep in mind that homosexuals do not receive the kind of support for their relationship that even unmarried heterosexual partners do.

As a life style, homosexuality entails special problems and difficulties. Working with a group of 54 men and 13 women homosexuals who wished to change to heterosexuality, Masters and Johnson reported success with 65 per cent [39a]. Help in accepting and respecting themselves is needed by some homosexuals who do not wish to change, or who cannot.

## Attitudes Toward Homosexuality

A polarization of societal attitudes toward homosexuality seems to be taking place in our society. In some parts of the country, conservatives have scored major victories over persons who champion homosexual rights, but in other parts of the country homosexuals are relatively free from harrassment. Other countries have been more tolerant to homosexuality in the past, and some are more tolerant now. In ancient Sparta, love between men was considered to be the ideal, and wives merely fulfilled the needed function of providing new citizens for the state. A man would have sexual intercourse with this wife for this purpose, but he lived with and loved his male companions.

In France, the *Code Napoleon* of 1810 allows all homosexual (and heterosexual) behavior between consenting adults [32]. The same has been allowed in England and Wales since 1971, and Illinois led the way in this regard in the United States [49].

Some persons still hold strong convictions, religious or otherwise, that homosexuality is unnatural, wrong, or sinful. The individual who is concerned about being homosexual and wishes to change can usually be helped to adjust [32]. However, it should be emphasized that one or two feelings of attraction to same sex, or even homosexual acts, do not mean that a person is a homosexual. During childhood and adolescence there is a developmental stage in which homosexual feelings and acts are especially likely to occur.

It is our belief that feelings of love and attraction for the same sex are normal throughout the lifespan. In our society it is permissible for women to show affection for one another, to hug and kiss. Most men hesitate to express their feelings in this way, although in Europe such behavior is considered natural. Body contact is essential for human life. Infants and children need to be held and cared for, and most adults feel the need for close contact with another human being. In our society, this need usually is fulfilled through heterosexual contact, but as we have seen, this has not always been the case in all societies.

Many homosexual groups have called themselves "homophiles," which means "one who loves the same sex." By putting the emphasis upon emotions rather than the genitals, they believe that they portray themselves more accurately.

**SUMMARY**  Cultures vary widely in their interpretation of sexuality and their regulation of its expression. Although most societies do not disapprove of both premarital and extramarital sex, sexual behavior is generally restricted in some way.

Premarital heterosexual activity varies widely between groups and individuals. American premarital sexual standards have been classified into the following four: abstinence, permissiveness with affection, double standard, and permissiveness without affection. In deciding upon the choice of a standard, the probable consequences of various courses of action (and inaction) are pertinent. Pregnancy, a possible result of sexual activity, is almost entirely preventable and also terminable, but when pregnancies are neither prevented nor terminated, the resulting babies must be cared for. And any one of these results of sexual activity may have a profound effect upon one or both of the couple involved. Another consequence, often preventable, is venereal disease. Guilt feelings may result. When heterosexual activity crowds out like-sex friendships in adolescence, development of the sense of identity may be curtailed.

Advantages of premarital intercourse include physical and psychological satisfaction. Premarital intercourse may also provide helpful experience and testing for compatability. Some groups look down upon virgins, although there are indeed many who do just the opposite. Before beginning a sex relationship, it is wise to think over possible consequences and plan to prevent undesired ones.

The twentieth century has seen a great change in women's sexual behavior in terms of acceptant attitudes and premarital intercourse, and in the frequency and number of partners. Although men have not changed as greatly as women in terms of frequency of premarital sex, their experiences must have changed because women have changed. Different behavior and attitudes have been noted in regard to social class, regions, and race. Adolescent peer groups exert strong influence on sexual practices.

Wives who discuss their sexual feelings with their husbands are more likely to say that they have good sex lives. The longer a woman is married, the more likely she is to have extramarital sex. A woman's sexual responsiveness increases throughout her twenties and thirties. A man's sexual responsiveness, however, declines slowly throughout much of adulthood.

Menopause, the cessation of menstruation, marks the end of fertility but not enjoyment of sex. Lowered estrogen levels may bring bodily aging changes and perhaps emotional upsets. Many women have no problems with menopause. Some welcome it.

Gender roles continue to be developed throughout life, with cultural forces molding the individual. In the nineteenth century, women gained some rights, some freedom from men, and a new point of view on gender roles. They suffered a setback after World War II, when the cultural ideal for women was focused on homemaking and having many children. The female role expanded again in the 1960s, through women's liberation and the development of new birth control methods. Women are seriously concerned now with working out appropriate new roles. Changes in women's roles have profound effects upon men's and children's roles, and hence upon the quality of life in the society. While women expand their roles, their self-esteem, and dignity, men are trying to retain their masculinity and feelings of self-worth. Gender roles within the family are not static, and can respond to the needs of family members.

Homosexuality is the sexual attraction to persons of the same sex. Bisexuals are attracted to both sexes. Homosexuality is interpreted variously as abnormal and a disease or as a normal variation of human behavior. Some but not all homosexuals are troubled about their condition. Some are well-adjusted, leading productive, happy lives. Increasing numbers of men and women are declaring themselves homosexual. Many homosexuals have heterosexual feelings and/or experiences at some time during their adolescent or adult lives. Homosexual life styles vary. Some are monogamous; others live with a partner and have outside relationships; others seem to be unable to find satisfying relationships. Societal attitudes toward homosexuality seem to be polarizing.

**REFERENCES**

1. Abrahams, Barbara, S. Shirley Feldman, and Sharon Churnin Nash. Sex role self-concept and sex role attitudes: Enduring personality characteristics or adaptations to changing life situations? *Developmental Psychology,* 1978, **14,** 393–400.
2. Anderson, Peggy. Pennsylvania: ERA in practice. *Ms.,* 1978, **7**:3, 92.
3. Bell, Alan P. Homosexualties. Lecture presented at the Institute for Sex Research, Bloomington, Ind. July 19, 1976.
4. Bell, Alan P. and Martin S. Weinberg. *Homosexualities: A study of diversity among men and women.* New York: Simon and Schuster, 1978.
5. Bell, Robert and Jay Chaskes. Premarital sexual experience among coeds, 1958 and 1968. *Journal of Marriage and the Family,* 1970, **32,** 81–84.
6. Bell, Robert R., Stanley Turner, and Lawrence Rosen. A multivariate analysis of female extramarital coitus. *Journal of Marriage and the Family,* 1975, **37,** 375–384.
7. Bonham, Scott Gordon. Who adopts: The relationship of adoption and social-demographic characteristics of women. *Journal of Marriage and the Family,* 1977, **39,** 295–306.
8. Boston Woman's Health Book Collective. *Our bodies, ourselves.* New York, Simon and Schuster, 1973.
9. Chesser, Eustance. *Strange loves: the human aspects of sexual deviation.* New York: Morrow, 1971.
10. Chilman, Catherine. Social and psychological aspects of adolescent sexuality: An analytic overview of research and theory. Milwaukee: School of Social Welfare. U. of Wisconsin–Milwaukee, 1977.
11. Christensen, Harold and George Carpenter. Timing patterns in the development of sexual intimacy. *Marriage and Family Living,* 1962, **24,** 30–35.
12. Christensen, Harold and Christina Gregg. Changing sex norms in America and Scandinavia. *Journal of Marriage and the Family,* 1970, **32,** 616–627.
13. Christensen, Harold T. and Leanor B. Johnson. Premarital coitus and the southern Black: A comparative view. *Journal of Marriage and the Family,* 1978, **40,** 721–732.
14. Davis, Peter. Contextual sex saliency and sexual activity: The relative effects of family and peer group in the sexual socialization process. *Journal of Marriage and the Family,* 1974, **36,** 196–202.
15. Dawson, John L. M., Y. M. Cheung, T. S. Lau, and F. Yue. The neonatal sex hormone reversal of cognitive skills in rats and men. U. of Hong Kong, 1972. (Mimeo.)
16. Erikson, Erik. *Identity, youth, and crisis.* New York: Norton, 1968.
17. Fisher, Peter. *The gay mystique: The myth and reality of male homosexuality.* New York: Stein & Day, 1972.
18. Ferrell, Mary Z., William L. Tolone, and Robert H. Walsh. Maturational and societal change in the sexual double standard. A panel analysis (1961–1971; 1970–1974). *Journal of Marriage and the Family,* 1977, **39,** 255–271.
19. Ford, Clellan and Frank A. Beach. *Patterns of sexual behavior.* New York: Harper, 1951.
20. Friedan, Betty. *The feminine mystique.* New York: Norton, 1963.
21. Gifford-Jones, W. *On being a woman: The modern woman's guide to gynecology.* New York: Macmillan, 1971.

22. Gould, Robert E. What we don't know about homosexuality. *New York Times Magazine,* February 24, 1974, 12, 13, 15+.
23. Green, Richard. Atypical sex role development. Lecture presented at the Institute for Sex Research, Bloomington, Ind. July 26, 1976.
24. Hobart, Charles W. Sexual permissiveness in young English and French Canadians. *Journal of Marriage and the Family,* 1972, **34,** 292–304.
25. Hole, Judith and Ellen Levine. *Rebirth of feminism.* New York: Quadrangle, 1971.
26. Hornick, Joseph. Premarital sexual attitudes and behavior. *Sociological Quarterly,* 1978, **19,** 534–544.
27. Hunt, Morton M. *The affair.* New York: American Library, 1971.
27a. Hutt, S. J. and Corinne Hutt, *Early human development.* London: Oxford U. P., 1973.
28. Kaplan, Helen Singer. The new sex therapy. New York: Brunner/Mazel, 1974.
29. King, Karl, Jack O. Balswick, and Ira E. Robinson. The continuing premarital sexual revolution among college females. *Journal of Marriage and the Family,* 1977, **39,** 455–459.
30. Kinsey, Alfred C., Wardell B. Pomeroy, Clyde E. Martin, and Paul H. Gebhard. *Sexual behavior in the human female.* Philadelphia: Saunders, 1953.
31. Kinsey, Alfred C., Wardell B. Pomeroy, and Clyde E. Martin. *Sexual behavior in the human male.* Philadelphia: Saunders, 1948.
32. Kogan, Benjamin. *Human sexual expression.* New York: Harcourt, 1973.
33. Levin, Robert J. The *Redbook* report on marital and extramarital sex. The end of the double standard? *Redbook,* 1975, **145**:6 38–42+.
34. Levin, Robert J. and Amy Levin. Sexual pleasure: The surprising preferences of 100,000 women. *Redbook,* 1975, **145**:5 51–56+.
35. Lott, Bernice. Sex role barriers to liberated parenting. Paper presented at *Parents and Children,* Conference at State University of New York at Stony Brook. November 11, 1977.
36. Lott, Bernice. Who wants the children? *American Psychologist,* 1973, **28,** 573–582.
37. Lozoff, Marjorie. Changing life styles and role perceptions of men and women students. Paper presented at *Women: Resources for a changing world.* Conference held at Radcliffe Institute, Radcliffe College, Cambridge, Mass. April 17, 1972.
38. Masters, William and Virginia Johnson. *Human sexual inadequacy.* Boston: Little, Brown, 1966.
39. Masters, William and Virginia Johnson. *Human sexual response.* Boston: Little, Brown, 1970.
39a. Masters, William and Virginia Johnson. *Homosexuality in perspective.* Boston: Little, Brown, 1979.
40. Mayo, Julia. The new black feminism: A minority report. In Joseph Zubin and John Money (Eds.). *Contemporary sexual behavior: Critical issues in the 1970s.* Baltimore: Johns Hopkins, 1973, 175–186.
41. Osmond, Marie Withers and Patricia Yancey Martin. Sex and sexism: A comparison of male and female sex role attitudes. *Journal of Marriage and the Family,* 1977, **37,** 744–758.
42. Parelius, Ann P. Emerging sex role attitudes, expectations, and strains among college women. *Journal of Marriage and the Family,* 1975, **37,** 146–154.
43. Perlman, Daniel. Self-esteem and sexual permissiveness. *Journal of Marriage and the Family,* 1974, **36,** 470–474.
44. Ramey, James W. Emerging patterns of innovative behavior in marriage. *Family Coordinator,* 1972, **21,** 435–456.

45. Reiss, Ira. *Premarital sexual standards in America.* New York: Free Press, 1960.
46. Reiss, Ira. *The social context of premarital sexual permissiveness.* New York: Holt, 1967.
47. Reiss, Ira and Brent C. Miller. A theoretical analysis of heterosexual permissiveness. *Technical Report No. II.* Minnesota Family Study Center, University of Minnesota, 1974.
48. Robinson, Ira, Karl King, and Jack Balswick. The premarital sexual revolution among college females. *Family Coordinator,* 1972, **21,** 189–194.
49. Rosenzweig, Saul. Human sexual autonomy as an evolutionary attainment, anticipating proceptive sex choice and idiodynamic bisexuality. In Joseph Zubin and John Money (Eds.). *Contemporary sexual behavior: Critical issues in the 1970s.* Baltimore: Johns Hopkins, 1973, 189–230.
50. Ross, Susan. *The youth values project.* Washington, D.C.: The Population Institute, 1978.
51. Scanzoni, John. Sex role change and influences on birth intentions. *Journal of Marriage and the Family,* 1976, **38,** 43–58.
52. Singh, B. Krishna, Bonnie L. Walton, and J. Sherwood Williams. Extramarital sexual permissiveness: Conditions and contingencies. *Journal of Marriage and the Family,* 1976, **38,** 701–712.
53. Sorensen, Robert C. *Adolescent sexuality in contemporary America.* New York: World, 1973.
54. Staples, Robert. Race, liberalism-conservatism and premarital sexual permissiveness. *Journal of Marriage and the Family,* 1978, **40,** 733–742.
55. Sutton-Smith, Brian. Sex differences in development. In Lee C. Deighton (Ed.). *Encyclopedia of Education,* Vol. 2., New York: Macmillan, 1971, 59–65.
56. Teevan, James, Jr. Reference groups and premarital sexual behavior. *Journal of Marriage and the Family,* 1972, **34,** 283–292.
57. Tomeh, Aida K. Sex role orientation: An analysis of structural and attitudinal predictors. *Journal of Marriage and the Family,* 1978, **40,** 341–354.
58. Udry, J. Richard, Karl E. Bauman, and Naomi M. Morris. Changes in premarital coital experiences of recent decade-of-birth cohorts of urban American women. *Journal of Marriage and the Family,* 1975, **37,** 783–787.
59. U.S. Bureau of the Census. *Households and families by type: March 1978* (Advance Report). Current Population Reports. Series P-20, No. 327. Washington, D.C.: U.S. Government Printing Office, 1978.
60. Vener, Arthur and Cyrus Stewart. Adolescent sexual behavior in middle America revisited: 1970–1973. *Journal of Marriage and the Family,* 1974, **36,** 728–735.
61. Walsh, Robert H., Mary Z. Ferrell, and William L. Tolone. Selected reference group, perceived reference group permissiveness, and personal permissiveness attitudes and behavior: A study of two consecutive panels (1967–1971 and 1970–1974). *Journal of Marriage and the Family,* 1976, **38,** 495–507.
62. Whiting, Beatrice. Work and the family: Cross-cultural perspectives. Paper presented at *Women: Resource for a changing world.* Conference held at Radcliffe Institute, Radcliffe College, Cambridge, Ma. April 17, 18, 1972.
63. Zelnick, Melvin and John F. Kantner. First pregnancies to women aged 15 to 19: 1976 and 1971. *Family Planning Perspectives,* 1978, **10,** 11–20.
64. Zelnick, Melvin and John F. Kantner. Sexual and contraceptive experience of young unmarried women in the United States, 1976 and 1971. *Family Planning Perspectives,* 1977, **9,** 55–71.

"Matchmaker, matchmaker, make me a match . . ." sing the daughters in *Fiddler on the Roof,* a musical play set in czarist Russia. They assume that their match will be someone handsome, kind, and a good provider. When their eldest sister reminds them that they could be married off to someone old and fat, or cruel, the younger girls decide that they would be better off single for a while. Matchmaking probably takes place in all societies. It may be formal, or informal.

**Traditional Matchmaking.** In societies such as India or traditional China, marriages are arranged by the families. The purpose of a marriage is to carry on the family name, and to build or strengthen an alliance between two families. The young couple is not supposed to get too close to each other, because a strong dyadic attachment would work against the cohesiveness of the family rather than for it. A prospective marriage partner is selected on the basis of qualities that would benefit the family: a beautiful girl with a large dowry, who is submissive and has learned the arts of homemaking and child care, would be the ideal bride. She would have to be of the same social standing as the boy's family. In traditional China, the aristocratic family would not consider a girl whose feet had not been bound when she was in infancy, making her unable to walk but erotically beautiful, and demonstrating that she was of high enough social standing to be carried about.

The matchmaking that takes place in India may be done by the families themselves, or through a village matchmaker who knows of a suitable young person in a neighboring village. Or, advertisements may be made in the paper. Figure 6-1 includes an example of such marriage advertisements. Beauty, caste, and education are all important bargaining points. But before a match can be made, an astrologer must determine whether or not the horoscopes of the young people fit together.

At times, matchmaking may be done by the whole community. Tara and Deepak were two young people of marriageable age in a modern Indian city. They met at a party, and Deepak was greatly taken with Tara. He thought about her a great deal during the several months that separated their first and second meetings. Meanwhile, many people in the community were starting to talk among themselves, saying how suitable a match the young couple would make. After their second encounter, Deepak was even more determined to "get things going" with Tara. He spoke to his mother, saying that he would like to marry Tara. Deepak was overjoyed when his mother replied that she had been thinking the same thing. We attended their wedding, which was a cause for great celebration for all.

The idea of marriages arranged by parents or an outsider goes against the feelings of people in our society. My (LSS) friends in India who attended a college in a large city had ambivalent feelings about arranged marriages. One girl sighed, "I do not know whether I will be happy or sad. My parents will try to find a good husband for me, but there is no way that I will know for sure before I marry him. They will let me meet him, and talk with him for fifteen minutes, but what can you learn about

Gorgeous guy, 22, white, college grad, very handsome, intelligent, honest, kind, thoughtful, warm, friendly. Tired of singles bars scene. Seek nice, friendly, down-to-earth, sincere, extremely attractive girl, 18–21, to date. Send foto: Get mine. Don. Box XXX

Source: New York, *Village Voice*, October 16, 1978. Vol. 23, No. 41.

I am expressive and alive, 35 yrs, educated. Terribly romantic, sensitive, perceptive and open white female who seeks a white man, 35–43, with same qualities to share this life with. Abundant enthusiasm for life not to be wasted. Box YYY

Source: New York, *Village Voice*, October 16, 1978. Vol. 23, No. 41.

WANTED for a 24 years old beautiful, good-natured Varshney girl, educated up to M.A., height 1.60m, fully accomplished in household affairs, a well-established, capable match of the same of Aggarwal caste. Preference to Engineer, Doctor or Industrialist. Girl's father and brother industrialists. Early decent marriage. Write to Box 000, Hindustan Times, New Delhi-1.

Source: New Delhi, *Hindustan Times*, January 20, 1974.

WANTED tall, charming, fair Medico match from respectable well-placed family for Army Captain Doctor, Punjabi Khatri, 26 yrs., 170 cm. tall, smart, getting Rs. 1350/-P.M. Girl's merits main consideration. Box 000, Hindustan Times, New Delhi-1.

Source: New Delhi, *Hindustan Times*, January 20, 1974.

**FIGURE 6-1**     Examples of marriage advertisements.

someone in that length of time?" And yet, these young women knew that they would marry someone, and that their parents would *try* to find them a suitable match. Furthermore, they insisted that their parents, being older and wiser, would probably be able to make a better choice of a mate than they could themselves.

**Modern Matchmaking.** Figure 6-1 also includes newspaper advertisements from an American weekly newspaper. Advertisements in magazines and newspapers is an increasingly frequent method of searching for a new data or mate. Writers of such advertisements almost always portray themselves as possessing socially desirable characteristics such as good personality, physical attractiveness, and recreational interests. Such characteristics are usually requested of potential dates as well. Women are more likely to stress their own physical attractiveness than are men, and men are more likely to request it in a potential partner. Women, on the other hand, are much more interested in a man's occupation than are men in a woman's [6]. Although newspaper and magazine advertisements are fairly new as a popular phenomenon in North America, traditional ideals of the attractive woman and the successful man are portrayed in the advertisements.

Friends are often unsolicited matchmakers. "How come a nice girl like you isn't married?" is a cliché, but the single woman is likely to hear it often. Amy, a career woman in her midforties, says that ten years ago her parents finally gave up trying to match her up with "nice boys" when she went home to visit them. Similarly the newly widowed man finds himself besieged with dinner invitations from well-meaning friends; when he gets there, there is invariably a single woman there for him to be nice to.

Not all single people resent being matched. Indeed, some people go to considerable trouble and expense in order to be matched with a stranger for an evening. Computer dating services abound in urban and college communities. These services are used more frequently by women than by men, because men still have the edge over women when it comes to initiating relationships. Computer dating services require that the applicants fill out questionnaires having to do with **demographic information,** the applicant's personality, interests, and preferences in a date.

A preliminary study of computer-matched marriages investigated the differences between the married individuals and others with whom they had been matched and had dated but had not married. All pairs of individuals, whether or not they eventually married, had been matched as closely as possible on forty variables having to do with personality and interests. The married group differed significantly from the nonmarried group on only six of the items. The most important variable was the expressed desire to marry; that is, if a couple that had been matched dated but did not marry, it was likely that one of them had a low desire to get married (to anyone) [29]. This important issue has not been given much attention in studies of mate selection: does one or both partners have a high desire to marry at the present time or in the near future? Figure 6-2 shows varieties of control over partner selection.

## DATING

After meeting, dating is usually the next step for a man and woman who are attracted to each other. (More about attraction will be said later.) In a closed field, of course, they may not date, but may be able to spend more time together on the job or in the club.

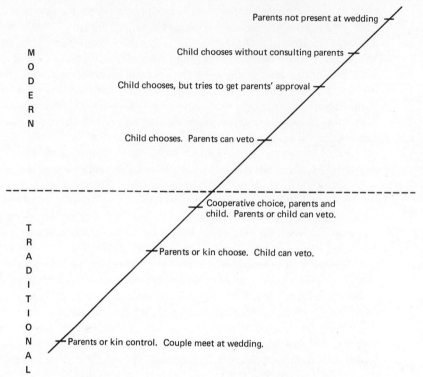

M
O
D
E
R
N

Parents not present at wedding

Child chooses without consulting parents

Child chooses, but tries to get parents' approval

Child chooses. Parents can veto

Cooperative choice, parents and
child. Parents or child can veto.

T
R
A
D
I
T
I
O
N
A
L

Parents or kin choose. Child can veto.

Parents or kin control. Couple meet at wedding.

**FIGURE 6-2**      From family control to couple autonomy in partner selection.


## Definition of Dating

Sometimes dating is courtship, sometimes it is not. For our purposes, *dating* refers to heterosexual social interaction entered into for one or more of the following purposes: fun, recreation, self-development, mutual-exploration, status-enhancement, exploitation, sex, and mate selection. This list, although not exhaustive of reasons for dating, is examined later. The possibility of homosexual dating is excluded from this definition in order to distinguish dating from friendship, but doubtless many of the same needs operate when homosexuals get together. Dating may involve groups of people, but these people are very often "paired off" in a way that is recognized by the group. Frequently, a date involves just two people.


## History of Dating

Dating for the purpose of recreation is a relatively recent phenomenon in the United States and Canada. Dating was widespread in the 1920s. My (LSS) Canadian grandparents and their friends dated in 1910, although they did not call it that. Previously, heterosexual interaction had more "serious" intentions and overtones; a young man and young woman who spent time alone together were on the road to marriage, assuming that the young man's intentions were "honorable." Relationships without the intent of marriage did, of course, occur, but almost always between a relatively upper-class male and a lower-class female. The double standard allowed such exploitation to take place with little cost to the young man's reputation.

A fascinating account of family life in the nineteenth century in the United States is gleaned from the accounts of European travelers at that time [11]. Many of the reports pictured young Americans as having astonishing amounts of freedom— before they married. However, a great deal of self-restraint was expected at the same time, especially on the part of young women, who were expected to remain chaste until marriage. Adolescents were permitted to be alone together; young women were permitted to travel alone. Some of the travelers complained that the freedom-with-restraint produced women who were cold. The travelers also noted that the age of marriage was extremely early, which could have been the result of the freedom-with-restraint.

Young people apparently had a great deal of freedom in choosing mates as well. In the 1830s, the dowry system was rare in the United States, and parents did not have much to say in the choice of a mate for their child. Mere lip service was paid to the parents' opinion, although it was formally required [11]. However, geographic mobility limited the choice of partners.

Evidence collected from the Hingham, Massachusetts, town records for the period 1635–1880 indicates a distinct shift from parental control of marriage in the seventeenth and early eighteenth century, to a stable, participant-run system in the nineteenth century, shortly after the American Revolution [30]. At this time, increased geographic mobility because of military service and college attendance helped to decrease parental control of marriage.

**Bundling.**   In Colonial New England and Pennsylvania there existed a fascinating courtship custom that literally kept young lovers warm on a wintry night. This custom was bundling. There were actually two kinds of bundling: (1) the bundling of travelers, and (2) the bundling of lovers. Because of a shortage of beds, a stranger who stopped at a village or farmhouse to spend the night would usually be invited to sleep with one or more members of the host's family. This invitation was literal; the guest was expected to do no more than share the bed of the family member. The second kind of bundling is what concerns us here.

Travel was slow in the early days of the Colonial period, and farmhouses were far apart. A young man who was courting a woman would have to walk through the snow on a winter's evening in order to visit his sweetheart. Shortly after the evening meal the family would prepare to go to bed, and if he were expected to leave, the young man would have had only a few minutes alone with the person whom he had walked miles to see. Fuel for warmth and light was scarce, and it would have been too costly and wasteful for a young courting couple to burn fuel just for their own comfort and convenience. And so, shortly after the parents and other family members went to bed, the couple would also retire. Frequently, all family members slept in the same room, but the daughter might have her own room. Outer garments, such as shoes, coats, and dresses, would be removed hurriedly, because the air was cold, and the couple would slip into bed beneath the blankets. There, they could talk softly late into the night.

A poem of the period shows the attitude of the country folk toward bundling:

> Nature's request is, give me rest
> Our bodies seek repose;
> Night is the time, and 'tis no crime
> To bundle in our clothes.
>
> Since in a bed, a man and maid
> May bundle and be chaste;
> It doth no good to burn up wood
> It is a needless waste.
>
> Let coat and shift be turned adrift,
> And breeches take their flight,
> An honest man and virgin can
> Lie quiet all the night. [9, p. 26]

Samuel Peters, writing in 1781, said that the custom of bundling had prevailed for 160 years in New England, and that it produced fewer "natural consequences" than did lovers courting on the sofa, which had been introduced into the cities of Boston, Salem, Newport, and New York in 1756 [25, p. 225]. He continues in defense of bundling:

> The custom prevails among all classes, to the great honour of the country, its religion, and ladies. Why it should be thought incredible for a young man and woman innocently and virtuously to lie down together in a bed with a great part of their clothes on, I cannot conceive. . . . Upon the whole, had I daughters now, I would venture to let them bundle upon the bed, or even on the sofa, after a proper education, sooner than adopt the Spanish mode of forcing young people to prattle only before the lady's mother the chichat of artless lovers. [25, p. 228]

As the country became more urbanized, the practice of bundling began to wane, although it remained in the rural regions for a much longer time than it did in the more urbanized regions. The prudery of the mid and late nineteenth century managed to stamp out most of the memories of bundling.* Bundling was simply not necessary if the young man could easily return to his own home, and if fuel was no

---

*For an interesting and brief account of a similar process at work in Victorian England, see Edward Brecher, *The Sex Researchers,* Boston: Little, Brown and Co., 1969, pp. 7–9.

longer at a premium. Courting moved from the bedroom to the parlor in the nineteenth century. In the twentieth century, modern dating developed.

**Factors Contributing to the Development of Dating.**   Industrialization led to the modern dating system. Increasing numbers of women working outside the home gave impetus to the Feminist movement. For the first time, women in the industrializing nations had an option other than becoming economically dependent upon men, and although the women were paid less than men, they had a bit of bargaining power that had previously been denied them. Industrialization also led to the development of the mass-produced automobile, which gave people, including lovers, a mobility that they had not had before. The automobile provided a sofa—or a bundling bed—on wheels.

A young man would now drive up to his sweetheart's door, park his car, and go inside to get her. Off they would drive for some form of entertainment. This was, and in many cases still is, the date. Dating of this kind began in colleges after World War I and spread into high schools in the following decades. It was viewed with alarm by some researchers, the most noted of whom was Willard Waller.

**The Dating—Rating Complex.**   Waller studied dating at the end of the 1920s at Pennsylvania State University [39]. It was the heyday of the fraternity house, and men outnumbered women six to one. Because of the university's geographic isolation, importing dates was difficult. These factors contributed to a system of competitiveness for dates, and what Waller called the dating-rating complex. Freshmen males simply did not date. After the freshman year, a man's ability to get high-prestige female dates depended upon the status of his fraternity, whether he had a "good line," was a good dancer, was prominent in school activities, had good manners, and was attractive, had plenty of money and access to an automobile. A popular girl was one who was attractive, had good clothes, a "smooth line," and could dance well.

Waller saw the dating system at Penn State as a departure from the formal courtship code, and as placing a tremendous emphasis upon thrill-seeking, exploitative relationships that could scarcely prepare the daters for marriage. Pretending that one was in love with one's partner was an important part of the game; each person wanted his partner to feel more involved with him or her than did she or he with the other. Waller's study was done at the end of the Roaring Twenties, at a particular university that might well have been unique, or at least different from other universities at the time. Since Waller's time, a number of other researchers have retested his ideas, both at Penn State and other places.

About twenty years later, Smith replicated Waller's study at the same campus. The male-female ratio had changed from six to one in the late twenties to three to one in 1950. When Waller did his study, almost half of the males lived in fraternities; at the time of Smith's study only a quarter did. The students were asked to agree or disagree with the 28 characteristics included in Waller's study. He found that his women subjects were less concerned than were Waller's as to whether men belonged to one of the better fraternities, or whether they had a great deal of spending money and access to a car. Eighty per cent of the men said that it was important for a woman to have good manners and be attractive. Smith concluded that a dating-rating complex still existed, but that the priorities had changed since Waller's day [31].

In the 1950s Blood tested Waller's and Smith's findings at the University of Michigan, using an instrument that included some factors that Smith had found to be significant, as well as some of Waller's items. About half of Waller's items were not supported by a majority of the sample. Blood's findings suggest that personality aspects were becoming more important than the more materialistic items that Waller had found in 1929 [3].


## Dating at the Present Time

Krain and his associates published a study of dating by University of Iowa students in 1977 [17]). A prestige ranking of fraternities and sororities existed, and dating was frequent between pairs of equal ranks. However, students also dated partners at other prestige levels. The authors concluded that the more competitive and materialistic aspects of dating in Waller's day had practically disappeared. They think relaxed and humanistic dating may be usual, although they caution that findings might be different in a noncollege sample.

Two studies of high school dating, one in Texas [8] the other in Florida [13] used both black and white subjects. Although their results are different, they give some notion of the usual ages and frequencies of dating behavior. The subjects in both studies were sophomores, juniors, and seniors. Table 6-1 gives this information. The figures for the Florida study are for whites and blacks combined, whereas the Texas figures are separate for the two groups. Although a sizable number of adolescents have begun to date by age 12, 14 or 15 is the year in which the largest number

**TABLE 6-1**   **Dating Ages and Frequencies in Two Southern High Schools: 1974**

|  |  | Texas (Dickinson) | |
| --- | --- | --- | --- |
| *Data Regarding Dating* | *Florida (Hansen)* | *White* | *Black* |
| Began dating at age 12 or younger | 10% | 15% | 17% |
| Modal age at first date | 15 years | 14 years | 14 years |
| Date at least once a week | 52% | 59% | 56% |
| Do not date, or almost never | 24% | 17% | 13% |
| Going steady | 27% | 80% | 68% |

*Sources:* George E. Dickinson. Dating behavior of black and white adolescents before and after desegregation. *Journal of Marriage and the Family*, 1975, **37,** 602–608.
Sally Hansen. Dating choices of high school students. *Family Coordinator*, 1977, **26,** 133–138.

begin dating. Over half of the students were dating at least once a week. Differences in the two schools were marked in age of beginning dating and in numbers going steady. All differences indicated more emphasis on dating in the Texas sample. We do not know what were the reasons for the differences, whether they were socioeconomic, regional, or other.

The most frequent types of activities for dates were going to movies and driving around. Blacks went dancing as often as they went to the movies. Parties accounted for a smaller number of dates. Whites reported more parental supervision than blacks, in terms of requirements for coming home at a certain time.

## Functions of Modern Dating

People still find marriage partners through dating. They also can date without any intention of finding someone to marry.

**Fun and Recreation.**   Having a good time is a common reason for a date. It is acceptable to most people to date just for enjoyment. Many kinds of recreation and social events are organized for couples. People committed to the single life, including homosexuals, may date with the opposite sex for recreational and social purposes.

**Companionship.**   A person may date because he is lonely and wants to spend time with a friend. Occasionally couples date over a long period of time for companionship, never moving toward marriage.

**Self-Development.**   Dating can increase a person's self understanding through interaction with another person, and perhaps a variety of others. Self-esteem grows through realizing that another person thinks well of one. Social skills grow with practice in dating situations. A sense of identity develops from self-revelations to a receptive and trustworthy person.

**Understanding of Others, and Mutuality.**   Increased human understanding can occur if dates listen to each other sincerely and each tries honestly to be understood by the other. Intimacy is in terms of thoughts and feelings, as well as sex.

**Exploitation.**   The dating-rating complex is still active at times. Status-enhancement is the motive when a person goes out with a date in order to gain prestige or look good to someone else. In the days of the double standard, the man was supposed to "pay" his date in expensive entertainment, while the woman (then called a girl) was expected to "pay" him in the form of sexual favors—kissing, petting, or sexual intercourse. Some of this kind of bargaining still goes on. Whatever the behavior, it is exploitation if one person uses another to gain her or his ends with disregard for the well-being of the partner and with deception. Communication is at a mini-

ELLEN S. SMART

mum in exploitative dating, although the two may be playing a game according to rules they both understand.

**Sexual Satisfaction.**   Whether it is exploitative or mutual, sexual interaction is a frequent feature of dating. A study of sexual expectations, although done in Australia, gives some indications of what the situation most likely is in North America [7]. University students were asked what sort of intimate behavior they would expect from dating partners at various stages in the relationship. Among the youngest, ages 17 to 19, more men than women expected intimacy beyond kissing, but at ages 20 to 30, expectations were about the same for men and women. Mutuality, rather than exploitation, is thus implied. Almost half expected that the first date would include prolonged kissing and cuddling, with stroking of hair and face. After several dates, about half expected heavy petting. When going steady, about two thirds expected intercourse.

**Looking for a Mate.**   The dating system allows for wide exploration in search of a mate. A man can date one woman after another and so can a woman date many men. The participants can break it up after the first date, or they can continue dating an indefinite number of times. Dating as mate-seeking is carried on by people at older ages, as well as younger. When divorced or widowed, an older person has to get back into the dating world if a new mate is desired. Some confirmed singles date for fun, then fall in love and realize they have found mates! Other daters want to marry but never find "the right one."

**Testing a Relationship.**   After locating a potential mate, there is still a long way to go before commitment. Dating affords a way of getting to know each other better.

**Changes in Dating.**   There is some evidence from research that at the college level, dating is becoming less important as a way for men and women to get to know each other. The coed dorm allows men and women to get to socialize without pairing, and may be a help particularly to shy individuals [19]. It appears that among high school students as well, it is no longer as important that the older, more rigid dating codes be followed. A woman no longer has to worry that if she accepts a date at the last minute, the man will think that she is unpopular. Indeed, she is free to extend invitations to men, something that was frowned upon or even forbidden when we were growing up in the early 1930s and the early 1960s.

The woman's liberation movement is doubtless responsible for this breaking down of traditional customs and roles. We think that the new dating is a good example of how men, as well as women, can benefit from the new freedoms accorded to women. Certainly many of the men that I (LSS) knew in college complained bitterly that they had to spend their money on women who never reciprocated. The women complained that they could not ask a man out without risking his scorn—and they were probably right. Today, it is still risky in some circles for a woman to play the "man's role"; but this is changing. Just how widespread and enduring these changes are remains to be seen.

## Courtship: Becoming Partners

When dating results in finding a marriage partner, then it is part of the sequence of courtship. Because partners can be nonmarital, also, it is not quite clear how permanent a relationship must be before the dating that led to it can be called courtship.

Courtship usually proceeds from dating to going steady to engagement to mar-

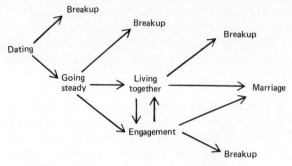

**FIGURE 6-3**   Varieties of pathways from dating to marriage.

riage. Choices at each stage are shown in Figure 6-3. Some couples skip parts of the sequence. Becoming partners involves a commitment. When two people tell each other, "I love you," they make some sort of commitment. Whether they say it or not, recognition of love means that the pair realize that they are attached to each other. Usually at this point, they redefine the way in which they are going to behave toward each other. Perhaps they know, from the social rules within which they operate, that when a couple love each other, they should date steadily or be engaged or get married or be exclusive sex partners or ask their parents if they may carry on any of these pair activities. Perhaps they have to talk it out, to find out what the other expects and what would be acceptable to both.

Since modern Western society is still essentially monogamous, the first form of pair commitment is usually steady dating. For many couples, casual dating gives way to steady dating while they are still quite young.

## Going Steady

Going steady usually means an agreement between a couple not to date others. This agreement is known by the peer group, and generally supported by it. In some cases, it is a kind of pre-engagement; the couple moves from going steady to engagement and then to marriage. In other cases, it is more a matter of convenience and security. When a deep emotional attachment is involved, and the couple thinks of themselves as a couple, they are said to be pair-bonded.

Some notion of the frequency of going-steady relationships can be gained from the Texas study reported on page 161 [8]. Over one decade, the percentage of white students going steady increased from 61 to 80 per cent, while that of black students increased from 54 to 68 per cent. Although more whites than blacks were going steady, more members of both groups were paired in steady relationships.

Going steady has been critized on the grounds that it limits the number of people that a person can get to know. The counterargument is that it allows the young person to get to know a person on a deeper level than is allowed in the casual dating relationship. Parents and clergy are often concerned that going steady will lead to sexual involvement that casual dating will not.

## Commitment to More Than One Person at a Time

An alternative to going steady with one person is "going steadily" with more than one person at a time. The college student who dates one person on campus and another at home is an example of a person with dual commitments. It is certainly possible, however, for an individual to date more or less seriously more than one person in the same locale. This kind of dating gives the advantages of both casual and steady dating, in that it allows a deeper knowledge of more than one person at a time.

## Pre-engagement

The business world has stepped in to assure that no young couple in love need be without symbols for their attachments. The exchange of high school and college class rings by going-steady couples is an old custom. The fraternity pin is still worn as a sign of commitment. More recently, the "pre-engagement" or "promise" ring has been pushed on adolescents, as a way of showing a level of commitment deeper than going steady, but not as deep as engagement.

## Engagement

Engagement usually involves a formal announcement by a couple or by the young woman's parents that they intend to marry. The man's parents usually acknowledge the engagement in some way, too. Sometimes the announcement is made at a party given for the purpose. A notice in the newspaper is often accompanied by a photograph of the prospective bride. A growing custom is to picture the prospective bride and groom together. The period after the decision to marry and before the wedding is the engagement period. Testing, planning, and preparation are the main purposes of engagement.

**Purposes of Engagement.** The relationship is developed further and tested further. Now that the two people are publicly committed, they are regarded as a couple by family and friends, and treated differently. The pair ask themselves, "How do other people regard us and react to us as a couple? Do they think we are suited to each other?" They find out whether his family and friends like her, whether hers accept him. Even though they do not need permission from anyone, they cannot help but be influenced by their reception as a couple.

There is still much to learn about one another, about experiences, ideas, and

Their engagement is announced.

values. Mothers get baby books out of storage to show to their children's fiancés. Siblings and old friends tell stories from childhood. The two confide information that they have not dared to tell before. They visit scenes of the other's earlier days and meet formerly important people, perhaps teachers or club leaders.

New roles must be explored and tried, some only through discussion and others in action. They begin to work out modes of dealing with sex roles, division of house-work and family business, responsibilities to parents and in-laws, having children, contraception, community obligations, and relations with friends and lovers after marriage. If they come from different ethnic, religious, or social class backgrounds, they will look for a life style that will satisfy both as to types of food, ways of serving meals, celebrating holidays, religious participation, earning money, and spending. Misunderstandings and conflicts inevitably arise. During exploration and resolution, modes of communication and problem-solving are developed. Goals are established.

Some of the preparation for marriage consists of finding a place to live and collecting some furnishings for it. In earlier times, much more was made of this phase of preparation. The bride traditionally assembled a trousseau, consisting of household linens and clothing for herself. She, her mother, and other women relatives embroidered the pillowcases and monogrammed the napkins. Today's bride-to-be does not feel the necessity of amassing textile goods to last a lifetime, realizing that storage will be a problem, styles change, and she can buy what she needs when the time comes. However, family and friends still give engagement and wedding presents that may amount to a substantial part of the furnishings for the new home. An avalanche of advertising descends upon the publicly announced bride, urging her to manage the gift-giving process in such a way that she receives a useful, prestigious collection and the stores make a good profit.

A third type of preparation, highly recommended, but often neglected, is *physical assessment* and *health planning*. Since health is strongly related to personal adequacy and partner relationships, a thorough premarital physical examination is an important way of determining the resources and liabilities that each partner brings to the family. The state requires a blood test for syphilis, but surely the absence of syphilis is not sufficient assurance of good health. Highly desirable as additional tests for venereal disease would be, ruling out gonorrhea and other venereal diseases, they would scarcely be adequate proof of physical health. In addition to a general physical examination that included venereal disease tests, we would recommend some exploration of the hereditary defects that each individual can be expected to carry. If the two people's genetic inadequacies match in such a way that their offspring would have increased chances of suffering from, say, hemophilia or phenylketonuria (PKU), then surely their premarital planning should include some joint decisions about these liabilities.

The premartial physical examination is an occasion when partners may get some sex education and information, although other opportunities also exist. Even if young people have enjoyed good sex education and an easy access to information, the prospects of marriage or living as a couple will bring up some new questions. Contraception will probably be one of them. Even if the physician is not able to do all of the education needed, he can make a contribution and can also direct his patients to other sources.

In Appendix A, we have provided the reader with a Premarital Questionnaire, to be filled out by the reader and her/his prospective partner, preferably prior to engagement. Use of this questionnaire should help the couple to determine possible areas of conflict that often remain undiscovered prior to marriage.

## PERMANENT VERSUS TEMPORARY MATCHING

An engagement used to be considered more of a permanent commitment than it is today. The breaking of a betrothal was a grave social, even legal, offense. "Better now than later" is a common modern attitude. In fact, marriage itself is less of a permanent commitment than it used to be. It has been said that all persons in our society, whether married or not, are available for marriage. Divorce, while not approved by everyone, does not incur the degree of censure that it did a generation ago.

## For Now or for Ever

The traditional marriage vow includes the promise to stay together "until death do us part." In spite of making this promise, many people get divorced. Many unmarried partners also vow to remain together. How many such promises are broken? Nobody knows.

The present generation of young people is placing less of an emphasis upon the "foreverness" of marriage, or of marriage-type relationships. Almost two decades ago, Hillsdale interviewed couples drawn at random from those who applied for marriage licenses ar the city hall of a large Midwestern city. He wanted to find out how many people " . . . bind themselves in a personal, existential commitment to *absolute marriage,* and how many to a *trial marriage*" [15, pp. 138–139]. He found that Catholics were overwhelmingly opposed to the idea of civil divorce and remarriage, and that non-Catholics were 84 per cent in favor of them. However, only 19 per cent of the males and 21 per cent of the females had considered the possibility of divorce for themselves [15].

It would be interesting to know whether any of the individuals interviewed by Hillsdale had previously considered the possibility of divorce, or if they thought of it later (for example, the night before the wedding ceremony). It would also be interesting to see if similar couples today have given more thought to the possibility of divorce. We suspect that they would.

Certainly, there are many engaged couples today who still believe that marriage can be broken only by death. Mormons choose between marrying for eternity and marrying only for life on earth. Even so, the divorce rate has risen to new heights, and half the states have changed to no-fault divorce, removing the stigma of guilt from one of the parties involved. The trend toward more and easier divorce reflects a more permissive attitude toward it by society.

We suggest that the question raised by Hillsdale is an important one that should be explored by couples who are considering marriage. How does each partner feel about the possibility of breaking up? Certainly, few people anticipating marriage would look forward to the demise of their relationship. But if one person believes that marriage is sacred, and that to break the marriage vow would mean an unpardonable breach of faith, and the other person believes that personal happiness and freedom are more important than a vow made at an earlier time, then perhaps the couple should reconsider their decision to marry.

## Breaking Up

Because young people have to find their own marriage partners, they have to explore the possibilities in various persons and pairings. Breaking up a pair relationship is common (see Figure 6-3). Such breakups incur little or no public censure, because they are recognized either as necessary preludes to finding a suitable mate, or as preventing the divorce that would happen if the pair were to marry.

How and why do breakups occur? A study of 103 breakups gives information about the process and also about progress in courtship [14]. The subject pairs of dating partners were juniors and seniors in four colleges in the Boston area. They answered questionnaires at the time, six months later, and two years later. At the end of the two years 45 per cent, or 103 couples, had broken up. Of those remaining, 65 were still dating, 9 were engaged, 43 were married, 10 had unknown status, and one person had died. Responses predictive of staying together included those showing closeness, expectation of marriage, love, longer period of dating, and exclusive dating. Having had sexual intercourse or having lived together had no relation to staying together or breaking up. Breakups were predicted by unequal involvement in the relationship, and differences in age, educational aspirations, intelligence, and physical attractiveness.

The timing of breakups showed a pattern. They occurred most often at points of change, such as going home for vacations, returning to school, starting a new semester. These points of time seemed to offer face-saving ways of changing or ending a relationship.

Breakups are rarely completely mutual. In reporting the reasons for the breakup, both men and women were likely to say 'I wanted it" or that it was mutual, even when the partner was the instigator. Apparently, it made it easier to bear. Women more often saw problems and precipitated the end. Men were likely to find it harder to break up than were women. Rejected men found it harder than rejected women to be friends after a breakup. When the man initiated the breakup, 70 per cent of the couples stayed friends, whereas when the women did, only 46 per cent were friends afterwards.

The authors suggest that women may be more practical about mate selection because they have fewer years for finding a husband, and because a wife's social and economic statuses are more dependent upon her husband's than are a man's on his wife's. A second possible reason is that women are more attuned to social-emotional life and therefore more discriminating and selective in relationships.

Although breakup before marriage is very different from divorce, because of its different social context, there are some similarities. One finding was that unequal involvement of partners is typical in the decaying stage of a relationship, while equal involvement occurs in the building stage. Divorce will be discussed in Chapter 9, which is devoted entirely to this important topic.

## "ASSORTATIVE MATING:" WHO MARRIES WHOM?

How do people sort themselves out into couples? There are some principles that are apparent in the formation of pairs.

## Homogamy

Like marries like. Since the early days of research on marriage, the principle of homogamy has been documented by many studies, showing that people usually marry mates similar to themselves in race, age, social class, and religion [16]. High correlations occur between spouses' IQs [37]. Attractiveness of appearance shows homogamy [35]. Steady dating partners were matched especially in social attitudes and values [14]. Homogamy in physical, psychological, and social characteristics was found in mate-selection preferences of high school students in Australia and university students in New Zealand [36]. Homogamy is generally taken for granted. It is the exception to the rule that is noticed and questioned.

## Mixed Marriages

An exception to the principle of homogamy is the mixed marriage. The participants are unlike in some noticeable way. All marriages represent mixed matches to one degree or another. Except for marriages between persons who grew up in the same household, which are extremely rare, each partner brings into the union a different cultural background, since no two families are exactly alike. Furthermore, individuals differ from each other in other ways: constitutionally ("night" people versus "day" people; persons who can eat anything without getting fat versus those who must count calories; people who like to live in a temperature of 78 degrees versus those who swelter unless it is below 68 degrees, and so on); age (May–December couples); politically; geographically; and in terms of values. And yet, interracial and interreligious marriages are what come to mind when one thinks of mixed marriages. Social class may also come to mind, but it is not considered as problematic. It is not unusual for a woman to marry "up" in terms of socioeconomic class, although it is somewhat deviant for a woman to marry "down."

Mixed marriages, of the religious and racial type, have long been considered a social problem in our society. Judaism, Catholicism, and Protestantism have all disapproved of mixed religious marriages. Americans appear to be intermarrying at an increasing rate, nonetheless, and a Gallup poll indicates increasing tolerance for mixed religious and racial marriages [24].

Within a community, interfaith marriage rates are influenced by the ratio of one religious group to another. For example, in Providence, Rhode Island, where a large, prestigious Jewish community exists, the intermarriage rate for Jews was only 4.5 per cent, whereas in Iowa, where the total Jewish population is only 10,000, the intermarriage rate was 50 per cent [27].

It is hard to find out how many marriages are religiously mixed. Only in Iowa and Indiana is information about religion required of persons applying for marriage licenses. Furthermore, a Protestant-Protestant marriage may be an interdenominational marriage that could actually be considered a mixed religious match. If one member of the couple converts to the religion of the other, it is difficult to say whether the marriage is mixed or not. It would depend upon the commitment of the convert to his new and old faiths.

Even in racially or ethnically mixed marriages, there are degrees of distance. Hawaii is known for high intermarriage rates and low levels of race prejudice. Even so, a study of mixed marriages showed that they tended to occur in certain groupings [18]. Japanese, Chinese, and Koreans were likely to intermarry, as were Caucasians, Hawaiians, Filipinos, and Puerto Ricans. Continental United States has a history of racism; as late as 1958 more than 30 states prohibited interracial marriages between blacks and whites. In many of these states a white was forbidden to marry an American Indian, a Chinese, a Hindu, a Japanese, or a Malaysian, as well. A few of these states maintained their laws until a 1967 Supreme Court decision struck them down [12]. The number of black men marrying white women has increased significantly since the 1950s and 1960s, although the number of white men marrying black women has not increased. The 1970 census showed more than twice as many black men marrying white women as did the earlier censuses [26].

In some cases of mixed marriages the ratio of available men and women within one's own group is a relevant factor. If, for example, there are few eligible men in one's own religious or racial group (eligible here means men of slightly higher social and educational standing, and slightly older, since women tend to marry "up" in regards to these variables), a woman may marry outside her group [38]. Servicemen stationed overseas are much more likely to marry members of another race (and probably of another religion, as well) simply because of propinquity [12].

In most cases, the mixed marriages occur because the partners are in love. Certainly this is the reason that most of them would give. And although mixed marriages have a higher divorce rate than do "homogamous" marriages, their success rates are higher than their failure rates.

## SOME THEORIES OF PARTNER SELECTION

Probably everyone has a theory of how partners find each other, or how they ought to go about it. The incidence of marital strife and divorce, however, suggest that many people hold inadequate theories or that they do not apply what they know! In this section, we describe some theories and principles of mate selection, ending with one that integrates much research on how people sort themselves into pairs.

**Romantic.** The romantic complex has already been described in connection with love, on pages 36-37. The mate selection principles of the romantic complex include: when the right person comes along, you'll know it, or you probably will; when the right person comes along, you'll be ready to get married. This is the mate selection theory that my (MSS) father says he holds, and no doubt most of his peers do and did. It worked well for him. He and my mother have just celebrated their sixty-fifth wedding anniversary. In marrying each other, they followed all the principles of homogamy without giving it a thought. Their year-long engagement was long enough to permit discussion of values and roles, especially when their similar backgrounds almost guaranteed few differences. They were of the average ages for marriage in their social group. It is not hard to explain their success, but why did he choose her instead of one of the other young women whose predictive value was just as great? The romantic explanation is a way of handling the mystery, and it has other benefits, too. If you marry The Right One, then you are almost bound to succeed! And it adds zest to living.

**The Ideal Mate.**    One way of looking at the ideal mate is as The Right One, the romantic notion of the one and only mate who exists and must be found. Probably developed from that notion, there is also the ideal mate who exists in the mind. Presumably, a person compares the real people with the ideal image, and accepts or rejects on the basis of how close the prospective mate comes to matching the ideal.

Many researchers have asked subjects questions about the qualities, characteristics, or competencies they desire in a mate. It is assumed that what people say they want will have some relation to their actual choices of partners. We do not know whether persons carry well-formed concepts of their ideal mates, or whether their answers to questions reflect thinking it out in response to the interviewer. Nor do we know how stable is an ideal-mate image, if indeed it does exist. It seems reasonable that ideals would be constantly adjusted to realities of personal growth and meeting new people. Following are examples of studies of characteristics in mates wanted by various persons.

A study of American and Canadian college students concluded that most students desired a mate with what the author called "Boy Scout characteristics"—that is, a person who is clean, honest, open, and reverent. The Americans made more direct reference to physical or bodily characteristics. American women, in particular, made specifications such as, "aggressive in lovemaking," "sensual," and "a good lover" [40].

When students and their parents were queried about mates for the students, both were far more tolerant of the idea of the student's marrying a person with a slight physical handicap than someone who is addicted to drugs or alcohol. The students were more selective for marriage partners than they were for dates. For example, 75 per cent would not date a drug addict; 85.1 per cent would not marry one. Approximately 39 per cent would not date a person who favored extramarital sex; about 72 per cent would not marry such a person [32].

Black and white college students were compared as to their desires for instrumental and expressive characteristics of mates [22]. Expressive (related to emotional satisfaction) characteristics were rated highest by both races. The five highest items were understanding, mutual affection, emotional maturity; kindness and consideration, dependability. There were some differences in the importance attached to instrumental functions (earning a living, homemaking, caregiving, and such). Black men placed more importance on instrumental characteristics of wives than did white men. Black men gave higher ratings to "desire to move ahead economically" and "willingness to work for the future." These findings are logical in light of the fact that black men have poorer opportunities than white men for earning a satisfactory family living wage. The men's ideals thus reflect their real experience.

## Family Structure

Sutton-Smith and Rosenberg, well-known for their studies on siblings, have evidence that both men and women tend to marry spouses from the same size families as the families in which they grew up [33]. Men with brothers are likely to marry women with sisters, whereas men with sisters tend to marry women with brothers. In regard to age, men marry women of the position they are used to, those with older sisters marrying first-born women and those with younger sisters marrying laterborns. The authors suggest that males with brothers make more use of cultural stereotypes in choosing mates, since they have no experience with girls in the family. The influence of the stereotype is indicated in their choosing girls with sisters, who may represent the most feminine type of woman to the naïve male. Trends in women's choices were in similar directions, but not so clear.

## Astrology

The most ancient theory of mate selection is the astrological theory. It is used today in India to assure that partners will be compatible. The correctness of fit between marriage partners is determined by the position of the stars at the moment that the individuals were born. We do not want to dismiss this as pure superstition, in spite of the lack of research evidence to support it.

## Stimulus-Value-Role

Murstein's theory of partner selection is the Stimulus-Value-Role theory of dyadic relationships [23]. These three words refer to overlapping stages of the courtship process, which is a "filter" process. (Incompatible couples are filtered out of the courtship process by screens that they encounter in the course of their interactions and experiences with each other and as a pair.) Other theories have assumed that the filters or tests of the relationship came in a regular order. For instance, after physical attraction would come testing for background and values, and if the pair were suited in those ways, they would go on to the next step of testing to see how well they got along together. Murstein thinks that several types of filtering or testing may operate at the same time, but that the emphasis changes as courtship progresses.

**Stimulus Stage.** When two people first encounter each other, especially in the open field situation (described on page 154), all the information they have about each other is what comes through their senses: appearance, voice, speech, nonverbal behavior, clothing. Although one can make some inferences from this information such as race and social class, probably the main message is in terms of physical attractiveness.

Physical attractiveness plays a big part in getting a pair together in the first place. Americans pay a great deal of attention to physical attraction, celebrating it in plays, stories, and songs, making money out of it in advertising and selling, and exploring it in research laboratories. From all three of these points of view, physical attractiveness is thought to be important in partner selection. Because of so many advertisements on the enchantment of white teeth, shiny hair, and thin bodies, and so many studies on the attractive powers of beautiful people, it is not easy to retain a perspective on this topic. Are good-looking people more loving in terms of care, respect, responsibility, and knowledge? Do they make better marriage partners? Better parents? Better homemakers? We don't know. We do know it is easier for them to attract people in the first place and that the initial liking persists through several meetings [20]. Attractive people tend to like themselves, too. Women of greater rather than lesser attractiveness reported more satisfaction with their own popularity, leadership ability, and self-consciousness [2].

A review of research shows that stereotypes about physical attractiveness are common [1]. In general, beautiful people are expected to be successful, talented, and good. Physical attractiveness is related to sex appeal, emotional arousal, and love. People tend to think that their own social status is enhanced by associating with an attractive person.

Although most studies of physical attraction deal with it as a whole, a significant difference in color preferences was found in a sample of 1,000 Caucasian students in Wyoming [10]. When asked about the features they preferred in men, women tended to choose darker eyes, hair, and complexion rather than lighter, while men preferred lighter eyes, hair, and skin in women. The authors note that these color preferences fit with cultural stereotypes. From the point of view of a person looking for a partner, however, it was encouraging to note that for each type of feature, there were some who preferred it.

Not only does a person notice whether others are attractive. He has an idea as to how attractive *he* is. Self-perceptions play a part in asking for a date, because nobody likes to be rejected. This topic was the focus of research on computer-dating at the University of Minnesota. The subjects were 177 male and 170 female students randomly selected from those freshmen and sophomores who had bought tickets for a computer dance at the university. The subjects were assessed by student accomplices for their level of physical attractiveness, and the subjects filled out a questionnaire about themselves, giving estimates of a number of their personal attributes and accomplishments, such as their own level of physical attractiveness and the number of dates that they had had in the past year.

The subjects were divided into two groups: those who were told that the person whom they selected as a date would definitely go out with them; and those who were told that their dates could refuse to go out with them after a brief meeting, and

that about 50 per cent of dates in the past had made such refusals. Results showed that a person's actual chances of rejection did not influence his choice of a date. The more physically attractive the subject was, the more desirable a date he or she requested [2].

Murstein [23, p. 182] concluded from his research that in the Stimulus stage, courtship was likely to progress when the man thought the woman better-looking than himself, or even more, when he thought he had got the best possible deal in regard to attractiveness. In addition to beauty, perceived status and group member-ship affect pair formation in the Stimulus stage. A person may be reluctant to approach a person of another race or ethnic group. A person of high social status may look unattainable and therefore unapproachable to a person of lower rank. Great good looks may offset low social class, or high social class may offset lesser good looks. Attractiveness is a help in gaining higher social status through marriage [34].

TWO FIND EACH OTHER                                                    **177**

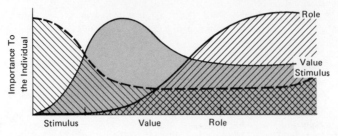

**FIGURE 6-4**

Murstein's diagram of the stages of courtship in Stimulus-Value-Role Theory.

*Source:* After Figure 7.2, Stages of courtship in SVR theory, in Bernard Murstein. *Who Will Marry Whom?* New York: Springer, 1976.

In early encounters, a person wants to be liked and approved. Self-esteem and feelings of comfort increase with expressions of liking and affirmation from the other one. Not yet having built a foundation of trust, it is risky to declare much affection or to be too enthusiastic. Here is a place where the language of behavior (see pages 55-57) comes in handy. Gazes, facial expression, gestures, posture, and movement are all safe ways of expressing interest, sexual excitement, admiration, and invitation, without commitment.

**Value Comparison Stage.** After some experience in the Stimulus stage, the couple exchange views on a variety of topics. They talk about interests, attitudes, and beliefs, gathering information about each other as persons. A process of give and take occurs as each discloses more about himself (herself). Intimacy develops as the two talk and listen, reveal and accept. Three of Fromm's aspects of love (mentioned on pages 28-29, 33-34) can be seen in this process: respect, knowledge, and response. A sense of intimacy and feelings of comfort result from this mutual disclosure and acceptance.

Value comparison may reveal differences that one or both cannot accept in a prospective mate. He believes in sexually open marriage, whereas she wants monogamy. She wants childfreedom, but he wants to have children. Discomfort ensues. Intimacy does not build up. The couple does not move toward marriage. They may break up.

Value comparison may start early, while the Stimulus stage predominates. It begins as the couple discuss interests, friends, associations, recreation, families, and such. As self-disclosure and mutual acceptance proceed, stimulus variables become less important. Murstein's diagram* of the stages of courtship in SVR theory, shown in Figure 6-4, depicts Stimulus starting out high in importance and decreasing as Value becomes more important. Where the two lines cross, the couple changes from the Stimulus stage to the Value stage. Stimulus continues to play some part in the

*Murstein cautions that the diagram is tentative. The sequence of stages is quite well established, but the height of the curves is not known.

third stage. When a certain level of disclosure and acceptance have resulted in considerable feelings of comfort and intimacy, value comparison becomes less critical to the relationship and role compatability becomes most salient.

**Role Stage.**   When the value comparison stage is satisfactorily completed, the couple know a lot about each other, but they have not yet learned much about how well their behaviors will fit together. The Role stage is the time when they try out their expectations of each other with how each behaves in various roles. Many of their roles must fit together if they are going to be compatible in marriage. She already knows how he dances and behaves on a date, but she has to find out whether he will act in ways consistent with what she expects of a husband. A husband has many roles. How will he be as a companion, lover, worker, host, father to her children, son-in-law to her parents, and so on? In other roles, compatability may mean similarity rather than reciprocity. Similarity might be desired in roles connected with social class, interests, recreation, politics, and religion.

It takes longer to explore role compatibility than to judge physical attraction and to compare values. Engagement offers rich opportunities for role exploration, because the two are treated as a couple and expected to behave in reciprocal roles.

Note that the SVR diagram shows Stimulus increasing during the Role stage. Murstein suggests that when the couple consider marrying, which they are most likely to do in the Role stage, they become more aware of physical attractiveness. When they commit themselves publicly to marriage, others will be appraising them as a couple, and they know it. Their children will probably resemble both. Therefore, they may become more aware of how the partner looks. Of course value comparison continues during the Role stage, as it does to some extent throughout marriage.

## PUTTING TOGETHER LOVE AND PARTNER SELECTION

As we showed in the chapter on love, a person goes through several stages of learning to love before she falls in love and becomes a lover. The love career is strongly dependent upon the culture in which it develops. The selection of a partner, in any culture, consists of a series of steps, not just one event. In Figure 6-5, we sketch some of the important steps in feeling and thinking that go into partner selection in our culture, bringing together some of the content of the *love* chapter with this chapter. Although a couple may become committed (select each other) without taking all of these steps, research and theory suggest that the processes pictured here are functional in selecting a compatible mate in our culture. Like Murstein, we think that the feelings and thinking of the early stages occur also in later stages, when new interactions, feelings, and thoughts are salient.

Potential pairs obviously have to meet each other, which they may do by chance or arrangement. At that point, perceptions of self and other are important. Whether or not he approaches her depends partly on how she looks and partly on

| | Feeling | Thinking |
|---|---|---|
| 1. Meeting | Attraction<br>Comfortable | Interesting<br>Good looking |
| 2. Getting Acquainted | Liking<br>Happy, comfortable<br>Stimulated, interested | Applying standards of class,<br>    ethnicity, religion, education,<br>    surface behavior |
| 3. Developing Attachment | Affirmed<br>Fulfilled<br>Desire to be close<br>Caring | Mutual revelation<br>Discussion and approval of<br>    values, behavior |
| 4. In Love | Esteemed<br>Cherished<br>Interdependent<br>Constant awareness<br>Heightened desire for close-<br>    ness and physical intimacy | Mental intimacy<br>Heightened communication<br>Trying out roles<br>Planning partnership |
| 5. Partnership Love | As a pair<br>Care, respect, responsibility | Mutual commitment<br>Knowledge |

**FIGURE 6-5**    Partner selection: Steps in feeling, thinking, and action; three paths to marriage.

whether he sees himself as attractive to the opposite sex. The feelings that lead one toward partner selection include being attracted and being comfortable. At the same time, the person is thinking that this is an interesting person and is planning to find out more. The next step is getting acquainted, possibly dating, or perhaps talking at work. They exchange information about themselves, their values, beliefs, experiences, group memberships, interests, abilities, and achievements. They observe each other in different situations and roles. They feel happy together and stimulated by each other. If all this continues, they become attached to each other. The thinking side of the relationship involves further self-revelation and mutual understanding and approval of what the other person is perceived to be, to do, and to believe. The feeling side involves a desire for closeness, and efforts to stay together. The fourth step in this series is being in love, feeling it and knowing it. Feelings include a constant awareness of being in love, a strong desire to be close, interdependence, and physical intimacy. Thoughts include concentration on the partner, making plans for and as a pair, trying out pertinent roles, and striving for mental intimacy. The fifth step, partnership love, is marked by commitment to each other, feeling and knowing themselves to be a couple, establishing the attitudes and actions that constitute partnership love: care, respect, responsibility, and knowledge.

Progress toward partnerhood is affected by pair interactions. The relationship may move forward, stay in the same spot, or break up. Positive interactions between the pair, their feelings and thoughts, result in progress into the next stage. A setback may occur, such as in Stage 2, she discovers that his family is of lower social class than hers, or he learns that she is of a different religion and would never be willing to convert to his. They break up. A setback in Stage 3 might be a quarrel that reduces self-revelation, increases disapproval, and reduces feelings of fulfillment and desire for closeness.

If the couple's love career progresses, they reach partnership love and commitment. They may express the commitment as living together, becoming engaged, or marrying. As Figure 6-3 suggests, engagement may come before or after living together and either may lead to marriage. What triggers the decision to marry? Two people do not marry simply because they are compatible with each other, or even because they love each other; they have to feel ready to marry. When that readiness will occur depends somewhat on the personality maturity of both. Many pressures external to the individuals operate, however. Becoming a senior in college (or high school) leads some couples to get engaged. The death of a parent, pressures to marry from family or peers, or a personal crisis may actually be more important in crystallizing the decision to marry than other variables that have previously been identified [4].

Our review of theories of mate selection is not inclusive of all that have been formulated. It would certainly make finding a partner easier if we knew exactly how partner selection does take place. It is unlikely that we will ever have an all-inclusive theory, because of the tremendous variations in individuals. The best that we can do is set up a few basic guidelines that seem to apply to the majority of couples.

## SUMMARY

Partner selection is of concern to family and community, as well as to the couple. Family, friends, and others may assist in the meeting of potential mates and in their courtship progress or lack of it. Matchmaking can be either professional or informal. Meeting may occur in an open field, where only immediate impressions are available, or in a closed field, where much information can be gained before approaches are made.

Dating is heterosexual interaction involving one or more of several purposes. Dating has a particular history in the United States and Canada, stemming from social and economic development. In the 1920s and for some years following, college dating was exploitative. Dating seems to be becoming more honest. In dating,

TWO FIND EACH OTHER

persons sometimes look for mates and sometimes find them unintentionally. If a partner is found through dating, then dating is part of a courtship sequence. The next step is going steady and the next, engagement or living together, and finally, marriage. Pair-bondedness includes a deep emotional attachment and thinking of themselves as a couple. Engagement begins with a commitment to marry, usually made public. The period permits testing the relationship privately and publicly, getting to know more about selves and families, exploring values and roles, preparing a home, and preparing physically.

Breaking up is a possibility at any point in the courtship sequence or even after marriage. Certain factors predict breakup. Their timing shows a pattern in college students.

Most marriages are homogamous in many ways, but all marriages are mixed in regard to some aspects. Mixing depends somewhat on availability of partners, although love is usually the reason perceived.

The romantic theory of partner selection includes a complex of ideas. One of them is the ideal mate, who must be found and recognized. There is also the notion that every person has an ideal mate in her (his) mind, which can be discovered by researchers. Family structure explains some partner choices. Astrology is used in Asia and elsewhere to insure correct choice of mates.

Stimulus-Value-Role theory integrates research on mate selection and provides a framework for research. The theory holds that courtship stages overlap and that incompatible couples are filtered out of the courtship process as it is carried on. In the first stage, the Stimulus stage, physical attractiveness plays a large part. Business and advertising exploit people in the Stimulus stage. There are stereotypes concerning beautiful people. Self-perceptions regulate dating aspirations in the Stimulus stage. Nonverbal behavior is used as a way of avoiding premature commitment.

The Value Comparison stage involves increasing exchange of information and self-disclosure. Acceptance and agreement produce feelings of comfort and intimacy. The Role stage is the one in which the couple discuss and try out behavior in a variety of roles with each other, and in settings of family, friends, community, home, work, and so on. The engagement period offers many such opportunities.

The feelings and thoughts developed in moving toward marriage are shown in a diagram (Figure 6-5). Partnership love includes the four elements of love: care, respect, responsibility, and knowledge. A feeling of readiness for marriage is also needed before marriage takes place.

**REFERENCES**

1. Adams, Gerald R. Physical attractiveness research: Toward a developmental social psychology of beauty. *Human Development*, 1977, **20,** 217–239.
2. Berscheid, Ellen, Karen Dion, Elaine Walster, and G. William Walster. Physical attractiveness and dating choice: A test of the matching hypothesis. *Journal of Experimental and Social Psychology*, 1971, **7,** 173–189.
3. Blood, Robert O. A retest of Waller's dating-rating complex. *Marriage and Family Living*, 1955, **17,** 41–47.

4. Bolton, Charles D. Mate selection and the development of a relationship. *Marriage and Family Living,* 1961, **23,** 234–240.

5. Bruce, John A. Intergenerational solidarity versus progress for women? *Journal of Marriage and the Family,* 1976, **38,** 519–524.

6. Cameron, Catherine, Stuart Oskamp, and William Sparks. Courtship American style: Newspaper ads. *Family Coordinator,* 1977, **26,** 27–30.

7. Collins, John K., Judith R. Kennedy, and Ronald D. Francis. Insights into a dating partner's expectations of how behavior should ensue during the courtship process. *Journal of Marriage and the Family,* 1976, **38,** 373–378.

8. Dickinson, George E. Dating behavior of black and white adolescents before and after desegregation. *Journal of Marriage and the Family,* 1975, **37,** 602–608.

9. Doten, Dana. *The art of bundling.* New York: Farrar, 1938.

10. Feinman, Saul, and George W. Gill. Sex differences in physical attractiveness preferences. *Journal of Social Psychology,* 1978, **105,** 43–52.

11. Furstenberg, Frank R. Industrialization and the American family: A look backward. *American Sociological Review,* 1966, **31,** 326–337.

12. Gordon, Albert I. *Intermarriage.* Boston: Beacon, 1964.

13. Hansen, Sally. Dating choices of high school students. *Family Coordinator,* 1977, **26,** 133–138.

14. Hill, Carles T., Zick Rubin, and Letitia A. Peplau. Breakups before marriage; the end of 103 affairs. *Journal of Social Issues,* 1976, **32,** 147–168.

15. Hillsdale, Paul. Marriage as a personal existential commitment. *Marriage and Family Living,* 1962, **24,** 137–143.

16. Hollingshead, August B. Cultural factors in the selection of marriage mates. *American Sociological Review,* 1952, **17,** 146–150.

17. Krain, Mark, Drew Cannon, and Jeffrey Bagford. Rating-dating or simply prestige homogamy? Data on dating in the Greek system on a midwestern campus. *Journal of Marriage and the Family,* 1977, **39,** 663–674.

18. Leon, Joseph J. Sex-ethnic marriage in Hawaii: A nonmetric multidimensional analysis. *Journal of Marriage and the Family,* 1975, **37,** 775–787.

19. Lozoff, Marjorie. *Changing life styles and role perceptions of men and women students.* Prepared for Women: Resource for a changing world. Conference held at Radcliffe Institute, Radcliffe College, Cambridge, Mass. April 17, 18, 1972.

20. Mathes, Eugene W. The effects of physical attractiveness and anxiety on heterosexual attraction over a series of five encounters. *Journal of Marriage and the Family,* 1975, **37,** 769–773.

21. Mead, Margaret. Marriage in two steps. *Redbook,* July, 1966.

22. Melton, Willie and Darwin L. Thomas. Instrumental and expressive values in mate selection of black and white students. *Journal of Marriage and the Family,* 1976, **38,** 509–517.

23. Murstein, Bernard. *Who will marry whom?* New York: Springer, 1976.

24. *New York Times.* Gallup study finds greater tolerance of mixed marriages. November 19, 1972.

25. Peters, Samuel. General history of Connecticut. New York: Appleton, 1877.

26. *Providence Journal-Bulletin.* More black men wed to whites. February 14, 1973.

27. Rosenthal, Erich. Studies of Jewish intermarriage in the United States. *American Jewish Yearbook,* 1963, **64,** 3–53.

28. Ryder, Robert G., John S. Kafka, and David H. Olson. Separating and joining influences

in courtship and early marriage. *American Journal of Orthopsychiatry,* 1971, **41,** 450–464.

29. Sindberg, Ronald, Allyn Roberts, and Duane McClain. Mate selection factors in computer matched marriages. *Journal of Marriage and the Family,* 1972, **34,** 612–614.
30. Smith, Daniel. Parental power and marriage patterns: An analysis of historical trends in Hingham, Massachusetts. *Journal of Marriage and the Family,* 1973, **35,** 419–428.
31. Smith, William M. Rating and dating: A re-study. *Marriage and Family Living,* 1955, **17,** 41–47.
32. Sullivan, Joyce A. *Selection of dates and mates: An intergenerational study.* Office of Educational Services: Ohio State U. Libraries, 1972.
33. Sutton-Smith, Brian, and Ben G. Rosenberg. Sex differences in the longitudinal prediction of adult personality. Paper presented at meetings of the Society for Research in Child Development. Philadelphia, 1973.
34. Taylor, P. A. and N. D. Glenn. The utility of education and attractiveness for females' status attainment through marriage. *American Sociological Review,* 1976, **41,** 484–498.
35. Terry, Roger L. and Elizabeth Macklin. Accuracy of identifying married couples on the basis of similarity of attractiveness. *Journal of Psychology,* 1977, **97,** 15–20.
36. Till, Amnon and Eric M. Freedman. Complementarity versus similarity of traits operating in the choice of marriage and dating partners. *Journal of Social Psychology,* 1978, **105,** 147–148.
37. Vandenberg, Stephen G. Assortative mating, or who marries whom? *Behavior Genetics,* 1972, **2,** 127–157.
38. Vincent, Clark E. Interfaith marriages: Problem or symptom? In Lloyd Saxton (Ed.). *The individual, marriage and the family: Current perspectives.* Belmont, Calif.: Wadsworth, 1970.
39. Waller, Willard. The rating and dating complex. *American Sociological Review,* 1937, **2,** 727–734.
40. Whitehurst, Robert N. Comparisons of ideal spouse conceptions of American and Canadian university students. Paper presented at meetings of the American Psychological Association, Montreal, 1973.

# CHAPTER 7

# PARTNERHood

In the previous chapter on partner selection, we explored how a couple moves from being strangers to considering themselves as a couple, or being *pair-bonded*. Pair-bonding is a special kind of attachment between two people who see themselves as a couple, whether or not the union is formalized in some way (for example, a going-steady couple, a married couple).

Partnerhood involves being pair-bonded, but cannot be explained entirely by saying that a couple sees themselves as a couple. For partnerhood as we define it to exist, there must be love between the participants, there must be an effective communication system, and there must be a kind of *reciprocity* [73]; that is, a mutual exchange, or a give-and-take. For reciprocity to exist between two people, they must remain separate entities; the notion that when two people love each other they "become one" means an end to reciprocity. (See Chapter 2, page 45.)

Partnerhood also implies a sense of commitment, but not a static kind that swears loyalty to the other person "right or wrong" or at any cost to the committed person. It involves instead a commitment to the other person, to the relationship, and also to one's own growth. Carl Rogers suggests the following definition of the relationship that we call partnerhood: "We each commit ourselves to working together on the changing process of our present relationship, because that relationship is currently enriching our love and our life and we wish it to grow" [66, p. 20].

This kind of partnerhood is probably achieved by only a tiny proportion of all the couples who become pair-bonded. Some couples may achieve it for a while, and then move on to another kind of relationship. Because of economic and other inequalities in our society, many couples never have the chance to form a partnership, because they are concerned with day-to-day survival. A starving person or one whose survival is constantly threatened is not able to expend the time and energy necessary to develop an intimate, reciprocal relationship [51].

MOLLIE S. SMART

## VARIATIONS ON PARTNERHOOD

Different kinds of partnerships are appropriate in different kinds of cultural environments. Mr. and Mrs. Kavoori, who live in India, perform *pujas* (ritual prayers) together each morning and have a special kind of religious partnership, each receiving spiritual benefits from the cooperative participation. Because he is a married Hindu, Mr. Kavoori cannot perform *puja* alone. The Kavooris have a type of closeness that is not felt by the more secularly oriented.

A few attempts have been made by persons interested in family theory to classify marriages into types. These types could conceivably apply to other relationships as well. A basic distinction set forth by Burgess and Locke was that of the *institutional* versus *companionship* marriage [10]. In institutional marriage, roles are clearly differentiated along sex lines, and the husband's status is higher than the wife's. By contrast, companionship marriage is democratic, innovative in respect to roles, and permissive; the emphasis is on personal happiness rather than on fulfilling one's duty.

## An Upper-Middle-Class Typology

In a study of upper-middle-class marriages, Cuber and Harroff identified five types of stable (not divorced or separated) marriages [18].

1. The conflict-habituated marriage that revolves around constant bickering and fighting.

2. The devitalized marriage in which the partners at one time were in love, but now have only memories of these more exciting times. Some devitalized couples accept the change in their relationship; others wish they could bring back the good old days.

3. Passive-congenial couples are very similar to the devitalized, except that their relationship has been that way from the beginning. Theirs was and is a marriage of convenience: for example, a business executive needs a charming, socially adept wife, and she wants the comfort and security of a man's salary. Affection may exist between them, but the "bells have never rung."

4. The vital relationship exists when the partners are involved in each other's lives, both in what they do and how they feel about each other. It is a vibrant, growing relationship, but does not exclude certain separate spheres in their lives.

5. The total relationship is like the vital, only more so. Some of these couples are so wrapped up in each other that they have no separate lives or identities. There are no serious differences, although there may have been in the past.

## A Black Ghetto Typology

Schulz distinguishes between four different kinds of relationships between black ghetto *boyfriends* and their women and the woman's children [70].

1. The quasi-father gives financial and emotional support to a woman and her children over a period of time, getting in return his meals, washing and ironing, sexual satisfaction, and familial companionship.

2. The supportive biological father supports his children economically, but he may be married to someone other than their mother.

3. The supportive companion provides a woman with weekends away from her children. He does not support her children and would be very unlikely to support a child conceived as a result of their relationship.

4. The pimp lives off the labors of one or more prostitutes.

PARTNERHOOD                                                                                          **187**

Many other typologies of relationships could be drawn up. We present several in order to give the reader the idea that stability and adjustment (which are not the same, and are explained in this chapter and the next) can exist in different types of relationships. Not all persons have the same expectations for a close relationship, or the same needs or capabilities.

## GENDER ROLE AND PARTNERHOOD

As cultural structuring of relationships becomes looser, there is less need for the adherence to strict definition of gender roles. In many parts of our society today, women are feeling more able to challenge the traditional ideas concerning woman's place and are striving to enter professions that were previously closed to them. Some men are involved in the equally difficult process of becoming more able to feel and express tenderness and caring toward their women, their children, and their male friends.

In many families, one partner is more willing and/or able to meet the challenge of gender-role flexibility than is the other partner. More usual is the man who has held onto the family reins for so long that he is angered and perplexed at his wife for the new demands that she is placing on him. *She* wants to develop her own creative and expressive talents, and to help him to become a more accepting person, both of her and of the changes that she sees going on around them. *He* thinks that he has too much to lose, and he feels outraged by her impudence. But there certainly are families today in which the man perceives how he and the whole family could benefit from a less structured situation, and the woman does not want to change because being supported by a man is too comfortable a situation to exchange for the unknown.

Rogers [66] sees the dissolution of gender-stereotyped roles as a necessary ingredient of partnerhood, and we agree that this is necessary for some people. For others, however, roles provide varying degrees of structure security and predictability to their lives and relationships. We see the dissolution of roles as an evolutionary process that can be hastened by thoughtful effort and facilitated by the cooperation of women and men. We have discussed this controversial issue more fully in Chapter 5.

## PARTNERSHIP INTERACTION

The development of a partnership takes place across a span of time. It may begin when two people are attracted to each other, or it may have a more formalized beginning, for example, when a traditional Indian couple (who have not met before) are married. In our society, partner selection is part of the process of developing a partner relationship. Once the selection is mutually made, and the couple are pair-bonded, partnership may exist. But in order for it to continue, it must develop and not stagnate or "unwind." In this chapter, we examine the interaction of partners, both married and unmarried.

## Love

In Chapter 2, we discussed the individual's lifetime experience with love. In order for love to exist, there must be *attachment* between the two. Attachment is a special kind of *bond*, or tie between people. We elaborate further on bonds in a later section. *Care*, the promotion of the loved one's life, growth, and well-being, is another essential of love. *Respect*, also a part of love, involves the realization that the loved one is a separate person with his own needs and wants. Love involves *knowledge* of the other person, and a *responsibility* toward him or her.

Love is greatly emphasized in our society as an essential ingredient of marital and family life. Although the choice of a partner is influenced by such mundane things as homogamy, attractiveness, agreement on values, and role compatibility, most of those who marry are convinced that they marry for love. When love no longer exists, many believe that there is no point in continuing a relationship.

As we have seen, love comes in many colors, and markings. The definition of love depends upon the cultural environment and specific experiences of the person who defines it.

## Bonds

A group such as the family or even a couple are kept together by **bonds.** "A bond, or tie, exists when a value of the individual—shared or unique—is felt to be fostered by association or interaction with some other person or group" [81, p. 41]. In other words, if I feel that something important to me is allowed to exist and grow because I am involved with a particular person (I like having a companion; my husband is such a companion) or group (a political party; a bowling league), then I feel *bonded* to that person, or that group. A bond can be one-way, such as when an adolescent has a crush on a movie star.

Many bonds hold a couple together. Indeed, the more bonds there are, the less chance there is that the couple will break up. Some bonds exist only momentarily; two strangers in a crowd lock eyes briefly and then go their separate ways. Others may exist for a short time and then dissipate: two recent divorcees may have much in common while they are still having a hard time adjusting to their divorces, but when they are readjusted the bond breaks easily. A couple on their first date may be amazed by the similarity of their outlooks: they both love basketball and hate baseball; they like the same music; they love Italian food. These bonds may endure, or they may later prove superficial.

The kind of bond that continues to grow, a **crescive bond** [81], is the most flexible and strongest bond of all. If the bonded individuals believe that something that they share (their special way of communicating, for example) is growing or "getting better," then that shared "something" is a crescive bond. It is essential for the continued functioning of a group (even a two-person group) that at least some of the bonds that exist continue to grow.

As Chapter 2 showed, love includes bonds of attachment between people. Attachment is a very durable, often permanent, bond by which one person (or animal) is tied to another. If both are tied to each other, the attachment is mutual, which is the case in pair-bonding. An attachment is built through the exercise of biologically based behavior patterns in which some mutuality is involved, such as the suckling and sucking of mother and infant, and talking, looking, touching, and sexual intercourse of adults. In the presence of the attachment object (the person to whom one is attached), an individual has a feeling of security, well-being, and happiness. The infant or child is more able to explore and to face frightening situations. The adult, also, can face crises and threats better in the company of the attached partner.

When attached persons are apart, they keep in contact by whatever sort of communication they can devise, whether it be looking across the room at each other, waving from the train window, telephoning, writing letters, or attempting extrasensory perception. They plan to get back together again, to regain the presence of the beloved. When love declines, it is because the bonds of attachment that hold the lovers together have become ineffective.

When people interact, bonds develop. For this reason, the jealous husband does have reason to fear his wife's interaction with her co-worker; the jealous wife has reason to fear her husband's interaction with fellow members of his Players group, as they rehearse for the play. Whether or not such bonds will replace the marital bonds depend upon many factors.

The chart on page 180 in Chapter 6 depicts partnership love as developing as bonds of attachment are built, as the couple feel themselves to be in love, and as they feel like a pair. As partnerhood develops, all sorts of mutual experiences and interactions contribute new sources of bonding. Their attachment grows stronger. In the beginning of a relationship, the bonds are not as many or as strong as they may be later on. The widowed bride is tragic, but it is easier for her to go on with her life than it is for the person who is widowed after many years of interaction. Even the person who reports his marriage as not particularly satisfying may be unable to function without his spouse, because over the years he has become dependent upon his spouse to play certain roles in relation to him. For example, each week before he did the grocery shopping, Mr. Alpert used to ask his wife if there was anything she felt like having for dinner. She would always say, "you buy whatever looks good to you." He became so dependent upon her reassurance that he had a very difficult time shopping after she died. A woman who kept her house neat and clean because her husband liked it that way may be unable to do so when he is no longer there to chide her when it begins to get messy.

**Sex.**   The sexual relationship is usually, but not always, a bond between partners. Its importance in a marital or quasi-marital relationship depends upon the sexual needs of the partners, and the relative strength of other bonds. Desire for sexual activity and frequency of participation vary from one stage of life to another. For the newly in love, living together, engaged, or married couple, sexual activity may be a consuming passion. Or interest and pleasure in sex may grow with time, decline temporarily, and then experience a renaissance. We explore that subject further in the section on marital adjustment and satisfaction.

## Jealousy

Traditional monogamous marriage has long been buttressed by jealousy [19], the fear of losing one's partner to a rival. Jealousy is experienced as well by persons in nontraditional relationships such as group marriages and sexually open marriages (see pages 466—470), although such feelings do not support these new kinds of marriage. Although the popular press has dealt with the subject of jealousy, social scientists are just beginning to study it. In a study of 80 undergraduate couples at the University of Connecticut who had been dating for at least two months, Teismann [78] found no sex differences in the way that men and women behave when dealing with a jealousy issue with their partners. He found that couples who role-played a discussion of a jealousy issue were more rejecting of their partners and used more guilt-induction than couples who role-played a discussion of a relationship-issue that did not involve jealousy. The relationship-issue group used more cognitive, reconciling, and appealing acts.

However, when it came to conceptualizing jealousy, Teismann did find a sex difference. Females tended to be jealous of the time that their partners would spend with another woman, or attention that the men would pay to her. The men conceptualized jealousy in terms of sexual contact that their partners might be having with other men. A possible explanation for this sex difference is that men are taught to see their partners as their sexual possessions, whereas women are not.

## Bargaining

Bargaining begins early in a relationship. When looking for a dating partner, for example, a person does not usually choose someone who is perceived as "too good" in relation to himself. Each person has an idea of what he or she has to offer, and although dreams are free, the cost of rejection often seems high enough to inhibit acting on one's fantasies. The individual's self-conception may or may not be accurate, however. A person with a low self-concept may not play all the cards he has, because he is unaware that he has them!

**Quid Pro Quo.** As two people associate closely with one another over a period of time, reciprocal behavior patterns develop, although in most cases each person is unaware of how predictable his behavior is. Lederer and Jackson call these reciprocal behavior patterns **quid pro quo,** which means "something for something." The *quid pro quo* pattern becomes a set of ground rules for interaction. As such, it provides predictability and security for the persons who share the response pattern [41].

On an elementary level, a *quid pro quo* held by many spouses is that the husband provides the income and the wife raises the children. On a smaller level, the wife may bake her husband's favorite dessert (which takes considerable time and effort), and he may respond by offering to clean the car, which is something that his wife usually does. He is probably not aware that the extra effort on his wife's part motivated him to do something that pleases her.

Bargaining behavior that is not immediately time-bound provides for the smoothest transition in a relationship. In other words, each partner needs to recognize that if one spouse does something for the other, the act need not be returned immediately. However, the repayment of the debt must not be postponed indefinitely, or the relationship will lose its balance.

Bargaining operates when rules are broken, as well as when extra kindnesses are given. When an unwritten, unspoken rule is broken, the other person may retaliate in kind. The violated individual is likely to feel betrayed without knowing why. Retaliation can lead to a negative cycle of more retaliation.

Another kind of bargaining may also be used by one or both persons in a relationship. When one person consciously attempts to make a deal, bargaining is brought from a nonconscious to a conscious level. It may be done with the intention to assure that a fair balance of give-and-take is maintained, or it may be used as a power weapon or as retaliation. "If you buy that camera, I'm going to get the stereo." The husband who finds out about his wife's secret affair consciously seeks out a lover for himself.

Although conscious and nonconscious bargaining goes on in all relationships, some persons are more concerned than others are with keeping the balance even. Such persons may be said to have high exchange orientation. Husbands with high exchange orientation were found to have lower marital satisfaction scores than husbands who were less concerned about the marital balance sheet [53]. Exchange orientation was measured by questions such as these: "If I do the dishes three times a week, I expect my spouse to do them three times a week," and "It does not matter if the people I love do less for me than I do for them." High exchange orientation would be indicated by agreement on the first item and disagreement on the second. The researchers did not attempt to determine why some people were higher in exchange orientation than others. It might be that individuals who think that they are getting less than they are giving would score higher on exchange orientation.

## Power

Whether or not the people are concerned about who gets more in the marital exchange, all marriages have a power structure. It may heavily favor one spouse, or be egalitarian, or be somewhere in between. Determining the power structure of a relationship is difficult, and when family power is considered, the task is even harder.

Although marital power has been studied for a long time, methodological problems have limited the value of what has been found. Many researchers interviewed only the wives, and assumed that the wives' perceptions of power would be accurate, when it has been shown that even when both husbands' and wives' perceptions are used, they do not measure up to their actual behaviors [55]. Relying only on the wife's perceptions compounds this error. But an even more basic problem is that "power" has been defined and measured in a number of different ways. Usually, the respondents have been asked to tell who makes particular decisions, such as what job the husband should take, or who plans family vacations. Possible answers might be husband always, wife always, sometimes wife, and sometimes husband.

Thorough criticism of power studies is not our purpose here. However, "power" covers a lot of territory. Results from different studies are not always strictly comparable, nor are all aspects of family power tapped by available studies.

**A More Comprehensive Typology.** Many different kinds of power exist in a family. Children, as well as parents, have power, and coalitions are often formed among family members to counterbalance the power of another person or coalition.

Safilios-Rothschild suggests the following typology to explain family power [68]. We present it here in an oversimplified form, in order to give an idea of the complexity of family power.

1. Legitimate power or authority is entrusted to a family member by societal norms, such as legal codes. In the United States and most Western societies, it is entrusted to the husband.

2. Decision-making power is held by the individual who makes decisions.
   (a) Major decision-making power, usually entrusted to the husband, concerns major issues that affect the family's life style; for example, the kind of job that the husband has.
   (b) Everyday decision-making power is usually entrusted to the wife, and involves routine decisions such as what to cook for dinner.

3. Influence power is the degree to which pressure, either covert or overt, is successfully used by one spouse so that his or her view is imposed on the spouse, in spite of the spouse's initial opposition. Influence power, although thought of as being more the woman's realm than the man's, was found in a study by Safilios-Rothschild to be used by both men and women, but along sex-stereotyped lines. Men relied more on persuasion and discussion, whereas women used "sweet talk and affection . . . anger, crying, pouting. . . ."

4. Resource power is power held by a person because he offers the other a highly desirable or necessary resource. The homemaker's resource power is low, because the resource of being a homemaker is not highly valued. On the other hand, a woman whose job has about the same prestige as her husband's has resource power. In subsistence societies, or even in most traditional societies, women hold power through their control over two important resources, food and the birth of children. Mead has pointed out that in industrialized nations, especially in the United States, women no longer control food and birth. Men have taken over the leading positions in the food industry and in obstetrics, making women's power subject to theirs [52].

5. "Expert" power is granted to a spouse who has special expertise. A woman accountant may be given power to make major financial decisions, even though this is normally the husband's realm.

6. Affective power is yielded by the spouse who has more to lose in terms of affection. The spouse who is less "in love" has more power. The woman who does not work outside the home is more dependent upon her husband for affection than he is on her, because she has fewer relationships than he.

7. Dominance power belongs to the more physically powerful spouse who uses violence or the threat of violence. This resource is more available to men than to women because of the greater physical size and strength of men.

8. Tension-management power is obtained by the spouse who can manage existing tensions and disagreements, even if these cannot be solved. In a family with children, one child may become the peacemaker among family members, or a clown who can get the others to laugh in spite of their problems.

9. Moral power may be claimed by a spouse who takes recourse to more "legitimate" and "respectable" set of norms. For example, a wife may be able to obtain more equitable division of labor by taking recourse to the norms of the women's liberation movement. This power exists only to the extent that the other spouse agrees [68].

Three other kinds of power have been identified by other researchers [61].

10. Coercive power is granted by spouse 1 to spouse 2 when spouse 1 believes that spouse 2 can punish spouse 1 for doing something that spouse 2 does not like.

11. Reward power is based on spouse 1's expectation that spouse 2 will reward spouse 1 if spouse 1 complies with spouse 2's wishes.

12. Referent power goes to spouse 2 when spouse 1 gets a feeling of satisfaction out of being a part of a unit with spouse 2. For example, if a person says, "I go along with my spouse because we are members of the same family," that person's spouse has referent power.

Most kinds of power can be exercised at different levels. If one person decides who will make all the other decisions, that one has a great deal of power even though much of the routine decision-making is carried on by someone else.

It is difficult to assess who has power in a family situation for a number of reasons. Different kinds of power do not have the same weight. In the same family, the dominance patterns change over time in both the long run and the short run. Also, it is often difficult to asses who has the power in a given situation because of the time lag between the decision-making and the enactment, but also because different family members may be using different kinds of power simultaneously. Perceptual distortions further complicate the picture: the wife may believe that she has little or no power, when she really has as much as or more power than her husband.

**Findings of Power Studies.**   Keeping in mind that the power studies have not included all of these dimensions of power, we now summarize some of the findings regarding marital power.

The husband usually has more decision-making power than the wife, in that he makes the more major decisions. Even when an egalitarian power distribution is espoused, family power is not evenly distributed. Stereotyped ideas restrict the realms of men and women [6, 57, 68]. Women gain power when they live in a culture that supports egalitarian norms. Even when decision-making power of wives is high, wives feel subservient when cultural norms prescribe that husbands are more powerful [37, 63]. The working wife has more power than the nonworking wife [5]; this is more true for the working-class wife than for the middle-class wife, probably because the former contributes proportionately more to the family income [32]. However, differences in family power occur in middle-class families as well. Professional husbands with employed wives were more likely than husbands with nonemployed wives to report that when disagreements occurred they were solved by mutual give-and-take, rather than by one person giving in [12]. These husbands were less concerned with power and authority than were husbands of housewives [13].

Husbands and wives were asked to give reasons why they would give in to their spouse on various issues. Differences were found by sex and social class. Women were more likely than men to attribute expert power to their spouse; husbands were especially likely to attribute referent power to their wives. Working-class spouses were more likely to attribute reward-coercive power to their partners than were middle- or upper-class respondents [61].

Power distribution in black families, like white families, varies by social class [48a, 83]. Intact black families varied from egalitarian (working- and middle-class) to patriarchal (lower-class) [36]. Black women who want love and companionship may lose power in relation to their men because of the relative scarcity of black men [74]. Egalitarian power is associated with high companionship and low sex-role differentiation [60].

**Parents, Children, and Power.**   The individual characteristics and resources of each member will combine with those of others and with many other factors to produce a unique power pattern in each family. Age of child and social class differentiated between dominance patterns in 44 families consisting of mother, father, and son of either 11 or 16 years of age [35]. The lower-class and middle-class families were not different in size, child's IQ, father's age, mother's age, family religion, and birth order of participating child. The individuals first filled out a questionnaire about their families and then, as family groups, filled it out again so as to represent the family's opinion. These data yielded scores of dominance, interruption, disagreement, and talking time. In summary, the power pattern was similar in both classes when the son was younger, with relatively equal parents, both more powerful than the son. With an adolescent son, the middle-class father retained his dominant status but the mother became more nearly equal with the son, whereas in the lower class, the common pattern was egalitarian among father, mother, and son.

If power relationships were considered in families with several children, the results would be even more complicated than those stated in the preceding paragraph. Children often form coalitions against other siblings and/or parents. One child may line up with one or both parents. And alliances change in time and in situations. Everyone develops and changes in the resources she brings to the family group and in the demands she makes upon it. The more immature a family member, the more limited the decisions she can make independently. The parents of an infant hold great authority, which they exercise constantly in caring for the baby.

**Power and Bargaining.**  If one person wields a disproportionate amount of power over the other, the situation may become intolerable for the dominated spouse. The spouse who finds the marital situation intolerable often has recourse to the last "card" of bargaining: threatening to leave, or simply leaving. But in many cases, even if one spouse obviously has a great deal more power than the other, the subordinate spouse does not leave, and may not even actively object, because the subordinate spouse supports the idea that the dominant spouse has *legitimate power*. The subordinate spouse may feel that the bargain is even, because even though she doesn't have a great deal of power in the family situation, she also has less responsibility.

## Conflict

Marital conflict has often been regarded as entirely destructive to a relationship. We believe that conflict, when engaged in with respect for one's "opponent" (as one must when playing football or tennis) can contribute to the growth of the relationship. No two people are exactly alike, and it is highly unlikely that two people will ever agree on everything, unless one person submerges his identity and needs to those of the other person.

**Action-Oriented versus Personality-Oriented.**  Conflict, although not inherently bad or harmful, is also not inherently good. The two people may differ over a course of action and engage in a struggle in which one person wins and the other loses a certain amount (action-oriented conflict). On the other hand, the conflict may take the form of hurting the other person, in an effort to protect one's own self-image (personality-oriented conflict). In the second case, the opponents use "dirty fighting": "You're sick!" "Your parents sure did a lousy job in raising you!" The digs may be much more subtle, however, perhaps having a double meaning. Action-oriented conflict may produce positive solutions; personality-oriented conflict is almost always destructive [69].

One study of intact couples who were parents of college students found that "gut-level communication" often escalated into physical violence, but that "rational" or planned communication (see Chapter 3, pages 68-70) did not. These findings were especially true for working-class couples [76].

**Basic and Nonbasic Conflict.**   Conflict may also be seen as basic or nonbasic [69]. Basic conflict involves changing basic rules in the game: one member of a previously monogamous couple decides that they should both be free to have deep, possibly sexual relations with other persons. If the basic values of the other partner are challenged by this change in the rules, basic conflict results. Or, if a husband in a traditional marriage decides that he will no longer provide for the family, the result is basic conflict. For many couples, a wife's decision to have a career in addition to her family results in basic conflict.

Nonbasic conflict takes place within a shared set of values, or frame of reference. A husband may agree that it is his wife's right to have a job that she enjoys, but he may object to her working late several nights a week because it means that they cannot eat together. Or, to borrow an example from Scanzoni, the partners may agree that sexual intercourse is good and necessary for their relationship, but may disagree on how often it should take place.

Basic conflict represents a more serious challenge to a relationship than does nonbasic conflict, although the "tremendous trifles" of nonbasic conflict can be extremely irritating if not resolved. Both kinds of conflict can be positive to a relationship, if they are brought into the open and dealt with at the action-oriented level rather than the personality level. As we said in Chapter 3, problems should not be stored away or "gunnysacked" and then dumped on the unknowing partner when the burden becomes too much to bear.

**Habituated and Situational Conflict.**   A third distinction that may be made is between *habituated conflict,* an established interaction pattern, and *situational conflict,* which arises because of a situation or event [69]. Some individuals and couples get feelings of fulfillment from conflicting and expressing negative feelings. The "conflict habituated" couples described earlier may pick a fight or resort to violence such as hitting each other or their children. Rose, a young bride married to an easy-going man, habitually picks fights with her husband explaining that "things were going too smoothly" before the fight.

Situational conflict results, for example, when a couple disagrees concerning whether or not to take a vacation, or how to discipline a child. Systems outside of the relationship can cause or tremendously influence situational conflict: the family that is forced to live in a slum tenement, and has little income to meet its needs, lives in a stress situation that is likely to generate situational conflict.

**Bonds and Conflict.**   In order for conflict to exist, the sparring parties must care enough to continue the relationship. Disagreement, even basic disagreement, will not result in conflict if one person disengages from the other. If there are no bonds between two people, holding them together in the same arena, there can be no fight. For the conflict-habituated, conflict itself is a bond; personality needs are fulfilled by conflict. For most people, however, conflict alone is not a strong enough bond to hold them together. Persons who love, or hate, are kept in conflict by these bonds.

## Communication

Conflict and communication are intimately related, but they are not the same. A person may have conflicting feelings within himself, but this is not what we mean by conflict. Communication may take place in which there is no element of conflict; that is, when two people agree with each other. A difference of opinion that is com-municated, however, is conflict.

In Chapter 3, we discussed the elements of effective communication. Nonverbal communication, when it is incongruent with the verbal messages, can deepen conflict by confusing the listener. A message that is too threatening to the listener's self-image, whether or not it is intended to be so by the speaker, can cause the listener to *not hear* what the speaker is really trying to say. By repeating what the speaker has said in his own words, the listener can clarify the message both for himself and the speaker, facilitating communication. Although honesty is important in communication, if tact is not used as well, conflict can be escalated, perhaps becoming destructive.

Learning how to communicate, and how to engage in constructive conflict, is not a simple matter. A couple who engage in nonconstructive conflict can be taught how to "fight positively" if their differences are not basic, or if these differences can be resolved. For the couple who need therapeutic help, as well as the couple who already communicate and conflict fairly effectively and want to improve their effectiveness, the learning and working process takes time and dedication. Fictionalized accounts of problem-solving, such as are seen on television, give the viewer the idea that relationship problems can be solved in an hour. This is not usually the case.

Through effective communication, conflict can be used for the growth and enrichment of the relationship, and of the individuals as well. By bringing differences out into the open, conflict that is adequately communicated can cause positive change. Adaptability is basic to life; it is the key to survival. It is especially important in cultures experiencing rapid cultural change, such as ours. It is important to individuals, because as they grow up, mature, and age, their own needs, their associates, and their environment all change.

## Growth of Partnership

Change is an inherent part of growth. And yet, threads of stability run through the growth of an organism. I am a different person from the one I was five years ago, and yet I am still the same person. Likewise, threads of stability run through a relation-ship, although the relationship may change radically from one time to the next. As long as crescive bonds continue to grow, or if new bonds are formed that replace the old (with the same person), a relationship will continue.

Just as no two persons are exactly the same, no two relationships are exactly the same. Basic to close relationships are the existence of bonds, bargaining, and (with perhaps a few rare exceptions) conflict. Love, which is a special kind of bond, serves as a mediator for the bargaining and conflict that occur in a relationship.

A partnership is a special kind of relationship between pair-bonded individuals. Although conflict may be rare or not basic, partners do not fear either the idea of conflict, or handling it when it exists.

## THE WEDDING: A TRANSITION POINT

A wedding is a ritual and a celebration, with a promise at its core. The promise may be called a vow, bargain, contract, or pledge, according to its context and meaning. Essentially, though, two people, usually a woman and a man, commit themselves to each other in an enduring relationship that is spelled out in the presence of their kin and community. A wedding has layer upon layer of meaning. No matter how sin-cerely a young couple might try to make it a straightforward declaration of theirs alone, eons of human culture have produced weddings. The particular culture in which this wedding occurs determines whether it is expected to last for eternity, for life, or as long as they shall love, whether the ceremony is holy or purely legal, whether it is primarily a union of a couple or of two families. Even in modern North American society, the meaning of a wedding varies considerably. When a young couple start to plan their wedding, they are often surprised at the complexities they encounter. Many reach a point of bewilderment at which one, usually the man, says, "This is supposed to be *our* wedding, but everybody is trying to run it. Why don't we cut out all this big fuss and just go off by ourselves to get married?"

Older studies have indicated that the couple who wed in church have a greater chance of surviving in marriage than a couple married in a judge's chambers. Of course, a church wedding does not guarantee permanence, or even harmony. It is possible for a couple to live in genuine partnerhood without ever having had a for-mal ceremony. The wedding ceremony does, however, have important influences that are both psychological and sociological.

### Social Meaning

A wedding to which friends, relatives, and members of the community are invited serves the purposes of publicly sanctioning the marriage and establishing the couple

in new roles and statuses in the community. Approval is given to the match and the gifts given by the guests help the couple get started in setting up a home of their own. The marriage of a woman and man unite their families, although this is less important in our society, with the exception of the upper class.

To the middle and working classes, the wedding provides a time to be extravagant, to live beyond one's means, to have a good time with all the people who have social meaning to the family [72]. The bride has been fed on dreams of a magnificent wedding since early childhood, and may desire such an occasion. The parents of the bride certainly have opinions as well, which in some cases run contrary to the bride's. We have known many young women who have complained that their weddings were really ''their mothers'.'' It was the mother who wanted the bride to have a fancy wedding gown and three hundred guests. In the end, it was the parents' friends who were invited, and not many of the young couple's.

## Psychological Meaning

Ideally in our society, the ceremony of the wedding expresses the love that the two people have for each other and the plans that they have for conducting their future life together. If it is a religious ritual, and both are in harmony with the religion, then the ceremony unites them as a pair and also integrates them with philosophy and beliefs, their God or gods, their ancestors, descendants, and fellow human beings. Thus the wedding strengthens the pair relationship by weaving it into a larger spiritual existence.

What about those couples who do not belong to a particular religion? Many of them go part way, perhaps enlisting the services of their parents' church, a friend who is a clergyman, or a nondenominational chapel. Even though unfocused, they have some feeling of their love and partnership being related to a religious, mystical, unifying force. Some couples turn to nature for the beauty that will make their wedding meaningful. Their processional is a walk down a beach or through a forest of autumn leaves, their music from a guitar or a flute, their ceremony written by themselves, with help from Gibran or a friend. The personalized, do-it-yourself wedding has become popular enough to inspire the writing of books such as *Getting Married the Way You Want* [20].

A wedding ceremony serves as an important **rite-de-passage,** especially for the bride. Traditionally in our society the bride has changed her last name to that of her husband. In some states at the present time she may keep her maiden name, but often this may take permission from a court. It is becoming increasingly frequent for the couple to change their name to a hyphenated form of both names (Anne Michalski and James Sander become Anne and James Michalski-Sander. . . . or Sander-Michalski). Not all names sound harmonious together, and two long names wedded can make for nightmares when one has to sign checks. Besides, what name should their offspring, Brian Michalski-Sander and his bride, Penny Vierra-McLaughlin choose? Instead of using a hyphenated name, some couples choose a completely new last name.

The woman who takes her husband's last name has a change in identification and identity. It implies that she is "his" more than he is "hers." The couple who uses a combination name share their old identities, and their new. The couple who choose a new name dissociate themselves from either of their families of orientation and make it hard for old friends to keep track of them. No method is perfect.

Getting married changes a person's self-concept in other ways as well. Commitment between the partners is tightened, and for each partner individual sets of feelings, ideas, and models of relationships that came from his or her family of origin are brought into play.

> Hitherto repressed or in some instances merely ignored feelings and conceptions about relating to a mate are brought into effect when one marries and thus is propelled into the same kind of structure that one's parents or surrogate parents had. [54, p. 188]

Even couples who have lived together for a year or two may find that their feelings change subtly (and mysteriously) when the legal knot is tied. Anne and Art had lived together for two years before they were married. Even though it was Anne's second marriage, she was shocked by the changes in herself during the month after the wedding. Whereas she had previously been happy living with Art, she was now miserable. She found herself feeling more responsible for household chores, and thereby trapped in the marriage. When Anne realized that her unhappiness stemmed from responsibilities that she felt because she was a *wife* rather than a live-in friend, her panic subsided. Upon discussing her feelings with Art, she found that he did not expect her to take over chores that previously had been his. Anne might have been headed for a second divorce, however, if Art believed that a wife should do all the housework.

Marriage may mean the granting of adult status to young people who before were previously thought of as adolescents. In this way, also, it can be important psychologically.

## Legal Meaning

A wedding involves a contract, as well as a promise and an expression of a relationship. In fact, a marriage may be performed without invoking any sort of religious or loving sentiments, on a pure contractual basis. In France, the civil and religious ceremonies are separated and may even be carried out on different days.

Each province and state makes its own laws concerning marriage, specifying the ages of brides and grooms, with and without parental consent, period of waiting between getting a license and marrying, and conditions of common law marriage. The usual ages for marrying without parental consent are 18 and 21. When a difference is made between male and female, the most common specification is that women may marry at 18 and men at 21 [80, 85]. With parental consent, minimum ages for marriage vary from 13 for the bride and 14 for the groom in New Hampshire to 16 and 18 in most states. Some marriages of persons below the legal limits are permitted, especially if the girl is pregnant. Close relatives are not allowed to marry. Some states consider first cousins too close to marry, whereas others permit them to do so. Until 1967, interracial marriages were forbidden in some states. In all but Maryland, Minnesota, Nevada, and South Carolina, blood tests for syphilis are required. The waiting period, between license and ceremony, varies from none to seven days, three days being the most usual period.

Almost any sort of ceremony can tie a legal knot, as long as the couple, who are legally free to marry, state their intention to take each other as husband and wife for life. Witnesses are required, one of whom is a clergyman or state official.

A *common law marriage,* in which there is neither license nor ceremony, is legal in thirteen states and the District of Columbia. Table 7-1 shows which states are common-law. The basic requirements of a common law marriage are that the couple be legally free to marry and that they agree to consider themselves husband and wife. In some states, another requirement is some sort of public acknowledge-

**TABLE 7-1**    **States That Have Common-Law Marriage and Community Property**

| Common-Law Marriage | Community Property |
|---|---|
| Alabama | Alaska |
| Colorado | California |
| Georgia | Idaho |
| Idaho | Louisiana |
| Iowa | Nevada |
| Kansas | Texas |
| Montana | Washington State |
| Ohio | |
| Oklahoma | |
| Pennsylvania | |
| Rhode Island | |
| South Carolina | |
| Texas | |

*Source:* Adapted from Laurel Leff. You, living together and the law. *Cosmopolitan*, 1978, *185*:6 (December), 194–200.

ment or recognition of their status, such as registering in a motel as Mr. and Mrs., having a joint charge account, or simply telling their neighbors that they are married. With the current practice of living together before marriage, some couples are getting themselves legally married without intending to do so, as did Fern and Vern in Rhode Island. They lived together for only a month, with a sign on their door saying *Fern and Vern Stern*. Neither of them knew that they were really married, but when Fern left Vern and announced her engagement to Walter, Vern found out about the common law and informed Fern that she would have to divorce him before she could marry anyone else. Even if Fern had married Walter before Vern learned that she was legally his wife, the marriage to Walter would have been void.

There are legal and financial advantages and disadvantages to being married. These have been summarized for Canadians and, in general, the same is true for Americans and, in fact, for most people [85]. Marriage restricts the freedom of all participants, placing the main financial burden on the husband and limiting the mobility of the wife. More obligation for sexual faithfulness is placed on the wife than on the husband. Wives gain rights to support, inheritance, and, in the case of separation or divorce, alimony or maintenance. In a partnership or living together without legal marriage, neither person has any legal claim to sexual exclusivity. Children belong to the mother; the father cannot legally control their upbringing, education, or religion. If a man is proved to be the father, in Family Court, or if he agrees in writing that he is the father, then he must support his children.

**Duties of Wives and Husbands.** With the current rapid change in gender roles, some of the existing laws on duties of spouses are out of date and not usually invoked. For example, few people would support the law that says the husband may decide where they will live and that the wife must live with him. However, desertion for a certain period constitutes grounds for divorce.

Different states have different laws concerning the property of a married couple. Before marrying and moving to a new state, it is a good idea to find out what the laws are. For example, some states have community property laws, by which the couple jointly own everything that they acquire during their marriage. (See Table 7-1.)

A couple or their families can make a contract at marriage. Although such a custom is not common in North America, it is growing in popularity. Influenced by women's liberation, a number of couples have decided that it would be sensible to spell out ahead of time the rights and responsibilities of each person. Sometimes contracts are made for definite time periods, with the plan that they will be reviewed and renegotiated at the end of that period. Unfortunately, such contracts would probably not be recognized by the courts [82]. Nonetheless, a contract may compensate for some of the diverse expectations that many couples have. As sex roles, age roles, and other roles become more flexible, people have to work harder at communicating their expectations, understandings, and plans. Disappointment, disillusionment, and severe conflict could be minimized by the interaction involved in making a contract and by having the contract to refer to. The Premarital Questionnaire in Appendix A could form the basis of such a contract.

Personal marriage contracts represent a new custom that is a variation on an old one. In historic societies and in tribal cultures, the families and kin make the contracts, but now the two persons do it. A pilot research project indicates that contracts include a wide range of provisions, of which the major ones are *economic,* the division and pooling of resources and income before and after marriage; *children,* whether to have them, responsibility for birth control, responsibility for care and support; *career-domicile,* relative importance of each person's career and what shall enter into choices regarding them; *relationships with others,* with friends, relatives, and sexual partners outside the marriage; *household responsibilities,* how work shall be shared; *evaluation, continuation and termination of contract* [77]. One purpose of the research project is to find out how many pairs, married and unmarried, are approaching partnership on a contractual basis.

## Homosexual Weddings

Although no legal sanction is given to marriage between members of the same sex, the fact that some homosexual couples wish to marry shows that a desire for deep, sanctioned commitment is not limited to the "straight" world. For the homosexual and her or his associates, the wedding has social and psychological meaning.

# MARITAL SATISFACTION

At the beginning of this chapter we discussed various kinds of relationships that remain stable. Similarly, different kinds of relationships satisfy different people. An outsider cannot look at a marriage that would make her unhappy and decide that the wife is unhappy. Some researchers have concluded that women were maladjusted in their marriages because the women did not fit into the researchers' preconceived molds of what a wife should be [40]. Therapists at times have made the same mistake, calling women who opt for a career rather than homemaking maladjusted, cold, or "masculine." Today, even the homemaker is not immune from being called names by some feminists who refuse to believe that being a mother is a satisfying career for many women.

## Work Roles

Because the work roles of family members both in the place of employment and in the home are so important to family functioning, we have devoted the next chapter to this topic. In this section we are concerned with the effect of work roles upon marital satisfaction. Marital satisfaction is associated with congruence between role perception and performance. In other words, if a man performs his role in the way that his wife thinks he should, and she performs her role in the way that he thinks she should, they will report high marital happiness. It appears to be more important for the husband to perform his work role adequately [34]. As women become dissatisfied with their roles, and strive to have more egalitarian roles in relation to their husbands, role strain may result. The husband who does not think that his wife is performing her role in the way that she should (perhaps, the way she used to) will feel dissatisfied with the relationship.

A study of working-class families in the Pacific Northwest illustrates that husbands and wives may find different aspects of the husband's role performance to be problematic. Couples were defined as "unstable working-class" if the husband had been unemployed for more than three months in 1973 and had earned less than $6500 that year. Among "unstable" working-class couples, dissatisfaction with marriage was related to unhappiness with the family's standard of living, especially among wives, and to quarrels about the husband's job (or lack of it), especially among husbands. Among "stable" working-class couples, economic issues were not related to marital satisfaction. Instead, marital satisfaction was related to satisfaction with communication and companionship. Additionally, wives in stable working-class couples who were satisfied with their marriages were also satisfied with the division of household tasks [9].

Low sex-role differentiation (that is, husband and wife roles that are similar rather than very different) has been found to be associated with high health, high companionship, and egalitarian power in the marital relationship [60].

**Working Wives.** In a study of upper-middle-class couples in Ontario, husbands of working wives reported lower marital and job satisfaction and more life pressures than husbands of housewives. The working wives, however, reported higher marital and life satisfaction, and fewer life pressures than did housewives. Working wives exhibited greater psychological and physical health than did housewives, but among husbands the opposite was again found. When the wife was employed, husbands and wives reported more communication [12].

The evidence concerning the relationship between employed wives and marital satisfaction is not clear-cut. A review of studies from the 1960s concluded that women who work full-time appear to have lower marital satisfaction than those who work only part-time, but women who work by choice do not appear to have lower satisfaction than those who stay home [34].

Data from the two national studies [73a] mentioned in the preceding paragraph reveal even more of the complexity of the relationship between employment and wives' marital satisfaction. No differences were found among employed and unemployed wives when they were asked how satisfied or how happy they were with their marriages. However, when they were asked if they had ever wished that they had married another man, and when they were asked if they had ever thought of getting a divorce, differences emerged between the two groups of wives. Among wives with less than a high school education, and wives with preschool children, employed wives were more likely than unemployed wives to answer "yes" to the questions concerning marital choice and having considered a divorce.

Is there a unifying explanation for the findings regarding wives' employment and marital satisfaction? We can only speculate. Less educated wives are more likely to be married to men with less education who earn less. One would expect that such wives would have lower evaluations of their husbands' role performance, and would therefore be more likely to wish they had married someone else and to consider divorce. Employed wives with preschool children are likely to feel considerable pressure from their own role demands, and to think that if they were married to someone else, or not married at all, there might be fewer demands made on them.

**Job Satisfaction and Marital Adjustment.** Is the person who likes his job more likely to like his marriage than the person who dislikes his job? Over the years, few researchers have probed this important question. In a review article, Kanter [39a, p. 47–48] notes that men's job satisfaction has been found to be related to happier family life among urban Australians and among American blue-collar workers in a college town. In a study of teachers and their employed husbands, it was found that the husband's job satisfaction, but not the wife's, was related to marital adjustment. Low job involvement was related to medium-to-high marital adjustment [64]. The relationship between job satisfaction and marital adjustment has not been adequately explored. Does the husband's job satisfaction influence the nonworking wife's marital satisfaction? Is job satisfaction more or less influential upon the marital satisfaction of persons in various jobs and careers? What is the relationship among income, job satisfaction, and marital satisfaction?

## Perception of Self and Others

Among a group of couples who had been married at least fifty years, satisfaction with marriage was found to be related to perceiving oneself as similar to one's spouse's self-perception [72a]. This finding is similar to the findings of Luckey [47] with a younger sample.

## Income and Education

Persons with low incomes and little education are more likely to report low marital satisfaction. The depressing effect of low income on marital satisfaction is stronger for blacks than it is for whites [34], probably because of the various types of discrimination that blacks endure.

## Children

Lower marital satisfaction is associated with having children and bringing them up. Children themselves may be gratifying, but studies consistently indicate that marital happiness is depressed when the couple are also parents. In their recent summary of this question, Harold and Margaret Feldman point out some ways in which parenthood and partnerhood can be made more compatible [23]. Chapters 9 and 10 deal further with this topic.

## Sexual Experience

Lovemaking is adult (and adolescent) attachment behavior. Sexual interaction per se may or may not be attachment behavior. Physical sharing and tenderness can be a temporary bond, or it can become crescive. What both partners think at the time is a "one-night stand" can become a lifelong sharing; what both think will last "forever" may quickly fade.

Good sex will not ensure that a relationship will continue; bad sex will not ensure its demise. In this section we discuss some of the research findings regarding the association of premarital sexual experience with later marital adjustment and the association between sexual adjustment and marital satisfaction. We again caution the reader that one factor does not "cause" the other.

**Premarital Sexual Experience.** Although older studies report that wives who engaged in premarital coitus had better *sexual* adjustment in marriage [29], those husbands and wives who married as virgins were a bit more likely to achieve high marital adjustment and stability [11, 79]. It was not concluded from these studies that premarital sexual experience *caused* (or causes) sexual adjustment in marriage;

rather, it is thought that women who had premarital coitus were more likely to be interested in sex, and more responsive, than those who resisted. Those persons who refrained from premarital intercourse had another characteristic that contributed to their later marital adjustment: responsivity to social requirements and expectations. For example, engaged couples who attended church regularly were less likely to be premaritally sexually experienced than were nonregular attenders [38].

Whether or not these findings would hold true today remains to be tested. We cannot say for sure if premarital sexual experience today is associated with more or less sexual adjustment in marriage. Among some groups today, a person who is responsive to social requirements and expectations would engage in premarital sexual activity, rather than refrain from it as she would have a generation or two ago.

Many, although not all, societies place a premium on female virginity. A virgin is worth more in the "marriage market." Americans, however, have found a way to circumvent the issue of virginity by "doing everything but" have coitus. From the traditional Danish point of view, the American who pets with many partners, but does not have intercourse, is more promiscuous than the Dane who has intercourse with a partner with whom he or she is serious [15].

The definition of virginity has been shown to be a variable concept; that is, not all persons agree that the absence of a hymen, or penetration of the vagina by the penis, marks the end of virginity. When asked if the concept of virginity made sense, 47.4 per cent of the female respondents and 40.5 per cent of the males said "no." The concept of male virginity did not make sense to 57 per cent of the female respondents and 56.2 per cent of the males. [2]. This study suggests that virginity is becoming less important in our society, but it does not support the idea that it is becoming totally irrelevant.

**Marital Sexual Adjustment.** Marital satisfaction studies have found a strong association between sexual and marital satisfaction. However, the woman's sexual satisfaction and adjustment have usually been measured by asking how frequently she has orgasms from coitus. The possibility of sexual satisfaction from other forms of lovemaking was ignored. Furthermore, a basic assumption underlying most discussion of marital sexual adjustment has been that the male's sex drive is higher, or more pressing, than the female's. That sexual maladjustment can result because the woman desires more sex than the male has, until recently, been ignored [22].

**Extramarital Sexual Involvement.** It is commonly assumed that extramarital sexual involvement means that the marriage is in trouble. In a study of women, 20 per cent of those who reported happy or very happy marriages had at least one extramarital coital experience, compared to 55 per cent of those who rated their marriages as fair to very poor [1]. Another study, using a sample of *Psychology Today* readers (who as a group are younger and better educated than the adult population in general) had different findings. Marital satisfaction was lower among subjects who had experienced extramarital sex, with the exception of women who had been married two or fewer years [24]. In a second survey of magazine readers, women readers of *Redbook* reported lower marital satisfaction if they had experienced extramarital sex. Nonetheless, half of the wives that had experienced extramarital sex said that they had happy marriages and that their sexual relationship with their husbands was good [43]. Interpreting the findings on marital satisfaction and extramarital sex is difficult. When measuring marital satisfaction, there is always great danger of over-reporting marital satisfaction, because to have a happy marriage is socially highly desirable. Thus, in several surveys, more than two thirds of respondents rated their marriages as "very happy" [26]. It may be that people who have engaged in extramarital intercourse inflate the reported happiness of their marriages in order to justify what is still socially disapproved behavior. On the other hand, the increased prevalence of extramarital intercourse may mean that disapproval of this behavior has decreased, especially among younger women. It may be that among increasing numbers of people, extramarital sexual involvements do not mean that the marriage is unhappy.

## Health

The relationship of health and marital satisfaction has not been given much attention by researchers. In a large area probability sample survey in California, it was found that unhappy marriage was correlated with poor health, social isolation, emotional problems, and low morale. Marriage was associated with better health only when the respondent reported a satisfactory relationship. Divorced persons were, on the whole, healthier than those who remained in an unhappy marital relationship [62].

## Companionship

Companionship means enjoying each other's company, having good times together, sharing activities, and being friends. A person who enjoys companionship with a spouse sometimes comments, "He (she) is my best friend." Companionship has the elements of love that we have discussed as attachment, response, and knowledge. Care and respect may also be involved in helping one another to enjoyment and in recognizing the individuality of each other. The in-love element is not part of the meaning of companionship, but companions can certainly be in love. Many happily married couples and unmarried partners, also, are companions in love.

It is commonly assumed that families that share many activities and interests are happy families. Companionship, satisfaction with marriage, and marital happiness have been found to be closely related [50]. Spouses who reported that their partners helped them to cope with life's tensions reported fewer stresses in their lives, more positive attitudes toward marriage and life in general, and higher marital satisfaction [14]. An important part of marital companionship thus seems to be "marital helping."

In another study it was reported that shared activities in leisure time were associated with marital satisfaction, but not equally for husbands and wives, and not equally at all stages of the life cycle. The husband's satisfaction was associated with shared activities during the first five years of marriage, and the wife's between the eighteenth and twenty-third years of marriage [56].

Companionship in marriage has been found to be correlated with high levels of health, health care practices, and health knowledge [60]. Since health and marital satisfaction have been shown to be associated [62], this finding suggests that all three factors, companionship, health, and marital satisfaction, are related.

In contrast, another study found that marital satisfaction was more strongly related to the absence of hostility than to the presence of companionship. That is, marital satisfaction was negatively correlated with hostility, defined as "the degree of mutual expression of overtly hostile activity, angry outbursts aimed at deflation of [the other's] status and self-regard, and dramatic acts aimed at symbolizing the breakdown of solidarity" (what we have called *personality conflict*). Marital satisfac-

tion was positively correlated with companionship, defined as "the degree of mutual expression by the spouses of affective behavior, self-revelatory communication, and mutual participation in other informal non-task recreational activities" [31]. In other words, in this study hostility accompanied low marital satisfaction more consistently than companionship accompanied high satisfaction.

Another investigation indicated that personal involvement with the partner was associated with marital happiness. Those who reported happy marriages concentrated on the relationship aspects of the marriage, whereas those who were less happy in their marriages focused on situational aspects (children, home, social life) as the sources of happiness in their marriages. When asked about sources of unhappiness in their marriages, those who reported happier marriages focused on the situational aspects and those who were less happy in their marriages cited relationship aspects as the source of unhappiness. It was found that those who were satisfied with the relationship aspects were satisfied with the marriage [28].

**Class Differences.**   When divorce applicants were questioned about causes for their marital failure, middle-class spouses reported themselves as more concerned with the quality of their emotional and psychological interaction, whereas lower-class divorce applicants saw their problems as stemming from financial problems and their partner's unstable physical interaction [44]. The findings of this study are consistent with a study reported in the section on work roles in this chapter [9]. Marital dissatisfaction among lower-working-class husbands and wives was related to problems over the husband's employment and the couple's standard of living, whereas among stable working-class couples marital dissatisfaction was related to problems about communication and companionship.

## Life Satisfaction

Family life appears to contribute significantly to the overall happiness with their lives that people report. While Bernard offers impressive evidence that marriage is more beneficial to men than it is to women [3], a recent national survey indicates that married women are most likely to report that they are "very happy" overall [21]. Forty per cent of married women, compared to 34 percent of married men, reported that they were "very happy." See Table 7-2 for the figures on single, divorced, and widowed men and women. In 1976 married people were most likely to report high overall happiness, followed by singles, widowed women, divorced men, widowed men, and divorced women.

When freedom from depression is used as a measure of life satisfaction, the married again have advantages over the unmarried. A study of residents in the Chicago area found that these respondents were least likely to be depressed if they were married, and most likely to be depressed if they were divorced, separated, or widowed. Among persons who were experiencing life strains such as economic hardship, social isolation, and burdensome parental responsibilities, the married were less likely to be depressed than were formerly and never married persons [58].

**212**     FAMILIES

TABLE 7-2     **Relationship Between Marital Status and Overall Happiness, by Sex and Year**

| | Year | N | Overall Happiness | |
| --- | --- | --- | --- | --- |
| | | | *Very Happy* | *Not Too Happy* |
| Married Men | 1957 | (904) | 36% | 8% |
| | 1976 | (686) | 34 | 8 |
| Married Women | 1957 | (960) | 43 | 7 |
| | 1976 | (732) | 40 | 6 |
| Single Men | 1957 | (82) | 11 | 12 |
| | 1976 | (125) | 26 | 11 |
| Single Women | 1957 | (75) | 27 | 11 |
| | 1976 | (125) | 27 | 14 |
| Widowed Men | 1957 | (47) | 13 | 40 |
| | 1976 | (43) | 14 | 21 |
| Widowed Women | 1957 | (232) | 19 | 24 |
| | 1976 | (253) | 20 | 19 |
| Divorced Men | 1957 | (40) | 22 | 20 |
| | 1976 | (86) | 15 | 19 |
| Divorced Women | 1957 | (111) | 18 | 27 |
| | 1976 | (174) | 13 | 20 |

*Source:* Elizabeth Douvan. Data presented at the symposium "Current state of American families: Implications for policy." Groves Conference on Marriage and the Family, Washington, D.C., 1978.

**Men's Life Satisfactions.**    Factors important to men's happiness with life have been found to vary with stage of the life career. In one study, men were not included in the sample if they were single and 35 or older; were divorced, widowed, or separated; or who had a child who was born when the respondent was 42 or older. The remaining men, who fit a normal life career pattern, defined happiness in terms of family when they had preschool or school age children, or when their children were grown. Men in other stages of their life careers (that is, single men, newly married men, or men with teen-age children) defined happiness in terms of sources outside the family [30].

Another way of looking at life satisfaction is to question people who are in later stages of life about their satisfactions throughout their lifetimes. When asked what was most important in their lives, a sample of 486 gifted middle-class men aged 52 to 72 were closely divided between occupation and family. Satisfaction with family was slightly more important, indicating that the middle-class male is not as obsessed with work as "the popular" stereotype would have it [71]. Additional evidence against this stereotype comes from a study of men and women employed by a large

**213**

corporation in the United States. Sales representatives were much more likely to indicate that their family was among the most important things in life (62 per cent) than they were to say that their career was (17 per cent) [39].

**Women's Life Satisfactions.** Women, too, apparently get satisfaction from home and employment. Data from six large national surveys indicate that housewives and employed women are about equally satisfied with their lives. When housewives were asked if they had ever wanted a career, over half (in both the working and middle classes) said that they had not. Employed women were asked which was more personally rewarding, housework or their employment. Thirty-nine per cent said that housework was more rewarding, 31 per cent said that the paid job was, and 29 per cent said that both were equally rewarding. Housework was disliked by fewer than 20 per cent of respondents who were questioned, although working women were less enthusiastic about housework than were housewives. Middle-class employed women were somewhat more satisfied with their employment and with being a housewife than were working-class women [84].

**Class Difference.** Thus, it seems that class is a more important factor in determining women's life satisfactions than is employment versus nonemployment. Even so, the class differences in reported life satisfaction are not large according to evidence from these surveys. No doubt members of each class compare their own lives to the lives of others whom they know. Rubin's study of working-class family life, mentioned on pages 71-72, indicates that life *is* harder in the working class, but that it is painful to recognize how difficult one's own life is. Rubin asked some of her respondents to read the manuscript of the book that she was writing, which described the respondent's lives. Although the people that she interviewed commented that the lives of their friends sounded just like the people described in the book, they failed to recognize their own lives, even when their own comments were extensively quoted. Rubin asked one woman if any of the book seemed like her own family. At first, the woman looked startled and confused. Then she replied haltingly:

> "Yes, I suppose so. But I really don't like to think about it. I guess nobody does. Bobby, he read that chapter and got mad at those alcoholic people, just ranted and raved about them. I thought he was off because he didn't recognize his own father there. I did, but he didn't . . . " [67, p. 214].

## MARITAL SATISFACTION AND LIFE SATISFACTION: CONCLUSIONS

Many factors contribute to how well each person adjusts to being married to his spouse, and how satisfied each spouse is with the relationship. Social support to the relationship affects not only stability but adjustment and satisfaction as well. Adjustment and satisfaction are highly personal and usually cannot be defined effectively for an individual or couple by an outside observer.

A person's satisfaction with other aspects of his life is likely to affect his satisfaction with and adjustment to his marriage, although the relationship is not always clear-cut. We would expect that a person who is happy with his job and children would be more satisfied with his marriage, but the opposite might be true in some cases.

Marital satisfaction is not static, even within a short time period such as a few weeks or months. Studies of marital satisfaction have been concerned with differences in satisfaction by stages in the marital career or parent-child career. Most couples, however, do experience minor fluctuations in the amount of satisfaction that they feel in their marital relationships. Just as some individuals fluctuate more in their feelings of life satisfaction, so do some couples change more in their relationship satisfaction than do other couples.

Low income is associated with less marital satisfaction. Children can be sources of disagreement and sources of pleasure in a marriage, even at the same time. Sexual adjustment is associated with marital adjustment, but we cannot be certain which causes which. Most likely, sexual and marital adjustment interact. Health and marital satisfaction have been found to go together. The relationship between extramarital sexual involvement and marital satisfaction is not clear. In one study, absence of hostility was found to be more closely related to high marital satisfaction than was companionship. Other studies, however, have found a relationship between companionship and marital satisfaction.

Married people report the highest life satisfaction, followed by the never-married, and then by the widowed and divorced. Men's definitions of happiness change over a man's life career, being more family-centered when children are school-age and younger. Both men and women find satisfactions in family life. Life satisfaction is lower at lower economic levels.

In sum, many complexly interrelated factors contribute to marital and life satisfaction.

## COHABITATION

Since 1960 the number of unmarried American individuals living with a member of the opposite sex has more than doubled, from an estimated 439,000 in 1960 to an estimated 957,000 in 1977. (See Table 7-3.) In 1977, nearly two million persons were living unmarried in the same household with someone of the opposite sex. Although some of these couples were tenant and landlady or landlord, or housekeeper and employer, most couples were about the same age and were living as roommates, friends, companions, or partners [27]. Exactly how many lived as partners cannot be determined from the census data. As we use the term, cohabitation refers to the living together of unmarried couples who are partners or quasi-partners.

Interest in the phenomenon of cohabitation rose in the early 1970s when it became apparent that it was becoming increasingly prevalent among college students [59]. While the cohabitation of college students has attracted more attention

**TABLE 7-3**  **Unmarried Couples Living Together, United States, 1960, 1970, and 1977**

| Year | All Unmarried Couples | In Two-Person Households | In Households of Three or More Persons |
|---|---|---|---|
| 1960 | 439,000 | 242,000 | 197,000 |
| 1970 | 523,000 | 327,000 | 196,000 |
| 1977 | 957,000 | 753,000 | 204,000 |

*Source:* Paul C. Glick and Arthur J. Norton. Marrying, divorcing, and living together in the U.S. today. *Population Bulletin,* 1977, **32**:5, Table 17.

than living together among other age groups, cohabitation is not unusual among divorced men [17, 27], and senior citizens are known to live together in unmarried pairs, too [46].

Census figures on cohabitation, such as those given in Table 7-3, provide a "snapshot" of the number of couples living together at given times. Because cohabitation relationships are generally rather short-lived, ending in either breakup or marriage, it might be more relevant to ask how many people have *ever* cohabited. In Table 7-4 a comparison is made by age group of men aged 20 to 30 who have ever cohabited and who are currently cohabiting. As can be seen, "snapshot" census figures do not reveal a person's *past* experience with cohabitation.

## Among College Students

Cohabitation involves varying degrees of commitment, from "friend" relationships, to dating relationships, to trial marriage [59]. There are different motivations for entering a cohabitation relationship, including wanting to escape from parental moral standards, emotional security, convenience, and desire to test a relationship [65].

Little is known about how widespread cohabitation is among college students. Students in marriage and family courses were surveyed in a number of states.

**TABLE 7-4**  **Cohabitation Experience by Age, Men Aged 20–30**

| Birth Year | Age in 1974 | N | Ever Cohabited Per Cent Yes | Currently Cohabiting Per Cent Yes |
|---|---|---|---|---|
| Before 1947 | 28–30 years | 541 | 17 | 6 |
| 1947–1949 | 25–27 | 692 | 21 | 5 |
| 1950–1952 | 22–24 | 740 | 19 | 5 |
| After 1952 | 20–21 | 537 | 12 | 3 |

*Source:* Richard R. Clayton and Harwin L. Voss. Shacking up: Cohabitation in the 1970s. *Journal of Marriage and the Family,* 1977, **39,** 273–283. Table 2.

Twenty-five per cent reported current or past cohabitation, with men reporting slightly higher rates than women [8]. A national sample of draft registrants aged 20 to 30 revealed that 15 per cent of respondents (all males) who were college students were currently cohabiting. Among student and nonstudent respondents combined, five per cent were currently cohabiting [17]. In a review of research on cohabitation among college students, Macklin [49] concludes that about 25 per cent of undergraduates have cohabited, an additional 50 percent would cohabit if they were to find an appropriate relationship and situation, and the remaining 25 per cent would not, for various moral, religious, and personal reasons.

## Among Young Men

What about cohabitation among young people in general, who are not necessarily in college? Little is known about noncollege women who cohabit, but there are some data regarding men aged 20 to 30, from the study of draft registrants cited earlier [17]. Cohabitation was found to be more frequent among city-dwellers, among blacks, among men with at least a high school education, and among men who had experienced sexual intercourse by the age of 15. Men aged 22 to 24 were the most likely to have cohabited, and those who were 20–21 were least likely. See Table 7-3 for a breakdown by age.

## Legal Aspects

In twenty-one states, cohabitation is against the law. Fornication is a crime in seventeen states. Table 7-5 shows which states these are.

Although people who cohabit avoid making a legal commitment to each other, they nonetheless may become legally entangled, especially when either or both partners acquire property. In states with common law marriage, a couple may even unwittingly end up married if they live together, as did Vern and Fern (see pages 3-4).

In the event of a breakup of a cohabitation arrangement, problems over property are common. If an unmarried couple acquires property in the name of one person, and that property appreciates over time, it may be difficult from a legal standpoint to determine who has rights to the property. A jury can decide a case either way, because there are no laws to protect the rights of either party. Even couples who rent rather than own their dwelling acquire property such as hi-fi equipment, records, and washing machines. A lawyer [4] suggests that cohabiting couples make "yours" and "mine" lists of property as it is acquired. Another method is for each partner to retain the bills of sale of items to which he or she is entitled. With either method, determining ownership in the event of dissolution is made easier.

In order to protect one's partner in the event of one's death, it is essential that

**TABLE 7-5**     **States in Which Cohabitation and Fornication Are Against the Law[1]**

| Cohabitation | Fornication |
|---|---|
| Alabama | Florida |
| Alaska | Georgia |
| Arizona | Hawaii |
| Arkansas | Idaho |
| Florida | Illinois |
| Idaho | Indiana |
| Illinois | Massachusetts |
| Indiana | Mississippi |
| Kansas | New Jersey |
| Kentucky | North Carolina |
| Massachusetts | Rhode Island |
| Michigan | South Carolina |
| Mississippi | Utah |
| Nebraska | Virginia |
| New Mexico | West Virginia |
| North Carolina | Wisconsin |
| South Carolina | Washington, D.C. |
| Virginia | |
| West Virginia | |
| Wisconsin | |
| Wyoming | |

[1]Adapted from Laurel Leff. You, living together and the law. *Cosmopolitan*, 1978, *185*:6 (December) 194–200.

cohabiting individuals make wills. The spouse of a person who dies without leaving a will receives a portion of the estate, but the live-in friend does not.

## Cohabitation and the Future of Marriage

There is evidence that cohabiting college women tend to be more marriage-oriented than are cohabiting men [48, 59]. Marriage after college is a highly popular choice, especially for women, but cohabitation is preferred by some, especially men. However, among college students, cohabitation is unlikely to be a permanent replacement of marriage. Ninety-nine per cent of those who had not cohabited, and 96 per cent of those who had, said that they eventually wanted to marry [8]. It should be remembered, however, that the students in this survey were sufficiently interested in marriage to take a course in marriage and the family. College students in general might be slightly less marriage-oriented.

There is little evidence concerning the relationship between premarital cohabitation and the quality of subsequent marriages. Many similarities have been found between married couples who had previously cohabited and those who had not [49]. In one study, couples who had cohabited were less likely to give in when they disagreed; were less dependent upon their spouses; disagreed more often regarding matters such as household tasks, recreation, and finances; had broken up more often; and were more likely to have sought marriage counseling [16].

## THE MIDDLE AND AGING YEARS

The excitement of being in love calms down as the years go on, even though it recurs at memorable times. Although a good sex life can continue into old age, frequency of desire usually decreases with passing years. Companionship, however, need not diminish at all. In fact, middle-aged and older couples may have more fun and enjoyment as a couple than they have had during many previous years. With more leisure, perhaps more money, and years of experience in knowing each other and responding to one another, the stage is set for better companionship. This is the time to rework old interests, to develop new shared activities, and to build more satisfying patterns in life.

The term *empty nest* has been applied to the home from which children have departed, leaving only aging parents (who may actually be in their forties). This period is sometimes considered a crisis, since the mother no longer has children to care for. Instead of a time of gloom, it is often an opportunity for new creativity, loving companionship, partner activities, and enjoyment of freedom. The launching of children is not always abrupt and not always a crisis. In fact, some parents may even be delighted to find themselves "alone at last!" Indeed, a national survey found that women in the postparental stage reported more marital happiness than those with children still at home [25]. Women whose children had left home some time ago were happier in their marriages than women whose children had departed more recently [23].

Persons whose marriages are satisfying in the later years have usually had satisfying marriages since the beginning. Those persons whose needs continue to be satisfied in marriage in the later years report high levels of morale and activity in the later years [75]. Among lower socioeconomic groups, and among marriages with small amounts of companionship and satisfaction in the early years, satisfaction declines in the later years.

Especially for women, when marriages are unhappy, morale is low. Men's morale seems to be more related to having a spouse present, rather than the quality of the marriage. Health and satisfaction with one's standard of living also are related to high morale in later life [42].

## Roles and Power Among the Aging

After the husband's retirement, the husband and wife experience a shift in roles, as the husband becomes more involved in homemaking tasks. This shift in roles has been found to be associated with more companionship [45]. Because of the relative scarcity of men in the aged population, husbands in intact couples tend to gain power. Patriarchal control in the aged population exists because old people have been affected less by cultural change than have younger people [6]. Many old widows possess money that could be a source of power to them, but they often give over its management to a male relative or a trust company run by men.

## Problems Associated with Aging

For many aged persons after retirement, money becomes more of a problem. It may be difficult to find adequate housing on a limited budget. Poor health is often troublesome [75]. Widowhood, which is more likely to happen to women but appears to have a more devastating effect upon men [7, 42], will almost always be a problem for one spouse or the other. Although widowhood is usually a crisis of great significance, steps can be taken prior to its occurrence to make the transition less difficult. We elaborate further on this subject in Chapter 14, pages 428–429.

## "The Golden Years"

For the couple, or individual, with good health and adequate income or savings, the years after 60 or 65 need not be "declining" years. Forced retirement can be a problem for the individual whose entire life revolved around a job, or it can be a time to develop old and new interests. Even individuals with health problems, such as stroke and coronary victims, can learn new skills and make new friends through geriatric day care centers that are available in some communities. By loving and being loved, along with doing something that seems worthwhile, an older person has a good chance of maintaining an adequate sense of self-esteem.

**SUMMARY**  Partnership is achieved when a pair-bonded couple have mutual love, effective communication, reciprocity, and commitment to growth of their relationship and of themselves as individuals.

Some of the partner typologies that have been conceived by American researchers are the following: institutional companionship; middle-class types of conflict-habituated, devitalized, passive-congenial, vital and total; ghetto types of boyfriends, quasi-father, supportive biological father, supportive companion, and pimp.

Gender-role stereotypes may block the development of partnership, if the two

MOLLIE S. SMART

people vary greatly in flexibility. Some satisfactory partnerships are organized around traditional sex roles, but for extensive freedom, considerable loosening is needed.

In our society, most people agree on the importance of love in the formation and duration of marital parnerships. Attachment, a component of love, is a special kind of bond. Many different bonds hold couples together. Crescive (growing) bonds, resulting from pair interaction, give strength to a partnership. The presence of an attached partner contributes to feelings of security and courage to face threats. When strong, long-standing bonds of attachment are disrupted, the individual has difficulty in many areas of functioning.

Bargaining, or give-and-take according to understood rules, is part of pair interaction. Violation of rules may result in retaliation and the beginning of a series of negative interactions. High exchange orientation, or emphasis on bargaining, makes for less satisfaction in marriage.

PARTNERHOOD

Power is exerted in different forms and contexts: authority or legitimate, decision-making (major and everyday), influence, resource, expert, affective, dominance, tension-management, and moral. Balances tend to occur in favor of husbands versus wives and working versus nonworking wives. Power has been classified also as coercive, reward, or referent. Power relationships become more complicated as children are added to a family. Responsibility goes with power.

Marital conflict is inevitable if both people are free to react and express. Action-oriented conflict focuses on issues resolutions; personality-oriented conflict tears down the other person. Basic conflict threatens values and previously agreed upon procedures; nonbasic conflict involves small issues within a shared value system. Conflict may be habitual or situational. Conflict can be constructive when communication is honest.

A wedding is a ritual commitment of two people to a bonding that has social and legal sanction. The particular ideals and expectations of the culture are embodied in the ceremony, for both the pair and the community. The social function includes a celebration and a happy time for all. Religion, either traditional or personal, is usually invoked. A change in social status occurs, often more for the bride than for the groom. The legal aspects of marriage may include a contract.

Marriage laws include minimum ages for marrying with and without parental consent, restrictions on blood relationships between spouses, health requirements, waiting requirements, and content of ceremony. Common-law marriage is legal in some states but not in others. Laws concerning responsibilities of spouses and property rights vary from state to state. Although they may not hold up in court, marriage contracts can be helpful to couples in spelling out duties, expectations, and agreements.

Marital satisfaction has a variety of sources and forms. Work roles and their performance are very significant to satisfaction in marriage. Salient factors include the ways in which work is divided between home and job and between husband and wife, income, and satisfaction on the job. Marital satisfaction is often depressed by parenthood. Sexual satisfaction contributes to marital satisfaction. The meaning of extramarital sex is not clear; it varies and it seems to be changing. Health is related to happy marriage. Companionship is related to satisfaction, health, egalitarianism, and low sex-role differentiation. Middle-class partners view satisfaction differently from working-class partners. Marriage contributes to a person's overall estimate of life satisfaction.

Cohabitation, or living together, is an increasingly popular partnership arrangement, involving a variety of motivations and degrees of commitment. Parents often disapprove. Legal aspects and property rights can be problematic. Breakup occurs much more frequently in cohabitation than in marriage.

The middle and aging years often bring great satisfaction, especially when marriage was satisfying previously. When children leave home, parents have opportunities for freedom and enjoyment. Problems of the later years are more associated with work, income, and health than with marriage relationships.

**REFERENCES**

1. Bell, Robert R., Stanley Turner, and Lawrence Rosen. A multivariate analysis of female extramarital coitus. *Journal of Marriage and the Family,* 1975, **37,** 375–384.
2. Berger, David and Morton Wenger. The ideology of virginity. *Journal of Marriage and the Family,* 1973, **35,** 666–676.
3. Bernard, Jessie. *The future of marriage.* New York: Bantam, 1972.
4. Bernstein, Barton E. Legal problems of cohabitation. *Family coordinator,* 1977, **26,** 361–366.
5. Blood, Robert O. and Robert Hamblin. The effect of the wife's employment on the family power structure. *Social Forces,* 1965, **43,** 59–64.
6. Blood, Robert O. and Donald Wolfe. *Husbands and wives.* New York: Free Press, 1960.
7. Bock, E. Wilbur. Aging and suicide: The significance of marital, kinship, and alternative relations. *Family Coordinator,* 1972, **21,** 71–79.
8. Bower, Donald W. and Victor A. Christopherson. University student cohabitation: A regional comparison of selected attitudes and behavior. *Journal of Marriage and the Family,* 1977, **39,** 447–453.
9. Brinkerhoff, David B. and Lynn K. White. Marital satisfaction in an economically marginal population. *Journal of Marriage and the Family,* 1978, **40,** 259–267.
10. Burgess, Ernest and Harvey J. Locke. *The family, from institution to companionship.* New York: American Book, 1945.
11. Burgess, Ernest and Paul Wallin, *Engagement and marriage.* Philadelphia: Lippincott, 1953.
12. Burke, Ronald J. and Tamara Weir. Relationship of wives' employment status to husband, wife, and pair satisfaction and performance. *Journal of Marriage and the Family,* 1976, **38,** 279–288.
13. Burke, Ronald J. and Tamara Weir. Some personality differences between members of one-career and two-career families. *Journal of Marriage and the Family,* 1976, **38,** 453–459.
14. Burke, Ronald J. and Tamara Weir. Marital helping relationships: The moderators between stress and well-being. *Journal of Psychology,* 1977, **95,** 121–130.
15. Christensen, Harold and Christina Gregg. Changing sex norms in America and Scandinavia. *Journal of Marriage and the Family,* 1970, **32,** 616–627.
16. Clatworthy, N. M. and L. Scheid. *A comparison of married couples: Premarital cohabitants with non-premarital cohabitants.* Unpublished manuscript, Ohio State U., 1977. Cited in E. M. Macklin, Nonmarital heterosexual cohabitation. *Marriage and Family Review,* 1978, **1,** 2: 1–12.
17. Clayton, Richard R. and Harwin L. Voss. Shacking up: Cohabitation in the 1970s. *Journal of Marriage and the Family,* 1977, **39,** 273–283.
18. Cuber, John F. and Peggy B. Harroff. *The significant Americans.* New York: Appleton, 1966.
19. Davis, Kingsley. *Human society.* New York: Macmillan, 1950.
20. Dobrin, Arthur and Kenneth Briggs. *Getting married the way you want.* Englewood Cliffs, N.J.: Prentice-Hall, 1974.
21. Douvan, Elizabeth. Current state of American families: Implications for policy. Paper presented at meeting of the Groves Conference on Marriage and the Family, Washington, D.C., 1978.
22. Ehrlich, Carol. The male sociologist's burden: The place of women in marriage and family texts. *Journal of Marriage and the Family,* 1971, **33,** 421–434.

23. Feldman, Harold and Margaret Feldman. Effect of parenthood at three points in marriage. Paper presented at meeting of the American Orthopsychiatric Association, New York, 1977.

24. Glass, Shirley P. and Thomas L. Wright. The relationship of extramarital sex, length of marriage, and sex differences on marital satisfaction and romanticism: Athanasiou's data reanalyzed. *Journal of Marriage and the Family,* 1977, **39,** 691–703.

25. Glenn, Norval D. Psychological well-being in the postparental stage; some evidence from national surveys. *Journal of Marriage and the Family,* 1975, **37,** 105–110.

26. Glenn, Norval D. and Charles N. Weaver. The marital happiness of remarried divorced persons. *Journal of Marriage and the Family,* 1977, **39,** 331–337.

27. Glick, Paul C. and Arthur J. Norton. Marrying, divorcing, and living together in the U.S. today. *Population Bulletin,* 1977, **32:**5.

28. Gurin, Gerald, Joseph Veroff, and Sheila Feld. *Americans view their mental health.* New York: Basic, 1960.

29. Hamblin, Robert and Robert O. Blood. Premarital experience and the wife's sexual adjustment. *Social Problems,* 1956, **3,** 122–130.

30. Harry, Joseph. Evolving sources of happiness for men over the life cycle: A structural analysis. *Journal of Marriage and the Family,* 1976, **38,** 289–296.

31. Hawkins, James. Associations between companionship, hostility, and marital satisfaction. *Journal of Marriage and the Family,* 1968, **30,** 647–650.

32. Heer, David. Dominance and the working wife. *Social Forces,* 1958, **36,** 341–347.

34. Hicks, Mary and Marilyn Platt. Marital happiness and stability: a review of the research in the sixties. *Journal of Marriage and the Family,* 1970, **32,** 553–574.

35. Jacob, Theodore. Patterns of family conflict and dominance as a function of child age and social class. *Developmental Psychology,* 1974, **10,** 1–12.

36. Jackson, Jacquelyne Johnson. Marital life among aging blacks. *Family Coordinator,* 1972, **21,** 20–27.

37. Johnson, Colleen L. Authority and power in Japanese-American marriage. In R. E. Cromwell and D. H. Olson (Eds.). *Power in families.* New York: Wiley, 1975.

38. Kannin, Eugene and David Howard. Postmarital consequences of premarital sex adjustments. *American Sociological Review,* 1958, **23,** 557–562.

39. Kanter, Rosabeth Moss. *Men and women of the corporation.* New York, Basic, 1977.

39a. Kanter, Rosabeth Moss. *Work and family in the United States: A critical review and agenda for research and policy.* New York: Russell Foundation, 1977.

40. Laws, Judith Long. A feminist review of the marital adjustment literature: The rape of the Locke. *Journal of Marriage and the Family,* 1971, **33,** 483–516.

41. Lederer, William and Don Jackson. *The mirages of marriage.* New York: Norton, 1968.

42. Lee, Gary R. Marriage and morale in later life. *Journal of Marriage and the Family,* 1978, **40,** 131–139.

43. Levin, Robert J. The *Redbook* report on premarital and extramarital sex. *Redbook,* 1975 (October), **38.**

44. Levinger, George. Sources of marital dissatisfaction among applicants for divorce. *American Journal of Orthopsychiatry,* 1966, **36,** 803–807.

45. Lipman, A. Role conceptions and morale of couples in retirement. *Journal of Gerontology,* 1961, **16,** 267–271.

46. Lobsenz, Norman. Sex and the senior citizen. *New York Times Magazine,* January 20, 1974, 8–9.

47. Luckey, Eleanore B. Marital satisfaction and its concomitant perceptions of self and spouse. *Journal of Counseling Psychology,* 1964, **11,** 136–145.
48. Lyness, Judith, Milton Lipetz, and Keith E. Davis. Living together: An alternative to marriage. *Journal of Marriage and the Family,* 1972, **34,** 305–311.
48a. Mack, Delores. The power relationship in Black and white families. In R. Staples (Ed.). *The Black family: Essays and studies.* (2nd Rev. Ed.) Belmont, Calif.: Wadsworth, 1978.
49. Macklin, Eleanor D. Nonmarital heterosexual cohabitation. *Marriage and Family Review,* 1978, **1,** 1–12.
50. Marini, Margaret Mooney. Dimensions of marriage happiness: A research note. *Journal of Marriage and the Family,* 1976, **38,** 443–448.
51. Maslow, Abraham. *Motivation and personality.* New York: Harper, 1970.
52. Mead, Margaret. Speech to the College of Home Economics, U. of Rhode Island, Kingston, 1969.
53. Murstein, Bernard, Mary Cerreto, and Marcia G. MacDonald. A theory and investigation of the effect of exchange orientation on marriage and friendship. *Journal of Marriage and the Family,* 1977, **39,** 543–548.
54. Nichols, William C. The marriage relationship. *Family Coordinator,* 1978, **27,** 185–191.
55. Olson, David. The measurement of family power by self report and behavioral methods. *Journal of Marriage and the Family,* 1969, **31,** 545–550.
56. Orthner, Dennis. Leisure activity patterns and marital satisfaction over the marital career. *Journal of Marriage and the Family,* 1975, **37,** 91–103.
57. Parsons, Talcott and Robert Bales. *Differentiation in the nuclear family.* New York: Free Press, 1955.
58. Pearlin, Leonard I. and Joyce S. Johnson. Marital status, life strains and depression. *American Sociological Review,* 1977, **42,** 704–715.
59. Peterman, Dan J., Carl A. Ridley, and Scott Anderson. A comparison of cohabiting and noncohabiting college students. *Journal of Marriage and the Family,* 1974, **36,** 344–354.
60. Pratt, Lois. Conjugal organization and health. *Journal of Marriage and the Family,* 1972, **34,** 85–89.
61. Raven, Bertram H., Richard Centers, and Aroldo Rodrigues. The bases of conjugal power. In R. E. Cromwell and D. H. Olson (Eds.). *Power in families.* New York: Wiley, 1975.
62. Renne, Karen S. Health and marital experience in an urban population. *Journal of Marriage and the Family,* 1971, **33,** 338–348.
63. Richmond, Marie LaLiberte. Beyond resource theory: Another look at factors enabling women to affect family interaction. *Journal of Marriage and the Family,* 1976, **38,** 257–266.
64. Ridley, Carl A. Exploring the impact of work satisfaction on marital interaction when both partners are employed. *Journal of Marriage and the Family,* 1973, **35,** 229–237.
65. Ridley, Carl A., Dan J. Peterman, and Arthur W. Avery. Cohabitation: Does it make for a better marriage? *Family Coordinator,* 1978, **27,** 129–136.
66. Rogers, Carl. *On becoming partners: Marriage and its alternatives.* New York: Delacorte, 1972.
67. Rubin, Lillian Breslow. *Worlds of pain: Life in the working-class family.* New York: Basic, 1976.

68. Safilios-Rothschild, Constantina. The dimensions of power distribution in the family. In Jacob Christ and Henry Grunebaum (Eds.). *Marriage problems and their treatment.* Boston: Little, Brown, 1972.

69. Scanzoni, John. *Sexual bargaining: Power politics in the American marriage.* Englewood Cliffs, N.J.: Prentice-Hall, 1972.

70. Schulz, David. *Coming up black: Patterns of ghetto socialization.* Englewood Cliffs, N.J.: Prentice-Hall, 1969.

71. Sears, Robert R. Sources of life satisfactions of the Terman gifted men. *American Psychologist,* 1977, **32,** 119–128.

72. Seligson, Marcia. *America's way of wedding.* New York: Morrow, 1973.

72a. Sporakowski, Michael J. and George A. Hughston. Prescriptions for happy marriage: adjustments and satisfactions of couples married for 50 or more years. *Family Coordinator,* 1978, **27,** 321–327.

73. Sprey, Jetse. On the management of conflict in families, *Journal of Marriage and the Family,* 1971, **33,** 722–731.

73a. Staines, Graham, Joseph Pleck, Linda Shepard and Pamela O'Connor. Wives employment status and marital adjustment: Yet another look. *Psychology of Women Quarterly,* 1978, **3,** 90–120.

74. Staples, Robert. The myth of black matriarchy. In Robert Staples (Ed.). *The black family: Essays and studies.* Belmont, Calif.: Wadsworth, 1971.

75. Stinnett, Nick, Linda Mittelstet Carter, and James Montgomery. Older persons' perceptions of their marriages. *Journal of Marriage and the Family,* 1972, **34,** 665–670.

76. Straus, Murray. Leveling, civility and violence in the family. *Journal of Marriage and the Family,* 1974, **36,** 13–29.

77. Sussman, Marvin B. Personal marriage contracts: Old wine in new bottles. Cleveland, Ohio: Institute on Family and Bureaucratic Society, Case-Western Reserve University, 1974 (mimeo).

78. Teismann, Mark. Jealous conflict: A study of verbal interaction and labeling of jealousy among dating couples involved in jealousy improvisations. Unpublished doctoral dissertation, University of Connecticut, 1975.

79. Terman, Lewis M. *Psychological factors in marital happiness.* New York: McGraw-Hill, 1938.

80. Thompson, David S. and David G. Paulsen. The family. In John Dille (Ed.). *The Time-Life family legal guide.* New York: Time-Life Books, 1971.

81. Turner, Ralph. *Family interaction.* New York: Wiley, 1970.

82. Wells, J. Gipson. A critical look at personal marriage contracts. *Family Coordinator,* 1976, **25,** 33–37.

83. Willie, Charles V. and Susan L. Greenblatt. Four "classic" studies of power relationships in Black families. A review and look to the future. *Journal of Marriage and the Family,* 1978, **40,** 691–694.

84. Wright, James D. Are working women *really* more satisfied? Evidence from several national surveys. *Journals of Marriage and the Family,* 1978, **40,** 301–313.

85. Zucker, Marvin A. and June Callwood. *Canadian women and the law.* Toronto: Copp Clark, 1971.

# CHAPTER 8
# PARTNERS AT WORK

It takes a great deal of work, as well as love, to make a home and family, and to keep them going. Partners have to work outside the home and within it in order to provide the care that all family members need. Work can be satisfying in many ways, including its enabling the worker to express love through care. It can also be a burden, as when a person must work at a hated job because he wants to care for his family. Similarly, with work inside the home. It is an expression of love through care, but it may be perceived as drudgery or as fulfilling.

Members of families are both consumers and producers of goods and services. In most families in our society, at least one member is gainfully employed (or, in the case of retired families, has been in the past). Through his or her employment, the employed member(s) produce goods and services that are consumed by others in the society. The employed person is generally paid in cash, which is exchanged for goods and services desired by the employed person and/or her family. Thus, an employed person is both a consumer and a producer of goods and services.

Additionally, goods and services are produced in the home, even though no cash is exchanged. When a meal is cooked and the dishes are washed, an economic function is performed. Buying groceries may be seen as both production and consumption: buying groceries, bringing them home, and putting them away is a service needed by all families. At the same time, grocery shopping is consumption, since goods are purchased. *Family economics* is the managing within the family of input and outgo of goods and services. It includes the input of cash into the family through the employment of family members, the services performed within the family (such as dishwashing), goods produced within the family (such as meals), financial planning and spending.

The family system interacts with society in a number of ways. The employment of family members brings them into direct contact with other parts of society. Employed individuals contribute to societal economic functioning, and also to the economic functioning of their families. Homemaking (housework and child care) is not counted as part of the Gross National Product, but nonetheless it is an important contribution to the economic functioning of the family and of society as well.

The employment of family members and the dividing up and performance of household tasks have a number of direct and indirect influences upon the functioning and interaction patterns of the family. We have discussed the relationship of employment to marital satisfaction in Chapter 7. In this chapter, we will examine forces from inside and outside the home that influence family economic functioning. Society at large influences family economics, both by setting limits on the kind of employment available to a given individual and through attitudes and norms that structure people's behavior. Within such limits, however, people have more choices than they may realize. We turn first to influences on family economics that are

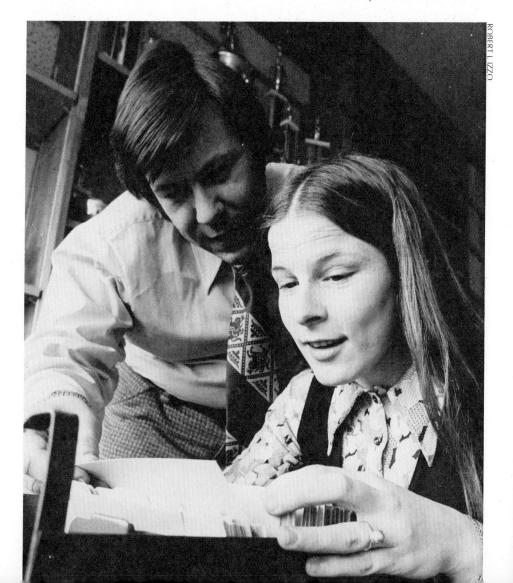

largely beyond individual control. We then examine areas in which people have choices.


## FACTORS BEYOND INDIVIDUAL CONTROL

The individual has nothing to say about the part of the world where she is born and grows up, the education available to her, inflation, the ups and downs of the stock market, the deterioration of a neighborhood, property values, and so on. The more flexible and resourceful the person, the better that person can adapt to change and make the best of what happens. It would be a mistake, however, to think that personal effort alone can make a great change in the individual's economic status, especially at the lowest levels. In North America and throughout the world, families vary enormously in financial resources, which make significant differences in the options available to them.


### Financial Status and Social Class of One's Parents

The individual has no choice in who his parents will be. Although in the United States social mobility (upward and downward) is less unusual than it is in many parts of the world, very few people move up or down more than one class level in their own lifetimes. Families that can afford to send their children to college (and perhaps to graduate school) make it easier for the children to obtain jobs with high social standing and pay. People who work their way through college must divert time and energy to earning money, while more privileged students can devote all of their time to earning high grades. Attending a more prestigious university (which costs more than the local community college) can help a person get into a more prestigious graduate school, which helps in getting a better paying job. While scholarship help is available to some deserving students from less wealthy backgrounds, competition for such help is keen. Coming from a middle-class (or higher) background is helpful in other ways, too. Parents who have gone to college are likely to be more intellectually stimulating and are more likely to understand the young person's need for quiet study-time.

Moving up from the lower class to the working class entails problems similar to those involved in moving from the working class into the middle class. In the lower class, individuals are often underemployed, and may lack values necessary for steady working-class employment.


### Gender

Women's average earnings have been less than men's for the same work, at all levels of occupation. Over the last twenty years most full-time women employees have earned only 60 per cent of what full-time male workers have earned. Almquist argues that

> . . . employer discrimination is the chief factor which produces wage gaps between men and women. Entry jobs are important steps in the process of discrimination. Men and women arrive in the labor market with essentially equal skills and competencies and yet they are typically assigned different jobs even within the same firm. [Men are assigned to higher level positions; women with equal qualifications are assigned to lower level positions.] However, the process of differentiation continues beyond the point where men and women are assigned to different jobs on different pay scales . . . As men mature, their earnings rise dramatically, while women do not have a steepening wage profile. The problem is *not* that women drop out of the labor force but that employers fail to pay them properly regardless of whether they drop out and return or stay in the labor force over a lifetime. [1, pp. 852–853]

## Race

Race differences, too, continue to exist. With both husband and wife working, the black family earns 98 per cent of what a white husband alone earns [16]. In 1977, the median income of white male-headed families was $17,848; of female-headed white families, $8799. For black families, the median income of male-headed families was $13,037 and for female-headed, $5454 [23]. Blacks thus suffer the double disadvantage of having fewer financial resources and of being subjected to racial discrimination. Other racial minorities also suffer from discrimination.

## Age

The age of the family head (a term used by the U.S. Bureau of the Census) is related to amount and timing of income [22]. In the U.S. population, when the head of the family was under 25, income was low. Income increased steadily to the 45–54 age bracket, after which it declined steadily to the lowest point of all, at 65 and over. This means that many older people are poor, often with fixed incomes from pensions or Social Security, or both. Inflation may be disastrous, changing the old person's economic status from moderate or low to extreme poverty.

Rise and fall of income varies with different occupations. Therefore, in making life-career plans, a couple would base them on what they can expect from their particular situation. A craftsman might reach his peak of earning at an age when a physician would be hardly beyond his lowest point. Professionals, especially the self-employed, reach earning peaks late in life and may taper off very little until well over the age of 65.

## Functioning of the Workplace

The workplace exerts many influences upon the functioning of a family. It obviously influences the amount of *income* and *benefits* a worker and his family will receive. When income is inadequate (as perceived by family members), stresses will exist within the family.

The workplace also dictates how much *free time* the worker will have, and what portion of the day this free time will be. Whether a normal work week is 35 or 60 hours will certainly influence the amount of time a worker can spend with his or her family in work and leisure. Related to free time left from the work week is *energy*. A person who dislikes his work, finds it stressful or boring, will come home from work needing refreshment and relaxation. Tim feels so drained by his job, which requires standing up for nine hours a day, that when he comes home he is too tired to do anything except watch TV. He also worries that his life isn't going anywhere, and he is starting to develop high blood pressure. Bob, on the other hand, enjoys his work. Although he often comes home physically tired at the end of a day, he is generally refreshed enough by eating dinner that he wants to go for a walk and do some work around the house. His work does not drain him emotionally; he comes home feeling good about himself and the world in general. *Childrearing practices* are affected by the workplace. Parents prepare their children for life as the parents know it. The business executive father who spends his days making decisions will expect and encourage more autonomy in his children than will the assembly-line worker who spends his days doing a routine task in a manner that has been determined by someone else [17]. How much free time and energy a parent has will certainly affect relationships with children. Tim is often cranky with his children; Bob enjoys playing with his and teaching them.

## State of the Economy

Needless to say, the functioning of the larger economic system is beyond individual control. When a family member is laid off because of cutbacks at her place of employment, the family usually suffers. If both husband and wife are employed, the lay-off of one member is likely to have less economically disastrous results, especially if the laid-off person is covered by unemployment compensation. Because lay-offs are most common among persons with the least stable employment records, the same group of individuals is most likely to be laid off again and again. This is the group that we have called "unstable blue-collar workers" in the previous chapter. For this group especially, changes in the economy mean the difference between employment and no employment.

The economy affects all of us. Even persons with steady employment must deal with the effects of inflation. The price of interest on bank loans can determine whether a family can afford to take out a mortgage on a house, or whether they must continue to pay rent. Owning a house provides an inflation-proof investment for a family.


## FACTORS UNDER INDIVIDUAL CONTROL

Given the variables over which the individual and family have little or no control, what are the areas in which families have real choices? We first examine some of these choices, and then turn to family economic decision making in the next section.


### Occupational Choices

Within limits imposed by intelligence, skills, educational availability, and the state of the economy, people have choices regarding their occupations. The choice that is made has many implications for the life style of the individual and his family. Some people carefully consider these implications before choosing an occupation or beginning a family, and others make career changes when it becomes apparent that their family life is suffering because of their job. Very frequently the job choice involves a trade-off between money and autonomy or responsibility, or between money and free time. A tradesperson may have the choice of more varied work in a small business for lower wages or work in a union shop with higher wages but with less responsibility. A research worker may choose to work in private industry for a higher salary or at a university for less money but for more free time or more flexible time. After a general area of occupation is selected, the individual often makes choices regarding how much time is allocated for employment and for other pursuits, and perhaps which portion of the day will be used for employment. Industrial workers who work at night often get a "shift bonus," an increase in their hourly wage. Night work may, however, limit the amount of time that one can spend with one's spouse and/or children. Within the family, decisions must be made regarding who will earn the money and who will do the homemaking. First, we look at homemaking and the costs of employment. Then, we discuss family decision making.


### Who Does the Homemaking?

What kinds of activities go into making a home? Such things as paying bills, deciding which insurance best suits family needs, sweeping the floor. In Appendix A we have included a lengthy list of tasks for the purpose of helping the reader and a potential partner to determine who will do which tasks. Although we have tried to be inclusive, the reader may think of other homemaking activities that should be added to the list. Although it may seem boring to even think about who does the housework, a great deal of family activity (and conflict) centers around family maintenance.

When a young couple sets up a household, each partner comes with conceptions of not only who will do what, but the correct way of doing things. How thoroughly rinsed must a dish be? Is it more important to have a clean sink or a vacuumed living room? Does the dog have the right to sit on the couch? And so on.

Traditionally, women have been responsible for most household tasks inside the house, and men have been responsible for outside tasks such as lawn mowing and snow shoveling. In the late 1960s, it seemed that women had taken over some of the outside work as well [15]. At that time, too, husbands of employed women did no more hours of housework per week than did husbands of housewives [25]. While employed wives and housewives alike still do the lion's share of homemaking tasks, there is some evidence that husbands of women under 35 are doing more tasks than was true a few years ago [12]. Whether or not this is a trend of the future remains to be seen. We now turn to homemaking in two kinds of two-parent families, the one-breadwinner family and the two-breadwinner family; and homemaking in the single-parent family.

**Two-Parent, One-Breadwinner Families.**   The "househusband" is a rare phenomenon in North America. When two parents are present, one-breadwinner families almost always consist of an employed husband and a housewife and their children, if any. Although this family has been thought of as the normative American family, it is normative only among families with very young children. In other words, only when children are very small are wives more likely to be housewives than to be employed wives. Overall, more than half of married women are breadwinners.

CRAIG M. SZWED

TABLE 8-1        **Work Experience by Presence and Age of Children, 1974**

| | Percentage of All Wives with Work Experience | Total | Worked Full Time (35 hours or more per week) | | | | Worked Part Time (fewer than 35 hours per week) | | |
| --- | --- | --- | --- | --- | --- | --- | --- | --- | --- |
| | | | Total | 50–52 Weeks | 27–49 Weeks | 1–26 Weeks | Total | 27 Weeks or More | 1 to 26 Weeks |
| Total | 52.2% | 100% | 68.9% | 43.4% | 13.4% | 12.1% | 31.1% | 19.4% | 11.7% |
| Presence and age of children. | | | | | | | | | |
| None under 18 years | 50.0 | 100 | 76.0 | 53.1 | 13.0 | 9.9 | 24.0 | 16.7 | 7.3 |
| 6–17 years only | 59.3 | 100 | 63.0 | 41.2 | 12.3 | 9.5 | 37.0 | 26.6 | 11.5 |
| Children under 6 | 41.2 | 100 | 63.3 | 27.4 | 15.8 | 20.0 | 36.7 | 16.2 | 20.5 |

Source: Howard Hayghe. Families and the rise of working wives—An overview. *Monthly Labor Review,* 1976, **99:5**,12–19. Table 6.

Among employed wives, 43 per cent have full-time, year-round jobs. Twenty-five per cent of employed married women work at full-time jobs for part of the year. Thirty-one per cent of employed wives work between one and 27 weeks out of the year [8] (see Table 8-1).

We do not know how many hours of housework per day the average "house-husband" and his employed spouse perform. There are data, however, on employed and nonemployed homemakers and their husbands. In the late 1960s, Walker found that women who worked 30 hours or more per week spent an average of 4 to 8 hours per day doing housework [24]. Whether or not their wives were employed, men spent an average of 1.6 hours per day doing household tasks. Nonemployed housewives tended to do about the same total amount of work (outside and inside the house combined) as their husbands, but wives who were employed at least 15 hours per week worked more than their husbands, especially when they had young children. Only the housewife with no children or with one child worked fewer total hours than her husband. Table 8-2 shows a breakdown of total hours of work per day, inside and outside the home, by husbands and wives. By looking at the middle columns of the table, it can be seen that women who were employed fewer than 15 hours per week did fewer hours of work per day than their husbands. Note that the housework hours logged by the women do not include supervising children or inter-actions that occur concurrently with the performance of other tasks. (For example, if the mother is preparing a meal while talking with a child, meal preparation is counted but talking is not. If the mother is reading a bedtime story to her child, it is counted.) Is it work or isn't it when a father suggests that his toddler get out of the pots and pans while he works at the sink? Is it work when a mother names objects for her toddler and suggests new activities while she is setting the table? These parents are performing important educational services and using emotional energy, but it may not show up in the work charts.

**Two-Breadwinner Families.** During any one year, about half of married women are employed. Thus, most families have two breadwinners for at least part of

TABLE 8-2

**Average Hours Per Day Used for Household Tasks and Employment by Family Composition and Employment of Wife, Syracuse, 1967–68**

| Family Composition Number of Children | All Work Per Day in Families with Wives Employed | | | |
| | 0–14 Hours Per Week | | 15 or More Hours Per Week | |
| | Wife's Work | Husband's Work | Wife's Work | Husband's Work |
|---|---|---|---|---|
| None | 8.7 hrs. | 9.2 hrs | 10.0 hrs | 9.0 hrs |
| 1 | 7.0 | 8.1 | 9.4 | 8.2 |
| 2 | 9.0 | 9.3 | 9.6 | 9.1 |
| 3 | 8.9 | 9.2 | 10.1 | 9.6 |
| 4 | 9.3 | 9.9 | 9.9 | 8.7 |
| 5 or more | 9.6 | 10.1 | 11.4 | 10.0 |

Source: Kathryn E. Walker. Time used by husbands for household work. *Family Economics Review,* 1970 (June), 8–10. Table 2.

their family career. As we have noted, most employed wives work part time or for part of the year. Thus, families differ in the amount of time that each breadwinner puts into earning cash. Families differ, too, in the amount of commitment that each earner has to employment. Employment may be either a "job," which implies low commitment to instrinsic aspects of the work, or a "career," which implies high commitment and usually more training.

The two-career marriage has special work-related problems not shared by the two-job marriage, or by the one-job/one-career couple, or by a marriage in which their is only one job or one career. Generally the husband is assumed to be the more committed, more expert partner [10], even when both partners are in the same field and have the same academic degree [9]. Finding two professional positions in the same geographic area can be such a problem that some couples set up two households and commute hundreds of miles on weekends. Figure 8-1 provides an illustration of such a couple.

Even when long-distance commuting is not necessary, household tasks must be divided. In one study of dual-career marriages, a number of techniques for dealing with the division of household tasks were noted [10]. Some couples used a flexible division that changed according to who was in town and who was out of town. Others hired work out, a solution that is more possible when the family income consists of two professional salaries. Efficiency might be increased, or housekeeping standards lowered.

Among dual professional couples, there is likely to be an equalitarian division of labor that is supported by the belief that when both partners have careers, the household tasks should be shared. However, the main *responsibility* for household tasks is more usually the wife's. When work is hired out, it is up to the wife to hire, fire, and supervise employees [11].

The dual-career family is still quite rare. It is much more usual that one or both

# How they deal with a weekend marriage

AMHERST, Mass. (AP) — The weekend marriage, once an arrangement limited mostly to movie stars and traveling salesmen, is now a challenge faced by a growing number of professional couples.

John and Adelle Simmons, for example, have been married 12 years. They have good jobs and two children.

But for the past five years they have lived in different cities, seeing each other only on weekends.

She is president of Hampshire College, a progressive liberal arts institution in western Massachusetts. He is an economist for the World Bank in Washington, D.C.

"When we started this I felt as if I were embarking on a grand experiment," said Simmons, 39.

\* \* \*

THE SIMMONSES meet almost every weekend — occasionally in Washington, but usually at their home in Amherst.

"If you only have weekends together, you don't let the little things bother you," said Mrs. Simmons, 35.

"I think John enjoys his private times in Washington," she said.

But don't other men grin, wink, poke him in the ribs and make sly jokes about his freedom?

"No," said John. "Most people see it as a substantial burden and are quite sympathetic."

He cooks his own meals in a two-room apartment and sometimes visits friends during the week.

When there are children in the family, having both spouses at home can become almost a mini-vacation.

"Last night, for instance, our one-year-old daughter was sick," said Mrs. Simmons. "So John spent half the night up with her, and I spent the other half."

\* \* \*

•WEEKEND FAMILIES must adjust. Parents can make it easier for children by assigning them tasks to facilitate the commuting and separation, and make them proud each parent has a good job.

\* \* \*

FIGURE 8-1    A dual-career couple live with long-distance commuting.

*Source:* Providence Evening Bulletin

partners work at a job. Such an employee may put in long hours, and may like his job, and yet not be preoccupied with it to the extent that many professionals are. At best, a job provides the employee with feelings of pride and satisfaction; at the least, it provides an income.

Women who are employed put in long work hours when work inside and outside the home are combined. We have already noted that one study showed little differences in the amount of household work performed by husbands of employed wives and husbands of housewives [24]. A more recent study, however, found that between 10 and 18 per cent of husbands of working wives aged 18 to 35 shared equally with their wives tasks such as shopping, cooking, washing dishes, and cleaning. Husbands of full-time housewives were much less likely to equally share cooking, dishwashing, and housecleaning [12]. See Figure 8-2. It is difficult to draw firm conclusions from these studies, since questions were not asked in the same way in each of them.

It seems likely that among younger husbands and wives there is more acceptance of the idea of sharing of household tasks when the wife is employed. A 1976 Gallup survey indicated that a majority of young husbands agreed that tasks should

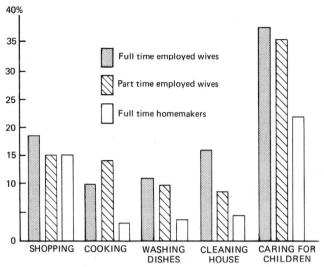

**FIGURE 8-2**     Per cent of wives aged 18 to 35 whose husbands share household tasks equally, 1977.

*Source:* M. Hunt. Making a living versus making a home. *Redbook,* April 1978. Pp. 70–73, graph 2.

be shared when the wife works, and most young employed wives in the 1977 survey thought that they gave their husbands and children as much attention as the housewives thought that they gave theirs [12]. In another national survey, this time of employed wives who were slightly older (in their 30s and 40s instead of 18 to 35), it was reported that between 55 and 65 per cent of the wives thought that their husbands disapproved of their working [2]. Of course, it is possible that husbands could *disapprove* of their wives' employment, while at the same time believing that when wives work husbands *should* share tasks equally, and yet *not* actually share the tasks in this way. We do not know the extent to which these attitudes and behaviors go together.

**Single-Parent Families.**   The breadwinner in a single-parent family has little choice concerning who will do the work that needs to be done. While children of school-age or older can take on the performance of household tasks, running the household is usually the responsibility of the adult breadwinner. The single-parent breadwinner is almost always strapped for time, energy, and/or money. We discuss the problems of the single parent in the next chapter.

## WORK DECISION MAKING

Who will do the housework? Who will care for the children? Who will bring home the paycheck? These questions once had easy answers, but not so today. Our society is in transition in a number of ways, gender-role attitudes and behaviors being an important one. We have seen that many women still think that their husbands are unenthusiastic about, or even disapproving of, the wife's employment. Nonetheless, women's commitment to their work has increased substantially over the past 20 years. In 1976, 82 per cent of working wives in a national sample said that they felt committed to their work, compared with 58 per cent in 1957 [13]. A Gallup survey of women aged 18 to 35 conducted in 1977 found that just over half of respondents said that they worked primarily for economic reasons, compared with two thirds of working wives in 1964. Forty per cent of working wives in 1977 said that the money they earned was less important than the pleasure, fulfillment, or recognition that they got from working. Two thirds of working women, even those working in low-paying jobs, said that they would feel bored and stifled if they did not work, and 80 per cent said that they would continue to work even if they did not need the money. House-wives, too, reported satisfaction with their lives [12]. Nonetheless, housewives in 1976 reported less enjoyment of housework than did their 1957 counterparts. In 1976, only half of respondents who were full-time housewives said that they felt positively toward housework, compared to two thirds in 1957 [13]. Thus, married women have changed in their feelings toward housework and employment. Although some men also have changed in their feelings, they don't appear to have changed as fast as women. There is bound to be conflict between many partners until a new balance is achieved.

However, just because many couples have conflict around work issues does not mean that each couple will be burdened with work-role related problems. Partners can communicate their wants and needs to each other, and they often can find solutions that each can live with, if not thoroughly enjoy. In order to make such decisions, some knowledge and forethought are necessary. Costs and payoffs of employment must be examined.

## Cost of Employment

It costs money to earn money. The employed person pays income taxes and usually Social Security taxes. Unless a uniform is supplied by the employer, it costs money to buy clothes for work and to keep them clean. Only people who live close enough to work to walk pay nothing to get to work. (Even a bicycle requires some upkeep!) Other things that eat away at paychecks are these: deductions for insurance and pension plans, union dues or fees for professional memberships, and lunches eaten out. And for many employed parents, child care is an additional expense. Thus, even if a salary or wage looks attractive, the would-be employee should consider the costs before taking a job. Does earning $50 more per week offset putting 150 extra miles on the car and spending four hours per week commuting? When taxes are subtracted from the $50, and then costs of extra transportation and child care, the $50 may disappear. See Figure 8-3 for some examples of how much it costs several employed

|  | Mrs. A. | | | Mrs. B. | | | Mrs. C. | |
|---|---|---|---|---|---|---|---|---|
| Wife's salary | $6000 | | Wife's salary | $11000 | | Wife's salary | $7000 | |

<table>
<tr><th colspan="3">Mrs. A.</th><th colspan="3">Mrs. B.</th><th colspan="3">Mrs. C.</th></tr>
<tr><td colspan="2">Wife's salary</td><td>$6000</td><td colspan="2">Wife's salary</td><td>$11000</td><td colspan="2">Wife's salary</td><td>$7000</td></tr>
<tr><td colspan="3">Taxes</td><td colspan="3">Taxes</td><td colspan="3">Taxes</td></tr>
<tr><td>Wife's income and</td><td>Social Security</td><td>1470</td><td>Wife's income and</td><td>Social Security</td><td>3190</td><td>Wife's income and</td><td>Social Security</td><td>1680</td></tr>
<tr><td colspan="2">Husband's additional</td><td>480</td><td colspan="2">Husband's additional</td><td>1650</td><td colspan="2">Husband's additional</td><td>715</td></tr>
<tr><td colspan="2">Transportation</td><td>300</td><td colspan="2">Transportation</td><td>150</td><td colspan="2">Transportation</td><td>500</td></tr>
<tr><td>Lunches (brought from</td><td>home)</td><td>-----</td><td colspan="2">Lunches</td><td>500</td><td>Lunches (supplied by</td><td>employer)</td><td>-----</td></tr>
<tr><td colspan="2">Additional clothing and upkeep (uniforms supplied by employer)</td><td>-----</td><td colspan="2">Additional clothing and upkeep</td><td>500</td><td colspan="2">Additional clothing and upkeep</td><td>300</td></tr>
<tr><td>Child care (mother babysits</td><td>for free)</td><td>------</td><td colspan="2">Child care</td><td>1500</td><td colspan="2">Child care</td><td>-----</td></tr>
<tr><td colspan="2">Cleaning help</td><td>-----</td><td colspan="2">Cleaning help</td><td>500</td><td colspan="2">Cleaning help</td><td>450</td></tr>
<tr><td colspan="2">ACTUAL NET INCOME</td><td>$3750</td><td colspan="2">ACTUAL NET INCOME</td><td>$3010</td><td colspan="2">ACTUAL NET INCOME</td><td>$3355</td></tr>
</table>

**FIGURE 8-3** The costs of being employed of three wives.

*Source:* Leonard Sloane. Does it pay a wife to get a job? *Women's Day,* 1976, **40:** 3, p. 70.

wives to work. Mrs. B., whose salary is nearly twice the salary of Mrs. A., has *less* net income than Mrs. A because of additional expenses for lunches, clothing, child care, and cleaning. It might be possible for Mrs. B. to bring her lunch instead of buying a sandwich, but it would be difficult for her to reduce her child care expenses. Her husband might do the cleaning that she hires out, saving that expense.

## The Payoffs of Employment

Although it may cost the second earner a considerable amount of dollars to begin employment, there may be hidden benefits down the road. Child care is expensive when children are young, but children grow up and leave home. Mrs. C above started work in a day care center when her children were of school age. Her starting salary was $3500 per year. Ten years later, however, when her children are in college and high school, she earns considerably more, even when inflation is taken into account. Were she starting in the same job today, she would be ten years behind professionally.

Other payoffs cannot be measured in dollars and cents. While housewifery may satisfy a number of women, other women prefer even a low-level and repetitive job to being at home all day [12, 20]. Having a change of scenery, meeting people, feeling responsible and that one is making a small dent somewhere in the world are payoffs that only the individual can measure. The devaluation of housework has deprived women of a certain amount of respect from themselves and others that used to go with the housewife role.

## Communication

It is possible for family decisions about division of tasks and production and use of family resources to be made by one person, or such decisions may be shared between or among family members. For real sharing of decision making to take place, communication among family members is essential. As we have seen in Chapter 3, communication takes place even when no words are spoken. When mother decides that Sandy will wash the dishes and Pat will vacuum, Sandy's shoulders slump and Pat's brows furrow. Neither child protests, but if mother is perceptive she will see that neither child is happy at the idea of performing the assigned task. Mother might have asked which child would prefer to do each task. Given a chance to choose, the chosen task might seem less unpleasant. Some families have a formal weekly meeting at which the division of household tasks is discussed. A structured meeting can make it more easy for more quiet or timid members to speak their minds. Another method of dividing tasks is to make a list of all tasks that need to be done during the next week. Family members choose tasks in turn, with the order of tasks rotated each week. Family members can discuss whether tasks are worthwhile doing at all, and if so, why. When Robby complained that drying the dishes was a waste of time, it was agreed that dishes could be left to air-dry as long as the person who washed them put them away when they had dried.

Communication is important for the planning of family finance. Short-range and long-term goals must be decided upon. Is it more important to take expensive vacations, or to save money for a house or a vacation home? Will money be put away for the children's college educations? Should the wife get a job as a typist now, or should she get training to be a legal secretary and go back to work later? If mother is offered a job for more money in another part of the country, should she take it? Questions involving the earning and spending of money involve many other areas of people's lives. Arguments about family finance are often arguments about many other things as well.

Somewhere during the process of becoming a couple, the topic of money can be explored in depth. Like mutual revelations about other important beliefs and attitudes, exchanging ideas on financial matters can be helpful in building the relationship or cutting it off after a few dates. If the pair continue into partnership, communication about finances grows more important. The partners and their children, if any, will set small and large goals throughout the life of the family. Marriage counselors and teachers often use inventories and questionnaires in order to help students, especially engaged couples, to explore their attitudes together. By comparing answers, they can see where they disagree on financial values and can then talk about their recognized problems [19]. The Premarital Questionnaire in Appendix A could be used to start an exploration of attitudes toward earning and spending. Another way for two people to begin communicating with each other as to financial goals is this: Each person should list five necessities and five luxuries; compare lists and discuss discrepancies.

# FINANCIAL PLANNING

In the remaining part of this chapter we discuss family financial planning. Because money has different meanings to different people, we begin with a discussion of some of the meanings of money.

## Meanings of Money

The significance of money for an individual or family depends first of all upon the level of needs being met. Then values determine meanings of money. Values, being products of the whole life experience, vary in time and space, between individuals and between families. Some examples of the meanings of money follow.

**Survival.**   For people who are poor and living precariously, *survival* is the basic meaning of money. To an Indian sweeper and his family, money means eating *today*. To Abdul, a jewelry salesman in the Vale of Kashmir, it was the wherewithal to flee from the Chinese, whose attack he considered imminent. To 5.3 million families below the United States poverty line, as to all poor families, money is subsistence. Especially to the 2.6 million poor women who head families, more money than their present income would mean some freedom of choice as to where to live and how to take care of their children. These women, like other poor people, realistically think that they have little control, power, or freedom of choice because survival has to be their first goal.

**Security.**   Although most people agree that money gives security, some individuals are much more concerned than others with having enough money to last for the rest of their lives. To the generation that struggled through the Depression of the 1930s, money is likely to be important as security. Young mainstream North American adults had no experience with financial depressions during their childhood and adolescence. Conflict is practically inevitable when money means earning and saving to parents, but spending and enjoying to teen-agers.

**Freedom of Choice.**   Even when people are as poor as the black women mentioned previously, cash in hand gives them some power and freedom of choice. They may not be free to buy steak, but they can go to the grocery store and select tunafish or chicken, a course of action generally preferred to receiving a package of food chosen by an agency.

Freedom of choice increases with affluence. As smaller proportions of family income are needed for the basic supports to life, more can be used as resources for reaching other goals. With a little more money than what is needed for subsistence, the poor family heads could have more control over where they live. They would look for more comfortable quarters to rent. With additional funds they might buy a house, and this step would open up many choices for arrangements and making improvements in home management. Freedom to buy a house could mean having a wider choice of neighborhoods and schools. Money could mean all of this!

Children's freedom of choice is also affected by the amount of money available to them. At six or seven years of age, a universal time for transition into middle childhood, experiences with money and choice begin to form the child's foundations of money management.

**Pleasure.**   Enjoy yourself! You can't take it with you! Money is only a means to an end, and that end is having a good time and making others happy, provided they have access to unlimited funds. Since few people are so affluent, the goal of *happiness today,* with money as the means, can precipitate financial crises and disasters.

**Unimportance.**   Money does not matter. The Lord will provide, or someone else will. This meaning is similar to the meaning of money as pleasure, in that management does not enter significantly into the picture. One life style in which this meaning is truly functional is that of the religious ascetic. The cloistered nun and the holy beggar do not need to plan because money has no meaning for them and someone else does the managing and providing that sustains their lives. For a family, however, money cannot be stripped of significance, but it can be given more or less emphasis. When counterculture families choose a simple, rural, perhaps communal life style, they minimize the importance of money.

**Power.**   Money can be the means of dominating other people. Money is power to the industrialist who enjoys managing a business empire, to the old person whose heirs are submissive in anticipation of future gain, and to the child who can buy treats for docile peers. Research suggest that in some cultures (but not others) high earnings increase a husband's decision-making power [21] and that the same is true for wives [18].

**Prestige.**   Similar to power, but not identical, prestige means being recognized as important, being looked up to, being respected. When a person thinks of money as bringing prestige, he has to have some way of letting other people know that he has money. He can carry out conspicuous consumption or flashy spending, make well-publicized contributions to charity, and let the amount of his earnings be known. Prestige was found to be a key to satisfaction of highly paid executives, most of whom were dissatisfied with salaries of less than $50,000 [14]. At any income level, some persons try to gain prestige by buying things that will impress other people. One buys an expensive car, another clothing, another a color television, and another an elaborate barbecue. Living in a particular neighborhood, or going to an expensive college, may be a dominant goal. Often when buying for prestige reasons, people buy on time, go into debt, and otherwise strain their financial resources. Many women, suffering from low self-esteem, find that when they earn a good income from a job they gain prestige with other people and thereby think more of themselves.

**Compensation.** Although the ordinary meaning of compensation is pay for work done, money may also mean compensation for deprivation, jealousy, and other hurt feelings. The young woman who marries a rich old man gives up the possibility of marrying a young, vigorous husband, but is compensated by more luxurious support and the prospects of a large inheritance. The secretly unfaithful man buys present for his partner. The neglected wife spends recklessly on clothes, make-up, and expensive furnishings, partly to make herself feel better and partly to punish her husband. She thus compensates herself for deprivation by him.

**Self-Development.** When growth of the individual personality is important, money may be looked upon as a means to this end. A person might use money to pay for taking courses, getting a degree, learning a skill or sport, taking a trip, purchasing books or materials for arts and crafts, or going to concerts and plays.

## Earning and Producing

Income is important to satisfaction! If any reader is doubtful of this, research shows that as income increases so does the homemaker's satisfaction with her level of living [7]. It is also no surprise to find that if she thought she had enough money, she felt good about it. Satisfactions connected with earning and producing include more than getting the money or things needed and wanted. Satisfactions depend on the meanings of money, as outlined in the first section of this chapter, and also upon the special interests, skills, tastes, and needs of the individuals involved. I (MSS) knit socks and sweaters and sew my own dresses because I enjoy producing these items. Since it would cost more to buy them than to make them, I am producing the equivalent of money. If my purpose were to make as much money as I could, however, I would do better to spend the time teaching or writing, instead of knitting and sewing. The satisfaction brought by my handwork makes it worthwhile, even though it represents a deplorable hourly wage.

The same could be said of a person's choice of jobs or of life style. Evelyn graduated with honors and a teacher's certificate, but she went to work and lived in a rural commune, where she earned no money and received only bed and board. Carlos turned down a promotion with a big raise because the new job would have required him to be away from home frequently. Being with Margarita and the children was more satisfying to him than the extra money, prestige, and power offered by the new position.

**Income Is More Than Money.** Economists define **real income** as "a flow of commodities and services available for the satisfaction of human wants and needs over a given period of time" [6, pp. 487–493]. Thus, a family might have a very comfortable real income even when its cash earnings were small. As Figure 8-4 shows, real income includes social income, barter, fringe benefits, cash, and home-produced services. *Social income* is income provided by the community, paid for by the taxpayer. It includes clinics, schools, museums, police, fire protection, municipal garbage collection, and so forth. *Fringe benefits* are provided by the employer in lieu of a larger salary or wage. Because the employee does not pay taxes on fringe benefits, and because benefits usually include insurance that is costly for the individual to purchase, a good fringe benefits package is valuable to the employee. Cash income comes from *wages, interest,* and *profits,* and is used to purchase *durable goods* such as a house, car, and appliances; *consumable goods* such as food, restaurant meals, and bought clothing; and services such as legal, medical, and repair services. *Home-produced services,* too, are a part of real income, and include housework, child care, maintenance, gardening, and the construction of homemade clothing. An alternative method of acquiring goods or services is through *barter,* in which a good or service is exchanged for either a good or a service from another person.

For example, Beth and Larry earn cash (part of their market income) by teaching and by selling maple syrup, hay, and lambs. They produce goods for their own use that include maple syrup, all the vegetables they eat, lamb to eat, flowers, Christmas trees for themselves and their friends, wood for the fireplaces, and some clothing. The services they perform include cooking, dishwashing, cleaning, laundering, child care, painting, carpentering, snow shoveling, and entertaining. The children, too, perform some services, such as table-setting, dishwashing, and emptying sap buckets during the sugaring season. The durable goods that they own are also producers of real income, since without their house, two cars, barns, farmland, tractor, freezer, washer, and so on, they would have to spend a great deal more cash in order to live

**FIGURE 8-4**    Real income comes from many sources.

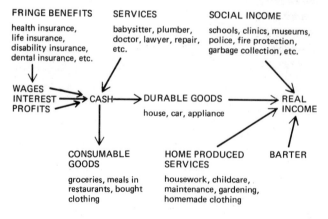

Community activities, such as this travelling theater, represent one form of social income!

as they do. Social income consists of facilities provided by the community or the environment, such as parks, schools, police protection, and libraries. Living in a rural area, Beth and Larry are limited in such facilities, but they have a county agent who helps them with farming problems, state parks, a good road that is plowed after snowstorms, and a free view of beautiful mountains. In addition to their money income from their salaries and the fringe benefits that go with their salaries, their income also includes the products of *barter*. Both give services to a cooperative school, where other parents also give of their talents to all the children enrolled. They exchange goods and services with their neighbors, making deals on the use of land, barns, farm machinery, and labor.

Every family can identify some income that is not money. Many people do not realize that services are equivalent to money. If they did, then the housework that women do would be regarded more highly and people might feel more worthwhile for doing it. By estimating what it would cost to hire someone else to perform those services, investigators at Cornell University figured that when only the husband was employed outside, the household work of both was worth $8800, of which $7600 was contributed by the wife and $1200 by the husband [4]. When the wife also had an outside job for fifteen hours or more weekly, her contribution through work at home was worth $6200 and the husband's $1300. Since estimates were based on 1967 prices, the amounts would be much greater today. And these were modest estimates. For example, pay for child care was figured at the rate of a low-paid worker rather than a skilled teacher, which many mothers are.

## Planning and Spending

What shall we buy? How much shall we pay? Who will purchase what? These are decisions that have to be made, based on the family's goals. An overall plan, designed to fit the *real income,* has to answer these questions for both the short term and the long term. Policies cover general methods of procedure, such as that one person will be responsible for day-to-day decisions about buying food, but that the couple or the family will make joint decisions about large items, such as cars and furniture. A budget is a plan for spending and saving money. Since saving is usually done in order to have something to spend in the future, a budget is a way of allocating money and timing its use.

**Budgeting.** When a couple first establish a partnership and begin living together, they have to take some actions with cash income. As we have discussed in an earlier section of this chapter, decisions must be made regarding who will earn the cash income and who will do the household tasks. If children are added to the family, who will care for them?

The necessity of allocating resources continues throughout all stages of life. The following procedures in budgeting are recommended by Gross, Crandall, and Knoll [6, pp. 554–577]: estimate funds available for spending, estimate expenditures, compare requirements and resources, review the plan as a whole. A year is a convenient time interval for planning, since some types of income and outgo occur on a yearly rather than a monthly or weekly basis. Detailed plans can be made by week, month, or pay period, more general plans for a year, and some plans for the whole family-life career. Indeed, some plans will even be made for the lineage family, but more likely by older families rather than younger.

When *estimating funds* available for spending, all sources should be included. Salaries and wages form the bulk of income for most people, but there may also be pensions, Social Security, disability payments, and interest from investments. We are assuming that the family budget reflects a partnership and that the couple pool what each earns, rather than thinking of any income as "my money." Since most family incomes fluctuate from year to year, the best estimate will probably not be exact.

Overestimation of income leads to overspending. Therefore, it is better to err on the low side.

The *estimation of expenditures* is more complicated than estimating income, since it covers such a multitude of goods and services. One way to begin is to delay making a budget until a record of expenditures has been kept for a few weeks or months. Fixed items, of course, must be listed first and classified in terms of time: monthly items, such as rent and essential transportation, and yearly amounts, such as insurance and taxes. Debts must be paid on a regular schedule. Appendix C, on pages 500–501, is a form developed at Cornell University for organizing payments that must be made and relating them to expected income [25]. All promised payments are to be listed at the times when they must be paid. When the list of promised payments for each pay period is subtracted from the income expected, the remainder is what is available for other purposes. It may be more convenient to divide the promised payments differently, so as to even out the remainders from each pay period.

Remainders can then be divided into amounts, needed regularly for food, clothing, personal allowances, recreation, education, contributions, savings, transportation, insurance, and miscellaneous. Some families will have additional categories. If a record of expenditures has been kept, amounts needed in each slot will be easy to estimate. If they add up to more than the remainder of income after deducting promised payments, some categories must be reduced.

*Balancing the budget* means working out a harmonious relation between requirements and resources. Upon adding both columns, if requirements exceed resources, then requirements have to be cut down or resources increased, or both. Expenses may be cut down by making use of social income or by using human resources. For example, money that was spent on movies could be channeled for basic necessities, and books taken from the library could provide entertainment. Instead of using packaged frozen cooked chicken, whole chicken could be purchased, cooked, and frozen to be thawed out when needed. Resources might be increased by the employment of additional family members, or by moonlighting by family members who are already employed. The benefits of added income must be weighed against the additional expenses incurred, as we have discussed on pages 238–239. Of course, some families' resources are so minimal that standards can't be further reduced.

Relations between present and future must also be kept in some sort of balance. A disastrous, and not-too-infrequent, solution to present imbalance is heavy use of credit that piles up an even bigger load of requirements for the future. Using credit means using goods or services now and paying in the future. Credit is, in effect, borrowing money, and charges are made for it just as interest is normally charged on any loan. Lenders are legally required to tell borrowers how much interest they are charging and what is the rate of interest, not just the lump sum. The borrower can then decide whether the extra cost of buying the car or television on credit is worth it. If a family decides to buy on credit, then its budget will have to include interest charges. If the family can wait to accumulate enough money for cash payments, or payment at the end of the month of purchase, it will be able to get along with lower expenditures.

There are some exceptions to the rule of saving by paying cash. Many sellers who accept credit cards or offer charge accounts do not give reductions for cash payment, even though it costs them more to have a customer charge an item than to have him pay cash. The result is that the customer can delay payment for a month or more without extra cost and actually has more money available to use. The drawback for many people is that they yield to impulse buying when the money does not have to be paid immediately. With strong-mindedness and careful planning, however, credit cards and charge accounts can be made to give a family financial flexibility without extra cost. Additional advantages include accurate records and protection in case of faulty merchandise. Therefore, credit must be included in considering funds available for spending. In order to open a charge account or obtain a credit card, an individual has to have a good credit rating, a way of showing that he is likely to pay his debts. A previous record of paying bills promptly is the quickest path to a good credit rating.

Sometimes present debt is offset by reduction of future requirements, as in buying a washing machine on credit in order to save paying a diaper service and making trips to a laundromat. A house mortgage is often an economical debt, the means of saving money that would have been spent in rent. A loan for further education is likely to result in a larger income.

Savings can also be considered as available for spending, if deemed necessary. Because savings are usually accumulated for emergencies and long-term goals, there would have to be a careful assessment before spending them on daily living.

*Evaluating the budget* means reviewing the whole plan from time to time, to see if it is satisfying family and personal needs in the best ways possible. As conditions change in the family and in the systems outside the family, changes in the budget are required. When a new baby is planned, or expected even if unplanned, all categories need adjusting, not only the cash expenditures but also the use of human resources or services. Likewise, when children grow up and the mother can spend more hours in a job, a complete reassessment of the flow of commodities and services is in order. A continuing question is that of sharing work in such a way that burdens and responsibilities are fair to all, to the couple and to the children.

The budget can serve as the focus for communicating and deciding about all sorts of matters basic to satisfying family life. In coordinating the flow of commodities and services from resources into family action, family members have recurring chances to consider everyone's present and future needs as well as attaining a degree of financial security.

## Savings and Investments

During times of crisis, a family has to call upon special ways of coping. A financial crisis occurs when there is not enough money to take care of present needs. Unemployment or illness can precipitate a financial crisis.

In an extended family or in closely knit communities, relatives or neighbors take care of the family in crisis. They give food, nursing care, shelter, or whatever is needed, even though they may share at some inconvenience and cost to themselves. The young man who was helper to our Indian cook had two younger brothers living with him, his wife, and his baby in a one-room shack. In justifying the large families in Samoa, the father of eleven children explained, "Here, our children are our treasure. We don't put our money in banks but into our families." In traditional societies such as Samoa, younger generations and kin assume responsibility for the aged.

North American nuclear families help their needy relatives, but not to such a great extent, and with less feeling of duty. There is a fairly strong feeling among young couples that they would like to stand on their own feet financially if they possibly can, although they would probably ask for help from their parents if they were in great need.

Savings, money set aside for future use, are used by some families to tide them over a period of crisis. Others borrow. An educational loan may be had for little or no interest while a student equips himself for a job that will enable him to repay the loan. A family may mortgage its house or put a higher mortgage on it in order to get money for an emergency.

## Insurance

When major financial crises occur, few families have enough saved to avoid financial disaster through their own efforts. Therefore, families must depend upon insurance to protect them against the risks that they are not willing or able to assume themselves. Many employees have varying kinds and amounts of insurance included in their fringe benefits packages. Persons who do not receive insurance as fringe benefits find that insurance requires heavy expenditures for the individual buyer.

*Group health insurance plans* are provided by many employers, unions, credit unions, colleges and universities, and other organizations. The employer or organization may pay all or part of the premiums, or may simply make the plan available for purchase by the individual or family. The extent of paid coverage provided by an employer is as important to consider as the salary or wage that is provided, since the employee does not have to pay taxes on fringe benefits.

A major principle of buying insurance is that the buyer should try to purchase as much protection for as little money as possible. Insurance policies vary widely in premium costs and in the kinds of risks that are insured against. Comparison shopping and careful reading of policies are important. Large deductibles and many exclusions render a policy less valuable but also less expensive. The cost of purchasing broader protection should always be considered relative to the probability of a given risk's occurrence, as well as the insured person's ability financially to handle a given expense should it occur.

For example, consider automobile insurance. If you have a fixed amount in mind to spend on car insurance, it is a wiser choice to buy more liability insurance and somewhat less collision. Imagine that in the same year you are at fault in two accidents. In the first accident, you cause damage of $150,000 in medical expenses to another person. If your liability insurance is for $75,000, you will probably be in debt for the rest of your life, since you would be personally responsible for the balance not paid by your insurance company. Your second hypothetical accident is less tragic. This time, you back your car into a telephone pole and must replace a fender. If you had purchased $100 deductible insurance, the insurance company would pay a larger proportion of the cost of a new fender than it would if you had purchased $200 deductible. But you would be better able to afford paying $200 toward a new fender than you would be able to afford paying many thousands of dollars of medical expenses for which you would be liable in the first accident.

The purchase of insurance can be confusing to even the well-informed buyer. Our main purpose here is to alert the reader to the necessity of having some insurance protection in order to avoid financial disaster should a major fiscal crisis occur. We recommend that before insurance is purchased, the reader look further into the topic. A personal finance textbook or consumer-oriented publication is suggested. Most insurance agents are not unscrupulous, but they *are* in business to make a profit. It will benefit the consumer to be well-informed. We now discuss some of the major kinds of insurance available to the consumer.

**Health Insurance.** Hospitalization/medical insurance pays for expenses due to illness or accident. The costs of an accident can strain or ruin a family budget, and catastrophic illness incurs costs that are almost incomprehensible. Costs of health care have risen out of proportion to the rest of inflation, making some kinds of health insurance essential for all individuals and families. Many people and their families are covered by insurance packages that come as part of their fringe benefits from employment. Such packages vary in their coverage, and it may be necessary for additional coverage to be purchased privately. We list and briefly describe some of the most common kinds of health insurance.

1. *Hospitalization* insurance is the most common kind of health insurance in the United States. It pays a portion of per-day hospital charges and of expenses such as use of the operating room, laboratory tests, X-rays, and medicine taken while in the hospital. It may also pay for some outpatient care [5, p. 514].

2. *Surgical expense insurance* covers all or part of surgical expenses. By paying a higher premium, a larger portion of the expense of surgery is covered.

3. *Regular medical expense insurance* provides for the cost of a physician's nonsurgical services in a hospital, at home, in a clinic, or in the doctor's office. First visits are usually not covered.

4. *Major medical insurance* provides coverage for relatively large amounts resulting from accidents or sickness. Three out of four Americans are covered with some kind of major medical insurance. Because of the large coverage provided by major medical insurance, the deductible is large ($500 to $1000 per accident or illness) [5, pp. 516–517]. In addition, the insured individual pays a portion of the expense (10–20 per cent).

5. *Comprehensive major medical insurance* combines basic hospital, medical, and surgical expenses with major medical protection. The deductible is usually relatively small, $100 or less. This kind of insurance is usually available under a group plan.

6. *Dental insurance* covers dental health care and care of dental injuries, and like comprehensive major medical insurance is available through group plans.

The above kinds of health insurance coverage are provided by commercial insurance agencies, by nonprofit Blue Cross and Blue Shield plans, and to a lesser extent by consumer cooperatives and community organizations. A new but growing trend in the American health insurance picture is the Health Maintenance Organization (HMO), a group medical practice that provides health maintenance and remedial care to members who pay a monthly fee. The fee entitles them to checkups and services as needed. Members pay the monthly fee (which ranged from $50 to $70 per month in 1975) whether or not they use the services. HMOs provide preventive medicine, and studies indicate that preventive care *is* better than treatment-oriented cure. Members of HMOs have better health, fewer premature deaths, and lower perinatal mortality rates [5, p. 530].

The U.S. Federal Government also provides insurance benefits to some citizens. *Medicare,* a part of Social Security, provides basic hospital insurance and supplementary medical insurance for persons over 65. There are many exclusions in coverage and large deductibles, and the insured person is required to pay a portion of the costs. Elderly persons who can afford to purchase supplementary coverage privately should consider it. *Medicaid* is provided by the federal and state governments for the very poor, primarily recipients of cash assistance benefits. Covered services are highly variable among the 50 states.

As can be seen, health coverage is available from a number of sources. Many individuals have some protection from one type of plan, and other protection from other plans. Frequently, coverage has some overlap and some gaps. In planning a health insurance program, the kind of benefits that the individual already has from various plans should be listed. Dual coverage should be avoided if possible, and gaps should be filled. In addition, particular health needs of the individual or family should be considered, as should the expense of the entire plan.

**Unemployment Insurance.**   When a family breadwinner is unemployed owing to sickness, disability, accident, or lay-off, other sources of income are needed for family maintenance. It may be possible for another family member to work, or the employee may be covered by various kinds of unemployment insurance. Some employers provide disability insurance, which pays all or part of the wage or salary when absence from work is caused by disability, sickness, or accident; others provide a given number of days annually for sick leave. Workmen's compensation pays part of lost wages when a work-related injury has been sustained. Unemployment insurance pays part of lost wages when an employee has been laid off (and, in some states, dismissed).

Social Security is usually thought of as a retirement system. However, it provides coverage for losses due to disability. When a worker who is insured under Social Security suffers total disability that has lasted at least five months and is expected to last at least 12 months, he or she will receive Social Security payments that will equal between 40 and 80 per cent of the lost salary or wages. When the above kinds of protection are not available, an individual should consider purchasing a disability income insurance policy from a commercial insurance agency. Although these policies are expensive, they make good sense for some individuals, particularly the self-employed.

**Life Insurance.** The most important aspect of life insurance is the provision of protection against financial loss incurred by the death of the breadwinner or home-maker. Some insurance policies provide other benefits as well, such as being able to cash the policy in for money while the insured person is still living. This kind of protection is more expensive than basic protection against loss of the breadwinner or homemaker.

The lowest cost protection is provided by *term insurance,* which pays a certain amount of money if the insured person dies during the term or period of coverage. At the end of the term, coverage ceases. Term insurance is especially useful to cover a family when the loss of the breadwinner would be a special financial hardship, for example, when children are growing up and one parent stays home to care for them. Even when both parents are employed, the death of one is likely to impose a financial hardship; hence, the lives of both might be insured. A couple may plan that if an employed spouse dies, the children will pay for their own college expenses. Or, 25-year term insurance might be purchased when the first child is born, to make sure that if a breadwinner dies at any time during the child's first 25 years, a payment will be received by the family. Term insurance might also be purchased on the life of a homemaker whose services to the family would be expensive to replace, especially when children are young.

*Whole life insurance,* more expensive than term coverage, offers financial protection for the individual's entire life. As with term insurance, a payment is made in the event of the insured person's death. In addition, the policy has a *cash value* which is based upon the amount paid in by the insured person, plus interest. The cash value increases the longer a policy is held. Insurance salesmen point out to potential buyers that it is possible for the insured person to borrow money against the insurance policy, and that a whole life policy is a form of savings. Both statements are true, but a price is paid in each case. If Ms. Cameron borrows $5000 against the cash value of her insurance policy in order to buy a car, and is then killed in an accident, her beneficiary gets the face value (the amount for which her life was insured) *minus* the $5000 that she has already borrowed. In order for Ms. Cameron to borrow $5000, the cash value of her policy must be slightly more than that. She will still pay interest on the loan, between 5 and 8 per cent per year [5, p. 484]. The savings feature of whole life insurance also has a cost. The interest rates paid by insurance companies are always lower than interest rates available for passbook savings accounts at bank and credit unions. The savings feature of whole life insurance is beneficial only to those persons who can't discipline themselves to save otherwise.

As with other kinds of insurance, the type purchased should fit the needs of the family. Protection should be largest when the death of the breadwinner or homemaker would be particularly difficult financially. Life insurance plans are often included as a part of fringe benefits of employment. Most life insurance policies are variations or combinations of term and whole life insurance.

**Loss of Property Insurance.** When a person owns property, whether it is a house, household furnishings, a car, or a valuable stamp collection, it is a good idea to have protection against its loss from fire, theft, and other perils. The greater the value of the property, the more hardship is likely to be caused if it should be lost. When a large purchase such as a house or car is made "on time," lenders insist that such insurance be purchased, since the buyer is responsible for payments even if the property is destroyed. Renters policies are also available.

**Liability Insurance.** Most states require that automobile owners purchase liability insurance to protect themselves in the event that the car owners are at fault in an accident. As we have noted, it is important to purchase adequate automobile liability insurance, because being at fault in an accident can financially ruin a non-protected individual. Owners of land, homes, and buildings may purchase liability insurance to protect against being sued by someone who is injured on the property. Other forms of liability insurance include protection against libel and slander, and malpractice insurance.

## Financial Security in Old Age

Part of every savings program should be geared toward financial protection for old age. Although Social Security benefits provide about a third of a retired couple's income [3], most people need additional resources. Pension plans from places of employment provide support for some persons, but such incomes are *fixed;* that is, there is no allowange for inflation. Many other workers are not protected by employee pension plans. Such persons may plan on their own through saving, investing, and insuring. If plans are made in accord with requirements of the U.S. government (Keogh plans for the self-employed, Individual Retirement Accounts for wage earners and homemakers), American individuals are eligible for income tax benefits during their working years.

## Some Persons Lack Protection

Through no fault of their own, some individuals and families are unable to respond to financial crises or to save for old age. Sometimes families whose resources are adequate find themselves similarly unprotected. Here, the problem may be attributed to poor planning. Few families, however, can save enough money to tide them over when a real financial disaster strikes, such as catastrophic illness. Illness cannot cause a financial disaster in England, New Zealand, Canada, and other places where medical and hospital services are underwritten by the government. In the United

States public assistance provides a minimum support for some families and individuals, but the official poverty line is extremely low. The only universal benefit is food stamps, but most food stamp users purchase the stamps with cash. Many people think that there is a stigma attached to welfare and find the conditions of receiving it humiliating or at least annoying. They would prefer to receive unemployment insurance, sickness insurance, or some sort of support to which they feel entitled.

**SUMMARY**  Family members both consume and produce goods and services. Work inside and outside of the home influences family members. Factors outside of individual control that influence family economic functioning include the financial status and social class of one's parents, gender, race, age, the functioning of the workplace, and the state of the economy. Women and racial minorities suffer from job discrimination. Income varies by age of worker. The work place influences the amount of income and benefits a worker will receive, how much free time and energy will be left from the job, and childrearing practices. The economy affects all persons.

Factors under individual control include occupational choices and the division of household tasks. Much family interaction is concerned with household work. Employed wives generally have worked longer hours per day than have employed husbands, and usually have responsibility for household tasks even when the tasks are performed by another person. Younger husbands are more likely to have egalitarian attitudes than are older ones. Among wives, work commitment has increased and enjoyment of housework has decreased.

Being employed costs money, but has benefits other than increased family income. Family members must communicate about task division and production of family resources.

Good financial planning is important for family functioning. Money means different things to different people, and can be a source of conflict. Real income, however, is more than money, and includes social income, fringe benefits, wages, interest, profits, durable goods, home-produced services, and barter.

A budget is an orderly way of allocating resources for both short-term and long-term use. Setting up a budget is one of the important economic tasks of new partners. Maintaining it is a continuing responsibility. Both processes require identifying joint goals, making plans and decisions, acting, and evaluating. The welfare of the family is heavily dependent on the adequacy of financial management, as well as upon the size of real income.

Financial crisis often can be avoided through savings, investing, and insurance. Families need adequate health insurance to cover possible expenses from illness and accident. Other important kinds of insurance are unemployment insurance, life insurance, loss of property insurance, and liability insurance. Many employers supply health, unemployment, and life insurance, but additional protection may be needed. The most important years for having adequate life insurance protection are those in which children are growing up. It is also important to plan for financial security in old age.

**REFERENCES**

1. Almquist, Elizabeth M. Women in the labor force. *Signs,* 1977, **2,** 843–855.
2. Andrisani, Paul J. Job satisfaction among working women. *Signs,* 1978, **3**:3, 588–607.
3. Cohen, Jerome. *Personal finance: Principles and case problems.* Homewood, Ill.: Irwin, 1975.
4. Gauger, William. Household work: Can we add it to the GNP? *Journal of Home Economics,* 1973, **65**:7, 12–15.
5. Gitman, Lawrence J. *Personal finance.* Hinsdale, Ill.: Dryden, 1978.
6. Gross, Irma H., Elizabeth W. Crandall, and Marjorie M. Knoll. *Management for modern families.* New York: Meredith, 1973.
7. Halstrom, Jeanne L. and Marilyn M. Dunsing. Level of living: Factors influencing the homemaker's satisfaction. *Home Economics Research Journal,* 1973, **2,** 119–132.
8. Hayghe, Howard. Families and the rise of working wives—An overview. *Monthly Labor Review,* 1976, **99**:5, 12–19.
9. Heckman, Norma A., Rebecca Bryson, and Heff B. Bryson. Problems of professional couples: A content analysis. *Journal of Marriage and the Family,* 1977, **39,** 323–330.
10. Holstrom, Lynda Lytle. *The two career family.* Cambridge, Mass: Schenkman, 1972.
11. Hopkins, Jane and Priscilla White. The dual-career couple: Constraints and supports. *Family Coordinator,* 1978, **27,** 253–259.
12. Hunt, Morton M. Making a living versus making a home. *Redbook,* 1978, **148,** 70–73 (April).
13. Igelhard, Alfreda. Married women and work: 1957 and 1976. Unpublished PhD. dissertation, U. of Michigan, 1978.
14. Lawler, Edward E. How much money do executives want? In Helena Z. Lopata (Ed.) *Marriage and families.* New York: Van Nostrand, 1973.
15. Lopata, Helena Z. *Occupation: Housewife.* New York: Oxford U.P., 1971.
16. McAdoo, Harriette Pipes. The impact of upward mobility on the reciprocal obligations of kin-help patterns in Black families. *Journal of Marriage and the Family,* 1978, **40,** 761–776.
17. Miller, Daniel and Guy Swanson. The changing American parent. New York: Wiley, 1958.
18. Oppong, Christine. *Marriage among a matrilineal elite.* London: Cambridge U.P., 1974.
19. Rolfe, David J. The financial priorities inventory. *Family Coordinator,* 1974, **23,** 139–144.
20. Rubin, Lillian Breslow. *Worlds of pain: Life in the working class family.* New York: Basic, 1976.
21. Safilios-Rothschild, Constantina. The study of family power structure: A review 1960–1969. *Journal of Marriage and the Family,* 1970, **32,** 539–552.
22. U.S. Bureau of the Census. *Current population reports.* Series P-60, No. 83. Washington, D.C.: U.S. Government Printing Office, July 1972.
23. U.S. Bureau of the Census. *Money income and poverty status of families and persons in the United States: 1977* (Advance Report). Current population reports. Consumer income. Series P-20, No. 116. Washington, D.C.: U.S. Government Printing Office, 1978.
24. Walker, Kathryn E. Household work time: Its implication for family decisions. *Journal of Home Economics,* 1973, **65**:7, 7–11.
25. Wiegand, Elizabeth. *Preview your spending.* Cornell Extension Bulletin 1143. Ithaca, N.Y.: Cornell U., 1968.

# CHAPTER 9
# splitting and splicing

Many persons who are concerned that the family is becoming obsolete point to the divorce rate as incriminating evidence. It is true that a large number of families are touched by divorce. It is also true that divorce is hard on adults and children alike. However, since most divorced persons eventually remarry, those people who end one marriage usually want to be married, although to a different person. In this chapter we examine divorce and remarriage.

## PROBABILITY OF DIVORCE

Exactly what a person's chances are of being divorced cannot be predicted safely for a number of reasons. It is common to read that one in two marriages end in divorce. These figures, however, are misleading. They are arrived at by comparing the number of marriages in a given registration area (or the entire nation) with the number of divorces during the same time period.

For example, last year in a given city 1000 persons married, and 400 persons obtained a divorce. The figures 400/1000 equals two fifths, or two divorces per five marriages. However, the 400 persons who obtained a divorce represent marriages that began many years earlier, two years ago, five years ago, fifteen years ago, and perhaps even fifty years ago. These marriages from previous years represent a different population (group) of people from the marriages of last year, and cannot be compared with each other.

To further illustrate this point, consider the divorce and marriage rates in a second hypothetical city. In this city last year, there were 1000 marriages and 1500

divorces. From these figures, can we conclude that each marriage ended in divorce one and a half times? Of course not!

A more accurate way of determining the probability of divorce is to follow each person through her various marriages, counting the times the person is married and divorced. We might thus examine the marital record of a woman who married in 1910. When this individual dies, we will know her marital record. Unfortunately, we cannot accurately predict for other persons from this person's record, because the group of persons who married for the first time in 1920, most of whom are dead by now, cannot be compared with this year's crop of brides and grooms. Those married in 1920 were culturally different from the new spouses of today, and experienced different events, such as World Wars I and II and the Depression.

Another method is to count the number of marriages and divorces among a group of persons who were married a given number of years. A 1971 study found that of persons married at least 20 years, four out of five had been married only once. Ninety per cent of the men and 80 per cent of the women were still married after at least 20 years of marriage.* About 15 per cent of the men, and 17 per cent of the women under 70 who had been married at some point had also been divorced [24]. These figures cannot be used with accuracy to predict the present generation's probability of getting a divorce, but they can be used to show the danger of predicting divorce with the present-divorce-to-present-marriage ratio.

*The difference in the numbers of still married persons results from the fact that men tend to die before their wives.

Another way of reporting divorce statistics is number of divorces per 1000 population (the *divorce rate*). We cannot predict future number of divorces from such statistics, but we can observe past trends. Table 9-1 shows the number of divorces per 1000 population from 1935 to 1977. The 1935 figure, 1.7 divorces per 1000 population reflects the low divorce rate during the Depression, and the 3.5 figure in 1945 reflects the high divorce rate following World War II.

Over the past 50 to 60 years, the number of divorced persons and the divorce rate have increased. As can be seen by looking at Figure 9-1, the divorce rate has had dips and peaks since 1921. The high rate of divorces in 1945–46 reflects the return of servicemen from World War II. Similarly, the increase of divorces that began in the 1960s and continued until 1977 was due in part to the liberalization of divorce laws in many states.

## FACTORS RELATED TO DIVORCE

Such explanations, however, are overly simple. Many other factors have contributed to the overall rise in divorce, and to its various peaks and dips. The age make-up of

**TABLE 9-1**      **Number of Divorces per 1000 Population, United States, for Reporting States and Divorce Registration Areas**

| Year (12-month period ending August) | Divorces per 1000 Population |
|---|---|
| 1977 | 5.0 |
| 1976 | 5.0 |
| 1975 | 4.9 |
| 1974 | 4.6 |
| 1973 | 4.4 |
| 1972 | 4.1 |
| 1970 | 3.5 |
| 1965 | 2.5 |
| 1960 | 2.2 |
| 1955 | 2.3 |
| 1950 | 2.6 |
| 1945 | 3.5 |
| 1940 | 2.0 |
| 1935 | 1.7 |

*Source:* U.S. Department of Health, Education and Welfare and Public Health Service Vital Statistics of the United States.

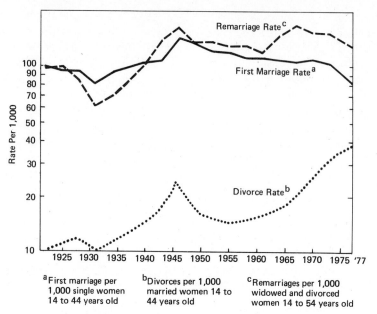

**FIGURE 9-1**    Rates of first marriage, divorce, and remarriage for U.S. women: 1921–
1977.

*Source:* P. C. Glick and A. J. Norton. Marrying, divorcing, and living together in the U.S. today. *Population Bulletin,*
1977, 32:5, Figure 1.

the population and the number of marriages in the previous decade both influence
the divorce rate. Since the divorce rate is the number of divorces per 1000 people,
the number of married people in the population influences the divorce rate. As we
shall see, young marriages are most vulnerable to divorce. Therefore, when there are
many young people in the population, we would expect a high divorce rate, since
half of all divorces occur within the first seven years of marriage.

Changes in attitudes have doubtless contributed to the overall trend toward
more divorce. The disgrace that accompanied divorce 50 or even 25 years ago is no
longer as severe. The divorcing person is likely to know someone who has been
divorced, or even to have a family member who has been divorced. Women, more
able to earn their own livings than they were a generation ago, are less likely to stay
in an unhappy marriage because of being economically trapped.

In the late 70s there was evidence that the divorce rate was leveling off.
Although the reasons are not clear, the 10 per cent drop in the marriage rate since
1972 is probably a factor [33]. The divorce rate may drop further as the "baby
boom" generation ages. People born between 1943 and 1957 have reached their
mid-20s and beyond. As the youngest of the "baby boom" generation reaches 30
and more, there will be fewer high-risk marriages in the population. We will now
elaborate on factors associated with divorce, beginning with age at marriage.

## Age at Marriage

It has been well established by research that persons marrying below the national average age (about 21 for women, 23 for men) have higher chances of divorce than those who marry when older.

Table 9-2 shows the **median** (the point that divides a group in half) ages of brides and grooms by previous marital status during the years 1963 to 1975. It can be seen the the median age of brides and grooms at their first marriage has risen, and that age of remarriages has dropped.

A nationwide survey made for the Office of Economic Opportunity in 1967 reported that 27 per cent of women who married in their teens, as compared with 14 per cent who married after they had reached their 20s, were divorced within 20 or more years of marriage. The comparable figures for men were 28 per cent who married before the age of 22, versus 13 per cent who married after age 22 [30].

However, women who marry for the first time after age 30 are more likely to divorce within the first 10 years of marriage than are women marrying for the first time in their 20s. Women marrying in their 30s are, however, less likely to divorce than women who marry for the first time at 20 years of age or less [25].

**Reasons for the Failure of Young Marriages.**  It is not the age of the spouses at marriage per se that causes divorce. Those who marry young are more likely to be

TABLE 9-2    **Median Ages of Bride and Grooom by Previous Marital Status, 1963–75**

|  | Median Age of Bride | | | Median Age of Groom | | |
|---|---|---|---|---|---|---|
| Year | Total | First Marriage | Remarriage | Total | First Marriage | Remarriage |
| 1975 | 22.4 | 20.8 | 32.0 | 24.7 | 22.7 | 35.5 |
| 1974 | 22.0 | 20.6 | 32.1 | 24.2 | 22.5 | 35.7 |
| 1973 | 21.9 | 20.6 | 32.3 | 24.1 | 22.5 | 36.3 |
| 1972 | 21.7 | 20.5 | 32.8 | 23.8 | 22.4 | 36.5 |
| 1971 | 21.7 | 20.5 | 32.9 | 23.7 | 22.5 | 36.9 |
| 1970 | 21.7 | 20.6 | 33.3 | 23.6 | 22.5 | 37.5 |
| 1969 | 21.6 | 20.6 | 33.8 | 23.5 | 22.4 | 38.2 |
| 1968 | 21.5 | 20.6 | 33.8 | 23.6 | 22.4 | 38.3 |
| 1967 | 21.4 | 20.5 | 35.0 | 23.8 | 22.6 | 39.1 |
| 1966 | 21.5 | 20.3 | 35.2 | 23.8 | 22.6 | 39.2 |
| 1965 | 21.4 | 20.4 | 35.5 | 23.6 | 22.5 | 39.6 |
| 1964 | 21.4 | 20.4 | 35.6 | 23.6 | 22.4 | 39.7 |
| 1963 | 21.3 | 20.3 | 35.6 | 23.7 | 22.5 | 39.8 |

*Source:* National Center for Health Statistics. *Monthly Vital Statistics Report: Advance Report, Final Marriage Statistics, 1975.* Rockville, Md., U.S. Department of Health, Education, and Welfare, (HRA) 77-1120, Vol. 26, No. 2, Supplement. May 9, 1977, p. 3.

premaritally pregnant, or are more likely to cut short their educations before graduating from high school or college. Not all premaritally pregnant couples are doomed to marital failure, of course, but some marriages that would not have taken place otherwise are forced by an unplanned pregnancy. Furthermore, it is not education that appears to be a crucial factor in determining chances for divorce, but income, which is usually (but not always) linked to the amount of education of the spouses, particularly the male [24].

Teen-age marriages, particularly those begun in high school, are not generally given much social support. Families may give some financial support to the young couple (for example, providing room and board), but if the families of orientation are limited in financial resources, the new family of procreation only can be an added strain. One exploratory study of high school marriages in rural Pennsylvania noted that the young spouses saw themselves as nobodies in the community. They were seldom in trouble with the law, but they just didn't matter much [17].

Early marriage is more prevalent among lower socioeconomic groups than it is among groups of a higher socioeconomic level. Those individuals who go on to college and graduate school are more likely to defer marriage than are those who terminate their formal educations with high school. Deferred marriage gives the couple more time for varied dating experience, which may be a factor in marital success. [5].

Those who marry early express less satisfaction with their marriages than those who marry later. It may be that people who marry young are more divorce-prone because they are not mature enough to handle the responsibilities of marriage. Another explanation, as yet untested by research, is that early marriages that are unhappy are more likely to be abandoned because the individuals involved realize that their chances for remarriage are good [37].

## Length of Marriage

Early marriages are most vulnerable to divorce. The median length of first marriage is around 7 years. This means that half of all divorces occur before 7 years, and half after 7 years. See Table 9-3 for a breakdown of median duration of marriages ended by divorce, by state. Since the divorce process itself takes up to two years, it is apparent that many marriages that end in divorce show signs of trouble quite early. Some people even say that they knew it was a mistake on their wedding day.

## Timing of the First Birth

Couples who conceived their first child before marriage have been found to have a higher divorce rate than those who were not pregnant at the time of marriage [12]. In addition, those who waited to marry for several months after the pregnancy was

**TABLE 9-3**  **Median Duration of Marriage Prior to Divorce or Annulment: Divorce Registration Area and Each Registration State, 1973–75**

[Based on sample data. Medians computed on data by single years, excluding duration of marriage not stated. The divorce-registration area included 29 States in 1973, 1974, and 1975]

| Area | Median Duration of Marriage | | | Area | Median Duration of Marriage | | |
|---|---|---|---|---|---|---|---|
| | 1975 | 1974 | 1973 | | 1975 | 1974 | 1973 |
| Divorce-registration area | 6.5 | 6.5 | 6.6 | Montana | 4.7 | 4.8 | 4.8 |
| | | | | Nebraska | 5.9 | 5.9 | 5.7 |
| Alabama | 4.7 | 5.0 | 5.3 | New York | 8.0 | 8.0 | 8.7 |
| Alaska | 5.1 | 5.1 | 5.3 | Ohio | 6.0 | 6.3 | 6.2 |
| California | 6.8 | 6.7 | 6.9 | Oregon | 5.8 | 5.8 | 5.8 |
| Connecticut | 8.2 | 8.1 | 8.4 | Pennsylvania | 7.7 | 7.7 | 7.6 |
| Georgia | 5.2 | 5.2 | 5.2 | Rhode Island | 7.8 | 8.0 | 8.4 |
| Hawaii | 5.4 | 5.3 | 5.6 | South Carolina | 6.6 | 6.8 | 6.9 |
| Idaho | 4.8 | 4.7 | 4.5 | South Dakota | 5.6 | 5.6 | 5.9 |
| Illinois | 6.1 | 6.1 | 6.5 | Tennessee | 5.3 | 5.2 | 5.2 |
| Iowa | 5.5 | 5.6 | 5.6 | Utah | 4.9 | 4.9 | 4.8 |
| Kansas | 5.2 | 5.2 | 5.2 | Vermont | 7.5 | 7.9 | 7.9 |
| Kentucky | 5.9 | 5.5 | 5.5 | Virginia | 7.7 | 7.8 | 7.9 |
| Maryland | 8.3 | 8.5 | 9.0 | Wisconsin | 7.0 | 7.2 | 7.4 |
| Michigan | 6.8 | 6.7 | 6.6 | Wyoming | 4.7 | 4.8 | 4.5 |
| Missouri | 5.6 | 5.5 | 5.4 | | | | |

*Source:* National Center for Health Statistics. *Vital statistics report. Advance Report: Final divorce statistics,* 1975. U. S. Department of Health, Education, and Welfare, Rockville, Md. (HRA) 77-1120, Vol. 26, No. 2, Supplement 2, May 19, 1977, p. 4.

known had a higher divorce rate than those who married as soon as the pregnancy was confirmed [10]. Those who conceived immediately after marriage had a higher divorce rate than those who waited for several months or years. The longer the interval between marriage and the first birth, the less was the probability of divorce [12].

Black working- and lower-class women who married when already pregnant were twice as likely to divorce within the first two years of marriage as were their classmates who were not premaritally pregnant. Of those women who were pregnant at marriage, marrying the baby's father rather than another man decreased the chance of divorce. Couples who had a close, exclusive relationship prior to pregnancy were also less likely to divorce. These findings suggest that the effect of premarital pregnancy on marital stability must be considered in light of a number of other variables [22].

The long-term effects of early pregnancy (pre- or postmaritally conceived) appear to be less important in terms of whether or not the woman in question is married. Although she may have been divorced and remarried, a mother of a child conceived out of wedlock is about as likely as other mothers to be married and living with her husband, who may or may not be the father of her first child [15].

## Length of Engagement

Older studies, done between the 1930s and the 1950s, indicated that the length of engagement was related to marital success. Couples with no engagement, or an engagement of less than six months, were found to be more likely to have poor marital adjustment if married, or to be divorced, than those who were engaged for over six months [58, pp. 179–180]. Unfortunately, these studies did not control for income level. It is likely that many of those couples who had short engagements also had low incomes, and we cannot be certain which variable (length of engagement or income) had a greater effect on marital stability.

**Purposes.** The purposes of an engagement in our society are to give test to the relationship, both publicly and privately, and to plan and prepare for marriage (see Chapter 6, pages 167–169). Such testing does go on before the formal engagement, but is intensified as the couple moves closer to marriage. Perhaps it is the intensity of the interaction that matters more than the formal engagement. If this is the case, then we speculate that the couple who publicly live together before marriage could achieve the testing purpose, as long as the length and quality of the relationship were adequate, and if the individuals were oriented toward marriage. Some planning would be done on the spot, or perhaps omitted. Preparation would also be curtailed. Physical examinations *could* be made a part of the living together period. Heredity counseling, also, could precede any decision about childbearing.

## Previous Marriage Record

Does having been divorced before increase a person's chances of divorcing a second time? A generation ago, the answer to this question was probably yes [46]. More recent data taken from census figures indicates that second marriages are only slightly less likely to survive than are first marriages. Glick and Norton [25] estimate that about 38 per cent of women now in their late 20s eventually will divorce, and that about 44 per cent of that group will redivorce.

It takes two people to make or break a marriage, although there certainly are cases in which one person contributes more to the breakdown of a relationship. However, it is possible that a quality in a husband that would cause one woman to want a divorce would make another woman happy. The individual who is contemplating marriage with a divorcé should take into consideration the financial and emotional strain that might be caused if the divorcé has another family. On the bright side, remarriages of older persons have been found to be more successful than first marriages, in part because the spouses know what to look for when they choose each other [40].

## Income and Education

Men who have graduated from college or who have gone to graduate school have the greatest marital stability. Similarly, men with higher incomes are less likely to divorce than are men with lower incomes. These relationships do not hold for women. Women with higher incomes and graduate school education are *more* likely to divorce than are women who have income lower than their husbands, or who have not gone to graduate school [25]. One explanation of these differences might be that men do not like being married to women whose earning power threatens theirs. However, a study by Levinger [38] suggests another possible explanation. Levinger found that women whose incomes compared favorably to their husband's were less likely to drop a divorce suit once they had initiated it in court. It is likely, therefore, that women with high earning power are less willing to stay in an unsatisfying marriage because they have more attractive alternatives open to them. Women's increased earning power compared to a generation ago is a commonly cited reason for the rise in divorce [25,32,65].

## Family of Origin's Influence

Children who grew up in families disrupted by death or divorce are more likely to divorce than are children who grew up in intact homes. The differences, however, are not large [52]. Further examination of the data revealed that if a girl's parents divorce, and she has no siblings, she is no more likely to divorce than is a girl whose parents remain married [47]. To explain this finding, the researchers suggest that divorced parents with more than one child have a more difficult time supervising the dating and mate selection activities of their daughters. The single parent with only one daughter is about as able to supervise the daughter as are parents who are still married. The daughter of divorced parents from a multichild family is more likely to choose a less than adequate spouse, and is therefore likely to divorce.

Another influence from the family of origin is social mobility. Men who have less education than either parent are less likely to marry, and to remain married, than are men whose education is equal to their parents' or greater than their parents' [24].

## Number of Children

Data from the 1970 National Fertility Study indicate that women with no children or with large numbers of children are more likely to divorce than are women with moderate numbers of children. Women of both races are especially likely to divorce if they are childless [60]. Having no children does not "cause" divorce. Marriages are most likely to end in the early years of marriage before the birth of children.

## Traditional Values

Persons who actively practice their religion, and who have traditional values, were found in the older studies to be less divorce-prone. Formal weddings were associated with greater marital stability than civil weddings, for example [39]. Values are changing today, more rapidly among some groups than among others. In a society that is moving away from some old traditions, it may be that such old values are no longer as important in determining marital stability. There is evidence that flexibility in the marital relationship is associated with marital *satisfaction,* at any rate [14]

## Mixed Marriages

When marriages do occur across religious and racial lines, are the chances for marital stability affected?

**Religious Intermarriage.**  Since a religion prescribes ways of behaving, as well as interpretations of life, it is logical that spouses from different religions would have more disagreements, conflicts, and problems than a pair of the same religion. Older studies on mixed marriages seemed to bear out this common-sense point of view, generally showing lower survival rates in mixed marriages than in homogamous unions. Nevertheless, mixed religion marriages have increased in frequency and acceptability. More recent and more carefully controlled studies have shown *slightly* higher divorce rates among interfaith marriages in contrast to intrafaith ones, but factors other than religious differences are seen as operating through association with mixed marriage [11]. The following conditions, which are more frequent in interfaith marriages, are also associated with above-average chances of divorce: youth of bride and low income [9], premarital pregnancy, civil marriage ceremony and urban residence, and previous divorce [11, 55]. On the other hand, some people in mixed marriages were older and had higher occupational status. These two characteristics are associated with lower divorce rates. Thus, it would seem that many of the people who enter into mixed marriages are different in background and personality from those who marry within their religion.

**Racial Intermarriage.**  Since the 1967 Supreme Court decision that declared miscegnation laws unconstitutional, there has been a rise in marriage across race lines [2]. The rise in interracial marriages has been especially great for couples consisting of black husbands and white wives. In 1970 there were more than twice as many such couples than there were in 1960 [53].

Divorce rates for black-white marriages are higher than for white-white marriages [51], although a study in a Midwestern state indicated that black-white marriages were more stable than black-black marriages [45]. Once again, however, we need to know the income levels of the couples involved before we can attribute the relative instability to racial combination alone. If we could compare black-black marriages with black-white marriages of the same income level, we might find that their success rates are similar, or, we might not. It may be that black-white couples give more consideration to the suitability of their match than do racially homogamous couples. The interracial couples may "try harder," too.

Hawaii has the highest proportion of interracial marriage in the United States, about 20 per cent. It also has the highest rate of divorce among interracial marriages, also 20 per cent [51]. Since space does not permit an adequate discussion of the dynamics of interracial marriage, the interested reader is referred to two books on the subject [16, 59].

## CHANCES OF DIVORCE: CONCLUSIONS

What causes a marriage to go "on the rocks?" In this section we have briefly noted a number of factors that are associated to varying degrees with broken marriages. Clearly, few if any marriages break up as a result of just one of these factors. There are countless "tremendous trifles" that, when added up, become intolerable to some persons. There is extramarital involvement, which may be a cause or a symptom of marital discord.

The factors that we have described do not necessarily *cause* divorce; no one has proved that they have caused it. They are merely "associated with" divorce: persons who divorce may also happen to be of a different race (or the same race), or have had unhappy childhoods (or happy childhoods). One or the other does nothing to guarantee success or failure. Keeping a marriage afloat takes a great deal of work, caring, and communication on the part of both partners, although again, even these factors do not guarantee success!

We will now take a closer look at failing marriages to learn more about the internal dynamics of marital breakdown. Studying how a marriage fails is difficult. Virtually all studies that deal with the breakdown process have been done retrospectively, that is, after the breakdown process has begun. When asked to report how the marriage began to fail, people's accounts are colored by what has happened since that time.

### Coming Apart

Divorce is usually, but not always, a crisis for those who are involved. Most North American marriages are based on passionate love, with partners who are heavily invested in each other, at least for a while. When such marriages end, the divorces are passionate also. Childless couples who have been married for a short time, however, may escape having a "passionate divorce" [36]. Couples who do not divorce with strong feelings probably were not very heavily invested in the beginning of their marriages. Our discussion of the psychological aspects of divorce are concerned mostly with people who experience "passionate divorce," probably the majority of divorcing persons.

**The Account.** How does it happen that people who mean much to each other become less important to each other? The whole process is so complex that it is almost impossible to describe [62, p. 104]. Accordingly, partners develop what Weiss [65] calls an "account" of what happened. From all of the hurtful interactions that lead to the end of the marriage, some are selected that when put together seem to give a coherent picture of what happened. Persons with more education give more sophisticated explanations of what went wrong with their marriages [32].

Individual members of the same divorcing pair may give such different reasons for the divorce that an outside observer would not realize that the two are talking about the same marriage. Weiss gives the following example:

> In one instance the wife complained that her husband had tried to stop her from improving herself by taking college courses and had attacked her love of books. . . . Her husband, she said, could not comprehend her wanting to stay up to work on a paper or to finish a book. But her husband complained not about her studiousness nor about her passion for literature but about her flirtatiousness. . . . He said that [when they went to parties] he was constantly competing [with other men] for her attention and that sometimes he lost the competition. None of the events significant to him appeared in her account, nor were any of the events significant for her included in his account. [65, p. 15].

Accounts may put all of the blame on the other partner; blame may be shared; or occasionally a divorcing person will take all of the blame. In the Hunts' survey, most respondents placed more blame on the spouse than on themselves, but the blame was stated in terms of incompatibility in tastes, habits, or emotional and sexual needs. Forty per cent of divorced persons gave as an explanation for their divorce that they had drifted apart. Many felt that their marriage had functioned smoothly at first but began to fall apart when the power distribution or roles changed. For example, a wife noted that when she and her husband had a baby, she had less time for her husband and wanted more emotional support from him, which he was unwilling to give. Some respondents placed the blame on "women's issues" such as the wife wanting to further her education or to begin a career, or the wife demanding that the husband share home tasks equally.

Very rare in the 1960s but more common today is a group of divorced persons who give equal blame to each partner. Such persons are more likely to be highly educated and to have had psychotherapy. This group of divorced persons gave reasons such as defective or neurotic interactions between the partners, changes due to personal growth, or incompatibility. Blame for the breakup was viewed with compassion for self and for partner [32].

Weiss [65 p. 15] believes that the construction of an account is "of major psychological importance" to the divorced because it organizes what happened into a unity that is conceptually manageable. What *really* happened is too complex to comprehend. Persons who do not construct accounts remain confused as to what happened, and have a more difficult time recovering from the divorce.

### Deciding to Separate

As marriages fail, marital tensions and dissatisfactions increase for one or both partners. Many couples become quarrelsome. The quarrels have a circular nature. They do not serve to clear the air, but rather to hurt one's partner and increase the partner's pain and/or desire for revenge [62, 65]. Marital intimacy declines. At the same time, partners may want the marriage to continue. Many forces keep marriages together. Among them are the fear of being alone; fear of reactions of one's family, friends, and colleagues; fear of hurting one's children; financial insecurity [65].

The decision to separate may be a mutual agreement that is worked out after the couple decides that the marriage cannot be saved. It may be approached tentatively, or be blurted out during a quarrel, or it may simply happen when one spouse departs. Even when both spouses agree that separation is the best solution, it is usually approached with anxiety [65]. A spouse may move out temporarily, come back, and then leave again. Some couples begin their separation by first moving to separate bedrooms, moving later to separate dwellings.

Once the decision is made by at least one partner, one or both partners may feel a sense of relief or even exhilaration. Interspersed with positive feelings are feelings of anxiety and panic. There may be a period of renewed marital "intimacy," which in reality is the dependent clinging of each partner to the other because of separation anxiety. However, quarrels soon break out again, forcing the partners to accept the inevitability of divorce [36].

### Aspects of the Divorce Process

Divorce is not merely the legal step that renders a married couple unmarried. Bohannan [7] has outlined six "stations" or aspects of the divorce process, which overlap and do not necessarily come in any particular sequence. The *emotional divorce* begins when the partners grow more distant from each other (or, in some cases, when one partner grows more distant from the other). The *legal divorce* occurs in the courtroom, making the husband and wife no longer married. The *economic divorce* is the separation of money and property. The *coparental divorce* deals with custody, visitation, and new styles of parenting. The *community divorce* is concerned with new interaction styles with friends and acquaintances. And finally, the *psychic divorce* involves the separation of one's identity from one's former spouse, and the development of a separate identity. We will now go into each aspect of the divorce process in some detail.

### Emotional Divorce

Emotional divorce is the inverse of the process of falling in love. It has been called "the erosion of love" [65] and "the process of alienation" [62]. Feelings of pleasure that used to come from being near one's spouse become replaced by annoyance, indifference, or hostility. The emotional divorce is usually a gradual process, and may be described as "drifting apart" [32]. It generally precedes the actual separation, and to the extent that both partners have little emotion invested in each other when separation occurs, the separation is made more easily. If one partner leaves the other suddenly, the shock of separation can be as great to the partner left behind as if the leaving partner had died.

The emotional divorce is complicated by the persisting feelings of attachment to the spouse [62, 65]. As discussed in Chapter 2, attachments are formed early in life and continue to be important throughout life. Children whose parents have abused them often express feelings of attachment as well as negative feelings, and the same is true of divorcing adults. An expectation of marriage is the permanent availability of an attachment figure, and the destruction of a marriage leads to distress that the attachment figure is no longer accessible [65, p. 42].

The persistence of attachment becomes especially troublesome after separation. Spouses call each other on the telephone to talk about dividing property, problems with the children, and so forth. They end up talking for half an hour, perhaps quarreling, or perhaps talking only in pleasantries. Or, the spouse who has moved out may come back to pick up an item, to visit the children, or to do a chore. Sometimes the couple will end up in bed with each other, making love, and then fighting. It is all very confusing to those involved.

### Legal Divorce

Legal divorce is an action by a court that terminates a valid marriage. (A valid marriage is a marriage that is recognized in the particular state.) Usually, but not always, questions of child custody, visitation, support, and property are decided at the time of the legal divorce. Legal divorce is easier to obtain when the spouses can agree upon these questions beforehand. Divorce laws vary tremendously from state to state. We can present here only a brief description of legal divorce.

**The Marriage Contract.**   As described on pages 203-205, persons who legally marry (or who live in common-law marriage in the states that recognize such unions) enter into a contractual agreement not only between themselves but with the state as well. Termination of this contract can be done only by the state; that is, by the court. The precise content of the marriage contract is determined by the state in which the couple lives. If a couple are married in Michigan and move to Idaho, the laws of Idaho apply once the couple are residents of that state.

At the present writing, the Equal Rights Amendment has not been ratified by a sufficient number of states to make it a part of the Constitution of the United States. Under ERA, marriage and divorce would require the same responsibilities and give the same rights to men and women. At present in non-ERA states, for example, the wife is required to live in any "suitable" domicile provided by the husband. If he moves to another state and she refuses to follow, it is the wife who has deserted and not the husband [48].

**Separation Agreements.**   In some states, a separation agreement is the first step in the legal divorce process. In other states, couples can divorce without having agreed on division of property, custody, visitation, and support [67]. A separation agreement is a formal document that describes the legal consequences of separation. It is a legally binding private contract that describes the division of "assets and responsibilities accumulated during the marriage" [67, p. 152]. It is also an agreement that the husband and wife will live apart *as if* they are unmarried. For example, each spouse relinquishes the right to entrance into the other's dwelling without the spouse's permission. The separation agreement also determines who will have custody of children, what the visitation rights of the noncustodial parent will be, and how much support is to be paid by whom and when, who will live in the family dwelling and who will move out, and how the family assets will be divided.

If the husband and wife agree beforehand, the judge will base his official order upon this agreement. If they cannot agree, the judge decides the terms. In some states, the separation agreement precedes the divorce, and in others it is a part of the divorce proceedings, or it may become a part of the proceedings upon the request of either party [67, p. 154].

**The Divorce.**   There are two basic kinds of divorce: fault and no-fault. Under fault divorce laws, one spouse is the defendant and the other the plaintiff. The plaintiff must prove that the defendant has broken the matrimonial law of the particular state. For example, if the grounds for divorce in a particular state are (1) adultery and (2) desertion for two years, the plaintiff must prove the defendant guilty of one or the other offense. Furthermore, the plaintiff in a fault divorce case must not be found guilty of the same or another matrimonial offense. If Mrs. X is filing for divorce against Mr. X on the grounds that he has committed adultery, the divorce will not be granted if Mr. X can support his claim that his wife has also committed adultery, or one of the other offenses in their state. Under such a divorce law, the two spouses who so offend each other "deserve each other" and not a divorce! Even when the defending spouse does not file a counterclaim, fault divorce is more difficult in a number of ways. If both spouses want the divorce, the judge may refuse to grant it on grounds of "collusion." For couples who have reached a relatively harmonious agreement concerning the necessity of ending their marriage, it is painful to have to decide who will be the "guilty" party. Another difficult aspect of fault divorce is that the plaintiff must go to court and "hang out the dirty laundry" in order to get the divorce.

In true no-fault divorce, there is no plaintiff and no defendant. Instead, one or both parties state that the marriage has broken down irretrievably. No blame is necessary and no one is found "guilty." Some states have grafted no-fault grounds onto a basically fault system of divorce. For example, in Connecticut, one ground for divorce is irretrievable breakdown of the marriage, but although no one is found "guilty" or "innocent" there is still a plaintiff and a defendant.

**Do-It-Yourself Divorce.** When there are no minor children involved and no disputes over property, it is possible for people to avoid paying an attorney's fee by doing the work of getting the divorce themselves. In some states, *pro se* (representing oneself) divorce kits are available from women's centers and other sources. The divorcing individual must fill out the appropriate forms and may need the signature of an attorney, will have to pay court costs and the cost of having the divorce notice served on the other spouse. Some lawyers argue that *pro se* divorce is fraught with many difficulties, but many individuals who have done it say that it gives a feeling of autonomy and directing one's own fate. At any rate, it saves lawyers' fees of $400 or more. *Pro se* divorce is not recommended when the divorcing partners are arguing over property. It might also be worth it to hire a lawyer who is sympathetic to *pro se* divorce in order to briefly discuss the case before going ahead with attempting the divorce.

## Economic Divorce

The economic divorce is the separating of the spouses' property and income. In *community property* states (see Table 7-1 on page 204), husband and wife have equal interest in all income and assets except those brought into the marriage and inheritances. In these states, property would be divided equally at the time of divorce. In other states, wives have the right to a third or more of the assets of the marriage.

**Alimony.** It is a myth that most divorced women collect alimony. In 1975, fewer than 125,000 of the 3.25 million divorced women received alinomy, and the average (mean) amount was $5790 per woman [34].

**Child Support.** Child support, too, is received by relatively few divorced women. It has been estimated that in 1974 5.8 million nonwelfare families and 2.9 million welfare families in the United States were not receiving all of the court-ordered child support payments to which they were entitled [13]. Although intending to support his children, a man finds that two households cost more than one. When he remarries, he often turns away from his other children as he attends to his new family. Only a high income permits child support without great strain.

## Co-parental Divorce

Only couples with children experience the co-parental divorce, the aspect that deals with custody, visitation, and styles of parenting. Considering the numbers of children involved in divorce, the average per divorce decreased from 1.32 in 1965 to 1.08 in 1975, but the total number increased each year through 1978, excepting 1977 [61]. See Figure 9-2, on page 274. It has been estimated that between 20 and 30 per cent of children would experience parental divorce during their childhood [4]. About 11 million U.S. children are being raised by one parent, over 9 million by mothers, and 800,000 by fathers [61, Table 66]. In the United States in 1971, 90 per cent of white children and 64 per cent of black children were living with their two parents [19]. In 1976, 80 per cent of white children and 50 per cent of black children were living with both parents [61], a considerable drop in five years.

Childless couples who divorce are able to part permanently without having to see each other again. But although one may become an ex-spouse, becoming an ex-parent is impossible unless one deserts and disappears. Some form of parental obligation continues after divorce. The custodial parent, in nine cases out of ten the mother, becomes responsible for daily care of and decision making about the children. The noncustodial parent bears some financial responsiblity and usually has visitation rights of some kind. For both parents, styles of parenting must change radically at the time of separation.

**Children's Reactions to Divorce.** When compared to the reactions of adults to divorce, childrens' reactions are much more tied to their developmental stage, their relationships with each parent, and the child's environment [63]. The immediate reaction of the child to the news of divorce will depend also upon how much the child knew and understood of parental problems. For children who had previously believed theirs to be a happy home, the news of divorce can be a terrible shock. Older children, especially adolescents, may express relief if they have been aware of parental fighting [65]. Preschool children have an especially difficult time adjusting to parental separation, because they often believe that the reason Daddy moved out was that they were bad. They are not yet able to understand complex explanations, and need reassurance that the custodial parent will not depart also, and that they will remain in contact with the noncustodial parent. School-age children often show behavior or learning problems at school, although they may not appear to be

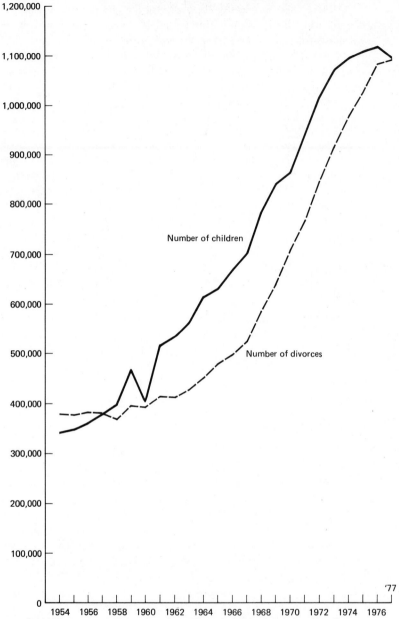

**FIGURE 9-2**    Number of divorces each year and number of children involved in divorces
in the United States.

*Sources:* Alexander A. Plateris. *Divorces: Analysis of changes.* Washington, D.C., U.S. Department of Health, Education,
and Welfare Publication No. (NSM) 73-27753. 1973.
*Statistical Abstracts of the United States.* U.S. Department of Commerce, Bureau of the Census. 1973.
*Statistical Abstracts of the United States.* U.S. Department of Commerce, Bureau of the Census. 1977.
New York Times, June 19, 1979, Changing patterns in U. S. divorce.

distressed at home. Older children and adolescents are more likely than younger to show intense anger, which although it may hide great sadness, still can serve to "galvanize them into activities that appear to ease the divorce distress" [63, p. 26].

The most important support to the child is his current relationship with each parent [29, 63] During the divorcing period, parent-child relations are fluid, changing a great deal in character [63]. The parents' relationship with each other has great importance for the child. When parents are supportive of each other's childrearing, the child's security is greatly increased [29]. Relationships with siblings can be helpful or can add to a child's distress. Only children are often under greater stress than children with siblings, but siblings can displace anger felt toward their parents onto their siblings, especially younger siblings [63]. Similarly, grandparents and other extended family members can add to a child's security or increase the child's conflicts, even when living far away. When grandparents insist that a child reject the grandparents' son- or daughter-in-law, the grandparents' "support" is destructive [63].

**Parent-Child Interaction.**  An extensive study of parent-child interaction in divorced families has been reported by Hetherington and associates [27,29]. The study began when a group of white, middle-class parents of preschool children had been divorced for two months. All parents had been separated for at least a year before the divorce occurred. The children were four years old at the beginning of the study, and six years old when it ended. Divorced families were matched with intact families.

When compared with intact families, interaction patterns between divorced parents and children were different, especially during the first year after divorce:

> Divorced parents make fewer maturity demands of their children, communicate less well with their children, tend to be less affectionate with their children and show marked inconsistency in discipline and lack of control over their children in comparison to parents in intact familes. Poor parenting is most apparent when divorced parents, particularly divorced mothers, are interacting with their sons [29, p. 20]

Children in divorced families, especially boys, exhibited more negative behavior than children in intact families. They were more dependent, obeyed less, showed less affection for their mothers, nagged, and whined more than children from intact families. Boys from divorced families showed more aggression and were less accepted by their peers [27]. Boys were less compliant to parental demands than were girls, and their fathers were more effective in getting a boy to comply. By two years after the divorce, the mother's parenting practices had improved, but fathers had become more distant. At two years, girls from divorced families were very similar to girls from intact families, but boys from divorced families still had more problems.

Parental reactions also showed variation by sex of parent, sex of child, and amount of time elapsed since the divorce. During the first year after the divorce,

divorced parents felt increasingly incompetent as parents, anxious, depressed, angry, and rejected. Divorced mothers, especially mothers of boys, had more intense and prolonged reactions. Fathers initially had a greater change in self-concept than did mothers, since all of the fathers in this study were noncustodial. The fathers complained of feelings of rootlessness, not knowing who they were, great feelings of loss, guilt, anxiety, and depression. Many fathers felt that they had lost their children. For most, this feeling declined with time, but for some, the pain continued at a high level.

At two months following the divorce, a third of the fathers and a quarter of the mothers in the Hetherington study "reported an ebullient sense of freedom [which] alternated with and by one year had largely been replaced by depression, anxiety, or apathy" [29, p. 13]. At two years after the divorce the negative feelings had markedly decreased.

Other studies of divorce report similar findings. Weiss notes that the initial adjustment to separation is less for the custodial parent, who still lives with a part of his or her family. Having to make all of the decisions about childrearing is both a burden and a benefit [20,65]. However, never having relief from the children is trying. The custodial parent's schedule may be too hectic to permit loneliness—until the children are in bed.

**The Single Parent.** Because the custodial parent is most often the mother, the pronoun "she" will be used in this section unless custodial fathers are specifically referred to.

Custodial parents of both genders share many common problems. Most divorced parents work outside the home, which means that job and child care must be juggled successfully. How difficult a feat this dual role will be will depend in part on how many children there are and on how old they are. Adolescents and older school-age children can get themselves ready for school, but younger children require more elaborate and constant attention. If the mother begins to work around the time of the divorce, young children react especially badly. If she has been working before the separation occurs, adjustment to the new life situation caused by the divorce is less radical and therefore easier [27]. Not surprisingly, Hetherington's research has shown that parent-child problems that occur around the time of divorce are interactive. When the children behave badly, the parent feels incompetent, angry, or depressed, and her behaviors toward the child are affected.

Custodial parents of both sexes must perform tasks that their spouse used to do, or they must hire a substitute. Whether or not they have children living with them, divorced men often initially have some difficulty with traditionally "feminine" tasks such as shopping, cooking, cleaning, and laundry [29,35]. Custodial fathers, like custodial mothers, must usually juggle child care and employment. They must take responsibility for meeting their children's emotional needs [41], a task that has traditionally fallen more to mothers than to fathers. There is concern about the single father's ability to rear daughters both among single fathers themselves [41] and in the divorce court [49]. Many fathers who win custody of their children are nonetheless quite enthusiastic about the experience. Strongly motivated to gain custody, such men want to be with and have responsibility for their children. One custodial father says

> I realized how important a part of my life my children were. It took me almost six months to figure out I wanted *them*, not the carefree life of a bachelor. . . . Yes, it was terrifying to think of raising them alone, because as men we're not raised to think we can do it.

But I found delight in being a single parent. Not that it wasn't difficult and horrible in all sorts of mechanical ways. But I found I actually liked all that dumb stuff—wiping noses, just being there for my daughters. And they were there for me. Having them helped keep me together after the marriage broke up. [44, p. 16]

Fathers with custody see themselves as more expressive and sensitive than they were before the divorce. As the primary caregivers, they must become more demonstrative of love and affection [1]. Hetherington [27,28,29] has shown that divorced mothers with preschool boys have a particularly hard time with parenting. To date no comparable study has been done of single fathers with daughters, although 20 single fathers whose daughters were of varying ages reported in a smaller study that they felt "quite successful" in rearing their daughters [49].

**Visitation.**   While the custodial parent cannot get away from the children, the noncustodial parent misses seeing the daily accomplishments of the children. At two months after the divorce, fathers in the Hetherington study were having almost as much contact with their children as fathers in intact homes who are often not available to their children. However, this level of interaction rapidly decreases. At two months about a quarter of the fathers reported that they were having more face-to-face interaction with their children than they had had before the divorce. Motivation for the contact varied. Sometimes the father was expressing a close attachment to the child or to the ex-wife; frequently it was based on a sense of duty toward the child; often, it was motivated at least in part by a desire to "annoy, compete with, or retaliate against" the ex-wife [29, p. 20]. By two years after the divorce, roughly 40 per cent of the fathers were seeing their children at least once a week; about 30 per cent saw them every two weeks; about 15 per cent saw them every three weeks; and about 15 per cent saw them once a month or less. Hetherington reports that it is very difficult to predict father-child contact at two years from the contact at two months. Some of the fathers who were most involved at two months found it too painful to have contact with the children, and stopped seeing them [27]. The ending of each visitation period hurts, reminding both father and children that they no longer live together [65].

**Divorce No Cure-All.**   A current myth is that divorce can banish all family and individual problems. Titles of books such as *Creative Divorce* [35] and *Divorce: The New Freedom* [21] and articles such as "Divorce: Chance of a new lifetime" [20] imply that one can shed an old marriage the way a snake sheds a skin; one may be painful and vulnerable for a while, but the new life style is more "self-actualizing" than the old. Although this idea may be true for some people, the reality portrayed by research is not so positive. The period of adjustment to divorce is a long, painful process for parents and children (and even for nonparents). At two years after separation, Hetherington's parents felt worse than they did at one year after separation [28]. Weiss [65] estimates that the recovery period from divorce is three to five years or more. Having divorced parents is easier on children today because their situation is shared by more of their peers than it was in the past, but, there are still many stresses.

## The Community Divorce

If they did not know it before, the divorcing couple soon discovers that a divorce tears a hole in the social fabric of which they have been a part. Friends, kin, and co-workers must be told about the person's change in marital status. It becomes apparent that other people feel that they have a stake in one's marriage. The community divorce is concerned with the divorcing person's relationships with other people.

**The Divorced Person and Friends.** Like the divorcing individuals themselves, friends of the couple go through different kinds of reactions to the news of divorce. Learning that the marriage of a friend is breaking up very often provokes anxiety and fear, especially among people who are themselves married [43]. The well-meaning but anxious friend may comment to his about-to-be-separated friend, "From what you say about your marriage, it doesn't seem that much worse than mine." Many divorcing persons report that friends are very supportive—at first. When first told that a couple is spearating, friends may not choose sides, but offer consolation to each partner separately. However, this period of support to both parties does not usually last long. Eventually, friends take sides and then may "fade away" [27, 65]. In a classic study of divorced women, Goode [26] reported that slightly over half of his respondents retained the same friends through the separation and divorce process. Hetherington [29] reports that divorced fathers were more likely to keep the same friends than were divorced mothers. Not suprisingly, when friends choose sides, they usually choose the person who was "their" friend. Friends made by either partner at her place of work tend to stay friends with their co-worker [65]. Thus, divorceés are likely to lose as friends the wives of their husband's co-workers.

Even when contacts with married friends are not severed completely, the quality of the relationship changes. The divorced person is an outsider in the world of couples. That married men make passes at divorced women is a cliché; the divorced man is also not immune from such advances by women. Eventually, if the separated or divorced person is to fit in, he or she must begin to associate with other separated and divorced persons. Hunt's term for separated and divorced persons is "formerly marrieds" or FMs [31,32]. In order to become adjusted to life as an FM the individual must learn the new social role. Hunt maintains that a kind of subculture exists in which the new FM is immediately recognized, accepted, and understood by others who have had the experience of separation and divorce. By living for a while in this subculture, the divorcing person can feel accepted as he is, learn new ways of behaving, and recover from the trauma of the divorce [32]. Some of the divorced person's new friends will be members of the opposite sex. Dating, sexual activity, and finding a new partner are closely related to recovering from divorce [32, 65]. These topics are covered in a later section of this chapter.

**The Divorced Person and Family.**   Telling one's family about an impending separation or divorce is often one of the most difficult steps that a divorcing person has to take. The reactions of family members will, of course, vary tremendously. One's children may have been very aware that their parents' marriage was in trouble, or they may have been unaware. The same is true of the married couples' parents, siblings, and other kin. Even when family members have been aware of trouble, the news may come as a terrible blow. Parents may believe that they have failed in bringing up their children correctly. Once convinced that the separation is inevitable, parents usually will support their child's decision. Most people probably expect their parents to support them when the going is rough. However, telling one's parents-in-law can be difficult if one has had a close relationship with them. Contact with in-laws usually decreases after divorce. When children are involved in the divorce, the amount of contact with their kin is related to the amount of contact they have with their father [3].

## Psychic Divorce

When two people have lived together for a number of years, they become accustomed to thinking of themselves as a couple. Their identities become somewhat fused. When they divorce, each former partner must begin to see himself or herself as an individual. This is the *psychic divorce*. Like other aspects of divorce, psychic divorce is not an easy process. It is especially difficult for wives who have not been employed outside the home, since the identity of such a wife is more likely to be bound up in her roles of wife and mother. Psychic divorce is also difficult for the noncustodial parent, usually the father. He must redefine his fathering role more radically than does the custodial parent, whose initial transition into separation is eased by the continuing presence of children.

When a person separates, he or she loses roles and aspects of self-definition. A separated person is in limbo, not really married and not really divorced. For a time there are no new self-definitions to take the place of the old ones [65]. It is only with time and perhaps with contact with other divorced and separated persons that the newly separated individual begins to construct a new identity [32].

Even when the divorce is final, one's identity does not change immediately. There are many daily reminders of the absence of one's spouse. Tasks that were done by the other spouse may remain undone, either from one's lack of skill or because the task is a painful reminder of one's new status. Also, being married had conferred status upon the individual. When a person gets married, his place in the social network changes. When the person divorces, he is again different. Marriages that have lasted at least two years deeply "inflitrate" one's life and identity [65].

Psychic divorce is concerned with the rebuilding of one's feelings of autonomy. The divorced person must answer the questions, "Why did I marry?" and "Why did I divorce?" [7, p. 61]. In the service of answering these questions, the divorcé may obsessively review events that led up to the divorce. Eventually, the events get sifted and sorted into an "account" (p. 268) that makes sense out of all that happened [65].

## Recovery from Divorce

By now it should be clear to the reader that divorce is a complex topic and a complex event. For most people it is a major trauma. Recovery is slow, and seems to happen in spirals. Many of life's problems have to be reworked [57]. The recovery process is assisted by finding and creating new social roles, learning how to take care of oneself, separating one's identity from one's former spouse's identity, dating, and becoming involved with new potential partners. The event that seems to be most related to recovery-from-divorce is finding a new mate [27]. We now examine the dating and sexual behavior of the divorced.

## Dating

Dating? The divorced person finds the word and the idea a bit ludicrous. Persons who were married only briefly and who have no children may fade easily into the singles scene, but those who have been married for a number of years and those who have children find dating difficult, at least initially. Divorced persons have been rejected by their spouses, and may wonder if they are attractive to anyone of the opposite sex. If a man has been married for five or ten years, it has been a long time since he has asked a woman out on a date. The pain of rejection is no less simply because he is no longer a teen-ager. A woman may wonder how to let men know that she is interested in dating them, or wonder if it is all right for her to ask out a man.

Some people are too hurt to begin dating right away; others have begun dating even before the separation. The person who is in the midst of separation and divorce needs to talk about it, as we have noted. The Hunts [32] maintain that separated and divorced persons find it easy to talk with each other about their situations. And yet, being too open too soon can frighten one's date and scare him or her away.

Hetherington [29] found that during the first year after divorce men were in a "frenzy" of social activity; dating and casual encounters at bars, clubs, and parties, as well as taking various courses and lessons. Women at this time were less active socially than their husbands were. During the second year after divorce, the men's social pace declined to the level of the women's.

## Sex

After having had a regular sex partner for a number of years, the idea of finding a new one can be exciting, frightening, or both. Hetherington [27] reports that men

### She doesn't want children to wake up to a stranger

Dear NEIGHBORS,

I am a young woman, divorced, with a boy and a girl in the lower elementary grades. I am seeing a fine man whom I enjoy. There are times when it would be nice if he could stay the night. But I am in a dilemma as to explain his pressence to my children in the morning. I feel it is only fair to give them an explanation. I'm sure that in this day and age many a young woman has this problem. If you've handled a similar situation, can you give me any suggestions?

BETSEY

**FIGURE 9-3**    A problem in establishing intimacy with a new partner.

*Source:* Providence Evening Bulletin, July 25, 1978.

usually enjoy their sexual freedom in the early months following divorce, but that women find casual sex to be degrading. Weiss [65] found that women are more cautious than men about getting sexually involved, and when they got involved in casual sex they were more likely to become distressed. The Hunts [32], however, say that women are becoming increasingly comfortable with casual sex. Although the majority of FM women have a more conservative outlook on postmarital sex, the number of new FM women who enjoy casual sex is rapidly increasing. The Hunts note that there is much more openness about postmarital sex than there was in the mid-1960s, when FMs took great pains to conceal their sexual activities from friends and neighbors.

It seems likely that enjoyment of casual sex is a temporary phase for both men and women. Hetherington [27] found that for people involved in a "meaningful" (emotionally intimate) relationship, more sexual activity was related to more happiness. However, for those involved in casual sex, more sex was related to unhappiness, feelings of being externally controlled, and depression. Data taken from diaries kept by the divorced respondents showed that depression increased after casual sex. Since most divorced people remarry sooner or later, again settling down with one sexual partner, casual sex may be seen as an interlude rather than as a permanent life style change for most divorced persons. In the early stages of separation it builds self-esteem for some persons, especially for men, but also for increasing numbers of women.

### Finding Someone New

For most divorced people, recovery from divorce is associated with finding a new intimate partner [29,62]. Although most divorced persons remarry, the decline in

**282**    FAMILIES

the remarriage rate means that more divorced persons are delaying marriage, if not putting it off permanently. A reason for the decline in the remarriage rate may be that more options are open to people now than previously. Either cohabitation or "going with" another person satisfies the needs of some individuals: they can have the security of a regular relationship without the permanent commitment of marriage [65]. We further discuss the topic of new heterosexual relationships in the section on remarriage later in this chapter.

## Divorce Groups and Therapy

In recent years more services have become available that are designed specifically for the separated or divorced person. The services may take the form of ongoing individual or group therapy, encounter groups, adult education, or parent education. Divorce therapy may take place before the couple has divorced, and be aimed at helping them to decide whether or not to divorce and at guiding them through the separation and divorce process. A second kind of divorce therapy is aimed at the divorcing *individuals* rather than at the divorcing couple. The main purpose of this kind of therapy is to help the individual recover from the divorce.

The early separation period has been targeted as a critical time for family therapy. A study of therapy for divorced families reports long-term success with time-limited therapy aimed for the early separation period [64]. Both parents and child or children were seen separately for between three and six sessions. The specific interventions used varied by family, but were of three basic types or combinations of the three types: child-centered, relationship-centered, or adult-centered interventions. In dealing with children in divorce, it comes as no surprise that the developmental level of the child has much to do with the kinds of problems encountered by the child and parents. Parents often needed help in responding to the child's needs in ways that were appropriate for the child's developmental stage. Because it takes several years for a family to recover from divorce, a large proportion of a child's life may be disrupted by parental conflict and divorce.

Adult education groups for divorced persons are another new service for separated and divorced persons. An example of divorce education is offered by Weiss [65]. Divorced and separated individuals meet once a week for eight weeks, each meeting lasting about two and a half hours. During the first hour, a lecture is given on an aspect of divorce. During the remaining time, participants are divided into discussion groups of no more than ten persons. Efforts are made to group members as closely as possible with respect to age, length of marriage, and age of youngest child. Whenever possible, half of the group members are male and half are female. Each group is led by an experienced group leader, whose role is to facilitate discussion among group members. The purpose of the lectures and discussions is to help people deal with their changing circumstances. Weiss notes that this form of divorce intervention seems most useful for persons who have been separated for less than a year. Persons who have been separated for more than a year are in a different phase of recovery, having already met many of the circumstances that are new to other group members.

Group therapy for children of divorce is available in Rhode Island and elsewhere. Many divorced parents are reluctant to let their children participate in such groups, probably because they see it as an admission that their divorce has caused their children problems that are not soluble at home. However, when children join such a group, they express the anger, fear, and pain that they are experiencing. They find that other children feel the same way, and they learn ways of handling their emotions and their new life situations.

## The "Good Divorce"

Is it possible to have a "good divorce"? Family therapists with extensive experience doing divorce therapy were questioned about divorce therapy and the divorce process. There was some variation in their responses, but some general conclusions emerged. In order to have a constructive divorce, both partners must want to end their relationship. Both partners must actively negotiate a settlement of property and children's affairs. It is important to have a sense of fair play and to be able to assess one's own needs. If a divorce is successful, each partner will have a feeling of psychological closure, and a balanced view of the marriage [36]. Additionally, the former marriage partners will be able to work with each other with civility on matters of mutual concern, especially the children. Some couples "hang on" to each other through their children or through continued haggling over property. Working civilly with each other is not the same as mutual dependence. When children are not involved, it is unlikely that divorced spouses have any real need for continued contact.

A "good" divorce means that psychic injury to children is minimal, and children understand to the best of their ability what the divorce means for them. Children need to feel free to be close to each parent. Very common among children of divorce is the fantasy that they can bring their parents back together. In a constructive divorce, such fantasies among children are minimized.

Finally, the divorcing individuals must be free of strong feelings of failure and self-disparagement. In a "good" divorce, each person gains greater self-understanding, increased personal competence, and the ability to form satisfying new relationships that do not repeat former mistakes [36].

## REMARRIAGE

Marriage itself is an extremely complex subject, about which it is risky to generalize. Remarriage, involving one or more persons who were previously married, is even more complex. Former spouses, whether dead or alive, exert an influence upon the

new union. When children exist from a former marriage, they too exert an influence upon the new marriage.

## Remarriage Rates

The marriage rates for divorced persons are considerably higher than are rates for singles, especially for individuals in their early twenties. (See Figure 9-1). However, remarriage rates have dropped since the mid-1960s. People are delaying both their first marriage and also subsequent marriages after divorce. Only half of persons who remarry after divorce do so within three years. Glick and Norton [25] report that 1975 data showed that four out of five divorced persons had remarried by middle age, but they predict that this proportion may decline in the near future. Between 1970 and 1975, the proportion of ever-divorced people in the population rose from 17 to 20 per cent.

## Second Marriages: Stability and Happiness

As noted previously, second marriages have almost as good a chance as first marriages of surviving until the death of one partner [25]. In her thorough study of many aspects of remarriage, Bernard [6] points out that the higher divorce rate among remarrieds in the 1940s served to weed out the less happily married among them, leaving as a residue a *more happily* married population than the once-married pop-

SPLITTING AND SPLICING

ulation. In a more recent survey, it was concluded that remarriages that are not quickly ended by divorce are about as happy as first marriages. Marital happiness was higher among never-divorced women than among women in remarriages, but no differences were found for men [23]. A consistent finding over the years has been that remarried widowed persons have happier marriages than remarried divorcées [6,18,39].

**Similarity of First and Second Spouses.**   It is popularly thought that when people remarry they repeat their mistakes, marrying someone who is similar to the former spouse. Little is known about how accurate this stereotype is. The Hunts [32], however, maintain that most divorced persons marry someone who is *different* from the first spouse. Persons who remarry quickly might be more likely to repeat their earlier mistakes. The delay in remarriage may help more divorced individuals find a new spouse who meets more of their needs.

**Involvement of Children.**   When children are included in a remarriage, the establishment of the new family is much more complicated than when childless people remarry. We use the term *reconstituted family* to refer to a family that includes a stepparent. Of the 65 million children under 18 years of age in 1967, 8.75 million were living in reconstituted families [25]. It is hard to find out how many persons over 18 also had stepparents, but there are many. Before a reconstituted family can feel and act like an integrated unit, the members must work out many new roles with each other and their extended families and friends. Because there are only vague guidelines for these roles in our society, it often takes a lot of effort to create the roles.

**Stepmothers and Stepfathers.**   In folklore, the stepparent, especially the step-mother, is a cruel and crafty ogre, bent on the destruction of the stepchildren. Is her reputation worse than his simply because stepmothers used to be more common when marital breakup was more often due to death than to divorce? Or is her role basically more difficult? Or less frequent, since women are awarded custody of children more often than men?

Studying divorced parents and their children, Hetherington [27] found that divorced women felt more animosity toward their spouse's new partner than divorced men did. This was true even when the ex-wife had previously remarried. Although some ex-husbands felt animosity when their wives remarried, this was much less likely to happen. Stepmothers, in turn, stirred up more bad feelings in the former relationship than did stepfathers. Some stepmothers wanted custody of the children, and others wanted their husbands to move far away from their ex-wives and children by the former marriage. Stepfathers, however, did not interfere in these ways, feeling less animosity toward the visists of their stepchildren's natural father.

Why would women feel hostility toward the remarriage of their former spouse, and why would stepmothers stir up more trouble than stepfathers? Hetherington does not give an explanation, but we offer the following. Fathers in the Hetherington study tended to withdraw from their children over the two-year period following divorce. Feeling less invested in their children, the remarriage of the former wife might be less threatening. The custodial wives, however, remained highly invested in the children. The husband's remarriage might make the former wife worry about the continuation of child support and the father's emotional support of the children.

Stepmothers might be more interfering than stepfathers simply because the latter live with the children and have more control over them. Stepmothers who don't live with their stepchildren have to take care of them and put up with them when they visit, but know that the loyalty of the children is with their mother. Stepmothers would therefore be motivated either to gain more control by getting custody of the children, or to shirk all responsibility for the children by moving far away where visitation would be less frequent.

Some stepmothers get along well, developing warm relationships with their stepchildren. When fathers are in close contact with their children (as some in the Hetherington study were not), the child is included in the courtship process and forms bonds of affection with the potential stepmother before the marriage takes place [56].

## Problems of Reconstituted Families

Raising children in a reconstituted family is even more difficult than primary parenting (raising one's own children). In a "primary family" (a husband and wife in their first marriages with their own children), children are added to the family as infants, and the family evolves slowly. The bringing together of half-grown children with a stepparent or stepparent and stepsibs is a more complex undertaking. It takes more work to get the families to blend into one unit that feels like a family. The problems of reconstituted families have been summarized by investigators in two studies: Duberman [18], who included stepmothers as well as stepfathers, and Bohannan and Erickson [8], who interviewed mothers, stepfathers, and stepchildren.

**Money.** Money is a problem in remarriages partly because of the existence of children. Noncustodial parents often resent paying child support when their children are living with a stepparent [18,42]. If child support payments are late or do not come, the budget of the reconstituted family is strained. The stepfather may have payments of his own to make to his children who live with his ex-wife, thus depleting the money supply for his second family.

**Self-Consciousness.** Reconstituted families, especially the stepparents, are self-conscious. Duberman maintains that society views them as deviant. People ask them embarrassing questions, such as which children belong to whom, how they get along together, and whether the divorced parent visits. In this manner, they are frequently reminded that they are different. In reality, however, there are enough reconstituted families that they are no longer unusual. But a stepparent knows he is different from the natural parent, and he thinks more about what he is doing, wondering if he is being a good father and if family conflicts and difficulties are those of most families, or if they are the result of his fathering.

**The "Real" Parent.** The natural parent may get in the way of a child's adjustment to a stepparent, especially if the child has regular contacts with the former. Because there is no socially prescribed behavior pattern for a stepparent, neither the child, the stepparent, nor the parent knows just what the stepparent should do. It takes time for the stepfather to work out his own role. The questions of name changes and adoption come up. Should the children continue to be called by the name of their natural father, or should the members of the reconstituted family have the same name? Again such decisions take a lot of discussion and thinking within the family.

**Hidden Agenda.** When a stepparent joins a family, all concerned may have expectations that they do not express. They may not be fully aware of what they want from one another. As we mentioned in Chapter 6, the role stage of courtship is important and complicated, because the couple must try out many roles in regard to each other. When the marriage involves children, as well as a couple, the number of new roles is much greater. Some role exploration can be accomplished before the marriage, but much more must be done when the reconstituted family starts living together. Good communication will bring out expectations and conflicts arising from them.

**Entering a Group.** The stepparent enters an established group. Usually, the stepfather enters a group consisting of a woman and her children. During the time that they lived as a one-parent family, they worked out ways of getting along together, probably starting from a period of turmoil after a divorce. Disorganization is likely to be most severe one year after a divorce and equilibrium to be established by two years [28]. Single parents take pride in their ability to run a household without a partner [44,56].

**Rivalry and Competition.** Children may act as rivals with the stepparents for the affection of the parents, especially if the children are older and have been living for some time without the second parent. Or, the child may compete with the parent for the affection of the stepparent. Sexual relations between adolescent girls and stepfathers sometimes occur, as in the novel *Lolita*. Incest taboos between children and stepparents are not as strong as in the case of natural parents.

**Everyday Sources of Friction.** Conflicts often arise over food, the division of labor, personal space, and discipline [8]. The same is true when children live with both natural parents, but in reconstituted families, there are more opportunities for these conflicts. The stepparent enters a group with established food habits. There is bound to be some readjusting of the group to his preferences and of him to theirs. If one or more are fussy eaters, or if they have unusual practices, problems will be frequent.

New patterns of doing the housework have to be established when a new family member comes in. Discussion and work charts were found most helpful in solving problems over who should do the various jobs at home.

Questions of space can be hard for those who move in and for those who have to move over. In one newly reconstituted family, the mother and her two young children have moved into the father's house, where he has lived alone except for weekend visits from his adolescent children. The two little children now sleep in the room that used to belong to the teenage girl, who must sleep on a day bed in the study when she visits. She resents her father's new wife and her stepsisters who have taken her space.

Discipline is especially difficult for stepparents. Wanting to be liked and accepted by their stepchildren, they often hesitate to do anything to arouse hostility. The problem is especially difficult for stepmothers, who play a more concentrated and intense role than stepfathers. The same principles of discipline apply to reconstituted families as to other families, but the necessity for communication and cooperation between parents is even greater.

**Adult Stepchildren.** Adults are sometimes glad when their lonely parents remarry. Older widowed men have many opportunities for remarriage, and a new wife solves problems of companionship and homemaking. However, an adult child usually resents a stepparent who seems likely to inherit money or goods that the child was expecting to receive at the death of the parent. The older bridegroom or bride can do much to alleviate this problem by discussing it openly before the marriage. If the fiancée has other means of support and agrees, she can legally renounce claim to her future husband's estate. Or the agreement may spell out a division of resources satisfactory to all. Failure to face this problem has made it difficult for many older stepparents to relate to their adult stepchildren.

## Successes in Reconstituted Families

Recent studies show that many stepparents make very positive contributions to their families. College men who were stepsons showed psychosexual development as adequate as that of biological sons, and better than that of father-absent sons [50]. Certain social and psychological characteristics in high school boys showed no differences between those who had grown up with stepfathers and those who had lived with their natural fathers [66].

Children's happiness, problems, and relationships with fathers and stepfathers were the focus of questions that Bohannon and Erickson asked of children and parents [8]. On all their measures, stepchildren compared favorably with children of natural parents. The children and their mothers thought that the stepfathers were just as good as the natural fathers. The stepfathers, however, did not think they were that good, nor did they think that their children were as happy as did natural fathers. The myth of the inept stepparent seems to have depressed the self-concepts of the stepfathers.

Family integration (feeling and acting like a family) was the theme of Duberman's interviews with 88 reconstituted families [18]. The integration score was derived from ratings by husband, wife, and interviewer. High ratings were obtained by 45 per cent, moderate by 34, and low by 21. When death had terminated the previous marriage, integration was likely to be higher than it was when divorce had ended it. Husband-wife solidarity had a strong effect on family integration. Stepparent-stepchild relationships were rated good or excellent in 82 per cent of cases. These relationships were important for integration, but not as important as the husband-wife relationship. Stepfathers tended to have better relationships with children than did stepmothers. Stepchildren's relationships with each other were better when both sets lived in one house.

As reconstituted families become more common, it seems likely that their self-consciousness will decrease. Perhaps the roles of stepfather, stepmother, and stepchild will grow clearer. We have heard of stepchildren rejoicing in having four sets of grandparents, instead of two. Very helpful guidance for stepfamilies is available in *Living in step: a remarriage manual for parents and children* [54].

## SUMMARY

Divorce frequency is expressed in various terms. A meaningful approach is to count the number of divorces among a group of persons married a certain number of years previously. Divorce has been more frequent than a generation ago because of changing attitudes toward divorce and because there have been more persons in the age group that is most at risk for divorce. Predictions of marital permanence are lower than average for teen-age marriages, premaritally pregnant couples, low-income couples, and couples with no children or large numbers of children.

Divorce is usually a crisis for those involved. Divorcing individuals develop an explanation or "account" for the divorce. This explanation is a simplification of the tangle of causes for the failure of the marriage. Construction of the account helps the individual to recover from the divorce.

Six aspects of the divorce process have been identified: the emotional divorce, the legal divorce, the economic divorce, the coparental divorce, the community divorce, and the psychic divorce. The emotional divorce begins when the partners grow away from each other. It is complicated by continued feelings of attachment to the spouse. The legal divorce is the legal action that makes a husband and wife no longer married. Divorce laws vary by state. In some states, there are fault divorce laws; in others, there are no-fault laws; and in still others the divorce laws are combinations of the two. Economic divorce is the separation of property and income. Not all children receive the child support to which they are entitled, and alimony is received by a small fraction of divorced wives.

The coparental divorce involves learning new ways of parenting by both the custodial and noncustodial parent. Because children's reactions to divorce are tied to their developmental stage, children need explanations that are appropriate to their level of understanding. They also need to express their feelings about the divorce. Mothers of preschool boys have a particularly difficult time with their sons and with their own divorce adjustment. The single parent has a task overload but may feel proud of managing alone. Noncustodial parents have a harder time in the initial stages of separation.

The community divorce is concerned with the divorced person's relationships with friends and acquaintances. The divorced person, especially the woman, often loses old friends. Making new friends, including others who have been divorced, is important for recovery. Telling one's family about the divorce is often difficult. The psychic divorce entails learning to see oneself as an individual who is separate from one's former spouse. Psychic divorce is especially hard for nonemployed women.

Dating is often difficult at first. Finding a new sex partner can be both frightening and exciting. Divorced men are more likely than women to enjoy the sexual freedom of divorce. Even those who have enjoyed casual sex usually settle down with one person after a while. Finding someone new is associated with recovery from divorce. Divorce groups and therapy also help divorced persons and their children.

Remarriage rates have dropped since the mid-1960s, but remain higher than rates for first marriages. When children are involved in a remarriage, building a sense of family is complicated. Reconstituted families are becoming common. Their particular problems include self-consciousness, the natural parent, hidden agenda, entering an established group, rivalry, conflicts over food, questions of space, division of labor, and discipline. Conflicts between older stepparents and adult stepchildren often have a financial basis.

**REFERENCES**

1. Albin, Rochelle. New looks at single parenting: Focus on fathers. *APA Monitor,* 1977, **8:**6, 7–8.
2. Aldridge, Delores. The changing nature of interracial marriage in Georgia: A research note. *Journal of Marriage and the Family,* 1973, **35,** 641–642.
3. Anspach, Donald F. Kinship and divorce. *Journal of Marriage and the Family,* 1976, **38,** 323–330.
4. Bane, Mary Jo. Marital disruption and the lives of children. *Journal of Social Issues,* 1976, **32:**1, 103–118.
5. Bayer, Alan. Early dating and early marriage. *Journal of Marriage and the Family,* 1968, **30,** 628–632.
6. Bernard, Jessie. *Remarriage: A study of marriage.* New York: Dryden, 1956.
7. Bohannan, Paul. The six stations of divorce. In P. Bohannan (Ed.) *Divorce and after: An analysis of the emotional and social problems of divorce.* Garden City, N.Y.: Anchor, 1970.
8. Bohannan, Paul and Rosemary Erickson. Stepping in. *Psychology Today,* 1978 (January), 53–54.
9. Burchinal, Lee G. and L. E. Chancellor. Survival rates among religiously homogamous and interreligious marriage. *Social Forces,* 1963, **41,** 353–362.
10. Christensen, Harold T. Scandinavian and American sex norms: Some comparisons, with sociological implications. *Journal of Social Issues,* 1966, **22,** 60–75.
11. Christensen, Harold T. and Kenneth E. Barber. Interfaith versus intrafaith marriage in Indiana. *Journal of Marriage and the Family,* 1967. **29,** 461–469.
12. Christensen, Harold T. and Hanna M. Meissner. Studies in child spacing: III. Premarital pregnancy as a factor in divorce. *American Sociological Review,* 1953, **28,** 641–644.
13. Committee on Finance, United States Senate. *Child support data and materials.* Washington, D.C.: U.S. Government Printing Office, November 10, 1975.
14. Crouse, Bryant, Marvin Karlins, and Harold Schroder. Conceptual complexity and marital happiness. *Journal of Marriage and the Family,* 1968, **30,** 643–650.
15. Cutright, Phillips. Timing the first birth: Does it matter? *Journal of Marriage and the Family,* 1973, **35,** 585–595.
16. Day, Beth, *Sexual life between blacks and whites.* New York: World, 1972.
17. deLissovoy, Vladimir. High school marriages: A longitudinal study. *Journal of Marriage,* 1973, **35,** 244–255.
18. Duberman, Lucile. *The reconstituted family.* Chicago: Nelson-Hall, 1975.
19. Dullea, Georgia. U.S. Statistics show single-parent families growing 7 times as fast as 2-parent ones. Toronto: *Globe and Mail,* December 4, 1974.
20. Feldberg, Roslyn, Elizabeth M. Fox, and Janet Kohen. Divorce: Chance of a new lifetime. *Journal of Social Issues,* 1976, **32:**1 119–133.
21. Fisher, Esther Oshiver. *Divorce: The new freedom.* New York: Harper, 1974.
22. Furstenberg, Frank, Jr. Premarital pregnancy and marital instability. *Journal of Social Issues,* 1976, **32:**1, 67–86.
23. Glenn, Norval D. and Charles K. Weaver. The marital happiness of remarried divorced persons. *Journal of Marriage and the Family,* 1977, **39,** 331–337.

24. Glick, Paul C. and Arthur J. Norton. Frequency, duration, and probability of marriage and divorce. *Journal of Marriage and the Family,* 1971, **33,** 307–317.
25. Glick, Paul C. and Arthur J. Norton. Marrying, divorcing, and living together in the United States today. *Population Bulletin,* **32:**5. Washington, D.C.: Population Reference Bureau, 1977.
26. Goode, William. *After divorce.* Glencoe, Ill: Free Press, 1956.
27. Hetherington, E. Mavis. The aftermath of divorce. Colloquium presented at the U. of Connecticut, April 13, 1978.
28. Hetherington, E. Mavis, Martha Cox, and Roger Cox. Beyond father absence: Conceptualization of effects of divorce. In Russell C. Smart and Mollie S. Smart (Eds.) *Readings in child development and relationships.* New York: Macmillan, 1977.
29. Hetherington, E. Mavis, Martha Cox, and Roger Cox. The aftermath of divorce. Address presented at the meetings of the American Psychological Association, September 1976.
30. Hetzel, Alice and Marlene Capetta. *Teenagers: Marriages, divorces, parenthood, and mortality.* Rockville, Md.: National Center for Health Statistics, Series 21, Number 23, 1973.
31. Hunt, Morton M. *The world of the formerly married.* New York: McGraw-Hill, 1966.
32. Hunt, Morton M. and Bernice Hunt. *The divorce experience.* New York: McGraw-Hill, 1977.
33. Hyatt, James C. Divorce rate is leveling off and may even fall, population experts say. *Wall Street Journal,* June 27, 1978.
34. Internal Revenue Service. *Individual income tax returns. Preliminary statistics of income, 1975.* Washington, D.C.: U.S. Government Printing Office. Publication No. 198 (2-77). 1977.
35. Krantzler, Mel. *Creative divorce.* New York: Signet, 1975.
36. Kressel, Kenneth and Morton Deutsch. Divorce therapy: An in-depth survey of therapists' views. *Family Process,* 1977, **16,** 413–443.
37. Lee, Gary R. Age at marriage and marital satisfaction: A multivariate analysis with implications for marital stability. *Journal of Marriage and the Family,* 1977, **39,** 493–504.
38. Levinger, George. Marital cohesiveness on the brink. In G. Levinger and O. C. Moles (Eds.), *Divorce and separation.* New York: Basic Books, 1979.
39. Locke, Harvey J. Predicting adjustment in marriage: *A comparison of a divorced and a happily married group.* New York: Holt, 1951.
40. McKain, Walter. A new look at older marriages. *Family Coordinator,* 1972, **21,** 61–69.
41. Mendes, Helen A. Single fathers. *Family Coordinator,* 1976, **25,** 439–444.
42. Messinger, Lillian. Remarriage between divorced people with children from previous marriages: A proposal for preparation for remarriage. *Journal of Marriage and Family Counseling,* 1976, **2,** 193–200.
43. Miller, Arthur A. Reactions of friends to divorce. In Paul Bohannan, (Ed). Divorce and after: *An analysis of the emotional and social problems of divorce.* New York: Anchor, 1970.
44. Molinoff, Daniel D. Life with father. *New York Times Magazine,* May 22, 1977.
45. Monahan, Thomas P. Are interracial marriages really less stable? *Social Forces,* 1970, **48,** 461–473.
46. Monahan, Thomas P. The changing nature and instability of remarriages. *Eugenics Quarterly,* 1958, **5,** 73–85.
47. Mueller, Charles W. and Hallowell Pope. Marital instability: A study of its transmission between generations. *Journal of Marriage and the Family,* 1977, **39,** 83–92.

48. Myricks, Noel. The Equal Rights Amendment: Its potential impact on family life. *Family Coordinator,* 1977, **26,** 321–324.
49. Orthner, Dennis, Terry Brown, and Dennis Ferguson. Single-parent fatherhood: An emerging family lifestyle. *Family Coordinator,* 1976, **25,** 429–438.
50. Oshman, Harvey P. and Martin Manosevitz. Father absence: Effects of stepfathers upon psychosocial development in males. *Developmental Psychology,* 1976, **12,** 479–480.
51. Plateris, Alexander. *Divorce: Analysis of change.* Rockville, Md.: National Center for Health Statistics, Series 21, Number 22, 1973.
52. Pope, Hallowell and Charles W. Mueller. The intergenerational transmission of marital instability: Comparisons by race and sex. *Journal of Social Issues,* 1976, **32:**1, 49–66.
53. *Providence Journal-Bulletin.* More black men wed to whites. February 14, 1973.
54. Roosevelt, Ruth and Jeanette Lofas. *Living in step: A remarriage manual for parents and children.* New York: McGraw-Hill, 1976.
55. Rosenthal, Erich. Divorce and religious intermarriage: The effect of previous marital status upon subsequent marital behavior. *Journal of Marriage and the Family,* 1970, **32,** 435–440.
56. Rosenthal, Kristine and Harry F. Keshet. The not-quite stepmother. *Psychology Today,* July 1978, 82–86+.
57. Smart, Laura S. An application of Erikson's theory to the recovery-from-divorce process. *Journal of Divorce,* 1977, **1,** 67–79.
58. Stroup, Atlee. *Marriage and the family: A developmental approach.* New York: Appleton, 1966.
59. Stuart, Irving R. and Edwin A. Lawrence. *Interracial marriage: Expectations and realities.* New York: Grossman, 1973.
60. Thornton, Arland. Children and marital stability. *Journal of Marriage and the Family,* 1977, **39,** 531–542.
61. U.S. Bureau of the Census. *Statistical Abstracts of the United States, 1977.* Washington, D.C.: U.S. Government Printing Office, 1977.
62. Waller, Willard. *The old love and the new.* New York: Liveright, 1930.
63. Wallerstein, Judith S. and Joan B. Kelly. Brief interventions with children in divorcing families. *American Journal of Orthopsychiatry,* 1977, **47,** 23–29.
64. Wallerstein, Judith S. and Joan B. Kelly. Divorce counseling: A community service for families in the midst of divorce. *American Journal of Orthopsychiatry,* 1977, **47,** 4–22.
65. Weiss, Robert S. *Marital separation.* New York: Basic, 1975.
66. Wilson, Kenneth L., Louis A. Zurcher, Diana C. McAdams, and Russell L. Curtis. Stepfathers and stepchildren: An exploratory analysis from two national surveys. *Journal of Marriage and the Family,* 1975, **39,** 526–536.
67. Women in Transition, Inc. *Women in transition: A feminist handbook on separation and divorce.* New York: Scribner, 1975.

# CHAPTER 10
# PARENThood: A MATTER of choice

Since antiquity, human beings have made efforts to control the birth of children, but only recently has birth control technology become highly effective and widely available. Parenthood is no longer taken for granted as the result of marriage. Although there are some pressures on a young couple to have children, other pressures make them think it over carefully. An increasing number of couples are remaining childless, while an increasing number of couples are having larger-than-average numbers of children 49 . The two groups seem to be balancing each other, as to total number of children born. If most of them are truly choosing, then it looks like a very fortunate state of affairs for children. More children are being born to people who really want to be parents!

What happens to people who do not become parents, by either choice or chance? Erik Erikson, in a recent speech to the International Psycho-Analytic Association, warns that stagnation and self-absorption result from denying and repressing the urge to procreate. Childfree people can, however, face the fact that they have not produced and nurtured their own children. They can express the urge to procreate by nurturing and working for the good of some other children or for all children. Other kinds of nurturant social creativity may also prevent stagnation and self-absorption.

## MAJOR DECISIONS

The biggest decision regarding parenthood is whether or not to become a parent. The dropping birth rate, shown in Figure 10-1, indicates that individuals are becom-

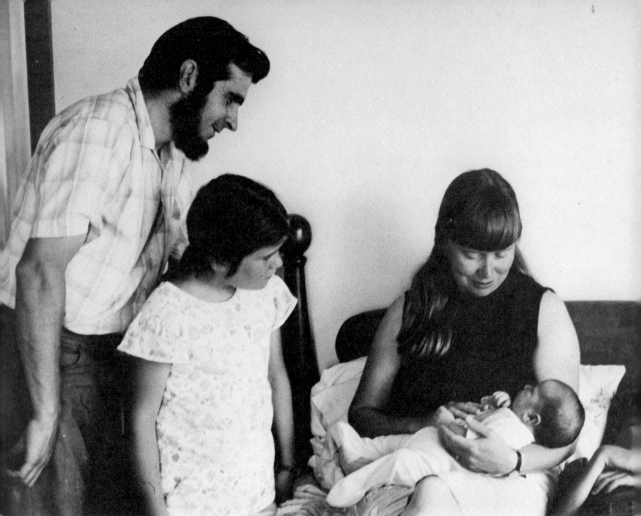

MOLLIE S. SMART

ing more reluctant to enter the parent-child career or to add children to those they already have.

If a person does not enter the parent-child career, no further decisions about parenthood are necessary. If the parent-child career is chosen, the next question is *when* to begin it. After the first child is born, the parents then face the question of whether to have another and, if so, when, and when to stop having children. Leaving the first question for a later section, we now discuss the questions of when to have children and how many children to have.

## When to Start the Parent-Child Career

In thinking about when to start a baby, there are many considerations. Physical readiness is very important. So also are experience with children, knowledge about

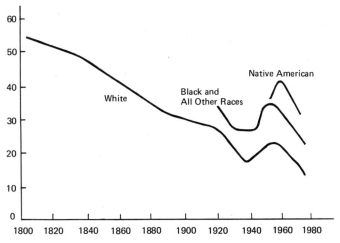

**FIGURE 10-1**     Birth rates in the United States from 1800 to 1980.

*Source:* Kurt J. Snapper. The American Legacy, Figure 2. In Edith H. Grotberg (Ed.) *200 Years of Children.* (DHEV Publication No. (OHD) 77-30103.) Washington, D.C.: U.S. Department of Health, Education, and Welfare, Office o Child Development, 1976.

children, emotional readiness, and planning for children. While physical readiness is usually achieved in the early 20s, it often takes a few years longer to achieve sufficient knowledge, experience, and emotional maturity.

**Physical Readiness.**   A girl is not ready to be a mother until she completes her own growth and lives a few years longer. The most favorable age for childbearing (as judged by infant mortality rates) is between 20 and 24 years of age, although the years between 19 and 35 are adequate [23]. Physical readiness also requires both partners to be in good health, including a state of excellent nutrition. Although couples rarely consult doctors for preconception advice, to do so would be to give their baby the best chance for a good start. Genetic counseling is helpful when partners have any knowledge of hereditary diseases in their families.

**Experience with and Knowledge of Children.**   Many young adults have had very little experience with babies and young children. Even those who have done baby sitting have rarely had the responsibility of 24-hour care of a baby. They often don't realize how much new babies cry, how many messy diapers must be changed, what it's like to get up in the middle of every night for weeks or months, and how it is to be interrupted no matter what one is doing. Although people cannot experience all of parenthood ahead of time, they can find out a great deal by getting to know parents with new babies, taking care of babies, seeing films, reading about children, and even taking classes for prospective parents. To gain such experience and knowledge *before* conceiving a baby would make it possible for a couple to judge whether they were ready to become parents.

**Emotional Readiness.**    On the basis of real experience with children, partners could examine their feelings about parenthood. Do they want to give care? Do they feel tender, loving, and patient? Are they frightened at the prospect of being completely responsible for another human being? Are they willing to put a baby's well-being ahead of their own wishes and needs? Have they ideas about what kind of child they want and will they happily accept a boy or girl, a baby who is not good-looking, or one with a handicap? Can the partners talk about all these questions and make plans and feel confident about their own relationship? And do they feel that they want a baby very much?

**Making Plans.**    Good management is an important part of getting ready to have a baby. Costs of prenatal care and birth have to be paid. Resources for caring for the baby require some financial planning and home management. It requires money to buy space, furniture, equipment, and clothing, and having a child often means a rearrangement of ways of earning, spending, and living. If both partners hold jobs, then the woman probably has to plan to stop her career for at least a few weeks or months, if not years. How will the family get along with less money? How will the new mother feel about giving up her occupational career to a greater or lesser degree? Will the new father take time off, too, in order to share the transition to parenthood and child care? Are grandparents going to help? What other sources of help will be used? In planning for parenthood, a person will have some individual problems to be solved, as well as these more general questions. If she is going to be a single mother, she will need a set of resources different from those of a wife. If one of the couple has a particular disability or if they carry a special responsibility, then plans for having a child are affected. These are questions of readiness for having a baby, since plans must be made to answer them.

## How Many Children?

Should we have another child? And another? Intended numbers, as well as actual births, have decreased. A U.S. Government survey in 1974 found that among wives between 18 and 39 years of age, every 1000 of them intended to have 2,550 children, in contrast to 3,118 intended children in 1967 [47]. A 1978 report on married women puts the average number of children desired at about two [31].

Sometimes couples have a second child out of a sense of duty and obligation, rather than because they really want another. A persistent myth says that there is something wrong with having an only child. Part of the myth is that only children are spoiled, selfish, and lonely. Another part of it says that parents are selfish if they do not provide a playmate for their first child. A study of social stereotypes showed parents of only one child, as compared with people who had or wanted more than one, to be thought more independent, autonomous, rebellious, nonconventional, self-centered, immature, and less friendly, wholesome, and good-natured. One-child fathers were viewed with even less favor than one-child mothers [36]. As we read the research literature, there are advantages and disadvantages to each position in the family. It is doubtful whether the advantages of having a younger sibling generally outweigh the advantages of being an only child. It is highly questionable whether the advantages of giving the older child a playmate outweigh the costs to parents who do not really want another child or who do not have personal and financial resources adequate for a second (or third) child. There are many other ways of finding playmates for one's child. It hardly seems fair to the second child to be given birth for the good of the first one, and not because of being wanted for himself. In fact, if people gave birth only to children *they* really wanted, many human problems would be prevented, perhaps even the population explosion.

Fortunately, the number of offspring does not have to be decided when the partnership is set up. If marriage required a contract specifying the number of children, there would probably be more mistakes in childbearing than there are today! When a couple first declare their love for each other and begin making plans for marriage, they often say something like this: "Let's have six children. They'll all be beautiful with you for a father (mother)." At this stage of life and love, an expansive statement about the number of desired children is often just a way of saying, "I love you very, very much and I want to share the rest of my life with you."

Couples differ in the number of children that may be appropriate for them. Before making any major change in life, it is wise to take stock of the present situation and weigh possible courses of action in regard to aims and goals. Because most couples would plan carefully before changing jobs, buying a house, or even buying a car, it makes sense for them to give even more thought to conceiving a baby. The baby causes bigger, more permanent changes and greater responsibilities than do most other new steps in life. Therefore, questions about the present and the future need to be considered each time a child is planned.

Sometimes couples disagree as to having a baby, or another baby. For the sake of the child itself, it seems to us that the veto power should be stronger, because we think a baby should be wanted by *both* parents. However, some such conflicts are solved by having the baby for the sake of the one parent who wants it, as in the case of Rob, who very much wanted a son, even though he had four girls, and Jean, who felt that she had already more than enough children. Rob told Jean that if she would try again, with the use of new techniques for controlling the sex of the fetus, he would change his mode of life to help a great deal more in caring for all the children. (In this family, income was more than adequate.) Jean wanted Rob to be fulfilled. The two of them discussed ways of rearranging their lifestyle in order to keep from overtaxing Jean. They had a son. Now, five years later, the seven of them are doing well, although Jean is more tired than she would like to be. Rob has kept up his part of the agreement. Both Jean and Rob put a great deal of time and energy into parenting. One of their minor problems is social disapproval for having so many children in an overcrowded world. They do not believe they have done wrong, however, because they planned for all their children, they love them dearly, and they do a good job as parents.

The question of population trends is discuussed in Chapter 15. Readers may question whether Jean and Rob should have had five children. The situation could be viewed from the standpoint of the couple, the family, the community, the United States, or the world.

## TRANSITION TO PARENTHOOD

The process of giving birth is described in the next chapter. This section is concerned with taking on parental roles, how people respond to their children, how it feels and what it means to become parents.

Becoming a parent includes four stages, pregnancy, delivery, recovery, and being at home with the baby. Each one of these stages involves a set of changes and strong emotions, some of which are positive and some negative [51]. Reactions to the various stages of transition into parenthood depend upon the body, personality, and experiences with which pregnancy is begun, the marital relationship in which the events occur [51], the type of assistance and support given, early contacts with the baby and its responses, and the wider social environment [43].

### Parenthood as Crisis

Becoming a parent involves many changes in behavior. When the individual is unprepared or unable to make the necessary changes, then a great deal of stress occurs. New parents, especially mothers, usually need some help from other poeple in taking on their new roles and responsibilities. Becoming a parent is both biological and social, since other people help the biological process to go along smoothly. The educator teaches the pregnant pair about the bodily changes they are feeling and seeing. The doctor or midwife helps the mother to deliver the baby; perhaps the father helps, too. A nurse-educator shows the mother how to help the baby in his efforts to find, suck, and swallow his food. In learning to care for and educate infants and young children, parents receive inputs from many sources, including kin, friends, professionals, and the media. Some of these inputs are truly helpful. Much of the outcome depends upon the personal resources of the couple and the use that they are able to make of the proffered help.

The other important person in this picture is the baby herself. What kind of baby is she? She makes the transition easy for her parents if she takes her food easily, rarely regurgitates, sleeps continuously for several hours, seldom cries, and responds to comforting. When 296 first-time mothers and 272 first-time fathers answered questionnaires about their young infants, 8 per cent of the women and 5 per cent of the men said that the baby interrupted their sleep and rest very much [42]. Physical tiredness and fatigue were felt somewhat by 64 per cent of mothers, and very much by 14 per cent. The majority of babies, then, were not very troublesome at night, but caused some fatigue to mothers, whereas a small minority placed considerable physical strain on the parents.

The ease and difficulty of making the transition to parenthood was studied, as mentioned, by looking for conditions associated with the parents' perceptions of bothersome change [42]. Transition to parenthood was found to be less stressful for both women and men when the child was planned, and when the child had not been conceived before marriage. The longer the women had been married, the better her health, and the easier her pregnancy, the less was she likely to report a crisis. Relatively little stress was felt by men who were older rather than younger and who reported that the role of father was important to them, as compared with other roles. Less than average crisis was experienced by women and men who had quiet babies who were healthy and ate and slept well.

In summary, people can get along better as parents if they prepare themselves for it and begin it at a suitable time. Satisfactory parenthood also depends upon social supports and upon the children themselves. When parents have a hard time, it is not always the result of something they did or did not do.

## JOYS AND SATISFACTIONS OF PARENTHOOD

When a group of California women rated benefits and costs of parenthood, the chief positive items were giving and getting love, enjoying children's activities, observing development, and helping and guiding growth. The costs included loss of freedom, privacy, and mobility, foregoing opportunities, worrying about children's health and well-being, and economic costs [4].

The feelings of a group of Australian mothers were found to be ambivalent, showing both anxieties and satisfactions [50]. Many of these women spoke of the pleasure they experienced when breastfeeding. "Breastfeeding really made me feel like a mother. That seemed to bring out this tremendous feeling that started down in my groin and worked up towards my head. Every time I saw her at the breast it was terrific."

In another exploration of the satisfactions that new parents experienced, 12 items were used: pride in the baby's development; less boredom; closer relationships with relatives; more appreciation of family and religious tradition; more interaction with neighbors; more to talk about with spouse; closer to spouse; fulfillment; appreciation of own parents; fun playing with baby; purpose in life; enjoyment of baby's company. Certain characteristics distinguished parents who felt more or less of these gratifications with their babies. The less educated the parents, the more pleasure they indicated. Men in occupations of lower prestige indicated more pleasure. This finding is hard to interpret. Perhaps it means that the less educated parents had fewer opportunities for interesting, pleasant experiences and therefore enjoyed their babies more fully. Or possibly, the more educated people were more aware of

problems and worried more about being parents and about their children's development. Other findings were that women under age 23 reported more maternal pleasure the longer they had been married, whereas women over 23 reported less pleasure the longer they had been married. Women's gratification was associated with placing high importance on the mother's role, high marital adjustment, and improved marriage. Men's pleasure in the baby was associated with having gone to parent classes and read books or cared for young children, placing the father role high in importance, and seeing a positive change in the marriage [42].

Many of the pleasures mentioned could apply to later stages in the parent-child career, when children are older. Playing with the child and enjoying his or her company may increase as children are more able to share activities with parents. Many fathers have more gratification from playing ball, boating, and camping with children than they do from playing with infants. Mothers, too, may enjoy sharing their work and recreation with children more than they enjoy the interaction with babies. If parents have to work very hard, and opportunities for recreation are limited, then they may not have many experiences of enjoying play with their children.

Even so, there are still many ways of being gratified by parenthood. We turn, now, to some of these satisfactions that do not come from parent-child interaction, but that still constitute some of the reasons why people have children. In thinking about these reasons for childbearing, we hope that our readers will evaluate them and decide for themselves whether they are good reasons.

## Doing What Comes Naturally

Growing up in a family, a young child sees family living as the way life is. A boy learns that he will be a daddy and a girl learns that she will be a mommy. What else could they expect other than to act like this daddy and this mommy? There has to be a baby, or several, to complete the picture. In imaginative play, the young child pretends parenthood, rehearsing future roles, being daddies and mommies, having babies, nursing, diapering, bathing, feeding, hugging, kissing, singing, spanking, scolding.

As the child grows older, he forgets many of the details of his preschool years, but he retains feelings about his experiences in the parent-child relationship and as a family member. College students remember the school-age period very well, however. Their memories of parental care and devotion have been found to be related to their attitude toward becoming parents [26]. Undergraduate men and women were divided into a group having highly positive attitudes toward having and rearing children and a contrast group with moderate to low attitudes toward parenthood. They were asked, "How much energy did your mother devote to your care and well-being (when not at work)?" and the same question in regard to their fathers. Highly positive attitudes toward childbearing and childrearing were more typical of students, both male and female, who remembered mothers and fathers as highly nurturant.

Thus, the child is oriented toward parenthood because his first experience shows him family life as the only way of living. The anticipated rewards are then influenced by the extent to which his parents are concerned and nurturant toward him. During the adolescent years, experiences outside the family make their impact. The young person talks with friends, reads, and views television. Expanded intellectual powers permit reasoning and thinking about parenthood. Even when careful thought points to one conclusion about childbearing and childrearing, the thinking is overlaid upon a core of emotional experience as a young child. And the most common attitude in young adults is, "Of course I want to have children. It's the natural way to live."

## Proving Oneself

Many people feel great satisfaction in knowing that they have made a baby and knowing that other people know it. Perhaps it is a special kind of competence, biological or reproductive competence, the exercise of certain bodily powers. The existence of the baby shows that its parents are sexually mature, fertile, and competent biologically. Sometimes one child is enough to prove this point for the parents, but there are people, probably more men than women, who like to prove it repeatedly. The Spanish word *macho* means a "virile, strong, brave man." The machismo pattern means that the male repeatedly seeks sexual conquests and, when married, tries to prove his continuing virility by siring many children. (Machismo is by no means confined to Latin cultures, nor is it universal in Latin countries [24].)

There are many good reasons for keeping the lid on machismo and letting one or two children prove the point. However, in thinking about reasons for having children, machismo is a powerful one. To a person whose self-esteem depends upon demonstrated virility, the rewards of reproduction are good feelings about himself.

## New Roles and Privileges

The role of new mother looks highly desirable in the enchanting pictures of mothers and babies shown in American magazines. Soft pink cheek rests on soft pink cheek. Shimmering golden hair trails over peach fuzz. Tiny fingers rest on a round breast. The scene gives promise of a new starring role that rivals the joys of a bride walking down the aisle. A romantic picture with slightly less impact is that of new parents standing beside the crib, watching their beautiful baby sleeping. It is almost as good as cutting the cake.

"When I am a mother (or a father), I'll be *really* grown up." Western civilization has no consistent way of conferring adult status. Is a child to consider himself a man, herself a woman, upon confirmation or Bar Mitzvah, on getting a driver's license, graduating from high school or college, voting, getting married, getting a job? (A Melanesian boy becomes a man when he moves into the men's clubhouse.) It is rewarding to know definitely that you have become an adult. If having a baby makes you feel grown up, then having a baby is rewarding. (In actuality, having a baby may or may not launch an individual into adulthood.)

Parenthood sharply changes the status of individuals in some societies. In India, a bride occupies a very lowly position in the family. Her status rises markedly when she bears her first baby, especially if it is a boy. Subsequent births improve her position. Her power increases enormously when her son marries, and this increase in power is implied in the birth of that first son. A new Indian father also advances in status, although the change in his position is not as marked as the mother's. The father does gain social approval for developing in the approved direction, in the stage of the householder. In Western society, there is a similar but weaker version of status advance through parenthood. The young couple usually feel social approval of their taking on parental roles and "settling down" into homemaking, childrearing, and community participation. Social approval and increased esteem are rewarding.

## Doing One's Duty

**Family Duty.** Parents of young marrieds are often eager to be grandparents. The paternal side wants its name carried on. Both sides want their genes passed along. They think it will be rewarding to have grandchildren to watch, care for, give to, boast about, and eventually perhaps leave some money to. The young couple may feel the pressure exerted subtly, or their parents may simply urge them to have children. In bearing a baby, many a young woman feels that she is giving her mother a gift, perhaps giving all four grandparents a gift. Sometimes it is an offering with which she hopes to obtain more love than she has heretofore had from her mother.

To a Hindu, family duty is also a religious duty. In order for the dead male ancestors to advance from one stage of being to a higher stage, they must have the prayers of their male descendants. A father needs a son to pray for him and for his father and grandfather. The male line msut keep going, and as it flows on unbroken, the wives receive spiritual benefits as part of the husbands' salvation. Therefore, bearing a son, or enough sons to surely have one who will discharge the religious duty, is a solemn family duty for a young couple. They understandably feel fulfilled when they perform this essential service to the husband's father, all his male ancestors and their wives.

**Duty to Church or State.** Duty toward a group can also motivate reproduction. When a minority group wants more power, or perhaps just to maintain its position, an obvious way is to increase its numbers. A steady increase can be assured by convincing members that their duty is to reproduce. "Be fruitful and multiply" is a command from the Lord, recorded in the book of Genesis, first spoken to Adam and Eve and later to Noah. Since that time, the same command has been given by various religious bodies. A young modern couple may feel satisfaction in doing their duty as Catholics, Jews, or Mormons when they produce another baby to join the church or temple. The group may be a racial minority. Many American blacks oppose birth control for black people because they want their numbers to increase. Nations, especially in wartime, have often promoted childbearing as a patriotic duty. Hitler exhorted "Aryans" to reproduce as a duty to Germany and to a particular physical type of German. Sometimes a political, religious, or racial group rewards mothers for repeated childbearing by giving them medals and public notice, or designating them as "Heroines of the Republic." Long ago in French Canada, it was the custom to give a couple a farm for every dozen offspring. Thus, doing one's reproductive duty to the group can bring all sorts of rewards, from satisfaction and recognition to substantial material benefits.

## Immortality

Less specific than the Hindu reason for wanting sons, but still powerful, is the notion of living on through one's children. It may be in terms of genes being passed along

in an endless chain, or it may be influence, in terms of knowledge and behavior patterns passed from parent to child.

## A Source of Help and Support

Children help with the work on farms and in other family businesses. To an American pioneer family, the rewards of childbearing were economic, as well as personal and emotional. Parental assessments in Panama, the Dominican Republic, and Yugoslavia led to a conclusion that when children are economic assets, they raise their parents' regard for themselves [7]. In addition to feeling satsifaction with their child helpers, such parents would look ahead to their own old age, when children's efforts in the family business would provide security for them. The Indian joint family described on page 8 is an example. When Mr. Patel retired from managing the family's textile mill, he continued to live from the income it produced while his sons ran the business. Indian college women expressed a long-term time orientation when asked to finish sentences concerned with the satisfactions of having children. They talked mainly about the time 25 years hence, when adult children would offer pleasure, help, and support [30].

An analysis of parental evaluation of children in six countries (Japan, Korea, the Phillippines, Taiwan, Thailand, and the United States) showed the economic value of children to be strongest in rural areas and weakest among the urban middle class [21].

Intergenerational help, economic and otherwise, is given in the United States, as shown by a study of 85 sets of three-generation families in Minnesota [20, pp. 64–66]. All the help given and received was analyzed as to sources, which included immediate and extended kin, peers, church, social agencies, private specialists, and commercial sources. The grandparent generation received 65 per cent of its help from the other two generations; that is, their own children and grandchildren. For the parent generation, familial help was 53 per cent of all help received and for the married child generation, it was 44 per cent. Of total help given, the percentage given to the other two generations was 47 per cent for grandparents, 44 per cent for parents, and 28 per cent for married children. These proportions of help given and received within three-generation families show a high level of transactions between generations. A young adult, aware of all the cooperation between his parents and grandparents, would be realistic in thinking that by having children, he was producing a future source of help and support for himself.

Another situation in which financial aid comes to parents through children is when welfare assistance is given to parents who cannot earn enough to support their families. Since public assistance is given in proportion to the number of dependent children in the family, each child actually does increase the family income, small though it is.

## Pride and Vicarious Satisfaction

One of the pleasures of parenthood is, beyond a doubt, being proud of one's off-spring. What does it take to make a parent proud? It varies with the parent. One may be bursting with pleasure over a normally developing infant or a child who learns to read at age seven and passes each grade at the end of the year. Another parent may require the child to win a medal, get the highest marks, or look like a fashion model before that parent is proud. Similar to feeling proud is living one's life over through the child. Many parents seek pleasure in having their children do well where they failed, solve problems that stumped them, or win the recognition that was withheld from them. Even successful adults enjoy all over again the particular delights of stages that they have passed through and that their children are now living.

As with other anticipated pleasures of parenthood, pride and vicarious satisfaction may or may not be realized, depending on the child and on what pleases the parent. The desire for these pleasures is neither good nor bad. The way in which these desires are expressed can be either positive or destructive to the child.

# THE PARENT-CHILD CAREER

Since children grow up and parents grow, too, any parent-child relationship is constantly changing. Not only is it changing within itself but also in relationship to the other careers of the parent and the child.

## Marriage Affects Children

Both common sense and research [11, 18, 52] say that a loving, happy, strongly committed married couple are more likely than their opposites to provide a good atmosphere for rearing healthy, competent children. Women who were competent, involved mothers were found to have husbands who were competent and involved fathers who were doing well vocationally and who had warm relations with family and friends. Maternal involvement and competence were correlated with marital happiness and skill in communication [18]. Such men and women can talk over questions of childrearing and at the same time trust one another to do well in caregiving, teaching, setting limits, and loving. Another study showed that when a mother and father were highly hostile to each other, they were likely to use a great deal of punishment, little reasoning, and encouragement of dependency in bringing up their children [11]. Thus studies show the effects of extremes of the marriage relationship upon the ways in which parents behave toward their children.

## Parents' Perceptions of Children: Ups and Down

As adults look forward to parenthood, they may expect some stages to be more or less rewarding than others, but they cannot be sure until they get there. Whether or not children turn out to be sources of pleasure, most prospective parents surely hope that they will be so, and they look upon that pleasure as a reward of parenthood. The extent of the pleasure, its timing, and its balance with pain are all very difficult to predict.

### Relation to the Marital Career

It is commonly believed that having children makes a marriage stronger and more lasting. When ethnic differences were measured in a working-class sample, it was found that 70 per cent of the black group agreed strongly with this belief, whereas 58 per cent of the chicanos and only 28 per cent of the whites did so [19].

The research evidence on this question does not lead to a yes-or-no answer. It may be that children strengthen some kinds of marital relationships and weaken others. There is no good reason to think that children will improve a poor marital relationship. Research has shown, however, that children may be the only source of pleasure in an unhappy marriage [27]. Sometimes divorce statistics are used to support the notion that a marital relationship will be improved if the couple have a child or another child. The argument will be advanced that there are more divorces among childless couples and couples with few children than among couples with larger numbers of children. Actually, divorce is more common in the early years of marriage, when couples obviously have no or few children, as compared with later years. It is likely that couples who are not getting along well together do not have children, or do not add to the children they already have, rather than that the absence of children causes the breakup. However, some unhappy couples do stay together "for the sake of the children" until the children are old enough to leave home.

Many researchers have tried to find out what effects children have on parents. Because there are so many ways of approaching this broad question, the results of the research do not give a clear answer. A parent can experience problems and satisfactions at the same time, stemming from the same child. The results of children upon the marital relationship can be quite different from the satisfaction felt with the child. Several studies examined marital satisfaction in relation to stages of family life (defined according to ages of children). Using middle-class samples, two United States interview studies [8, 40], one United States questionnaire study [39], and one New Zealand questionnaire study [45] showed general satisfaction to be high in the beginning of marriage and parenthood, declining as the children got older, and increasing as the children left home. In a sample with above-average educational level, marital communication and adjustment were found to decrease as children were born and to increase when children left home [14]. Marital happiness of women with very young children was found to be low [17]. Correlates of dissatisfaction in marriage were examined in a large sample that included the proportions of social classes existing in one county. Results showed childless marriages to be more satisfactory. In contrast to nonparents, parents, especially those currently raising children, were less likely to be satisfied with their marriages. This was true regardless of sex, race, age, or income [38].

After summarizing many studies that show the negative effect of parenthood upon marital satisfaction, the Feldmans suggest ways in which the strain of childrearing upon marriage could be alleviated [13]. Supports for parenthood would include training ahead of time and on-the-job, time off for mothers, pay and pensions, help in conflict resolution, and more active parenting by fathers. Although we cannot ignore what research is telling us about the depressing effect of children upon marital happiness, childfreedom is not the only way of reversing this effect.

## Growth Through Parenthood

Another common belief is that persons increase in self-esteem through being parents. Research has confirmed this notion for men but not for women. The study of parenthood in Panama, the Dominican Republic, and Yugoslavia showed that for married people between 20 and 40, self-esteem was higher for childless women than for women with children, but that the opposite was true for men [7]. Apparently, men were built up by parenthood and women were not. Similar findings were reported in the United States by a review of literature on the transition to parenthood. In the early and middle adult years, women decreased in self-esteem and personal development whereas men increased [41]. Although these results may look like a large black mark for motherhood, the responsibility for them need not fall on the children. Quite possibly the role of homemaker and mother is held in low social esteem and the woman, therefore, sees herself as unworthy while performing in that role. It is at this time of life that many women are cut off from the occupational career that formerly gave them status and satisfaction. The homemaker role is often very burdensome, with little help in doing the dull and hard tasks. As the next chapter shows, parenting is an activity in which tremendous creativity and all sorts of talents can be used to the great advantage of children. Quality of care-giving, socializing, and teaching has direct effects on the child's physical, social, emotional, and intellectual development. Surely, if women and the rest of society appreciated these facts, women would derive more self-esteem from being competent mothers. However, some of the best educated women may reject motherhood because they do not understand all that goes into doing it well, and they do not wish to put out all that effort in the face of a general lack of appreciation.

Children do cause a great deal of work, but, at the same time, they stimulate parents to grow. Different stages of child growth call for different kinds of development in parents. Each state of parenting has its own special ways of growing and of failing to grow, and its own frustrations and satisfactions. As parents face the demands children place upon them, they experience both hope and fear. During pregnancy and at birth, as we have already discussed, transitions to new roles mean a shakeup of established routines and attitudes. Such growth is both painful and pleasant. Having a baby means knowing something one did not know before, having a special experience that makes a person different. Being parent to an infant, for most people, is the first time for being primarily responsible for a completely dependent person. It is a matter of life and death! First-time parents may feel overwhelmed when this thought hits them. It is suddenly very important to understand nonverbal communication and to communicate through physical channels. The baby offers chances for having new feelings and new transactions. It may be difficult to realize that the new baby is a unique and separate individual. Doubts arise. Will I be able to give the right kind of care?

**Early Childhood.**   As the child develops his conviction of being a distinct person and agent, the parents have to seek a balance between setting him free and providing the nurturance and limits that will keep him safe. This complicated process requires empathy, vigilance, patience, planning, and inventiveness. The toddler tackles problems of learning to walk, and talk, to manage for himself at table and toilet, to manipulate his toys. As he grows older, he explores, asks questions, starts new tasks, intrudes, and imagines. If the parent is open-minded and ready to grow, he will see some of what the child is trying to do and be. Again, the child's growth needs make pressures on the parent, and if the parent can respond to these needs, finds new ways of being creative. By this time, parents, most likely now deeply attached to their children, want to help the children develop. Hence they try to change their own behavior in ways that will be good for the child. But parents also experience frustration, anger, and feelings of inadequacy while socializing young children.

**School Age.**   The process of letting go, of course, continues when the child goes to school. As he or she learns skills and rules, parents both teach and learn from him. For all parents, but especially for immigrant parents, the child teaches new things learned in school, from friends, and from other contacts that the parent does not have. I (MSS) learned the states and capitals of the United States with my children. Later, living in India, the two of us (MSS and LSS) learned the geography of the country together.

Children push and pull their parents into community involvement that requires parents to learn and develop. Girl Scouts, Boy Scouts, parents' and teachers' (PTA) meetings, Sunday School, and so many more expect some commitment from parents. One does not have to be a parent in order to participate in such organizations, but for parents, the pressure is turned on. And, reluctant or eager, parents find themselves in new worlds where they have to adapt. Beginning in the school years and continuing even throughout life, children enlarge their parents' social contacts, bringing home friends, instigating contacts between families, showing parents new places to go for fun, and getting involved with social agencies. When a family moves to a new community, as does the average American once in five years, children are often the first links between the family and the new neighbors. At this stage of life, parents are most likely to learn more about children, in general, and to be able to see their own children in relation to others.

At the time that children are opening new worlds of activity and interest to parents, they also are more independent and may even contribute some help with housework. Thus, parents gain in freedom and also have more choices of activity open to them. There are possibilities for new friends, new social organizations, new skills, and new work. There are also possibilities for parents to feel like failures in launching their children into school and community.

**Adolescence.**    While the adolescent is struggling with his problem of separating himself further from his parents, alternating between wanting to be close and wanting to be independent, his parents suffer, too. Even when they realize that the child is ambivalent, and normally so, it is hard to keep trusting and loving, letting him make mistakes, neither hanging onto him nor pushing him out. The patience, self-control, and empathy needed are like the demands of preschool years, but new in scope. There is also a new pleasure, the adult thinking of which adolescents are capable. In spite of their sometimes babyish emotions, teenagers are capable of logical thought. They have interesting ideas on all sorts of problems that adults are also interested in, and discussions between the generations can be stimulating and rewarding to parents. Parents may doubt their own capacities for accepting their children's achieving of sexual and social maturity. They may fear having their own inadequacies exposed as their children's minds mature.

**Adulthood.**    Grown children can be tremendously growth-promoting to their parents especially if they are friends who enjoy each other's company. Adult children have all the advantages of adolescents and none of the disadvantages. They are like close friends, if parents realize that they actually are adults. But they are friends who have access to another universe of ideas, people, and experiences, all of which they can share with their parents. Thus, adult children represent a very important pathway of communication with the changing world as parents grow old and encounter the dangers of rigidity. With the shared past and long-standing intimacy and affection as a background, adult children are well fitted to know their parents' needs and potentialities, and to offer opportunities for growth that parents can use.

When parents grow old, they are likely to become more dependent upon their children than they have ever been before. They may need and receive economic aid, as well as assistance in planning and making decisions, in everyday tasks such as shopping and home maintenance. Grown children are very important sources of care, respect, and response. Since old people in Western society occupy a marginal position, with respect and recognition hard to obtain, the esteem of their grown children can contribute enormously to the parents' feelings of being worthwhile. Parents may fear being unloved, abandoned, or dominated by adult children.

## ADOPTIVE PARENTS

When people want to be parents but cannot give birth to children, they may acquire offspring through adoption. Or the couple may adopt because they can give birth

only with difficulty. More rarely, parents adopt children for other reasons, as they do when they feel needed by a child who has no parents or whose parents cannot care for her. Parents may add to the children they already have by adopting another child. Sometimes a man adopts children belonging to the woman he marries, in order to feel completely a father to them and to have the same legal obligations as a biological father. About 4 per cent of United States women eventually adopt a child [5]. About half of these women also bear children of their own. The average age of the adoptive mother is around 30.

Adoptive parents are definitely parents by choice, since it usually takes a great deal of persistence to get a child from an agency and a great deal of money to get one on the black market. An estimated 5000 babies a year are sold for up to $25,000 each [3]. An attempt to make this practice illegal is presently under way. Adoptive parents can receive most of the ordinary rewards and pain of parenthood, although they miss out on the pleasure of proving themselves biologically and thinking about their genes being passed on indefinitely. One of the drawbacks of adoptive parenthood (although some people think it an advantage) is not experiencing pregnancy, delivery, and the postpartum recovery period. As mentioned earlier, these physical experiences serve to break up routinized behavior patterns, to focus the parents on the new child, and to provide a setting in which parent-child bonds can most readily be established. As one adoptive father put it, "For months, I could hardly realize that we had a daughter. Suddenly, one day, she was here in the midst of us and we never really got ready for her. When she cried at night, I was always surprised."

People who adopt are not always married couples. Single people adopt children, often older children. Occasionally, homosexual pairs act as parents. Adoptive agencies used to insist upon the utmost conventionality in would-be adoptive parents, but now the agencies have relaxed on many of their regulations.

Adoptive parents face the task of dealing with the existence of their child's biological parents. In some cultures, such as traditional Hawaiian and Afro-American, a child can acknowledge and know both his biological parents and his adoptive parents, and the parents know and accept the reality. Not so in most cases of American adoption. Many adoptive parents would like to forget that they did not give birth to their child, and until recently agencies aided them by keeping the source of the child a deep secret. Upon reaching adolescence, children are concerned with their own identity and they search out all sorts of information about it. The adopted child wants to know about his biological roots and about why his parents did not keep him. He does not love his adopted parents less even though he wants to meet his own parents. If adoptive parents realize the normality of their child's desires, they can accept them more comfortably and can even help the child to learn what he wants to know. If they face the situation from the time the child enters their family, they can speak casually and truthfully of the adoption and answer the young child's questions as they arise.

## SINGLE PARENTS

Of the 4 million single-parent families in the United States, 90 per cent are headed by women [1]. A 1977 U.S. government report on the status of children says that 9.4 million children under 18 are living in female-headed families and 710,000 in male-headed families [46]. The report also notes that there has been a steady increase in numbers of children in female-headed families. Some single parents have never been married; others have lost a partner through divorce, separation, or death. Just about the only experience they all have in common is bringing up children without the help of a partner. Many single parents are poor and many are young. Figure 10-2 shows age trends in unwed motherhood.

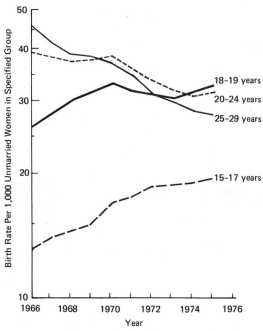

FIGURE 10-2     Age trends in unwed motherhood.

*Source: Monthly Vital Statistics Report,* Figure 2, **26:**5, Suppl., DHEW Publication No. (HRA) 77-1120, Washington, D.C., September 8, 1977.

**Unwed Mothers—by Choice.**    Unwed mothers who choose to have children can be divided into two main classes. First there is a small but growing number of well-educated, liberal women who plan to conceive and to provide a home and excellent care for the child. Figure 10-3 is from a newspaper article describing some of these unwed mothers, their problems and joys. Usually these mothers are unmarried because they have not found men they wanted to marry before they reached the age when they considered they should start childbearing. Because of their earning ability and social resources, they usually can meet most of their children's needs very well. However, the child of an unwed mother sees that other children have fathers and asks, "Where is my daddy?"

Second, about 10 per cent of teen-age out-of-wedlock pregnancies are intended [2]. Some girls wish to become pregnant in order to have a baby whom they can keep and love, and who, they think, will give them love and comfort in return. Most of these young mothers have no idea of what babies are like, how to care for them, and what it is like to be constantly responsible for another human being. Their physical and mental growth incomplete, their education unfinished, they have neither skills nor resources for meeting the needs of infants. These mothers, and all the other teen age mothers, are presently giving great concern to many people, including gov-

# Out of Wedlock

## Women Who Choose Unwed Motherhood Face Unusual Problems

### Some Career Women Stop Waiting for 'Right' Man; Social Scientists Worry

#### 'The Right to Have a Daddy'

By Deborah Sue Yaeger
*Staff Reporter of The Wall Street Journal*

Norlishia Jackson always had planned to have a child before she turned 30. As her 28th birthday approached, she still wasn't married. So she made a calculated decision: She got pregnant. Her daughter Kandi now is six.

"I wanted to experience motherhood and feel what it was like to have a baby growing inside me," says Miss Jackson, who is the holder of a bachelor's degree in psychology and a master's in counseling and guidance, and currently is director of a center for homeless girls in Washington, D.C.

In practical terms, Miss Jackson's situation now doesn't differ markedly from that of thousands of young mothers who are separated or divorced, the victims of unwanted pregnancies, or single adoptive parents. But the deliberate choice of single motherhood puts her among a small but growing number of women who are stirring curiosity and controversy among counselors, doctors and sociologists.

**FIGURE 10-3**    Unwed, and mothers by choice.

*Source: The Wall Street Journal, September 12, 1977, p. 1.*

ernment officials. Plans are being made for programs to help both mothers and babies and to prevent teen-age pregnancy.

**Teenage Parents.**    Half of all out-of-wedlock births in one year are to teen-agers [2]. More than 600,000 babies were born during a recent year to women between 15 and 19 years of age, one third of the babies to unmarried mothers and one third to mothers who had married after conception [2]. Two thirds of the total number of pregnancies were not intended. (The survey questions were asked *after* the babies were born, and probably show a higher rate of intended pregnancy then was actually the case.) Over 13,000 babies were born to mothers younger than 15.

(The United States has one of the world's highest rates for teenage childbearing.) Of the unmarried teenage mothers, 87 per cent kept the child. Consequently a large number of teenage mothers are bringing up children whom they did not intend to have. The majority of sexually active teenagers, especially the younger ones, do not use contraceptives. Many have vague and faulty notions as to how pregnancy occurs. Many have no access to contraception, or if they do, fear discovery by parents. Many feel that contraception spoils spontaneity, and makes a girl seem calculating, unromantic, or not nice. Among those who bring their infants to term and keep them, both the mothers and fathers have the handicaps of immaturity and lack of education and earning power. Teenage mothers, and often fathers, too, never catch up with their classmates who postponed childbearing until later [33]. Some teen-age parents get help from programs designed to help them learn and grow up. They are often a drain upon their own parents and cause disruption in their marital and family careers. They cost taxpayers billions of dollars [38a].

**Widowed, Separated, or Divorced Parents.**  Over half of the widowed, separated or divorced mothers work outside their homes [46]. Many of them are poor. Among them, they have over 5 million children. Even if a mother does receive enough money to support her family, the combined jobs of earning and childbearing are a crushing burden to carry. When mothers have to rely on unpredictable and/or stigmatizing sources of income, they suffer from feelings of being unable to control their own fate [6]. Since many single mothers do not have enough financial and emotional support, new policies and services are needed.

Single fathers are not very numerous, but they have recently become more noticeable through the fathers who seek and gain custody of children after divorce. Since men tend to earn more money than women, financial problems are not prominent for single fathers. Rather, they have to learn more about home management and child care [16]. Interviews with single fathers showed their problems to include dating and sex, finding time and patience for the children, making decisions alone, and finding caregiving facilities [35]. Parents and relatives were usually helpful. The fathers reported that they had become less discipline-oriented, more concerned about good day care and education, and more protective of their children.

# PATHS TO REJECTING PARENTHOOD

If people choose parenthood for its expected rewards, then they reject it because they do not expect it to be rewarding or not rewarding enough to offset the disadvantages. Although social pressures still impel many young couples toward parenthood, counterforces have been at work, starting in 1963 with Betty Friedan's blast, *The Feminine Mystique* [15]. Since that time, many feminist writers have pointed out the disadvantages of parenthood, especially motherhood.

Childlessness is increasing [49]. A recent study in the Northeast showed 17 per

cent of wives between 25 and 34 to be without children [32]. Among college graduates of the same age range, 35 per cent were childless.

A group of early decision-makers were studied by interviewing college students who wished to remain childfree and contrasting them with a group who wanted to have children [22]. The women planning to be childfree were more autonomous; although they were aware of social pressures to have children, they were less concerned about the disapproval they would encounter. They also had some support from others who accepted childfreedom.

Cooper and her associates [9] interviewed 44 couples who had decided to remain childfree. The main motive of the childfree couples was to have more personal freedom. Other important motives were having fewer responsibilities, and lack of interest in being a parent. Wives reported much interest in careers and in having greater time and intimacy with their husbands. Six of the couples had decided independently, before marriage, to be childfree. Most of the rest came to the decision through thoughtful discussion of life styles, taking an average of 2.3 years to arrive at an explicitly stated agreement. In half of these couples, the decision was entirely mutual, and with the other half, one spouse pushed more than the other for an agreement on childfreedom. Almost every person expressed enthusiasm and satisfaction over having chosen to be childfree. Although most perceived some pressure from other people to change their decision, they did not think that their childfreedom affected their relationships with parents, in-laws, friends, acquaintances, clergy, physicians, and workmates. They did, however, tend to seek childfree friends and associations.

The question of couple disagreement on childfreedom was examined in a sample of 40 couples. When it was the husband who first opted for childfreedom, the wife was likely to come over to the same point of view. If, however, the wife wanted no children and the husband did want children, he was likely to divorce her unless she gave in to his wishes. The author concluded that because the husband's marital power is usually much greater than the wife's, childfree marriages may not differ much from traditional ones. Wives have fewer alternatives to their present marriages than husbands do. Therefore, wives are more likely to accommodate themselves to their husbands's wishes [28].

## DETERRENTS TO REPRODUCTION

The burdens of motherhood have received a great deal of attention lately and many disadvantages may apply somewhat more to mothers than to fathers. However, offspring bring disadvantages to men, too, as some of the following will show.

### Restrictions

Children tie you down! Nobody doubts it. Even partners who are sure they want children will postpone pregnancy for a few months or years. They want to be free to have fun together, to advance in their work, to assemble a pleasant place to live, to travel. Society generally approves of a period of freedom for newlyweds.

If the first baby brings an end to carefree recreation, travel, and spending and severely limits the mother's job potential, then can the second be even more restricting, and the third . . .? Yes. Each child adds to the work load of the parents, using an additional portion of their time, energy, and opportunities for being alone together [25]. Figure 9-1 shows the total hours of daily household work done in families with none to nine children. It is harder to get an adequate baby-sitter for two children than for one. A friend or relative may be willing to mind one child but not two. Whereas a couple might take one small child backpacking or bicycling, two are likely to be backbreaking, and three impossible. One child can sleep on a cot in a motel room or in the grandparents' spare bedroom; two might squeeze in; three would spill over. For a women who wants to have a job or to study, every additional baby poses more problems.

**Expenses**

Everyone knows that children cost money, but nobody knows just how much each one is going to cost before he reaches the point of earning his own living. Partners contemplating parenthood will note that the mother will have to give up her job at least temporarily and that child care will cost something either in lost income or hired services. Medical care will also cost, but it may be scaled to their income. If the prospective parents do not look beyond the first year or two, they may think that babies don't eat much and that many of their clothes will come from presents. When a child approaches adolescence, however, he needs *more* food than an adult. His clothes cost more because he grows out of them quickly and also gives them hard wear. And actually, new babies do cost a great deal in terms of medical fees, housing, equipment, loss of income, and increased need for insurance.

Using data gathered by the U.S. Department of Labor, a study of expenditures per family member shows the following: a family with a disposable income between $10,000 and $15,000 spent $840 per person on food when it consisted of two members (a family total of $1680) but only $462 per person when there were five members (a total of $2310). For housing and utilities, the two-member family spent $1219 per person ($2438, total), the five-member family $535 ($2675, total). Figures for the three-member family were $549 for food and $875 for housing, per person [10]. Each addition to a family in a given income bracket thus means less spent on basic items for each individual in it. Any projection of costs over the next 18 years would of course be in today's dollar values. However, let us take a modest estimate of the average yearly cost of a present-day child, $4000. Multiply this figure by 18 years and it can be seen that the child costs $72,000. Send the child to college and you will add 4 × $6,000 or $24,000, for a total cost of $96,000. Give her a fancy wedding or buy him a car and the investment approaches $100,000.

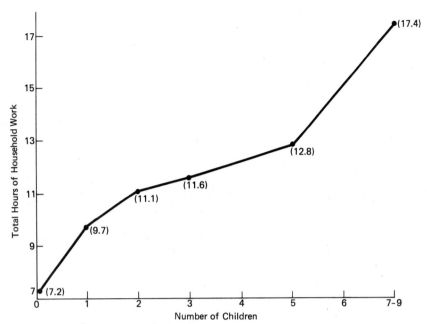

**FIGURE 10-4**   Total hours of daily household work by all workers in families where the homemaker is not employed outside the home.

Data from Katherine E. Walker. Household work time: its implications for family decisions. *Journal of Home Economics,* 1973, **65** (7), 7–11.

## Children Not Enjoyed

As mentioned previously, it is hard for parents to know whether they will enjoy their children or not, and whether they will enjoy then at all ages and stages. If a person feels definitely negative toward children, including potential offspring, it surely will be a deterrent to reproduction. But social pressures from family and friends being what they are, some child-dislikers succumb and produce children.

Women's liberation and other social forces are making it more comfortable for those who wish to resist pressures toward parenthood. Books and magazine articles analyze these pressures, urging women (rarely men) to be individuals and do what they themselves really want to do. For example, *Life* magazine published the following:

> The eight years before we had children were glorious. I had an enjoyable career, an idyllic home life. But friends pitied us, undoubtedly worried that we would continue living hedonistic, meaningless but terribly comfortable lives until we became parents .... You don't have to justify being childless. It's no one's business but your own if your ovaries don't work or if they do. If you are pressured to "prove yourself," take it from one who has been there [37].

PARENTHOOD: A MATTER OF CHOICE                    **321**

### Fear of Being a Bad Parent

A person can like children and yet not feel suited to being a parent. He (or she) may not want the restrictions on time, money, and freedom to move. A woman may feel physically inadequate for pregnancy, labor, and child care. Noncommitment to permanent marriage may look like an obstacle to being a good parent. A person may wish to remain single. A history of depression or emotional instability can make a person cautious about his potential as a parent. One of the pair may worry that the other one would not be a good parent, even though quite *self*-confident.

### Fear of Effect on Marriage

A couple may want to keep their pair relationship just the way it is, not risking it with the introduction of a third member. If they know something of the research on child-bearing as a crisis, they may choose to avoid that crisis.

### Concern with Population

A few years ago a young woman received national notice for her valedictory speech at a college graduation. Pretty and talented, the very picture of an ideal American girl, she announced that she had regretfully given up any plans to bear children. Her reason was her worry over the population explosion. At present, there is nothing remarkable in young women and men rejecting parenthood because they believe that the earth already has too many people. It is all too obvious that the increasing population is an important cause of food shortages, crowding, pollution, and the ravaging of land and sea.

There are, however, many couples who are not directly influenced in their reproductive behavior by the threat of overpopulation. Perhaps those who give it as a reason for childlessness are using it to rationalize, or more likely, as a valid additional reason to support their decision.

### Social Disapproval

Although all the voluntarily childless wives studied by Veevers [48] felt social disapproval directed against them, a growing number of people do not disapprove of childlessness but rather disapprove of people who bear many children. In crowded parts of the world, such as Indonesia, Tonga, and India, government officials post signs saying that two children are enough. In the United States and Canada, voluntarily childless people support each other and are approved by many individuals and some organizations, such as NAOP, the National Organization for Optional Parenthood. An example of NAOP's positive approach is their use of the attractive term *childfree,* instead of the negative *childless.*

## REASONS WHY PARENTHOOD IS DIFFICULT

In addition to the reasons implied in the previous section, "Deterrents to Parenthood," are some others that make parenthood less than blissful.

### Complication of Relationships

As Figure 9-5 shows, the husband-wife dyad involves only one relationship. When one child is added, the relationships are represented by a triangle instead of a straight line, because they include husband-wife, father-child, and mother-child. With the birth of the second child, the number of relationships jumps from three to 6, because the newcomer relates to three people. A family with four children includes 15 different relationships. If one adds groups, such as Child 1 and Child 2 in relation to Child 3 and Child 4, the relationship network becomes ever so much more complex. Often parents will notice that when just one family member is absent, the whole atmosphere changes, sometimes for the better, sometimes for the worse, but usually in the direction of tranquility.

## Permanence

There is no acceptable way to terminate American parenthood. If incompatible parents and children could divorce each other, the situation would be quite different. There are cultures where it is all right for children to wander off and live with relatives or friends for indefinite periods, which they may well do when things get tough at home. Or it may be permissible for parents to give out some of their children for adoption, as did the parents of an Indian friend of ours. In this case, the motivation was not to get rid of their lovely daughter, but to share their children with a brother who had none. In contrast, in the United States, there is practically no reason that would justify a couple giving up a child, except a serious abnormality of the child. Even parents who do not wish to shoulder the burden of caring for a retarded child are often told that the child will be better off at home and they should devote themselves to making the best possible life for him.

The state rarely steps in to rescue a child from inadequate parents, even though the parents' behavior is really a cry for help. Legally, and by custom, the rights of parents have been held to be more important than the welfare of children. Hence, child abuse often reaches extreme levels before a neighbor tells the authorities or the parents themselves take the child for treatment. Even then, the parent is not routinely given the chance to undo parenthood, but efforts are made to rehabilitate the person as a parent.

A number of fathers, and some mothers as well, try to escape parenthood by deserting. They may thus shift most of the burden to the other parent, but the deserting parent will still be required to pay for the support of children to the extent to which he possibly can.

## No Choice

In discussing reasons why people choose to be or not to be parents, we assumed that people actually were choosing. It is true that birth control technology is available in all parts of the world, but it is not available to all people. There are still many women who conceive without wanting to do so and men who impregnate without wishing to become fathers. A survey by the International Planned Parenthood Federation

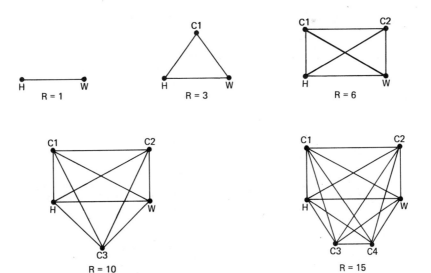

**FIGURE 10-5** Number of pair relationships in families of 2 to 6 members. H = husband. W = wife. C = child. R = number of 2-person relationships.

showed only one third of the world's adult population as knowing enough about birth control to plan their families [29].

Even the willing parent has little choice beyond being or not being. Technology that is basic to choosing the sex of one's child is not yet developed for ordinary use. There is as yet no way to choose a pretty, clever child, big or small, fair or dark, quiet or noisy, outgoing or inward-oriented. Children affect parents in different ways, as every parent of two children knows. Parenthood can be a delight to the willing parent who gets a compatible child; it can be frustrating and disappointing with a child who does not fit the parent's capacities and expectations.

### Social Nonsupport

In comparison with some other countries, the United States does little to assist parents in preparation for parental roles, in making choices as to becoming parents, or in performing as parents. For one reason, there is no overall family policy. States and local communities do as they see fit. The limited offerings in school are confined largely to girls, and in some school systems, to girls who are not very talented academically. Controversies rage regularly over whether sex education belongs in the schools, even though it is the only place where many future parents will ever have a chance to learn basic facts and technologies and to discuss implications intelligently. Education for child care and development has low status, is often dismissed as mere baby-sitting, is pinched on fundings, and its teachers are paid less than teachers of physics and computer science. Public provisions for health care, nutrition, and family-centered recreation are abysmal. But why go on with negatives? The following section illustrates some supports to parents that are offered in various parts of the world, including some enclaves in the United States.

## AIDS TO PARENTS

The following are examples from our reading and experience and are not at all exhaustive of the ways in which various societies support parenthood.

Supports to Latin American mothers have been required by law ever since the 1920s [24]. Privileges and protections include paid maternity leave, free medical care for mother and child, a layette and milk for the baby, a cash allowance for breast feeding, time off during work hours for nursing the baby, nurseries for infants located in factories and firms where women work.

Children's allowances are given to all mothers in Canada in amounts graduated to the age of each child. Although there is a question as to the wisdom of encouraging childbearing, it is still true that cash payments to mothers make it easier for women to carry on in the maternal role. Government-supported low-cost medical and hospital insurance are widely available, making it possible for most parents to get health care for their children.

The Swedish government set up the Royal Commission on Sex Education and paid for a comprehensive study of the Swedes' sexual knowledge, behavior, and attitudes. The results gave information on what had been accomplished to date by the official sex education program and how it might be made more practical. The study showed that 98 per cent of Swedes wanted unmarried mothers to have all the rights of married mothers, a situation that largely prevailed [34].

Free contraceptive services are provided for all who accept them in China, India, England and other countries. In China, a local health worker makes monthly visits to each woman of childbearing age, checking on her use of contraceptives and her satisfaction with them [44]. Although population control is an important aim of most government-sponsored birth control services, the quality of family life is also enhanced by family planning.

Milk and dairy products are subsidized by the New Zealand government, to the extent that everyone can afford them. Thus, the nutrition of children is underwritten. Government subsidies make physicians' fees very low, prescriptions free, and hospital care almost free. Financed by a combination of government payments and voluntary efforts, parent education if offered to all, not just in groups and classes but on an individual basis as well. Marriage counseling is available. Recreation facilities are within geographic and financial reach of almost all urban dwellers. Business and work hours are planned to permit maximum use of the many parks, swimming pools, courts, beaches, and playing fields.

College and university education is free in Sri Lanka and the U.S.S.R. for students who qualify for higher education. Competition is fierce for the few positions.

In the kibbutzim of Israel, all the work and responsibilities of parents are shared by the whole communal group. The parent-child relationship is one of enjoyment and emotional closeness. Parents are not involved with providing food, clothes, education, medical care, and discipline to their own children any more than they are in providing for all children in the kibbutz. Child care and responsibility are also shared widely in China [44].

On the island of Bali, villages put on dance dramas in the temple courtyards. In the village where we visited, the young mothers go together to these affairs, enjoying each other's company during the performance. The babies and toddlers go, too, as does everyone in the village, but the grandmothers, not the mothers, are in charge of the young children for the evening.

In Chapter 1, we wrote about how work is shared in joint families, as is common in Asia. Although many restrictions may be, and often are, placed upon young adults, the responsibilities and work of parenthood are shared, and loneliness is not a problem. Parents never experience the depths plumbed by the North American parents who believe that their children's shortcomings are the result of their own inadequacies as parents and as persons.

There are, of course, supports to American parents. The federal Department of Health, Education and Welfare disseminates information, sponsors research, and funds assistance programs within the limitations of its budget. Private voluntary agencies make many important contributions. For example, the Vanier Institute in Canada and the Child Study Association of America educate parents and parent educators. The Family Service Society provides a variety of programs, including group and individual counseling, day care, and family planning services and educates both clients and leaders.

**Parental Support in New Family Forms.**  Utopian societies are both old and new in the United States. They have come up with many imaginative and ingenious arrangements for sharing the burdens of parenthood. A longitudinal study of alternate family forms in California offers some concrete examples of efforts to relate practice to theory [12]. The 50 families in the study included unmarried couples and single mothers, many living in groups, and communal families. Perhaps the first sharing of parenthood is in giving birth, which is usually done at home, with the help of other members of the community, and with the attitude that the new baby is a treasure to all. Infants are held, carried, and breast fed for warmth, closeness, and "naturalness." Nursing mothers switch babies for feeding, sharing their gift of milk, caring for more than their own, and thus teaching the babies to trust adults in general. When infants reach two and a half or three years of age, they become members of children's groups, who do much to care for one another. Mothers are then freed from intense child care. Adults, as well as children, are seen as having rights.

**SUMMARY**  Figure 10-6 summarizes the two opposing sets of pressures on persons as potential parents.

Gratifying to some but not to others, parenthood is not the only path to challenge and growth. Having children is a personal choice, even though many outside pressures for and against childbearing are often exerted. After choosing to be a parent, the questions *when* and *how many* must be answered.

Readiness for parenthood involves many areas of life, including physical, financial, emotional, and occupational ones. Plans for each conception require evaluation of the whole family situation at that particular time.

The transition to parenthood may be a crisis, depending upon how difficult it is to make the necessary changes and adjustments. Degree of difficulty depends upon the parents themselves, their own resources, the social supports, and the baby. Pleasures with children vary between persons and from one time of life to another. Other satisfactions through parenthood involve meeting all sorts of expectations, proving oneself in various ways, discharging duties, achieving new status, religious values, pride, and vicarious satisfaction.

The parent-child career goes up and down in satisfactions, as does the marital career. Each career affects the other. The middle stages of both the parent-child and marital careers tend to be relatively low. Some of the pain of being a parent is associated with personal growth. Various demands for parental development are typical of different periods of child development. Although women's self-esteem tends to decrease in the middle years and men's to increase, it is not certain that parenthood is the reason.

Adoptive parents are parents by choice. They miss some of the experiences of

**FIGURE 10-6**     Pressures toward and against parenthood.

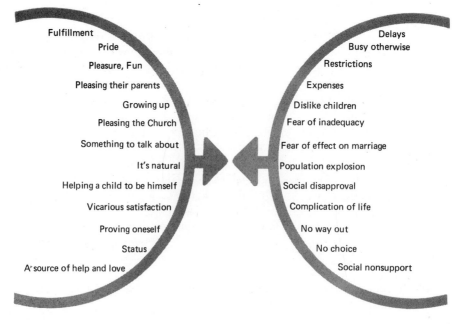

| | |
|---|---|
| Fulfillment | Delays |
| Pride | Busy otherwise |
| Pleasure, Fun | Restrictions |
| Pleasing their parents | Expenses |
| Growing up | Dislike children |
| Pleasing the Church | Fear of inadequacy |
| Something to talk about | Fear of effect on marriage |
| It's natural | Population explosion |
| Helping a child to be himself | Social disapproval |
| Vicarious satisfaction | Complication of life |
| Proving oneself | No way out |
| Status | No choice |
| A source of help and love | Social nonsupport |

biological parenthood but their responsibilities to children are the same as those of all parents. Some single parents are parents by choice and single by choice. They often get together in groups to help each other to meet the demands of parenthood. Most single parents are poor, young, and female. Teenage childbearing, a growing problem, curtails healthy development of both baby and parents.

A few voluntarily childless couples enter marriage with an agreement not to have children. The rest go through a lengthy period of discussion and decision-making. Deterrents to reproduction include restrictions on freedom to work, play, and travel; increased housework and hours spent in child care; the financial burden imposed by children; dislike or nonenjoyment of children; fear of parental inadequacy in self or partner; desire to keep the partnership relation as it is; awareness and concern with world population problems; social disapproval of childbearing, a recent reality for people who have more than two or three children.

Being a parent is often difficult. The addition of each child complicates the relationships in the family group. No matter how incompatible a particular child-parent dyad may be, Western society offers no acceptable way of severing the relationship. Even parents who have made a true choice of childbearing have little or no choice as to the characteristics of their child.

In many countries, including the United States, support offered to children and parents is not very substantial. In other countries, for example, China, childrearing is shared and parents are aided. In some of the new types of families, as well as in some of the older and rarer experimental forms, parents are assisted by the community.

**REFERENCES**
1. Albin, Rochelle. New looks at single parenting: Focus on fathers. *APA Monitor,* 1977, **8:6,** 7–8.
2. Alan Guttmacher Institute. *11 million teenagers.* New York: Planned Parenthood Federation of America, 1976.
3. Baby black market. *Marriage and Family Review,* 1978, **1:2,** 14.
4. Beckman, Linda J. Exchange theory and fertility-related decision-making. *Journal of Social Psychology,* 1977, **103,** 265–276.
5. Bonham, Gordon S. Who adopts: The relationship of adoption and social-demographic characteristics of women. *Journal of Marriage and the Family,* 1977, **39,** 295–306.
6. Bould, Sally. Female-headed families: Personal fate control and the provider role. *Journal of Marriage and the Family,* 1977, **39,** 339–349.
7. Bortner, R. W., Claudia J. Bohn, and David F. Hultsch. A cross-cultural study of the effects of children on parental assessment of past, present and future. *Journal of Marriage and the Family,* 1974, **36,** 370–378.
8. Burr, Wesley, R. Satisfaction with various aspects of marriage over the life cycle: A random middle class sample. *Journal of Marriage and the Family,* 1970, **32,** 29–37.
9. Cooper, Pamela E., Barbara Cumber, and Robin Hartner. Decision-making patterns and postdecision adjustment of childfree husbands and wives. *Alternative Lifestyles,* 1978, **1,** 71–94.

10. Cutright, Phillips. Income and family events: Family income, family size, and consumption. *Journal of Marriage and the Family,* 1971, **33,** 161–173.
11. Dielman, T. S., K. Barton, and R. B. Cattell. Relationships among family attitudes and child rearing practices. *Journal of Genetic Psychology,* 1977, **130,** 105–112.
12. Eiduson, Bernice T., Jerome Cohen, and Jannette Alexander. Alternatives in child rearing in the '70's. *American Journal of Orthopsychiatry,* 1973, **43,** 720–731.
13. Feldman, Harold and Margaret Feldman. Effect of parenthood at three points in marriage. Paper presented at meetings of the American Orthopsychiatric Association. New York, 1977.
14. Figley, Charles R. Child density and the marital relationship. *Journal of Marriage and the Family,* 1973, **35,** 272–282.
15. Friedan, Betty. *The feminine mystique.* New York: Norton, 1963.
16. Gasser, Rita D. and Claribel M. Taylor. Role adjustment of single parent fathers with dependent children. *Family Coordinator,* 1976, **25,** 397–401.
17. Glenn, Norval D. and Charles N. Weaver. A multivariate, multisurvey study of marital happiness. *Journal of Marriage and the Family,* 1978, **40,** 269–282.
18. Heath, Douglas H. Maternal competence, expectation, and involvement. *Journal of Genetic Psychology,* 1977, **131,** 169–182.
19. Heath, Linda L., Brent S. Roper, and Charles D. King. A research note on children viewed as contributors to marital stability: The relationship to birth control use, ideal and expected family size. *Journal of Marriage and the Family,* 1974, **36,** 304–320.
20. Hill, Reuben, *Family development in three generations.* Cambridge: Schenkman, 1970.
21. Hoffman, Lois W. A cross-cultural study of the value of children. Paper presented at meetings of the American Psychological Association, New Orleans, 1974.
22. Houseknecht, Sharon. Reference group support for voluntary childlessness: Evidence for conformity. *Journal of Marriage and the Family,* 1977, **39,** 285–292.
23. Illsley, Raymond. The sociological study of reproduction and its outcome. In S. A. Richardson and Alan F. Guttmacher (Eds.). *Childbearing: Its social and psychological aspects.* Baltimore: Williams & Wilkins, 1967.
24. Kinzer, Nora S. Priests, machos and babies: Or, Latin American women and the Manichaean heresy. *Journal of Marriage and the Family,* 1973, **35,** 300–312.
25. Knox, David and Kenneth Wilson. The difference between having one and two children. *Family Coordinator,* 1978, **27,** 23–25.
26. Lott, Bernice E. Who wants the children? *American Psychologist,* 1973, **28,** 573–582.
27. Luckey, Eleanore B. and Joyce K. Bain. Children: A factor in marital satisfaction. *Journal of Marriage and the Family,* 1974, **32,** 43–44.
28. Marciano, Teresa Donati. Male pressure in the decision to remain childfree. *Alternative Lifestyles,* 1978, **1,** 95–112.
29. McDonald, Corbett. Quebec birth rate drop "remarkable." *London* (Ontario) *Free Press,* October 24, 1973.
30. Mead, Robert D. and Labh Singh. Motives for child-bearing in America and in India. *Journal of Cross-Cultural Psychology,* 1973, **4,** 89–110.
31. Metropolitan Life Insurance Company. Average ideal family size of married women. *Statistical Bulletin,* 1978, **59:**1, 10–12.
32. Miller, Celia E. What's happening to the U.S. family size? *ZPG National Reporter,* July 1977, 8.
33. Moore, Kristin A. and Linda J. Waite. Early childbearing and educational achievement. *Family Planning Perspectives,* 1977, 9:5, 220–225.

34. Moskin, J. Robert. Sweden: The contraceptive society. In Arlene S. Skolnick and Jerome H. Skolnick (Eds.). *Family in transition*. Boston: Little, Brown, 1971.

35. Orthner, Dennis K., Terry Brown, and Dennis Ferguson. Single-parent fatherhood: An emerging family life style. *Family Coordinator,* 1976, **25,** 429–437.

36. Polit, Denise F. Stereotypes relating to family-size status. *Journal of Marriage and the Family,* 1978, **40,** 105–114.

37. Radl, Shirley. Mother's day is over. *Life,* May 19, 1972.

38. Renne, Karen S. Correlates of dissatisfaction in marriage. *Journal of Marriage and the Family,* 1970, **32,** 54–67.

38a. Rich, Spencer. Teen pregnancies in 1979 said to cost U. S. $8 billion. International Herald Tribune, May 15, 1979.

39. Rollins, Boyd C. and Kenneth L. Cannon. Marital satisfaction over the family life cycle: A reevaluation. *Journal of Marriage and the Family,* 1974, **36,** 271–282.

40. Rollins, Boyd C. and Harold Feldman. Marital satisfaction over the family life cycle. *Journal of Marriage and the Family,* 1970, **32,** 20–28.

41. Rossi, Alice S. Transition to parenthood. *Journal of Marriage and the Family,* 1968, **30,** 26–39.

42. Russell, Candyce S. Transition to parenthood: Problems and gratifications. *Journal of Marriage and the Family,* 1974, **36,** 294–302.

43. Rutter, Michael. Maternal deprivation, 1972–77: New findings, new concepts, new approaches. Paper presented at meeting of the Society for Research in Child Development, New Orleans, 1977.

44. Sidel, Ruth. *Women and child care in China*. Baltimore: Penguin, 1973.

45. Smart, Mollie S. and Russell C. Smart. Present, past, and projected satisfaction in stages of the family life cycle in New Zealand. *Journal of Marriage and the Family,* 1975, **37,** 408–415.

46. Snapper, Kurt J. and JoAnne S. Ohms. *The status of children 1977*. U.S. Department of Health, Education, and Welfare. Office of Human Development Services. DHEW Publication No. (OHDS) 78–30133. Washington: U.S. Government Printing Office, 1978.

47. *Toronto Globe and Mail*. U.S. couples plan fewer children. October 2, 1974.

48. Veevers, J. E. Voluntary childless wives: An exploratory study. *Sociology and Social Research,* 1973, **57,** 356–366.

49. Veevers, J. E. *Childless by choice*. Toronto: Butterworth, 1979.

50. Westbrook, Mary T. Analysing people's experience of events: A study of the childbearing year. Unpublished Ph. D. thesis, Macquarie U., Australia, 1975.

51. Westbrook, Mary T. and Linda L. Viney. The application of content analysis scales to life stress research. *Australian Psychologist,* 1977, **12,** 157–166.

52. Westbrook, Mary T. Reactions to childbearing in early maternal experience of women differing in marital relationships. *British Journal of Medical Psychology,* 1978 (in press).

# CHAPTER 11

# Living and Learning with Children

Parents and children affect one another throughout all of their interactions, starting with conception. As they enter parenthood, a woman and a man say good-bye to certain parts of themselves and hello to new ways of being, because a certain new individual has begun.

## HAVING A BABY

### Pregnancy

After the sperm penetrates the egg, the fertilized egg descends the Fallopian tube to float in the uterus. The fertilized egg divides into two cells, then four, and continues to divide. After about a week, when the organism has become a ball of cells, it attaches itself to the wall of the uterus. Meanwhile, in the ovary at the spot from which the egg burst forth, the *corpus luteum* (yellow body) is developing. If the egg had left the uterus instead of attaching itself to the wall, the *corpus luteum* would have regressed and disappeared. When the developing egg implants in the lining of the uterus, however, the *corpus luteum* continues to develop in the ovary, producing the hormones of pregnancy and thus taking part in the development of the bodies of the woman and embryo.

Throughout the whole period of pregnancy, the woman's body performs three functions in addition to all that it does in the nonpregnant state. It nurtures the organism that is to become a baby, it prepares for giving birth, and it prepares for breast feeding the future baby. Although all three functions proceed without any conscious effort or knowledge on the part of the women, she is involved as a whole person.

Pregnancy is an *experience,* different from all other experiences, just as each part of the sexual cycle is a unique experience. It has its own perceptions and emotions, strengths and vulnerabilities. Figure 11-1 shows the pregnant woman in the first, second, and third trimesters.

**Development and Experiences.** The first trimester (three months) is a time of reorganizing and rebalancing bodily processes. The **embryo** is much too small (about 10 grams weight and 22 millimeters length at six weeks) to be a drain on her nutrients or a strain on her abdominal muscles and pelvic organs. Why, then does the first stage of pregnancy often bring on a need for extra sleep and rest, emotional ups and downs, a finicky appetite and nausea? The best answer seems to be that the changeover of the body from nonpregnant to pregnant state requires considerable use of energy and resources. The nausea of pregnancy is most likely caused by the biochemical balance or imbalance that is typical at this time. The experience of the bodily state is probably similar to the experience of rapid growth during the pubescent growth spurt, when hormonal balances change, energy needs are great, and emotional reactions are often heightened.

The beginning of the second trimester usually marks a change in bodily functions and perceptions. At this time, the healthy pregnant woman feels well and vigorous. She looks pretty, with the "glow" of pregnancy. The changeover has taken

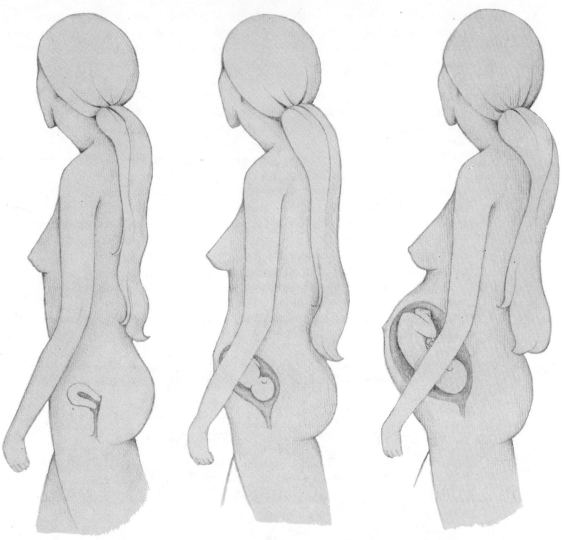

**FIGURE 11-1**     Three trimesters of pregnancy. Left to right: approximately one month, five months, and eight months.

place and her bodily systems have settled into their expanded functions that are basic to nurturing the fetus. (The embryo completed the structure of its basic systems at eight weeks and achieved the new name and status of **fetus.**) As the fetus increases in size, the woman's uterus grows larger. Early in the second trimester, the top of the uterus rises above the pelvis, making a little bulge in the abdomen. She looks pregnant, as well as pretty. The next important experience is **quickening,** feeling the fetus move. Of course, the fetus has been moving for a long time, but, floating freely in the amniotic fluid, the movements could not be felt. Only as the fetus grows big enough to push against the walls of the uterus can the pregnant woman feel what is inside her. At first it feels like a gentle fluttering. As the fetus grows bigger and stronger, pushing more vigorously against the uterine walls, the fluttering turns to squirming and thumping. Fetuses are individuals, just as infants and children are. Each fetus has its own pattern of moving and responding to stimulation.

By the end of the second trimester, the fetus is well finished as to bodily structures, but it must grow bigger and more mature before it will be ready to be born. The tasks of the pregnant woman during the third trimester are to carry an increasingly heavy load, to supply more and more nutrients, to remove more and more waste products, and to prepare for labor, birth, and lactation. Thus, all of her systems must work harder. Dramatic changes take place in some of them. Blood vessels and blood supply increase. The uterus and birth canal develop in size and functional capacities. Breast tissue increases and the breasts begin to secrete colostrum, the infant's first food. Many of the normal bodily changes require some adjustment, such as expanded clothing, more frequent urination, more rest, more bathing, and careful attention to eating enough of essential nutrients. And while bodily preparation for birth goes on spontaneously, psychological preparation is a matter of conscious effort and learning. During the third trimester, a North American woman has the option of taking a course that will teach her how to control her body and perceptions during the birth process (see pages 337–338). Since probably she has had little or no experience with birth and since the culture offers next to nothing in the way of preparation, this is her last chance to get ready for the enormous physical and emotional performance.

**Sharing Pregnancy as Partners.**   Until quite recently, a husband was an object of pity and the butt of jokes as he waited nervously in the waiting room, excluded from his wife in the labor and delivery room. The stress of fatherhood is real. An English study showed one in seven to nine suffering some symptoms in reaction to his wife's pregnancy, including nausea and expansion of the abdomen [52].

Americans and Canadians used to hold two strangely conflicting notions on the nature of pregnancy and childbirth. These were women's topics and women's business, to be discussed and performed by wives but not husbands. At the same time, childbirth was the province of male doctors, who were the real authorities and stars of the show. It was as though the obstetrician, not the mother, produced the baby. Although this situation still prevails for some women and men, it does not have to be so.

For couples who choose modern prepared childbirth, the man is an active participant in pregnancy and birth and the woman's performance is the center of interest. The doctor or midwife and nurses assist the mother to deliver the baby. When abnormal conditions occur, doctors diagnose and treat.

The first pregnancy brings new situations to the couple and requires them to grow and change by adapting to the new. The woman has experiences with her body that she can share through communication with her partner. Both are likely to have misgivings or fears or feel excitement and anticipation about the new roles and responsibilities that they are about to take on. Information about the developing embryo and fetus are interesting to both and make for strengthening the bonds between them. Although it is natural for the woman to be preoccupied with her perceptions and thoughts, her behavior may look like withdrawal from her partner, or a pushing aside. Her awareness and his understanding can serve as a bridge. So also does their joint planning for taking care of the child, both short-term and long-term.

Preparation for childbirth includes both expectant parents. Since the father can assist the mother at birth, he must learn along with her. As well as instruction in the processes and conduct of labor, prospective fathers are usually given a lesson or two in the special contributions of fathers to the heredity and development of the child. Childbirth preparation classes are held for groups of couples in about the same stage of pregnancy. Thus, they share one another's problems and anxieties, often finding reassurance and solutions. When the father is not available to share the pregnancy and birth, or does not choose to do so, the mother can still prepare herself and can even share it with another person. In the era before father participation, women were assisted by other women who *cared*. Nurses and midwives are worldwide helpers of women in labor.

## Preparation for Childbirth

Essentially, preparing for childbirth means learning about the physiology of labor and how to control and work with the natural processes. For this reason, it is sometimes called **natural childbirth.**

Different cultures have different ways of preparing individuals for childbirth. First of all, there is the basic attitude and interpretation that permeates the culture [35]. Pregnancy is considered an illness by the Cuna Indians of Panama, where a pregnant woman consults her medicine man daily and takes medicine throughout labor. Some societies see pregnancy as a sign of strength and sexual adequacy. Many cultures, including Judeo-Christian, have interpreted birth as defiling and have required women to be purified afterwards, through religious ceremonies. The Puritans, like their English forebears, thought that labor pains were the cross that God placed upon women for Eve's sin and that woman's honor could be recovered by the bearing of children. A sixteenth-century English writer published this quotation, ". . . we are conceived in filth and uncleanness, born in sin and care and nourished with pain and labor" [44]. The fear, shame, and guilt built up by such beliefs would practically guarantee painful and difficult childbirth! Pain is minimized in societies where childbirth is regarded as a natural event with which women are equipped to cope. This is not to say that birth is painless in any society. It can be more or less so. Some individuals report experiencing no pain at all. Pain can be dealt with in different ways that minimize or maximize, that blot it from memory through amnesiacs, or that eliminate it from perception through drugs or psychological training. Modern

Western culture has developed, in addition to drug-dependent methods, two main methods of controlling and sometimes preventing the pain of childbirth.

**Read Method.**    Grantly Dick-Read, an English physician, began in 1914 to develop his theory and method of childbirth without fear. He believed that pain resulted from tension caused by fear and anxiety. Instead of working in harmony, the muscles of the uterus work against each other and abdominal muscles may also hold back the birth process. Therefore, the pregnant woman is taught details of her reproductive system, the anatomy and physiology involved in labor. She does exercises to promote physical fitness and learns relaxation and controlled breathing. She learns of the experiences of other women, trained in this method, who found birth a supreme experience. During labor, she uses skills she has acquired under the guidance and support of doctors and nurses trained in the Read method. Their confident expectations are important in maintaining her own control and freedom from tension-causing pain. Although drugs are used only minimally in the Read method, they are not forbidden. They are used when the woman or the doctor sees a real need. The Read method and methods derived from it are commonly used in the United Kingdom today.

**Lamaze Method.**    During the 1950s, Russian obstetricians applied the conditioning principles of Pavlov to childbirth. Lamaze brought the method to France and from there it spread to the rest of the Western world. The Lamaze method is now the most widely used method of preparation for childbirth in the United States and Canada.

Lamaze training is given during the last two months of pregnancy to a woman and the partner who plans to help her during labor. As in the Read method, they learn the anatomy and physiology of reproduction. Then the woman learns to perform breathing and mental concentration that control her brain activity in such a way that pain sensations are blocked out [51]. By strongly activating one area of the brain, other areas are rendered inactive and do not respond to incoming stimuli. Emotions influence bodily functioning, and fear produces changes that create pain during labor. Words act as stimuli to produce emotional states and can thus create fear and pain. Through teaching, words can be used to produce positive emotional states and thus to eliminate fear and pain. Anesthetics are used, if needed, but the need is minimal, since prepared women wish to retain control and experience the birth.

Growing numbers of parents attest to the effectiveness of childbirth preparation, especially the Lamaze method. It is the standard birth method in the Soviet Union and China and is used in half the births in France [51, p. 253]. An American study contrasted women who followed the Lamaze method with a group who did not receive systematic psychological preparation. The outstanding findings were that the Lamaze group developed more positive attitudes toward pregnancy, had more positive experiences in labor and delivery, had less pain, and, after the birth of the baby, had more positive views of themselves. Husbands' participation during labor and

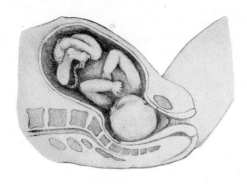

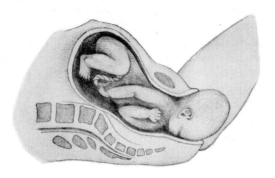

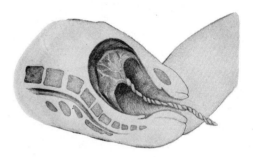

**FIGURE 11-2**     Three stages of labor.

presence during birth contributed greatly to wives' feelings of rapture. These wives perceived their husbands as strong and helpful, whereas wives in the control group often saw their husbands as weak and helpless [51].

      **The Birth Process.**   Labor is real muscular work, since it is the force that pushes the baby out of the mother's body. The first stage of labor serves to dilate, or open, the cervix, making a passageway out of the uterus into the vagina. The uterus contracts rhythmically, pushing the baby downward. At the same time, muscles surrounding the opening relax and are pulled upward, thus enlarging the opening. This stage lasts several hours, the length of time varying greatly from one woman to another and from one labor to another. As labor progresses, contractions become stronger and closer together. The traditional term for contractions is *labor pains*. Since contractions do not always hurt, and the word *pain* is likely to stimulate fear and pain, this word is not used by Lamaze and Read practitioners. During the first stage, the prepared couple put their knowledge into practice, breathing, relaxing, back-rubbing, and keeping up confidence and positive attitudes. The most difficult time in most labors is the end of the first stage, when the cervix is enlarging to its full opening.

The second stage consists of pushing the baby out of the uterus, through the vagina and out of the mother's body. Now the mother feels like pushing, and her efforts help, whereas in the first stage, the uterine contractions are not under her conscious control. The prepared woman has techniques for breathing, bearing down and relaxing that she can exert precisely. The husband coaches, as for an athletic event, which indeed it is. Doctors, midwives, and nurses direct them both, acknowledging the father as part of the team. As the baby emerges, the prepared mother feels a tremendous sense of achievement, even joy and rapture. Some women equate the experience with an orgasm. The father, acting in partnership at the birth, feels his own joy and catches the supreme emotion of the mother.

The placenta and membranes are expelled during the third stage, monitored carefully by the medical personnel but little noticed by the new parents. The traditional patient is usually anesthetised at this point, the father is still in the waiting room. The prepared couple is ecstatically greeting their new baby and telling each other how wonderful they are and how much they love each other. The prepared-for baby, usually alert now, may be put to the mother's breast for a welcoming few drops of colostrum. The new mother, of course, has already had some interaction with her infant before giving birth. The first three hours after birth have been shown to be an important time for mother-infant adaptation [25]. If the father is present at this time, he, like the mother, is fascinated with the baby and spends the same time touching, holding, and looking [37].

**Obstetrical Assistance and Intervention.**   Having a baby is not a very risky venture as far as the mother's survival is concerned. Today, the United States maternal death rate is less than 4 in 10,000 live births, whereas in 1930, it was 67 in 10,000 [50]. Childbirth is safe because of good obstetrical care. Although the great majority of births are normal and could be conducted without a physician, not all emergencies are predictable. For the safety of mother and baby, it is best to have the knowledge, skills, and equipment of modern medicine available. Every pregnancy should be monitored and supervised so as to apply the best knowledge and judgment to nutrition and to any irregularities or problems.

Qualified midwives can take care of a normal pregnancy and birth, but medical doctors are needed in abnormal cases. The skills and knowledge derived from Lamaze or other such preparation are not substitutes for qualified medical personnel but are useful in cooperation with them. Although it is true that babies have been born in taxis or at home without professional assistance, it is much safer for mothers and babies to use the advantages offered by modern medicine.

**Drugs for Labor and Childbirth.**   Sedatives induce calm, drowsiness, or sleep; amnesiacs make the patient forget; analgesics reduce pain; general anesthetics induce unconsciousness; local anesthetics block the transmission of impulses through nerves. A wide range of drugs is used to accomplish these purposes at different times, in various women. Research on infants has indicated that excessive use of drugs is harmful to embryos and fetuses and that infants may suffer from the effects of drugs given prenatally. A review of the effects of drugs on the neonate concludes,

> there is enough evidence to date that obstetric anesthesia in any form involves an element of calculated risk to the infant. Without denying the great beneficial possibilities of analgesia and anesthesia, one should consider carefully the alternative of natural childbirth, by means of hypnosis or one of the various relaxation techniques, whenever the physical and emotional condition of the mother allows it. [2]

Obstetricians are aware of these findings. Their responsibility is to judge the type and amount of medication that are most beneficial to mother and infant. Although the patient can talk over these matters with her doctor, she must trust his judgment when she is in labor, since the obstetrician, not the patient, has the training and experience that qualifies him to decide. When a complication requires a painful procedure, such as surgery, the doctor orders an appropriate anesthetic. The use of Caesarian section, although not a normal birth, is of tremendous benefit to mother

A prepared mother, fully awake, greets her daughter who was born a few minutes ago.

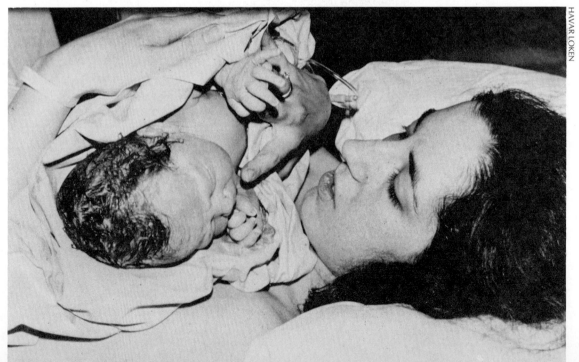

HAVAR LOKEN

and infant in cases where it is needed. When an abnormal birth occurs, the mother cannot have the experience of controlling her body. Some hospitals prepare both parents for a Caesarian delivery and permit the father to be present during the birth [26]. Mothers may be able to breastfeed on the delivery table, just as in a normal birth.

## Childbirth Services

In pioneer days in America, birth services were given mostly at home, by husbands, midwives, women friends, and occasionally doctors. In 1935, 35 per cent of babies were born in hospitals; in 1976, 95 per cent were [9]. A reappraisal of birth services is presently underway. More and more couples are looking for alternatives to hospital deliveries.

**Hospitals.**   Obstetricians and hospitals are prepared to deal with difficult cases and emergencies. They perform a growing number of Caesarian sections. They save the lives of premature babies and babies otherwise at risk. Often they are overe-quipped for normal cases. Although many hospitals are changing in response to patient demands, the general atmosphere of a hospital is likely to be that of a place where patients are sick and where established routines are followed. The use of medication in childbirth has been very common and almost routine. Mothers and babies have been kept apart, except for scheduled feeding times. Fathers have been permitted only to look through windows at their babies. Siblings were excluded entirely. Such treatment prevented the spontaneous bonding at birth between parents and infant, made it difficult or impossible for mothers to breastfeed, and cast a feeling of gloom and separation over a family. Some hospitals now keep parents and infant together for a while after birth and allow rooming in, where the baby stays in the mother's room. A few even let young brothers and sisters visit their mother and new sibling. A couple wanting such a modern hospital may have to hunt for one, but if they persist, they will probably find it.

**Home Births.**   More and more families are turning to home deliveries as a way of making birth more natural, shared, joyful, healthy, and inexpensive (55). Doctors, midwives, and nurses are involved. An obstetrician-midwife team, doing only *normal* deliveries at home, reports on 560 cases with no fatalities and only one serious problem. Ecstatic reports by several of their patients attest to the emotional satisfaction to the whole family when a birth is celebrated as a wondrous family event.

**Birth Centers.**   In an attempt to bridge the gap between hospital and home, birth centers offer both a homelike atmosphere and lifesaving equipment for use in case of emergencies. The Maternity Center, in New York City, is an established birth center that now serves as a model. Doctors consult during the pregnancy. Nurse-midwives deliver the babies, but doctors are available at the time of the delivery for consultation and emergencies. A quick transfer to a hospital is made on those rare occasions when it becomes necessary. The Maternity Center gives preparation for childbirth and supportive education after a baby is born. I (MSS) am currently involved with setting up a birth center in Rhode Island.

**La Leche League.** An association devoted to promoting breastfeeding, La Leche League International, Inc., has many local chapters. Prospective mothers learn to prepare for lactation and new parents receive help with breastfeeding. For instance, with a first baby, a mother can use some help from an experienced woman in positioning the baby, keeping his nose free for breathing, bringing up air bubbles, and expressing milk for use in a bottle when the mother wants or needs to be away for a feeding. La Leche colleagues promote pride and confidence in breastfeeding, helping a new mother to fully enjoy the experience and to appreciate its importance to her baby.

Today, new findings in nutrition and growth emphasize the physical benefits of human milk for human infants. Psychological studies indicate emotional benefits of breast-feeding to both mother and baby. Women's frank acknowledgement of sexuality includes recognition that breast-feeding is a stage in the sexual cycle and that it brings sensory gratification to the pair who participate in this symbiotic activity. Ethologists point out that sucking is attachment behavior, through which the infant builds the basis of a love relationship with his mother. Suckling is the reciprocal role, through which the mother strengthens her own attachment to the baby. The mother and baby on page 343 are here seen in a reciprocal relationship and mutual enjoyment.

**Help at Home.** Hospitals send mothers home three or four days after birth. Mothers go home from a birth center a few hours after delivery. New mothers need to rest in order to reorganize their bodies, recuperate from the fatigue of labor, and establish lactation. The rest period is recognized in the old terms "confinement" for a birth, and "lying-in period" for the time of recovery. In an earlier period in North America, the lying-in period was about two weeks, and extra rest was prescribed for at least six weeks, the period of the return of the uterus to normal. American women used to stay in hospital for ten days to two weeks. Women still do in New Zealand, but in the United States, the cost is prohibitive. No matter whether a short or long rest period after birth is deemed correct, the new mother needs several weeks of extra support from someone, as she takes care of the baby, establishes her breast milk, and reorganizes her body. Many new fathers are able to give considerable help and support at this time. Grandmothers often come to help, also, especially if there are other children in the family. Some professional help is highly desirable, even if it is just for reassurance and advice. Often it is possible to have visits from a nurse who is skilled in promoting the adjustments of infants and their families.

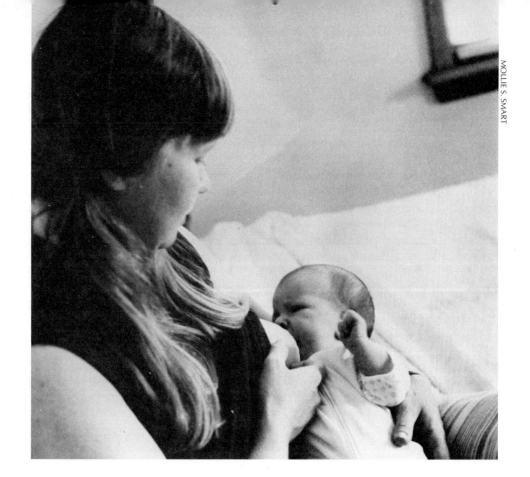

## PARENTING

Interaction and mutual influence continue throughout life with parents and children. Many studies show mutual influence over a short time, although long-term results of any specific behavior are hard to prove.

As parents, men and women make different contributions, as well as similar ones. For example, fathers are more visually attentive and playful; mothers do more caretaking and talking [37]. Babies with involved fathers are more able to cope with unusual situations and strange people. A mother's verbal stimulation is important in the infant's cognitive development.

### The New Look in Fathers

Recent years have seen a growing number of books and articles about fathers and their importance to children. Earlier studies dealt with father absence and what went wrong, but now fathers are being appreciated for their presence.

The Women's Liberation movement has led to a realigning of men's and women's roles [30]. While women are getting jobs and developing careers, men are expanding their lives and interests in children and homemaking. As men and women share more at home and at work, men are getting more involved with their children and enjoying it. Another influence is shared childbirth. When couples go together to prenatal classes that prepare them to give birth together, the father is included and important in childrearing from the prenatal period. Of course there have always been some fathers who took care of their babies and who spent a lot of high-quality time with their children, but now there are more such fathers. The involved father makes a double contribution to the baby, directly in his interactions, and also through the mother. His relationship with her affects her as a parent, and him, too. When a mother has intense, continuous interaction with her children, she is likely to feel fatigued and irritated, just as anyone would with any long-lasting, unrelieved responsibility. A review of worldwide anthropological literature concludes that children are more likely to be rejected when mothers and children are alone together all day than when fathers and grandparents are present [40]. When parents are hostile to each other, both are more likely to use much punishment and little reasoning with their children [17].

## Functions of Parents

While parents are performing their functions of caregiving, socializing, and teaching their offspring, they have feelings of love, enjoyment, pride, annoyance, fatigue, anxiety, and more. Children react to the feelings, as well as to what parents do and say.

**Caregiving.**   Care is one of the components of love. Taking care of children is, in almost all societies, considered the duty of parents. Sometimes parents get a great deal of help from servants, kin, or community. An extreme example is the Israeli kibbutz, where the bulk of care is given by adult members *(metaplot)* who specialize in the caregiving function.

When very immature persons give birth, as do many teenagers, they usually do not know how to care for a baby adequately, nor do they have the physical and emotional resources to do so. Often the grandmother provides the baby care, especially in black families. Some teenagers learn caregiving from programs given by schools or other agencies. Learning techniques of feeding, bathing, and diapering is not enough. Parents also have to learn what to expect of babies and children, how to interpret their behavior, and how to deal with their own feelings of frustration.

Child care means providing for safety, health, and growth through shelter, food, clothing, regulation of stimulation, sanitation, medical attention, and protection from noxious influences. To a degree, the child's health is a measure of the care given by his parents. A healthy child is not only free from illness and wounds but also has weight proportionate to his height, lively skin and eye color, shiny hair, firm muscles, balanced posture, abundant energy, curiosity, concentration, and resilient emotions.

In the area of child care, the family system has important interaction with the physiological systems of the child, on one hand, and on the other, with educational, economic, and political systems of the nation and the world. For example, poor children throughout the world are smaller than children whose families have adequate incomes. When income is adequate, then the educational and occupational level of parents shows up as an influence, as seen in a Danish study of the skeletal maturity of children 7 to 18 years old [3]. Thus if parents do not have the money to buy food, children will be undernourished; but even when money is available, educated parents will supply a better diet. The same point could be made in the area of keeping children free from infections. Where poverty prevails, children are often invaded by bacteria, viruses, worms, amoebas, bacilli, and toxic chemicals, because their parents have little power to keep hookworms out of bare feet, amoebas out of the drinking water, or lead paint off the walls. When parents can pay for better living conditions, their knowledge of child care makes an obvious difference in their children's health. If parents know how infections are carried, they can prevent them through cleanliness techniques and teaching. Parents can help the ill child to recover with minimal stress because they know that rest and high protein food will aid the child's resources in overcoming infection. Health care is discussed further in Chapter 14.

**Neglect and Abuse: the Negation of Care.**   The abusing parent is incompetent in the role of caregiver [20]. Abuse takes the forms of attack (verbal, physical, and sexual) and neglect (failing to give adequate food, protection, response, and stimulation). Although one parent, more often the mother, actually does the battering or starving, the problem is really one of family interaction and of interaction between the family and the other systems in the society [21].

When the interaction patterns of abusing and neglecting families were compared with those of normal families, a difference was found in the mothers [11]. Mothers in abusing families directed few contacts to other family members and accentuated the negative. Mothers in neglecting families also made few positive and many negative responses to their children. This is not to say that the mother is the cause of child abuse, but to show something of the kind of family interaction in which abuse is likely.

Figure 11-3 illustrates child abuse. The victims of abuse are often infants and young children, but children of all ages, including teen-agers, are abused by their parents. Many of these children who are abused are unwanted, often conceived out of wedlock by parents of low socioeconomic status. Some child abuse occurs at all socioeconomic levels, however. A nationwide survey of abused children revealed 29 per cent of them as deviant in social interaction and general functioning, 14 per cent with physical deviations, and 8 per cent with intellectual deviations [22] Although lack of care may have produced the deviations in the children, the fact

# Why do parents abuse their children?

By STEPHEN P. MORIN
Journal-Bulletin Staff Writer

PROVIDENCE — Louise S. began abusing Suzanne a few minutes after she was born.

"Everybody told me that a daughter would be beautiful and perfect," she recalled. "But when the nurse showed me Suzanne, she was all red and ugly and she was crying. I threw her at the nurse and screamed, 'Get her out of here. I don't want her.'"

Things didn't improve when they left the hospital. An unmarried mother living on welfare at only 18, Louise felt abandoned by her family and her boyfriend.

She took her frustrations out on her daughter. Before Suzanne could crawl, Louise routinely slapped and punched her for messing her pants or for crying.

\* \* \*

MARRIED LATER, LOUISE had two other daughters and remembers throwing them to floor and pummeling them with her fists "until I was completely exhausted."

When Suzanne was 2, her mother beat her so badly her face swelled like a red balloon. Louise packed her daughter's face in ice and took her to a doctor. She was worried about her daughter's condition. But Louise really wanted help for herself. The doctor's remedy was simple. "Next time," he told her, "get a punching bag."

Three years ago, Louise joined Parents Anonymous. Now, from a different perspective, she says: "I think the reason I hit my kids was because I was uncomfortable with myself."

\* \* \*

PUBLIC CONCERN has been heightened recently by a series of abuses that appeared to take the form of an epidemic. In March, 18-month-old Shawn W. was slain during a brief visit with his mother. His parents have been charged with the murder.

On May 10, a Warwick family was charged with sexually molesting three foster children in its care.

On May 14, five-week-old Tina D. died after being beaten on the head because her crying annoyed her mother's boyfriend, Warwich police said.

Three days later, Noel P., 7, of Central Falls, bled to death after allegedly being stabbed by his mother. She told police: "God made me do it."

On May 18, Warwick police arrested a man for twice throwing the 23-month-old-daughter of his sister in Narragansett Bay. The man was apparently angry because the baby had soiled her pants. Although she didn't die, the girl was hospitalized for bruises and human teeth marks on her body.

\* \* \*

FIGURE 11-3    Child abuse is more prevalent than many would like to think.

*Source:* Providence Evening Bulletin, June 7, 1978.

remains that the abused children presented great problems to their parents, in their undesired births and in problems of functioning. A substantial number of the parents were themselves unwanted and abused babies. Thus the parents already knew family violence, having experienced it from their own parents. When they became parents, they already had violent, aggressive behavior patterns available to use. When these parents met frustrations, often from being poor and having few resources of any kind, their difficult children made it all the harder to cope with their multitudes of problems. Not knowing how to get the baby to stop crying or the toddler to stay out of the way or the child to stop wetting the bed, the parent hurt the child instead of caregiving or teaching.

The two *essential* conditions for child abuse are, first, cultural justification for the use of force against children and, second, isolation of parents from support systems [20]. Thus our society makes child abuse possible, and even likely, by maintaining that parents, and even teachers, have the right to hit children. Lack of social, economic, and other support systems is illustrated in the preceding paragraph. Parents Anonymous is an organization designed to give the kind of support that helps parents who are incompetent in the caregiving role, or who fear that they could abuse their children. A recent evaluation has shown Parents Anonymous to be very successful in stopping child abuse and helping parents to gain in self-esteem and adequacy [12]. The organization has about 600 local chapters. The national office is at 2180 Artesia Boulevard, Redondo Beach, California 90276.

**Socializing.** Parents teach children how to function as members of their family, community, and society. The process of socialization results in the acquisition of the behavior patterns, values, beliefs, attitudes, knowledge, and skills of a particular culture. Through socialization, the child builds a concept of self as worthy or worthless, competent or incompetent, masculine or feminine, able or unable to exert control. Socialization orients the child to present, past, and future, determining to a large extent willingness to delay immediate pleasure for future gains, as well as evaluation of the past. Parents perform many socializing functions in regard to their children, but they obviously do not do the whole job. Nor does the family do it all. The younger the child the more the parents are likely to be the main socializers. Of course, there are exceptions, such as upper-class families who employ nurses and teachers as caregivers and socializers.

Strictly speaking, all teaching is socializing, but we plan to use the term *teaching* for parents' functions in purposefully helping their children to acquire intellectual and motor competencies. Under *socializing,* we are concerned with shaping the child's social and emotional behavior, his attitudes and values, and his assumption of the roles defined by his culture. Of all the roles that everyone must learn, sex role is one of the roles most strongly influenced by parents. The topic of gender-role learning is covered on pp. 82–90. Parents also act as socializers in the contexts of emotional expression and control and moral development.

**Outside Influences on Socialization.** In socializing, just as in caregiving, parents' behavior is influenced by social systems outside his family. The occupational and economic systems are linked to the family in modes of parent-child interaction. For example, observations of black parents with their fifth-grade sons revealed the more *educated* mothers as encouraging their children's autonomy more and as using more words [13]. When fathers came from higher *occupational* levels, mothers encouraged sons' autonomy. The more educated the fathers, the more love they expressed and the more words they used.

*Race differences* may be important in the socializing practices of parents. When black and white high school students of the same socioeconomic level were questioned, the black students reported more close relationships with both fathers and mothers than did the white students [49]. In an extensive study of the effects of parental authority patterns on preschool children, the black girls seemed to respond differently from white girls to authoritarian parental practices [4]. The black parents enforced directions firmly, did not encourage individuality, and often one of the pair

was rejecting. Compared with white girls whose parents behaved in this manner, the black girls were more domineering, independent, and very much at ease. The author suggests that since black women, as compared with white women, have outstanding competencies, their socialization practices most likely prepare their daughters for survival in a difficult world. "Perhaps the black girl admires and seeks to emulate her aggressive mother whose forcefulness assures her security." Thus the daughter, although made to conform as a child, would learn the adult role by watching her mother's performance and successes.

**Emotional Expression and Control.** Parent's personalities and childrearing practices are related to children's personality characteristics and emotional behavior. High self-esteem is more likely in children when family interaction is highly positive

[32]. Parental warmth, nurturance, supportiveness, acceptance, and love are all associated with healthy development of children [54].

A review of many studies of father-absent children brought out the important influence of fathers on their sons' emotional expression and self-control [7]. As a preschool child, the father-absent boy is likely to be more dependent, anxious, less aggressive, less masculine, and less mature than other boys. Studies of school-age father-absent children have revealed a high rate of behavior problems in regard to school adjustment [7, p. 77]. During the school years and adolescence, father-absent boys are more likely than other boys to be weak in peer relationships, conscience, impulse control, and delay of gratification, and thus to have problems in handling their aggressive impulses [7, pp. 63–68]. High aggression was found more typical of boys whose fathers were absent owing to divorce than of boys whose fathers were dead [41]. Some studies of father-absent girls have shown them as more dependent on their mothers and as having more difficulty in dealing with their aggressive impulses than girls with fathers at home [7, p. 111].

The mother is seen as an important influence on boys' self-control in several studies concerned with resistance to temptation. Interviews and family interaction observations were conducted with adolescent boys and their parents discussing typical discipline situations [31]. The boys were also tested on yielding to the temptation of touching objects that they had been punished for touching. Self-control was related to the degree of mothers' communicativeness, but not to that of the fathers, and not to general measures of discipline. The important contribution of the influential mothers was most likely their asking for information about the problem and then discussing and interpreting it. In other words, they reasoned with their sons.

**Moral Development.**   Children's goodness has been measured in terms of what they know and what they do. Tests of moral knowledge and judgment, such as Kohlberg's, use stories that present moral problems. The subject's solutions form the basis for locating him in a stage of moral development. Data from the longitudinal Berkeley Growth Study show that fathers' and mothers' moral judgment levels correlated with those of their sons over the age period 10 to 20 [23]. However, there was no significant relationship between parents' and daughters' scores [27]. A study of moral judgment in normal and delinquent boys and their mothers also showed results consistent with the Berkeley data. The mothers of nondelinquent boys, as well as the normal boys themselves, showed higher levels of moral judgment than the mothers of delinquent boys and their delinquent sons. New Zealand boys' moral judgments, as shown by a moral dilemmas test, were similarly related to the support that they thought they received from their parents [46]. The relationship did not hold for girls. The fact that these studies showed no relation between parents' and girls' moral judgments does not prove that there is none, but only that the methods used did not reveal any.

The action part of moral behavior includes doing what one knows to be right: telling the truth, helping, giving, being kind and generous, not hurting others, and respecting the rights and belongings of others. Studies concerned with moral action have examined some of these behaviors. Generosity and helping are of special interest. Research on all sorts of moral behavior shows that it is influenced by age, experience, and conditions of the experiment. Although much of the research on altruistic behavior has been done in laboratory experiments, the results have some implications for parents. Experiments have shown that in such situations as giving to charity or sharing treats with friends, children are most likely to do what a model does and to say what he says [10]. That is, if an adult makes a donation, so does the child, but if he tells the child it is nice and kind to give but does not give himself, the child will not give but will be able to say later that giving is good. The warmth shown by the model will increase the child's imitative actions, but only if given when the child imitates. Otherwise, the model's warmth is likely to make the child self-indulgent. The hypocrite, who practices selfishness and preaches generosity, loses ability to influence children as they grow beyond about nine years of age. When a selfish model praised chidren's donating, they gave less than when they were praised by a generous model or even by a neutral model [36]. The implications for parents are clear. If they want their children to be kind and generous, they will have to show them, as well as tell them, and it will help if they respond with warmth and praise when the child is doing right.

Research on helping or rescuing others from pain and peril suggests that children, as well as adults, are held back from action by fear that they will break rules or that other people will think poorly of them. For instance, when children were told that it was all right for them to leave the room, they were more likely to go to the aid of a child crying in the next room [47]. Sympathy for the person in distress probably plays an important part in a child's rescue attempts, since in so doing, he is trying to relieve his own upset feelings. It seems likely that parents promote children's helping behavior when they demonstrate it themselves and when they appear to get satisfaction out of doing so [10].

## Discipline: Practical Implications of Research on Socialization

The word *discipline* is sometimes understood as *punishment,* unfortunately. Like the word *love,* discipline has many meanings. To us, it means "teaching the child to control himself and to behave and feel as a cooperating member of his family and his society."

Discipline is closely related to love, since children want to please the people they love. Therefore, there is more power in a reason, rebuke, or reward from a loved one than from a person with no emotional meaning for the child. By being warm and loving, having good times with the child and meeting his basic needs, a parent lays down the foundation for discipline.

**Setting Limits.** Good discipline includes making clear what kind of behavior is permitted and what is not. Mrs. Katz arranged her kitchen cupboards with nesting pots, wooden spoons, clothespins, and plastic milk bottles in a large lower section. All foods and cleaning material are kept in high cupboards. Jerry, age one and a half, goes to his cupboard and plays with his toys. The kitchen is a place where the choices open to Jerry are mostly between one piece of "good" behavior and another piece of "good" behavior. At an older age level, say ten years, an environment that promotes good behavior might be a back yard with a basketball hoop and a tree, but no flower beds.

The child also needs to be told what he may do and what he may not do. It is not enough to say just *no* or *don't* but it is necessary. *Limits* are a line drawn around something that is right. "You may go out, but be home by 10 o'clock." "You can buy a jacket by yourself, but $—is all we can afford." "Yes, you can read to the end of the chapter before you turn the light out." In setting limits such as these, parents give children some freedom but they use their own wisdom and exert their authority in making decisions that their children are not mature enough to make.

**Reasoning and Talking It Over.**   There are two strong reasons for communicating with children as to why the parent sets certain limits or makes certain demands. First, the child is much more likely to cooperate when she knows the reasons. Second, reasoning helps to develop her own conscience and moral code, to make the good behavior truly a part of herself. In communicating reasons and explanations, frankness about feelings also helps. If the parent is a skilled listener, he will help his child to express what he feels along with what he thinks. "It was wrong to tell Joey to crawl out on the roof and then to shut the window so that he couldn't get back into the bedroom. Do you want to tell me anything about what happened before that?"

In expressing their own feelings to a child, parents accomplish several important ends. They make the present issue more understandable. They make themselves more understandable, as human beings with feelings. They show children how to express feelings and imply that it is all right to do so. We are assuming here that the parents are not expressing themselves violently or explosively, but rather along these lines, "I'm feeling pretty upset, too. When I saw Joey up on the roof in his pajamas, I was afraid that he would slip on the ice and fall off, or at least that he would catch cold. And then when I saw you holding the window shut, it made me very angry. Being so frightened made me more angry than if you had done something wrong but not dangerous."

**Rewards, or Positive Reinforcement.**   Children, like other people and animals, tend to repeat acts that are rewarded. What is a reward? The approval of a loved person is one of the strongest rewards, even if it is only expressed in a smile or a pat. A child will work, control himself, and try to do "right" for expected approval. Feedback, or information about results of one's actions, also acts as positive reinforcement, leading the child to repeat his successful actions or to take the next step.

Concrete rewards, such as money, candy, stickers, or even elaborate ones such as watches and cars, may be effective in themselves or for their symbolic value.

Unless the reward has some value other than the immediate pleasure it brings, it may soon wear out as a motivator of good behavior. Gold stars or candies may continue to move children to learn and act as desired because they give feedback and symbolize approval.

Good discipline includes rewarding the child for "good" behavior and not rewarding him for "bad" behavior. It sounds simple, but it is hard to carry out. When Dylan was sitting quietly in his room, hooking up wires to his dry cell, he got no positive reinforcement from his father, but when he enticed Joey onto the roof and shut the window, he received a great deal of attention. Sometimes any kind of attention, even disapproval, feels better to a child than getting no response.

**Punishment and Negative Reinforcement.**  Punishment is an action or occurrence that hurts or makes a person unhappy. If he learns from it, he learns *not to respond.* Thus he does not make the unpleasant stimulus occur. Negative reinforcement is an event leading to a response that ends the event or makes its recurrence less likely. Suppose that Dylan saw his father acting very angry and upset while Joey was out on the roof. If he had been negatively reinforced by his father's emotional behavior, he would have tried to terminate it, to make his father feel better. In order to end his father's anger, he would have opened the window and let Joey come in. Not wishing to make his father angry again, Dylan might never again close the window after suggesting that Joey climb out onto the roof. The negative reinforcement would be continuing to affect Dylan.

Withholding a reward can be negative reinforcement. The child does something in order to change the situation of no reward, such as washing the dishes in order to be able to go out to play. Often punishment is used intentionally as negative reinforcement. When parents punish by scolding, spanking, withdrawing privileges or giving tasks, they are often trying to change a child's behavior from "bad" to "good." When they withhold approval and ignore, however, they often are just not thinking about the child and not intentionally applying negative reinforcement. Very often, intentional punishment does not get the desired results, and neither does ignoring improve the child's behavior. Are punishment and negative reinforcement useless? It depends on the kind of punishment and the circumstances under which it is given. Intense punishment makes a person afraid and anxious. He is likely to resent and fear the person who punishes harshly and will not try to please him or imitate him. Mild punishment may be effective when given with reasons and explanation by a loved parent, especially if the parent also shows the child how to do right instead of wrong. Sometimes ignoring bad behavior acts as negative reinforcement, especially if desired behavior is rewarded.

**Setting a Good Example.**  Since children model their own behavior on that of people they love and admire, of people who seem to be powerful, and of people they see rewarded, parents stand a good chance of being imitated. Not only will a child do what his parents do, but he will also say what they say, even though the words do not agree with the actions. It can be very disconcerting to a parent to have his insincerity or bigotry reproduced. Sometimes children act as mirrors to parents who see their own weaknesses reflected. Luckily, reasoning can repair some of the damage. Overhearing Melinda saying, "Shut up, you old bat" to her grandmother, Glenna took her daughter aside, and said, "How dare you be so rude to your grandmother! What ever has got into you?"

"I didn't think you'd care, Mother! I know you say I should always be polite, but I heard you telling Dad on the phone that Grandma made you sick and tired and that you weren't going to listen to her talking and talking and talking."

Glenna suddenly saw herself being just as rude as Melinda had been. She explained, "I do care about Grandma. She is my mother and I love her even though she does talk a lot. I'll try to be more patient with her. Will you try with me?"

**Putting It All Together.**   In teaching a child to behave in the right ways and to gradually take responsibility for his own behavior, parents use various methods, in various combinations. Parenting is an art, not a science, since every child is unique and every situation is a new one. It is important to love the child and let her know it, to make clear what is approved and disapproved, to give opportunities for good behavior rather than bad, to listen to the child and encourage her questions and expression, to explain and reason, to be firm and yet flexible, to admit mistakes, to be consistent in words and actions, to reward frequently, especially with praise and approval, to punish lightly and with explanation. No parent has ever done all of this all of the time, since parents are not perfect. Like children, they are still learning and growing. In fact, helping a child to grow into a responsible adult is in itself a growth-producing process.

## TEACHING

Even in the early years, parents are teachers in the sense of stimulating their children's development. The kind of physical and social environment they provide will make a difference in the mental development of the child. For example, Yarrow and associates found that six-month-old infants' scores on mental and motor tests and on measures of goal-directed behavior and exploratory behavior all correlated with the quality of the stimulation from toys and people [60]. When parents (or anyone else) respond to what infants do, and when they arrange for babies to play with toys that they can manage and control, then the infants grow mentally and socially [56]. A study of adoptive mothers and their babies showed that infants' IQs tended to be lower when mothers were highly restrictive, talked little to their babies, and gave them little physical contact [5].

Many studies show that preschool children's intelligence, language development, learning style, and general competence are related to their mothers' methods of teaching them and guiding their daily lives. Children's competence and mothers' adequacy vary with socioeconomic level, but there are some excellent mothers in all levels. A vivid description of what these mothers actually do is given by White, [57, pp. 242–244]. He holds that the action of the mother directly to and with her child of one to three, especially two to three years, is the most important formative factor in his development; that the results of these actions form the basis for the child's behavior and success in school; that a good job of mothering can be done without a father in the home. The competent mothers talk a great deal to their children, most often in response to the child, encouraging, helping, stimulating interest, setting limits as to what he may do and not do, and making suggestions that will expand his play. The mothers are busy people, doing their other work while they also meet the needs of their children, pausing in other tasks briefly but sufficiently. They design environments for play that contain many interesting things to see, manipulate, climb, explore, and use imaginatively. They can say *no* without feeling guilty or anxious. They have high levels of energy. (This is a composite picture. Probably no individual woman is such a paragon.)

Father-availability has been found related to sons' cognitive functioning and school competence [7, pp. 55–63]. A study of father-son interaction indicated that fathers' methods of teaching, like mothers', affect the development of sons' IQs and related competencies. Paternal nurturance, support, expectations, and direct teaching all had positive relations to sons' intellectual development.

Class and ethnic differences in measured IQ, achievement, and cognitive style may arise largely from differences in parents as teachers of their young children. Many studies have shown class differences in mothers' interactions with infants and preschool children. Middle-class mothers generally exceed lower-class mothers in talking more responsively, asking questions that focus the child on the task, giving more praise, watching the child and returning his glances, and giving more things to play with [39, 42]. In a situation in which young middle- and working-class children had equal chances for achievement, the working-class parents expected less of their children than did the middle-class parents of theirs [33]. Both ethnic and class differences were demonstrated in a comparison of teaching styles of Anglo-, Mexican- and Chinese-American mothers [48]. Each mother taught a bean bag toss game and a color sorting game to her three-year-old. The Chinese mothers gave a high proportion of enthusiastic positive feedback and also fitted their responses very carefully to the child's demand for help. Mexican mothers gave much negative feedback and many nonverbal instructions. The differences were consistent with the mothers' concepts of their own parental roles. The Chinese mothers saw their instruction of young children as an important part of the mother's responsibilities. The Mexican mothers considered teaching to be the teacher's job, in the school. The Anglo mothers said that they were uncertain as to what they should be teaching.

Even though competence in teaching is more typical of mothers in higher socioeconomic positions and in certain ethnic groups, *anyone can learn* these competencies. Presumably fathers, as well as mothers, can learn to teach young children. The sort of excellence described by White and implied in these other studies is a human potential. Since the link between children's intellectual competence and parental teaching behavior is well established, many intervention programs are now in progress. Parents are learning how to be teachers [43].

## SUCCESS, FROM THE PARENTS' STANDPOINT

Successful parenthood is defined differently by different societies, but from the viewpoint of parents themselves, a feeling of success comes from a good fit between their goals for their children, their own resources, and the development of the children. Actually, parents probably have less influence than they think they do on the sorts of adults their children become.

### Parents' Values and Goals for Children

Parents have many hopes and dreams for their children. Their goals are both big and small. What the parent wants is a product of his own time in history and his place in

This father is available for play, instruction, and protection.

a particular society, as well as of his own particular experiences. Goals for their children are derived from what parents believe to be fundamental human nature, and of course these beliefs come from the society in which they live. The ways in which parents use affection and control are strongly influenced by their views of mankind, what children are like at birth, and how they learn [8]. Is the child seen as inherently bad, good, or neutral? Records from seventeenth-century France, for example, show parents as being very concerned with making their children obedient and dependent [28, pp. 146–158]. Obedience or "breaking the will" was also a big issue with parents in the seventeenth-century Plymouth Colony [16, pp. 80–191]. An observer wrote, "And surely there is in all children . . . a stubbornness, and stoutness of mind arising from natural pride, which must, in the first place, be broken and beaten down; that so the foundation of their education being laid in humility and tractableness, other virtues may, in their time, be built thereon . . . " [16, pp. 182–183].

Considerable research has been done on the socialization value of obedience or conformity [18]. It seems likely that parents try, probably without much awareness of their motivation, to prepare children for life as they have experienced it.

Many modern parents, living in a rapidly changing society, are not sure of what they want for their children, or they may hold conflicting goals, for instance, "I want my child to be always happy and I want him to grow up into a responsible person." Goals also include physical attributes, such as strength and beauty, and achievements, such as getting high marks or earning a million dollars. In daily life, parents set goals for small pieces of behavior, as well as broad goals of socialization. Mrs. A. tries to get Joe to wipe his feet before he enters the house. Mr. B. urges Leon to swallow that mouthful of food before he takes a drink of milk. Mrs. C. insists that Lisa greet people by name, instead of just saying, "Hi."

## Parents' Resources

Resources include everything that parents can bring to bear upon their children in order to impel them toward the goals they have for them. As mentioned previously, nations and communities vary greatly in how much help they offer to parents. The extreme example is the kibbutz, where nation and community have similar aims, and where parents participate in setting goals and working toward them for all children. In many times and places, schools and churches are resources for parents, but sometimes parental goals do not jibe with those of the social institutions. Resources also exist in the family as a whole, in the parents as a pair, and in the individuals. Since mothers' and fathers' resources tend to strengthen and complement each other, the single parent usually needs to find some source for supplementary resources.

No matter how strongly one might believe in a particular method of teaching children, one must be *able to apply it* before it can work. Parents may feel able to give positive reinforcement but unable to ignore undesirable behavior, even when they think that negative reinforcement or nonintervention might be effective. They may find it difficult or impossible, often, to modify the situation in ways that they believe would be helpful. For instance, a different neighborhood or a room for each child could reduce behavior problems but might be unattainable. In such cases, the parents' limited *resources* make it impossible to apply the learning theories that they hold.

### Child Development and Behavior

The proof of the parents' success is the child himself, or so it seems to the parents, and, to a large degree, to kin and community. The child's health and growth show parental care; her manners and character reveal parental socializing; her intelligence and achievement reflect the parents as teachers. When they judge their child adequate, satisfying, or excellent in all these ways, then parents feel that their theories were valid, that they applied them correctly, and that they did right as parents. Thus there is a fit between development of the child and the parents' goals and resources.

Rarely do the child, the goals, and the resources dovetail perfectly. Many parents feel somewhat unsuccessful and some feel that they are failures. Some parents are judged failures by the community.

## PARENT EDUCATION

In traditional societies, families teach children to be parents. In complex, rapidly changing cultures, children's early experiences in family living are not sufficient to equip them for parenthood [58]. Potential parents have to learn from other systems in addition to the lessons they learn from their parents and kin. Being a parent is not just using a set of skills, although "parenting skills" are needed. So are feeling and intuition, since parenting is also an art. New mothers' feelings of competency, or lack of them, are very important to their functioning, and probably depend upon a variety of experiences, situations, and competencies [15].

Ideally, education for parenthood is both preparental and on the job. Some girls and very few boys are fortunate enough to have high school courses that prepare them for parenthood. A study of existing programs led to the recommendations that school programs should include the following: discussion of alternatives for guiding children's behavior; communication skills; children's effects on marriage relationships; exploring personal values and their impact on parent-child relationships; the commitment needed for parenthood; and supervised interaction with young children [14].

During pregnancy, many couples have some instruction on the care of infants. When the baby is born, the time when the sudden change is made from nonparent to parent, much day-to-day education could be used, and often none is available. Hospital personnel, midwives, or baby-care nurses can be very important teachers at this time. In New Zealand, specially trained nurses offer their services to new mothers, 95 per cent of whom accept. The Plunket nurse goes to the home several times during the first few weeks, giving advice and support to the mother. Later the mother takes the baby to the nurse's office for individualized service during the first five years of life.

Parents of preschool children may be educated in connection with the day care centers or nursery schools that their children attend. Parent-teacher organizations sometimes offer courses for parents. Social agencies are also sources of education. Authorities speak to parents through books, magazines, and television. Classes and study groups provide support that only personal interaction can give. Many types of courses are offered. They may stress treatment, enrichment, or prevention, and may be given prenatally or postnatally [19]. They may be oriented toward the family, the marriage, parenthood, the fetus, or children. A course may stress *behavior modification,* or *communication,* or *self-development,* reflecting the theories of learning and development held by its originator. Since parents can help each other to grow and learn, parent educators usually structure the group in such a way that sharing is most helpful. Some parent-run groups operate for years, with members contributing ideas, leadership, information, materials for discussion, and support for one another as they develop parental competencies and philosophy.

## PARENTS AND ADULT OFFSPRING

Longitudinal data at both Berkeley and Harvard have recently been analyzed in attempts to find adult behavior that could be linked with the ways in which the adults had been treated as children by their parents [34, 45]. Both studies showed that very little in adult behavior could be directly attributed to parental practices in childhood. Children's development is affected by many, many influences in addition to what their parents do. This knowledge should help to free parents from feelings of guilt and self-reproach when their adult children fall short of perfection. Attachments or ties of love continue to bind grown-up children and parents in many, probably most, cases. A study of young adults' kinship relations revealed them as feeling that relationships with their parents were closer than relationships with their siblings and best friends. They also felt more obliged to parents [1, pp. 78–83, 114].

Women tend to feel kinship ties more strongly than men, or at least to take responsibility for maintaining relationships [53]. The mother-daughter attachment in adulthood is usually stronger than the mother-son attachment, and the sister-sister attachment tends to be stronger than attachments involving brothers. There may even be a biological basis for mother-daughter closeness, since the mother-daughter attachment is strong in many adult mammals, including sheep as well as primates.

Ethnic groups vary in the way relationships within the family are structured, and in the way that the family is seen in relation to kin and nonkin. For example, among black and Irish Americans, the ideal relationship between parents and adult children is a relationship between equals. By contrast, in Mexican-, Japanese- and Italian-American families, the father remains in a position of authority within the family until he ceases to be able to carry out the role of family head. At this time, the eldest son takes over [59].

Some young adults find it a problem to establish satisfactory relationships with their own parents. In some cases, a parent tries to dominate the adult child. In other cases, the young adult has not taken the steps necessary to achieve emancipation. What kind of relationship will be considered satisfactory by the parent and by the child will be influenced by a number of factors, including the cultural expectations of the ethnic group and the life experiences of the individuals. When a parent tries to dominate an adult child, the child's reactions will be different according to whether the child sees her role in relation to her parent as one of submission or of equality. The Irish-American father whose son continued to act in a subservient role in relation to him would probably feel that he had failed as a father, as would the Japanense-American father whose son tried to act like a "buddy."

Relationships between adult children and parents are affected by individual life experiences as well. Thirty-five-year-old Meg complained: "My mother is always telling me what to do and what she thinks about everything I do. She keeps buying me stuff, buying clothes for me, and even wants to help my friends. If only she wouldn't phone me every day."

For Meg, deepened insight into her mother was enough to give her a feeling of independence. In discussing her mother, Meg was able to give some reasons for her annoying behavior: "I'm all Mother has. Dad died when I was 12 years old and she had to work to take care of me. We were very close while I was growing up and we didn't have the usual adolescent-parent conflicts. I just can't hurt her feelings now."

Meg was helped to see that her mother had potential for growth, just as she herself had, and that the two of them could continue to love each other while changing. She also came to realize that she must accept her mother as a human being, with imperfections, instead of expecting her to be completely competent and adequate (which she seemed to be to the 12-year-old Meg). Meg decided that she must make certain decisions in order to be her own self and that she could trust her mother to accept her as an adult instead of as an adolescent or little girl.

In some cases, open discussion between parent and child about problems of relating may be helpful. In other cases, it may be futile for a child who wants a relationship-between-equals to achieve his goal. In such a case, moving away may be a solution. By doing thus, frequency of interaction is decreased, perhaps making it possible for the child to fulfill occasionally the parents' desires for a continued unequal relationship. Such a solution will probably not be an ideal one for either person; it is actually a coping mechanism rather than a true solution.

Parents continue to give care to their grown children and also to receive care from them. Thus, there is mutual dependence in many parent-offspring pairs. One-directional dependence usually occurs only when the parents are very old. Almost 2½ million elderly persons live with their adult children [6]. The Minnesota study of three generations showed that the oldest and youngest generation turned to each other for help with problems more than did the middle generation [24, pp. 63–67]. The kinds of help given and received included economic, emotional gratification, household management, child care, and illness assistance. Parents gave the most economic aid and married grandchildren received the most.

Caregiving patterns might be expected to vary from one culture or subculture to another. A study of family and friend relationships among older black women revealed patterns of children's giving to married and spouseless mothers [29]. Gifts were given to about 64 per cent of all the women but the spouseless mothers received more economic and health assistance. Younger children gave more care to spouseless mothers than to married mothers. Eldest children gave care equally.

SUMMARY

The fertilized egg divides to form a ball of cells that implants in the lining of the uterus, grows into an embryo, and then into a fetus. The *corpus luteum* in the ovary that produced the egg directs the development of the pregnant woman's body. Her physical reorganization and development are focused on nurturing the embryo and fetus, preparing to give birth and preparing to breast feed. Her experience, which is different in each trimester, is absorbing and may result in some exclusion of the husband unless efforts to share are sincere.

A modern revolution in methods of conducting childbirth has given women more control over the process and has placed importance on the family interaction involved. The importance of medical skill and technology is acknowledged, since childbirth is a tremendously complicated although normal event. Constructively handled, childbirth is a cooperative achievement between the parents, the infant, and the medical and hospital personnel. During the recovery period, kin and friends also play a part. Continuing support and education are needed by the new parents. A revolution in childbearing is under way.

Family and other social systems affect the ways in which parents and children influence one another. Fathers are becoming more salient as parents.

Children's health is partly the result of care given by parents, whose caregiving capacities are limited by both economics and education. When parents abuse, neglect, and injure their children, family pathology is indicated, as well as pathological interaction between family and society.

As socializers, parents teach children to function as members of their culture and to think, believe, and feel in appropriate ways toward other people and toward themselves. Healthy child development is associated with parental love, warmth, nurturance, and support. Parents' level of moral development is related to children's, with mothers' reasoning being an important influence, especially with boys. Helping and giving are stimulated when parents help, give, and appear to feel good about doing so.

Discipline is the operation of teaching a child to control himself, to behave responsibly, and to cooperate with his fellow beings. A loving relationship is a good foundation from which to discipline a child. Methods include setting limits verbally and environmentally, reasoning and explaining, expressing feelings and encouraging the child to express hers, giving frequent rewards, especially approval, giving information about success, punishing seldom and lightly, with explanation, setting a good example, being consistent in words and deeds, admitting mistakes, and not expecting perfection in child or self.

Mental development is influenced by parents' teaching and guidance. Although there is a class difference in adequacy of teaching style, competence as a teacher can be taught and learned.

Parents feel successful when they are able to implement the goals they have for their children and when the children develop and behave in accordance with the parents' goals. All parents hold learning theories that they try to apply. Parent education can be done before people become parents and at any time during parenthood. Parents can help each other to develop competencies and philosophies.

When children grow up, friendship and enjoyment of companionship with parents is possible but not inevitable. Interdependencies are common between generations, with the middle-age generation contributing the largest share of help, but the older generation still giving. When very old, parents often become more dependent on their children.

**REFERENCES**

1. Adams, Bert N. *Kinship in an urban setting.* Chicago: Markham, 1968.
2. Aleksandrowicz, Malca K. The effect of pain relieving drugs administered during labor and delivery on the behavior of the newborn: A review. *Merrill-Palmer Quarterly,* 1974, **20,** 122–141.
3. Andersen, E. Skeletal maturation of Danish school children in relation to height, sexual development and social conditions. *Act. Paed. Scand.* Supplement 185, 1968. (Quoted in *Dairy Council Digest,* 1969, **40:** 2, 10.)
4. Baumrind, Diana. An exploratory study of socialization effects on black children: Some black-white comparisons. *Child Development,* 1972, **43,** 261–267.
5. Beckwith, Leila. Relationships between attributes of mothers and their infants' IQ scores. *Child Development,* 1971, **42,** 1083–1097.
6. Benedict, Robert, The family and long term care alternatives. Paper presented at meeting of the Groves Conference, Washington, D.C., 1978.
7. Biller, Henry B. *Father, child, and sex role.* Lexington, Mass.: Heath, 1971.
8. Borstelmann, L. J. Public and professional childrearing concepts: Spock and beyond. Paper presented at meeting of the American Orthopsychiatric Association, 1977.
9. Brew, James D. An obstetrician's point of view. In Charlotte and Fred Ward (Eds.), *The home birth book.* Garden City N.Y.: Dolphin, 1977.
10. Bryan, James H. Why children help: A review. *Journal of Social Issues,* 1972, **28,** 87–103.
11. Burgess, Robert L. and Rand D. Conger. Family interaction patterns related to child abuse and neglect. Paper presented at meeting of the Society for Research in Child Development, New Orleans, 1977.
12. Bush, Sherida. Parents Anonymous: A program that works. *Psychology Today,* 1978, **11,** 109–110.

13. Busse, Thomas V. and Pauline Busse. Negro parental behavior and social class variables. *Journal of Genetic Psychology,* 1972, **120,** 280–294.
14. Coward, Raymond T. and Florence Kerckhoff. Parent education in the public schools. *Journal of Home Economics,* 1978, **70,** 24–27.
15. Coward, Raymond T. and Judith A. Myers. Factors associated with self-perceptions of parental competency in postpartum mothers. Paper presented at meeting of the American Orthopsychiatric Association, New York, 1977.
16. Demos, John. Infancy and childhood in the Plymouth Colony. In Michael Gordon (Ed.). *The American familty in historical perspective.* New York: St. Martin's, 1973.
17. Dielman, T. E., K. Barton, and R. B. Cattell. Relationships among family attitudes and child rearing practices. *Journal of Genetic Psychology,* 1977, **130,** 105–112.
18. Ellis, Godfrey, J., Gary, R. Lee, and Larry R. Petersen. Beyond class and conformity: A cross-cultural analysis of parent socialization values. Paper presented at meeting of the National Council on Family Relations, San Diego, 1977.
19. Figley, Charles R. The transition into parenthood: An overview of intervention programs. Paper presented at meeting of the American Orthopsychiatric Association, New York, 1977.
20. Gambarino, James. The human ecology of child maltreatment: A conceptual model for research. *Journal of Marriage and the Family,* 1977, **39,** 721–35.
21. Gelles, Richard. Child abuse as psychopathology: A sociological critique and reformulation. *American Journal of Orthopsychiatry,* 1973, **43,** 612–621.
22. Gil, David G. Violence against children. *Journal of Marriage and the Family,* 1971, **33,** 637–648.
23. Haan, Norma, Jonas Langer, and Lawrence Kohlberg. Family patterns of moral reasoning. *Child Development,* 1976, **47,** 1204–1206.
24. Hill, Reuben. *Family development in three generations.* Cambridge, Mass.: Schenkman, 1970.
25. Hopkins, John B. and Peter M. Vietze. Postpartum, early and extended contact: Quality, quantity or both? Paper presented at meeting of the Society for Research in Child Development, New Orleans, 1977.
26. Hotchner, Tracy. Special deliveries: The new hospital birth. *New West,* April 24, 1978.
27. Hugins, William, and Norman M. Prentice. Moral judgement in delinquent and nondelinquent adolescents and their mothers. *Journal of Abnormal Psychology,* 1973, **82,** 145–152.
28. Hunt, David. *Parents and children in history.* New York: Basic, 1970.
29. Jackson, Jacqueline J. Comparative life styles and family and friend relationships among older black women. *Family Coordinator,* 1972, **21,** 477–485.
30. Kearney, Helen K. The impact of the Women's Movement on parenting; Changing roles of men and women. Paper presented at meetings of the Groves Conference, Grossinger, N.Y., 1977.
31. LaVoie, Joseph C. and William R. Looft. Parental antecedents of resistance-to-temptation behavior in adolescent males. *Merrill-Palmer Quarterly,* 1973, **19,** 107–116.
32. Loeb, Roger C., Leslie Horst, and Patricia Horton. Family patterns associated with self-esteem in pre-adolescent children. Paper presented at meeting of the American Psychological Association, San Francisco, 1977.
32a. Marciano, Teresa D. Male pressure in the deicision to remain childfree. *Alternative Lifestyles,* 1978, **1,** 95–112.

33. Marcus, Terri L. and David A. Corsini. Parental expectations of preschool children as related to child gender and socioeconomic status. *Child Development,* 1978, **49,** 423–424.

34. McClelland, David C., Carol A. Constantian, David Regalado, and Carolyn Stone. Making it to maturity. *Psychology Today,* 1978, **12:** 1, 42ff.

35. Mead, Margaret and Niles Newton. Cultural patterning of perinatal behavior. In Stephen A. Richardson and Alan F. Guttmacher (Eds.). *Childbearing: Its social and psychological aspects.* Baltimore: Williams & Wilkins, 1967.

36. Midlarsky, Elizabeth, James H. Bryan, and Philip Brickman. Aversive approval: Interactive effects of modeling and reinforcement on altruistic behavior. *Child Development,* 1973, **44,** 321–328.

37. Parke, Ross D. and Douglas B. Sawin. Fathering: It's a major role. *Psychology Today,* 1977, **11:**6, 109–112.

38. Passman, Richard H. and Raymond K. Mulhern. Stress affects maternal punitiveness: A model for investigating child abuse. Paper presented at meeting of the American Psychological Association, San Francisco, 1977.

39. Pytkowicz, Ann S. and Helen L. Bee. Mother-child interactions and cognitive development in children. *Young Children,* 1972, **27,** 154–173.

40. Rohner, Ronald P. *They love me, they love me not: The worldwide study of parental acceptance and rejection.* New Haven: HRAF Press, 1975.

41. Santrock, John W. Father absence and sex-typed behaviors. *Journal of Genetic Psychology,* 1977, **130,** 3–10.

42. Schachter, F. F., R. Marquis, C. Bundy, and J. McNair. Everyday speech acts of disadvantaged and advantaged mothers to toddlers. Paper presented at meeting of the Society for Research in Child Development, New Orleans, 1977.

43. Schaeffer, Earl S. Parents as educators: Evidence from cross-sectional, longitudinal and intervention research. *Young Children,* 1972, **27,** 227–239.

44. Schnucker, R. V. The English Puritans and pregnancy, delivery, and breast feeding. *History of Childhood Quarterly,* 1974, **1,** 635–658.

45. Skolnick, Arlene. The myth of the vulnerable child. *Psychology Today,* 1978, **11:**9, 56ff.

46. Smart, Russell C., and Mollie S. Smart. Preadolescents' perceptions of parents and their relations to a test of responses to moral dilemmas. *Social Behavior and Personality,* 1976, **4,** 297–308.

47. Staub, Ervin A. A child in distress: The influence of age and number of witnesses on children's attempts to help. *Journal of Personality and Social Psychology,* 1970, **14,** 130–140.

48. Steward, Margaret and David Steward. The observation of Anglo-, Mexican-, and Chinese-American mothers teaching their young sons. *Child Development,* 1973, **44,** 329–337.

49. Stinnett, Nick, Sharon Talley, and James Walters. Parent-child relationships of black and white high school students: A comparison. *Journal of Social Psychology,* 1973, **91,** 349–350.

50. Swanson, Harold D. *Human reproduction.* New York: Oxford University Press, 1974.

51. Tanzer, Deborah and Block, Jean L. *Why natural childbirth?* New York: Doubleday, 1972.

52. Trethowan, W. H. Pregnancy symptoms in men. *Sexual Behavior,* 1972, **2:** 11, 23–27.

53. Troll, Lillian E. The family of later life: A decade review. *Journal of Marriage and the Family,* 1971, **33,** 263–290.

54. Walters, James and Nick Stinnett. Parent-child relationships: A decade review of research. *Journal of Marriage and the Family,* 1971, **33,** 70–111.
55. Ward, Charlotte and Fred Ward. *The home birth book.* Garden City: Dolphin, 1977.
56. Watson, John S. and Craig T. Ramey. Reactions to response-contingent stimulation in early infancy. *Merrill-Palmer Quarterly,* 1972, **18,** 219–221.
57. White, Burton L. and Jean C. Watts. *Experience and environment: Major influences on the development of the young child.* Englewood Cliffs:, N.J. Prentice-Hall, 1973.
58. Whiting, Beatrice B. Folk wisdom and child rearing. *Merrill-Palmer Quarterly,* 1974, **20,** 9–19.
59. Woehrer, Carole E. Cultural pluralism in American families: The influence of ethnicity on social aspects of aging. *Family Coordinator,* 1978, **27,** 329–339.
60. Yarrow, Leon J., Judith L. Rubenstein, Frank A. Pedersen, and Joseph J. Jankowski. Dimensions of early stimulation and their differential effects on infant development. *Merrill-Palmer Quarterly,* 1972, **18,** 205–218.

# CHAPTER 12

# sisters, brothers, and all the rest

Suppose a young adult looks back over his life and asks, "What made me the way I am today?" No doubt he will give some credit to his parents. If he has brothers and sisters, or only one sibling, he will probably see them as having been a great influence upon him. He may realize that a brother or sister, or several of them, are closely connected with many of his feelings about himself, his estimates of what he can do, his knowledge, skills, and interests.

Grandparents also may be seen as having played a part in the personality development of the growing person, especially if they lived near enough to him to have frequent contact. In sheer number of hours spent together, however, grandparents and other relatives have much less opportunity than siblings to be important influences. The network of kin may be small or large or strong or weak in regard to the nuclear family and its members.

## SIBLING RELATIONSHIPS

Siblings are the closest of relatives, since all of their genes come from the same two people. Not only do they draw upon the same sources of heredity but they also live in very similar environments and tend to spend a great deal of time together, sharing the intimate experiences of daily living. Siblings do not have the *same* sets of genes unless they are identical twins, nor do they have the same environments, even if they are identical twins. Each child contributes part of the family environment of every other child. Granted their similarity in heredity and environment, it sometimes seems surprising that siblings turn out as differently as they do.

## Ordinal Position

The child's position in the family is often thought to be important in shaping his personality. Everyone has her own experience of being in the particular spot of

**366**   FAMILIES

eldest, middle, or youngest, and in a special arrangement of boys and girls or all boys or all girls, or even in being an only child. Studies of large samples have generally indicated that firstborns and early-borns score higher on various measures of intelligence and achievement. A study of a sample of National Merit participants, drawn from 794,589 students, showed that firstborns from small families scored highest and lastborns from large families lowest on verbal tests [8]. The relationship did not hold for nonverbal tests. The results suggest that the advantage of the first-borns is due to the particular kind of language interaction they have in their families, talking on a high level with parents and then simplifying their own language for younger siblings. These findings fit with those from studies of infants, both full-term and premature, in which mothers were observed giving more responsive care and stimulation to firstborns than to laterborns [13]. Firstborn infants had more social transactions with anybody than did later-borns.

Firstborn children have been shown by various American studies to differ from later-borns on personality measures. For example, firstborns among college students were more aware of important political persons, suggesting more adult orientation and response to authority [23]. Especially among girls, firstborns have often been seen as more anxious, fearful, sensitive to pain, and desirous of love and friendship [15, 37, 47].

In their cross-culture study of child behavior, the Whitings found that only in their United States sample did the eldest child differ in these ways from middle children. Among their subjects in Africa, India, Okinawa, the Philippines, and Mexico, the youngest's personality was different. American eldest children were more anxious and sought attention more; non-American youngest children sought attention more [58].

The Whitings' study suggests that differences in childrearing affect the patterning of ordinal positions. A sample of thirty-nine societies revealed many differences in the ways that firstborns are treated. The birth of the first child, which frequently gave parents greater status and their marriage more stability, was often recognized in elaborate birth ceremonies. Firstborns were likely to have authority over their younger siblings and to be more respected by them in childhood and adulthood. In contrast, the North American ideal is to treat all children "fairly," dividing property and privileges equally among them. In practice, it often does not work out that way. For instance, in our family, as in many, the first child's baby book is bulging with photographs, whereas the last child's book is rather thin.

## Sibling Interaction

Sometimes I love you, sometimes I hate you! These feelings are true of most close relationships, but especially those of siblings. They did not choose each other, and yet they live in the closest proximity, often sharing a room, sometimes even a bed. They play with the same toys. One wears another's outgrown clothes. They have the same surname, parents, relatives, and family reputation. There are many chances for them to play together, to have fun with each other, to help each other, and to conflict, fight, and resent each other. In addition to loving and hating, siblings switch easily from cooperating to trying to control and trying to resist. The following discussion treats siblings in the various roles that they play with each other.

**Playmates and Companions.** Even though we said earlier that we think it unfair to have a child for the main purpose of being a playmate, it is still fun to have a playmate! One of the great advantages of having a sibling is to have someone to play with at any time of the day or night, while working, eating, going to school, or doing just about anything. It takes two or more to play games of chance and skill, to throw and catch a ball, to turn a rope for jumping, and to take roles in imaginative play. Two or more can think up new things to do much better than only one. Sometimes it is important to have a sibling for company, just to be together without doing anything in particular. It keeps a person from feeling lonely and alone. Since adults are bigger and stronger than children, a child companion often feels more comfortable and more like oneself. Even siblings who often quarrel may seek each other's companionship frequently, as do Rachel and Pat. They have many conflicts over toys, being first, sitting in the front seat, and so on, but when Pat takes a long afternoon nap and Rachel wakens early, she keeps asking, "Can I wake Pat up? I want to play with him. I have nothing to do."

Much important learning takes place through play, especially in young children. Before the age of six or seven, imaginative play, especially dramatic play, is the means through which children reflect upon their experiences, interpret them, and place them in meaningful contexts. Siblings are likely to resemble each other on tests of creative thinking. [41]. Through play, children develop motor coordination and intellectual skills. Thus, sibling play is an important mode of learning and one in which children teach each other. Enjoying play together and realizing the necessary contributions of others, siblings strengthen their attachments to each other and prepare for later group interactions.

In their study of families with six or more children, Bossard and Boll found that almost all of the informants reported a great deal of play between siblings. Excerpts from the interviews represent playing together as one of the best parts of living in a large family. An example follows:

"We rarely had outside company and did not feel the need of it. We had good imaginations and played many games, which were joined in by two dogs and a cat. This life continued for some years, and, as far as we children were concerned, it was the closest thing to heaven" [6, p. 168].

When Sutton-Smith and Rosenberg [55, p. 50] interviewed children in grades 3, 4, and 5, they asked, "How do you have fun with your sibling?" Over half of the answers involved playing games together. Girls, more than boys, mentioned a variety of pursuits including working, helping, teaching, reading, and going places.

Children's preferences in playmates were affected by the sex of siblings, according to Koch's findings on five- and six-year-olds from two-child families. Children generally preferred like-sex playmates. The child in a two-sex sibling pair was more

Brothers are playmates at hide and seek.

likely than the child of a like-sex pair to prefer opposite-sex playmates or to be indifferent as to the sex of his playmates [30]. Thus, the sibling inclined the child to increased acceptance of playmates of the same sex as the sibling.

Facilitation and inteference by siblings were also examined in the study of power and influence of siblings ages five and a half to thirteen and a half [4]. A facilitating comment was, for example, "You did that very well." An interfering comment was, "Give me that." Older siblings were seen very much more as facilitators than as interferers, and the overall perceptions assigned more facilitation than interference in sibling interaction. This result is heartening, when one considers the great attention paid to power and control by researchers and writers, and the few articles to be found on positive relationships between siblings.

Sibling relationships tend to last throughout life, even when contacts are not

SISTERS, BROTHERS, AND ALL THE REST

**369**

very frequent [2]. Sibling solidarity was found to be greater in the working class than in the middle class. A study of siblings in a metropolitan area found that even though they ordinarily had little interaction, they were likely to turn to each other when their marriages were disrupted [45]. The sister-sister tie is especially strong. Thus, kinship is seen to operate in a compensatory manner. We were interested to see our own experience reflected in this study. My (MSS) sister lived hundreds of miles away in Canada. When her marriage broke up, she and her sons came to live with us for a year. We renewed the companionship of our girlhood. Figure 12-1 shows six-year-old Laura's interpretation of this situation.

**Teacher-Learner.**   Younger children, even infants, watch, follow, and imitate their older siblings [31]. Younger siblings modify their behavior in response to an older sibling more often than do older to younger [46]. Older siblings are often in the position of teaching younger ones, both by acting as models and by controlling through dispensing all sorts of reinforcements. The eldest girl is most likely to be a teacher to younger siblings, not only in North America but also in many cultures. Among high school girls in South India, the eldest of several sisters was likely to have

**FIGURE 12-1**    When I (LSS) was 6 years old, I drew this picture of "My Family."

a position of honor, with minimal household work assigned to her. Her chief task was to be teacher to the younger children [17].

*Facilitation* is part of teaching, as well as of playing. The good teacher arranges an environment and tasks that make the pupil free to learn. Since younger children often perceived older siblings as facilitators, it seems likely that the latter were thus in their roles as teachers. Teachers also use control as a technique for focusing the learner's attention and efforts.

Firstborn girls, especially, show preference for teaching as an occupation, most likely reflecting their childhood experiences as teacher of younger siblings [55, p. 115]. Many studies have revealed firstborns as being more adultlike than later-borns, more anxious, achievement-oriented, affiliative, conservative, and controlling of subordinates. Firstborn girls were found to exceed other girls and boys in offering to help a child in distress [51]. These characteristics fit with the firstborn taking on an active role in teaching siblings. An analysis of scores on a college entrance examination showed higher results for closely spaced girl pairs than widely spaced girl pairs, and higher for girls with sisters than for girls with brothers. Results were different for boys, with secondborn boys scoring higher when widely spaced than when closely spaced. This study and others have shown the firstborn of a male pair to score higher than the second on tests of intellectual abilities [34, 44].

Teaching, learning, and conceptualizing of school-age sibling pairs were analyzed with older siblings present or absent while younger siblings sorted objects and attained concepts. Results confirmed the studies just mentioned, by showing girl siblings to be more effective teachers than boy siblings or nonrelated girls. (Boy and girl teachers were equally good with nonrelated children.) Not only did girl siblings learn better and attain more mature concepts but the girl siblings also exceeded the other child-teachers in the use of these techniques: reasoning from a general principle, explaining, defining, describing, demonstrating, illustrating, and selecting examples [9]. Boy siblings seemed to be more influential as models and stimulators [11] than as teachers. Children attained more mature concepts when siblings were four years older than when they were two years older [10]. The sibling structure of the family has an effect on the way in which children learn from their mothers, as well as in the teacher-learner relationships among siblings. Mother-child teaching and learning is different if the child has an older brother from the way it is when the child has an older sister [11].

Sex-role learning is strongly influenced by siblings in that secondborn children's behavior patterns resemble those of their older siblings, whereas firstborn children develop less of the behavior typical of the sex of their younger siblings [55, p. 154]. The mechanisms of these learnings are complex, no doubt including modeling, operant conditioning, and environmental factors, such as the presence or absence of gender-typed play materials (dolls, footballs, and the like).

When fathers are absent, older brothers have special significance for boys. Black, father-absent children between four and six years of age were assessed for aggressive and dependent behavior. Boys, but not girls, with older brothers were found to show more aggression and less dependency than boys without older brothers [60].

**Protector-Dependent.**  When Susan and Ellen were getting ready to go to school in the morning (to second grade and kindergarten, respectively), Susan would often assume a teacher role, telling Ellen to hang up her pajamas and showing her how to read a word or two. Then they might be playmates for a few minutes with the piano or the trapeze, scuffling as rivals when their desires conflicted. But when they walked up the street to school, Susan was the protector against teasing boys who threw snowballs, and Ellen was the dependent. Almost any mother of two or more children could tell such a story. The elder sibling typically defends the younger ones from outside attack, even though she may use aggression and control at home.

In non-Western cultures, older siblings often care for younger ones and may be literally burdened with them. When we met some children on a mountainside in Nepal, one little girl was carrying a baby. We asked the children to dance for us by first dancing for them. The child nurse put the baby down and did a lovely dance but stopped reluctantly as her little sister kept creeping into the dance and clutching at her. The role of the child nurse is also prominent in Africa. In Acholi, the *lapidi* or child nurse is usually a girl but may be a boy, between six and ten years of age. The *lapidi,* who starts to take care of the baby when he is as young as one month of age, follows the baby's mother to the fields. The young woman giving the information said that she had greatly enjoyed being *lapidi* for her cousin until he was a year old, when another cousin took over as *lapidi* and the first one went to school [3].

In Bossard and Boll's study of 100 large families (with six or more children), 91 of the families were reported to have sibling participation in childrearing, especially in discipline [6]. Of these, 82 families indicated that siblings were important as childrearers. There were three main types of delegation of responsibility: because of abdication or incapacitation of parents, siblings carried on the whole childrearing function; parents gave over a certain supervision and protection of younger children to older children; one or two older children functioned as assistants to parents. The reactions of the younger children to siblings' discipline was favorable on the whole. Comments indicated that 57 percent considered the discipline satisfactory, or very satisfactory, whereas only 11 per cent said that they resented it. What happens to the overburdened eldest child is another story. Bossard and Boll [6, pp. 262–284] found that these children were often reluctant to have children. As one of their informants put it, "By the time I was 18, I had changed so many diapers and blown so many noses that I wanted to do other things than marry and keep on doing more of the same." Apparently, the children in the dependent role like it, as they look back, for Sutton-Smith and Rosenberg found that youngest girls from large (four or more children) families were most likely to want to have many children [54].

When the dependent sibling is handicapped, the burdens carried by the protector are even heavier. Studies of the families of mentally retarded children have shown special kinds of personality development in the normal siblings. When normal girls had many interactions with retarded siblings, their mothers saw them as having more neurotic or negative traits than comparable girls outside the family. Normal boys and girls with retarded siblings were relatively disinterested in achieving personal success and more concerned with dedication, personal sacrifice, and contributing to the welfare of mankind [19, 20].

**Adversaries.**　　Rivalry and jealousy are common among siblings, even among playmates and good companions. Julia and Jack have always been exceptionally good friends, but their father recalls this incident. One day he came home with two identical trucks, except that one was red and one was blue. He said to two-year-old Julia, "You take first choice, dear. Do you want the red truck or the blue truck?"

Julia sized up the situation for a moment and then firmly announced, "I want Jack's."

The importance of the adversary roles is supported by studies of the ways in which children employ power tactics [55] and their perceptions of power and influence in siblings' interactions [4]. Sutton-Smith and Rosenberg asked questions about power relationships of sibling pairs at preadolescence and at college age. At both age levels, firstborns perceived themselves, and secondborns also saw them, as more bossy and exercising higher power. Firstborns commanded, reprimanded, scolded, and bossed, used more physical restraint and physical attack, gave more rewards, and deprived the sibling of more privileges. The secondborns pleaded, whined, sulked, harassed, pestered, bothered, asked for help and sympathy, got angry, and acted stubborn [55, p. 57]. Sex differences in children's use of physical power were significant. Boys were more inclined to hit, beat, wrestle, and chase, whereas girls scratched, pinched, and tickled. In general, boys more often used attack and offense; girls most often used reasoning, defense, and making the sibling feel obligated. Thus, boys behaved in more physical ways, girls behaved more symbolically. In same-sex sibling pairs, offense, sulking, and teasing were more frequent. In opposite-sex pairs, defense and making up occurred more often. The polite behaviors of explaining, asking, and taking turns were used much more by firstborn girls than by firstborn boys.

Perceptions of older and younger siblings' power and influence were studied in 498 girls and boys from 5½ to 13½ years of age [4]. Shown pictures of children in various age and sex combinations, performing social actions, the subjects were asked, "Who would say . . . ?" Examples of items indicating high power were, "You can have it" and, "Stop doing that." Low power was shown by, "Can I have this?" and, "No, I won't do it." Results showed that the older sibling was generally assigned high power and the younger sibling was assigned low power. Children with older male siblings saw higher power in the older sibling than did children with older female siblings.

In a review of studies on family violence, Steinmetz comments that Americans are complacent about violence between siblings, which is frequent and sometimes serious [53]. She estimates that during one year, about 138,000 children used a knife or a gun on a sibling! Since 5 per cent of surveyed families reported a sibling having used a knife or a gun at some time, she estimates that 2.3 million children have had the experience of being threatened or attacked thus. Steinmetz has found that siblings continue to have conflicts as they grow up, but they change their focus [52]. Young ones fight about possessions, teen-agers over responsibilities and social obligations, and those in between over personal space boundaries, touching, or "looking funny" at each other. The greatest degree of violence took place between girl-boy sibling pairs.

Sibling violence is encouraged by a family that accepts violence as a way of life, but how do rivalry and jealousy get started between siblings? The firstborn has about a year, at the very least, in which he or she does not have to share his parents' attention with other children. Although he may displace his father somewhat in the mother's attentions and later (according to psychoanalytic views) see the father as a rival to be displaced, no rival sibling threatens his early months. The birth of the second child is very significant, often disturbing, to most firstborns. In many cultures this event signals the end of his infancy. It may mean that he is weaned and must stop sleeping with his mother. Balinese mothers tease toddlers by paying attention to new babies. In Western cultures, mothers may try to ease the emotional shock of having a young sibling but they still give much time, attention, and energy to the new family member because she is physically dependent. The firstborn is likely to feel jealous on seeing the baby receiving a share of what used to be his alone.

A laterborn child has at least one sibling who is bigger, more powerful, and more able than herself. She does not know how it feels to be the only focus of parental attention but she soon realizes that her sibling is more powerful and influential than she is. Here, according to Adler, is an important source of the feeling of inferiority [1].

## Products of Sibling Interaction

From the research quoted previously and from other studies too numerous to mention, these conclusions follow: sibling interaction is one of the basic ways in which personality is shaped and culture is passed on; patterns of reaction and motivation are established; philosophies of life are begun; sibling interaction ordinarily takes place in conjunction with parent-child interaction, modifying, supplementing, and occasionally replacing it.

**Self-Concept.**   The ways in which a person sees herself (or theorizes about herself) are, in part, products of the roles she has played with siblings and reflections of siblings' perceptions of her. Self-concepts of kindergarten children were more positive when they came from small families. Older and only girls had more positive self-concepts or self-esteem than did middle and youngest girls [49]. It seems reasonable that an individual would think better of herself as a teacher than as a pupil, as protector than as dependent, and as the more powerful of adversaries.

Yet another aspect of self-theory is *locus of control,* or the extent to which one

374        FAMILIES

feels able to influence events versus the extent to which influence seems to reside in the world outside the self. Since siblings give each other frequent, repeated experiences with controlling and being controlled, the results of these encounters are bound to affect the child's convictions as to the degree to which he himself is in charge.

Another component of the self-concept is gender identity, the conception of oneself as female or male. Interactions with siblings have been shown to influence sex-typed behavior in general.

**Orientation to Family of Procreation.**   Many experiences in the family of origin shape not only the individual's behavior as a member of one sex or the other but also his notions of how family life should be conducted. The choosing of wives and decisions about how many children to have are influenced by the numbers and sexes of siblings. Apparently, people try to repeat social patterns that they are familiar with, other things being equal.

**Skills and Competencies.**   Siblings influence the choice and development of all sorts of competencies, cognitive, creative, motor, and social. Even in infancy, the presence of an older sibling made a difference in exploratory and social skills. As compared with only children, babies with siblings explored toys more, made more responses to toys, laughed and smiled more, and initiated more play with a stranger [14].

The interests and skills siblings learn together often have a direct bearing on occupational choice, as shown by the relationship between ordinal position and certain jobs and professions. In many ways, interactions in the wider world are reflections or outgrowths of the behavior patterns and interpretations that children learn in the home-based world of sibling interaction.

# INTERACTION WITH GRANDPARENTS

Grandparenthood may be reached in the 40s or even in the 30s, when teenage children have babies. Even when grandparents are in their 50s and 60s, they are usually vigorous and active, busy with work and interests. Grandmothers, as well as grandfathers, are likely to have jobs and careers. During the years of great-grandparenthood, living with adult children becomes more frequent.

## Availability

Most children have some experience with grandparents. Most grandparents of young children are alive and living within a distance that permits some interaction.

**Chances of Having Living Grandparents.**    Compared with the situation of 50 years ago, today's children are much more likely to have grandparents. A survey showed that 97 per cent of white 10-year-olds had at least one living grandparent and 74 per cent had all four living grandparents. Of 20-year-olds, 78 per cent had at least one and 7 per cent had four grandparents. Fifty years previously, the corresponding figures at age 10 were 79 per cent and 11 percent, and at age 20, the corresponding figures were 51 per cent and less than 1 per cent [38]. Grandchild availability is lower, however, in terms of number of grandchildren per grandparent.

In contrast to such high grandparent availability, consider the situation in poor countries where life expectancy is short. In Gabon, West Africa, where life expectancy for men is 25 years of age and women 45, there must be little opportunity for children to know their grandfathers [57, p. 746].

**Place of Residence.** When grandparents live nearby, they are likely to have closer affectional ties with grandchildren [7]. There is some evidence that young nuclear families are likely to live farther from the grandparents than are older nuclear units [56]. However, persons over 65 in six countries (Denmark, Britain, United States, Poland, Yugoslavia, and Israel) were found to have frequent contact with their children. About 50 per cent of those interviewed had seen one of their children within the past 24 hours and about 75 per cent had seen one of their children within the past week. It seems likely, then, that geographic factors do not keep the majority of grandparents and grandchildren from seeing each other regularly. A sizable minority of grandparents, however, live far apart from their grandchildren [50].

## Patterns of Relationships

What does a grandparent do? A carefully selected sample of Wisconsin grandmothers were agreed that a *good* grandmother does the following: loves and enjoys her grandchildren; sets good examples; helps grandchildren when asked; interferes little in grandchildren's lives; listens well; does not interfere with parents' upbringing of grandchildren; does not spoil grandchildren; disciplines grandchildren if necessary [43]. The activities the grandmothers carried out were mainly only three: Babysitting, recreation, such as reading stories and playing games, dropping in to visit. Their concepts of grandmotherhood included a large measure of restraint, because they placed considerable emphasis on what they should *not* do, as well as what they could properly do and should do. Their comments suggest that a modern grandmother may have to earn her place in the family.

Margaret Mead deplored the diminishing of grandparental roles in the United States in recent times [36]. When families move frequently and when they live in suburbia or other homogeneous communities, grandparents can be especially valuable links to history and original family culture. "The generation gap has been widened by America's cultural approach to the aged: grandmother's house with its myriad lessons becomes granny's condominium with vinyl furniture."

**Types of Grandparents.** Grandmothers play their roles in various ways, dependent partly on their own life style. In the Wisconsin study mentioned earlier [43], four types were distinguished. Twenty-six per cent were involved in social and vocational roles that were important, and although they described grandmothering as joyous, they did not interact a great deal with grandchildren. Among 17 per cent, who were older, less educated, and less involved with friends and community, grandparenting was very gratifying and involving. A third group, 29 per cent, blended attitudes and actions of the first two. The last group, 28 per cent, were remote from grandchildren, having little interaction, few expectations, and little involvement with grandchildren. These women were also lower than average in education and had few friends and few community involvements.

An older study that included grandfathers as well as grandmothers showed a third of grandparents to be conscientious in doing what they thought grandparents were supposed to do, and almost another third to play a lot while seeking mutual satisfaction with grandchildren [39]. This study also found remote grandparents in 19 per cent of the women and 29 per cent of the men.

These two studies suggest that grandparenting is more of a voluntary activity than an obligation. Here we see the other side of the coin of having to earn one's place in the family. A grandparent can choose to try to do so or can choose not to.

**Black Grandparents.** A comparison of kin relationships in black and white families showed that the black families had more contact with kin, received more help from them in childrearing, and were more likely to have them living in the home. Although this study does not discuss grandparenting in particular, it does suggest that black grandparents exceed white grandparents in interacting with grandchildren and helping parents in child care [24].

**Age Effects.** Just as the age of the grandparent seems to make a difference in the interaction with children, so does the age of the child matter. Whereas fun seeking with or caring for a preschool child requires a grandparent strong of wind and limb, being responsible for an adolescent may involve less bodily activity and more mental and moral fiber.

From the standpoint of children, perceptions of grandparents have been found to differ from age to age. Three age groups of white, middle-class children were interviewed and questioned. All groups reported more contact with maternal grandparents than with paternal grandparents. Of the four grandparents, the maternal grandmother was most often chosen as favorite, especially by the four- and five-year olds. (The fact that grown daughters are likely to maintain close relationships with mothers is consistent with closeness between maternal grandmother and grandchildren.) The youngest children saw their favorite grandparents almost entirely in terms of what the grandparents gave to them in the way of love and presents. The middle group (8- and 9-year-olds) gave some egocentric responses like those of the younger children, but also mentioned mutual enjoyments, such as playing games. In addition, the middle group told some of the good qualities of the grandparents. The oldest group (11- and 12-year-olds) also gave egocentric reasons and did not mention mutuality as much as did the middle group. There was some indication that the older children did not feel as close to the grandparents as did the youngest and middle groups [29]. However, a study of grandchildren 18 to 26 years old indicated that these young adults were in close touch with their grandparents, whom they felt to be important influences in their lives [42]. The grandchildren felt responsibilities toward their grandparents, in terms of giving emotional support and tangible help when needed. In common terms, they loved, respected, and enjoyed their grandparents!

## Emotional and Social Meanings

Of the 70 pairs of grandparents mentioned previously [39], the majority enjoyed those roles, but 36 per cent of the grandmothers and 29 per cent of the grandfathers

The Seder, a time when a Jewish family blends feelings of warmth, security, continuity of life, and renewal.

felt uncomfortable or disappointed. Some found it hard to think of themselves as grandparents, probably disliking the implications of age. Some conflicted with the parents as to how the children should be reared. Others felt indifferent and guilty about their indifference. How grandparenting compared with friendship was the subject of a study of life satisfaction in a representative sample of older men and women in a working-class area [61]. Although the subjects reported that their grandchildren were important to them, the extent of activities was rather limited. Life satisfaction was found to be more highly related to friends than to grandchildren.

In addition to being potential sources of mutual pleasure, love, and security, grandparents and children can help each other with developmental problems. Through their experiences with grandparents, children form concepts of what old age is like and attitudes toward it [25]. In playing the role of grandchild, the child learns the grandparent role, in anticipation, and therefore prepares himself for later life, just as he also learns how to be a parent by being a son or daughter.

The **sense of integrity,** according to Erikson, is "the acceptance of one's one and only life cycle and of the people who have become significant to it as something that had to be and that, by necessity, permitted of no substitutions" [18, p. 139]. It means feeling good about the time, place, conditions, and conduct of your own life, a feeling of belonging to a particular part of the human order, and that the whole and the part are worthwhile. Some of the grandparents studied said that their grandchildren helped them to feel biological renewal and to see themselves as going on into the future. Quite often, grandfathers expressed satisfaction in the emotional fulfillment of being with grandchildren, doing for them, giving to them, and teaching them.

The continuity of life can be enhanced for grandchildren, too. Although the study of grandparents showed that only a few thought of themselves as reservoirs of family wisdom, grandchildren might see them as playing such a role more frequently. I (MSS) recall many satisfactions when my grandmother was my reservoir of wisdom. She was in her seventies when I was born and could, therefore, remember events that I studied in history classes. Most excitingly, she sometimes spoke of Ontario as *Upper Canada,* because she could remember Confederation, when Canada became a nation. Grandma even provided a link with England, because she remembered her own mother going back to her home in Devon to visit my grandmother's grandmother. These reminiscences gave me a great feeling of belonging in the history of my family and my country when I was around ten years old.

When my eldest daughter was ten, we lived far away from both sets of grandparents, but she benefited from a friend's grandmother. With four friends, Sue used to meet each week with Barbie's grandmother, who taught them how to knit and told them stories about when she was young.

As Mead [36] has pointed out, it is even more important today for a child to have a grandparent who provides a sense of family and community continuity, because the parents, as well as the child, were born into a present-oriented and homogenous culture. "A young person sees his own future as he observes his grandparents, and he sees his own past, too, which is another word for a people's history. Continuity is the message of optimism civilization offers its discontents."


## IN-LAW RELATIONSHIPS

In-laws are widely recognized as potential sources of trouble. Many non-Western societies take care of the mother-in-law problem by *mother-in-law avoidance,* a requirement that a man keep from meeting his mother-in-law. In traditional Indian families, in-law conflicts are avoided by having the bride guided and taught by the mother-in-law. The bride must learn to cook, keep house, and generally behave in the manner of the groom's family. The daughter-in-law must also show respect to the father-in-law and older brothers-in-law, by careful avoidance behavior. According to the family, it may be by not being seen at all, by covering the face, or by covering the head. When one of my (MSS) daughters was ill in an Indian village home, she judged the seriousness of her condition by the fact that the wife of the middle son, while caring for her, did not realize that her sari had slipped off her head in the presence of Older Brother.

In modern Western societies, such as in North America, there are no firm rules for behavior with in-laws. We have mother-in-law jokes that depict her as troublemaker. Indeed, studies of in-laws have shown mothers-in-law to be the most difficult of all in-laws [32, p. 228; 16, p. 117]. The sister-in-law was consistently revealed as the second most difficult. Interestingly, in Duvall's study, most of the women who were judged difficult as mothers-in-law were not considered troublesome grandmothers, since only 7 of the 1,337 respondents mentioned grandparents as being difficult, whereas 491 named mothers-in-law. This finding points up the fact that in-law relationships differ at different times in the marital career of the couple.

## Premarital Stage

"I've just got a new son-in-law, if they ever get married." So said a middle-aged man in a cartoon. With living together more frequently preceding marriage, the term *son-out-law* might be considered, except for the fact that most cohabiting couples probably do not consider themselves committed to marriage. As mentioned in Chapter 7, of 1191 college students in various regions of the United States, 25 per cent said that they either were or had been living with a person of the opposite sex. Over half the respondents thought that their parents knew about their cohabiting. A large majority thought that the parents disapproved, or that they would disapprove if they knew about the relationship. About 90 per cent of females knew or thought that parents would disapprove, and over 70 per cent of males. Men were more likely to think that their mothers disapproved, and women were more likely to think that their fathers disapproved [5].

It seems likely that as cohabitation becomes more usual, it will be more acceptable to parents. Parents will be at a loss for a while to know how to behave as pre-in-laws or out-laws or whatever they may be called, since there are at present no such roles in our society. Although we cannot provide research data, I (MSS) can say from experience that when middle-aged parents get together with their close friends, a topic of conversation is how to feel, think, and act in regard to one's cohabiting children.

Engagement is the traditional time for in-law relationships to get started, and established customs are available to guide the participants. The form may vary from an elaborate engagement party to simply telling the news, but parental approval of the match is a positive support. For many couples, engagement is the time for getting to know one another's family of orientation and much of the kin network. Although the broad outlines of in-law roles are sketched, much of each relationship has to be worked out between the people involved. The more mixed the match, the more communication will be necessary for creating satisfying interaction.

## Early Marriage

Although Western culture generally holds the husband-wife relationship as being of primary importance, most people believe that a young couple has duties to parents-in-law. In the Minnesota study of three generations, only 14 per cent of the young married couples disagreed with the statement, "A young couple has a real responsibility for keeping in touch with parents-in-law" [26, p. 60]. The two generations usually help each other, the parent generation giving more [12, 26].

**Age of Couple.** The age of the bride was found to be related to the amount of in-law difficulty reported by young couples [32]. Of 544 women, excellent adjustment to in-laws was reported by 45 per cent of those who married between 17 and 19, and by 63 per cent of those married at 24 or older. This finding fits with the fact that the establishment of adult relationships with parents is a task of the late teens and early 20s. The younger the married couples, the more they would be engaged in the adolescent process of becoming independent financially and emotionally. Parent-adolescent problems would become in-law problems as well.

**The Mother-in-Law Problem.** Since the women complained more about mothers-in-law than did the men in Duvall's study, the husband's mother is implicated as the greatest troublemaker of all in-laws. Or could it be that the daughter-in-law is the problem? It is more likely that each contributes to the conflict. Women have more at stake than men in homemaking and childrearing. The husband's mother must give over the product of her parent-child career to a young, inexperienced woman who is likely to be less competent than herself. The younger the bride, the less competent she will seem, and the more she might learn and improve through advice and supervision. The young wife probably is not very good at homemaking and knows it. She may feel that she has to compete with her mother-in-law in homemaking and for her husband's esteem. Another factor may be that homemaking standards and techniques have changed since the time when the parents were first married.

Although each case is unique, some general principles often hold. The situation may be eased by making real attempts to communicate (see Chapter 3) and by showing respect through gaining knowledge of the other person as an individual. Since self-esteem is basic to being able to ask for help, to give and accept help, and to share a loved one, both the young woman and older woman would profit from facing problems of self-esteem. The young husband usually plays a crucial role in conflicts between his two important women. To make both feel loved and esteemed is ideal. To choose the wife, if choice is necessary, is to solidify the pair relationship and to give it primary importance. If the young husband is extremely attached to his mother and dependent on her, then his wife and his mother are very likely to have trouble with each other. On the other hand, if the young couple live far away from their parents, many of the troublesome conflicts will never occur. At the same time, mutual aid and loving contacts will also be reduced.

## The Middle Years

When a couple become parents, then in-law relationships involve relations with their children's grandparents. As the generation in the middle, the parents strongly influence the ways in which children and grandparents can relate to each other. Parents largely control the contacts that the younger and older generations have and they interpret them to each other. If Mother and Mother-In-Law are still locked in competition to be most esteemed by Father, then Mother is likely to set the stage for her children to dislike Paternal Grandmother. Happily, though, the most usual course of events seems to be for parents to accept the help and love that grandparents offer in this stage of life and to work out ways of getting along together. The mother has learned how to keep house and has developed her own style of homemaking, community activities, and perhaps a job. The father has had some experience and probably some success in his vocation. Some couple solidarity and nuclear family identity are established. Thus, many of the trouble spots of early marriage have disappeared, as far as in-law relationships are concerned.

When children reach adolescence, the parent couple often feel squeezed between the demands of their children and their parents. The financial cost of children goes up astronomically at this point, and grandparents may need support, too. Emotional demands may be even greater than economic, since the normal struggles of adolescents are fraught with difficulty for parents, whereas the adjustments required by aging grandparents may place additional burdens upon the parent generation.

In cultures where the grandparent generation retains strong authority in the family, the situation is, of course, quite different. In the extended family, the parent generation continues to defer to the elder generation and the mother-in-law can still direct the daughter-in-law, even when she is the mother of adolescent children. The middle-aged husband may quite properly continue to esteem his mother above all women.

## OTHER KIN

Since **kin** usually means all the relatives other than the nuclear family in which a person is living, we have already discussed some of the kin, for some nuclear members become kin. When a child grows up, leaves his family of orientation, and forms his family of procreation, then his parents may become "relatives" or kin to him, although he remains a child to them. He and his siblings are adult kin to each other.

Ethnic groups vary in closeness to kin. Italian- and Polish-Americans have a great deal of interaction among parents and adult children. Social events are usually gatherings of kin. Scandinavian Americans have the lowest rates of interaction with kin, but are very likely to belong to formal organizations [59].

There are various ways of ordering kin according to closeness and distance. Farber [21] has sescribed four kinship models, one of which has Jewish origins, and another Roman Catholic. Subjects revealed their beliefs about kinship by answering questions about how various kin should inherit when someone dies without leaving a will. He found that responses about rights and closeness were related to religion and to style of thinking, and of course to concepts of marriage.

STANLEY SUMMER

## Basic Family Units

The importance of kin varies inversely with the importance of marriage, for the society and for the individual. Where the marriage relationship is considered to be of primary significance, then kin relationships are not so important [22]. However, even in a society that stresses marriage, such as middle-class America, kin usually provide basic family relationships for those who have not married and those who are

**384**     FAMILIES

widowed or divorced. Sibling relationships are especially strong among older, unmarried people, with sister-sister ties being the strongest. Cousins, aunts, uncles, nieces, and nephews also serve as sources of help, love, and security for people who are not in nuclear units.

## Mutual Aid

Obligations and interactions among kin are especially strong in certain cultures. Black families tend to give more mutual aid than white families [59]. Interviews with middle-income black families revealed considerable support given and received by 66 per cent [35]. Only 10 per cent said that they had not received help. Aid included financial help that they had received from their families. In contrast to some earlier findings, families who had recently moved from the working class to the middle class were not cutting themselves off from their families of origin. Kin involvement was usually high. It was easy for relatives to visit in 65 per cent of the families. Visiting relatives was easy for 75 per cent. Others kept in touch through phone calls and letters.

Another example of strong kin interaction comes from Honolulu, where third-generation Japanese-Americans carry on many reciprocal relationships with siblings and cousins, in addition to helping their parents [28]. Although these people are not poor, it often happens that kin are more important in poor countries and in economically deprived groups than among prosperous people. A recent study of a representative group of Chicago widows shows practically no help coming from siblings, grandparents, aunts, uncles, cousins, nieces, nephews, or grandchildren [33]. Only their parents and their children contributed any economic, service, social, and/or emotional support. Indian kinship obligations contrast with the behavior of Chicago kin towards widows in the family. It is common for kin to have privileges and responsibilities to each other that seem incredible to a Westerner. For example, young Indian friends of ours live in a one-bedroom apartment with their two children. Whenever either set of grandparents wishes, they come and stay for two or three months. Grown siblings also visit freely.

## Belonging and the Sense of Integrity

An interesting kin behavior pattern is the family reunion. In this sense, the family is the large, ongoing entity that really does have cycles. (See page 15 for a distinction between cycles and careers.) Many families have reunions at weddings, anniversaries, and funerals. When my (MSS) parents celebrated their sixtieth wedding anniversary, 150 to 200 people came to greet them. Second and third cousins drove 200 miles to the event. Some families have formalized family reunions that are exactly that. Figure 12-2 illustrates such a reunion. Most large family groups, the kind that have reunions, boast of at least one family historian, who gathers vital information,

# 38 Kinfolk Hire Bus For Visit

LANSING, MICH.–(AP)–The 38 Michigan members of the Harr clan believe the energy crisis may keep them from driving to Wisconsin for their family Christmas dinner. So they've chartered a bus.

The Lansing branch of the family will be lead by Edwin Harr, in his 60s, when they board the bus next Saturday morning for the trip to the home of his daughter, Edna Huggett, and her husband, James, in Marshall, Wisconsin.

"The men are real happy about not having to drive. Everybody's real tickled about it. We can all sing and talk together. It wouldn't be as close if we took separate cars," said Doris Feldpausch about the trip to her sister's.

The charter with Indian Trails Bus Co. will cost $520, or $13.68 per person, Mrs. Feldpausch said.

The bus will leave Dewitt, just north of here, early Saturday morning to start the 600-mile trek. The family is to arrive at the Huggetts just in time for dinner.

**FIGURE 12-2**   The family reunion is still very much alive.

*Source: Providence Evening Bulletin. December 18, 1973.*

records it, saves clippings and photographs, and serves as a clearinghouse for kin communications.

Family reunions and family historians promote emotional security and the sense of integrity in all the members. Just as my (MSS) grandmother's true family stories did for me as a child, so does kin solidarity give individuals a feeling of belonging to present, past, and future.

## QUASI-KIN

"You are just like a sister to me!" "I feel as though you were my own parents." "A brother couldn't have done more." Many of us have such experiences. In our family, there are three biological daughters, plus an Indian daughter and a fourth American daughter. People use kinship terms to express love and closeness to those who are not biologically related but to whom they are attached.

Among black families, quasi-kin are often very important, just as blood relatives form a strong social network [59]. A study of black families in San Francisco revealed the salience of quasi-kin [40]. The author suggests that black kin networks stretch to include nonblood relatives, who become "almost indistinguishable" from biological and legal relatives. Parenting functions were shared by quasi-kin, as well as by grandparents, aunts, and older siblings. In contrast, Irish-Americans are likely to see adult members in terms of their ability to act as friends [59].

### Fictive Kin

Sociologists have studied the use of kinship terms in addressing nonrelatives. *Fictive kin term* is what they call it [27]. Fictive kin terms have been noted in Japan, Latin America, India, and the United States. It seems likely that they are used in most societies. In interviews with 115 American wives, 70 per cent reported that they or members of their family used fictive kin terms, some with only one or two people, some with a great many. *Uncle* and *aunt* were the most frequently used. More female than male terms were used. About 75 per cent of fictive kin were close family friends. Often the parents of the user were the ones who suggested the term, and children were the most frequent users. Fictive kin probably substitute somewhat for real kin or for kin living far away. Use of the terms also seems to strengthen friendships.

**Sororities, Fraternities, and Fraternal Orders.**  Quasi-sibling relationships are the core of sororities, fraternities and fraternal orders. Members call themselves and others brothers and sisters. They have duties and responsibilities to each other, such as offering aid for studies or business, reflecting glory upon the group through personal achievements, refraining from disgraceful behavior that would bring shame to the group, and contributing to the financial support of the group. Sororities and fraternities have also regulated mate selection for their members [48].

### Utopian and Religious Societies, Communes, and Others

Quasi-family describes many of the organizations in which unrelated individuals live, work, and love in close relationships. Family terms are often used. A commune may be "a family" and the leader a father or a mother to the group. In the Utopian societies of the past, the leader was often a strong, authoritarian man. Nuns are *sisters,* and heads of convents or orders are *mothers.* The *father,* of course, is God.

An even looser, more comprehensive use of fictive kin terms occurs among oppressed and/or militant people who feel kinship through devotion to a cause. Blacks may call one another *brother* and *sister* in order to express racial solidarity. Women call each other *sister* in the context of women's liberation.

**SUMMARY**  Age and position differences showed firstborns as superior verbally, receiving more stimulation, being more bossy, and exercising more power, whereas secondborns did more pleading, whining, and harassing. Boys used more physical means, whereas girls used more symbolic means. Conflicts were common.

As playmates and colleagues, siblings have good times together. Preference in friends is affected by experiences with siblings. Adult siblings, especially sisters, often turn to each other in times of stress. Siblings teach each other and learn from one another. Firstborn girls are likely to be good teachers and to help other children. Sex-role learning and marital choice are related to ordinal position and composition of the family. Siblings protect and care for younger siblings, who depend upon them. Playing a protector role often influences children later in their social and family behavior. Sibling interaction affects an individual's self-concept in terms of self-esteem, locus of control, and gender identity. Other results include orientation to family living, skills and competencies, and choice of occupation. Sibling interaction influences and is affected by parent-child interaction.

Four-generation families are now common in North America. Young parents and their children do not ordinarily live with the grandparents, but the various generations usually keep in touch. Types of grandparents show considerable variation because the grandparental role is restricted and voluntary. Grandparents can contribute to a child's understanding of history and sense of belongingness and integrity. Black grandparents help more with care of grandchildren than do white grandparents. From their interaction, grandchildren may prepare themselves by anticipating roles in later life, whereas grandparents may develop the sense of integrity.

Female in-laws cause more trouble than males, since the mother-in-law, especially the paternal one, ranks first and the sister-in-law second as sources of difficulty. Early marriage is the time when in-law problems loom largest, because of the young couple's establishing new relationships and their immaturity. If conflicts are solved at this stage, the middle years are likely to be easier. Grandparents are usually appreciated by parents.

Kin definitions and solidarity vary widely. Kin usually provide aid in cultures and situations of stress and deprivation. Belongingness and the sense of integrity are enhanced by kin gatherings, family history, and symbols of family continuity. Kin can be secured by means other than biological connections. Quasi-kin include those referred to as "just like" kin, adopted kin, those called by kin names, members of organizations that use kin names, and devotees to a cause who express solidarity through kin terms. Quasi-kin are often important in black families.

**REFERENCES**  1. Adler, Alfred. *Understanding human nature.* New York: Premier, 1959.
2. Allan, Graham. Sibling solidarity. *Journal of Marriage and the Family,* 1977, **39,** 177–184.
3. Apoko, Anna. At home in the village: Growing up in Acholi. In Lorene Fox (Ed.). *East African childhood.* New York: Oxford U.P., 1967.

**388**  FAMILIES

4. Bigner, Jerry J. Second borns' discrimination of sibling role concepts. *Developmental Psychology,* 1974, **10,** 564–573.

5. Bower, Donald W. and Victor A. Christopherson. University student cohabitation: A regional comparison of selected attitudes and behavior. *Journal of Marriage and the Family,* 1977, **39,** 477–453.

6. Bossard, James H. S. and Eleanor S. Boll. *The large family system.* Philadelphia: U. of Pa., 1956.

7. Boyd, Rosamonde R. The valued grandparent: A changing social role. In Wilma Donahue et al. (Eds.). *Living in the multigenerational family.* Ann Arbor, Mich.: Institute of Gerontology, 1969.

8. Breland, Hunter M. Birth order, family configuration, and verbal achievement. *Child Development,* 1974, **45,** 1011–1019.

9. Cicirelli, Victor G. The effect of sibling relationship on concept learning of young children by child-teachers. *Child Development,* 1972, **43,** 282–287.

10. Cicirelli, Victor G. Relationship of sibling structure and interaction to younger sib's conceptual style. *Journal of Genetic Psychology,* 1974, **125,** 37–49.

11. Cicirelli, Victor G. Effects of mother and older sibling on child's conceptual style. *Journal of Genetic Psychology,* 1977, **131,** 309–317.

12. Clark, Alma B. and Jean Warren. *Economic contributions made to newly married couples by their parents.* Cornell Agriculture Experiment Station Memoir 382. 1963.

13. Cohen, Sarale E. and Leila Beckwith. Caregiving behaviors and early cognitive development as related to ordinal position in preterm infants. *Child Development,* 1977, **48,** 152–157.

14. Collard, Roberta R. Social play and play responses of firstborn and laterborn infants in an unfamiliar situation. *Child Development,* 1968, **39,** 325–334.

15. DeFee, John F. and Philip Himelstein. Children's fear in a dental situation as a function of birth order. *Journal of Genetic Psychology,* 1969, **115,** 253–255.

16. Duvall, Evelyn. *In-laws, pro and con.* New York: Association Press, 1954.

17. Elder, Joanne F. Family patterns and adolescent girls in South India and the United States. Unpublished M.A. thesis. Oberlin, Ohio: Oberlin College, 1955.

18. Erikson, Erik H. *Identity, youth and crisis.* New York: Norton, 1968.

19. Farber, Bernard. Family organization and crisis: Maintenance of integration in families. *Monographs of the Society for Research in Child Development, 1960,* **25.**

20. Farber, Bernard. Interaction with retarded siblings and life goals of children. *Marriage and Family Living,* 1963, **25,** 96–98.

21. Farber, Bernard. Social context, kinship mapping, and family norms. *Journal of Marriage and the Family,* 1977, **39,** 227–240.

22. Gibson, Geoffrey. Kin family network: Overheralded structure in past conceptualizations of family functioning. *Journal of Marriage and the Family,* 1972, **34,** 13–23.

23. Hansson, Robert O., Warren H. Jones, and Mary E. Chernovetz. Birth order and political awareness. *Journal of Social Psychology,* 1977, **102,** 151–152.

24. Hays, William C. and Charles H. Mindel. Extended kinship relations in black and white families. *Journal of Marriage and the Family,* 1973, **35,** 51–57.

25. Hickey, Tom, Louise A. Hickey, and Richard Kalish. Children's perceptions of the elderly. *Journal of Genetic Psychology,* 1968, **112,** 227–235.

26. Hill, Reuben. *Family development in three generations.* Cambridge, Mass.: Schenkman, 1970.

27. Ibsen, Charles A. and Patricia Klobus. Fictive kin term use and social relationships: Alternative interpretations. *Journal of Marriage and the Family,* 1972, **34,** 615–620.
28. Johnson, Colleen L. Interdependence, reciprocity and indebtedness: An analysis of Japanese American kinship relations. *Journal of Marriage and the Family,* 1977, **39,** 351–363.
29. Kahana, Boas and Eva Kahana. Grandparenthood from the perspective of the developing grandchild. *Developmental Psychology,* 1970, **3,** 98–105.
30. Koch, Helen. The relation in young children between characteristics of their playmates and certain attributes of their siblings. *Child Development,* 1957, **28,** 173–202.
31. Lamb, Michael E. The development of sibling relationships in infancy: A short-term longitudinal study. *Child Development,* 1978, **49,** 1189–1196.
32. Landis, Judson T. and Mary G. Landis. *Building a successful marriage* (5th ed.), Englewood Cliffs, N.J.: Prentice-Hall. 1968.
33. Lopata, Helena Z. Contributions of extended families to the support systems of metropolitan area widows: Limitations of the modified kin network. *Journal of Marriage and the Family,* 1978, **40,** 355–364.
34. Lunneborg, Patricia W. Birth order and sex of sibling effects on intellectual abilities. *Journal of Consulting and Clinical Psychology,* 1971, **37,** 445.
35. McAdoo, Harriette P. The impact of upward mobility on the reciprocal obligations of kin-help patterns in Black families. *Journal of Marriage and the Family,* 1978, **40,** 761–776.
36. Mead, Margaret. Grandparents as educators. *Saturday Evening Post,* March 1977, 54–56.
37. Mealiea, Wallace D. and Frank H. Farley, The relationship between ordinal position in females and the expression of extreme fear. *Journal of Social Psychology,* 1973, **90,** 333–334.
38. Metropolitan Life Insurance Company. This age of grandparents. *Statistical Bulletin,* 1972, **53,** (September), 8–10.
39. Neugarten, Bernice L. and Karol K. Weinstein. The changing American grandparent. *Journal of Marriage and the Family,* 1964, **26,** 199–204.
40. Nobles, Wade W. Toward an empirical and theoretical framework for defining Black families. *Journal of Marriage and the Family,* 1978, **40,** 679–694.
41. Olive, Helen. Sibling resemblances in divergent thinking. *Journal of Genetic Psychology,* 1972, **120,** 155–162.
42. Robertson, Joan F. Significance of grandparents: Perceptions of young adult children. *Gerontologist,* 1976, **16,** 137–140.
43. Robertson, Joan F. Grandmotherhood: A study of role conceptions. *Journal of Marriage and the Family,* 1977, **39,** 165–174.
44. Rosenberg, Benjamin G. and Brian Sutton-Smith. Sibling age spacing effects upon cognition. *Developmental Psychology,* 1969, **1,** 661–668.
45. Rosenberg, George S. and Donald F. Anspach. Sibling solidarity in the working class. *Journal of Marriage and the Family,* 1973, **35,** 108–113.
46. Samuels, Helen R. The sibling in the infant's social environment. Paper presented at meeting of the Society for Research in Child Development, New Orleans, 1977.
47. Schacter, Stanley. *The psychology of affiliation.* Stanford, Calif.: Stanford U.P., 1959.
48. Scott, John F. Sororities and the husband game. *Trans-Action,* 1965 (September–October), 10–14.
49. Sears, Robert R. Relation of early socialization experiences to self-concepts and gender role in middle childhood. *Child Development, 1970, **41,** 265–289.*
50. Shanas, Ethel. Family-kin networks and aging in cross-cultural perspective. *Journal of Marriage and the Family,* 1973, **35,** 505–511.

51. Staub, Ervin. The use of role playing and induction in children's learning of helping behavior. *Child Development,* 1971, **42,** 805–806.
52. Steinmetz, Suzanne K. *The cycle of violence: Assertive, aggressive and abusive family interaction.* New York: Praeger, 1977.
53. Steinmetz, Suzanne K. Violence between family members. *Marriage and Family Review,* 1978, **1:** 3, 1–16.
54. Sutton-Smith, Brian and Benjamin G. Rosenberg. Sex differences in the longitudinal prediction of adult personality. Paper presented at meetings of the Society for Research in Child Development, Philadelphia, 1973.
55. Sutton-Smith, Brian and Benjamin G. Rosenberg. *The sibling.* New York: Holt, 1970.
56. Troll, Lillian E. The family of later life: A decade review. *Journal of Marriage and the Family,* 1971, **33,** 263–290.
57. *United Nations Demographic Yearbook.* New York: United Nations Publishing Service, 1972.
58. Whiting, Beatrice B. Folk wisdom and child rearing. *Merrill-Palmer Quarterly,* 1974, **20,** 9–19.
59. Woehrer, Carol E. Cultural pluralism in American families: The influence of ethnicity on social aspects of aging. *Family Coordinator,* 1978, **27,** 329–339.
60. Wohlford, Paul, John W. Santrock, Stephen Berger, and David Liberman. Older brothers' influence on sex-typed, aggressive, and dependent behavior in father-absent children. *Developmental Psychology,* 1971, **4,** 124–134.
61. Wood, Vivian and Joan F. Robertson. Friendship and kinship interaction: Differential effect on the morale of the elderly. *Journal of Marriage and the Family,* 1978, **40,** 367–375.

# CHAPTER 13

# HEALTH IS MORE THAN brushing your teeth

The United States pays more for health care than does any other country in the world. The total public and private expenditure in 1976 was $189 billion, over three times the health cost in 1966 [8]. Even these enormous and increasing outlays of money have not made health care as available to all Americans as it is, for example, to all people in Great Britain. Discontentment is growing. Many people resent not only the huge prices charged by doctors and hospitals, but some of their values and attitudes, the fragmentation of persons, and disregard for families. New approaches to health are based on several ideas: the wholeness of health; positive health; the individual's right to make choices; the potential of families for giving health care to their members; the relation of health to work and the community; the possibilities inherent in new kinds of health services; acceptance and dignifying of death.

Health is an important topic in the study of families, because a family can make its members sick or well. In turn, a sick or well family member influences family interaction for worse or for better.

## Wholeness of Health

Health is more than physical fitness and absence of disease. It also includes mental, emotional, and social functioning. René Dubos, a scientist-philosopher, says "For human beings, health is a measure of an individual's ability to function within his own set of values" [15]. This definition allows for differences in persons and in cultures, emphasizing that health involves ongoing adaptation. It includes not only a person's body, but the ways in which that person thinks, feels, and relates to other people. Mortality rates show that family living is positively related to health. Non-

married persons are more likely to die than are married persons, and married people without children have higher mortality rates than married people with children [23]. Marriage apparently does more for men's survival than for women's, because men living alone have the highest mortality rates. The women with highest mortality are those living as dependents in families. The authors conclude that family ties promote survival, but that low-status positions work against adults' survival.

Good health can make a big difference in the way a person handles crises and solves problems. When feeling good, with plenty of energy, it is easier to cope with hard times. This principle was illustrated in a reporting of crises by 500 women who had recently become first-time mothers [34]. The young mothers who said that they were in excellent health were less likely to report high levels of crisis than were those who said they were in less than excellent health.

Paying little attention to emotional and social aspects of health, Western medicine has been concerned mostly with curing and preventing specific diseases. Until recently, infectious diseases were the main focus. Now the emphasis is on preventing and treating chronic and degenerative diseases, such as cancer, heart problems, and genetic disorders. Almost all non-Western systems of medicine are based on an integration of body, mind, and environment [15]. The Chineses system studies interrelationships between different organs and systems and also between organism and place, seasons, weather, time of day, and social milieu. Indian yogis can control their heartbeat and other bodily processes through mental exercises. African healers treat illness not only with drugs but with what a Westerner would call psychotherapy [25]. Lambo, a Western-educated Nigerian psychiatrist, explains that health is not isolated, but reflects the integration of the community. When a patient comes to a healer, the latter looks for tensions and aggresssions in the patient's relationships with family and community, which he then treats with an appropriate ritual. The community may take part in a day and a half of ritual dancing. " . . . supernatural forces are regarded as the agents and consequences of human will. Sickness is the natural effect of some social mistake."

Long before Hawaii was part of the United States, a system of family therapy was based on wholeness of persons [33]. Ho'oponopono means to set right, to restore and maintain good relationships among family members, and family-and-supernatural powers. Ho'oponopono took the form of a family conference, led by a qualified senior member or healer, who followed certain procedures. Prayer was part of the process. The leader asked questions, channeled emotions and paced the proceedings, using periods of silence regularly. Participants answered truthfully, confessed, repented, made reparation, forgave, and were released from guilt and tension. Like the African concept of sickness described by Lambo, the Hawaiian concept included disturbed social relationships in illness. When such a disturbance was set right, the person usually felt better. Of course there was also a place for more physical treatment.

Healing is also carried on in some religious institutions in the United States currently, and in these situations the concept of health is more like that of non-Western medicine than it is like American medicine. In addition to the services of the fundamentalist churches, Roman Catholic and Episcopalian services of healing are offered. Mind-body relationships are also acknowledged by biofeedback therapy and by treatment in which patients visualize desired processes, such as the cells of the immune system destroying cancer cells.

The wholeness of health was the topic of a recent public policy conference in Washington [35]. The theme was integration of psychological, sociological, cultural, and spiritual health into a health care system with a biomedical and technological base.

## Positive Health

Many people are trying to achieve excellent health instead of just getting by. Efforts include jogging and other forms of regular exercise, going to health spas, attention to nutrition, yoga, support group, and rejection of pollutants such as food additives and cigarette smoke. Some people use the concept of the wholeness of health in their efforts to become as healthy as possible. Voluntary changes in life style often reflect a search for excellent health for a family. For example, Sue and Jack have just moved from Vermont to Virginia in order to establish a different way of life. They have left behind the long, cold winters, their jobs as college professors, their big old house and rocky acres. They are going to live as cooperating neighbors with a group of people who share their religion and values. They will be farmers, home when the children are home, working together.

## Making Choices

Even if health is considered in a narrow sense rather than in terms of wholeness, an individual makes many choices that affect him. Examples are choosing what and how much to eat, whether to smoke, drink, and use other drugs, whether and how to exercise, and when to rest. Information is needed on which to base choices, and often support and help in making decisions are also needed. Children learn in their families to make such choices; adults get help from family members, friends, and community.

Currently the United States is the scene of several struggles over choices that relate to health. Although there is general agreement that it is good for individuals to take responsibility for health decisions in a narrow sense, violent quarreling has erupted over whether a woman may choose to terminate her pregnancy. Heated disagreements also occur on concepts of death and whether the individual has a right to reject life-prolonging treatment for herself, her child, her spouse, or her parent. These struggles result from differences in meanings of life, death, individual, society—differences that are religious. In a concept of the wholeness of health, however, such decisions are also matters of health.

# FAMILIES AS GIVERS OF HEALTH CARE

Care, including health care, is an expression of love, according to the concept of love presented in this book. Traditional wedding ceremonies imply that health care should be an aspect of marital love. "I take thee . . . in sickness and in health, to love and to cherish. . . ." Children learn at home how to care for themselves and others. Following are some of the ways in which families deal with the health of their members.

## Life Style and Environment

When a life style promotes emotional fulfillment, it contributes to health. Hypertensive diseases are related to modes of living that produce stress. Families are not all the same in reactions to a given environment. Living in a city may be full of stress for the Saretzkis but enjoyably stimulating to the Beaudins. The Jacksons like living in different places as part of life in the armed services, but the Johnsons hated it. What is important for health is to live and work in ways that feel comfortable to the family. Families living in poverty have little choice in regard to life style, but many families have more choice than they realize.

Life style also includes modes of homemaking and home management, ways of eating, dressing, exercising, resting, and recreating. Peace or chaos can result from the ways in which these activities are planned and carried out. Well-being also depends on the home environment itself, the space provided, the cleanliness and tidiness maintained, but again, different families have different requirements for satisfaction. There is, however, a point beyond which elaboration of luxurious environments has no measurable influence on personal satisfaction or measures of family well-being [10].

**Nutrition.**   Bodies are constantly being built and rebuilt out of materials supplied by the family. Since bodies are important parts of persons, and persons make up families, the quality of family life is influenced by the food supplied and the eating patterns developed. Nutrition influences positive health and recovery from illness.

Poor nutrition and poor eating habits are very common in the United States, not primarily because of poverty, but more because of affluence, ignorance, advertising, and lack of food-related skills. The report of the Senate Select Committee on Nutrition and Human Needs states, ''The simple fact is that our diets have changed radically within the last 50 years, with great and often very harmful effects on our health. These dietary changes represent as great a threat to public health as smoking. Too much fat, too much sugar or salt, can be and are linked directly to heart disease, cancer, obesity, and stroke, among other killer diseases.'' [39]

The committee recommended these changes in diet: More fruits, vegetables, and whole grains; less fat consumption—eat less red meat, more fish and poultry; reduce saturated fats and substitute unsaturated fats; reduce cholesterol—eat fewer eggs, less butter; reduce sugar intake by 40 per cent, so that it is 15 per cent of daily caloric intake; reduce salt by 50 to 85 per cent. These recommendations apply to the whole family. Nutrition is important throughout life, but it has special significance during periods of rapid development, including the period of old age, when atrophy occurs.

Because the embryo and fetus are hidden and perhaps even secret, pregnant parents may be unaware of the far-reaching importance of what they provide at this time for their child-to-be. Nutritionists from many different countries have agreed that malnutrition during prenatal life and infancy had harmful effects on birth weight, survival, illness, growth, and behavior [11].

Prematurity and malnutrition of the mother are frequently noted when newborns weigh too little. Quality of nutrition is an important factor in the production of larger babies, who are more likely to survive and have better health [1]. The nutrition of the fetus depends not only on the quality and quantity of food eaten by the woman carrying it but also on the reserves in her body at the beginning of pregnancy. An old wives' tale holds that the fetus will take what it needs from the mother, no matter what she eats. Although there is some truth in this notion, it is also partly wrong. The fetus has priority on certain elements, such as iron and ascorbic acid, but the mother has priority on other elements, such as iodine and vitamin A. Under conditions of scarcity, both will suffer, but with different deficiencies.

Until quite recently, it was customary for obstetricians to try to limit the pregnant woman's weight gain severely. Many women were urged to keep the gain to around 15 pounds. The Committee on Maternal Nutrition of the National Research Council now regards this practice as dangerous to the life and health of mothers and babies. The committee emphasizes an intake of the appropriate nutrients without curbing calories and with careful attention to the needs and condition of each individual [36].

Since the brain develops early in life, it is especially affected by prenatal malnutrition. The most rapid brain growth takes place prenatally and during the first six months after birth, the time when new cells are added. The brain reaches 90 per cent of its adult size by three or four years of age. From the evidence available, it is likely that learning ability and various brain functions are depressed by prenatal malnutrition [41].

Breast-fed infants usually grow well in the early months, even if their mothers are not well nourished. For her own health, of course, the nursing mother requires extra calories rich in nutrients. For instance, if calcium intake is inadequate for milk production, some calcium will be drawn from her bones. The critical time for the infant is when the mother's breast milk dwindles and supplementary foods are needed. For poor babies, the earlier the weaning, the greater the risk of life and health. Damage results from infections as well as from inadequate nutrients.

Infancy can be a time of risk to the affluent, too, because overfeeding or giving excess sugar and fats can result in obesity and poor eating patterns that will persist. The preschool years are the easiest time to establish attitudes and practices that result in lifelong excellent nutrition.

Adolescence is a critical time for nutrition. Children grow very rapidly during the year in which puberty is reached. The majority of girls are growing at their fastest rate since early infancy when they reach a point about six months before their first menstruation. After puberty, the rate of growth slows down, until it stops. The time of the growth spurt depends more upon the nutrition of the children than upon any other factors, since it occurs when a child reaches a certain weight [19]. (For Caucasian girls, the average weight at menarche is 46 kilograms.)

During the growth spurt, large quantities of nutrients are needed for building and transforming the body of a child into that of an adult. The average girl of 12 and boy of 14 need more food, and high quality food, than they ever needed before. Since the boy has farther to go to reach his mature size, he needs more food than the girl, and needs larger quantities for a longer time. However, Henry, Zach, Yvonne, and Brenda are not "the average," just as no individual is. Each spurts, reaches puberty, and achieves mature status at a particular individual time. Zach grew 10 inches between ages 13 and 15; Henry grew six. Zach's mother complained that he made peanut butter sandwiches before she had finished the dinner dishes, whereas Henry waited until bedtime for his snack. Yvonne reached menarche at 11, Brenda at 14. Both are normal; neither is average.

As part of a study of the effects of mothers' employment, over 400 teen-age girls and boys were asked, "Did you have anything to eat this morning before school?" Eighty per cent of those with a nonemployed mother and 70 per cent of those with an employed mother answered yes [17]. Therefore, 20 to 30 per cent of this sample of adolescents went to school without eating any food. The study also showed that more boys than girls ate before going to school.

Adolescent girls' nutrition is especially important. For the girl herself, of course, it is good to have a strong, beautiful, well-functioning body. In addition, her nutrition during adolescence is fundamental to her future performance in pregnancy and childbirth. Her baby will be healthier and better developed if she begins pregnancy with a mature body, well stocked with all the elements that go into building a baby. Her own nutrition will contribute to success in labor, delivery, and lactation.

When the requirements of adolescence and pregnancy are added together, the result is a real problem [21]. It is *possible* for a pregnant teenager to eat enough of the needed nutrients and to avoid useless and harmful foods, but very often, in reality, she does not. Studies of poor pregnancy outcome show two outstanding causes, poor nutrition and youth of the mother. Many of the very young mothers are poor girls who have had inadequate nutrition and other care throughout their lives, including their own prenatal lives. Among the hundreds of thousands of births to teen-agers each year (see page 414), nutrition plays an important role, shown in the following comparisons of births to teen-agers compared with those to women between 20 and 24: Babies more likely to die during the first year; low birth weight twice as frequent; babies more likely to have neurological defects; maternal death risk greater; mother more likely to have toxemias, anemias, and birth complications [4].

Nutritional problems in old age are illustrated by the following incident. When Craig telelphoned Mrs. Baker, age 97, to tell her that the geriatric day care center would be closed because of the ice storm, she asked, "How will I get anything to eat?"

"Take some of the cans from your food shelf," Craig suggested, "Open them, warm up the food, and eat it."

"No, I won't," Mrs. Baker replied. "I just won't have anything to eat unless you take me to the day care center."

Mrs. Baker is extreme, in refusing to eat anything at all, unless the meal is served to her in a social setting. She insists upon living alone. She is probably starving to death. She has already suffered a spontaneous hip fracture. Many older people are like her to a lesser degree, eating far less than they need to maintain life and health. Their diets are usually deficient in both quantity and quality. Snack foods, such as bread, cookies, and tea are easy to prepare, relatively inexpensive and easy to eat. Proteins, minerals, and vitamins require more money, planning, and effort, in short, more *management*. An example of a nutritional problem of older people, especially older women, is bone loss, or *osteoporosis,* as its extreme form is called. Bone loss may result in loss of height, back pain, and easily broken bones. Many people suffering from osteoporosis have had a long-term diet deficient in calcium [14].

Insofar as nutrition determines the health level of the elderly, it is important in determining their whole life-style. In a long-range study of 1200 old people, half drawn from a California community and half from admissions to a psychiatric ward, it was evident that physical problems preceded mental ones for several years and that early retirement was often the result of poor health [40].

**Rhythms in Family Living.**    All animals have rhythms of activity and rest. As far as we can tell, only human beings have to plan their lives so as to carry out the rhythms. Marital harmony is affected by partners who work, play, and sleep at times not congenial to each other, by one or both being fatigued, irritable or lethargic, by one having tremendous, sustained energy while the other needs a frequent change of pace. When children are added to the family, rhythms become much more complicated. The disruption caused by the first baby is largely one of breaking the patterns of living already established by the parents. The hardest adjustment for many new parents is having to get up in the middle of the night and early in the morning.

## Managing Activity and Rest

For the sake of health and satisfying family interaction, homemakers plan and direct the rhythms of family members. If one person did exactly as he wished at each moment, the result would be chaos for all. Communication between family members is important in the planning stage. Since a tired person feels grouchy, he may keep quiet or snap at others when the subject of rest and activity comes up. Therefore, it helps to be aware of one's own state and its influence on communication. A discussion of some of the needs peculiar to various positions in the family follows.

If partnership is to develop, live, and grow, the couple need time alone together when both feel good. The honeymoon is traditionally a time to be alone together for sex, communication, and recreation. Since the need for such time continues throughout life, timing of family activities ideally includes regular privacy for the couple. In cultures where husband-wife roles are clearly defined, their need for regular times alone together is not so great. Since everyone knows what husbands and wives are supposed to do, there is less to talk over and less to decide. In Samoa, for example, one big *fale* (a beautiful, oval, one-room thatched house, open on all sides) shelters a couple, all of their children, perhaps nine or twelve, a grandparent or two, and possibly other kin. Privacy and secrets must be impossible.

The structure of the time plan for a family is usually strongly influenced by the occupational system, by the demands of the husband's job, and the wife's, if she has one. Then decisions have to be made about when to start and stop all the activities about which choice seems possible. In trying to work, study, communicate, and

have good times together, a young couple may deprive themselves of sleep and exercise, both of which are essential to health.

The person who comes closest to needing everything *his* way is the newborn baby. When he is hungry, he is very, very hungry, and totally dependent upon his caregiver to fee him. He moves from one state to another under the influence of his own physiological processes. He drowses, sleeps, wakens quiet and alert, and actively cries. The timing of good care fits what he needs, whether it be food, holding, rocking, washing, or letting him sleep. His mother and other caregivers have to adjust their own rest and activity patterns to his, but for just a little while. By three or four months of age, most babies are beginning to fit into family rhythms, having stabilized their own bodily processes. When caregivers try to understand what the baby wants and needs and to meet his needs during the first year, the year-old baby tries to cooperate with them [3]. Parents can then make use of the budding of respect (see page 28) in order to make changes in timing that are more convenient for other family member's activity-rest rhythms.

Because the essence of early childhood is curiosity, exploration, imagination, and action, the young child gets very tired. Whole health care involves planning for alternating quiet play and active play, regular, nutritious meals and snacks, quiet before meals and bed time, bed before exhaustion, much outdoor play, and opportunities for large muscle exercise.

Relatively slow growth allows more leeway in meeting the school-age child's needs for rest and food, but going to school means hours of physical inactivity.

*Me an My Little Sister*

**FIGURE 13-1**    Drawings by 11-year-old girls. a: An American. b: A New Zealander.

Inactivity at home, too, results in insufficient stimulation for muscular development and coordination, for exercise of heart, lungs, and all that goes into fitness and stamina. American children spend many hours watching television. They ride on buses instead of walking to school. We obtained evidence that they think of themselves as inactive. When we asked 100 girls and 100 boys in each of five countries to draw "a picture of yourself and someone else, anyone you like, *doing something,* anything you like" [38]. Pictures showing children engaged in games and sports were between 40 and 60 per cent of drawings in Australia, Canada, England, and New Zealand, but in the United States, they were only 15 per cent. Frequently, American children drew themselves and their friends "just standing." Figure 13-1 shows typical drawings.

For school-age children, healthy rhythms include regular daily hours of active play, much of it outdoors. Children also do some housework that contributes to the family. Among 1400 families in upstate New York, children between six and eleven worked, on the average, half an hour daily [42]. Children can take an active part in planning the use of time. Some families have regular meeting times when they talk over matters of concern. Some find that mealtime offers the right time and place for planning and deciding.

During their growth spurt, adolescents need more rest than they did as children, since growth makes heavy demands upon energy. Teachers and parents usually expect more work from adolescents than from children. Teen-agers contributed an hour of housework daily in the New York State study [42]. To complicate the picture, planning and deciding with teen-agers may be difficult because they are so involved in establishing their own identity and independence. The best insurance for effective family cooperation at this point is a history of planning together throughout childhood. Parents can still learn better methods of communication, though. They will probably need them in order to keep defining family goals and planning ways of reaching them.

Exercise stimulates bodily processes in such a way that the body can make full use of oxygen and of nutrients from food. Fitness and stamina develop as muscles, lungs, and heart are used to capacity. Exercise causes individual muscle fibers to increase in size and strength, building up the lean tissues, making bones more rugged and better mineralized and decreasing the more inert fat tissues. Even in adults, exercise increases the outpouring of the growth hormone that in turn mobilizes stored fat for fuel [24, pp. 180–185]. Thus, the body is built and rebuilt most efficiently as the organizing processes are called upon, and the building materials are available.

## Use of Medical Services

Families vary in the medical services they want, find, and use. There are some people who have a family doctor who has taken care of them for years, who knows them as members of a family and a community. Other people have no connections with a physician. Still others use a panel of specialists, according to the specific problem faced. Comprehensive health care and group practice provide yet another kind of care. So do clinics and emergency rooms, the main servers of the poor.

Poor people go less often to get medical services, both treatment and prevention, than do more affluent people. Common explanations are that their lack of money holds them back and that they have attitudes toward health that make them reluctant to get medical services. These two reasons are not sufficient, however [16]. The type of services available to the poor also account for their low use. Outpatient departments and clinics, the services used by most poor people, are often disease-oriented and dehumanizing. Patients have to wait for long periods in crowded, busy, impersonal, unattractive settings.

Availability of different types of services will, of course, limit the choices a family can make. Often a person does not look for a particular service until it is needed. For example, I (MSS) did not seek a breast cancer specialist until I learned that I had breast cancer. However, families need basic health services, such as dental care and immunizations. Because they are almost certain to suffer some illness, making plans for medical care is an important part of family health care. The choice of a physician, dentist, or clinic can be based on information gathered from several sources. Experiences of friends are important, as well as qualifications, practices, objectives, and fees. Although people often hesitate to see for themselves and to ask questions of the providers of health care, it can be done. My sister and I once called on a new physician in his office, to see whether we wanted him to be our family doctor. The result was good medical care for all of us and a satisfactory relationship with the doctor.

Whatever the type of care chosen, a family can best get good services by making their wants and beliefs clear and by making sure that they understand the information and treatment given. Too often patients and their families are intimidated by powerful medical figures who may not care or may simply not understand the needs and fears involved. The patient may need to have a family member stand up for what he needs and wants, acting as advocate with the doctor, hospital, or clinic. In India, Africa, and Polynesia, a family member is expected to go to a hospital and stay with a patient, giving constant support and care.

It is often hard to decide whether to seek medical help for the illness of one's child or oneself. Are the symptoms serious enough to merit the price of a doctor and the effort of getting an appointment and going to the office or clinic? Knowledge and health skills help a person to make this decision. Family members feel concerned and responsible for the health of other family members. They consult one another about how to treat illnesses and injuries, making extensive use of over-the-counter medicines. Americans do more self-medication than do families in countries where professional help is more available to all [32]. When the decision is to get medical help, the best use of it can be made by cooperating with the treatment plan by taking the pills, sticking to the diet, checking on blood pressure, or doing whatever has been prescribed. Because most health services are actually given to persons by themselves or by family members, the quality of care received depends upon the patient or family taking responsibility.

## Coping with Illness and Injuries

Even with positive health measures, people sometimes get sick and hurt. The family is the primary giver of treatment, as well as of preventive measures. Living in close everyday contact, parents and spouses are usually the first to see that something is wrong. A government survey showed the extent to which parents were concerned about health problems in their children. Figure 13-2 shows the extent to which the health of schoolchildren and adolescents is a problem, from their parents' point of view and from the findings of a health survey. The United States government conducted the survey on 7,119 children between the age of 6 and 11, and 6,768 youths between the age of 12 and 17, all of whom were representative of the population of that age. Parents of 19 per cent of the children were worried about some aspect of their children's health. The examining pediatricians found about 13 per cent of the children to have a significant abnormality. This represents 3.1 million children in the total population.

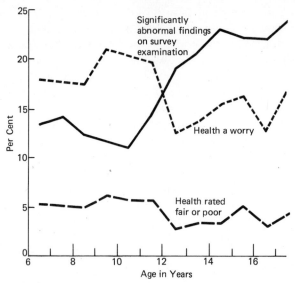

25 ┐

Significantly
abnormal findings
on survey
examination

20 ┤

Per Cent

15 ┤

Health a worry

10 ┤

5 ┤

Health rated
fair or poor

0 ┘

6      8      10      12      14      16

Age in Years

**FIGURE 13-2**

Per cent of U.S. children in 1963–65 and youths in 1966–70 with significantly abnormal findings on survey examination and parent ratings of fair or poor health or health a worry, by age.

*Source:* Jean Roberts. Examination and health history findings among children and youths, 6–17 years. Washington, D.C.: U.S. Department of Health, Education, and Welfare, Vital and Health Statistics—Series II-No. 129 DHEW Publication No. (HRA) 74-1611, 1973, Figure 1.

**Special Skills.** Nursing skills make a big contribution to family health. Many techniques are passed down from mother to daughter and perhaps to sons. A child may learn from direct experience how to take a temperature and pulse, give an enema, rub a back, and set up a room for a sick patient. Courses in home nursing teach these skills and more. Preparation for having a baby, or *post partum* classes, offer parents opportunities to learn how to tell when a baby is ill and how to give care that may prevent serious developments. For example, dehydration is one of the main reasons for hospitalizing infants, but the early stages of dehydration can be treated at home.

First aid and accident prevention courses give valuable knowledge and skills that can enhance health. Such courses are required for swimming teachers, group leaders, and such, but everyone needs to know about these matters. An important part of parental caregiving is to make the environment safe for children while still giving opportunities for exploration and learning.

**Infections: Prevention and Treatment**

A healthy body can put up a stronger fight against most disease organisms than one weakened by poor nutrition, physical or psychological stress, insufficient rest or lack of exercise. Immunization is required or recommended in the United States in order to prevent the following diseases: diphtheria, measles, mumps, poliomyelitis, rubella, tetanus, and whooping cough. Many communities provide free immunization programs for infants and young children, but parents have to plan to have it done. Middle- and upper-income parents also have to pay. After measles vaccine was introduced in 1963, the annual incidence of cases dropped from half a million to just over 22,000. Parents became complacent and many failed to have their children immunized. Upswings occurred, with a 69 per cent increase in a recent year [28]. A significant increase in rubella cases occurred in high school and college students in 1977. In Asia, Africa, and other parts of the world, additional immunizations are needed. Health care includes protection against cholera, yellow fever, malaria, plague, and typhoid. Adequate health services include immunizations against diseases as recommended by public health authorities.

Environment and life style are pertinent to disease prevention. A family can live in a hookworm-infested area and yet prevent hookworm infection by wearing shoes. There may be amoebas in the water and on the vegetables, but amoebic dysentery can be avoided by boiling all drinking water, eating only freshly cooked food, and careful handwashing after toileting and before eating. Amoebas, and other intestinal parasites, hookworm, and the common cold are diseases that cannot be prevented by immunization. They have to be halted before they enter the body, and that is what cleanliness techniques do. When children grow up in a locality where such diseases are common, they learn from their parents how to manage. When adults move into the area of a health threat that is new to them, they must learn new management skills if they decide that it is worthwhile to prevent illness.

Venereal disease cannot be prevented by immunization, but only by keeping the organisms out of the body. Venereal diseases include all infections transmitted by sexual contact, but the best known are syphilis and gonorrhea. Because venereal disease has such far-reaching effects upon reproduction and health and because its spread depends upon interpersonal relationships and life styles, we discuss it in Appendix D.

**Treating Illness.**   Home nursing makes it possible for the patient to be treated as a whole person within his family. Love, expressed as care, contributes to healing, along with confidence in recovery and sympathy for the discomforts the patient feels. Recovery is aided by pleasures such as an orderly room, interesting activities, flowers, and messages.

Special nutrition aids recovery. The body's reaction to stress is to break down some of its protein and other essential elements. Such stress can be caused by infections (especially gastrointestinal), surgery, accidents, and drugs. Therefore, the ill and recuperating patient needs extra protein, minerals, and vitamins [13]. And since rest aids in body building, it is also necessary for recuperation. Prompt treatment for infections and other illnesses leads to quicker recovery and hence conserves the family resources of money, energy, and time.

## Preventing Accidents and Injuries

In a recent two-year period there were, on the average, 295 deaths from accidents daily in the United States [29]. Motor vehicle accidents were the first cause of death. Falls ranked second.

Physical safety is an impotant consideration in planning where to live and in setting up and running a home. Are the community and neighborhood sites of violence and crime, polluted air, loud noise, or congested traffic? Is fire protection adequate and available? As mentioned previously, the physical features of the house may be safe or dangerous. Often a family has to balance one disadvantage against another, deciding which goal is more important.

In planning space and home operations for maximum safety, the special characteristics of various family members are significant. For instance, because preschool children are likely to be more impulsive and curious than older children, they need more protection from access to fires, machines, cleaning materials, medicines, garden tools, and trash. Accidents occur less frequently to elderly adults than to younger ones, but older people take a longer time to recover [30]. Two thirds of accidents to people over 65 occur at home. Older women have more accidents than older men and are disabled longer. Because of poor eyesight, unsteadiness, and vulnerability to falls, older people probably need uncluttered passageways and handrails on steps and bath facilities. Safety in the kitchen is promoted by sturdy equipment, convenient storage arrangements, and work space planned to fit the tasks and the person performing them. If partners and children are flexible enough in sex roles and communication, all together may do better in planning and arranging for use of space, especially kitchen space.

In educating children for safety, parents' teaching and behavior are influential in many areas of life, incuding driving a car, wearing seat belts, walking in traffic, handling weapons, and engaging in sports, especially water sports. Basic attitudes of self-esteem and respect for the individual come through in the way adults take care of themselves and their children. Children most readily acquire the behavior patterns of parents who are consistent in what they say and what they do.

## Living with Genetic Defects and Handicaps

Family planning can prevent the birth of many children with hereditary disorders, but not all such children. At present 6 per cent of infants are born with some sort of genetic defect. This incidence is increasing, as a result of modern medicine that makes it possible for children with various defects to grow up and reproduce. It is estimated that all human beings have twelve or more disadvantageous genes [20].

The Bureau of Education for the Handicapped estimated that over 7.8 million persons between birth and 19 years of age have some sort of handicapping condition. About 6 per cent of preschool children and 12 per cent of children 6 to 19 were estimated to have handicaps. Table 13-1 shows the percentages of children having various kinds of handicaps.

**TABLE 13-1**      **Estimated Percentages of Children between Birth and 19 with Selected Handicaps**

| Type of Handicap | Estimated percent |
|---|---|
| Speech impaired | 3.5 |
| Learning disabled | 3.0 |
| Mentally retarded | 2.3 |
| Emotionally disturbed | 2.0 |
| Crippled and other health impaired | .5 |
| Hard of hearing | .5 |
| Visually handicapped | .1 |
| Deaf | .07 |
| Deaf, blind, and other health impaired | .06 |

Source: Snapper, Kurt J. and JoAnne S. Ohms. *The status of children* 1977. U. S. Department of Health, Education, and Welfare. Office of Human Development Services. DHEW Publication No. (OHDS) 78-30133. Washington, D. C.: U.S. Government Printing Office, 1978, Exhibit 4-10.

## Controlling Drug Use

Drugs contribute to a tremendous health problem and at the same time, drugs are the means of relieving all sorts of illness and pain and of correcting bodily deficiencies. Drugs are everybody's problem, not only the individual's and the family's but also the world community's. But here we are concerned with what families and individuals can do to preserve and promote the health of their members.

Medicines, especially pills, are very much a part of everyday life in the Western world, particularly in the United States. Young infants receive vitamins in drops and as soon as they can pick up bits of food and chew them, chewable vitamin pills are one of their daily pleasures and benefits. Adults toss down various food supplements and medication with breakfast and casually take a couple of aspirin tablets if bothered with a headache. Television commercials laud and illustrate a huge succession of pills, liquids, and sprays for all bodily parts from head to toes. A clear messsage is delivered every day, even every 20 minutes; solve your problems by swallowing or squirting something. It is not a very big jump for a 10- to 12-year-old to accept a pill or a sniff from a friend who tells him it will make him feel great.

As with the other health problems discussed in this chapter, drugs pose the greatest threats to the person at times when growth is rapid. Those periods are prenatal life, infancy, and adolescence.

**Prenatal Life and Infancy.**    Many drugs endanger the fetus and future child if taken by a pregnant woman. Such drugs include not only tranquilizers and hard drugs, but medicines such as quinine and social drugs such as cigarettes and alcohol [37]. Damage to the fetus includes deafness, defects in limbs and other deformities, prematurity, small size, irritability, excitability, retardation, and cognitive defects. The safest rule for the pregnant woman to follow is to take no drugs unless ordered by a doctor who can show why it is necessary.

At first glance, it might seem that there is little chance of infants ingesting drugs, and yet there are several ways in which they do. Breast-fed babies receive a share of the drugs taken by their mothers, either voluntarily or in the form of pollutants. Some drugs pass into the breast milk more readily than others. Since new medications are being constantly produced and prescribed, research can hardly keep pace enough to give information about all. The director of a poison control center gives this rule of thumb for judging whether to give a particular drug to a nursing mother: if $\frac{1}{15}$ or $\frac{1}{12}$ of the dose would not be suitable for a baby, then do not give the drug to the mother [5]. Existing evidence indicates that oral contraceptives, nicotine, and marijuana will be transmitted to the baby and that they are probably harmful.

Young children sometimes swallow pills, medicines, cosmetics, or cleaning materials that they find. The best management of such situations is *prevention*, through careful storage of harmful materials, as well as supervision of children.

Sometimes parents give drugs to their children, either because they do not believe that the substance is harmful to anyone or because they believe that children and adults should be treated alike. Parents have been known to share their "joints," LSD, or alcoholic drinks with their very young children. Such practices are likely to endanger the child's present health and set the stage for future habituation. The danger is greater in the case of some drugs, such as cocaine or LSD, than others. However, alcohol is highly dangerous for some individuals. Families that incorporate alcohol into a cultural or religious ritual teach their children to use it moderately Such teaching, however, does not guarantee that the child will not become addicted.

**Adolescence.**    Adolescence and perhaps the preceding year or two are the time of life when most people think of drug problems as pertinent. Looking for new experience and asserting their independence of adults, the preadolescent is likely to try cigarettes, alcohol, marijuana, and other drugs. Where he goes from here depends upon many factors, including his self-esteem, his parents' behavior, his peers' behavior, and the availability of the various drugs.

Considering drugs (including alcohol and cigarettes) as a health management problem, the first thing for individuals and families to do is to get full information on the action of drugs that they use or consider using. Good communication patterns are very helpful in family discussions of this topic, on which many adolescents and parents have trouble talking with each other. Other tensions and conflicts are often reflected in an abuse of drugs. When one member of a family is habituated or addicted, it is likely that the family needs outside help in order to solve the problems that led to it and to change present behavior patterns. Sources include professional therapy, groups, and individuals that have experienced the same problem, and combinations of these agents.

## Recreation

Recreation means continuing renewal of the person, in body, mind, and feeling. *Play*, the normal means of recreation, is any activity carried on with pleasure, for its own sake. Physical health is enhanced by active motor play, as in sports and outdoor games. Mental and emotional refreshment come from artistic creating and experiencing, social play, humor, and enjoyment of nature, as well as from sports and games.

In planning for recreation, family members have to take into consideration time, place, money, and everyone's abilities and preferences. Often play can be a part of more serious or humdrum processes. A creative act can transform a meal into recreation, something as simple as an interesting conversation, some jokes or funny stories, or a heart-shaped red gelatin dessert on Valentine's Day. In New Zealand, most families have easy access to a beach, camp grounds, skiing, bowling, cricket, and many more outdoor activities. Since all places of business are closed on Saturdays, couples and families often go on weekend expeditions. When getting acquainted with people, they often ask, "What are your sports?" Everyone is expected to enjoy some sort of outdoor exercise and to take part in it frequently. Americans may be headed in this direction, although they have been generally relatively sedentary. However, outdoor active recreation has had an impetus from the energy crisis, from renewed interest in fitness by health-conscious young adults, and from increased amounts of leisure time. This is not to say that jogging for weight control is exactly play and recreation, but jogging is definitely exercise in the service of health. And perhaps those who jog will sometimes hike or play golf for fun.

At the same time that recreation is contributing to health, it can be strengthening the bonds of partnership, parent-child relations, sibling relations, and even kin relations. Mutual enjoyment, sharing, and cooperation of an experience result in positive feelings between the participants.

ROBERT J. IZZO

# THE COMMUNITY'S ROLE IN PROMOTING HEALTH

The wider environment determines to a large extent what the family can make of their life style. A look backward into medical history shows that a substantial decline in mortality rates occurred in the nineteenth century in both Europe and the United States. The decline, due to decreases in infectious diseases, came about through the introduction of basic community hygiene: purification of water, sewage disposal, pasteurization of milk, and other food hygiene [27]. Before the introduction of these community hygiene measures, a family would have little chance of controlling infectious diseases through its own life style.

## Medical Services

Communities usually offer some public and some private or voluntary services. National and state policies determine to a large extent what is available locally. In Great Britain, every resident has accesss to nationally financed physicians and hospitals. In New Zealand hospitals, prescription drugs, and children's dentistry are free, but adults may pay small fees to doctors. In Ontario compulsory insurance pays for doctors, prescription drugs, and hospitals. The insurance is free to older citizens. In the United States occasional services, such as immunization clinics, are free to everyone. Some medical services are given to the poor in established hospitals or in community clinics. Well-baby clinics and family planning clinics may be offered under community, state, or national auspices. Voluntary health organizations, such as Planned Parenthood, offer services on a sliding scale of fees.

## Sanitation

Clean water has been taken for granted by most North Americans, but those who have had to boil drinking water will always appreciate the comfort and security of potable tap water; the same is true with milk. After having to boil milk before using it, pasteurized milk and powdered milk seem like the greatest luxuries. Modern industrialized nations ordinarily provide sanitation of milk, water, and foods through legislation, inspection, and taxes. Communicable diseases are controlled through both prevention and detection, isolation and treatment. Efforts are mounted against carriers, such as malaria mosquitoes and rabid animals. Garbage and trash are collected and disposed of. Public toilets are provided. In very poor countries, most of these amenities are either lacking or inadequate. Especially in very crowded cities, such as Calcutta and Jogjakarta, educated, wealthy people provide their own sanitation, whereas the poor have no choice.

## Safe Streets

Pedestrians can walk along most North American streets wihout falling into holes, tripping over loose pieces of sidewalk, stumbling into the wares of a sidewalk shopkeeper, or slipping in fresh cow manure. However, an American strolling in a big city, especially at night, stands a greater chance than a Canadian of getting mugged, robbed, raped, and/or killed. Where bicycle riding is concerned, North Americans have a long way to go to equal the networks of safe paths provided in the Netherlands and other advanced European countries.

## Nutrition

Although much remains to be done, North Americans have made efforts to feed people through a variety of programs. The school hot lunch program is one of the most important ones because it reaches over 25 million children annually, 11 million receiving lunch free [39]. Many children need it tremendously. When breakfast is also given to hungry children, they benefit greatly, both physically and mentally. In some schools, only subsidized milk is given. Food stamps and surplus foods have been used to supplement the diets of the poor. There have been occasional programs to improve the intake of pregnant and nursing mothers. *Meals on Wheels,* a combined public and voluntary service, is invaluable to invalids and old people. Some schools, as well, provide meals for the aged.

Milk and milk products are subsidized by the New Zealand government. Everyone can afford generous quantities of these highly nutritious foods.

## Education

Health education is a vital public health service, covering many different kinds of programs to all sorts of people. It cannot be done once and for all in the schools, although the foundation is laid by sound health courses in school. However, health sciences are constantly yielding new knowledge, requiring people to update their education.

Even more important, a person needs education on special topics at certain points in life. Sometimes the appropriate education can come from the family and a public program is not necessary, as with preschool children's sex education. At other times, public programs are the only way in which most will be reached, as in adolescents' education for family planning and venereal disease control. Education for childbirth and infant care is a necessity to prospective parents and new parents. Although a few may get sufficient education privately, the need for public services is great in this area. The greatest need is among single pregnant girls and adolescent parents. A recent social action program for this population includes health services along with educational programs [12]. Another great need is for adult education in regard to aging.

An expansion and revamping of nutrition education is needed in order to motivate people of all ages to eat what is good for life, growth, and health. Traditional nutrition education could be supplemented with teaching based on cultural food imagery and emotional play upon such themes as survival, minimizing suffering, parental love and duty, success, achievement, and beauty [7].

## NEW DIRECTIONS AND CONCERNS IN HEALTH CARE

Dissatisfaction with traditional health care has led to new attitudes, ideas, and solutions. More change can be expected at national levels, where health problems are being addressed seriously.

In a 1978 Government report on the status of children, descriptions of many programs reflect concern with the wholeness of health, positive health concepts, and the caregiving functions of families. Comprehensive programs include: income assistance and maintenance programs; Child Welfare Services, designed to prevent neglect, abuse, exploitation, and delinquency; Indian Social Services; Appalachian Child Development Program; Youth Challenge Program; Supplementary Food Program for Women, Infants, and Children, which serves pregnant and lactating women and their children up to five years if they are identified as being at risk; programs of the Bureau of Education for the Handicapped; Community Mental Health Centers Comprehensive Services Support program; Child Development-Head Start Program. The Government also sponsors research and publishes information concerning health. Officials point out needs and trends in efforts to stimulate communities, families, and individuals to provide appropriate care. Some new developments and pressing health-related concerns include the following topics.

## Self-Care

Some families provide most or all of their own health care services, such as those who live in an area of Northern California 50 miles from a clinic or hospital. The help they do accept is from a Maternity Outreach Project and a lay midwife [31]. Even among families who consult physicians, hospitals, and clinics, there is much self-medication and caring for illness at home.

*The Family as Healer* is the title of a new book by Harold Wise, a physician who believes that the family's potential for self-care should be maximized by physicians and other health workers [43]. Wise recognizes the interaction of health and illness on marriage and family life. By involving families in plans for treatment, Dr. Wise and his associates strengthen family members' coping abilities. This approach contrasts sharply with that of the old-fashioned authoritarian doctor who simply gives orders to his patients, nurses, and other workers.

### Availability of Comprehensive Health Services

How can everyone have access to adequate medical care at affordable prices? A recent answer to this question is the Health Maintenance Organization, a service designed to keep people well in addition to treating them when they are ill. Users pay a fixed sum whether they are sick or not. The price is kept down not only by preventing costly illness, but by using a variety of medical personnel, most of whom are paid less than self-employed physicians.

Comprehensive services are offered also at neighborhood clinics, where a few physicians are supplemented by nurses, social workers, midwives, physicians' assistants, nutritionists, volunteers, and others. Government grants, community and private support, and sliding fees may finance these clinics.

Compulsory health insurance is presently recommended by some as a way of providing health care to everyone. The government would pay some of the cost, or perhaps all of it for some people. One of the difficulties with this idea is that it does

**Figure 13-D**    The support of the visiting nurse enables families to care for patients at home.

ZETTE EMMONS

not include ways to reduce or control costs. Nobody seems to be able to find a way to deliver medical services as inexpensively as do governments that have been providing care and controlling costs for many years.

See pages 251–252 for descriptions of types of health insurance.

## Family Planning

Contraception is becoming more and more accepted. Only a few years ago, services and education were given by a voluntary agency, Planned Parenthood, but now the federal government assists in giving services and education for fertility control. Poor women and young women are not yet adequately served. Government officials and publications [9, 39], along with many private organizations and persons, express deep concern over adolescent pregnancy (See pages 316–317). Although research and constructive action have probably been held back by reluctance to face the reality of adolescent sexuality, programs are now being constructed. Universal education, as well as family planning services, is greatly needed. Isolated family planning clinics are certainly useful, but have their limits. If family planning were integrated into comprehensive health care, then more people would receive help with it when they need it.

## Teenage Parenthood

As discussed previously, teenage parenthood, a growing problem, strains the health, resources, and life opportunities of the young parents, their babies, and their families of orientation. Preventing the problem is ideal, but services are needed by those who encounter it. Needs are financial, educational, medical, nutritional, psychological, and social. A model program is conducted at Johns Hopkins Medical Center, where 1,400 mothers have been assisted and compared with a similar group not in the program [22]. Their average age was 15½. The program mothers have had few subsequent pregnancies and have gone back to school in greater numbers. More of their babies were normal at one year of age. The cost of the model program is $2000 per mother per year. Only 30,000 mothers could be included in national programs of this type, out of the 600,000 teen-agers who give birth, if the sum originally planned in the late Spring of 1978 is made available by Congress [2]. And then there would be nothing left to pay for prevention! Suppose, however, that appropriations were made with the idea of lowering the annual outlay of $8.3 billion that is actually spent on support payments, medical costs, social services, and related costs [33a]. Surely then it would seem worth while to spend millions to prevent teenage pregnancies from occurring in the first place as well as to prevent pregnancies beyond the first.

## Venereal Diseases

Gonorrhea has increased in prevalence for a number of years, and genital herpes has become an epidemic. It is estimated that sexually transmitted diseases cause the death and/or lifetime disability of 100,000 babies and young women every year [18]. These diseases are, of course, related to the increase of sexual activity outside marriage, especially among teen-agers. Although education and services are indicated, solutions must be sought in research, too. There is no sure way to prevent sexually transmitted diseases other than abstinence or monogamous sex. In other words, life style is the basic source of this growing health problem. Venereal diseases are discussed in more detail in Appendix D.

## Childbirth

In Chapter 11 we discussed new trends in childbirth. Briefly, normal births are being freed from the domination of a medical orientation through home births, birth centers, midwives, education for childbirth, and new knowledge about infants' capabilities and the bonding process. The problematic aspect is how to retain the safety factors from the medical model while developing the psychological and social benefits from the new.

## Caring for the Elderly

People over 65 now number close to 10 million in the United States. As the numbers of old people increase, as they will for the next 50 years, so will costs of caring for them and problems related to care. Government payments for the elderly, now amounting to $112 billion, are estimated at $635 billion for the year 2035 [6]. Half of the long-term care of older people is now provided by families. Most adult children care about the well-being of their parents. About 600,000 people need nursing homes. Much of the care received is minimal or poor, centered on physical needs and neglecting psychological and social aspects of health. The care of old people places burdens on many families.

Robert Benedict, U.S. Commissioner on Aging, lists some important questions regarding care of the elderly [6]. Should there be explicit government policies on long-term care of the aged? Should the policy be to assist adult children to care for parents? Can society guarantee quality in services? Can stigma be removed from government assistance? Should all older people receive community help, regardless of financial need? Should care for the elderly be nonprofit? Can neighborhood facilities be developed? Should there be a single system of care?

**Death and Dying**

Death and dying will be discussed in Chapter 16. Here they are mentioned only as an area of concern in health. Dying has been removed from family and home and tucked away in hospitals and nursing homes. There is now a movement to humanize dying, to treat the dying as whole persons, giving them loving care in their families. As young people learn to accept death as the inevitable part of life that it is, they are able to live creatively with dying family members. Another part of the humanizing of death is to let persons die when they are ready, instead of prolonging dying through the use of machines and devices. Wholeness of health includes a dignified death.

**SUMMARY**

Health and family interaction mutually influence each other. Health refers to mental, emotional, and social functioning, as well as to physical. A positive concept of health includes standards of excellence. Individuals and families make many choices that affect health, sometimes conflicting with political and religious institutions.

Families provide much health care for their members. Care is an expression of love. Health is enhanced by life styles that promote emotional fulfillment, as well as adequate physical surroundings, nutrition, and rhythms of exercise and rest. Times of rapid growth are especially critical for nutrition. These times include prenatal life, infancy, and adolescence. For other reasons, old age is also a time for special concern about nutrition. The management of exercise and rest requires careful planning and communication, because it is involved in family interaction and satisfaction.

Families choose medical services from among those available to them. Money determines to a large extent what kind of medical care a family can get. Even when money is not a barrier, people tend to avoid large, busy, unattractive, impersonal settings. A satisfactory choice is more likely if a person has some medical knowledge, information about resources, and enough self-assurance to keep looking and asking for what she wants. Because it is difficult for a patient to be assertive, it helps to have an advocate or family member along to see that needs are met and to give emotional support.

Families give care for most illnesses and injuries. The better the nursing and diagnostic skills, the better the care. The ill person can be treated at home as a whole person. Home management and life style are significant in prevention of illness and accidents. Family planning, with genetic counseling can prevent the occurrence of many genetic defects. Families with handicapped members need extra supports from outside.

Drug-related health problems are more serious at some stages of life than at others. Prenatal life, infancy, and adolescence are times of potential danger.

Recreation through play is renewing to body and mind, and integrating to families. Life style sets the stage for the types of recreation available. The community also contributes recreational opportunities, as well as various health services, both preventive and therapeutic.

New ideas about health are being translated into programs on national and community levels. The family is receiving recognition as a provider of health care. Better methods of health-care delivery are being sought and explored. Problems of reproduction and sex are causing concern. There are new trends in childbirth, care of the elderly, and the conduct of death.

**REFERENCES**

1. Ademowore, Adebayo S., Norman G. Courey, and James S. Kime. Relationship of maternal nutrition and weight gain to newborn birthweight. *Obstetrics and Gynecology,* 1972, **39,** 460–464.
2. Adolescent pregnancy bill. *Washington COFO Memo,* Summer 1978, p. 6.
3. Ainsworth, Mary D. Salter. The development of infant-mother attachment. In Bettye M. Caldwell and Henry Ricciuti (Eds.). *Review of Child Development Research,* Vol. 3. Chicago: U. of Chicago, 1973.
4. Alan Guttmacher Institute. *11 million teenagers.* New York: Planned Parenthood Federation of American, Inc., 1976.
5. Arena, Jay M. Contamination of the ideal food. *Nutrition Today,* 1970, **5:** 4, 2–8.
6. Benedict, Robert. The family and long term care alternatives. Paper presented at meeting of the Groves Conference, Washington, D.C., 1978.
7. Berg, Alan. *The nutrition factor: Its role in national development.* Washington, D.C.,: The Brookings Institution, 1973.
8. Califano, Joseph A., Jr. What's wrong with U.S. health care? *Washington Post,* June 26, 1977.
9. Chilman, Catherine S. *Social and psychological aspects of adolescent sexuality: An analytic overview of research and theory.* Milwaukee: Center for Advanced Studies in Human Services, U. of Wisconsin, 1977.
10. Chilman, Catherine S. Habitat and American families: A social-psychological overview. *Family Coordinator,* 1978, **27,** 105–111.
11. Coursin, David. Maternal nutrition and the offspring's development. *Nutrition Today,* 1973, **8:** 2, 12–18.
12. Cromwell, Richard E. and Joan L. Gangel. A social "action" program directed to single pregnant girls and adolescent parents. *Family Coordinator,* 1974, **23,** 61–66.
13. Dairy Council. Nutrition in illness. *Dairy Council Digest,* 1969, **40:** 5, 25–28.
14. Dairy Council. Nutritional implications of osteoporosis. *Dairy Council Digest,* 1970, **41:** 5, 25–28.
15. Dubos, René. Health and creative adaptation. *Human Nature,* 1978, **1:** 1, 74–82.
16. Dutton, Diana B. Explaining the low use of health services by the poor: Costs, attitudes, or delivery systems? *American Sociological Review,* 1978, **43,** 348–368.
17. Feldman, Margaret and Harold Feldman. *Sexism in the family.* Ithaca, N.Y.: Unpublished manuscript, 1974.
18. Franck, Phyllis and Diana S. Hart. VD: The neglected epidemic. *Washington Post,* September 12, 1977.
19. Frisch, Rose E. Weight at menarche: Similarity for well-nourished and undernourished girls at differing ages, and evidence for historical constancy. *Pediatrics,* 1972, **50,** 445–450.
20. Handler, Philip (Ed.). *Biology and the future of man.* New York: Oxford U.P., 1970.

21. Hurley, Lucille S. The consequences of fetal impoverishment. *Nutrition Today,* 1968, **3:** 4, 3–10.
22. Kennedy, Edward M. Congressional concerns and activities to nurture and sustain the economic, social well being, and health of families. Paper presented at meeting of the Groves Conference, Washington, 1978.
23. Kobrin, Frances E. and Gerry E. Hendershot. Do family ties reduce mortality? Evidence from the United States 1966–1968. *Journal of Marriage and the Family,* 1977, **39** 737–745.
24. Krogman, Wilton M. *Child growth.* Ann Arbor: U. of Michigan, 1972.
25. Lambo, Thomas A. Psychotherapy in Africa. *Human Nature,* 1978, **1:** 3, 32–39.
27. McKeown, Thomas. Determinants of health. *Human Nature,* 1978, **1:** 4, 60–67.
28. Metropolitan Life Insurance Company. Measles, mumps, and rubella. *Statistical Bulletin,* 1977, **58:** 11, 3–4.
29. Metropolitan Life Insurance Company. Seasonal variation in mortality from accidents. *Statistical Bulletin,* 1977, **58:** 12, 8–9.
30. Metropolitan Life Insurance Company. Health of older persons. *Statistical Bulletin,* 1978, **59:** 1, 14–15.
31. Mills, Nancy. A midwife's story. In Charlotte and Fred Ward (Eds.). *The home birth book.* Garden City, N.Y.: Doubleday, 1977.
32. Pratt, Lois. The significance of the family in medication. *Journal of Comparative Family Studies,* 1973, **4,** 13–31.
33. Pukui, Mary K., E. W. Haertig, and Catherine A. Lee. *Náná I ke kumu (Look to the source).* Vol. 1. Honolulu, Hui Hánai, 1972.
33a. Rich, Spencer. Teen pregnancies in 1979 said to cost U.S. $8 billion. *International Herald Tribune,* May 15, 1979.
34. Russell, Candyce S. Transition to parenthood: Problems and gratifications. *Journal of Marriage and the Family,* 1974, **36,** 294–301.
35. Scardino, Katherine. "Holistic Health"—Equal to the sum of its parts. *APA Monitor,* 1978, **9:** 6, 4.
36. Shank, Robert E. A chink in our armor. *Nutrition Today,* 1970, **5:** 2, 2–11.
37. Smart, Mollie S. and Russell C. Smart. *Children: Development and relationships.* (3rd ed.) New York: Macmillan, 1977.
38. Smart, Russell C. and Mollie S. Smart. Group values shown in preadolescents' drawings in five English-speaking countries. *Journal of Social Psychology,* 1975, **97:**1, 23–37.
39. Snapper, Kurt J. and JoAnne S. Ohms. *The status of children 1977.* U.S. Department of Health, Education, and Welfare. Office of Human Development Services. DHEW Publication No. (OHDS) 78–30133. Washington, D.C.: U.S. Government Printing Office, 1978.
40. Spence, Donald L. and Betsy C. Robinson. Patterns in retirement. In Frances Carp (Ed.). *The retirement process.* Public Health Service Publication No. 178. Washington D.C.: U.S. Government Printing Office, 1968.
41. Vore, David A. Prenatal nutrition and postnatal intellectual development. *Merrill-Palmer Quarterly,* 1973, **19,** 251–260.
42. Walker, Kathryn E. Household work time: Its implications for family decisions. *Journal of Home Economics,* 1973, **65:** 7, 7–11.
43. Wise, Harold. *The family as healer.* New York: Harper, 1979.

# CHAPTER 14
# COPING WITH CRISES AND PROBLEMS

A **crisis** occurs in a person or group when a sudden, highly significant change produces a situation that the person or family cannot handle effectively. The crisis requires the application of behavior patterns or resources that are not available. The person or group is in disequilibrium and thus to restore equilibrium, habitual modes of response must change quickly. Very often, because the resources at hand are insufficient for producing new responses, new sources of help, support, teaching, and problem-solving must be sought. The individual may turn first to his family or perhaps to a friend. The family in crisis may turn to friends or relatives or to another social institution, such as the church, school, or hospital. Because change in modern life is rapid, families in crisis often do not know how to get help. History and past experience are either not known or not adequate for this particular problem.

Limited in time, a crisis represents a turning point for the individual or family. Persons in crisis are more likely to reach out for aid, because their own resources are not adequate for coping. A successful dealing with the crisis, whether with help from the intervention of others or by working it through by oneself, can upgrade the individual or family interaction patterns. The newly formed behavior patterns may improve present ways of living. The experience may also prepare the members of the family to cope better with future crises. Failure to resolve the crisis can start a pattern of overlapping crises, or chronic problems. Very prompt intervention may result in very quick and easy resolution.

An example of very early successful crisis intervention is a case handled by a nurse in New Zealand [48]. Ray Taylor recognized a sudden behavioral and physical change in a nine-week-old infant as indicating a crisis caused by the mother's withdrawal. When the mother, guided by the nurse, restored her loving attention, in extra measure, the infant promptly recovered. Being very immature, the infant reacted as a whole to the threat. Because he was in a stage of rapid development, his reorganization and recovery were very swift. This case documents the importance of dealing with mental health problems at an early age and of having community support systems available to parents.

Some problems are not limited in time, but continue for a long period, even over the lifetime family career. This type of situation will be discussed later in the chapter, under the heading Ongoing Problems.

## CRISES

A crisis is usually named in terms of the stressor event that precipitates it. Although there are many, even an infinite, number of events capable of causing crises, certain types are common. They have been classified in various ways. The list of events and classifications that we give here could be expanded. There are certain principles of crisis resolution that hold from one stressor to another.

### Types of Stresses that Precipitate Crises

Certain kinds of events usually result in crises in families. The severity of a particular crisis, however, depends upon details of the event and the family itself. Table 14-1 follows some classifications of crisis-producing stresses suggested by Reuben Hill [20]. Reading down, events or situations are listed. Reading across, events are classified as to whether they originate within the family or from outside. It is likely to be harder to cope with crises due to within-family events, such as out-of-wedlock births and divorce, than to cope with events arising from outside, such as floods and forced migrations. The former result from inadequacy within the family system, the latter from forces outside it. The next classification is in terms of effects upon families. Under *dismemberment* are events that remove a member from functioning in the family. Looking down the column under *dismemberment,* some of these events are death, hospitalization, and divorce. When the event adds one or more persons to the family, it is classified as *accession.* The accession column includes undesired pregnancy, remarriage, and taking an old person into the family. *Demoralization,* the third category under *effect on family,* means that the family's role patterns and unity are disrupted and a period of confusion is created. Coping with the crisis requires establishing new role patterns. Demoralization can occur with either dismemberment or accession.

Two additional columns show two further ways of classifying stressor events. *Status shifts,* sudden changes in family status, occur with sudden impoverishment or wealth, sudden fame or notoriety, refugee migrations, and other war-related deprivations, disasters, and political declassing. The last column, *Conflict in role conception,* refers to clashes between family members over what is right for the other to do.

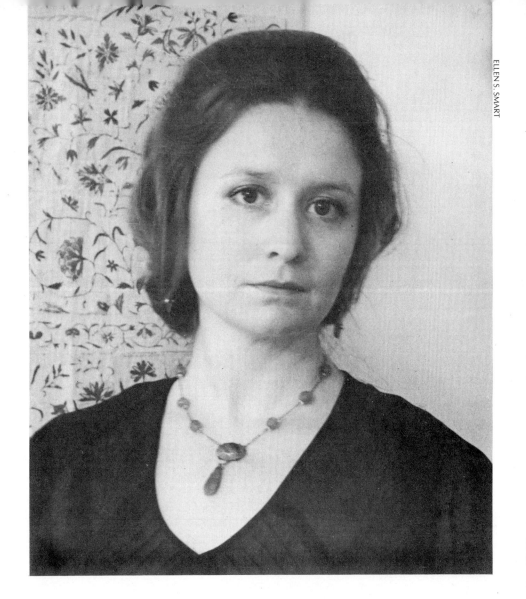

Parents and adolescents often conflict over role conceptions, but sometimes the conflict reaches crisis proportions when the family has had a status shift or when social change is rapid. We urge our readers to add items to the *Stressor Events* column and to fill in checks opposite their additions.

Some crises have already been discussed in previous chapters. Divorce, the very disruptive crisis that has received checks in five columns, has had a whole chapter devoted to it. We have also discussed unwanted births, child abuse, remarriage, and some aspects of hospitalization. After some general comments on coping with crises, we shall discuss death, mental illness, rape, moving, and disasters.

TABLE 14-1      Ways of Classifying Stressor Events Leading to Family Crises

| Stressor Event | Source | | Effect on Family | | | Status Shift | Conflict in Role Concept |
|---|---|---|---|---|---|---|---|
| | Within Family | Outside Family | Dismemberment | Accession | Demoralization | | |
| Death | X | | X | | | | |
| Hospitalization | X | | X | | | | |
|   For mental illness | X | | X | | X | | |
| War separation | | X | X | | | | |
| Job loss | | X | | | | X | X |
| Unwanted pregnancy | X | | | X | | | |
| Out-of-wedlock birth | X | | | X | X | | X |
| Birth of handicapped child | X | | | X | | | |
| Divorce | X | | X | | X | X | X |
| Violence | | | | | | | |
|   Beating | X | | | | X | | X |
|   Rape | X | X | | | X | | X |
| Incest | X | | | | X | | X |
| Remarriage | X | | | X | | | X |
| Addiction | X | | | | X | | |
| Desertion | X | | X | | X | | X |
| Suicide | X | | X | | X | | |
| Delinquency | X | | | | X | | X |
| Running away | X | | X | | X | | |
| Aged kin move in | X | | | X | | | X |
| Arrest, imprisonment | | X | X | | X | | |
| School failure | X | X | | | | | X |
| Disasters | | X | X | | | X | |

*Source:* Reuben Hill. Generic features of families under stress. In Howard J. Parad (Ed.). *Crisis interventions: Selected readings.* New York: Family Service Association of America, 1965.

## Vulnerability to Crises

Some families have more crises than others. Different families react differently to what looks like the same situation. For example, Mr. Agnelli's family became severely disorganized when he was sent to prison, but Mr. Haupt's family carried on effectively while he was imprisoned. In analyzing the reasons why some families are more vulnerable to crises than others, Hill finds two main factors: first, the family's resources for meeting stressor events; and, second, the family's modes of defining stressor events [20].

**Resources for Coping with Stressor Events.** One type of resource for coping is material or physical, such as income, space, equipment, credit, and health. Education, experience, ideas, intelligence, are another type of resource. The possession of the first kind of resources is related to socioeconomic status, with lower-class people having less.

Family *integration* is another type of resource that explains differences in vulnerability. An integrated family feels like a unit, with members attached to each other and to the family as a whole. There are family goals, values, loyalty, and patterns of communication and cooperation. Members' needs are satisfied in the family. The section on stepparents and stepchildren (pp. 286–290) told of a study in which family integration was the criterion used for successful family reconstitution. The crisis of putting together new family members (a crisis of accession) was resolved when a high degree of integration was achieved. The integrated family is able to deal with many stressor events without experiencing crises, or with the effects of crises being minimal.

*Adaptability* is also a family resource that helps in avoiding crises and in solving them when they do occur. An adaptable family is organized in such a way that it can think up ways of meeting challenges and problems, can put new behavior patterns into effect, and can change goals realistically. Such abilities are likely to be based on good communication, trust in one another, and family integration, as well as upon the resources mentioned in the first paragraph of this section.

**Defining a Crisis.**   A family may react to a stressor event as a challenge or as shattering. If it is a challenge, of course, it is not a crisis, because one of the essentials of a crisis is that it be a situation with which the person or group does not have any way of coping. For a while, they do not know what to do, and during this time, they have very upset emotions.

An outsider, looking at a family under stress, may say that they are having a crisis, because most families do have a crisis when faced with hospitalization, delinquency, disaster, or any of the other items in Table 14-1. Also, there are cultural definitions of what should cause a crisis for a family. For example, when a child runs away from a North American home, the family usually defines it as a crisis. In some African societies, children may leave home to stay with friends or relatives when they want to get away from the family, and nobody is upset. Another example is out-of-wedlock birth, which is likely to be much more stressful to a middle-class white family than to a lower-class black family, because of the way in which it is defined by social class and ethnic group.

## The Experience of Crisis

Two main stages of crisis are impact and coping.

**Impact.**   When the stressor event occurs, there is a period of impact. One gets *hit* or *struck* with an illness or disaster! Emotional tension rises rapidly. Some efforts are made to deal with the problem. If the problem persists, tension increases and a second level of attempts at solution occurs. The problem may be solved, redefined, or avoided [43]. If none of these efforts works, then the problem is insoluble and a state of crisis exists. Mental confusion and feelings of upset, helplessness, and exhaustion are experienced by the persons involved.

**Coping.**   The family or person in crisis has three main tasks to perform in resolving the crisis in a healthy way:

1. Keep the problem in focus. Face it. Keep it in consciousness, rather than avoiding, ignoring, withdrawing. Seek information about the problem and strive for objective understanding.

2. Deal with the emotional upset that is part of crisis by acknowledging feelings, talking about them, awareness, acceptance. Expression of upset feelings in an art form is helpful to some individuals, especially to children. Unhealthy alternatives to acknowledging feelings are ignoring, denial, magical thinking, excessive fantasy, excessive sleeping, regressive behavior, and development of physical symptoms.

3. Look for help and learn how to use it in dealing with tasks and feelings. The main sources of help are kin, friends, and institutions. [43]

### Helping Persons and Families in Crisis

Among the professionals trained in helping are social workers, psychologists, psychiatrists, nurses, and counselors. Many individuals do not realize how important an untrained ordinary person can be in aiding friends and relatives who are under stress. A troubled person usually takes the problem to a friend or family member before seeking a professional, and often it is enough.

**Friends as Helpers.**   A friend can be most helpful by responding *now*. A person in crisis feels desperation and urgency. He wants help with his perceptions of the problem and with managing his feelings. A helping friend listens, asks questions that clarify the problem for himself and the others, encourages expression of feelings, reassures in regard to normality of reactions and eventual outcome, and assists in getting further information or directions toward professional help. Overall, the friend's behavior says, "I care about you. I believe in your ability to find solutions. You can count on me."

Family and friends often help in situations commonly defined as crises, sometimes through established rituals, such as funerals. When a family member is ill, friends assist with managing feelings when they bring flowers and visit, and with performing tasks, as when they bring food to the family and offer to do errands. After a disaster, friends help by offering shelter and giving furniture, clothing, and such. Customary helping responses are not well established in many crises where disgrace is involved, such as rape, addiction, and imprisonment. Only very intimate friends are likely to help at times like these.

**Professional Help.**   If a person or family in crisis turns to other individuals who are closely involved in the problem, their own feelings may be stirred up to the extent that they cannot be of much help in identifying the problem and searching for a solution. An uninvolved, trained person may be useful in this kind of situation. Such a person will have empathy, but not sympathy, as defined on pages 62–63. Some professionals are prepared to assist in a variety of crisis situations. Social workers and clergymen, for example, deal with personal, marital, and family crises. Clergymen are particularly likely to help with death and dying. A counselor may devote her practice to marriage and divorce counseling or to parent-child problems. Some professionals work only with rape cases or cases of child abuse. Whatever the crisis may be, a professional will assist the persons in crisis with facing and managing feelings during the periods of impact and coping, and with performing the tasks necessary for coping.

Some methods of crisis intervention are discussed in connection with particular stressor events in the sections that follow. Family therapy, which we describe in the context of mental illness, is applicable to other crises, as well.


## Dying and Death

Dying causes a family crisis of major proportions. Everyone is affected, first of all the dying person, and then all members of the family that is being dismembered. All experience mental and emotional upset, feelings of helplessness and not knowing what to do, necessity for changing role behavior, and need for help.

Because death is universal and inevitable, all societies have ways of coping with the crises caused in dying individuals and their families, and in families after bereavement. In North America social customs and interpretations of dying and death are undergoing change.

**Death Awareness Movement.**   When I (MSS) was a child, in the 1920s and 1930s, my friends and I were familiar with death. People of all ages died, even my contemporaries. My mother took me to call when friends and relatives died. I remember seeing people I knew in their coffins, at home, looking very beautiful, surrounded by flowers and weeping relatives. Laura (LSS) was a child in the 1950s and 1960s. She has never seen a dead body. She has been to only two funerals, those of her grandparents, one of whom was cremated and the other of whom had a closed casket. Our experiences are typical of our generations. Death has been taken out of the family and hidden away, as though people could escape death by pretending it did not exist. At the same time, death was being pushed on into old age, rather than being something that could and did happen at any time to anybody, young or old. Youth can hardly imagine being old, let alone dying. Yet another trend altered the face of death. Dying was stretched out. Life-prolonging technologies now can keep people alive, or not dead, for long periods. A crisis, by definition, lasts only

a limited time. So what could families do when an old person lingered for months or years, not very alive, but not dead?

New ways of coping with new conditions of dying had to be found. The death awareness movement represents modern ways of coping with the crisis of death. Dying and death are subjects of study (the field of thanatology) by medical personnel, psychologists, educators, clergy, and lay people, especially those who are dying. Psychiatrist Elisabeth Kübler-Ross, one of the leading thanatologists, has done much to promote death awareness and positive ways of dealing with the crises involved.

**The Dying Person.**   Although every person knows that some day she will die, death precipitates a crisis when it becomes imminent. The stressor event is a diagnosis, or the realization that one has a condition that will probably soon cause death. The most common of such events are a heart attack and the diagnosis of cancer. As with other crises at impact, the person first tries to find ways of avoiding death. Through medical, religious, or other means, the patient may recover from this attack, and the crisis is averted. If, however, the prognosis is death within a limited time, tension increases, with feelings of confusion and helplessness. The person facing death may deal with it by denial, acting as though the condition did not exist, not talking about it, going about living as usual. Or, she asks, "Why me?" and feels angry at the unfairness of it. Then gradually facing the truth, she grieves. Great waves of sadness and crying are part of grieving. It is so painful to face the fact that one is going to stop *being,* to leave family and friends, to stop seeing, hearing, and feeling. It hurts to talk about it, and yet it helps. A person cannot talk about it alone, though, and he needs to talk with someone who cares what is happening to him. He wants to know, and to be *told* that his loved ones love him. Even though he wants his family to be able to get along all right after he dies, he also wants to know that they will miss him and that they will grieve.

The dying have tasks, as well as feelings to manage. When death is acknowledged as coming soon, the goal is no longer avoiding death, but making plans for its conduct and plans for using the time between now and then. The dying person needs other people to help with the planning and carrying out of the tasks of dying, just as he needs people to share his grieving. Family and friends are the first line of support, but further support from community sources is almost always needed.

**The Family with a Dying Member.** Family members go through the stages of crisis when one of their members is dying. The impact causes great tension, fear, anger, confusion, efforts to avoid the death, sadness, and grief. Avoidance is one way of handling the pain, not talking about it, pretending that the person is not going to die. Sometimes families think that they are easing the burden of the dying member by not mentioning it, but really, they are making it harder for all concerned. If feelings and tasks are to be handled, goals redefined, and the remaining time used rewardingly, then the family has to get together in expressing grief and making plans. They are more likely to do well if they are an integrated family, with established ways of communicating clearly with each other.

Tasks to be done include caring for the ill person. Most people want to die at home, in the midst of family, although few are fortunate enough to do so. Can the family manage to give care at home? It takes physical work, which could be shared by several family members, and even friends. It takes rearrangements, such as renting a hospital bed. Someone will have to do more laundry, make special foods, and give medications. Perhaps even more, it means that the dying person is part of everyone's awareness.

The other type of task is "winding up one's affairs," planning for the funeral, and making some plans as to how the family shall carry on afterwards. Is the will in order, the way the dying person wants it, and understood by the family? Are there business affairs to be put in order? Families can help with these matters, bringing peace to all concerned, as the redefined goals of the dying are reached.

In the time that is left, the dying person may enjoy parts of living that are still possible. Adequate medication can do a lot to ease pain. Pleasure can come from visits from intimates, music, being read to, flowers, a view, and more. Most important is to feel and be with people who care. To be isolated and alone is tragic.

**The Community and Death.** For many people, the church is the source of help in dying, bridging the gap between life and afterlife. Priests and ministers help the dying and their families, and perform the funeral rituals. Many clergy are aware of the findings of thanatology and use the new knowledge in their ministrations. In some religions, such as Judaism, mourning is ritualized in ways shown to be helpful by modern thanatologists.

Even though churches teach that there is a heaven, many people have been looking for extra reassurance that they will continue to exist after death. Such assurance is given by Elisabeth Kübler-Ross [27], Raymond Moody [38], Robert Monroe [37], and others who have investigated out-of-body experiences and the experiences of people who have technically died and were then resuscitated. Books, lectures, and courses and coaching on these topics have helped many people to accept the inevitability of their own death and of the deaths of family members.

Even if people cannot die at home, their are ways of bringing compassion to institutional care. The hospice movement has influenced families, hospitals, and nursing homes to manage the crisis of dying in positive ways. A multiple team deals with physical, emotional, and spiritual needs of patients in the hospice or at home, sharing knowledge and responsibilities with families. Another creative service is a telephone service or hot line to deal with problems of death and dying. The original one is the Shanti Project, in San Francisco [14], where it offers free counseling. *Shanti* means inner peace. Through the telephone, even the most isolated person can immediately contact someone who cares and who knows ways of coping with the crisis of death.

**The Bereaved Family.**   At the death of the member, the family suffers a crisis of dismemberment. Anticipation and planning during the dying period will perhaps soften the blow of the death, but it is still a crisis. Emotional and mental upset occur after the impact, and perhaps disbelief, anger, and denial. Coming to terms with the crisis requires mourning, or "grief work," which takes time. Sighing, crying, exhaustion, and lack of appetite are symptoms of normal grief [30].

A ritual mourning period provides a time and opportunity for grief work. The family receives friends and other mourners at certain hours on certain days. They talk about the death and the deceased, recalling episodes from the past, discussing how much they will miss the person, crying. Thus they go over and over the fact of the death and they experience the sadness again and again, facing it with many different people. Friends also help with tasks, bringing food, keeping records of flowers and other offerings, giving tangible support and evidence of caring.

A bereaved person may be strongly preoccupied with thoughts of the one who is dead, and may show coldness, even hostility to friends and relatives, even to family members. Other symptoms include restlessness and searching for something to do, along with inability to start and maintain an activity. Recovery comes after sufficient grief work, but many bereaved persons do not get enough opportunity for mourning. Going back again to the death customs of my (MSS) childhood, a mourning period of one year was prescribed for all bereaved family members, and for the death of a spouse, two years were sometimes kept for mourning. Women wore black clothing and men, black arm bands. Toward the end of the mourning period, women changed from black to gray, and in summer, white. Mourners neither went to parties nor entertained, but friends called often. They had plenty of time and plenty of recognition and sharing of grief, sometimes even too long. Today, only Judaism marks a year of mourning. Everyone else has no defined period, and many feel pressured to "snap out of it" before they have finished mourning. Widows often feel that friends are embarrassed by their grief and that they try to discourage expression of it [32, 45]. Incompletion of grief work can lead to psychiatric problems in the bereaved [40].

Roles suddenly change when a spouse dies. A person becomes a widow instead of a wife, a widower instead of a husband. In India a new widow must take off her jewelry and wear a white sari, making her status clear to all. Although American customs no longer impose a black dress, there is a status change nevertheless. Widows report that they feel like "fifth wheels" socially. They are left out of couple affairs. Married friends may consider them a threat to their own marriages [32, 45]. Although a widow may continue to cook and keep house, these tasks no longer have the meaning they did when her husband was alive. She may have a hard time coping with the homemaking tasks that he used to do, probably maintenance work and financial matters. The widower is likely to have trouble with cooking and house-keeping. Even though he has better chances of remarriage than a widow has, and is invited out more, the widower is likely to find his new status even more difficult than is a widow [3,5,17]. For one thing, he probably did not anticipate being a widower.

Adjustment to widowhood will of course depend upon the flexibility and resources of the person, upon family integration and adaptability, and upon opportunities offered by friends and community. One community meets some of the problems of widowhood through a widow-to-widow crisis intervention program. Soon after she is bereaved, the new widow is contacted by a woman who was widowed previously. The widow aide offers help to the new widow in adjusting to her situation. Not all widows want or need assistance, but the adjustment of many that do is facilitated by such a program [45].

## Mental Illness

The onset or recognition of mental illness usually acts as a stressor event for a family crisis. When one person acts strangely or disruptively, or seems to be out of touch with reality, then everyone becomes upset and the stages of crisis ensue. During the crisis, professional help is needed. Although friends and relatives may give support, they can rarely give enough to solve the crisis. Even less can they give the sort of help needed for making changes in the conditions that are the basic causes of the mental illness.

Life style and the family play crucial roles in prevention, causation, treatment, and recovery. (The wholeness of health, and the contribution of a healthy life style were discussed on pages 393-402.) Mental illness is a frequent result of crises that are not handled in positive, adaptive ways. The life histories of mentally disordered persons often show sudden deterioration after crises that were beyond the person's capacities [7, p. 201]. The disorder is actually a response to the problem, the best response that the person can make at the moment. During a crisis time, help in finding effective responses can make the difference between health and illness.

The causes of a mental illness can be physical, such as poisoning from lead paint or pellagra caused by a vitamin B deficiency. Some mental illness is genetically based. Severe developmental crises sometimes occur when individuals change from one stage of life to the next, as during adolescence. A role change can precipitate a crisis, as may the change into parenthood or widowhood. Disorders may result from the straining or breaking of family relationships, as in hospitalization, divorce, and death. Interpersonal problems can arise within the family, or outside of it. But no matter what the source of the basic cause of mental disorder, when one person suffers, so does the rest of the family. From that time onward the rest of the family also continues to be involved with the illness.

The significance of the family is recognized to some extent by psychiatric programs that include the families of patients who are undergoing treatment. In this situation, families are helped to understand the patient's illness and what they can do to promote his or her health. They may also discuss their own feelings and benefit from sharing with other families of mentally ill patients. Developed in the 1960s family therapy is different from programs that focus on one patient. In this approach, the pathology is seen as a product of group interaction, as well as of individual disruption [1,36]. The family is regarded as a behavior system and not just a number of individuals. The adaptive responses of family members are strongly related to the ways in which the group functions as a whole. When psychiatric help is first sought, it is usually for one member of the family whom the others consider ill or disturbed. When the therapist talks over the problem with the whole family, he often finds that several or even all of the members are disturbed and that their difficulties are interlocking. Often, the problem has existed for some time, but was contained by some sort of balance in the family. When the equilibrium was upset, perhaps by the breakdown of one member, the others assumed that all their trouble was caused by the ill person.

It is easy to see how family therapy could be applied to conflicts between husband and wife or between parents and children. It also seems logical that it would help the family to understand a member who had been hospitalized and to integrate the recovering patient into the family in a healthy way. If family interaction contributed to the illness, then family interaction would have to change in order to support the members instead of tearing them down.

Pages 393-394 told of Hawaian family therapy and of African community psychotherapy, in which concepts of unity of life prevail [28]. The mentally ill patient is seen as disordered in his relationships to one or more of family, friends, community, nature, his dreams, the dead, and the spirit world. There are some movements in our society toward treating mental illness in a broad context of relationships. In Hawaii, the Queen Liliuokalani Children's Center makes use of some of the traditional wisdom in the context of today [41].

## Rape

A violent crime, rape causes a crisis in the victim and her family. Only in recent years has it been possible to study rape in terms of crisis. The Women's Movement has brought this crime out into the open, whereas it used to be hidden away under the disgrace it brought to a woman and her family. Now help is available for victims.

**Stages of Crisis in Victim's Reaction to Rape.** A mental health team studied the reactions of rape victims to the experience and to the assistance given them [13]. The responses formed a predictable patterns of three states.

*1. Immediate acute reaction, lasting several days.* Victims felt shock, disbelief and dismay, then anxiety and fear. In this stage, the woman needs to talk about the experience to encouraging, sympathetic listeners. Without such listening, she is likely to think that friends and relatives are ashamed or that they want to punish her for what has happened. (Indeed, shame and punishment are the traditional lot of the rape victim.) The professional helper is able to reassure her that her responses are similar to other women's, that she will feel less troubled in several days or weeks, and that she will probably go through a third stage of reaction.

As with all crisis intervention, there are tasks, as well as feelings to cope with. The tasks of the rape victim in this phase include getting medical attention, including tests for venereal disease and pregnancy; legal matters and police contacts; telling family and/or friends; practical matters, such as canceling engagements and notifying employer of absence; clarifying information. A rape crisis center helps clients to take care of all these tasks, and to contact the needed resources, in addition to dealing with their emotional upset.

*2. Outward adjustment.* The victim goes back to her regular activities, says she feels all right and seems recovered. She has little desire to talk about the rape. This period usually represents denial and rationalization, normal defenses against emotional pain. During this period, the woman may need to be encouraged to keep follow-up medical appointments. If she first goes for help at this time, likely owing to pressure from a friend or relative, then she is likely to be unresponsive. A professional worker will tell her that she may have more severe reactions later, and that she may return when she wishes.

*3. Integration and resolution.* The victim again wants to talk about the experience. She is depressed. Phase 3 is often precipitated by a particular incident, such as finding she is pregnant or infected, or being called to court. Before she can resolve the crisis by integrating the experience, she has to deal with her feelings about herself and her feelings about her assailant. She may feel guilty, unclean, and/or damaged. She feels anger toward the rapist and perhaps toward herself. This phase is usually completed by several weeks after the rape, but if it is not, professional help should be sought.

**The Families of Rape Victims.** A crisis is usual when a family member is raped. Family members feel upset, afraid, angry, confused about what to do. Perhaps they interpret it as a brutal attack that causes pain and fear to one of their members. Then they would react as a family would to an accident or sudden illness. If, however, they see the episode bringing disgrace to the family, "ruining" the woman, and even the fault of the victim, then their reactions will hurt the victim even further.

Families need help in coping with this crisis, especially if their interpretation is in terms of disgrace and guilt. They need to express their feelings and to get more information about what really happened, about how the victim feels, about the tasks that must be done. They need help in performing the tasks, or in assisting the victim to do so. The husband of a victim may be in special need of counseling.

## Moving

If moving precipitates a family crisis, it is a very minor one, compared to those we have just discussed. The feeling side of the crisis is one of upset and loss of social relationships, in addition to the confusion of reorganizing life in an unknown context. The tasks of moving, of course, are enormous. An integrated family has resources for dealing with both. They communicate with each other about their feelings of loss and anxiety, searching for ways of minimizing these feelings. Someone suggests a regular newsletter. Mother says that the children can invite old friends to visit. They look for information about the new place, its history, geography, and what the Chamber of Commerce says about places of local interest. They make plans for exploring the new place, joining a church, finding clubs, and starting activities. The tasks of packing, transporting, and settling the new home can be done cooperatively, in such a way that the family feels drawn together by doing a hard job well. Geographical mobility is a fact of life in the United States. One out of five families moves each year. Families who move frequently learn how to cope with the stresses of moving and are able to settle into a new community without much difficulty [29]. Wives who moved frequently reported that frequent moves did not diminish the number or quality of the social relationships that they had, but that they had grown in their skills of making close friends [23].

Children, however, appear to be more able to adjust to moving than do parents. Furthermore, children under the age of 11 generally have the easiest time adjusting. In one study, it was reported by mothers that 90 per cent of their children between the ages of 6 and 11 made friends easily in the new community, and 69 per cent of those between 11 and 18 years of age did [46]. Perhaps mothers' reports do not tell the whole story. An autobiography written by my (LSS) sister at age 11 expressed her grief at moving to a home in a new state. She told of her happy former life with a group of friends who had a bicycle club, a sewing club, and a Girl Scout troop. Then, she wrote, "My life was shattered. I had to leave everything." At age 10, I (LSS) was sick and miserable for the first two months after our move to India.

Adjustment to the new community is facilitated by the arrival of furniture and other familiar objects, by the return to a "normal" schedule, by friendly neighbors in the new neighborhood, and by the presence of familiar chain stores and restaurants in the new community [23].

**Maladaptions to Moving.**    Incomplete resolution of the crisis of moving is associated among middle-class wives with the wife's not taking part in planning the move. Persons with less income perceive their neighbors as being less helpful [23], and since neighbors play a significant role in whether the newcomers feel welcome or not, it is likely that adjustment is more difficult for persons with lower income.

Military families move frequently, usually without having a choice regarding where they are going or when. A study of military wives found that those who identified with military life were able to adjust easily to frequent moves, and that their children adjusted well. Women who did not want to be military wives did not adjust to moving. The researcher writes: "Having been forced to move, they apparently experience the event as a major problem-ridden life crisis in the midst of an already wretched existence, cut off from and unable to reach out to informal or formal support" [34].

The military families just described involved people from a lower-class background who were generally upwardly mobile socially. Indeed, geographic mobility is very much tied in with class mobility; a move to a new community is very often undertaken as an effort to raise the family's level of living. In reality, this may not occur, especially among the rural poor who go to the city in search of work [15]. Adjustment to moving for these families is made much more difficult because of the number and complexity of changes that they must make. They must change from rural to city living; they must learn new job skills; they lose the support of kin and neighbors; they must learn new management skills such as shopping and food storage in the city; they must learn how to find their way around a strange city; they are unaware of recreational and cultural opportunities such as libraries and museums, and they have left behind their rural pastimes.

For an aged person, being moved against her wishes may precipitate an earlier death. Patients in a home for the aged were more likely to die during the first year of their stay there; after the first year death rates stabilized. An eighty-year-old patient who had been there for ten years was no more likely to die than if she had been there two years. When an employees' strike forced the relocation of 57 patients, their mortality rate rose significantly for the first three months after relocation and then dropped to the earlier rates [26].

## Disasters

Tornadoes, floods, earthquakes, fires involving large areas, plane crashes, shipwrecks, and acts of terror or violence against large numbers of people (such as the dropping of an atomic bomb on a city) cause crises on a very large scale. Because of their intensity and the large number of people involved, they are called disasters. A whole community, including the usual help agents, may be destroyed or badly damaged during a disaster. An individual in a disaster may lose all of his personal possessions, including perhaps even his clothes; his loved ones may die or be badly injured; he himself may be injured. Friends may have all they can do to handle their own needs. Famine in a widespread area may also be seen as a disaster, although it lacks the suddenness that characterizes most disasters.

**Phases of Disasters.**   Three overlapping phases of reaction to community disasters have been identified: (1) a period of impact, (2) a period of recoil, and (3) the posttraumatic period [49]. The first period is characterized by the impact of stress, and it continues until the stresses no longer operate. A tornado destroys a home in a matter of minutes; a flood may take hours or days. The period of recoil begins with the suspension of the initial stressor event. Further stresses may continue, but their intensity is not as great. After the flood has swept through the town, the waters remain high but do not flow as swiftly. In the posttraumatic period the stresses are more social in nature. During this period people begin to realize what the disaster means in terms of loss.

**Psychological Reactions.**   During the impact period, reactions vary. Some individuals remain "cool and collected"; others experience states of confusion, paralyzing anxiety, and hysterical crying. About three quarters of the survivors, however, are stunned and bewildered by the disaster. During the recoil period, most survivors seek shelter, sit or pace about, are in ambulances, or are telling someone about their experiences. At first, they are not very aware of what they are doing and exhibit dependent behaviors. Within one or two days, however, most survivors are unwilling to talk as freely as they were at the beginning of the recoil period [49].

During the posttraumatic period, many survivors have reactions of anxiety, fatigue, depression, recurrent dreams, and the like. Children are likely to be especially disturbed by disasters, fearing their return. Adults, as well, may find that they never completely get over the feelings of terror brought on by the disaster. Survivors are subject to "acute episodes of *symbolic reactivation* of their entire constellation of death anxiety and loss" [31, p. 485]. Survivors of Nazi concentration camps and of the atomic bombs dropped on Hiroshima and Nagasaki report an increased awareness of their own mortality. Those survivors who cannot complete their "grief work" are especially susceptible to mental disturbance [31].

Even the children of survivors of the Nazi holocaust continue to be affected by it, because of the continuing effects upon their parents. All these years after the tragic events, support groups and therapy groups are getting together to share their trauma and to help one another to integrate the experience. The severity of the results of the holocaust can be understood when it is seen as a combination of many extreme stressors: death, dismemberment of various types, injury, violence, moving, status shift, imprisonment, and more.

# ONGOING PROBLEMS

Some families live with difficulties that continue a long time, perhaps throughout the whole family life career. Such a problem may get started through a crisis that is not resolved. For example, the birth of a brain-damaged child is a stressor event that causes a family crisis, but there is no really satisfactory solution. The family cannot regain its former equilibrium. The new family member continues to be a source of stress. The family must work out modes of living that can contain the succession of stressor events. In the following section, we discuss several ongoing family problems: chronic illness and disability, mental retardation, addiction, aging, and poverty.

## Chronic Illness and Disability

Most acute illnesses progress into a milder stage that lasts for a while, perhaps for a very long time or forever. A permanent disability can occur anytime, as a result of an accident, disease, or war. Disabled war veterans suffer a precipitous change from vigorous fitness to being permanently handicapped. A disability may be present from birth. Dealing with a temporary impairment is, of course, different from integrating a permanently handicapped person into family living.

The "sick role" is a pattern of behavior expected of an ill person, varying with the nature and circumstances of the illness and with other roles played by the person. The sick person is generally regarded as needing special care and help, which he should accept in order to speed his recovery. Since he has diminished strength and is in need of extra nurture, the patient is relieved of some of his ordinary obligations and responsibilities. Immature behavior is tolerated, not only in children but also in adults. "He's like a big baby when he's sick." Sometimes patient and family do not agree on how the sick role should be played. Conflicts may arise over how much the patient should do for himself, whether he should stay in bed and take medicine.

In order to support one or more members in the sick role, a family has to make changes in the behavior of all members. One or more of the well members will take on the role of nurse, giving care that will help the sick one to recover. "Moral support," helping the patient to feel more cheerful and confident, is given by family and friends who offer evidence of love and concern by visiting, entertaining, and bringing offerings of flowers, food, books, and so on. In addition to offering the patient care, respect, response, and knowledge, family members must make additional adjustments to the illness. Someone has to take over the work that the patient would ordinarily do.

When an adult is sick for a long time, or permanently disabled, the family will most likely have to adjust to a lower income and to spending portions of its income on therapy, equipment, and other supports for the disabled member. If it is the father who is incapacitated, the mother may have to carry a paid job without much help with the housework and childrearing. Psychological adjustments to such situations are often difficult, not only for the person who cannot live up to the ordinary role expectations for his age and sex but also for the rest of the family, whose roles are also altered and who must often live within unusual constraints. There is also the problem of accepting the attitudes and behavior of other people, who regard the disabled and his family as different, inferior, or pitiable. When community supports are necessary, there are requirements of dealing with the clinic, the welfare department, the Veterans' Administration, and other bureaucracies that may add strains as they give help. And all too often, the assistance is not sufficient for completely satisfactory solutions.

Family strains occur when a child has learning disabilities or developmental

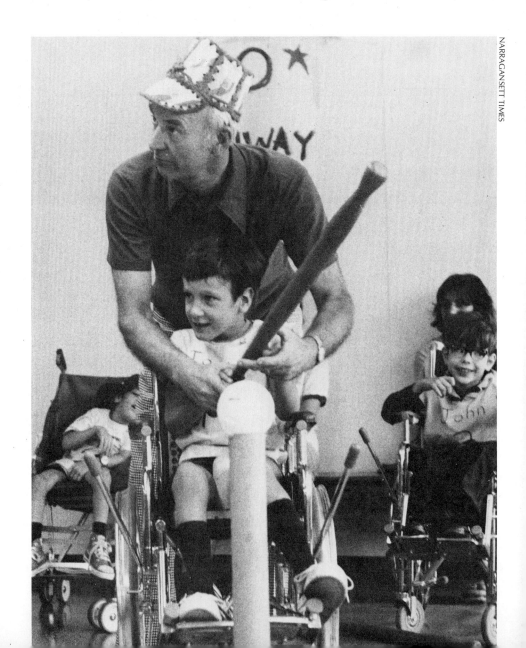

disabilities. Such children need expert teachers and families need explanations, reassurance, and coaching in how to encourage their children. When a handicapped child is born to or adopted into a family he brings special health care problems to be solved. Special arrangements are necessary if a family member has been disabled by an injury, or has a speech defect or a metabolic problem. Expert help is usually needed with such problems, in teaching methods of care and coping to the person affected and to the family. The treatment and teaching include what to do to help the person physically and educationally, how to manage a household with a handicapped member, and to deal with the social-emotional effects on all members of the family.

Parents of handicapped children may feel guilt as well as sorrow. They are likely to isolate themselves from normal community contacts. For this reason, there are associations of parents of retarded children, alcoholics, families of alcoholics, overweight people, single parents, and many other groups who have physical, mental, or social problems. Such groups supply opportunities for sharing, expressing, giving and receiving sympathy, understanding, and techniques for dealing with mutual problems. They are important, often essential, supplements to professional advice and treatment for physicians, psychotherapists, physical therapists, and social workers.

Adjustments of families with retarded, epileptic, or cerebral palsied members were studied among a poor, rural, largely black population in Alabama [10]. Interviews did not reveal concern over family closeness and happiness, sibling adjustments, or social stigma. The main problems were concerned with time, money, and physical effort. These people had little knowledge of social services and expressed little need for them. The researchers, however, concluded that the families did need supportive services to help them cope with the demands created by handicapped members. Such services are available in cities and suburban areas. Interestingly, the University of Alabama does provide a service available to rural and urban citizens alike. *On Your Own,* a monthly bulletin for the handicapped, is mailed to anyone who requests it.*

## Mental Retardation

Among the many kinds of disabilities that affect family life, mental retardation stands out as a particularly difficult one. A crisis is precipitated when a retarded or abnormal child is born, or when the condition is diagnosed. Expectations and behavior patterns must be changed on many levels. In an immediate context, the child needs care that is modified to suit her special needs. Special treatment and services may have to be sought and bought. Long-term planning may be even more difficult. The family's relationship to the community is likely to be affected.

The heartbreaks, fears, and frustrations of having a retarded child are expressed very movingly by the journalist father of a boy called Noah [16]. Read it and weep!

*Continuing Education in Home Economics, P.O. Box 2967, University, Alabama 35486.

It begins, "He is a tyranny you will never quite learn to live with, an obsession you will never learn to live without. He is a brain-damaged child. He belongs to you. And you are angry."

The presence of a retarded child poses many questions in family management. One difficult decision is whether to keep the child at home or to put her in an institution for the retarded. It may also be possible to combine living at home with day care or day school. Sometimes foster home placements are made. In making such a decision, parents usually need counseling. In fact, they can hardly avoid it, since facilities for retarded children almost always have professional social work services as part of the program. However, the decision is the parents' responsibility. When a plan has been made for care and education, much additional planning remains to be done. Although many retarded children can eventually earn their living, they may need continuing help in managing their affairs. Some will not be able to earn their living. Parents realize that the child will probably outlive them. How will they provide for the child's supervision and care after their death? Only the most affluent can set up trust funds and arrange for paid guardians. Sometimes siblings and kin accept future responsibility for the child. Some families must rely on social institutions outside the family in order to provide future care.

In addition to the stress of caring for, obtaining services for, and making future provisions for the retarded child, families are subject to additional stress from the behavior of other people, and often from their own fears, guilt, and anxieties concerning the causes of retardation. Siblings, as well as parents, suffer from these social and emotional disturbances connected with the retarded member.

Families of retarded children have been studied in order to understand the nature of their peculiar stresses and their reactions to them [12]. The effects of home and institution were compared by studying, over the period of a year, the functioning of families who kept their retarded children at home and families whose retarded children were placed in institutions. Prior to institutionalizing their child, families functioned less adequately than the families who kept their retarded children at home. Since the former families felt more stress from their retarded children, it is hard to say whether the children were the cause of poorer functioning or whether the lower level of family functioning resulted in more difficult retarded children. More significant was the finding that over the year, the families with retarded children at home deteriorated. In this group the siblings appeared to suffer most. As far as the functioning of retarded children were concerned, no differences were found between those who were institutionalized and those who remained at home. In interpreting the results of this study, it would be easy to conclude that all retarded children should be sent to live in institutions. There are, however, other solutions that might turn out to be just as satisfactory for siblings and parents. A day-care center offers enough support to some families.

Social interaction in 281 families with one or more retarded children was shown to be different from that of 754 families with normal children [33]. Interaction within the family, indicated by reading and talking with children, was less in families with retarded children. Such families visited less with people outside the immediate family, especially in the neighborhood. The results of this study suggest that parents of retarded children may be timid in making social advances or that neighbors may not be as friendly with these parents as with others. In either case, the study points up the value of an association for parents of retarded children. By socializing with families who have similar problems, interaction would be increased and families may also gain emotional support from one another.

## Drug Use and Addiction

In extreme stages of dependence on any drug, the individual is disrupted and his condition is certainly a problem to his family. Drug use is not a clear-cut behavior, however. I (MSS) feel that I need two cups of coffee in order to wake up completely in the morning, but I do not think of myself as a drug addict. Is a person alcohol-dependent if he looks forward greatly to a drink before dinner every night? What about the light smoker who cannot give up his daily consumption of ten cigarettes? Is a weekly marijuana party a sign of dependence? Surely drugs are an area where the definition of problem behavior is very salient. Definitions vary widely. The individual and his family may take a different view of drug use. The community may tolerate what the law forbids. Therefore, we confine the discussion to situations where the disrupting influence of drug use is obvious and acknowledged, although we recognize that more subtle problems also occur. It is also possible for people to use drugs without getting into difficulties. Examples include the moderate smoking of the Hunzas of Pakistan who may live to well over one hundred years, the ritualized moderate drinking in many cultures, and the religious use of hallucinogens by the Peyote Indians.

Drug use becomes problematic when it results in harm to body, mind, family relationships, and social behavior. Family, kin, and community are also involved in causing the behavior, treating it, suffering from disturbed relationships, and establishing a new equilibrium. Since alcoholism is the most widespread drug problem, its treatment is probably more advanced than treatment of other types of drug abuse. The role of the family is clearly recognized in the treatment of alcoholism, particularly in terms of the husband-wife relationship. Family therapy may be effective. When the alcoholic is beginning to gain control of his drinking, changes occur in relationship with the spouse and a new balance must be achieved. Alcoholics Anonymous have a companion organization for the families of alcoholics, to which children, as well as spouses, belong.

Addiction to hard drugs, such as heroin, places an even greater strain on family relationships than does dependence on nicotine and alcohol. Because hard drugs are illegal, users may be socially stigmatized, prosecuted, and even imprisoned. In order to maintain themselves on hard drugs, many users commit crimes and thereby bring financial and legal disasters upon themselves and their families. Addicts and their families urgently need expert help in dealing with the addiction, the sources of its occurrence, the crises and chronic problems caused by it, and in the establishment of healthy patterns of living. Research into methods of treating heroin addicts gives some information on the changes that methadone therapy made in the patients and their families [8]. Reports were obtained from the wives of 72 men who had remained for a year on the methadone program of the drug abuse research team. Of these wives, 22 had also been heroin addicts and were on methadone. Results showed that after entering the methadone program, regular employment and time spent with the family increased and sexual relations improved.

Persons seeking help with drug problems can get information from regular sources, as mentioned earlier. Such agencies and individuals will recommend groups, organizations, and therapists who specialize in the particular problem.

## Aging

Aging is problematic in an industrialized society largely for two reasons. Most basic is the fact that in modern societies with good sanitation, nutrition, and health care, more and more people survive until old age. From 1970 to 1978, the number of people over 65 years of age increased by 20.6 per cent [20a]. Another factor is the industrialized society's emphasis upon productivity: the individual's sense of self-worth is largely tied up in what he *does* rather than what he *is*. The retired person is likely to feel cast aside and worthless.

However, aging does have certain inherent problems that are largely culture-free. The body atrophies and becomes less resilient and resistant to disease. For example, bones become less dense and more likely to break; connective tissue becomes less elastic; the working capacity of the heart decreases; the nervous system deteriorates [6]. Many of these problems can be delayed by proper diet, rest, and exercise.

Some societies venerate age, equating it with wisdom. Although Western society worships youth, the age group of 40-to-60 years holds a great deal of power [39]. People of this age control business, and have much influence in law, medicine, education, the financial world, and politics. Retirement usually precipitates a loss of power. influence, and prestige.

**Life Satisfaction while Aging.** Health was found to be most highly associated with satisfaction in living, among variables that were also correlated with satisfaction, including income, marital status, education, and employment. The subjects were people over 60, living in Chicago [4]. An English study of persons between 62 and 86 years of age showed that those who were most active in social life reported most satisfaction with life and that the less active people experienced less life satisfaction [25]. Common sense would also suggest that when a person feels good and is able to be active, he enjoys living much more than if he is uncomfortable, suffering, and lacking in energy.

Spence [47] suggests looking at activity or disengagement from activity in old age in terms of careers. On page 15 we mentioned the concept of family careers as including marital, parent-child, adult-parent, and sexual experience. Like occupational careers, family careers move forward; they are not cyclic. Individuals enter a given career at some point and leave it at another point. Spence points out that as people age, certain careers decrease in importance and end, while others begin and increase in importance. A key to understanding a person at a given moment is his **career set,** or his present engagement with his various careers. How does he see himself in his social and historical context? A widow is disengaged from her marital career but still engaged in her parent-child and grandparent-grandchild careers. A retired biology teacher is disengaged from his professional teaching career but pursues a recreational career of identifying birds and collecting shells and mushrooms. The career set of an older person will be different from his career set of a decade or two ago, but it can be active and satisfying in the context in which he lives. Erikson's notion of the sense of integrity is illustrated by the older person who looks back on his various careers with satisfaction and looks forward to his daily activities as worthwhile and good [11, pp. 268–269].

**Income and Aging.** Both engagement and activity theories imply that the individual has a choice in his or her life style. However, poverty is a fact of life for many of the elderly. Retirement almost always means a loss of income that is not ade-

quately offset by pensions and Social Security. In 1978, the Census Bureau listed 25,000 people over 65 as being *without* income [51]. Less than $1000 was the income of 88,000 old people, while 173,000 received between $1000 and $1500. On the other end of the scale were 366,000 older persons with over $25,000 income. The median income for those over 70 was $5007.

**The Importance of Work.**   With the recent and continuing rise in numbers of older people, the group over 65 has gained some political power, and with it, some recognition and benefits. Twenty four million votes carry some weight! And so do the American Association of Retired Persons, the Gray Panthers, the National Council on the Aging, and the National Council of Senior Citizens, through which many older people work together to improve life for themselves and their age mates. They have succeeded in modifying mandatory retirement laws, securing greater flexibility and more opportunities to work and earn.

As we have pointed out in regard to young adults, self-concepts and self-fulfillment depend somewhat on work. At any age, a person needs to produce in some way that is satisfying to himself and respected by other people although it need not be on a paid job. In earlier times, people continued to work until they became ill or died. Only since the United States Social Security system was established in 1935 have people thought that everyone should retire at 65, and even then, some have kept on working. Forced retirement has made many people feel useless, worthless, and old, as well as poor. For some, a part-time job, or a new type of work represents a chance for renewal. Others want to keep on with their old jobs as long as they can. Some really want to retire. And why shouldn't all have a choice that would let each older person work in the way he wants? It is a complex topic, because some youth will be deprived of jobs they want if the elderly are employed.

**Families and Older Persons.**   Several researchers have asked what contributes to positive relationships between the elderly and their adult children. An analysis of information from adult child-parent pairs showed that health and attitude toward aging were most closely associated with good relationships in these pairs [22]. Interviews with 90 pairs of older mothers and daughters yielded data showing that attitude toward aging and the living environment had direct effects upon the mother-daughter relationships [21]. Health and finances contributed indirectly to the relationships.

Just as age does not change a person's need to work, so it makes no difference in the need to love and be loved. The older a person becomes, the more friends and family members she loses through death. If she is entirely segregated within her age group, then death comes more often to the people near her. The older person who lives in a family, in an ordinary community, has contacts and ties with people of all ages, and hence relatively fewer contacts with death and more chances for love. In a family, too, there are opportunities for doing small pieces of useful work, even after a person is no longer able to handle a paid job. Nearly 80 per cent of older persons

have children. Why then do 8 million persons live alone and only 3.6 million old people live with their children and grandchildren?

Public assistance, or societal assumption of responsibility, makes it possible for most older people to live on their own. (The cost to the federal government in 1978 was $112 billion [2]). To the resources they already have, they can add Social Security, Medicare, perhaps housing for the elderly, Meals on Wheels, and other services. About 40 per cent of people over 65, and not in institutions, or between 9 and 10 million people, need some such supportive services in order to remain independent [2]. Usually the older generation wants to live independently (but often with societal help) as long as possible, and the younger generation also wants them to do so. Adding an aged member to the family household can precipitate a crisis of acces-

**TABLE 14-2**     **Living Arrangements of Persons over 65 (United States)**

| Living Arrangement | Approximate Number (in millions) |
|---|---|
| Alone | 8.0 |
| With spouse only | 6.0 |
| With spouse and others | 1.5 |
| With children and grandchildren | 3.6 |
| With sibs, grandchildren, and non-related | 1.4 |
| In nursing homes | 1.3 |
| In institutions | 1.2 |

*Source:* Robert Benedict. The family and long-term care alternatives. Paper presented at meeting of the Groves Conference on Marriage and the Family, Washington, D.C. 1978.

sion (see page 420). Grannie requires space, care, and role changes on the part of everyone! As Hess has said, '' . . . when one no longer *must* care for aged parents, one is faced with the moral choice of doing so or not, and much will depend upon the psychic costs involved [18].'' Most adult children do show concern for the well-being of their parents and grandparents [2]. Some adult children give a great deal of care to parents who still live in their own home, but who must have much help in order to do so. An increasingly popular arrangement among middle-class families is to build or remodel part of the children's house as a living unit for older parents. Another solution is side-by-side apartments. Children may be able to give adequate care if they get some help from siblings and community agencies. Geriatric day care centers make it possible for some old people to live with their families if the aged person is taken to the center during the day. Here he receives meals, health care, and appropriate therapy and counseling. There are social and recreational activities. It is much more interesting and stimulating than sitting home alone, and it gives the family some freedom from responsibility. Family living can also be done in foster families, as illustrated in Figure 14-1.

About 2 million people are being cared for in nursing homes or other institutions [2]. It is estimated that about 3 million more need long-term care that they are not getting, 600,000 of them needing nursing homes.

No matter what the living arrangements, family members can help an older person to have a sense of belonging and a feeling that her life is worthwhile. Expression of love is much more than care, even though quite a lot of care may be needed. The younger adult has knowledge of the older one, going back through the years. Responding can be on the basis of shared memories, as well as in terms of the present. Even though capacities are diminished, respect is shown for the person as he is. When the younger one must make a decision for the elder, it can be done lovingly, by listening to his comments, being sensitive to his feelings, and saving his dignity.

# 'The Ladies' Are Doing Fine In Their New Foster Family

### By GEORGIA DULLEA

Having a spare room but no resident grandmother, Ruby Gibbs and family went looking for one, five years ago, through the city's Foster Homes for Adults program. This led them to Edna Baumgarten, a tiny sweet-faced woman in her 60's with no prior experience as a grandmother, but with lots of natural talent. Soon she was playing Scrabble with the children, drying the supper dishes and making music on the organ in the living room.

"It's not the same as being a boarder." Miss Baumgarten was saying at the dining table the other morning. "I don't feel like a boarder here. It's like we are part of the family."

She meant, besides herself, Sophie Mieslich and Claire Katz. They are also in their 60's and they joined the Gibbs family in Queens after she did. Nobody calls them boarders. To the social worker who visits twice a year, they are "client residents" living in the home of "paid proprietors." To the Gibbs family, they are "The Ladies."

"Have a good day, ladies," calls Walter Gibbs as he heads for work in Long Island City as a junior high school science teacher.

"How are the ladies?" asks Gregory Gibbs, who is 20 and the eldest of the three children, when he phones home from college in South Carolina.

Usually, Ruby Gibbs is happy to report that "the ladies are fine, just fine."

Not all of the city's 1,012 foster homes for adults are as warm and loving as the one Mrs. Gibbs runs. Hers is a model home, caseworkers say. Demographically speaking, however, it is fairly typical.

Like Ruby Gibbs, two out of three proprietors are black. And like "the ladies" she cares for, two out of three residents are white. This ratio of black proprietors to white residents puzzled social workers at the Division of Foster Homes for Adults, which is part of the Human Resources Administration, the agency that made a study a few years ago.

According to Rita Galvin, the program's senior caseworker, it was found that older blacks in the city were more likely than whites to remain in the family home, where they were needed to mind the grandchildren while the mothers worked.

**FIGURE 14-1**  Foster homes provide care and family living for some older people.

*Source: New York Times, February 27, 1978.*

## Poverty

Being poor means not having enough to live on, not enough of what it takes to live in ways considered normal and adequate by the society in which one lives. The official United States definition of poverty is based on income. In 1977, 11.6 per cent of the population, 24.7 million persons, were living below the official poverty line of $6191 for a family of four [51]. Old people and children are poor more often than young and middle-aged adults. Among people over 65, 3.2 million were poor, and among children under 18, 10.2 million, or 16.2 percent. Figure 14-2 shows the distribution of types of families in those below the poverty level in 1959 and 1976. Note the increased proportion of poor families headed by a woman. Figure 14-3 shows percentages and numbers of poor people by ethnic group and age group.

The problems of poor people are chronic, since they go on and on. Crises happen often as food runs out, the rent comes due, payments of income are held up, a

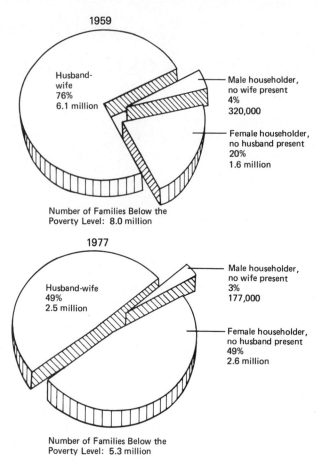

1959

Husband-
wife
76%
6.1 million

Male householder,
no wife present
4%
320,000

Female householder,
no husband present
20%
1.6 million

Number of Families Below the
Poverty Level: 8.0 million

1977

Husband-wife
49%
2.5 million

Male householder,
no wife present
3%
177,000

Female householder,
no husband present
49%
2.6 million

Number of Families Below the
Poverty Level: 5.3 million

**FIGURE 14-2**    Types of families below the poverty line: Proportions and total numbers within 5.3 million poor families.

Sources: U.S. Bureau of the Census, Current Population Reports, Series P-60, No. 115, "Characteristics of the Population Below the Poverty Line: 1977" (Advance Report), U.S. Government Printing Office, Washington, D.C., 1978.
U.S. Bureau of the Census, Current Population Reports, Series P-60, No. 116, "Money Income and Poverty Status of Families and Persons in the United States: 1977" (Advance Report), Washington, D.C.: U.S. Government Printing Office, 1978.

family member becomes ill, another gets into trouble at school or with the police, the man of the family deserts, or an unwanted pregnancy occurs. Characteristics of the urban poor in Western societies include these: a large proportion of mother-headed families, high rate of desertion by men, belief in male superiority, fighting, physical punishment of children, wife-beating, early sex activity, and living together without marriage [19, p. 47].

Poverty affects an individual during prenatal life and continues for the rest of his life. A malnourished mother has less to give to her embryo and fetus and is more

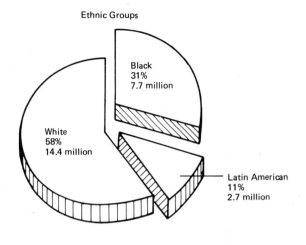

Ethnic Groups

Black
31%
7.7 million

White
58%
14.4 million

Latin American
11%
2.7 million

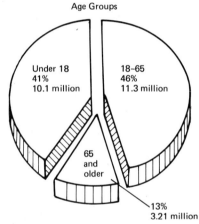

Age Groups

Under 18
41%
10.1 million

18–65
46%
11.3 million

65
and
older

13%
3.21 million

**FIGURE 14-3**     Distribution of the 24.7 million poor people of the United States in ethnic groups and age groups.

*Sources:* U.S. Bureau of the Census, *Current Population Reports,* Series P-60, No. 116, "Money Income and Poverty Status of Families and Persons in the United States: 1977" (Advance Report), Washington, D.C.: U.S. Government Printing Office, 1978.

likely to damage her baby through a difficult delivery than is a well-nourished mother. Poor babies and children receive less adequate medical and dental care than do richer children. They have worse housing, clothing, food, toys, and schools, fewer chances for trips and varieties of experiences.

And what of the other big group of poor people, the aged? Their deprivation is also physical, mental, and social. Unable to pay much rent or to finance and perform repairs, they often live in squalid quarters. Rooms are drafty in winter, hot in summer, paint peeling, faucets dripping. A handicapped older person may be unable to navigate the stairs and is hence confined indoors, with never a change of scene or breath of fresh air. No wonder many of the aged go downhill mentally, with no stimulation and no new ideas brought in. Poor nutrition is almost inevitable in poor, old people, especially those who live alone. They lack the money and opportunities to buy food, the equipment and ability to cook it, and perhaps even the teeth needed to chew it. And besides, who has any appetite for eating under these conditions? Poor, old people often lack medical care. They may be unable to go to clinics to get attention; they may feel that it is not worth the effort.

The public has a generally negative attitude toward those people who must live on public funds. Furthermore, the recipients of public assistance tend to feel disparagement and hopelessness toward themselves. These negative attitudes contribute to the impotence of poor people, adding to the multitude of factors that prevent them from improving their socioeconomic status. Among people with low incomes, there are important differences between those who manage to live without public assistance and those who cannot, perhaps because of the low esteem in which welfare recipients are usually held. And among all low-income people, there are large individual differences in behavior, probably greater than differences between people who have moderate and high incomes.

**Adaptations to Poverty.** The responses and behavior patterns of poor people have common elements, because many of their efforts are directed toward survival in a harsh environment. The very poor are more likely to believe that success is due to luck or fate, rather than to hard work. Quite logically, the poor cherish toughness and endurance, qualities necessary for survival in the world of poverty. Much of the behavior that is adaptive to poverty is also behavior that prevents the achievement of higher financial and social status. Thus, they are caught in their efforts to survive, unable to develop strategies that would help them in the long run. Poor children live with danger, both physical and social. Skills needed for survival in that world include defensiveness and suppressing curiosity, which make it difficult for them to get ahead in school or in the mainstream of society [24]. Seeing their parents and relatives in badly paying, low-status jobs, they cannot hope for more for themselves. They become locked into poverty.

Most very poor people share the overall cultural high esteem for a stable marriage and childbirth within marriage. However, the ideal is not always achievable, and being unmarried is also acceptable. As expressed by a Harlem mother, "If you want somebody—oh, you *want somebody*—to help you—and there's the children and the rent—well maybe then it doesn't seem all that important whether you're married or not" [19, p. 10]. Similarly, poor people tend to regard out-of-wedlock births less negatively than do the affluent, but they still prefer that parents be married. Poor women, in general, would like a good marriage to a good man, but good men are hard to find and most men are seen as unpredictable, controlling, and difficult to understand. As one woman put it, "Men folks are rotten these days. You got to lick 'em to get along with them. You got to take so much off 'em" [19, p. 50].

Every day is a struggle for poor parents, a struggle to earn money, to obtain and prepare enough food, to keep children clean and safe in a dirty and dangerous environment. When mothers have jobs, as many do, their work load is enormous. What few labor-saving devices they have are old and rickety. They do not have the aids that middle-class working mothers have, such as self-cleaning ovens with timers, dishwashers, and food processors. There is neither time nor inclination for reading and getting ideas to discuss with children, or for aiding and encouraging children in intellectual and artistic pursuits. There isn't even money for going to the movies.

Maladaptive behavior in childrearing methods is most serious, since poverty is perpetuated through this channel. During the past 15 years, many research studies have focused upon relations between the parent behavior and children's intelligence, learning, and achievement motivation. Physical care, including nutrition and control of illness, is often inadequate because parents lack both material resources and knowledge. Growth of children's bodies, and most important, their brains, is depressed by malnutrition and disease. Beginning in infancy, the teaching style of the parents, mostly the mother, is a vital influence on the child's personality and intelligence. The mother, or principal caretaker, arranges a stimulating, orderly, responsive environment or permits barren or chaotic surroundings. She encourages questions, exploration, and initiative, setting up situations where the child can succeed in choice-making, problem-solving, and creating, or she ignores him until he gets into trouble, when she punishes him or tells him to shut up. She gives out information, names objects, directions, numbers, and colors, reads stories, points out interesting events, takes the child on outings and trips, shows him how to act with friends, plays imaginative games, role plays, pretends, shows him how to help her, explains how to do things right and what went wrong, generalizes on a level that the child can understand, or she does not teach in these ways. The television is making too much noise, the light is dim, and the mother is too tired, too busy, or even absent. (Working mothers include 2.5 million women with children under 3, 5.4 million women with children under 6, and 9.2 million women whose children are between 6 and 17 [52]. Among black women, 42 per cent of mothers of preschool-children were employed in 1972. Numbers of children with employed mothers have risen since then.) Although the affluent mother may be employed and still interact with her children, the poor mother has too much to do at home and too little support in doing it. She teaches that being good is being quiet, not talking back, not asking questions, and obeying the rules set by adults. These teachings make the child easier to live with at home and fit him for school *as it looks to the mother*. In reality, such a child goes to school without basic cognitive concepts; with language and social behavior inappropriate to the classroom; lacking in achievement motivation, curiosity, impulse control, and self-esteem.

Are race differences in behavior really only socioeconomic differences? Most childrearing studies have suggested that poverty is much more salient than race. However, an analysis of *very poor* versus *moderately poor* mothers and children shows some differences that are more pronounced in the very poor [42]. The subjects came from several preschool programs in which mothers, as well as children, were taught. Mothers' attitudes and behaviors were measured before and after the educational programs. Child measures included IQs, IQ gains, and motivation. *Authoritarianism* was higher in black mothers than in white mothers. The difference increased among the very poor. Highly authoritarian mothers were likely to express approval of strictness and to have unrealistically high expectations for their children in school. (Other studies have found that poor black children's low achievement aspiration is expressed in statements of unachievable goals.) Highly authoritarian mothers less frequently expressed nurturance, as shown by meeting their children's needs, communicating, and sharing. After the mothers had finished the educational program, the white mothers decreased in authoritarianism and increased in egalitarianism. The black mothers did not change in mean scores on authoritarianism. Increases in egalitarianism appeared in mothers of girls, but not of boys. Egalitarianism in mothers was related to their children's IQ, IQ gains, and behavior leading to cognitive development. These results suggest that the black mothers, especially the poorest ones, were trying very hard to make their children obedient. In the dangerous life of the black ghetto, obedience to the mother has survival value, but in school and in the mainstream of North American life, a serious deficit results from the tactics through which the mothers taught their children obedience.

**What Can Be Done.**  We have tried to show that dwellers in poverty have developed ways of meeting crises and solving problems that make survival possible but that perpetuate their poverty. The cycle of poverty is a cycle of the lineage family, in which each generation contributes to the entrapment of the next. Individuals, nuclear families, and lineage families are locked in. The community, on local, state, and national levels, has made attempts and is still trying to find the keys to freeing the poor and letting them join the mainstream. Many keys are needed, because the solutions have to be on many levels.

The 1960s saw a blossoming of programs to help the poor. Then came a reaction against programs, and the assertion, often by the poor themselves, that all they needed was jobs and income. The way it looks to us is that both are needed. Certainly an adequate income is essential if a person is not going to be poor, and jobs are necessary for feelings of adequacy as well as for earning money. Children and the aged cannot support themselves with jobs, and persons who have been socialized to poverty cannot earn much under our present conditions. Therefore programs are needed, along with jobs and income maintenance, in order to alleviate present distress and to prepare both children and adults to enter the mainstream of the social and work world.

A long-term follow-up of 14 infant and preschool experiments shows that these programs do have positive, lasting effects [9]. Children who went to these programs were better able to meet school requirements. The children themselves, now adolescent, rated their own school competence higher than did adolescents who did not have preschool education. Intelligence tests showed significant increases in intellectual functioning of children who had attended preschool programs. The increases lasted at least through the primary grades in school. These findings justify further programs for young children and their parents. The authors point out that day-care programs should include well-planned educational components.

Surely there is now little question but that infant and preschool programs help poor children to enter the mainstream of society. Much research remains to be done to show the mechanisms through which these programs succeed, and to delineate more programs at different ages. Health and nutrition programs have also been shown to improve poor children's physical status, and much remains to be done in expanding and improving such programs.

The U.S. Commissioner on Aging has said that current programs for the aging are inadequate, and often inappropriate [2]. "My personal vision of the future is federally supported, state administered, community operated comprehensive systems of services embracing a full continuum of services, spanning health and social services, which would include assessment and diagnosis, community linkage services, in-home services, community and neighborhood services, living arrangements such as special housing and skilled and intermediate long-term services."

To sum it up, the ideal is to help the poor in such a way that they will not be poor any more. The approach is twofold, to make jobs and income available, and to offer opportunities for learning behavior and attitudes that will enable people to work and interact in such ways that they will obtain and have adequate resources for living.

**SUMMARY**    Occurring in response to a stressor event, a crisis is a situation requiring unavailable responses and having feeling and cognitive components. Stressor events can be classified in several ways. Vulnerability to crises varies with a family's resources and definitions. Crises occur in two main stages, each of which requires certain kinds of coping and helping. Helpers can be family, friends and/or professionals.

Dying and death cause major crises. The feeling side of dying usually includes denial, anger, confusion, helplessness, grieving, and acceptance. Tasks include work, care, and planning. Dying and death are presently fields of study and new developments that are proving helpful to people who are dying and to their families.

Mental illness involves the whole family and life style. Such a crisis usually requires professional help, often family therapy.

Crises resulting from rape have been the topic of recent study and of innovations in treatment. The responses of victims and their families follow predictable patterns, requiring specialized help.

Moving, a frequent stressor event, may precipitate minor crises. Adverse reactions are most frequent in persons who have no part in the decision to move, and in older people.

Reactions to disasters follow regular patterns, often resulting in lasting anxiety. Results are severe and long-lasting when several stressor events are combined, as in the Nazi holocaust.

Crises are of limited duration, but some family problems last for long periods, even throughout the family life career. When a family member is chronically ill or disabled, physically or mentally, the whole family must make many adjustments and efforts in order to support the one with the disability. They need help from relatives, friends, and community.

Drug addiction places a great strain on the whole family, as well as upon the afflicted individual. Family therapy may be effective. Even if the problem is not cured, all family members benefit from supportive treatment.

Aging tends to be a problem in our society, where there are many old people and age is not venerated. Life satisfaction at later ages is much affected by health and also by income, marital status, education, employment, and activity. Poverty is often a problem. Older people have succeeded in making work choices more available. Although most adult children feel responsibility for older parents, it is difficult for many to give enough care. Community and federal programs help.

About 25 million people live below the official poverty line. The following are over-represented: old people, children, nonwhite people, and families headed by women. Poverty depresses physical development and cognitive development. Adaptations to poverty result in characteristics that depress motivation and school achievement, perpetuating poverty. Much can be done to help poor people join the mainstream of society.

**REFERENCES**

1. Ackerman, Nathan W. and Stephen W. Kempster. Family therapy. In Alfred M. Freedman and Harold I. Kaplan (Eds.). *Treating mental illness.* New York: Atheneum, 1972.
2. Benedict, Robert. The family and long-term care alternatives. Paper presented at meeting of the Groves Conference on Marriage and the Family, Washington, D.C., 1978.
3. Berardo, Felix. Survivorship and social isolation: The case of the aged widower. *Family Coordinator,* 1970, **19,** 11–25.
4. Bild, Bernice R. and Robert J. Havighurst. Senior citizens in great cities: The case of Chicago. *Gerontologist,* 1976, **16**:1, Part 2.
5. Bock, E. Wilbur. Aging and suicide: The significance of marital, kinship, and alternative relations. *Family Coordinator,* 1972, **21,** 71–79.
6. Bromley, D. B. *The psychology of human ageing.* Middlesex, England: Penguin, 1971.
7. Caplan, Gerald. *Support systems and community mental health.* New York: Behavioral Publications, 1974.
8. Clar, June S., William C. Capel, Bernard Goldsmith, and Gordon T. Stewart. Marriage and methadone: Spouse behavior patterns in heroin addicts maintained on methadone. *Journal of Marriage and the Family,* 1972, **34,** 496–502.
9. Consortium on Developmental Continuity. *The persistence of preschool effects.* Final Report, Grant No. 18-76-07843, to the Administration on Children, Youth, and Families. Office of Human Development Services. U.S. Department of Health, Education, and Welfare. Washington, D.C.: Government Printing Office, 1977.
10. Dunlap, William R., and J. Selwyn Hollinsworth. How does a handicapped child affect the family? Implications for practitioners. *Family Coordinator,* 1977, **26,** 286–293.

11. Erikson, Erik H. *Childhood and society.* New York: Norton, 1963.

12. Fotheringham, John B., Mora Slekton, and Bernard A. Hoddinott. *The retarded child and his family: The effects of home and institution.* Toronto: Ontario Institute for Studies in Education, 1971.

13. Fox, Sandra S. and Scherl, Donard J. Crisis intervention with victims of rape. *Social Work,* 1972, **17**, 37–43.

14. Goleman, Daniel. Help for the dying and their friends. *Psychology Today,* 1978, **11**:10, 34–35.

15. Gottlieb, David and Anne Heinsohn. *America's other youth: Growing up poor.* Englewood Cliffs, N.J.: Prentice-Hall, 1971.

16. Greenfeld, Josh. A place for Noah. *Psychology Today,* 1978, **11**:10, 46+.

17. Harvey, Carol D. and Howard Bahr. Widowhood, morale, and affiliation. *Journal of Marriage and the Family,* 1974, **36**, 97–106.

18. Hess, Beth. Working paper on grandparenthood. Paper presented at meeting of the Groves Conference on Marriage and the Family, Washington, D.C., 1978.

19. Herzog, Elizabeth. *About the poor: Some facts and some fictions.* Children's Bureau Publication 451-1967. Washington, D.C.: U.S. Government Printing Office, 1968.

20. Hill, Reuben. Generic features of families under stress. In Howard J. Parad (Ed.). *Crisis intervention: Selected readings.* New York: Family Service Association of America, 1965.

20a. Industrial National Bank of Rhode Island. Changing labor force patterns. *Quarterly Economic Review,* 1979, **10**:2, 4–7.

21. Johnson, Elizabeth S. Good relationships between older mothers and their daughters: A causal model. *Gerontologist,* 1978, **18**, 301–306.

22. Johnson, Elizabeth S. and Barbara Bursk. Relationships between the elderly and their adult children. *Gerontologist,* 1977, **17**, 90–96.

23. Jones, Stella. Geographic mobility as seen by the wife and mother. *Journal of Marriage and the Family,* 1973, **35**, 210–218.

24. Keniston, Kenneth. *All our children: The American family under pressure.* New York: Harcourt, 1977.

25. Knapp, Martin R. The activity theory of aging: An examination in the English context. *Gerontologist,* 1977, **17**, 553–559.

26. Knight, Aldrich C. and Ethel Mendkoff. Relocation of the aged and disabled. In Bernice Neugarten (Ed.). *Middle age and aging.* Chicago: U. of Chicago, 1968.

27. Kübler-Ross, Elisabeth. *On death and dying.* New York: Macmillan, 1969.

28. Lambo, Thomas A. Psychotherapy in Africa. *Human Nature,* 1978, **1**:3, 32–39.

29. Landis, Judson and Louis Stoetzer. Migrant families: An exploratory study of middle-class migrant families. *Journal of Marriage and the Family,* 1960, **28**, 51–53.

30. Lindemann, Eric. Symptomology and the management of acute grief. In Howard J. Parad. *Crisis intervention: Selected readings.* New York: Family Service Association of America, 1965.

31. Lifton, Robert Jay. *Death in life: Survivors of Hiroshima,* New York: Vintage, 1969.

32. Lopata, Helena Z. *Widowhood in an American city.* Cambridge, Mass.: Schenkman, 1973.

33. McAllister, Ronald J., Edgar W. Butler, and Tzuen-Jen Lei. Patterns of social interaction among families of behaviorally retarded children. *Journal of Marriage and the Family,* 1973, **35**, 93–100.

34. McKain, Jerry Lavin. Relocation in the military: Alienation and family problems. *Journal of Marriage and the Family,* 1973, **35,** 205–209.
35. Metropolitan Life Insurance Company. Widows in the United States. *Statistical Bulletin,* 1977, **58**:9, 8–10.
36. Minuchin, Salvador. *Families and family therapy.* Cambridge, Mass.: Harvard U. P., 1974.
37. Monroe, Robert A. *Journey out of the body.* New York: Doubleday, 1973.
38. Moody, Raymond A., Jr. *Life after life.* New York: Bantam, 1976.
39. Neugarten, Bernice. The awareness of middle age. In Bernice Neugarten (Ed.). *Middle age and aging.* Chicago: U. of Chicago, 1968.
40. Parkes, C. Murray. *Bereavement: Studies of grief in adult life.* New York: International Universities, 1972.
41. Pukui, Mary K., E. W. Haertig, and Catherine A. Lee. *Nānā I ke kumu (Look to the source.)* Vol. 1. Honolulu: Hui Hānai, 1972.
42. Radin, Norma and Paul Glasser. The utility of the Parental Attitude Research Instrument for intervention programs with low-income families. *Journal of Marriage and the Family,* 1972, **34,** 448–458.
43. Rapoport, Lydia. The state of crisis: Some theoretical considerations. In Howard J. Parad. *Crisis intervention: Selected readings.* New York: Family Service Association of America, 1965.
44. Schlesinger, Ben. The one-parent family in Canada: Some recent findings and recommendations. *Family Coordinator,* 1973, **22,** 305–309.
45. Silverman, Phyllis. Widowhood and preventive intervention. *Family Coordinator,* 1972, **1,** 95–102.
46. Smith, Ramona, and Victor Christopherson. Migration and family adjustment. *Journal of Home Economics,* 1966, **58,** 670–671.
47. Spence, Donald. The meaning of engagement. *International Journal of Aging and Human Development,* 1975, **6,** 193–198.
48. Taylor, Ray and Mollie S. Smart. Depression and recovery at nine weeks of age. *Journal of the American Academy of Child Psychiatry,* 1973, **12,** 506–510.
49. Tyhurst, J. S. The role of transition states—including disasters—in mental illness. Paper presented at the Symposium on Preventive and Social Psychiatry, Washington, D.C., 1957.
50. U.S. Bureau of the Census. *Statistical abstract of the United States: 1977.* Washington, D.C.: U.S. Government Printing Office, 1977.
51. U.S. Bureau of the Census. *Money income and poverty status of families and persons in the United States: 1977* (Advance Report). Current Population Reports, Series P-60, No. 116. Washington, D.C.: U.S. Government Printing Office, 1978.
52. Women's Bureau. *Working mothers and their children.* Washington, D.C., 1977.

# CHAPTER 15

# down the road and around the world

Before we think about the future of family life, we must first consider the future of human life. What happens in Africa and Asia affects North America, and vice versa. People everywhere are responding to pressures from changes in the physical and biological world. Already, in Third World countries, famine is a reality. Affluent nations, as well as poor ones, are continually menaced by environmental deterioration and violence.

On the whole, people in affluent nations live as though their lands of plenty were eternal. Few have even thought of what it will be like to live in a world where millions of starving people beg for aid and we do not have enough to feed them and ourselves [26].

## WORLD POPULATION AND THE QUALITY OF HUMAN LIFE

Currently in the United States, the birth rate is sufficiently low that were it not for legal and illegal immigration, there would be a negative population growth rate (a decrease in the population of the United States) over time. Even with the current *legal* immigration rate, Westoff has estimated that the population of the United States should stop growing in about 50 years, stabilizing at 250 million persons, and then begin to decline [45]. However, because it is unlikely that illegal immigration will be eliminated, we can expect that the population will continue to grow even if the number of births remains below the number of deaths, as it was in 1977. It is dangerous to assume that birth and death rates will remain the same, and to project far into the future from present trends. During the Depression the birth rate was low, and demographers did not anticipate the "baby boom" after World War II, when birth rates soared.

**455**

The population growth rate of the world has begun to subside. In 1970 world population increased by 69 million, and in 1975 it increased by 64 million. In industrialized Western nations, stabilization of populations is expected within a number of years [38]. China encourages one-child families by giving them money, goods, land, and privileges, while penalizing families with three or more children [10a]. Birth rates have decreased in parts of Asia, and in some countries in Eastern Europe, Latin America, Africa, and the Middle East. Nonetheless, in many countries the decline in birth rate has been modest or offset by a decline in the death rate.

Although it is encouraging that availability of contraceptives is slowing the rate of world population growth, the problems of overpopulation have not been solved.

World population is still growing, and it is growing in the poorest countries. Further-more, children born two decades ago are entering the work force in huge numbers, worsening already desperate unemployment situations in many countries. By the year 2000, at least 800 million more people will be looking for work, mostly in developing countries [46]. As countries industrialize, jobs tend to become fewer as machines take over tasks once done by human labor. Schumacher has suggested that the solution to many ecological and human problems is the return to smaller, less centralized business enterprises that require more human labor and less wasteful use of raw materials [36].

DOWN THE ROAD AND AROUND THE WORLD

**457**

## Family Relationships Still Important

No matter how dire the threats posed by the biological world or how upsetting the new ideology to the established order, human beings continue to live in families of one kind or another. In fact, the more difficult the world seems, the more a person feels in need of a few other people with whom he can work and love. The intimates who compose a family may be the common grouping of man, woman, and their children, or they may be one of many types of combinations. Most importantly, they meet each other's needs, especially emotionally. The needs to be met, and the ways of meeting them, are affected by the prevailing physical, biological, and social conditions.

Although human beings have made some terrible problems for themselves by interfering with the balance of nature, the large-scale bungling was possible because of flexible thinking, reasoning, and innovation. People are now applying these very human resources to solving their problems by developing new ways of interacting with each other. Even though physical and biological scientists continue to work in their areas, they, along with social scientists, recognize the need for widespread changes in human interaction. Many, but not all of the constructive changes in human interaction, will be in intimate, primary relationships. It is here that personalities are shaped and values created, in the arena known as family living.

And so we have come full circle from Chapter 1, where we examined the kinds of families that people live in. We have found that not everyone is living in a marriage or a family, as marriage and family have been defined in the past. Some persons are living in a variety of relationships in which they are emotionally close to other people who are adults and/or children. They are not always related by blood or by law. The group usually performs several functions typical of families in the old sense. We call these new types of groups different forms of the family. The most common family form remains the nuclear family, a married man and woman and their child or children. Other traditional family forms, such as the extended family, also continue. Many innovative family forms are being tried, some on a large scale, some on a small scale. In North America, a large number of people are living in nontraditional styles, but it is very hard to find out just how many. It is said that when 7 to 10 per cent of a population practices an innovation, the custom becomes accepted by the mainstream of society [30]. Therefore, it is possible for the traditional mode to continue while other customs practiced by a small minority are also permitted.

Among family innovators, motivations vary from self-interest to sincere attempts to solve human problems. No matter what the reasons for the new family forms, all of them are potentially valuable as experiments in human relationships. They offer the means of learning more about human potential and the possibilities for restructuring modes of living. The main part of this chapter deals with family innovations in North America and ways in which family life could be supported and improved. But first we want to discuss the world wide concern with equality and some orientations that are newly important in North American thought. These orientations are significant in family innovation.

# NEW ORIENTATIONS TO LIFE

Many young adults, and some not-so-young ones have adopted new values and adapted old ones, based on different interpretations of reality and philosophies of life.

## The Notion of Equality

Around the world, people are thinking about equality and feeling the effects of this heady idea. The *notion of equality* is operating in many contexts, including the following: equality among nations (one vote in the United Nations, equal respect, equal access to food and other resources); equality among races and ethnic groups (equal opportunities for education, jobs, housing, and respect); equality among classes (an adequate income for all, equal treatment by the legal and educational institutions); equality between age levels (children's right to be protected under the law to the same extent that adults are protected, adolescents' rights to meaningful work and a place in society, the rights of the aged to use their abilities productively and to have care and respect); equality between the sexes (in pay scale, job opportunities, education, politics, religion, law, and work within the home).

## Time Orientation

The present is very important. Less emphasis is put on the future and the past. For other people, the change is to vast units of time, or even timelessness, rather than counting time in hours, days, and years. Existential philosophy has contributed to the present-orientation. This point of view has much to contribute to the improvement of family relationships, since it can mean cherishing each day, each encounter, each experience, and making them all as good as they can be. It implies shedding the burdens of inadequacies and guilt from the past, as well as the possibility of becoming different in the future. Although emphasis on the present has many positive influences on relationships and experiences, it also may take away from other aspects of life. Immediate gratification may prevent building long-term relationships and other investments, such as economic and educational ones.

## Sources of Knowledge

Science is mistrusted, instead of being considered the fountain of wisdom that it once was. Part of the argument against science is along the lines of, "Look what a mess the world has got into through the use of science. The technology of war has been developed by science and yet the world's hunger cannot be appeased." People express horror of a computerized society, with surveillance of individuals and domination by an intellectual elite. (There are many others with an opposite view, who look forward to a technological society, the postindustrial era, where everyone is affluent, educated, and happily employed in interesting, nontaxing work.)

Instead of getting information from science and using its methods for exploring, some young people are turning inward to find knowledge through intuition, meditation, and drug-induced states. They also turn outward, in the opposite direction from science, to find reality and meaning in religion, mysticism, extrasensory perception, and charismatic leaders. A young friend recently explained to us, ''Science is only a phase in human thinking. Man has lost the ability to receive revelation of truth from God, but he will regain it. We must take a time perspective of eons rather than years. We now have some revelations, through prophets.''

At the same time, scientists and technologists are discovering and producing at a fast pace. Their products have revolutionized life through changes that continue. Scientists are also probing the sources of the mystics and prophets. Sometimes science fiction points the way to new knowledge. There is an open-mindedness that admits the possibility of learning from nonscientific sources.

## Power versus Love

The reality of power is very obvious on the national level, in politics and war; within nations, in politics, revolution, and crime; between classes and races and sexes; and

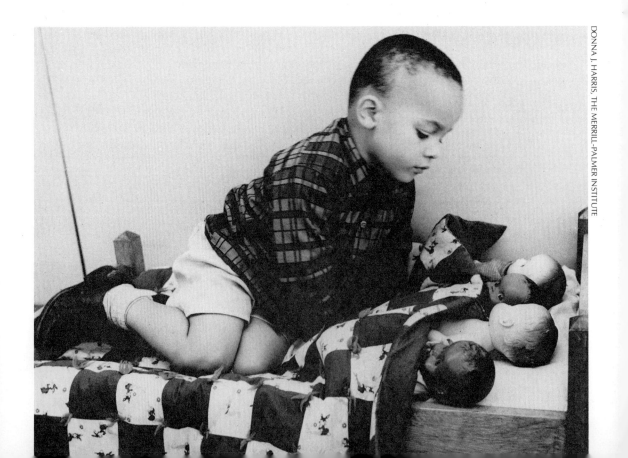

between persons within the family. On all these levels, people are questioning the morality of power and how to limit it. If people are to be equal in important ways, than one cannot overpower another. Actually, it is not new for religious leaders to look to love as a way of restricting power orientation, but the application to family life is new. Never have we had so many women questioning and challenging the right of men to control them through power. Nor have the rights of children ever been so clearly distinguished from the rights of adults over them.

## Roles versus Individuality

Probably most people believe as we do, that roles are necessary as guides to behavior and expectations in daily life. A person would be paralyzed a good deal of the time if he had to have intimate knowledge of every individual before he could interact with him. In other social institutions, as well as in the family, many persons are objecting to having to play roles, however, because they feel too restricted in them.

**Occupational Roles.** Some factory workers do not want their roles restricted to tightening a nut or coming to work at a moment determined by the head office. They want to take part in planning what work shall be done, who shall do what, and when they shall do it. Other factory workers prefer the old way, finding satisfaction not in the repetitive work that they do, but in the socializing with fellow workers that is made possible by doing the same task over and over [35]. Ideally, workers would be allowed to choose the kind of occupational role that would best suit their needs. Some could work as craftspersons, starting with raw material and ending with a finished product. Others could work on assembly lines.

**Gender Roles.** As with work roles, some persons are rejecting the traditional roles that prescribed one set of behaviors and attitudes to males and another to females. Many women want access to all kinds of work, equal pay for equal work, free choice as to whether and when to bear children, and opportunities for true sharing in housework and childrearing. Many men want equal access to the world of feeling, emotion, and self-expression that is largely denied them in the traditional role. These men want free choice as to whether they may be dominant, aggressive, and competitive, achieving, and tough. For other women and men, many or all of the traditional roles are still comfortable and functional. Such women prefer to stay at home, perhaps even after the children have left home. If their husbands earn enough money, they do so.

An alternative kind of gender-role flexibility is one that responds to stage of the life career. It may be functional for the woman to stay at home when children are small, and she may prefer to do so. Later, when the children enter school, she may want to have a part-time job, and when the children leave home, she may want to work full time. While a 50-50 division of all breadwinning and homemaking tasks may seem to be an ideal, there are other alternatives that may better suit the needs of particular couples. What we advocate is that families have choices open to them.

**Age Roles.** The newly popular field of psychohistory reveals that age segregation has increased ever since the Middle Ages, when there was little difference between children and adults. Children and adults wore the same style of clothing, ate the same food, played games and took part in celebrations together, did similar work, and went to bed at the same time. This pattern holds true in most primitive societies. In industrial cultures, such as our own, children are different from adults in what they wear and eat, how they work and play, when they sleep, who takes care of them when they are sick, and in just about every aspect of their lives. The culture of childhood is separate from the culture of adulthood. Childhood, too, is differentiated into infancy, preschool, school age, adolescence, and youth.

Recently, social scientists such as Levinson have continued the differentiation of age roles into adulthood [18]. From the early 20s until around 28, the individual is concerned with "getting into the adult world." The "age 30 transition" occurs somewhere between 28 and 32, during which time persons who have remained single think about marriage; those who have not yet found a vocation make more concentrated efforts to do so, and those who are married or have a career reevaluate their marriage and/or career and either become more committed or make a change such as divorce or a career switch. Between 32 and 39 comes a period of "settling down," concerned with order, stability, "nest building" and "making it," concerned with striving, mobility, and achievement. Levinson's research, from which these adult age roles were derived, was concerned with men. Women's patterns would be more complex, because of the greater impact that childbearing decisions make on women's life patterns.

Youths and young adults are considered the most beautiful and attractive. Middle adults have the most power. People in other stages are objecting to having to play roles assigned to them. School-age children would like some choices in what they learn in school and how they spend their time. Adolescents would like to clear up many of the conflicts they experience from being defined as both dependent and independent. Old people do not want to be powerless, useless, and out of date. Middle-age adults would like release from some of the pressures and demands that come from being in the middle of the generations.

## Emphasis on Sex

Sex is very important in North America. Many industries, especially advertising, thrive on sex ideology. Many people believe that everyone needs sexual intercourse in order to be healthy, or that everyone has a right to it. Evaluations of social life, friendship, family life, and marriage are highly weighted in sexual terms. Preoccupation with sexual expression diminishes the amount of time and energy spent on other pursuits, such as intellectual, cultural, artistic, athletic, and community service activities. With some people, sex is an all-consuming hobby and anything goes.

## Emphasis on Growth

Continued personal growth is highly valued. There is nothing unusual about recognizing that individuals develop as they grow older. Hinduism outlines five normal stages of life and Shakespeare mentioned seven. But modern thought, typified by Maslow [22] and Rogers [34], holds that the individual personality can grow continually, through creative problem-solving and honest human interaction. This idea is a central one in encounter groups and some kinds of therapy. It has obvious significance in a rapidly changing culture.

# VARIANT LIFE STYLES

Both the United States and Canada are made up largely of peoples from other countries. The United States was characterized as a "melting pot," but in recent years many groups have experienced an upsurge in ethnic pride. Canada has long recognized the existence of cultural pluralism within its boundaries, but this coexistence has not always been easy. Currently, the United States is recognizing that it is not a monolingual, monocultural nation.

There has always been pluralism in these nations, but attention is currently being focused upon the new family forms that are, in some cases, emerging, and becoming more visible. In previous chapters we have discussed a number of variant life styles, including homosexuality (pages 140–146), cohabitation (pages 215–219), contract marriage (pages 205, 217), childfree couples (pages 317–319), and single parents (pages 11–12, 314–316, 414). In this section we briefly describe some other contemporary life styles, none of which are really new, but that are becoming more prevalent. Many of these forms are changing rapidly, and it is impossible to determine how many people are directly involved with them. Some of these life styles are temporary for large numbers of people, as indeed the nuclear family is a temporary life style for many. Much of what we say is speculative.

## Voluntary Simplicity

If everyone cut down on the use of the world's resources, then the depletion and pollution of the environment would be slowed down. There would be more food to go around if overfed people ate less, and those with just enough money made do with foods that are plentiful and cheap to produce. There would be more fiber for clothing and shelter if affluent people paid less attention to fashion and more to durability. If people stayed home more and enjoyed simple recreation, then the land would be less covered with the cement of highways and the fuel supply would last longer. Many more such statements can be made. These facts are taken seriously by a large number of people today. Nobody knows how many.

The term "voluntary simplicity" has been used to describe a life style in which the choice is made to consume fewer material goods, to live and work in a "human scale" environment (for example, to live in a small house and work for oneself or for a small rather than a large enterprise), to rely less on large institutions, to live in harmony with the environment, and to strive for personal growth [9]. This life style is not new, as it has been advocated by ancient and modern spiritual leaders such as Jesus, Buddha, Moses, and Gandhi, and is practiced today by some religious sects in North America, such as the Amish and the Mennonites. Voluntary simplicity is not an all-or-none life style. Almost everyone practices a few pet economies. Many people make some conscious effort to carry on certain practices that make their own lives healthier and that benefit their community, nation, or world. Growing and canning one's own food, taking the bus or walking instead of driving alone in one's car, recycling bottles and cans, making one's meal from scratch instead of buying pre-packaged foods—all these ways of economizing are in harmony with a life style of "voluntary simplicity."

Even those who strive for a high degree of simplicity must use some of the world's resources other than their own labor and their own land. As mentioned in Chapter 13 (pages 412–413), in northern California, a number of families live self-sufficient lives as far as most health services are concerned, but they accept mid-wives from a maternity outreach program sponsored by the federal government. Pioneers in Alaska are known to live alone and off the land for months at a time, but they use manufactured trucks, boats, and planes, as well as supplies brought from the Lower Forty-eight. The few people who live in extreme voluntary simplicity probably make little impact on the ecological problems of the world, but their examples may inspire significant numbers of people to make savings that add up.

For there to be a real *choice* of a simple life style, the person choosing must not be poor. It is unlikely that persons who have grown up poor in an affluent culture would voluntarily choose to live in a "simple" life style. Edward Abbey, who grew

NARRAGANSETT TIMES

up poor, enjoys his material luxuries now that he can afford them. He describes his childhood:

> One of my childhood chores was the drawing and carrying of water for the kitchen. In wintertime that meant heating a kettle of water—left over from the day before—on the wood-burning cookstove (I also hewed the wood), putting on hat, coat, gloves, and taking the kettle of boiling water out to the pump by the back door, pouring it slowly over the sheath of ice until I could work the handle, then thawing and priming the pump until the water began to flow, refilling the kettle and a couple of buckets, and lugging them all back into the warmth of the kitchen. It was a great day on the sub-marginal Abbey farm . . . when my proud, improvident father finally accumulated enough surplus capital to buy and install a hand pump *inside* the kitchen. With a sink! And a drain! Ask my mother about involuntary simplicity. [1]

## Communes

In Chapter 1, we noted that communes are not new to the United States in this century, and that other countries have and are experimenting with this life style. Communes vary tremendously in their purpose, size, and structure; the only generalization that applies to all communes is that they are cooperating groups of people committed to their group.

It has been estimated that there were at least 10,000 discrete communes in the United States between 1965 and 1975 [16], and in 1977 the number of persons living in communes was estimated to be under 250,000 [47].

Communes have been categorized in a number of ways, two of which we mention here. Ramey [30] breaks down communes into three types, the *religious*, the *utopian*, and the *evolutionary*. Religious communes are characterized by strong leadership and a faith that binds the members to the leader and group. Utopian communes, although often consisting of alienated youth grouped together in an unstructured way, may instead have a tight structure and a strong leader. The evolutionary commune, in contrast to the other two types, is not aloof from society but represents a group of people who are committed to each other and to coping with today's society in a more successful way than they could manage on their own.

Additional ways of characterizing communes make distinctions between *rural* and *urban* communes, and *creedal* and *noncreedal* [3]. Urban communes are more prevalent and easier to start; all that is needed is a place to live and a group of people. Membership is often fluid, In many college and university towns, "co-ops" are an established way of life. Some urban communes are what Ramey calls evolutionary communes. For others, the urban commune represents a means for poor (although generally middle-class) young people to share their resources while they break away from their families.

The rural commune, by contrast, represents a "purer" type of commune, since it entails more isolation from the members' former environment, and a bigger change in life style. The ideology of the rural commune stresses conservation and agriculture as a way of life. This attitude recognizes the reality of the wasteful, overdeveloped world. However, in the early stages of a rural commune, subsidization from benefactors or welfare is usually essential. Moving beyond this stage of dependence is difficult [3].

Sex roles in many rural communes are strongly traditional, not always happily so for women [10]. However, age roles are not characteristic of the rural commune. Children and adults are thought to have the same needs and abilities. Children are expected to contribute to the welfare of the commune through work that is the same as adult work, and are expected to solve their own problems. Adults tend to see themselves as "kids" [3].

Creedal communes are similar to Ramey's religious communes. They are organized around a formal structure of beliefs and have a strong leader. The Children of God and followers of the Guru Maharaj Ji are contemporary examples of the creedal commune, which has a long history on this continent. Creedal communes are generally more successful than noncreedal communes. Members of a noncreedal commune often share a set of unwritten beliefs and values, but are not so tightly bound together by these more loosely conceptualized beliefs.

The relative success of creedal communes, both historically and at the present time, indicates that when a group of people reject the structure and values of the larger society, they need to have a formalized set to replace them. A charismatic leader who sets forth this structure may provide the "glue" for a commune, as did John Humphrey Noyes, founder and leader of the Oneida Community established in 1848 in central New York State. The community lasted for about thirty years until the death of Noyes, and represents one of the most radical family experiments that this continent has seen. The community was based upon the values of economic communism, group marriage, sexual equality, and scientific breeding of children, and grew to include several hundred members. After puberty, much sexual freedom was allowed, although couples were not supposed to form attachments. An individual conveyed his desire for sexual relations with another member to the Central Committee, which decided whether or not to grant permission. Children were not to be conceived unless planned by the committee, and male continence was the form of birth control that was used [14].

We include this extremely brief description of one aspect of a nineteenth-century commune to show that radical family experiments are not limited to the present. Many other interesting examples could be given.

Communes exist in other countries as well. In Chippenham, a commune near Christchurch, New Zealand, men and women live in separate houses, with children in each house. The men chose to live apart from women in order to make themselves more nurturant. They believed that as long as they could do so, men would use women as emotional crutches, confiding their feelings, pain, and joy to women, not men. Now, in the men's house, they are learning to hug and to comfort, to encourage, to welcome guests, and to care for one another, for children, and for other people [33].

## Co-marital Sex

Consensual extramarital relationships, or co-marital sex, represents the flourishing of a type of relationship that has probably been practiced by a small number of persons in our society for many years. Havelock Ellis, one of the early sex researchers who lived from 1859 to 1939, had a version of a consensual extramarital sexual relationship with his wife Edith. Both Havelock and Edith had women lovers [4]. Today consensual extramarital relationships involve lovers of the same and opposite sex for both husbands and wives [31]. Co-marital sex has gained in popularity and practitioners, reflecting the increasing cultural emphasis on sex. It has gained impetus from the decline of the double standard and the blossoming of honesty and communication in marriage.

**Swinging.** The form of co-marital sex that first came to public attention is swinging. Swinging involves mostly white suburban couples with above-average incomes and educations. The numbers of swingers has not been determined, but a study using a probability sample of 579 married adults in a Midwestern university community found that 1.7 per cent of the respondents had participated in swinging, and that an additional 6.7 per cent said that they would if the opportunity arose [5]. In a survey of *Redbook* readers, 4 per cent of currently married women and of widowed, separated, and divorced women had participated in swinging. Half of these women had done so only once [17]. It seems that only a tiny proportion of people swing.

Swingers appear to have stronger needs for social-heterosexual interaction than do nonswingers [32]. When swingers were matched with nonswingers on variables such as age, income, marital status, neighborhood, education, and children, it was found that swingers began dating and courtship earlier, were more involved in their community but less religious, had much more frequent intercourse with their spouses, and were less bored with life [12].

Swingers claim that swinging makes a positive contribution to their marriage, helping them to feel closer not only sexually but in other areas as well. Communication is said to be facilitated. A study of dropouts from swinging shows that not all who try swinging are satisfied with it. Problems involved, in order of prevalence, were jealousy, guilt, feeling a threat to the marriage, the development of outside attachments, boredom, and loss of interest, disappointment, divorce or separation, and wife's inability to "take it" [8]. Some couples who drop out of swinging do so because they form *intimate friendships* ("an otherwise traditional friendship in which sexual intimacy is considered appropriate behavior" [30, p. 436]) with other swingers [27]. Most other literature on swinging notes that emotional involvement of any kind is taboo because it is considered a threat to the marriage [3,48].

Swinging reportedly makes a marriage more egalitarian [2, 6]. However, men initiate swinging much more frequently than do women [13]. Bartell found that men often "wanted out" sooner than did women, but Denfield [7] reports the opposite.

At any rate, the prevalence and significance of swinging cannot be determined accurately. Its emphasis upon purely recreational sex seems to us superficial and decadent.

**Sexually Open Marriage.** Sexually open marriage has been called intimate friendship by Ramey [30, 31] and interpersonal swinging by Varni [44]. Each term denotes a slightly different version of a co-marital sexual relationship. The most significant difference between sexually open marriage and swinging is that the former emphasizes friendship and emotional commitment, whereas the latter condemns it. Some persons in sexually open marriages have friendship circles that often include both spouses and singles as well [31]. Others prefer not to participate as couples, but instead form friendships with individuals whom they see without the presence of their spouse, but with the spouse's knowledge and consent. Jealousy is not unknown for persons in sexually-open marriages, but couples in one preliminary study tended to see the stresses and conflicts as potentially growth-promoting. Wives especially were motivated to form intimate friendships by a desire for more emotional fulfillment than they could get from one person [15].

## Open Marriage

Co-marital sex as a life style is not as pervasive as one might think, considering the amount of attention it has received. Open marriage, a life style publicized by George and Nena O'Neill in their book by that name [24], has probably won more to its side than have swinging and sexually open marriage. All but one of our list of new orientations to life are reflected in the book *Open Marriage*. It is present-oriented, emphasized individuality, growth, and to some extent, sex. The O'Neills believe that " . . . open marriage is designed to strengthen the individual in the marriage . . . The children of open marriages will tend to be responsible, confident, self-reliant individuals" [25].

The open marriage model is characterized by eight guidelines. The most important is open and honest communication between the partners, and between each partner and others outside of the primary relationship, including the opposite sex. Co-marital sexual involvement is an option that the O'Neills do not consider to be a crucial issue. The larger context of the open relationship is much more important.

Living for now, another guideline, involves relating to oneself and one's partner in the present rather than in terms of the past or distant future. Equality between the spouses involves relating to one's mate as a peer, instead of seeing one's mate in terms of the traditional roles of husband and wife. In order to achieve identity, each spouse must develop his or her own potentials instead of living life through the spouse or child. "Trust, growing through the utilization of these and other guidelines and based on mutuality and respect, creates a climate for growth. Liking, respect, sexual intimacy, and love grow through the dynamic interaction and use of these elements" [24].

We concur with the O'Neills on most of their guidelines; we differ with them on time orientation. Living for now is important in the emotional sense, but long-term planning and goals are important for family functioning, as we have tried to show in Chapter 8. We certainly do not endorse living solely for future economic gain, or thinking so much about the past and future that the present becomes unimportant. We believe that the future and the past each have their place in our lives: the past, to give perspective, and the future, to provide continuity and goals. But the present moment should be lived, not just endured.

## Singles

Until recently there was little interest in studying persons who did not marry. Most Americans eventually marry, but at any one time a substantial minority of adults are unmarried. Around 30 per cent of men and 37 per cent of women over 18 were unmarried in 1976. Some of these persons were never-married; others were separated, widowed, or divorced. Similarly, some currently unmarried persons are looking for a mate; others are "voluntarily single" and are not looking. Table 15-1 presents a typology of singlehood. A person may move from one category to the other as he becomes older. Some younger temporary singles marry; others are unable to find a spouse and become involuntarily single; still others may come to enjoy single life and become stable, voluntarily single. Some persons who marry become volun-

**TABLE 15-1**     **A Typology of Singlehood**

|  | Temporary | Stable |
|---|---|---|
| Voluntary | Younger never-marrieds who postpone marriage. | Men and women who choose to be single. |
|  | Recently divorced persons who are seeking new partners. | Single parents who do not seek spouses. |
|  | Never-marrieds who had not previously been interested in marriage but who are now actively seeking spouses. | Cohabitators who do not intend to marry. |
|  | Cohabitators who now want to marry. | Formerly marrieds who do not want to remarry. |
| Involuntary | Divorced, widowed, and deserted persons who seek remarriage. | Older widowed, divorced and never-marrieds who wanted to marry or remarry, who have not found a spouse, and who have accepted singlehood as a probable life state. |
|  | Single parents who seek spouses. |  |
|  | Younger never-marrieds who actively seek spouses. | Never-marrieds who have not succeeded in the marriage market because of physical or mental impairment. |

*Source:* Peter J. Stein. The lifestyles and life chances of the never-married. *Marriage and Family Review,* 1978, **1**:4, 1–11. Table 2.

tarily single again, whereas others who would prefer to remain married find themselves again without a spouse [42]. Whether being single is problematic to the individual depends largely upon how desired a state it is to that person.

**Rise in Numbers of Singles.**    A number of factors have contributed to there being more singles. The delay of marriage and the increase in numbers of young adults have swelled the ranks of singles in the United States. The rise in number of divorces has contributed also to the number of singles. Several researchers have concluded that marriage is becoming less desirable among both college and noncollege youth, in part because of the visibility of divorce, but also because of the orientation toward personal, individual growth [42]. In larger cities commercial interests cater to the needs of singles through singles bars, clubs, apartment buildings, and publications.

**Black Singles.**    A greater proportion of blacks remain unmarried throughout the life cycle until age 65. The differences are especially pronounced in young adulthood: Among 25- to 29-year-olds about a third of black men and a quarter of white men are unmarried; 30 per cent of black women and 10 per cent of white women aged 25–29 are single [42]. Staples notes that most middle-class single blacks see their single status as forced upon them [41]. Singles bars do not cater to blacks, and there are few singles organizations that provide opportunities for blacks to meet. Such black singles usually live in predominantly white areas and work largely among whites.

**Needs for Social Support Systems.** Although living within a family is not the only way to get social and emotional support, all persons need close, caring relationships, as singles themselves recognize [42]. Among young women it is common to seek such a relationship from a sister, mother, or woman friend, as well as from a male partner. It is not as common among American men to seek a close emotional relationship with another man [23]. More common now than in the past are men's and women's groups, therapy and encounter groups, and group living arrangements for singles. Such arrangements often help individuals make a transition to a paired relationship or to family living.

## Friendly Divorce

Some partners agree to end their primary commitment to each other while maintaining a cooperative relationship, usually because they think it is the best thing for their children. Some sadness is inevitable at the breakup of such an important attachment, but much trauma is avoided when the severed pair maintain a degree of respect and care. Property is divided fairly and business matters are worked out with full communication. If there are genuine affectionate relationships with in-laws, they can be maintained.

Since we do not have information about large numbers of friendly divorces, we only describe some cases. The first is a report of a divorce ceremony; the other two concern the ways in which divorced friends worked out their relationships.

The divorce of Anne and Matt was reported in an article in the *Christian Century* [37]. The couple told their friends that they were going to be divorced and invited them to a party at which the occasion was marked by cutting a cake. The "Service of Dissolution of Marriage" was performed at the couple's home. Matt responded "I do" to the question, "Do you release her with your love and blessing, in gratitude for the part she has played in your life, in knowledge that her part in you will never be forgotten or despised, and in faith that in separation as well as in union, you are both held in the grace and unity of God?" Anne was then asked the same question. Formal announcements of the "amicable divorce" were later sent out (see Figure 15-1).

Amy and Andy were married while both were in college. When they graduated, Amy worked as a secretary while Andy went on for his M.A. As soon as he got a teaching job, they had two children in rapid succession. Three years later, Andy said he wanted to live alone; he felt stifled by family life. He loved Amy and the children, but wanted to be free to date other women and to be himself. After a few months, Andy and Amy agreed to a divorce, since Andy did not think that he wanted to live with her again. Andy paid a reasonable amount for the children's support. Amy got a job and found day care for the children. Andy goes to see Amy and the children about once a week. Sometimes they have dinner at Amy's; sometimes Andy takes them all out. Occasionally, he takes Amy out on a date. Amy's friends have asked her why she puts up with Andy's desertion from the husband role and his assumption of a merely friendly role. She has explained that it is good for the children to have contact with their father and that for her, this arrangement is better than nothing. Andy represents present-orientation, rejection of roles, and emphasis on his own growth.

Bonnie and Buzz were happily married for ten years, during which time he did well in a professional career and she was a homemaker and mother of three children. Bonnie, feeling bored and restless, joined a women's liberation group and gained enough support and self-confidence to go back to college for a degree. Soon she found a job and did extremely well. Threatened by Bonnie's success and her contacts with other men, Buzz wanted out of the marriage. Bonnie had tried at first to change her husband's traditional concept of masculinity and femininity, but, by now, she was convinced that her new life style would not fit with his old one. Her role as his wife was too confining. She wanted to grow. He wanted her to stay as she was. They agreed that divorce was best but that they would continue to live near each other, since the children needed both of them. The children are based at Bonnie's house, but they go regularly to Buzz's. If Bonnie is going out for dinner, or away for a weekend, Buzz takes care of the children. They all spend Christmas and other family festival days together. The parents contribute equally to the economic support of the children, but each knows that the other would do more if necessary. Bonnie has turned down offers of better jobs because they would require moving away from Buzz. She would not separate the children from their father. Nor would she want to lose him as a partner in childrearing, even though he is no longer a partner in marriage.

## Viability of Alternate Forms

Most persons can expect to live at least a part of their lives outside a nuclear family. In one year (1978), 25 per cent of households were nonfamily [43]. As people move through their family careers, some persons move into, and some out of nuclear family living. The United States and Canada have always had some family forms other than the nuclear conjugal family. The number and proportion of people living in alternate family structures seem to be increasing. Although they will probably increase further, it is unlikely that nuclear families will be in the minority in the forseeable future. A large sample of students was drawn from seven universities,

*Matthew and Anne Surrey*
*Announce*

*An Amicable Divorce*
*Their friends and relatives*
*Are invited not to take sides*
*And to keep in touch*
*With both of them.*

*For the time being still*
*Both at home at*
*1492 Columbus Circle*
*Middle City, Midwest*

**FIGURE 15-1**    A Midwestern couple sent announcements of their amicable divorce to their friends and relatives.

*Source:* Mary M. Shideler, An amicable divorce. *Christian Century,* 1971, 88, 553–555.

representing five regions of the United States [8]. When asked questions about their attitudes toward various new life styles, 70 per cent said that they thought the traditional monogamous marriage the most fulfilling type of man-woman relationship. Two-stage marriage had the highest expression of favorable attitudes. 45 per cent. About one third had favorable attitudes toward cohabitation, communal living, and marriage between homosexuals. Only 6 per cent were favorable to group marriage and 13 per cent were favorable to extramarital sex with mutual consent. Lowest approval was given to extramarital sex without knowledge of mate.

Ramey suggests that the more complex a family form, the less likely it is that the life style will be adopted by a large number of persons [32]. As we have seen, swinging is practiced by only about 4 per cent of couples. Communes, too, are not extremely popular, and most are short-lived. The only published study on group marriage reported that somewhat more than a hundred group marriages had been found [6]. Open marriage (not sexually open marriage) is likely to become more popular as women gain more equality with men. Childfree marriage is an example of an alternate life style that is *less* complex than the traditional nuclear family. If Ramey is correct, we would expect more couples to choose childfree marriage. Some variant life styles are chosen for a time, and then abandoned. For many couples cohabitation is likely to remain a transitional stage from singlehood to marriage.

True acceptance of pluralism in family living would require facilitating constructive human relationships in a variety of ways. A program to help nuclear families to be more successful need not penalize other kinds of families and could even assist them. If some of the strains on individuals and nuclear families can be alleviated, the benefits will spill over to the minority of family forms, too. Nonnuclear forms can be thought of not only as alternates but also as backups to the nuclear family.

## SOCIETAL SUPPORTS FOR THE FAMILY

In Canada, the Vanier Institute of the Family actively leads in forming public opinion and public policy. The Institute advocates a "familial society," described in these words.

> A familial society is one in which the person and the quality of his immediate relationships—at home, at study, at work, and at play—are perceived as fundamental to the quality of the society and its institutions. It is a society in which all the arrangements and structures facilitate such relationships and serve to enhance them. . . . If children, parents, and grandparents are to grow up well, the basic requirement is a society that cares . . . The adults who care for children also need to be surrounded by persons who care deeply for them. [20]

In the United States opinions differ widely as to how family life ought to be conducted and as to what sorts of goals and actions should be supported by public funds and government effort. There is no overall family policy. Some officials wish to strengthen traditional nuclear families, but not the variant family forms. Many people shrink from frankly addressing the embarrassing problems of adolescent childbearing and family violence. Others call for a return to the good old days when sex was contained within marriage or practiced only surreptitiously otherwise, when homosexuals were strictly undercover, and when men, women, and children played their prescribed roles. Social change is a fact, and a restoration of the past is impossible, but traditions, ideals, and values can be used for guidance in planning the future. If Americans are to hold their rights to life, liberty, and the pursuit of happiness, then some supports for family living will be forthcoming from various institutions.

Will American political, legal, religious, and economic institutions be up to the challenge? The family now needs some strengthening, creative action from other social institutions, in addition to the efforts of individuals. On pages 412–416 we discussed changes in health care that would be supportive to families. In the following pages we suggest societal supports in the form of income, work-sharing, choices in regard to jobs, child care, homemaking education, social contacts, and legal reform. The list is only partial. It could be expanded.

## Economic Support

Enough food, clothing, and shelter are basic to satisfactory family life. North America has the resources necessary for meeting the physical needs of all its people but has failed in sharing and distributing. The family cannot solve this problem. The challenge could be met through combined efforts of government and industry.

## Work Sharing and Choice of Jobs

In Chapter 8 we explored the relationship between work inside and outside the family and family life. While family members have some choices regarding the division of work tasks, more support could come from various parts of society. Business and industry are run with little concern for human needs. Some branches of government are experimenting with "flextime," allowing workers to pick their own hours, and also with job-sharing. Although only a tiny percentage of workers are affected by these experimental programs, results are promising. Part-time work, however, is increasing in popularity. In 1977 a fifth of U.S. workers worked part time (fewer than 35 hours per week.) About half of the 16 million part-time workers in the United States now have at least some regular fringe benefits. Although part-time work has been usual in some occupations, unions are generally unenthusiastic about part-timers, and some professionals believe that persons in their ranks who would work part time would be those of lower capacity. Other professionals disagree, saying that two part-timers are more productive than one full-timer [21]. Husband-wife job sharing is satisfying to some couples. Some colleges have even come to realize that they get more for their money by hiring a couple to share a job [11].

## Child Care and Homemaking Support Systems

Another strain could be relieved by giving parents (chiefly mothers) some help in caring for their children. If a mother is going to go out to work, someone must look after the children. According to Stack, the children of black working mothers are reared at home, by kin [40]. "Shared adult responsibilities toward children in the black community are not only an obligation of kinship, they constitute a highly cherished right." These families do not want to have outsiders care for their children. Other families want and need assistance with child care from people outside the family, but they want it to be from caregivers whose values and practices match their own. A variety of child-care services are essential in order to meet the variety of needs that North American families have. Some children require all-day care every day, others for a few hours a week. Children who go to school may need a place to go in the late afternoon. Kindergarteners may need lunch and care for half a day.

Child development specialists know how to conduct excellent programs that will be good for children's physical, mental, and emotional development. Growth-promoting programs have been demonstrated at all age levels and for children with various capacities and limitations. An important part of most successful programs is parent involvement. Children are benefited when parents and teachers work together cooperatively and with mutual respect. Black parents are not the only ones who do not wish to send their children to day-care centers or university nursery schools. Family day care in their own neighborhoods is often satisfactory to parents who do not want their children exposed to alien values. At the same time, family day-care providers, if licensed, have received some training in child development and education and they are supervised by professionals.

Other types of day care are those provided by commercial firms, for profit, and those provided by industry as fringe benefits or as a means of gaining more workers. During World War II, the Kaiser Company delivered excellent day-care services to mothers who worked in the shipyards. Day-care facilities are attached to factories in other countries, including Russia, China, and India. Schools could do some of the job and benefit older children at the same time. Some schools already run nursery schools as laboratories. Churches and community agencies also provide day care. Much more is needed, in order to have enough places for all and to provide care for children whose parents cannot afford to pay. We believe that the government should give leadership and that public funds should be used for young children, just as they are for the education of older ones.

Although affluent parents often buy household services or provide their own through sharing of homemaking tasks, many women and almost all single parents must struggle with heavy household burdens. Child care centers could offer many aids in addition to supervising and educating children. The first nursery schools in England, around 1920, gave the children baths when they arrived. The Kaiser child-care centers used to prepare a main dinner dish that the parents could take home with their children at night. Children at the University of Rhode Island nursery school are taken to have their teeth cleaned at the University dental clinic. An obvious service is that of washing and mending clothing and exchanging clothing as children outgrow what they have. Food and clothing services could serve a double purpose if schools and universities used services to children for teaching older boys and girls. Older children could then use their homemaking skills to be more helpful in their families.

Some other homemaking supports exist but are not widely available. Geriatric day care centers (pages 398, 415) can keep an old person based at home without overburdening the family. Visiting homemakers help families in crises, as when the mother is ill, but there are not enough of them to go around. Visiting nurses help in

DONNA J. HARRIS, THE MERRILL-PALMER INSTITUTE

crises of illness, but they cannot go to all the families who could benefit from their services. Working mothers and single fathers urgently need help in caring for their children when they are ill. Only a minute proportion of day care centers have facilities for taking care of sick children.

Another type of homemaking support needed by many families is help in home maintenance and improvement. The poor, the aged, and single-parent family heads need it most. When people can neither pay a skilled workman nor do it themselves, what are they to do with a leaky tap, a stopped-up toilet, a burned-out element, or a broken stair tread? Although education for homemaking would be a long-term solution, communities might maintain home rescue squads for immediate action. If students were required to give a year or two of service to nation and community immediately after high school, there would be personnel available. The young people themselves would also benefit from learning skills and from doing constructive work for others.

Recreational services are another child care support that could be expanded to benefit families more. Many children need a safe place to play and opportunities to learn motor skills, games, and hobbies. Much is already done by voluntary organizations, such as Scouts, and by churches and community houses, but much more is needed. Poor families urgently need space, equipment, and teachers or leaders to promote constructive play. Families also need opportunities to play together and to enjoy recreation as families. Many commercial interests work against free, available, simple neighborhood recreation. As with child care, the knowledge is available. There are competent community planners and recreation professionals, who could deliver the services if they were given the financial resources to do so.

## Education for Human Living

Our fast-changing culture has not developed adequate ways of keeping up with its own newness. Some of our biggest problems come from not knowing how to communicate, relate, share, and care. In almost every spot in the family life cycle, people need to know more about how to realize their full human potential. We have to discard the notion that education begins in kindergarten and ends upon graduation from school or college. Lifelong, continuing education is a basic support to family living.

Throughout this book, we have advocated many educational measures. To summarize, we propose that everyone be educated in these areas: for self-understanding in terms of feelings, emotions, abilities, health, and growth; for communication; for planning and decision making; for homemaking; about sex; about childbirth and childrearing; about marriage and its alternates; for changing and growing old. There are other fields of education, too, but what we are recommending here is in connection with personal and family life.

Some privately endowed institutions, such as the Merrill-Palmer Institute in Detroit and the Clara Elizabeth Fund, in Flint, Michigan, are designed for education for human living. Some universities, such as Utah State University, have cooperated with a wide variety of community organizations to establish family life education that reaches beyond the student body and into communities [39]. Industry (Radio Corporation of America) and a community organization cooperated to create a family development training project that educated all family members in both job and home skills. The operation transformed 400 of 728 deprived seasonal farm worker families into self-supporting families, tripling their average income [28]. Canada's Vanier Institute could well be expanded in its scope and functions. Voluntary associations provide leadership and demonstrations. They include Child and Family Service Associations, the Child Study Association of America, the National Council on Family Relations, the Groves Conference, and the Association of Couples for Marriage Enrichment, founded by David and Vera Mace [19]. If such institutions and projects could be multiplied and their efforts expanded, family living would be greatly strengthened. Since all people need education for human living, occasional programs are not enough and a systematic delivery system is needed.

## Social Contacts

Social isolation is problematic to many members of nuclear families and to people living alone or in single-parent families. Many have moved away from kin and childhood friends. They need ways of finding friends and groups of congenial people. Church membership offers a path to sociability for those who accept it, but many people do not. Nor can everyone do volunteer work, join an interest group, or find enough friendship even if they do work and join. Continuing education will offer some opportunities for making friends, as will consciousness-raising groups. Family cluster programs, sponsored by the Unitarian Church, are useful to urban families as a way of creating a network of relationships that substitutes for absent kin, friends, and neighbors. Instead of supplying only individual friends, the system brings together groups that resemble the larger family. Participants reported that they experienced these benefits: relationships that were intimate, honest, and real; awareness of goodwill in others; contact with children for childless people; children relating to adults and children outside their immediate families; understanding of how other families operate [29].

## Legal Reform and Clarification

There are confusing and outdated laws regarding the family, marriage, sex roles, and children. Although laws of necessity lag behind the latest thinking, they should be kept up to date as much as possible. Then, too, marriage in two steps could be legalized, institutionalizing what many couples are in fact doing. Legal reform would make laws more functional and easier to understand and to apply. More uniformity between the states is highly desirable, as well as more cooperation in administering

**480** FAMILIES

the law. Members of the legal profesiion vary from very corrupt to highly moral and unselfish. Greater numbers of the latter are needed by all, but especially by poor families and minority group members. Equality before the law is a reality only when everyone has equal access to its power.

Basic legal equality between the sexes has been spelled out in the Equal Rights Amendment. The confirmation of the amendment would add greatly to the actual equality between men and women.

## In Conclusion

We believe that people will continue to need intimate relationships, and that most will have the experience of living in a nuclear family at some times during their lives. Most will experience other living situations as well.

Today it is not possible to talk about "the family." Rather, there are *families*— nuclear families, single-parent families, no-child families, extended families, and quasi-families.

We hope that individuals and families will be able to reach out to each other, both in good times and bad. Families that are cut adrift from the extended family and home town community need new supports, as we have shown. Such families have the advantage of being able to choose friends out of a wider population than was possible in the past. However, many people need to learn how to make deep, satisfying friendships more rapidly than was necessary in the past. North America needs people who care for each other, who cooperate willingly, and who often put the needs of the group ahead of individual desires. Because of the amazing flexibility of human beings, such adaptations are possible.

The United States has been, is, and always will be a pluralistic society, made up of many different kinds of people and kinds of families. We hope that our government will develop its capacities beyond responding to pressures from special interest groups. For continued societal strength and individual welfare, human resources, rather than material wealth, must increasingly be relied upon. We believe that human potential is best nurtured in families. The healthy development of individual, family, and society can be enhanced not only by voluntary efforts but also by government policies that support the strengths of a number of family forms.

## SUMMARY

The world population explosion continues to threaten human life. The United States, like other Western countries, shows promise of stabilizing its population in about 50 years. Family relationships, in various forms, will continue to provide emotional satisfaction as well as other necessities.

New orientations to life include equality in many contexts; more emphasis on the present, and changes in attitudes toward past and future; new uses of science and some rejection of it; reassessment of the morality of power use; rejection of role restrictions and redefinition of roles in regard to occupations, gender, and age; emphasis on sexual expression and satisfaction; belief in personal growth.

A variety of life styles exist in North America. Belief in the importance of voluntary simplicity is expressed in a range of life styles, making more or less contribution to the preservation of world resources. Communes, both old and new, include many different ways in which groups of people live together in commitment and cooperation. Main categories are religious, utopian, and evolutionary. Rural communes are among the minority of organizations in our society that are developing a mode of life compatible with the world's diminishing resources. Co-marital sex is extramarital sexual relations with one's spouse's consent. Sexually open marriages involve co-marital sex with emotional commitment. Swinging is organized co-marital sex that is usually done without emotional involvement, for purely recreational purposes. Co-marital sex may be included in "open marriage" but is not the main feature of it. The basics of open marriage are equality, identity, trust, communication, respect, honesty, personal growth, and present-orientation. The number of single people has recently increased greatly. Singles represent a variety of people: never married; separated; divorced; voluntarily single; temporarily single. Singles need close relationships, like everyone else. Friendly divorce is a style sometimes achieved by people who wish to continue cooperation in their roles as parents, even though they no longer wish to be marital partners. For most persons the family life career includes living in several different family forms.

The supports a society provides to its families vary with political and economic factors. American families need better ways of gaining economic support, as well as choices on how they will work and earn money. Many families need help with child care and homemaking. Because of rapid social change, continuing education is needed, especially education for family living and human relationships. Legal reform could clarify, improve, and strengthen families.

**REFERENCES**

1. Abbey, Edward. Voluntary simplicity. Follow-up and comment. *CoEvolution Quarterly,* 1977, **15,** 55.
2. Bartell, Gilbert. Group sex: An eyewitness report on the American way of swinging. New York: Signet, 1971.
3. Berger, Bennet, Bruce Hackett, and Mervyn Millar. The communal family. *Family Coordinator,* 1972, **21,** 419–427.
4. Brecher, Edward. *The sex researchers.* Boston: Little, Brown, 1969.
5. Cole, Charles and Graham Spanier. Co-Marital mate-sharing and family stability. *Journal of Sex Research,* 1974, **10,** 21–31.
6. Constantine, Larry L., and Joan M. Constantine. *Group marriage.* New York: Macmillan, 1973.
7. Denfield, Duane. Dropouts from swinging. *Family Coordinator,* 1974, **23,** 45–49.
8. Edwards, Maxine and Nick Stinnett. Perceptions of college students concerning alternate life styles. *Journal of Psychology,* 1974, **87,** 143–156.

9. Elgin, Duane and Arnold Mitchell. Voluntary simplicity (3). *CoEvolution Quarterly*, 1977, **14,** 4–19.

10. Estallechild, Vivian. Hippie communes. In Joann Delora and Jack Delora (Eds.). *Intimate life styles: Marriage and its alternatives,* Pacific Palisades, Calif.: Goodyear, 1972.

10a. For the first time, China encourages one-child family. *Wall Street Journal*, May 22, 1979.

11. Gallese, Liz R. Two for the price of one. *Wall Street Journal,* April 19, 1974.

12. Gilmartin, B. G. That swinging couple down the block. *Psychology Today,* 1975, **9:**4, 54–58.

13. Henshell, Anne-Marie. Swinging: A study of decision-making in marriage. *American Journal of Sociology,* 1973, **78,** 885–891.

14. Kephart, William. Experimental family organization: An historico-cultural report on the Oneida Community. *Marriage and Family Living,* 1963, **25,** 261–268.

15. Knapp, Jacqueline J. Co-marital sex and marriage counseling: Sexually open marriage and related attitudes and practices of marriage counselors. Unpublished Ph.D. dissertation, U. of Florida, 1974.

16. Koening, Peter. Communes in retrospect: A search for family ties. *APA Monitor,* June, 1977, 6+.

17. Levin, Robert J. The *Redbook* report on premarital and extramarital sex. The end of the double standard? *Redbook,* 1975, **145:**6, 38–42+.

18. Levinson, Daniel J. *The seasons of a man's life*. New York: Knopf, 1978.

19. Mace, David R. (Ed.). Marriage enrichment. *Family Coordinator,* 1975, **24,** 131–170.

20. MacKinnon, Fred R. Speech to a Conference on Family Policy, reported in *Transition,* 1977, **7:**1, 4–5.

21. Main, Jeremy. Good jobs go part time. *Money,* 1977, **10:**6, 80–86.

22. Maslow, Abraham. *Toward a psychology of being*. New York: Van Nostrand, 1962.

23. Nye, F. Ivan. Ambivalence in the family: Rewards and costs in group membership. *Family Coordinator,* 1976, **25,** 21–31.

24. O'Neill, Nena and George O'Neill. *Open marriage: A new life style for couples*. New York: Avon, 1972.

25. O'Neill, Nena and George O'Neill. Open marriage: Its implications for human service systems. *Family Coordinator,* 1973, **22,** 449–456.

26. Paddock, William and Elizabeth Paddock. *We don't know how*. Ames, Iowa: Iowa State University Press, 1973.

27. Palson, Charles and Rebecca Palson. Swinging in wedlock. In Henena Z. Lopata (Ed.). *Marriages and families*. New York: Van Nostrand, 1973.

28. Porter, Gwendolyn H. The family training concept. *Family Coordinator,* 1974, **23,** 171–174.

29. Pringle, Bruce M. Family clusters as a means of reducing isolation among urbanites. *Family Coordinator,* 1974, **23,** 175–179.

30. Ramey, James W. Emerging patterns of innovative behavior in marriage. *Family Coordinator,* 1972. **21,** 435–456.

31. Ramey, James W. Intimate friendship: Logical outcome of rejecting monogamy. *Family Coordinator,* 1975, **24,** 1975, **24,** 515–530.

32. Ramey, James. Experimental family forms: The family of the future. *Marriage and Family Review,* 1978, **1:**1, 1–9.

33. Reid, Mike. Lives apart. *Mushroom,* 1978, No. 14 (September), 20–22.

34. Rogers, Carl R. *On becoming a person*. Boston: Houghton, 1961.

35. Schrank, Robert. How to relieve worker boredom. *Psychology Today,* 1978, **12**:2, 79–80.
36. Schumacher, E. F. *Small is beautiful.* Perennial Library edition. New York: Harper, 1975.
37. Shideler, Mary M. An amicable divorce. *Christian Century,* 1971, **88,** 553–555.
38. Signs of hope, signs of stress. *People,* 1977, **4**:1, 27.
39. Skidmore, C. Jay and Jay D. Schvaneveldt. Reaching the community through a family life conference. *Family Coordinator,* 1974, **22,** 465–471.
40. Stack, Carol B. *Defining the family for the 21st century.* Durham, N.C.: Duke University, Center for the Study of the Family and the State, 1978.
41. Staples, Robert. Single and black in America. Unpublished manuscript, U. of California at San Francisco, 1977. Cited in Peter Stein. The lifestyles and life chances of the never-married. *Marriage and Family Review,* 1978, **1**:4, 1–11.
42. Stein, Peter J. The lifestyles and life chances of the never-married. *Marriage and Family Review,* 1978, **1**:4, 1–11.
43. U.S. Bureau of the Census. *Households and families by type: March 1978* (Advance Report). Current Population Reports, Series P-20, No. 327. Washington, D.C.: U.S. Government Printing Office, 1978.
44. Varni, Charles. Cited in James Ramey. Intimate friendships: Logical outcome of rejecting monogamy. *Family Coordinator,* 1975, **24,** 515–530.
45. Westoff, Charles F. Some speculations on the future of marriage and the family. *Family Planning Perspectives,* 1978, **10,** 79–83.
46. World's growing work force. *People,* 1978, **5**:3, 37.
47. Zablocki, Ben. *Alienation and investment in the urban commune.* New York: Center for Policy Research, 1977.
48. Ziskin, Jay and Mae Ziskin. *The extra-marital sex contract.* Los Angeles: Nash, 1973.

# appendix A
# PREMARITAL QUESTIONNAIRE

A couple contemplating marriage or a marriage-type relationship should spend time discussing values and goals. The Premarital Questionnaire provided here as a supplement to the text of *Families: Developing Relationships* can help this important process by raising a number of relevant issues.

**Instructions:** Each partner should have a copy of the questionnaire. Additional copies may be available from your instructor.

In the left column are questions to be answered either by checking the appropriate column or columns at the right, by writing in "yes" or "no," or by writing in a short answer, where appropriate.

You and your partner should each fill out one of these forms, without consulting each other or discussing the questions until you have finished. When finished filling out the forms, go over each question, reading your answers in turn, and discussing those that are problematic.

*Place an O* in the column or columns to show who did this task in your family of origin, which is the family in which you grew up. *Place an X* in the column or columns to show who will do this in your family of procreation (the new family that you and your partner are forming). *Note:* If more than one person did or will do a particular task, indicate all of the people who shared the responsibility.

**485**

| Place an O in the column or columns to show who did this task in your family of orientation. Place an X in the column or columns to show who will do this task in your family of procreation. | Wife | Husband | Child | Other | Outside paid help | No one |
|---|---|---|---|---|---|---|
| **Paid work** Who | | | | | | |
| 1. works for pay, full time? | | | | | | |
| 2. works for pay, part time? | | | | | | |
| **Unpaid work, in and around home:** **Care of the home** Who | | | | | | |
| 3. washes the dishes? | | | | | | |
| 4. puts away the dishes? | | | | | | |
| 5. plans the meals? | | | | | | |
| 6. cooks the meals? | | | | | | |
| 7. does cooking such as baking bread or preparing other staples? | | | | | | |
| 8. plans the shopping list? | | | | | | |
| 9. does the food shopping? | | | | | | |
| 10. puts food away after the shopping trip? | | | | | | |
| 11. cleans the refrigerator? | | | | | | |
| 12. cleans the oven? | | | | | | |
| 13. vacuums or sweeps? | | | | | | |
| 14. washes floors? | | | | | | |
| 15. washes windows? | | | | | | |
| 16. dusts? | | | | | | |

| Place an O on the column or columns to show who did this task in your family of orientation. Place an X in the column or columns to show who will do this task in your family of procreation. | Wife | Husband | Child | Other | Outside paid help | No one |
|---|---|---|---|---|---|---|
| 17. picks up commonly used rooms such as the living room? | | | | | | |
| 18. picks up privately used rooms such as individual bedrooms? | | | | | | |
| 19. washes clothes? | | | | | | |
| 20. puts away clean clothes? | | | | | | |
| 21. mends clothing? | | | | | | |
| 22. irons clothing? | | | | | | |
| 23. sets the table before meals? | | | | | | |
| 24. clears the table after meals? | | | | | | |
| 25. does minor repairs of plumbing? | | | | | | |
| 26. does minor repairs of furnishings? | | | | | | |
| 27. does minor repairs of appliances? | | | | | | |
| 28. does or is responsible for major household repairs? | | | | | | |
| 29. takes care of the garbage and trash? | | | | | | |
| 30. If hired help is used, who does the hiring, firing, and supervising? | | | | | | |
| Care of the yard Who 31. cuts the grass? | | | | | | |
| 32. shovels the snow? | | | | | | |
| 33. takes care of the garden? | | | | | | |

| Place an O in the column or columns to show who did this task in your family of orientation. Place an X in the column or columns to show who will do this task in your family of procreation. | Wife | Husband | Child | Other | Outside paid help | No one |
|---|---|---|---|---|---|---|
| *Care of yard, continued* <br> 34. rakes leaves? | | | | | | |
| *Care of car or other vehicle* <br> Who <br> 35. sees that it has sufficient gas and oil? | | | | | | |
| 36. cleans the exterior (or takes it to a carwash)? | | | | | | |
| 37. cleans the interior? | | | | | | |
| 38. sees that it is serviced or kept in good repair? | | | | | | |
| *Care of pet* <br> Who <br> 39. feeds it? | | | | | | |
| 40. exercises it? | | | | | | |
| 41. disposes of waste? | | | | | | |
| 42. brushes, washes, etc.? | | | | | | |
| *Financial management* <br> Who <br> 43. decides the family budget? | | | | | | |
| 44. pays the bills? | | | | | | |
| 45. makes major purchasing decisions? | | | | | | |
| *Choosing a home or place to live* <br> Who <br> 46. decides whether to live in a rural, suburban, or urban environment? | | | | | | |
| 47. chooses the actual dwelling? | | | | | | |

Short answer: answer *yes* or *no,* or fill in with your answer, as appropriate, for questions 48–51.

*Children, planning and care of.*

48. Do you want to have children? _____

49. Will you use contraceptives? _____

    If yes, what kind? _____

    If yes, whose responsibility is
    the use of contraceptives? _____

50. If you want children, do you want
    natural, adopted, or both? _____

51. Would you want to terminate an unwanted or unplanned
    pregnancy with an abortion? _____

    If you want children:

52. When do you want to start your family?

    _____

53. Will husband be present at birth of child(ren)? _____

54. Do you believe in day care for infants? _____

    for small children? _____

| Place an O in the column or columns to show who did this task in your family of orientation. Place an X in the column or columns to show who will do this task in your family of procreation. | Wife | Husband | Child | Other | Outside paid help | No one |
|---|---|---|---|---|---|---|
| *Child care:* Who cares for infant and toddler? | | | | | | |
| 55. diapers? | | | | | | |
| 56. feeds? | | | | | | |
| 57. bathes? | | | | | | |
| 58. plays with? | | | | | | |
| 59. disciplines? | | | | | | |
| 60. gets up at night with? | | | | | | |
| 61. tends when sick? | | | | | | |

| Place an O in the column or columns to show who did this task in your family of orientation. Place an X in the column or columns to show who will do this task in your family of procreation. | Wife | Husband | Child | Other | Outside paid help | No one |
|---|---|---|---|---|---|---|
| *Child care, continued.* Who cares for preschool child? 62. feeds? | | | | | | |
| 63. bathes? | | | | | | |
| 64. puts to bed at night? | | | | | | |
| 65. teaches skills? | | | | | | |
| 66. takes care of child's toys? (organizes, puts away, etc.) | | | | | | |
| 67. disciplines? | | | | | | |
| 68. gets up at night with? | | | | | | |
| 69. takes care of when sick? | | | | | | |
| 70. plays with? | | | | | | |
| Who cares for school-age child and teen ager? 71. sees that the child is fed and bathed? | | | | | | |
| 72. plays with and/or supervises activities? | | | | | | |
| 73. helps with homework? | | | | | | |
| 74. disciplines? | | | | | | |
| 75. takes care of when sick? | | | | | | |

Answer the following questions by writing in *yes, no,* or a short answer.
76. At what age will children be given household work responsibilities? _____
77. Will children be given an allowance? _____
   If yes, how much? _____
      at what age? _____
78. Will children be given formal religious instruction? _____

If yes, by whom and at what age? _____

79. Will you instruct your children about sex? _____

    If yes, at what age? _____

       who will do it? (mother, father, other?) _____

80. How will you express affection to your children?

    _____

    Will your way of expressing affection change as the children grow up?

    _____

81. Do you believe in physical punishment?

    If no, what kind of punishment do you think is appropriate?

    _____

*Marital relationship*

82. If your marriage becomes unbearable and cannot be saved, would you consider
    divorce? _____

83. How do your parents show affection for each other?

    _____

    How will you show affection for your spouse?

    _____

    After children are born, will you display affection
    for each other in front of the children? _____

84. How frequently do you expect to have sexual relations with your spouse? (times per
    week) _____

85. What kind of recreational activities will you engage in, without your spouse?

    _____

86. What kind of recreational activities will you engage in, with your spouse?

    _____

*Outside relationships*

87. Who will decide which other couples will be your friends?

    _____

88. Who will decide who each spouse's same-sex friends will be? _____

89. Will each spouse have friends of the opposite sex who are not necessarily the other
    spouse's friends?

    _____

90. If yes to 89, will these friends be strictly on a work or professional level? _____

91. If no to 90, will physical intimacy be a part of these relationships? _____

92. If yes to 91, will limits be placed upon the amount of physical intimacy? _____

93. Will friendships with members of the opposite sex be kept secret from the other spouse?

    _____         _____

*Religion*

94. Do you attend church or temple? _____

    If yes, which one? _____

           how often? _____

95. Do you expect your spouse to attend church or temple?

    If yes, the same as yours? _____

    How often? _____

96. Do you celebrate religious holidays?

    If yes, which ones?

_____

    How do you celebrate?

_____


*Work* (These questions apply to you and your spouse, not to people in general.

97. How do you feel about the wife working outside of the home after children are born?

_____

98. How do you feel about the wife earning more than the husband?

_____

99. How do you feel about the husband working for pay on a part-time basis only, or being a full-time house-husband?

_____

100. Whose career should come first? _____


*Miscellaneous*

101. How often will you visit your parents? (times per week, month, or year) _____

102. How often will your parents visit you?

_____

103. How much money will you give to charity? _____

104. How much time will you spend working for community organizations? _____

105. Where would you go for help if you had personal problems, marital problems, or problems with a child? (check appropriate answer or answers)

    [   ] counselor (individual, marriage, or child therapist)

    [   ] clergyman

    [   ] friend

    [   ] medical doctor

    [   ] relative

    [   ] I would try to read about the problem

    [   ] consult no one.

106. Rearrange the following items in terms of their importance, most important first. First, order them in the way that you would like your spouse to feel. Do this even if you have no intention to change your spouse.

Then, order them the way that you feel.

| | Spouse | Self |
|---|---|---|
| A. Devotion to your country | | |
| B. Family (including having children) | | |
| C. Personal growth of self as an individual | | |
| D. Religion | | |
| E. Work or career | | |
| F. Your relationship as a couple. | | |

# appendix B

# basic sex

## PRENATAL DEVELOPMENT

### Conception

Of the millions of **sperm** that flow from the father, only one fertilizes the mother's single egg. The sperm and egg provide materials that combine to make a unique individual, unlike anyone who has ever been born before. The individual's uniqueness is possible because of the possible combinations of genetic material from the mother and father.

Each cell of a human body, with the exception of the sex cells (sperm and ova) contains a total of 46 **chromosomes.** Chromosomes contain **genes,** tiny codes that determine how the individual will develop from one cell into a large organism containing billions of cells. Of these 46 chromosomes, two determine the sex of the individual. From the mother's ovum comes an X chromosome (so called because when viewed under a microscope it looks like an X); from the father's sperm comes either an X chromosome, which results in a female child, or a Y chromosome, resulting in a male child.

When a sperm penetrates an egg, 22 chromosomes plus one X or Y chromosome from the father unite with 22 chromosomes plus one X chromosome from the mother in a unique new cell that will divide and subdivide to become a new individual. Seventy-two hours after conception, the individual consists of a ball of 32 cells; after four days it is a hollow ball of about 90 cells. This hollow ball of cells normally attaches itself to the mother's **uterus,** where it will spend the next nine months.

### Embryo and Fetus

During the next period of development, the individual is called an **embryo.** It develops a face, neck, arms, legs, fingers, toes, functioning internal organs, and some bone calcification. The

494

head end develops faster than the tail end. At the end of eight weeks, with the basic structures laid down, the individual begins to look human. It is given a new name, **fetus,** which it keeps until it is born and becomes an infant (baby). During the third month of prenatal life, the first month of the fetus, the organism becomes differentiated as male or female. Other bodily systems also become more complex. At the age of five months, the fetus is about half as long as it will be at birth. At the age of seven months, it has a good chance of living outside the mother, should the fetus become an infant prematurely.

## Basic Sexual Anatomy

**Male.**    The most obvious difference between a male and female baby is, of course, the difference between the external genitals: the boy has a **penis** and **testes,** and the girl has a **vulva** (see Figures B-1, B-2). The penis is a complicated organ made of three cylinders of erectile tissue, two of which are nearly alike* and lie next to each other. The third cylinder lies beneath the two, and contains the urethra, the tube that at separate times carries urine, and in mature males ejaculate fluid or **semen** (the liquid that contains the male sex cells). The head or **glans** of the penis is also made of erectile tissue, but it is more richly endowed with nerves, making it extremely sensitive to touch. When the penis is flaccid (not erect), the head is covered by a loose ring of skin known as the **foreskin.** When the penis is erect, the foreskin pulls back to allow the sensitive head to receive the greatest stimulation.

All males are born with a foreskin, but it may be removed surgically in an operation called **circumcision.** This operation is performed ritually upon Jewish and Muslim boys, but may be performed routinely in some hospitals for "medical reasons." Actually, there is considerable difference of opinion as to whether or not circumcision has medical merit. It is true that it is harder to keep the uncircumcised penis clean, as a smelly substance called *smegma* forms under the foreskin if it is not drawn back and carefully washed daily. If left too long, the foreskin may stick to the glans. Opponents of circumcision claim that the individual can be taught to wash routinely, and that unnecessary surgery is never advisable.

Behind the penis is the **scrotum,** a loose sack of skin that contains a pair of testes. When it is mature, each testis is usually about an inch and a half long and an inch in diameter and ovoid in shape. From before the boy is born until the end of his life, the testes produce testosterone, the hormone that before birth literally makes him male. Should he lose his testes before reaching puberty, he will not develop into a normal adult male, but will instead be a *eunuch.* A eunuch retains a high voice, does not develop bodily hair, and is, of course, sterile. In the mature male, the testes also produce the male sex cells, **sperm.**

Sperm is made in the seminiferous tubules, tiny tubes within the testes. However, it is not yet mature when it is produced, and spends from two to four weeks in the **epididymis** or *collection tube,* during which time it becomes activated. The sperm is made of three parts: a head, containing the genetic material (chromosomes), which are the male contribution to the new life; a midsection, which produces chemicals that allow the sperm to convert materials in the seminal fluid into energy; and a tail section, for propulsion.

*It is not unusual for one of these cylinders to be slightly larger than the other, making the penis curve slightly.

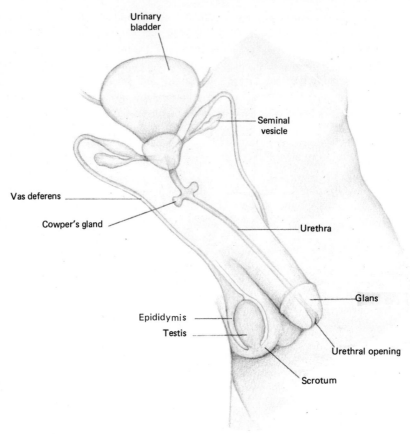

Urinary
bladder

Seminal
vesicle

Vas deferens

Cowper's gland

Urethra

Glans

Epididymis

Testis

Urethral opening

Scrotum

**FIGURE B-1**     Genital system of circumcised male.

From the epididymis, the sperm is pushed into the body cavity via the **vasa deferentia** (singular *vas deferens*), a pair of tubes about eighteen inches long that loop up around the urinary bladder and then down to the **ampulla,** an enlargement in the vas deferens, which serves as a storage place. After the ampulla are several glands that produce the largest part of the fluid that contain the sperm: first, the *seminal vesicles,* and then the *prostate gland.* Below the prostate gland are two Cowper's glands, which produce an alkaline substance during sexual excitement that neutralizes any urine that may still be in the urethra.

**Female.**   The female's external genitals are called the **vulva.** The vulva consists of the **mons veneris,** a small mound of fatty tissue located over the pubic bone; the **labia majora,** or outer lips, which when parted reveal the **labia minora,** or inner lips. The **clitoris,** the most sensitive part of a female's anatomy, is located where the inner lips join. It resembles a very tiny penis, although the urethra does not open through the clitoris, but is located instead below the clitoris in the **vestibule.** The clitoris does, however, have a glans and a tiny foreskin that, like the male's, should be carefully pulled back for a daily washing. Smegma may form around the clitoris and under the foreskin, eventually causing painful adhesions.

Into the vestibule opens the urethra, and also the **vagina** or birth canal. The newborn female may have a **hymen** or maidenhead, a fold of tissue that partly or completely covers the vagina. The thickness and appearance of this tissue varies widely from individual to individual: some females are born without one; others are born with one so elastic that it easily stretches out of the way during sexual intercourse. For other women, the hymen is so thick and tough that it must be removed surgically prior to sexual intercourse; for still others, the hymen may be broken easily through manual manipulation or even through strenuous exercise. Although the absence of a hymen has historically been taken as proof that a girl is not a virgin, its absence or presence *proves* nothing.

The vagina is a tube made of extremely elastic muscle. It is the passageway from outside

**FIGURE B-2**   Female genital system. A: External genitals. B: Varieties of hymens. C: Internal genital system.

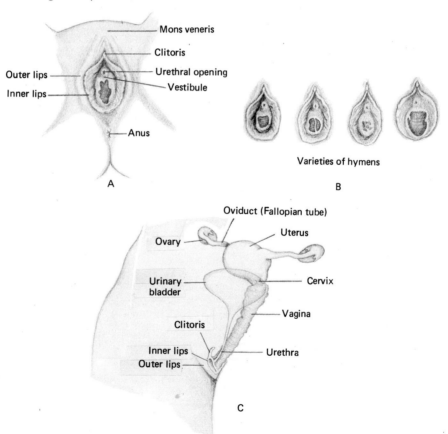

of the female's body to her **uterus,** a small, pear-shaped organ that is capable of stretching to hold a baby. The end of the uterus, the **cervix,** sticks down slightly into the vagina. The cervix is made of rings of strong muscle that dilate (open) when it is time for a baby to be born. At other times, the cervical opening is tiny and protected by a plug of mucus.

At the upper end of the uterus are two **Fallopian tubes** or **oviducts,** each of which opens into the uterus at one end, and at the other end forms finger-like projections reaching toward one of two **ovaries,** the female gonads or sex glands. A female is born with about 500,000 **ova,** (eggs, female sex cells), all that she will ever produce, unlike the male, who produces about a million sperm daily, once he matures sexually. The female does not release any ova until she reaches sexual maturity, about twelve or fourteen years after she is born.

# APPENDIX C

# budget

*Source:* Reprinted by permission from Elizabeth Wiegand, *Preview your spending.* Cornell Extension Bulletin 1143, Ithaca, New York: New York State College of Home Economics.

# RECORD OF PROMISED PAYMENTS

1. Write in the column on the left side the various things you have agreed to pay for in the next 12 months. Your list may include such payments as house rent, car loan, insurance, or phone service, as well as payroll deductions such as social security, health insurance, or taxes. List only those things you have actually promised to pay for. Do *not* list the food, clothing, toll calls, or haircuts you hope to buy. You are not committed to pay for these things *yet*.

2. At the top of the next 12 columns write the names of the months, beginning with the month when you are making this record; for example, March, April, May.

3. Fill in the amount which is due in the column when you agreed to pay it. For example, life insurance: March $46, Sept. $46.

4. When you have recorded all the year's promised payments, add up each column and write the totals on the last line.

| Promised payments | MONTHS OR PAY PERIODS | | | | | | | | | | | |
|---|---|---|---|---|---|---|---|---|---|---|---|---|
| | | | | | | | | | | | | |
| | | | | | | | | | | | | |
| | | | | | | | | | | | | |
| | | | | | | | | | | | | |
| | | | | | | | | | | | | |
| | | | | | | | | | | | | |
| | | | | | | | | | | | | |
| | | | | | | | | | | | | |
| | | | | | | | | | | | | |
| | | | | | | | | | | | | |
| | | | | | | | | | | | | |
| | | | | | | | | | | | | |
| Total promised payments | | | | | | | | | | | | |

# RECORD OF ESTIMATED INCOME

1. In the first column list the kinds of income you expect to receive: gross wages or salary, commissions, interest on savings accounts, dividends, sale of products. Do not include children's earnings unless they will be spent for the family as a whole.

2. At the top of the next 12 columns write the names of the months.

3. Now try to estimate your income for each month. If you work or sell irregularly, your estimates may be difficult to make.

4. When you have written in the amounts, add up each column.

5. Copy the monthly totals of promised payments from above onto this Record.

6. Subtract the total promised payments from the total estimated income and you will know the sum to be available each month for other wants and needs.

| Kinds of income | MONTHS OR PAY PERIODS | | | | | | | | | | | |
|---|---|---|---|---|---|---|---|---|---|---|---|---|
|  |  |  |  |  |  |  |  |  |  |  |  |  |
|  |  |  |  |  |  |  |  |  |  |  |  |  |
|  |  |  |  |  |  |  |  |  |  |  |  |  |
|  |  |  |  |  |  |  |  |  |  |  |  |  |
|  |  |  |  |  |  |  |  |  |  |  |  |  |
| Total estimated (gross) income |  |  |  |  |  |  |  |  |  |  |  |  |
| Total promised payments |  |  |  |  |  |  |  |  |  |  |  |  |
| Income available for other uses |  |  |  |  |  |  |  |  |  |  |  |  |

## Can You Divide Your Income Better?

Now study your completed Records of Promised Payments and Estimated Income. You may want to shift some payments from a month having heavy expenses to one with light expenses or larger income. Insurance premiums and church and charitable pledges are fairly easy to shift. Or you can level large payments by paying monthly or quarterly. During some months you may prefer to keep unpledged income high—around Christmas or vacation time, for example.

If you are wondering about new borrowing or credit buying, a glance at your present load of promised payments will indicate when you could begin and how long payments need to last, depending on the size of installment you feel you could assume. Or you may simply decide that additional debt is unwise this year.

If your Preview helps you to know what income you will receive and the way you have divided a chunk of it, it has proved to be a valuable tool. Keep it handy; refer to it often.

# Appendix D

# VENEREAL DISEASE

A venereal disease is a disease spread by sexual contact. Gonorrhea and syphilis are what most people mean when they say "V.D.," but there are other diseases as well, some dangerous and others merely irritating. In this appendix we briefly describe the more common venereal diseases.

## GONORRHEA

Although gonorrhea is curable by penicillin (and other drugs for those who must not use penicillin), recently strains that are resistant to treatment have evolved. The person who treats herself with nonprescribed penicillin may use the wrong type of the drug, or may stop taking the drug before all of the organisms that cause the disease have been killed. The surviving organisms are the strongest of those that caused the infection. The disease progresses in the infected individual, who passes the hardy strain of gonorrhea on to others through sexual contact.

### Transmission of Gonorrhea

The organism that causes gonorrhea can be transmitted only through sexual intercourse, including vaginal, anal, or oral-genital intercourse. Outside of the body, it dies almost immediately. A man has a 20 to 50 per cent chance of contracting gonorrhea from one act of intercourse with an infected partner; a woman has a more than 50 per cent chance after one act of vaginal intercourse with an infected man. A woman who takes oral contraceptives has a 100 per cent chance of contracting gonorrhea from an infected man.

## Symptoms of Gonorrhea

Although many men first notice symptoms of gonorrhea within three to five days after exposure to it, about 30 per cent of men do not show symptoms. Symptoms may appear as soon as one day or as late as two weeks after exposure. When symptoms appear in the male, he first has a thin, clear discharge seeping from the opening of his penis. After a day or two the discharge becomes heavy and creamy. It is usually white but may be yellow or yellow-green. The tip of the penis becomes swollen, with the lips of the urethral opening standing out from the glans. Urination is painful or causes a burning sensation and may become difficult.

If treatment is delayed for more than a few days, the infection spreads up the urethra, and may eventually invade the prostate gland and the epididymis, or the symptoms of gonorrhea may seem to go away. If untreated, however, the man can still spread the disease to his sexual partners. The untreated man may also become sterile.

Most women who contract gonorrhea experience no symptoms at all for the first weeks or months of their disease. Before the disease is discovered, permanent damage may be done to the Fallopian tubes, causing sterility. Some women, however, do notice a change in the vaginal secretions from the normal clear or white to a yellow-green or greenish color, and may experience abdominal pain or cramping. The gonorrheal discharge is rarely noticeable unless another infection is present at the same time.

## Complications of Gonorrhea

If left untreated, gonorrhea can cause severe pain and infection in both men and women. Damage to the reproductive system is not reversible, and sterility results. In women who have had such damage, the likeliness of an ectopic pregnancy (pregnancy that occurs outside of the uterus, in the Fallopian tube or abdominal cavity) is greatly increased. Fertilization occurs in the Fallopian tubes. If the tubes are partially blocked by scar tissue from the gonorrheal infection, the fertilized egg cannot pass to the uterus and develops elsewhere instead. Eventually, the area hemorrhages and the woman experiences severe pain and internal bleeding. If she does not receive immediate medical attention, she may die.

## Treatment of Gonorrhea

The best treatment for gonorrhea is penicillin, given in injections in the buttocks, accompanied by an oral dose of penicillin [2]. For persons allergic to penicillin, other antibiotics (spectinomycin or tetracycline) are substituted [3].

## Prevention of Gonorrhea

When having sex with a partner who has other sexual partners, it is a good idea to take one or more of the following precautions against contracting gonorrhea. Washing the genitals with soap and water after coitus is recommended even when another method is also used. Urination immediately after coitus helps to flush the urethra of any germs that may have entered. It may help to drink a glass of water before intercourse, so that there is sufficient urine in the bladder to allow for this. When properly used, a condom helps to prevent the spread of gonorrhea from one partner to the other. Contraceptive creams, jellies, and foams also act to kill gonorrhea bacteria [1; 2]. If all persons used these methods of gonorrhea prevention, the disease would be wiped out in a generation [1]. Unfortunately, many people still believe that fear of V.D. will keep people chaste.

# SYPHILIS

Although syphilis is not as widespread a disease as gonorrhea, it is more serious because of the extensive damage that it can do when untreated. It may affect any of the body's organs when in the late state. The diagnosis of syphilis is difficult because symptoms at various stages resemble the symptoms of other diseases.

## Transmission of Syphilis

Syphilis is highly contagious for about the first year of the disease, if untreated. It is most commonly passed from one person to another through vaginal, anal, or oral-genital intercourse. It can travel from one partner to the other through the intact skin of the sexual organs. A man wearing a condom can contract syphilis from his partner, if the organism enters where his penis joins his body. The syphilitic rash is also highly contagious. Within a few hours after the organisms enter the body, they are carried by the bloodstream to all parts of the body.

## Stages and Symptoms of Syphilis

**Primary Syphilis.**   Around three or four weeks after exposure to syphilis (or as early as ten days or late as three months), a chancre or sore appears on the body at the point of entry of the organism. On a man it is usually on the glans of the penis, but it may be elsewhere. A woman who has had vaginal intercourse usually does not notice the chancre, since it usually develops on her cervix or vaginal walls. Many women, therefore, are not aware when they have primary syphilis unless informed by their sexual partners.

When the chancre first appears, it is a dull red bump about as large as a pea. The bump's surface becomes eroded, and the chancre becomes a dull red, open sore that may be covered by a scab. The chancre does not hurt, and does not bleed easily. It may have a rubbery pink border. If left untreated, the chancre heals by itself within one to five weeks after its appearance.

**Secondary Syphilis.**   The infected person continues to infect his sexual partners, even when symptoms do not exist. The disease usually progresses to its second stage about six months after exposure, when a skin rash develops. The rash is extremely contagious to other people. It may not be obvious or may not appear at all. Nevertheless, the syphilitic person is still able to infect others.

### Latent Syphilis

If secondary syphilis is not treated, it may become dormant or hidden for many years. About a year after the initial infection, the individual is no longer infectious to others, with one exception. A pregnant woman passes the disease to her fetus.

### Late Syphilis

A number of years after exposure, the untreated individual may develop a number of complications, including heart disease, blindness, paralysis, insanity, and other serious complications.

### Prevention and Treatment of Syphilis

The method described earlier to prevention of gonorrhea also helps to prevent transmission of syphilis [1]. A complete physical examination should be given to persons who believe that they may have syphilis. If sores or a rash exist, fluid taken from them are examined under a microscope. For years, blood tests have been given routinely to persons applying for marriage licenses in most states. Such a test is required in all but two states.

As with gonorrhea, the first choice in antibiotics to treat syphilis is penicillin (though a different type than the type used to treat gonorrhea), and the second choice is tetracycline.

## GENITAL HERPES

A painful condition called genital herpes, or herpes type II, is a disease that is closely related to herpes simplex (herpes type I), which causes cold sores. Once a herpes virus invades the human body, it remains there for the duration of the individual's life. In most people, the virus remains dormant most of the time, but for unknown reasons it may become active again.

### Transmission

The transmission of the herpes virus is not completely understood. Usually, it is probably transmitted through vaginal, oral, or anal sexual intercourse with an infected partner. However, cases of herpes have been found in persons whose only sexual partner showed no signs of having herpes. Herpes affects women more commonly than men [5].

## Symptoms

Symptoms appear within a few days after the initial invasion of the virus into the body. The initial infection tends to be more extensive and painful than subsequent occurrences, and may take two to four weeks or more to heal. In women, blisters appear most commonly on the labia, but may also appear on the clitoris, outer part of the vagina, anal area, and cervix. In men, blisters appear most commonly on the glans or shaft of the penis. The blisters rupture, forming soft, extremely painful open sores. Sores that occur on the cervix are usually painless.

When genital herpes recurs in an individual, the sores tend to be smaller, less painful, and to heal more quickly (three to 10 days). The best way to avoid recurrences of herpes is to maintain a good state of health through good nutrition and adequate rest and exercise [5].

## Treatment of Herpes

Until recently, there was no effective treatment of herpes. However, in a recent experiment, an anti-viral agent, 2-deoxy-D-glucose, cleared up the lesions of most infected subjects in 12 to 72 hours [1]. Women treated with the locally-applied drug had fewer recurrences within two years than did a control group which did not receive the drug. Because the treatment does not appear to be effective for all persons, preventing the spread of herpes is important. The infected person may wish to avoid sexual contact if it is painful. Otherwise, to avoid spreading herpes, the male partner should wear a condom during sexual intercourse if one person is infected, and oral-genital sex should be avoided.

## Dangers of Herpes

Women who have had herpes are more likely to get cervical cancer than are women who have not been infected. Women who have had herpes should therefore have a PAP smear every six months for the rest of their lives, in order to detect possible cervical cancer as early as possible.

An additional danger of herpes is severe neurological damage to fetuses of women who have herpes while pregnant. The herpes virus may pass through the placenta to affect the fetus, although additional research is needed to verify this possibility. It is known that about half of infants exposed to herpes by birth through the vagina of an infected woman will have severe neuro-muscular abnormalities or will die [5]. Therefore, women with active herpes should be delivered through Caesarian section.

# VENEREAL WARTS

Venereal warts are caused by an organism that is similar to the organism that causes common skin warts.

## Transmission

Venereal warts are usually transmitted through oral, anal, or vaginal intercourse with an infected partner, although venereal warts have been found on persons whose only sexual partner has no sign of the warts. A person who has regular sexual intercourse with an infected person has a 60 to 70 per cent chance of developing the disorder [6].

## Symptoms

Venereal warts appear three weeks to three months after exposure. The most likely site of infection for men are the glans and foreskin, meatus (opening of the penis), shaft of the penis, and scrotum, in that order. In women, the most common sites are the vaginal opening, but the labia and deep parts of the vagina may also be affected.

In moist areas, the warts are white, pink, or red and are soft. The shape is like that of a cauliflower. The warts can grow together in a tissue mass that becomes quite large. On dry skin, such as the shaft of the penis, the warts are usually small, hard, and yellow-gray, looking much like common skin warts that occur on other parts of the body. If a person with venereal warts has another infection such as vaginitis or gonorrhea, the discharge may be increased by the warts.

## Treatment

Small warts may be easily removed by applying podophyllin, an irritating substance extracted from the mandrake plant. Because podophyllin is irritating and can cause a chemical burn if left on too long, it should be washed off with soap and water after four hours. If the warts are very large, surgical removal may be necessary. To avoid transmission of warts, a condom should be used.

## OTHER VENEREAL DISEASES

Both men and women may develop irritating genital diseases that may be spread through sexual contact or other means (such as a washcloth) as well. These diseases may be confused with gonorrhea and often develop in conjunction with it. In the male, the disease is known as *urethritis* (inflammation of the urethra), and in the female, *vaginitis* (inflammation of the vagina). The affected area burns or itches, and there may be an abnormal discharge from the male's urethra or female's vagina. Females may have itching or burning sores on the clitoris, inner lips, vestibule, cervix, or vagina. Urethritis and vaginitis are caused by a number of different organisms, and treatment for the different organisms varies. Therefore, medical examination and diagnosis are essential.

# CONCLUSIONS

Venereal diseases are usually spread by sexual contact, and vary in severity from being merely annoying to causing severe injury or death. Ignorance is the biggest factor in the spread of venereal disease, which is reaching epidemic proportions. The person who believes that he or she is infected with any kind of venereal disease should seek immediate medical attention and should inform his sexual partners when a disease is confirmed. Sexual contact should be avoided until the disease is cured.

By law, all information regarding the patient's condition is kept confidential. In all states it is unlawful for authorities to inform parents that their children, minor or otherwise, have a venereal disease. Most states have free VD clinics. To find out the laws and availability of clinics in a particular state, the reader should contact the state health service.

**REFERENCES**

1. Brecher, Edward M. Women—Victims of the V.D. rip-off. *Viva,* 1973, **1**:(2), 103, 104+. (November)
2. Contraceptive cream useful in helping prevent gonorrhea. *Family Planning Perspectives,* 1977, **9**, 34.
3. Fiumara, Nicholas J. The treatment of gonococcal proctitis. *Journal of the American Medical Association,* 1978, **239**, 735–737.
4. Hatcher, R. A., G. K. Stewart, F. Stewart, F. Guest, P. Stratton, and A. H. Wright. *Contraceptive technology 1978–1979.* New York: Irvington, 1978.
5. Herpes genitalia virus type II. Storrs, Conn: University of Connecticut Women's Health Clinic. Mimeo, 1978.
6. Venereal warts (condylomata acuminata). Storrs, Conn.: University of Connecticut Women's Health Clinic. Mimeo, 1978.

# appendix E

# glossary

**Adolescence**—Socially defined time of life, beginning with a biological event (pubescence) but ending when adulthood begins.

**Ambisexual**—See bisexual.

**Ampulla**—Enlargement in vas deferens in which sperm are stored.

**Annulment (of marriage)**—Declaration by the court or church that a valid marriage between two particular persons never existed.

**Assortative mating**—Formation of couples according to certain principles of selection.

**Attachment**—An enduring tendency to seek the presence of and to make and keep contact with a particular other.

**Basic conflict**—Conflict over basic values.

**Behavioral modification**—The gradual changing of response patterns through the planned use of reinforcements.

**Bisexual**—An individual who is sexually attracted to members of both sexes.

**Bond**—A tie that exists when a value of the individual is felt by him to be fostered by association or interaction with another person or group.

**Career**—An individual's or group's forward movement in time in certain activities and/or relationships, such as the occupational career, the marital career, and the parent-child career.

**Career set**—The total picture of a person's involvement with her various careers at a given moment.

**Caste**—Unit of stratification in a society wherein individual mobility is not allowed.

**Cervix**—End of the uterus that opens during the labor process.

**Chromosome**—A body within the cell carrying the material of heredity. Each egg and each sperm carries twenty-three chromosomes.

**Circumcision**—Surgical removal of the foreskin on the penis (or on the clitoris, in the case of the female).

**509**

**Class**—Unit of stratification in a society in which individual mobility is allowed.

**Climacteric**—See menopause.

**Clitoris**—The female homolog of the penis; the most sensitive part of female anatomy.

**Cohabitation**—The state of an unmarried, heterosexual couple sharing a bedroom.

**Coitus**—Sexual intercourse.

**Co-marital sex**—Extramarital sexual relationships based on mutual agreement of spouses.

**Communication**—The sending and receiving of messages in a social context through the use of words and nonverbal behavior.

**Congruent message**—A message conveyed through the use of words and nonverbal cues, both of which give the receiver the same meaning.

**Conjugal family**—Nuclear family in which the husband-wife relationship is of primary importance.

**Connotative meaning**—The implied meaning of a word; its emotional overtones.

**Consanguine family**—Family held together by "blood" ties.

**Control**—The setting of limits; curtailing child's autonomy; demanding compliance.

**Correlation**—When two conditions or events vary together.

    **Positive correlation**—When one variable increases, so does the other.

    **Negative correlation**—When one variable increases, the other decreases.

**Courtship**—A sequence of heterosexual interactions oriented toward marriage.

**Couvade**—Practice among some peoples in which a man, preceding the birth of his child, imitates the mother's pregnancy, the birth of the child and recovery from giving birth. He complains of, and probably experiences, labor pains.

**Crescive bond**—A growing bond.

**Crisis**—That which occurs when a sudden, highly significant change produces a situation that cannot be handled effectively.

**Dating**—Heterosexual social interaction entered into for one or more of the following purposes: fun, recreation, self-development, mutual exploration, status-enhancement, exploitation, sex, and mate selection.

**Demographic information**—Vital statistics, such as birthdate, place of birth, marital status, nationality of parents.

**Denotative meaning**—The meaning of a word as defined in the dictionary, devoid of emotional overtones.

**Divorce rate**—The number of divorces per 1000 persons.

**Embryo**—The unborn individual, prior to the eighth week after conception.

**Empathy**—Ability to accurately perceive another's feelings, without forgetting that the feelings are the other's and not one's own.

**Epididymis**—Collection tube, located in the testis, through which sperm pass after they are produced in the seminiferous tubules.

**Ethnic group**—A group of persons who share a culture.

**Exchange orientation**—A concern with keeping an even balance of give-and-take in a relationship.

**Extended family**—A family consisting of two or more nuclear units living in one home.

**Fallopian tubes**—Tubes through which ova pass from the ovaries to the uterus.

**Family career**—A set of family interactions and experiences that move forward in time, each career having a beginning and an ending.

**Family development**—The changes that take place in a nuclear family during the span of its existence. The changes that take place as a family continues, generation after generation.

**Family life cycle**—Processes of family development that repeat in one generation after another.

**Family of origin**—The family consisting of an individual's parents and siblings.

**Family of procreation**—The family consisting of an individual's spouse and children.

**Fecund**—Capable of producing children.

**Fetus**—The unborn individual, from the eighth week after conception until birth.

**Foreskin**—Loose ring of skin covering the glans of an uncircumcized penis (or clitoris, in the case of the female).

**Gender identity**—The conviction that one is a boy (man) or girl (woman).

**Gender role**—Behavior patterns that are culturally acceptable as sex-appropriate.

**Gene**—The functional unit of heredity, a segment of a chromosome.

**Generativity**—An investment of oneself and one's resources in the development of the next generation; a caring for ongoing creativity.

**Genitalia**—Sex organs.

**Glans**—The knob-like head of the clitoris, in the case of the female, or penis, in the case of the male.

**Gonads**—Sex glands (see also *ovary, testis*).

**Heterosexual**—An individual who is attracted to and possibly has sexual relations with members of the opposite sex.

**Homogamy**—Like marrying like.

**Homosexual**—An individual who is attracted to and possibly has sexual relations with only members of the same sex.

**Hymen**—Fold of tissue partly or completely sealing the vagina of most virgins.

**Incongruent message**—A verbal message accompanied by nonverbal cues that do not give the same meaning.

**Infant**—The human young from birth to two years of age.

**In love**—Includes feelings that accompany attachment behavior, efforts to attain and keep proximity to the loved one, and sexual response.

**Kin**—Relatives, both "blood" relatives and those acquired through marriage or legal adoption.

**Kinship web**—The particular pattern of connections with kin that each nuclear unit establishes and maintains.

**Labia majora**—Outer lips of the vulva.

**Labia minora**—Inner lips of the vulva, joining at the clitoris.

**Legal separation**—Agreement, affirmed by a court, for a married couple to live apart under specified conditions.

**Lesbian**—Female homosexual.

**Lifetime family**—A family consisting of one set of members who advance through their family life careers, without cycles and without repetitions.

**Lineage family**—The family over generations.

**Management**—The setting of goals and the process of organizing, directing, and using resources in order to reach those goals.

**Market income**—Barter and cash.

**Masturbation**—Sexual stimulation, usually referring to self-stimulation.

**Matrilineal family**—Family headed by a female; descent is traced through the female line.

**Median**—The number that divides a group such that half of the scores fall above it, and half below it.

**Menarche**—First menstruation.

**Menopause**—Cessation of menstruation.

**Menstruation**—Sloughing off of blood-rich uterine lining.

**Mons veneris**—Small mound of fatty tissue over the pubic bone.

**Natural childbirth**—Giving birth with understanding of and in harmony with natural bodily processes. Also called prepared childbirth.

**Negative reinforcement**—An event followed by a response that terminates the event or that makes its recurrence less likely.

**Nuclear family**—Father, mother, and children.

**Nurturant socialization**—Care and teaching of another (usually an infant or child) that nurtures. The implication of nurturant socialization is love.

**Nurture**—To promote the development of, by providing nourishment, support, encouragement, and so forth.

**Orgasm**—Peak of sexual excitement.

**Ovaries**—Female gonads that produce ova in the mature female before menopause and hormones through her lifetime.

**Oviducts**—See Fallopian tubes.

**Ovulation**—Release of an ovum by the ovary.

**Ovum** (*plural* ova)—Egg, female sex cell.

**Pair-bond**—Special kind of attachment between two people who sees themselves as a couple.

**Partnership love**—A mutual love, consisting of being in love, care, responsibility, respect, and knowledge.

**Patrilineal family**—Family, headed by a male; descent is traced through the male line.

**Penis**—Male sex organ.

**Polyandry**—Marriage of one woman to more than one man.

**Polygamy**—Marriage of one individual to more than one spouse. (See also *polyandry* and *polygyny*.)

**Polygyny**—Marriage of one man to more than one woman.

**Positive reinforcement**—An event that increases the probability that a certain response will recur.

**Prenatal**—Before birth.

**Propinquity**—Closeness in terms of space. When applied to partner selection, it means people tend to marry those who live close to them.

**Prostate gland**—A gland surrounding the neck of the bladder and urethra in the male.

**Puberty**—Period of development at which sexual maturity is reached.

**Puberty rites**—Ceremonies that mark the passage from child to adult status.

**Pubescence**—Series of bodily changes preceding puberty, lasting about two years.

**Punishment**—That event that makes a person hurt or unhappy.

**Quickening**—The first movement of the fetus that is felt by the pregnant woman.

**Real income**—Goods, services, fringe benefits, wages, interest, profits, and social income.

**Reconstituted family**—A family of which at least one member was previously married to someone else.

**Rite de passage**—Ceremony that marks an important period or change in a person's life.

**Role**—Behavior expected of a person who occupies a position. Roles are reciprocal (mother-daughter), and an individual has many roles (mother, teacher, wage-earner, friend, daughter, etc.).

**Romantic love**—Love based on a complex of beliefs, attitudes, and values including mystery, uniqueness, influence of fate, beauty, symbols, and jealousy.

**Scrotum**—Loose sack of skin located behind the penis and containing the testes.

**Semen**—Sperm-containing fluid.

**Seminal vesicles**—Paired structures opening into the urethra in the male.

**Sense of integrity**—Feeling of belonging in time and space, and in one's personal and social relationships; a conviction that one's life is meaningful, and an absence of any strong desire to have lived it differently.

**Sense of intimacy**—The capacity for knowing another person deeply and allowing oneself to be known deeply in a mutual relationship.

**Sexually open marriage**—Marriage of individuals who grant each other permission to have sexual and emotional relationships with others.

**Sibling**—Brother or sister.

**Social income**—Facilities provided by the community or environment, such as parks, schools, police protection, libraries.

**Socialization**—The process of learning a society's culture: values, behaviors, attitudes, knowledge, skills.

**Sperm**—Male sex cells.

**Spousefree parent**—An unmarried person who chooses to become a parent.

**Status, ascribed**—A status that a person acquires by right, as opposed to earning it. A child born to a king is a prince or princess. By contrast, one must earn the nonascribed status of doctor.

**Structure of a family**—Pattern of positions and roles in the family.

**Sympathy**—"Feeling with" another person; feeling the same as another, and (in contrast to *empathy*) not recognizing a difference between the feelings of other and self.

**Testis** (*plural:* **Testes**)—Male gonad or sex gland that produces both sperm and hormones.

**Testosterone**—A hormone produced by the testes in males, and by the adrenal gland in both sexes. It is the predominantly male hormone.

**Urethra**—Passageway from the bladder to the urethral opening, conducting urine in both female and male. In the male, the urethra also carries semen.

**Uterus**—The hollow organ in the female in which the young develops during gestation.

**Vagina**—Female organ of sexual intercourse; also *birth canal.*

**Vas deferens** (*plural:* **vasa deferentia**)—Tubes that carry the sperm from the testes to the base of the penis.

**Vestibule**—Area between the clitoris and the vaginal opening.

**Virgin**—A male or female not experienced in having coitus.

**Vulva**—External female sex organ, consisting of the mons veneris, labia minora and majora, clitoris, vestibule, and vaginal opening.

**Wet dream**—Ejaculation of semen during sleep.

# AUTHOR index

Entries in *italics* refer to pages on which bibliographic references are given.

Abbey, Edward, 446, *482*
Abrahams, Barbara, 135, *148*
Ackerman, Nathan W., 430, *452*
Adams, Bert N., 358, *361*
Adams, Gerald R., 176, *182*
Ademowore, Adebayo S., 396, *417*
Adler, Alfred, 374, *388*
Ainsworth, Mary D. Salter, 27, 29, 47, 48, 400, *417*
Alan Guttmacher Institute, 315, 316, *330*, 398, *417*
Albin, Rochelle, 278, *292*, 314, *329*
Aldous, Joan, 85, *115*
Aldridge, Delores, 266, *292*
Aleksandrowicz, Malca K., 340, *361*
Alexander, Jannette, 327, *330*
Allan, Graham, 370, 373, *388*
Almquist, Elizabeth M., 230, *256*
Ames, E. W., 8, *22*
Anderson, E., 345, *361*
Anderson, Peggy, 137, *148*
Anderson, Scott, 215, 216, 218, *225*
Anderson, W., 37, *47*
Andrisani, Paul J., 237, *256*
Anspach, Delores, 280, *292*
Anspach, Donald F., 370, *390*
Apoko, Anna, 372, *388*
Arceo, Rosalina, 105, *116*
Archer, Dale, 56, *75*
Ard, Ben N., Jr., 68, *75*
Arena, Jay M., 408, *417*
Argyle, Michael, 55, *75*
Arney, William Ray, 112, *115*
Avery, Arthur W., 216, *225*

Bach, George, 69, *75*
Bagford, Jeffrey, 162, *183*
Bahr, Howard, 429, *453*
Bain, Joyce K., 309, *330*
Bakan, David, 90, *115*
Bales, Robert, 196, *225*
Balswick, Jack O., 121, *149*
Bane, Mary Jo, 273, *292*
Barber, Kenneth E., 266, *292*
Bartell, Gilbert, 468, *482*
Barton, K., 308, *330*, 344, *362*
Bauman, Karl E., 126, 127, *150*
Baumrind, Diana, 348, *361*
Bayer, Alan, 262, *292*
Beach, Frank A., 13, *22*, 25, 47, 94, 95, *115*, 118, 129, *148*
Beckman, Linda J., 301, *329*
Beckwith, Leila, 353, *361*, 367, *389*
Bell, Alan P., 144, *148*
Bell, Robert R., 127, 130, *148*, 209, *223*
Benedict, Robert, 359, *361*, 415, *417*, 443, 444, 451, *452*
Berardo, Felix, 429, *452*
Berg, Alan, 412, *417*
Berger, Bennet, 466–68, *482*
Berger, David, 209, *223*
Berger, Stephen, 372, *391*
Bernard, Jessie, 212, *223*, 285, 286, *292*
Bernstein, Barton E., 217, *223*
Berscheid, Ellen, 176, 177, *182*
Bigner, Jerry J., 369, 373, *389*
Bild, Bernice R., 440, *452*
Biller, Henry B., 84, 85, *115*, 349, 354, *361*
Birdwhistell, Ray L., 51, 61, *75*

Block, Jean L., 237, 238, *363*
Block, Jeanne Humphrey, 80, *115*
Blood, Robert O., 162, *182*, 196, 208, *220*, *223*
Bock, E. Wilbur, 220, *223*, 429, *452*
Bohannon, Paul, 269, 280, 288, 290, *292*
Bohn, Claudia J., 307, 310, *329*
Boll, Eleanor S., 368, 372, *389*
Bolton, Charles D., 181, *183*
Bonham, Gordon Scott, 122, *148*, 313, *329*
Borstelmann, L. J., 356, *361*
Bortner, R. W., 307, 310, *329*
Bossard, James H. S., 368, 372, *389*
Boston Woman's Health Book Collective, 132, *148*
Bould, Sally, 317, *329*
Bower, Donald W., 217, 218, *223*, 381, *389*
Bowlby, John, 27, *47*
Boyd, Rosamonde R., 377, *389*
Brecher, Edward, 468, *482*
Breland, Hunter M., 367, *389*
Brew, James D., 341, *361*
Brickman, Philip, 350, *363*
Briggs, Kenneth, 202, *223*
Brinkerhoff, David B., 206, 212, *223*
Britton, James, 65, *75*
Bromley, D. B., 440, *452*
Brown, Charles T., 55, *75*
Brown, Terry, 317, *331*
Brownfield, E. Dorothy, 62, *75*
Bruce, John A., 153, *183*
Brucken, Laura, 83, *116*
Bryan, James H., 350, *361*, *363*
Bryson, Heff B., 235, *256*
Bryson, Rebecca, 235, *256*
Bundy, C., 354, *363*
Bureau of the Census. *See* U.S. Bureau of the Census
Burchinal, Lee G., 266, *292*
Burgess, Ernest, 186, 208, *223*
Burgess, Robert L., 345, *361*
Burke, Ronald J., 196, 207, 210, *223*
Burr, Wesley R., 309, *329*
Bursk, Barbara, 442, *453*
Bush, Sherida, 347, *361*
Busse, Pauline, 348, *362*
Busse, Thomas V., 348, *362*
Butler, Edgar W., 438, *453*
Butterworth, Charles E., 108, *115*
Byrne, Donn, 38, *47*

Califano, Joseph A., Jr., 392, *417*
Callwood, June, 204, *226*

Cameron, Catherine, 157, *183*
Cannon, Drew, 162, *183*
Cannon, Kenneth L., 309, *331*
Capel, William C., 440, *452*
Capellanus, Andreas, 39, *47*
Capetta, Marlene, 261, *293*
Caplan, Gerald, 430, *452*
Carlier, Auguste, 39, *47*
Carter, Linda Mittelset, 219, 220, *226*
Cattell, R. B., 308, *330*, 344, *362*
Census. *See* U.S. Bureau of the Census
Centers, Richard, 195, *225*
Cerreto, Mary, 193, *225*
Chancellor, L. E., 266, *292*
Chaskes, Jay, 127, *148*
Chernovetz, Mary E., 367, *389*
Chesser, Eustace, 145, *148*
Cheung, Y. M., 142, *148*
Chilman, Catherine S., 85, *116*, 124, 125, 127, 142, *148*, 396, 414, *417*
Christensen, Harold, 120, 128, *148*, 209, *223*, 262, 263, *292*
Christopherson, Victor, 217, *223*, 381, *389*, 432, *452*
Cicirelli, Victor G., 371, *389*
Clar, June S., 440, *452*
Clark, Alma B., 381, *389*
Clatworthy, N. M., 219, *223*
Clayton, Richard R., 216, *223*
Cohen, Jerome, 254, *256*, 327, *330*
Cohen, Sarale E., 367, *389*
Cole, Charles, 468, *482*
Coleman, Daniel, 428, *453*
Coles, Robert, 19, *22*
Collard, Roberta R., 375, *389*
Collins, John K., 164, *183*
Conger, Rand D., 345, *361*
Connor, Jane M., 88, *115*
Consortium on Developmental Continuity, 450, *452*
Constantine, Joan M., 10, *22*, 468, 475, *482*
Constantine, Larry L., 10, *22*, 468, 475, *482*
Constantian, Carol A., 358, *363*
Conte, Hope, 38, *47*
Cooper, Pamela E., 319, *329*
Corrales, Ramon, 65, *75*
Corsini, David A., 354, *363*
Coursin, David, 396, *417*
Coward, Raymond T., 357, *362*
Cox, Martha, 277–79, 289, *293*
Cox, Roger, 277–79, 289, *293*
Crandall, Elizabeth W., 244, 246, *256*
Crawford, Susan Heffernan, 112, *116*

Cromwell, Richard E., 412, *417*
Crouse, Bryant, 266, *292*
Cuber, John F., 69, *75,* 187, *223*
Cumber, Barbara, 319, *329*
Curtis, Russell L., 290, *294*
Cutright, Phillips, 113, *115,* 264, *292,* 320, *330*

Dairy Council, 399, 405, *417*
Datan, Nancy, 83, *117*
Davis, Keith E., 218, *225*
Davis, Kingsley, 191, *223*
Davis, Peter, 128, *148*
Dawson, John L. M., 142, *148*
Day, Beth, 267, *292*
DeFee, John F., 367, *389*
deLissovoy, Vladimir, 262, *292*
Demos, John, 356, *362*
Denfield, Duane, 468, *482*
Deutsch, Morton, 268, 269, 284, *293*
Dickinson, George E., 162, 166, *183*
Dielman, T. E., 308, *330,* 344, *362*
DiMatteao, M. Robin, 56, *75*
Dion, Karen, 176, 177, *182*
Dobrin, Arthur, 202, *223*
Doran, Louise, 112, *116*
Doten, Dana, 160, *183*
Douvan, Elizabeth, 212, *223*
Duberman, Lucile, 286, 288, 290, *292*
Dubos, René, 392, 394, *417*
Dullea, Georgia, 273, *292*
Dunlap, William R., 437, *452*
Dunsing, Marilyn M., 243, *256*
Dutton, Diana B., 402, *418*
Duvall, Evelyn M., 15, *22,* 380, *389*

Edwards, Maxine, 468, 474, *482*
Ehrhardt, Anke A., 83, *116*
Ehrlich, Carol, 209, *223*
Eiduson, Bernice T., 327, *330*
Elder, Joanne F., 371, *389*
Elgin, Duane, 464, *483*
Ellis, Godfrey, 356, *362*
Erickson, Rosemary, 288, 290, *292*
Erikson, Erik H., 31, 33, 34, *47,* 123, *148,* 379, *389,* 441, *453*
Estellechild, Vivian, 467, *483*

Fagot, Beverly I., 83, *115*
Farber, Bernard, 373, 383, *389*
Farley, Frank H., 367, *390*
Farrell, Warren T., 89, 105, *115*
Fein, Ellen, 85, *115*

Feinman, Saul, 176, *183*
Feldberg, Roslyn, 277, 278, *292*
Feldman, Harold, 15, *22,* 208, 219, *224,* 309, 310, *330, 331,* 398, *417*
Feldman, Margaret, 15, *22,* 208, 219, *224,* 310, *330,* 398, *417*
Feldman, S. Shirley, 135, *148*
Ferguson, Dennis, 317, *331*
Ferrell, Marcia M., 79, *116*
Field, Sheila, 212, *224*
Field, Tiffany, 29, *47*
Figley, Charles R., 309, *330,* 358, *362*
Fish, K. D., 85, *115*
Fisher, Esther Oshiver, 278, *292*
Fisher, Peter, 145, *148*
Ford, Clellan, 13, *22,* 94, *115,* 118, 129, *148*
Fotheringham, John B., 438, *453*
Fox, Elizabeth M., 277, 278, *292*
Fox, Sandra S., 431, *453*
Francis, Ronald D., 164, *183*
Franck, Phyllis, 415, *417*
Freedman, Eric M., 172, *184*
Friedan, Betty, 136, *148,* 317, *330*
Frisch, Rose E., 93, *115,* 397, *417*
Fromm, Erich, 29, 30, 33, *47*
Furstenberg, Frank, Jr., 112, *115,* 159, *183,* 263, *292*

Galat, Joanne P., 87, *116*
Gallese, Liz R., 476, *483*
Gambarino, James, 346, *362*
Gangel, Joan L., 412, *417*
Gary, J., 356, *362*
Gasser, Rita D., 317, *330*
Gauger, William, 246, *256*
Gebhard, Paul H., 99, *116,* 125, 127, 129, *149*
Gelles, Richard, 345, *362*
Gibran, Kahlil, 45, *47*
Gibson, Geoffrey, 384, *389*
Gifford-Jones, W., 131, *148*
Gil, David G., 345, *362*
Gill, George W., 176, *183*
Gilmartin, B. G., 468, *483*
Gitman, Lawrence J., 251–53, *256*
Glass, Shirley, P., 209, *224*
Glasser, Paul, 449, *454*
Glenn, Norval D., 177, *184,* 210, 219, *224,* 286, *292,* 309, *330*
Glick, Paul C., 5, *22,* 215, 216, *224,* 261– 62, 264–66, 285–86, *293*
Goldsmith, Bernard, 440, *452*
Goode, William, 279, *293*

Gordon, Albert I., 173, *183*
Gordon, Michael, 39, *47*
Gottlieb, David, 433, *453*
Gould, Robert E., 141–43, *149*
Gottman, John, 56, *75*
Green, Richard, 120, 134, *149*
Greenblatt, Susan L., 196, *226*
Greenfield, Josh, 437, *453*
Gregg, Christina, 120, *148*, 208, *223*
Griffitt, William, 38, *47*
Groeneveld, Lyle Peter, 113, *115*
Gross, Irma H., 244, 246, *256*
Guest, F., 103, 106, 108–110, *115*
Gurin, Gerald, 212, *224*
Gusdorf, Georges, 52, *75*

Haan, Norma, 349, *362*
Hackett, Bruce, 466–69, *482*
Haertig, E. W., 394, *418*, 430, *454*
Hainline, Louise, 85, *115*
Haley, Jay, 52, *75*
Hall, Judith A., 56, *75*
Halstrom, Jeanne L., 243, *256*
Hamblin, Robert, 196, 208, *223*
Handler, Philip, 406, *417*
Hansen, Sally, 162, *183*
Harroff, Peggy B., 69, *75*, 187, *223*
Harry, Joseph, 213, *224*
Hart, Diana S., 415, *417*
Hartner, Robin, 319, *329*
Harvey, Carol D., 429, *453*
Hatcher, Robert A., 103, 106, 108, *115*
Havemann, Ernest, 102, *115*
Havighurst, Robert J., 18, *22*, 440, *452*
Hawkins, James, 71, *75*, 212, *224*
Hayghe, Howard, 234, *256*
Hays, William C., 378, *389*
Heath, Douglas H., 308, *330*
Heath, Linda L., 309, *330*
Heckman, Norma A., 235, *256*
Heer, David, 196, *224*
Hefner, Robert, 88, *115*
Heinsohn, Anne, 433, *453*
Hendershot, Gerry E., 393, *418*
Henshell, Anne-Marie, 468, *483*
Herzog, Elizabeth, 446, 448, *453*
Hess, Beth, 444, *453*
Hetherington, E. Mavis, 85, *115, 277, 278,*
    282, 287, 289, *293*
Hetzel, Alice, 261, *293*
Hickey, Louise A., 379, *389*
Hickey, Tom, 379, *389*

Hicks, Mary, 206–208, *224*
Hill, Carles T., 171, 172, *183*
Hill, Reuben, 307, *330, 360, 362, 381, 389,*
    420, 422, *453*
Hillsdale, Paul, 170, *183*
Himelstein, Philip, 367, *389*
Hobart, Charles, 71, *75*
Hoddinott, Bernard A., 438, *453*
Hoffman, Lois W., 307, *330*
Hogan, Robert, 29, *48*
Hole, Judith, 135, *149*
Hollingshead, August B., 172, *183*
Hollinsworth, J. Selwyn, 437, *452*
Holstrom, Lynda Lytle, 235, *256*
Hopkins, Jane, 235, *256*
Hornick, Joseph, 112, *116*, 127, *149*
Horst, Leslie, 349, *362*
Horton, Patricia, 349, *362*
Hotchner, Tracy, 341, *362*
Houseknecht, Sharon, 319, *330*
Howard, David, 209, *224*
Hughston, George A., 208, *226*
Hugins, William, 349, *362*
Hultsch, David F., 307, *329*
Hunt, Bernice, 265, 268–70, 279–82, 286,
    *293*
Hunt, David, 356, *362*
Hunt, Janet G., 85, *116*
Hunt, Morton M., 130, *149*, 233, 236–39,
    *256*, 265, 268–70, 279–82, 286, *293*
Hurley, Lucille S., 398, *418*
Hutt, Corinne, 79, *116*, 134, *149*
Hutt, S. J., 134, *149*
Hyatt, James C., 260, *293*

Ibsen, Charles A., 387, *390*
Igelhard, Alfreda, 238, *256*
Illsley, Raymond, 297, *330*
Institute for Educational Leadership, 14, *22*
Internal Revenue Service, 272, *293*

Jackson, Don, 63, *75*, 192, *224*
Jackson, Jacqueline J., 196, *224, 360, 362*
Jacob, Theodore, 196, *224*
Jankowski, Joseph J., 353, *364*
Johnson, Colleen L., 196, *224, 385, 390*
Johnson, Elizabeth S., 442, *453*
Johnson, Joyce S., 212, *225*
Johnson, Leanor B., 128, *148*
Johnson, Virginia, 97–100, *116*, 125, 131,
    133, 145, *149*
Jolly, Alison, 5, *22, 25, 47, 57, 75*

Jones, Elise F., 112, 113, *117*
Jones, Stella, 432, 433, *453*
Jones, Warren H., 367, *389*

Kafka, John S., 153, *183*
Kahana, Boas, 378, *390*
Kahana, Eva, 378, *390*
Kahn, Alfred J., 8, *22*
Kalish, Richard, 379, *389*
Kannin, Eugene, 209, *224*
Kanter, Rosabeth Moss, 207, 214, *224*
Kantner, John F., 112, *117*, 122, 127, *150*
Kaplan, Helen Singer, 97, 98, 100, *116*, 133, *149*
Karlins, Marvin, 266, *292*
Karlson, Georg, 71, *75*
Katz, Robert, 62, *75*
Kearney, Helen K., 344, *362*
Keller, Helen, 50, *75*
Kelly, Joan B., 273, 283, *294*
Kempster, Stephen W., 430, *452*
Keniston, Kenneth, 448, *453*
Kennedy, Edward M., 414, *418*
Kennedy, Judith R., 164, *183*
Kennell, John H., 27, *47*
Kent, Ronald N., 87, *116*
Kephart, William, 467, *483*
Kerckhoff, Florence, 357, *362*
Kertesz, Andrew, 287, 289, *294*
Keshet, Harry F., 287, 289, *294*
Khatri, A. A., 8, *22*
King, Charles D., 309, *330*
King, Karl, 121, *149*
Kinsey, Alfred C., 99, *116*, 125, 127, 129–31, 140, 143, *149*
Kinzer, Nora S., 304, *330*
Klaus, Marshall H., 27, *47*
Klausner, William, 71, *75*
Klobus, Patricia, 387, *390*
Knapp, Jacqueline J., 469, *483*
Knapp, Martin R., 440, *453*
Knight, Aldrich C., 433, *453*
Knoll, Marjorie M., 244, 246, *256*
Knox, David, 320, *330*
Kobrin, Frances E., 393, *418*
Koch, Helen, 369, *390*
Koenig, Peter, 466, *483*
Kogan, Benjamin, 142, 146, *149*
Kohen, Janet, 277, 278, *292*
Kohlberg, Lawrence, 349, *362*
Komarovsky, Mirra, 71, *75*
Krain, Mark, 162, *183*

Krantzler, Mel, 277, 278, *293*
Kressel, Kenneth, 268, 269, 284, *293*
Krogman, Wilton M., 402, *418*
Kübler-Ross, Elisabeth, 428, *453*
Kuhn, Deanna, 83, *116*

Lamb, Michael E., 370, *390*
Lambo, Thomas A., 394, *418*, 430, *453*
Landis, Judson, 380, 382, *390*, 432, *453*
Landis, Mary G., 380, 382, *390*
Lane, Mary E., 105, *116*
Langer, J. W., 112, *116*
Langer, Jonas, 349, *362*
Lau, T. S., 142, *148*
LaVoie, Joseph C., 349, *362*
Lawler, Edward E., 242, *256*
Lawrence, Edwin A., 267, *294*
Laws, Judith Long, 206, *224*
Lederer, William J., 63, *75*, 192, *224*
Lee, Catherine A., 394, *418*
Lee, Gary R., 219, 220, *224*, 262, *293*
Lee, Patrick C., 86, *116*
Lee, R., 356, *362*
Lei, Tzuen-Jen, 438, *453*
Lenneborg, Patricia W., 371, *390*
Leon, Joseph J., 173, *183*
Levin, Amy, 128, 130, *149*
Levin, Robert J., 128, 130, *149*, 210, *224*, 468, *483*
Levine, Ellen, 135, *149*
Levinger, George, 212, *224*, 265, *293*
Levinson, Daniel J., 463, *483*
Liberman, David, 372, *391*
Lifton, Robert Jay, 434, *453*
Lindemann, Eric, 428, *453*
Lipetz, Milton, 218, *225*
Lipman, A., 220, *224*
Lobsenz, Norman, 216, *224*
Locke, Harvey J., 71, *75*, 187, *223*, 266, 286, *293*
Loeb, Roger C., 349, *362*
Lofas, Jeanette, 290, *294*
Lonner, Thomas D., 16, *23*
Looft, William R., 349, *362*
Lopata, Helena Z., 233, *256*, 385, *390*, 429, *453*
Lorenz, Konrad Z., 25, *47*
Lott, Bernice E., 83, *116*, 139, *149*, 303, *330*
Lozoff, Marjorie, 127, *149*, 165, *183*
Luckey, Eleanore B., 208, *225*, 309, *330*
Lyness, Judith, 218, *225*

McAdams, Diana C., 290, *294*
McAdoo, Harriette P., 230, *256*, 385, *390*
McAllister, Ronald J., 438, *453*
Mace, David R., 480, *483*
Mace, Vera, 480, *483*
McClain, Duane, 157, *184*
McClelland, David C., 358, *363*
McDonald, Corbett, 325, *330*
MacDonald, Marcia G., 193, *225*
McGlone, Jeanette, 80, *116*
Mack, Delores, 196, *225*
McKain, Jerry Lavin, 433, *454*
McKain, Walter, 265, *293*
McKeown, Thomas, 410, *418*
MacKinnon, Fred R., 475, *483*
Macklin, Eleanor D., 172, *183*, 217–19, *225*
McNair, J., 354, *363*
Madsen, C., 67, *75*
Main, Jeremy, 476, *483*
Marciano, Teresa Donati, 319, *330*
Marcus, Terri L., 354, *363*
Marini, Margaret Mooney, 210, *225*
Markham, Howard, 56, *75*
Marquis, R., 354, *363*
Martin, Clyde E., 99, *116*, 125, 127, 129–31, 140, 143, *149*
Martin, Patricia Yancey, 139, *149*
Maslow, Abraham, 185, *225*, 463, *483*
Masters, William, 97–100, *116*, 125, 131, 133, 145, *149*
Mathes, Eugene W., 176, *183*
Mayo, Julia, 137, *149*
Mead, Margaret, 41, *47*, 152, *183*, 194, *225*, 336, *363*, 377, 380, *390*
Mead, Robert D., 307, *330*
Mealiea, Wallace D., 367, *390*
Mehrabian, A., 54, 58, *76*
Meissner, Hanna M., 262, 263, *292*
Melton, Alfred, 97, *116*
Melton, Willie, 174, *183*
Mendes, Helen A., 277, *293*
Mendkoff, Ethel, 433, *453*
Menken, Jane, 113, *117*
Messinger, Lillian, 288, *293*
Metropolitan Life Insurance Company, 298, *330*, 376, *390*, 405, 406, *418*
Midlarsky, Elizabeth, 350, *363*
Millar, Mervyn, 466–68, *482*
Miller, Arthur A., 279, *293*
Miller, Brent C., 127, *150*
Miller, Celia E., 319, *330*
Miller, Daniel, 231, *256*

Miller, Sherod, 65, 68, *75*
Mills, Nancy, 412, *418*
Mindel, Charles H., 378, *389*
Minuchin, Salvador, 430, *454*
Mitchell, Arnold, 464, *483*
Mitchell, Edna, 87, *116*
Molinoff, Daniel D., 278, 289, *293*
Monahan, Thomas P., 264, 267, *293*
Money, John, 83, *116*
Monroe, Robert A., 428, *454*
Montemayor, Raymond, 65, *75*
Montgomery, James, 219, 220, *226*
Moody, Raymond A., Jr., 428, *454*
Moore, Kristin A., 317, *330*
Morgan, Edmund S., 40, *47*
Morris, Naomi M., 126, 127, *150*
Moskin, J. Robert, 326, *331*
Mueller, Charles W., 265, *293*, *294*
Murdock, George P., 14, *22*
Murstein, Bernard, 33, *47*, 153, 175, 177, *183*
Myers, Judith A., 357, *362*
Myricks, Noel, 271, *293*

Nash, Sharon C., 83, *116*, 135, *148*
Navran, Leslie, 71, *75*
Neugarten, Bernice L., 378, *390*, 440, *454*
Newton, Niles, 336, *363*
Nichols, William C., 202, *225*
Nobles, Wade W., 387, *390*
Nolan, John D., 87, *116*
Noller, P., 71, *76*
Norton, Arthur J., 5, *22*, 215, 216, *224*, 258, 261–62, 264–65, 285, 286, *293*
Notarious, Cliff, 56, *75*
Nye, F. Ivan, 472, *483*

O'Connor, Pamela, 207, *226*
Ohms, JoAnne S., 317, *331*, 396, 411, 414, *418*
O'Leary, Daniel, 87, *116*
Oleshansky, Barbara, 88, *115*
Olive, Helen, 368, *390*
Olson, David, 153, *183*, 193, *225*
O'Neill, George, 469, *483*
O'Neill, Nena, 469, *483*
Oppong, Christine, 16, *22*, 242, *256*
Orthner, Dennis, 211, *225*, 277, 278, *294*, 317, *331*
Oskamp, Stuart, 157, *183*
Osmond, Marie Withers, 139, *149*

Paddock, Elizabeth, 455, *483*
Paddock, William, 455, *483*

Palson, Charles, 468, *483*
Palson, Rebecca, 468, *483*
Pam, Alvin, 38, *47*
Parelius, Ann P., 120, 127, 139, *149*
Parke, Ross D., 29, *47, 73, 76,* 339, 343, *363*
Parkes, C. Murray, 429, *454*
Parson, Talcott, 196, *225*
Patterson, G. R., 83, 86, *115*
Patty, Rosemarie A., 79, *116*
Paulsen, David G., 203, *226*
Pearlin, Leonard I., 212, *225*
Perlman, Daniel, 120, *149*
Pedersen, Frank A., 353, *364*
Peplau, Letitia A., 171, 172, *183*
Peterman, Dan J., 215, 216, 218, *225*
Peters, Samuel, 160, *183*
Petersen, Larry R., 356, *362*
Plateris, Alexander, 267, *294*
Platt, Marilyn, 206–208, *224*
Pleck, Joseph, 207, *226*
Plutchik, Robert, 38, *47*
Polit, Denise F., 298, *331*
Pomeroy, Wardell B., 99, *106,* 125, 127, 129–31, 140, 143, *149*
Pope, Hallowell, 265, *293, 294*
Porter, Gwendolyn H., 480, *483*
Prabhu, Pandharinath H., 42, *47*
Pratt, Lois, 196, 206, 210, *225,* 403, *418*
Prentice, Norman M., 349, *362*
Pringle, Bruce M., 480, *483*
Pukui, Mary K., 394, *418,* 430, *454*
Pytkowicz, Ann S., 354, *363*

Radin, Norma, 449, *454*
Radl, Shirley, 321, *331*
Ramey, Craig, T., 353, *364*
Ramey, James W., 11, *23,* 123, 130, *149,* 458, 468–69, 474, *483*
Rapoport, Lydia, 424, *454*
Raven, Bertram H., 185, *225*
Ray, Dixie L., 71, *75*
Rebecca, Meda, 88, *115*
Regalado, David, 358, *363*
Reid, Mike, 467, *483*
Reiss, Ira, 14, *22,* 120–21, 124, 127–28, *149*
Renne, Karen S., 210, *225,* 310, *331*
Reusch, Jurgen, 53, *76*
Rich, George W., 8, *22*
Rich, Spencer, 317, *331,* 414, *418*
Richmond, Marie LaLiberte, 196, *224*
Ridley, Carl A., 207, 215–16, 218, *224*

Roberts, Allyn, 157, *184*
Robertson, Joan F., 377–79, *390*
Robinson, Betsy C., 399, *418*
Robinson, Ira S., 121, *149*
Rodrigues, Aroldo, 195, *225*
Rogers, Carl R., 45, *48,* 185, *225,* 463, *483*
Rogers, Peter L., 56, *75*
Rohner, Ronald P., 344, *363*
Rolfe, David J., 240, *256*
Rollins, Boyd C., 309, *331*
Roosevelt, Kristine, 290, *294*
Roper, Brent S., 309, *330*
Rosen, Lawrence, 130, *148,* 209, *223*
Rosenberg, Ben G., 174, *183,* 368, 371–73, *390, 391*
Rosenberg, George S., 370, *390*
Rosenthal, Erich, 172, *183,* 266, *294*
Rosenthal, Kristine, 287, 289, *294*
Rosenthal, Robert, 56, *75*
Rosenzweig, Saul, 146, *150*
Ross, Dorothea M., 87, *116*
Ross, Sheila A., 87, *116*
Ross, Susan, 127, *150*
Rossi, Alice S., 310, *331*
Rothman, David J., 39, *48*
Rothman, Sheila M., 39, *48*
Rubenstein, Judith L., 353, *364*
Rubin, Lillian B., 71, *76,* 214, *225,* 239, *256*
Rubin, Zick, 38, 43, *48,* 171, 172, *183*
Russell, Candyce S., 300–302, *331,* 393, *418*
Rutter, Michael, 300, *331*
Ryder, Norman B., 113, *116*
Ryder, Robert G., 153, *183*

Sabagh, Georges, 71, *75*
Safilios-Rothschild, Constantina, 194-96, *226,* 242, *256*
Samuels, Helen R., 370, *390*
Santrock, John W., 349, *363, 372, 391*
Satir, Virginia, 60, *76*
Sawin, Douglas B., 29, *47,* 339, 343, *363*
Scanzoni, John, 139, *150,* 197, 198, *226*
Scardino, Katherine, 394, *418*
Schacter, F. F., 354, *363*
Schacter, Stanley, 367, *390*
Schaeffer, Earl S., 355, *363*
Scheid, L., 219, *223*
Scherl, Donald J., 431, *453*
Schnucker, R. V., 336, *363*
Schrank, Robert, 462, *484*
Schroder, Harold, 266, *292*

Schulz, David, 187, *226*
Schumaker, E. F., 457, *484*
Schvaneveldt, Jay D., 480, *484*
Scott, John F., 387, *390*
Seamans, Barbara, 99, 100, *116*
Sears, Robert R., 213, *226*, 374, *390*
Self, Patricia A., 83, *117*
Seligson, Marcia, 201, *226*
Serbin, Lisa A., 87, 88, *115, 116*
Shanas, Ethel, 377, *390*
Shank, Robert E., 397, *418*
Shephard, Linda, 207, *226*
Shideler, Mary M., 472, *484*
Sidel, Ruth, 326, 327, *331*
Silverman, Phyllis, 429, *454*
Sindbert, Ronald, 157, *184*
Singh, B. Krishna, 129, *150*
Singh, Labh, 307, *330*
Skidmore, C. Jay, 480, *484*
Skolnick, Arlene, 358, *363*
Smart, Laura S., 281, *294*
Smart, Mollie S., 309, *331*, 349, *363*, 401,
    402, *418*, 419, *455*
Smart, Russell C., 309, *331*, 349, *363*, 401,
    402, *418*
Smith, Daniel, 159, *183*
Smith, Harold E., 8, *22*
Smith, Ramona, 432, *454*
Smith, William M., 162, *184*
Snapper, Kurt J., 317, *331*, 396, 411, 414,
    *418*
Sobrero, Aquiles J., 105, *116*
Sorensen, Robert C., 124, 128, *150*
Spanier, Graham, 468, *482*
Sparks, William, 157, *183*
Spence, Donald L., 16, *23*, 399, *418*, 440,
    *454*
Sporakowski, Michael J., 208, *226*
Sprey, Jetze, 185, 188, *226*
Stack, Carol B., 476, *484*
Staines, Graham, 207, *226*
Staples, Robert, 128, *150*, 196, *226*, 472,
    *484*
Stass, A. W., 43, *48*
Staub, Ervin, 350, *363*, 371, *391*
Stayton, Donelda J., 29, *48*
Stein, Peter J., 471, 472, *484*
Steinmetz, Suzanne K., 373, 374, *391*
Stekton, Mora, 438, *453*
Sternglanz, Sarah H., 87, *116*
Steward, David, 354, *363*
Steward, Margaret, 354, *363*
Stewart, Cyrus, 127, *150*

Stewart, F., 103, 106, 108–10, *115*
Stewart, G. K., 103, 106, 108–10, *115*
Stewart, Gordon T., 440, *452*
Stewart, Mollie K., 86, *117*
Stinnett, Nick, 219, 220, *226*, 348, 349, *363,
    364*, 468, 474, *482*
Stoezer, Louis, 432, *453*
Stone, Carolyn, 358, *363*
Stratton, P., 103, 106, 108–10, *115*
Straus, Murray, 69, *75*, 198, *226*
Stroup, Atlee, 264, *294*
Stuart, Irving R., 267, *294*
Sullivan, Joyce A., 174, *184*
Sussman, Marvin B., 205, *226*
Sutton-Smith, Brian, 134, *150*, 174, *184,
    368, 371–73, *390, 391*
Swanson, Guy, 231, *256*
Swanson, Harold D., 339, *363*
Switzer, Ellen, 100, *117*

Talley, Sharon, 348, *363*
Tanner, James M., 93, 94, *117*
Tanzer, Deborah, 337, 338, *363*
Taylor, Claribel M., 317, *330*
Taylor, P. A., 177, *184*
Taylor, Ray, 419, *455*
Teevan, James, Jr., 128, *150*
Teisman, Mark, 192, *226*
Terry, Roger L., 172, *183*
Terman, Lewis M., 208, *226*
Thomas, Darwin L., 174, *183*
Thomes, Mary Margaret, 71, *75*
Thompson, David S., 203, *226*
Thornton, Arland, 266, *294*
Till, Amnon, 172, *184*
Tolone, William L., 121, 127, 128, 139, 148,
    *150*
Tomeh, Aida K., 139, *150*
Tonick, Illene J., 87, *116*
Trescher, William H., 112, *115*
Trethowan, W. H., 335, *363*
Troll, Lillian E., 358, *363*, 377, *391*
Truseel, James, 113, *117*
Turner, Ralph, 189, 190, *226*
Turner, Stanley, 130, *148*, 209, *223*
Tyhurst, J. S., 434, *454*

Udry, J. Richard, 14, *23*, 126, 127, *150*
U.S. Bureau of the Census, 5, 11, *23*, 124,
    *150*, 230, *256*, 442, 445, *454*, 473, *484*

Vandenberg, Stephen G., 172, *184*
Van Riper, Charles, 55, 61, 62, *75*

Varni, Charles, 469, *484*
Vaughan, Barbara, 113, *117*
Veevers, J. E., 295, 317, 323, *331*
Vener, Arthur, 127, *150*
Veroff, Joseph, 212, *224*
Vietze, Peter M., 339, *362*
Vincent, Clark E., 173, *184*
Viney, Linda L., 300, *331*
Vore, David A., 397, *418*
Voss, Harwin L., 216, 217, *223*
Vygotsky, Lev S., 54, *76*

Wackman, Daniel, 65, 68, *75*
Wadsworth, Benjamin, 40, *48*
Waite, Linda J., 317, *330*
Walker, Kathryn E., 234, 236, *256*, 401, 402, *418*
Waller, Willard, 161, *184*, 268–70, 282, *294*
Wallerstein, Judith S., 273, 283, *294*
Wallin, Paul, 208, *223*
Walsh, Robert H., 121, 127, 128, 139, *148*, *150*
Walster, Elaine, 176, 177, *182*
Walster, G. William, 176, 177, *182*
Walters, James, 348, 349, *363*, *364*
Walton, Bonnie L., 129, *150*
Ward, Charlotte, 341, *364*
Ward, Fred, 341, *364*
Ware, Helen, 11, *23*
Warren, Jean, 381, *389*
Watson, John S., 353, *364*
Watts, Jean C., 354, *364*
Weaver, Charles N., 210, *224*, 286, *292*, 309, *330*
Weinberg, Martin S., 127, 144, *148*
Weinstein, Karol K., 378, *390*
Weir, Tamara, 196, 207, 210, *223*
Weisberg, Carol, 71, *75*
Weiss, Robert S., 265, 268–70, 273, 277–83, *294*
Wells, J. Gipson, 205, *226*
Welter, Barbara, 40, *48*
Wenger, Morton, 209, *223*

Westbrook, Mary T., 300, 301, 308, *331*
Westoff, Charles F., 112, *117*, 455, *484*
Wheeler, Ella W., 32, *48*
White, Burton L., 354, *364*
White, Lynn K., 206, 212, *223*
White, Mary A., 87, *116*
White, Priscilla, 235, *256*
Whitehurst, Robert N., 174, *184*
Whiting, Beatrice, 137, *150*, 357, *364*, 367, *391*
Wiegand, Elizabeth, 248, *256*
Wilkinson, Melvin L., 36, 37, *48*
Will, Jerrie A., 83, *117*
Williams, J. Sherwood, 129, *150*
Willie, Charles V., 196, *226*
Willis, F. N., Jr., 43, *48*
Wilson, Kenneth L., 290, 294, 320, *330*
Wise, Harold, 412, *418*
Woehrer, Carole E., 359, *364*, 383, 385, 387, *391*
Wohlford, Paul, 372, *391*
Wolfe, Donald, 196, 220, *223*
Wolinsky, Annie L., 86, 87, *116*
Women in Transition, Inc., 271, *294*
Women's Bureau, 449, *454*
Wood, Vivian, 379, *391*
Wright, A. H., 103, 106, 108–10, *115*
Wright, James D., 214, *226*
Wright, Thomas L., 209, *224*
Wyden, Peter, 69, *75*

Yankelovitch, Skelly and White, Inc., 83, *117*
Yarrow, Leon J., 353, *364*
Yeung, David, 108, 109, *117*
Yue, F., 142, *148*

Zablocki, Ben, 466, *484*
Zelnick, Melvin, 112, *117*, 122, 127, *150*
Zimmerman, Carle C., 13, *23*
Ziskin, Jay, 468, *484*
Ziskin, Mae, 468, *484*
Zolotow, Charlotte, 87, *117*
Zucker, Marvin A., 204, *226*
Zurcher, Louis A., 290, *294*

# subject index

Abortion, 111–12
Abuse of children, 345–47
Accident prevention, 404, 406
"Account" of divorce, 268–29
Activity, 399–402
Adolescence
    drug use, 408
    gender roles, 134–40
    nutrition in, 397–98
    parenthood, 316–17
Adoptive parenthood, 312–14
Adult children and parents, 358–60
Adulthood, gender roles, 134–40
After-the-fact birth control, 110–112
Age and finances, 230
Age roles, 462–63
Aggression, 69–70
Aging, 440–45
    family living, 442–45
    health care, 415
    income, 441–42
    life satisfaction, 440–41
    work, 442
Aging couples, 219–20
Alternate lifestyles, 327, 464–66
Assistance, public, 254
Assortative mating, 171–79
Astrology, 175
Attachment, infant, 27–28
Attraction, studies on, 38–39

Bargaining, 192–93
Barter, 244
Being in love, 31–33

Bereavement, 427, 429
Birth center births, 341–42
Birth control, 101–12, 324–26
    after-the-fact, 110–12
    chemical barriers, 106
    condom, 105–106
    continence, 102–103
    decision-making, 112–13
    diaphragm, 104–105
    douches, 110
    historical, 101–102
    intrauterine devices, 107–108
    mechanical methods, 105–106
    menstrual extraction, 110
    natural methods, 102–103
    oral contraceptives, 108–109
    preventive methods, 104–10
    rhythm, 103
    sterilization, 109–10
    withdrawal, 102–103
Birth process, 338–39
Black feminism, 137
Black singles, 471–72
Bonding, 33, 189
Breadwinners, 233–37
Breaking up, 170–71
Breastfeeding, 103, 301
Budget form, 499–501
Budgets, 246–49
Bundling, 159–61

Care, an aspect of love, 30–33
Caregiving, 344–45
Career, family, 15

Caste, 17–18
Chemical methods of birth control, 106
Child care, 321, 476–77, 489–91
Childbearing, 332–42
Childbirth, 336–42, 415
    medical assistance, 339–42
    methods, 336–38
    natural, 336
    preparation, 336–38
    process, 338–39
Childfreedom, 317–19
Childlessness, 317–19
Childrearing, 72–73
Children
    abuse of, 345–47
    and divorce, 273–78
    and marital satisfaction, 208
    cost of, 320
    neglect of, 345–47
    planning for, 488–91
    support from, 307–308
Choices, occupational, 232
Circumcision, 495
Class differences, 18–20, 71–72, 187, 214, 229, 354
Climacteric, 94
Cohabitation, 215–19
    legal aspects, 217–18
Co-marital sex, 468–69
Common law marriage, 203–204
Communes, 203–204, 387, 466–67
Communication, 48–76, 100–101, 199, 240
    clarifying, 64
    codes, 67–68
    congruent messages, 57–59
    effective, 62–64
    family, 65–73
    honest, 66–68
    incongruent messages, 57–59
    language, 50–51, 72–73
    looking, 55
    marital, 51–52
    meaning, 60
    mutuality, 61–62
    nonverbal, 55–59
    partner, 70–72
    planned, 68–69
    problems, 63–64
    reality, 58–59
    roles, 52–53
    status, 53
    symbols, 57

    uses for, 49–53
    working class, 71–72
Community property, 204
Community's role in health care, 410–12
Companionship, 210–12
Compatibility, sexual, 99–100
Competency, 375
Competition in remarriage, 289
Conception, 494
Comprehensive services in health care, 413–14
Condom method of birth control, 105–106
Conflict, 197–99
Congruent messages in communication, 57–59
Conjugal family, 5
Consanguine family, 8
Consumers, 227
Continence, 102–103
Contraception. See Birth control
Contracts, marriage, 205
Cost of children, 320
Courtship, 165–71
Credit, 248–49
Crisis of parenthood, 300–301
Crises, 419–34
    classification of, 422
    definition, 419–20
    financial, 254–55
    health, 393
    impact of, 423–24
    intervention, 419, 424–34
    precipitation, 420–23
    stages of, 423–24
    vulnerability, 422–23
Cross-cultural comparisons, 8–11, 34, 43, 95–96, 118–19, 456–57
Custody of children, 273–78

Dating, 157–65
    after divorce, 281–82
    definition, 158
    factors influencing, 161
    first, 162–63
    frequency of, 162–63
    functions, 163–65
    history, 158–62
    rating and, 161–64
Death, 425–29
    awareness movement, 425–26
Decision-making, 112–13
    work and, 237–40

Deterrents to parenthood, 319–23
Development
    during pregnancy, 333–36
    family, 15–16
    love, 25–34
    prenatal, 494–95
Diaphragm method of birth control, 104–105
Difficulties of parenthood, 323–26
Dilemmas of love, 45
Disagreements, 69–70
Disasters, 433–34
Discipline, 65, 73, 350–53
Disease, venereal, 502–507
Divorce, 257–84
    "account" of, 268–69
    chances of, 257–59, 267
    children and, 273–78
    do-it-yourself, 272
    factors related to, 259–66
    family and, 280
    fault laws, 271
    friends and, 279
    friendly, 472–73
    no-fault laws, 272
    numbers of, 274
    processes, 269–84
        community, 279–80
        coparental, 273
        economic, 272–73
        emotional, 270
        legal, 270–72
        psychic, 280–84
    recovery from, 281–84
    therapy, 283–84
Drug use, 407–408
Drugs for labor and childbirth, 340–41
Dual-career marriages, 234–37
Dying, 425–27

Earning, 243–46
Economic system, 231
Economics, family, 227–29
Education, 208
    for human living, 479–80
    health, 411–12
    parent, 357–58
Effective communication, 62–64
Embryo, 494–95
Empathy, 62–63, 425
Employment, 231–40, 243–46
    cost of, 238–39
Empty nest, 219

Engagement, 167–69
Environment and health care, 395–96
Equal Rights Amendment, 137
Equality, 459
Ethnicity, 18–20, 354
Evolution of love, 24–26
Expression of love, 35–43
Extended family, 8–10
Extramarital sex, 209–10

Family
    and divorce, 280
    career, 15
    communal, 11
    communication in, 65–73
    conjugal, 5
    consanguine, 8
    development, 15–16
    economics, 227–29
    extended, 8–10
    forms of, 5–13, 458
    functions of, 13–14, 458
    homosexual, 12–13
    lifetime, 15–16
    lineage, 15–16, 385–86
    matrilineal, 9
    nuclear, 5
    origin, 1, 7
    procreation, 1, 7
    one-parent, 11–12
    patrilineal, 9
    polygamous, 10–11
    poor, 11
    reconstituted, 286–90
    role in health care, 394–410, 414
    societal supports for, 475
Family planning and health care, 414
Family reunion, 385–86
Family structure, 5–13
Family studies, 2–21
Family therapy, 394, 430
Family uniqueness, 20–21
Family violence, 373–74
Father-infant love, 29
Fathers, 343–44
Fears regarding parenthood, 322–23
Female sexual anatomy, 496–98
Femaleness, 77–90
Femininity, 77–90
Feminism, 135–37
Fetus, 494–95
Fictive kin, 387

Fidelity, sexual, 129–30
Fighting, marital, 69–70
Finances
   age and, 230
   gender and, 229–30
   planning, 241–55
   race and, 230
Forms of family, 458
Friends
   and divorce, 279
   love of, 30–31
Fringe benefits, 244
Functions
   dating, 163–65
   family, 13–14, 458
   parents, 344–56

Gender
   and finances, 229–30
   differences, 78–90
   differentiation, 78–90
Gender role, 82–90, 134–40, 188, 462,
      486–87
   adoption of, 84
   attitudes, 139–40
   identity, 84
   learning, 371–72
   learning theory, 82–90
      cognitive, 88
      dialectic, 88–89
      psychoanalytic, 82–83
      social learning, 83–87
Genetic defects, 406
Going steady, 166–67
Gonorrhea, 502–504
Grandparents, 375–80
   ages of, 378
   availability, 375–77
   black, 378
   patterns of relationships, 377–78
   types of, 377–78
Growth through parenthood, 310–12

Handicaps, 406
Health, 210, 392–418
Health care
   childbirth, 415
   community's role, 410–12
   comprehensive serives, 414
   elderly, 415
   family planning, 414
   family's role, 394–410

   new directions in, 512–16
   of dying, 416
   self-care, 412–13
   standards of, 394–95
   teenage parents, 414
   venereal disease, 415
Health insurance, 251–52
Helping in crises, 424–34
   friends, 424
   professionals, 425
Herpes, genital, 505–506
Historical birth control, 101–102
Home births, 341
Home maintenance, 479
Home management and health care, 396
Home nursing, 404–405
Homemaking, 228, 232–40, 244, 486–87
   and health care, 396
   support systems, 477–79
Homogamy, 172
Homosexual
   behavior, 143–44
   family, 12–13
   life styles, 144–45
   marriage, 205
Homosexuality, 140–46
   attitudes, 145–46
   theories, 141–43
Honesty in communication, 66–68
Hormones, 142
Hospice movement, 428
Hospital births, 341
Households, types of, 7
Househusband, 233–27
Housework, 138–39, 233–37, 486–87

Ideal mate, 174–75
Identity, 202
Illness
   and injuries, 403–406
   mental, 429–30
Income, 208, 243–46
Incongruent messages in communication,
     57–59
Individuality, 461–62
Infant, 72–73
Infant-father love, 29
Infant-mother love, 27–29
Infanticide, 112
Infatuation, 32
In-laws, 380–83
Insurance, 250–54

health, 251–52
liability, 254
property, 254
Interaction between partners, 188–200
Integrity, sense of, 379
Interaction, parent-child, 275–78
Intrauterine devices, 107–108
Investments, 248–50
Isolation, social, 480
IUD's, 107–108

Jealousy, 191–92
Job satisfaction, 207
Jobs, choice of, 476

Kin, 365–87
    as socializers, 85
Knowledge, an aspect of love, 30–33

La Leche League, 342
Lamaze method of childbirth, 337–38
Laws, divorce, 271–72
Learning, gender role, 371–72
Learning to love, 25–34
Legal aspects of cohabitation, 217–18
Legal reform, 480–81
Liability insurance, 254
    life, 254
Life insurance, 253–54
Life satisfaction, 212–15
Life styles, 464–66
    alternate, 327
    and health care, 395–96
Lifetime family, 15–16
Ligation, tubal, 109
Lineage family, 15–16, 385–86
Love, 24–47, 189, 460–61
    and partner selection, 179–81
    being in, 31–33
    care, 30, 33
    development of, 25–34
    dilemmas of, 45
    evolution of, 24–26
    friends, 30–31
    in ancient world, 39
    in India, 42–43
    infant-father, 29
    infant-mother, 27–29
    infatuation, 32
    knowledge, 30, 33
    learning to, 25–34
    Middle Ages, 39–40

partnership, 33
Puritan, 40
regulation of, 44–45
respect, 30, 33
romantic, 36–37, 173–75
Samoan, 41
self, 30
unconditional, 30
universal aspects, 43
varieties of expression, 35–43
Victorian, 40–41

Male sexual anatomy, 495–96
Maleness, 77–90
Marital career and parenthood, 309–10
Marital communication, 51–52
Marital relationships, 491
Marital satisfaction, 206–15, 219
Marriage
    advertisements, 156
    alternate forms, 473–75
    and parenthood, 308–10
    Black ghetto, 187–88
    common law, 203–204
    companionship, 187
    contracts, 205
    dual-career, 234–37
    duties, 205
    financial aspects, 204
    homosexual, 205
    institutional, 187
    legal requirements, 203–205
    mixed, 172–73
        racial, 266–67
        religious, 266
    open, 469–70
    relation to cohabitation, 218–19
    sexually open, 469
    types of, 186–88
    upper middle class, 187
Masculinity, 77–90
Matchmaking, 155–57
    modern, 156–57
    traditional, 155–56
Mate selection. See Partner selection
Matrilineal family, 9
Media as socializers, 87
Medical services, 402–403, 410
Medicine, non-western, 394
Menarche, 93–94
Menopause, 94, 131–33
Menstrual extraction, 110

Menstruation, 94
Mental illness, 429–30
Mixed marriages, 172–73
Money
    in remarriage, 288
    meanings of, 241–43
Moral development, 349–50
Mother-infant love, 27–29
Mothers-in-law, 382
Moving as crisis, 432–33
Mutuality in communication, 61–62

Natural childbirth, 336–38
Natural methods of birth control, 102–103
Neglect of children, 345–47
Nonverbal communication, 55–59
Nuclear family, 5
Nutrition
    and health care, 396–99, 411
    in adolescence, 397–98
    in old age, 398–99

Occupation, choice of, 232
Occupational roles, 462
Old age, financial security in, 254
    nutrition in, 398–99
    See also Aging
One-parent family, 11–12
Oral contraceptives, 108–109
Ordinal position, 466–67
Orgasm, 97–99
Orientations to life, 459–64
Origin, family of, 1, 7
Ovulation, 94

Parent education, 357–58
Parent-child career, 308–27
Parenthood, 295–331
    adoptive, 312–14
    and marriage, 308–10
    choice of, 295–300
    crisis of, 300–301
    decisions, 295–300
    deterrents to, 319–23
    difficulties of, 323–26
    duty, 305
    fears regarding, 322–23
    growth through, 310–12
    marital career and, 309–10
    pressures for and against, 328
    readiness for, 297–98
    rejection of, 317–19
    teenage, 316–17

transition to, 300–301
    unwed, 315–16
Parenting, 343–60
Parents
    and adult children, 358–60
    as socializers, 83–85
    as teachers, 353–55
    development during pregnancy, 333–36
    functions of, 344–56
    roles of, 304
    single, 277–78
    values, 355–57
Partner selection, 151–84
    breaking up, 170–71
    closed field, 154
    couple autonomy, 158
    family control, 153–56, 158
    love and, 179–81
    open field, 154
    social control, 151–53, 155–58
    theories, 173–81
Partnerhood, 185–225
    during pregnancy, 335–36
    financial obligations, 204
    gender roles, 188
    growth of, 199–200
    interaction, 188–200
    middle and aging years, 219–20
    typologies, 186–88
Partners, 70–72
Partnership love, 33
Patrilineal family, 9
Peer group, influence of, 128
Pension plans, 254
Perception of self and others, 208
Permanence in pair relationship, 54, 169–71
Person-oriented family, 65
Planning
    financial, 241–55
    for children, 488–91
Polyandry, 10
Polygamy, 10–11, 118
Polygyny, 10
Poor family, 11
Population, world, 455–58
Postmenopause, 132–33
Poverty, 445–51
    adaptations to, 448–49
    age groups, 447
    ethnic groups, 447
    programs, 450–51
    types of families, 446
Power, 193–97, 460–61

Pre-engagement, 167
Pregnancy, 332–36
    development during, 333–36
Premarital sex, 208–209
    consequences of, 122–25
    premarital questionnaire, 485–93
Preparation for childbirth, 336–38
Problems of families, 435–51
    aging, 440–45
    chronic illness, 435–37
    chronic disability, 435–37
    drugs, 439–40
    mental retardation, 437–38
    poverty, 445–51
Procreation, family of, 1, 7, 375
Producing, 227, 243–46
Property insurance, 254
Puberty, 93–96
    cross-cultural perspective, 95–96
Pubescence, 93–94

Quality of human life, 455–58
Quasi-kin, 386–87
Questionnaire, premarital, 485–93

Race and finances, 230
Race differences, 348
Rape, 431–32
Read method of childbirth, 337
Readiness for parenthood, 297–98
    emotional, 298
    physical, 297
Reconsitituted families, 286–90
    problems of, 287–90
    success of, 290
Recovery from divorce, 281–84
Recreation, 408–409, 479
Regulation of love, 44–45
Rejection of parenthood, 317–19
Relationships
    grandparent, 377–78
    in-law, 380–83
Religion, 202
Religious societies, 387
Remarriage, 284–90
    children in, 286–90
    happiness, 285–86
    rates, 285
    stability of, 285–86
Respect, an aspect of love, 28–30, 33
Rest, 399–402
Rhythm method of birth control, 103
Rhythms in family living, 399–402

Rivalry in remarriage, 289
Roles, 65, 179, 461–62
    age, 462–63
    gender, 462, 486–87
    in communication, 52–53
    occupational, 462
    of parents, 304

Safety, 406–410
Sanitation, 410
Satisfaction, marital. See Marital satisfaction
Satisfactions of parenthood, 301–308
Savings, 248–50
School-age children, activity and rest, 400–401
Science, 459–60
Self health care, 412–13
Self love, 30
Self-concept, 202, 374–75
Self-esteem, 348–49
    women's, 137–39
Self-expression, 53–55
    processing, 53–54
    tension relase, 54–55
Sense
    of integrity, 379
    of intimacy, 33–34
    of trust, 72
    parental, 295
Separation agreements, 271
Services, 244
    recreational, 479
Sex, 77–150, 191, 463
    after divorce, 281–82
    co-marital, 468–69
    education, 90–92, 96
    information, 494–98
Sexual adjustment, 209
Sexual anatomy, 495–98
Sexual attitudes and behavior
    changes in, 125–28
    extramarital, 129–30
    group differences in, 128
    marital, 128–30
    older people, 131–33
    postmarital, 129–31
    premarital, 119–28
Sexual behavior, 92–100
    childhood, 92–93
    adolescence, 93–96
Sexual compatibility, 99–100
Sexual development, 93–94
    female, 93–94
    male, 94

Sexual fidelity, 129–30
Sexual intercourse, 96–100
Sexual response, 96–100
    female, 96–97
    individual differences, 99–100
    male, 96–97
Sexual revolution, 125–28
Sexual standards, 120–21, 129–30
    choice of, 121–25
Sexuality, aging and, 131–33
Siblings, 365–75
    as socializers, 85
    companionship, 368–70
    conflict, 373–74
    dependency, 372–73
    interaction, 367–75
    jealousy, 373–74
    learning, 370–72
    play, 370–71
    power, 373
    relationships, 367–75
Single parents, 277–78
Singles, 470–72
Simplicity as life style, 464–66
Social stratification, 17–20
Socialization, 347–53
    discipline, 350–53
    influences on, 348
    moral development, 349–50
    race differences in, 348
Spending, 246–49
Standards of health care, 394–95
Status, 203
    financial, 229
    in communication, 53
Status-oriented family, 65
Stepparents, 287–90
Sterilization, 109–10
Stimulus-Value-Role theory, 175–78
Stratification, social, 17–20
Structure, family, 5–13
Support
    for parents, 325–27
    from children, 307–308
    systems, homemaking, 477–79
Supports for the family, 475
Sympathy, 62–63, 425
Syphilis, 504–505
System
    economic, 231
    family as a, 16–20

Teachers as socializers, 85–87
Teaching, parental, 353–55
    class differences in, 354
    ethnic differences in, 354
Teenage parenthood, 316–17
Terms use of, 1–2, 5–12
Therapy
    divorce, 283–84
    family, 430
Time orientation, 459
Transition to parenthood, 300–301
Trust, sense of, 72
Tubal ligation, 109

Unconditional love, 30
Unemployment insurance, 252–53
Uniqueness of family, 20–21
Unwed parenthood, 315–16
Utopian societies, 387

Values, 2, 178–79
    parental, 355–57
Vasectomy, 109–10
Venereal disease, 502–507
    health care, 415
Violence, 69–70
    family, 373–74

Warts, venereal, 506–507
Wedding, 200–205
    legal aspects, 203–205
    meanings of, 200–204
    rite de passage, 202
Widowhood, 220, 317, 429
Withdrawal as birth control, 102–103
Women's Liberation, 344
Women's movement, 135–39
Work, 138–40, 227–56, 486–87
    and decision-making, 237–40
    employment, 231, 232–40, 243–56
    homemaking, 228, 232–40, 244
    housework, 233–37
    of childcare, 321
    producing, 243–46
    roles, 206
    sharing, 476
Working class, 71–72
Working wives, 207
Workplace, 231